BRADY

Scott Foresman - Addison Wesley

MATH

AUTHORS

RANDALL I. CHARLES

Carne S. Barnett **Diane J. Briars** **Warren D. Crown**
Martin L. Johnson **Steven J. Leinwand** **John Van de Walle**

Charles R. Allan • Dwight A. Cooley • Portia C. Elliott
Pearl Ling • Alma B. Ramírez
Freddie Lee Renfro • Mary Thompson

Scott Foresman
Addison Wesley

Editorial Offices: Menlo Park, California • Glenview, Illinois
Sales Offices: Reading, Massachusetts • Atlanta, Georgia • Glenview, Illinois
Carrollton, Texas • Menlo Park, California

http://www.sf.aw.com

The friendly characters who help you in this book with math tips, remembering, and problem solving are Zoombinis™. They are used with the permission of Brøderbund Software and can be found in the interactive problem-solving software, *Logical Journey of the Zoombinis®*, © 1996 Brøderbund Software and TERC, available from Brøderbund Software, Novato, California. For more information, write Brøderbund at P.O. Box 6125, Novato, CA 94948-6125, or call (415) 382-4740.

Cover artist Robert Silvers was taking photographs and playing with computers by the time he was ten. Eventually he melded his interests in computer programming and photography to produce a program that divides images into a grid and matches them with images from a database. The results are mosaics such as the one on this cover.

2001 Impression

Printed in the United States of America

ISBN 0-201-36391-7

9 10–VH–02 01

CHAPTER 1 Data, Graphs, and Facts Review 6

Theme **ANIMAL NETWORK**

SECTION A Reading Graphs and Facts Review 9

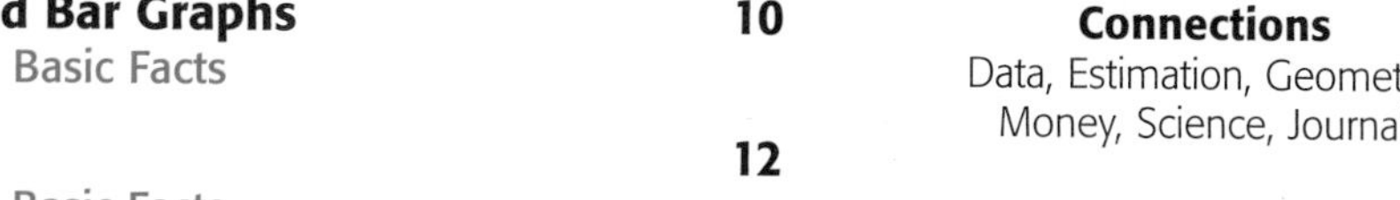

Connections
Data, Estimation, Geometry, Money, Science, Journal

SECTION B Making Graphs, Describing Data, and Facts Review 25

Problem Solving
Draw a Picture,
Look for a Pattern, Make a Table,
Use Objects/Act It Out

Connections
Data, Science, Recreation, Journal

Chapter Resources

Review and Maintenance appears in green type; **Problem Solving** in red type

CHAPTER 2 Place Value and Time 48

Theme Amazing Facts

CHAPTER 3

Adding and Subtracting Whole Numbers and Money 90

Theme ON THE JOB

Problem Solving
Look for a Pattern, Use Objects/Act It Out

Connections
Algebra, Data, Geometry, Logic, Mental Math, Money, Time, Careers, Fine Arts, Health, History, Science, Journal

Connections
Algebra, Calculator, Data, Geometry, Logic, Measurement, Mental Math, Money, Patterns, Time, Careers, Geography, Music, Science, Social Studies, Journal

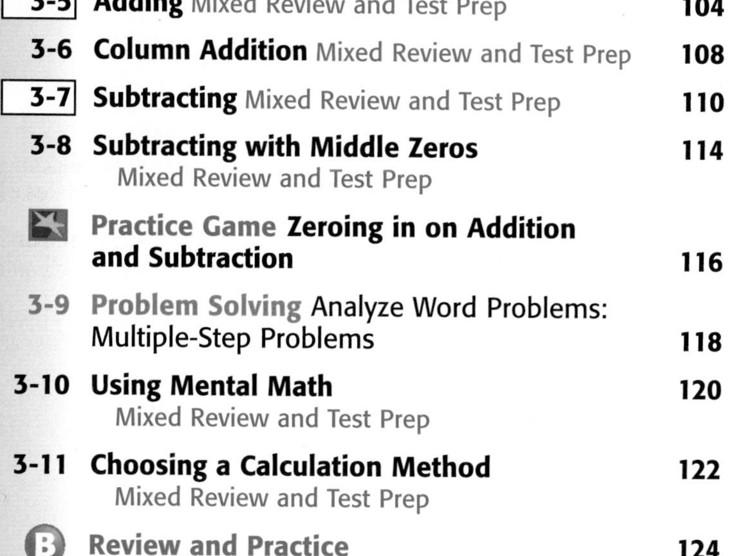

Problem Solving
Use Objects/Act It Out

Connections
Data, Mental Math, Patterns, Time, Careers, Journal

Chapter Resources

CHAPTER 4

Multiplication and Division Concepts and Facts 144

Theme KEEPING FIT

SECTION A Understanding Multiplication 147

Problem Solving
Look for a Pattern, Make a Table

Connections
Algebra, Data, Measurement, Mental Math, Money, Patterns, Time, Health, History, Social Studies, Journal

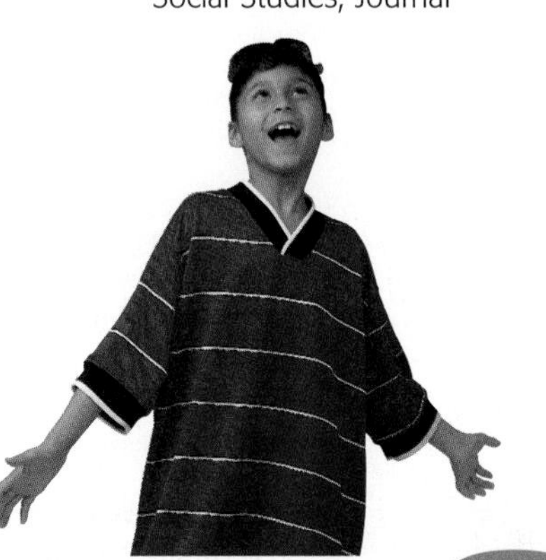

SECTION B Understanding Division 165

Problem Solving
Work Backward

Connections
Algebra, Data, Mental Math, Money, Time, Health, Science, Sports, Journal

SECTION C Extending Multiplication and Division 175

Problem Solving
Look for a Pattern, Make an Organized List, Use Objects/Act It Out

Connections
Algebra, Data, Measurement, Money, Patterns, Time, Health, History, Science, Sports, Social Studies, Journal

Chapter Resources

CHAPTER 5

Multiplying by 1-Digit Factors 196

Theme TIME OUT FROM School

CHAPTER 6

Multiplying by 2-Digit Factors 246

Theme 

Section A Multiplication Number Sense 249

Problem Solving
Draw a Picture, Look for a Pattern, Use Objects/Act It Out

Connections
Algebra, Data, Estimation, Geometry, Measurement, Mental Math, Money, Time, Careers, History, Journal

Section B Multiplying 259

Connections
Data, Estimation, Geometry, Measurement, Mental Math, Money, Probability, Time, Geography, History, Math History, Social Studies, Journal

Section C Extending Multiplication 273

Connections
Algebra, Data, Money, Time, History, Journal

Chapter Resources

Review and Maintenance appears in green type; **Problem Solving** in red type

CHAPTER 8

Using Geometry 340

Theme **Artist at Work!**

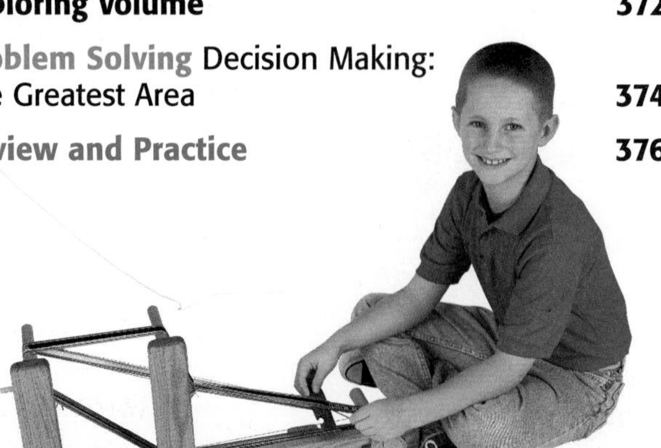

CHAPTER 9

Fractions and Customary Linear Measurement 382

Theme **Getting Involved**

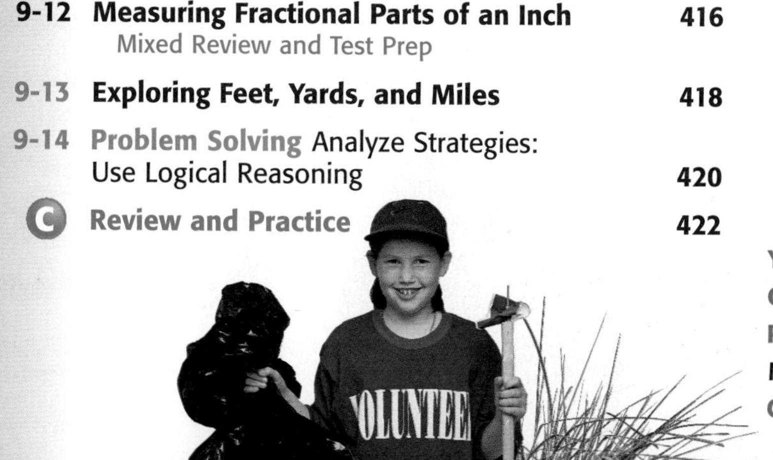

Chapter Resources

CHAPTER 10

Fraction Operations and Customary Measurement 428

Theme Fun IN THE City

CHAPTER 11

Decimals and Metric Measurement 472

Theme GOING FOR THE GOLD

CHAPTER 12

Dividing by 2-Digit Divisors and Probability 524

Theme THAT'S ENTERTAINMENT

Welcome to Math Class

Welcome back to math class! I'm the **Get Ready** Zoombini. My friends and I are here to help you this year in math class.

Remember, practice really can make perfect!

My helpful **math tips** cannot be beat!

I have good ideas for **problem solving.**

Did you know? Come to me for fun facts!

Math doesn't only happen in math class! Math helps us understand what we see and do every day.

Have you ever:

- made sure a blue damsel fish has a big enough tank at the aquarium?
- discovered patterns in Hmong (MAWNG) clothing?
- figured out how many strokes a dragon boat racer paddles in a race?
- found out how far you travel on a roller coaster?

We will do that and more as we explore the math that real students use every day.

Reviewing Skills

You Will Meet real people like these who use math skills in their everyday lives

On page 539, meet Reginald who plays video games. He also enjoys reading and sports.

Liesl is a member of the International Wheelchair Aviators. She flies airplanes. See her on page 259.

You already know lots of math!
Let's review some basic facts.

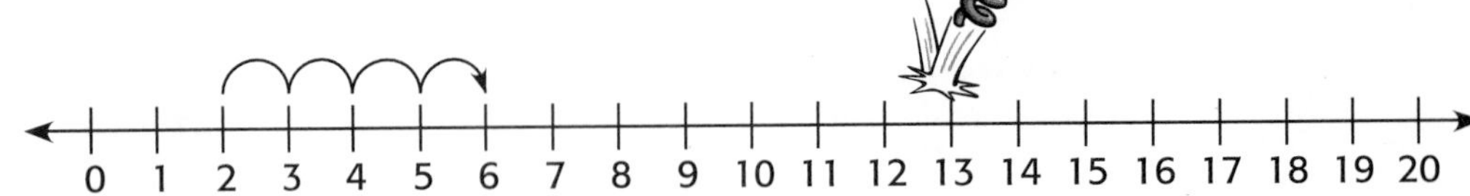

Review addition facts. Find each sum. You may use the number line to help.

1. 2 + 4	**2.** 3 + 7	**3.** 5 + 6	**4.** 8 + 8	**5.** 6 + 2
6. 9 + 7	**7.** 4 + 3	**8.** 7 + 7	**9.** 1 + 9	**10.** 5 + 3
11. 8 + 4	**12.** 6 + 7	**13.** 5 + 5	**14.** 9 + 3	**15.** 6 + 6
16. 5 + 8	**17.** 4 + 6	**18.** 7 + 2	**19.** 6 + 1	**20.** 4 + 9
21. 4 + 4	**22.** 5 + 7	**23.** 6 + 9	**24.** 4 + 7	**25.** 9 + 9

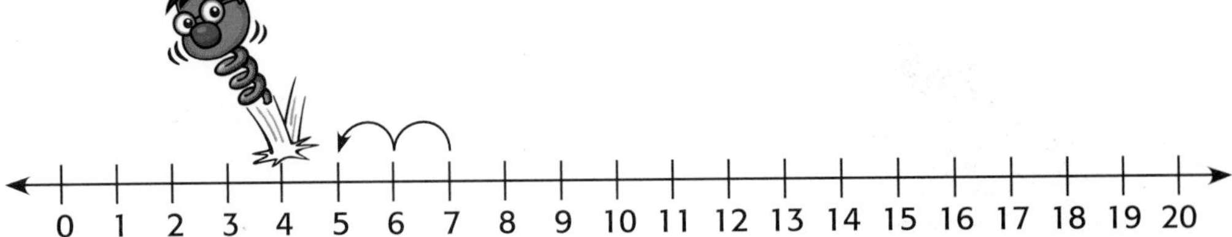

Review subtraction facts. Find each difference. You may use the number line to help.

26. 7 − 2	**27.** 6 − 4	**28.** 8 − 7	**29.** 11 − 3	**30.** 10 − 5
31. 13 − 6	**32.** 10 − 7	**33.** 14 − 7	**34.** 15 − 9	**35.** 13 − 8
36. 10 − 2	**37.** 17 − 8	**38.** 16 − 9	**39.** 15 − 7	**40.** 9 − 9
41. 7 − 6	**42.** 14 − 5	**43.** 18 − 9	**44.** 12 − 4	**45.** 13 − 5
46. 11 − 8	**47.** 12 − 6	**48.** 14 − 8	**49.** 11 − 4	**50.** 16 − 8

Review skip counting. Copy and complete each pattern.

51. 6, 8, 10, ■, ■

52. 40, 50, 60, ■, ■

53. 35, 40, 45, ■, ■

54. 18, 15, 12, ■, ■

Complete the pattern.

55.  __ __

56. 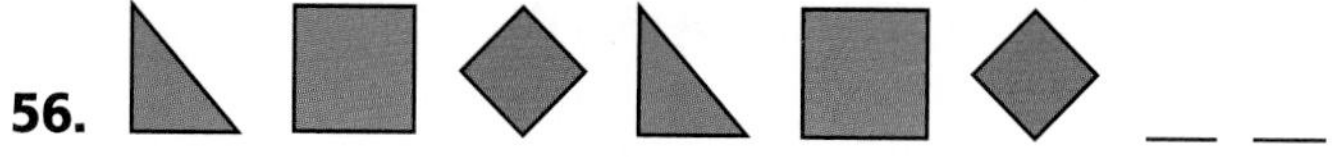 __ __

Add and subtract to solve the riddle. Match each letter to its answer in the blank below. Some of the letters are not used.

57. $3 + 2$	[S]	**58.** $12 - 5$	[A]	**59.** $5 + 4$	[C]
60. $10 - 8$	[L]	**61.** $9 + 9$	[O]	**62.** $15 - 5$	[D]
63. $5 + 9$	[O]	**64.** $16 - 7$	[R]	**65.** $7 + 8$	[N]
66. $7 + 5$	[V]	**67.** $3 + 8$	[N]	**68.** $10 - 9$	[I]
69. $3 + 3$	[I]	**70.** $9 - 6$	[I]	**71.** $9 + 8$	[G]

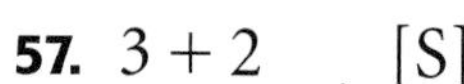

2 14 11 17

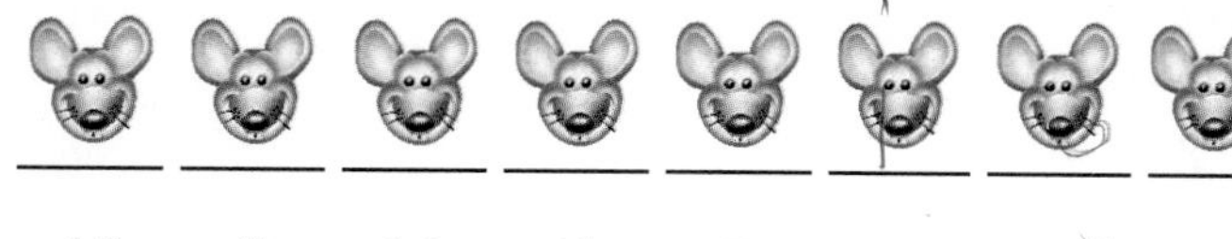

10 3 12 6 5 1 18 15

PRACTICE AND APPLY

Problem Solving

Introduction to Strategies

Problem Solving Strategies

- Use Objects/Act It Out
- Draw a Picture
- Look for a Pattern
- Guess and Check
- Use Logical Reasoning
- Make an Organized List
- Make a Table
- Solve a Simpler Problem
- Work Backward

Choose a Tool

There are many ways to solve a math problem. One way is to think of facts as if they are clues in a mystery. Using different ways or **strategies** to organize the clues can help you see patterns.

A biologist thinks she has discovered a new kind of fast-growing plant. She looks for a pattern in how the plant grows. How many stems will grow by the fourth week?

Ann and Victor solve the problem in different ways.

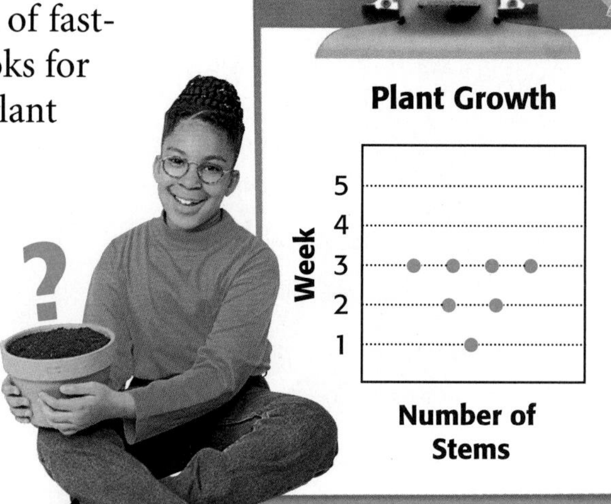

Draw a Picture and Look for a Pattern

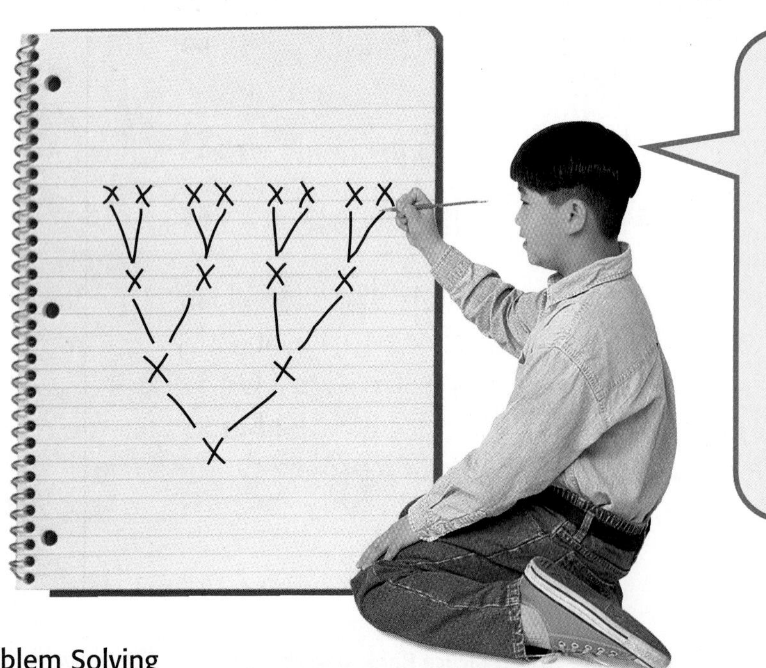

I'll draw an X to show the number of stems there are each week.

Each week there are two times as many stems. So by the fourth week, there will be 8 stems.

I'll make a table.

On the second week, 1 stem is added.

On the third week, 2 stems are added.

So, I think 4 more stems will be added on the fourth week. There will be 8 stems by the fourth week.

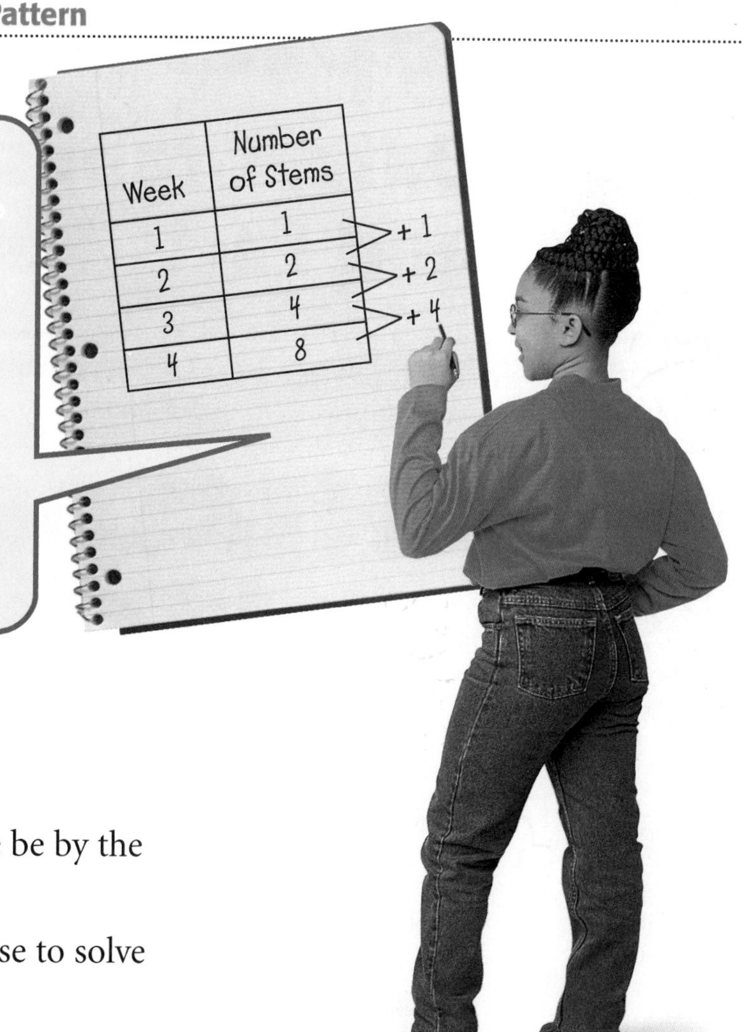

Week	Number of Stems
1	1
2	2
3	4
4	8

Talk About It

1. How many stems will there be by the fifth week?
2. What strategy would you use to solve this problem? Why?

Try These

Use any strategy to solve.

1. The library charges 1 cent for the first day a book is late. It charges 3 cents the second day, 6 cents the third day, 9 cents the fourth day, and so on. How much will Sarah have to pay if she returns her book 5 days late?
2. Sam likes collecting. Every time he collects 10 insect stickers, he can send in for a spider sticker. If Sam has 6 spider stickers already, how many insect stickers has he sent in?
3. **Journal** Have you ever kept a journal about what you do every day? You can also keep a journal about math. Start by writing about your favorite kinds of math problems. Or, write about what you would like to learn this year. Remember to check your journal throughout the year to see your progress!

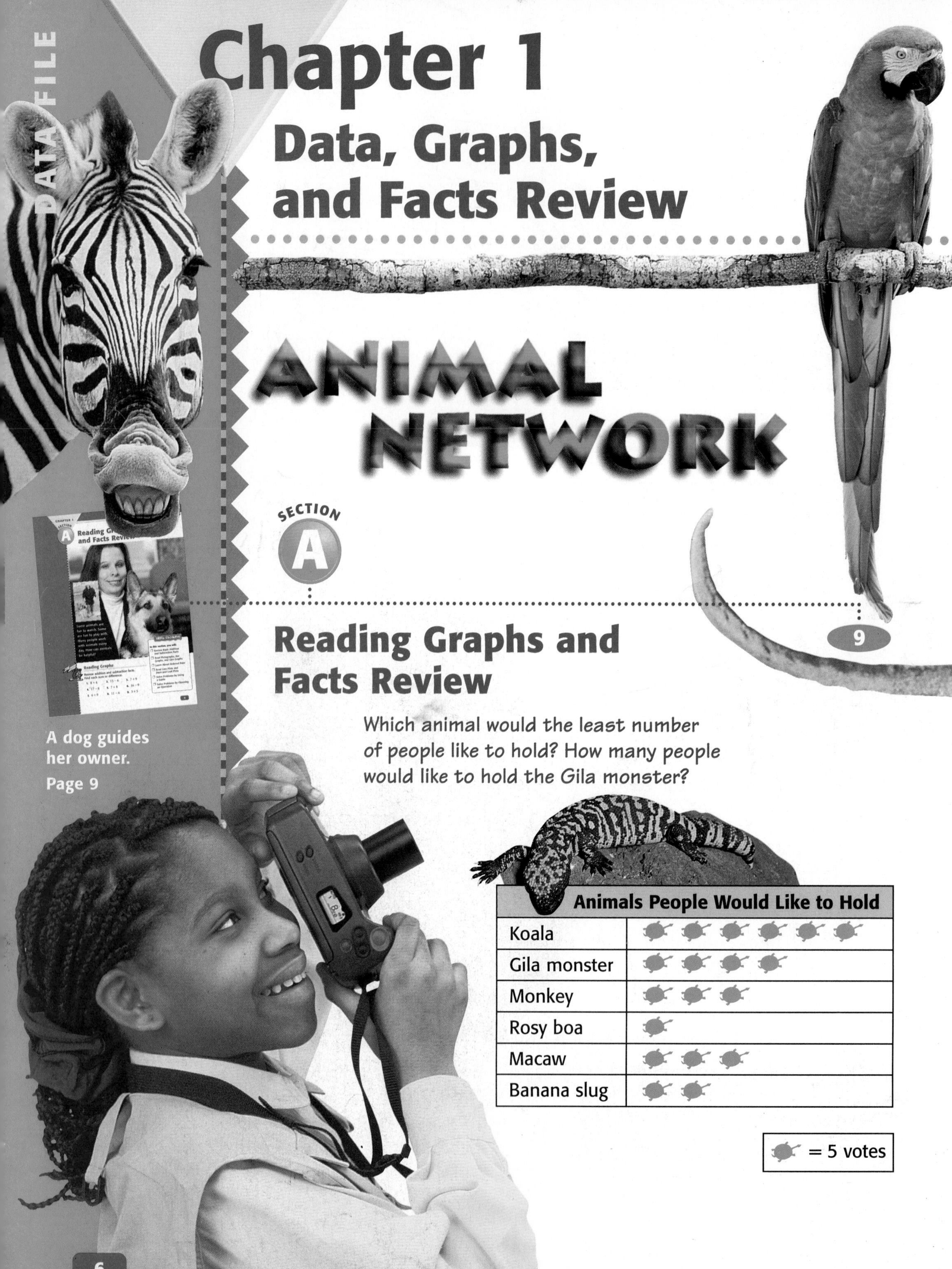

Chapter 1

Data, Graphs, and Facts Review

ANIMAL NETWORK

SECTION A

Reading Graphs and Facts Review

9

Which animal would the least number of people like to hold? How many people would like to hold the Gila monster?

Animals People Would Like to Hold	
Koala	🐢🐢🐢🐢🐢🐢
Gila monster	🐢🐢🐢🐢
Monkey	🐢🐢🐢
Rosy boa	🐢
Macaw	🐢🐢🐢
Banana slug	🐢🐢

🐢 = 5 votes

A dog guides her owner.

Page 9

Making Graphs, Describing Data, and Facts Review

25

Each tally mark stands for one kangaroo.
How many kangaroos jumped 39 feet?

Distance Jumped (ft)	Number of Kangaroos
36	𝍷
37	𝍷𝍷𝍷𝍷
38	𝍸 𝍷
39	𝍸 𝍷𝍷𝍷
40	𝍸 𝍷
41	𝍷𝍷𝍷𝍷
42	𝍷

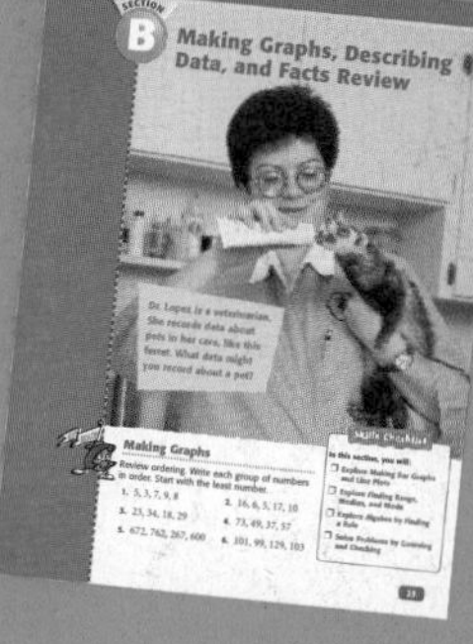

Dr. Lopez at work
Page 25

Surfing the World Wide Web!

Choose your favorite animal from the list at **www.mathsurf.com/4/ch1**. Compare your choice with other students' choices. Make a graph of the data.

TEAM PROJECT
ANIMAL calendar

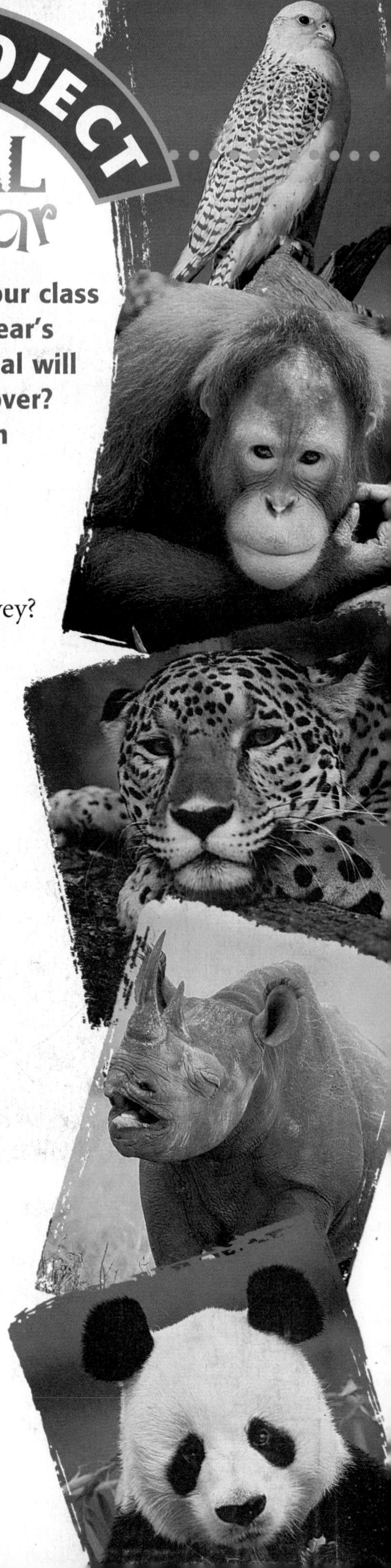

Materials
colored markers

A wildlife club has asked your class to design a cover for next year's animal calendar. What animal will your class choose for the cover? Take a class survey and then design a cover.

Make a Plan

- What questions will you ask in your survey?
- Will you give people a list of animals to choose from?

Carry It Out

1. Write your questions. Then survey your class.
2. Use the data you collect to figure out which animal to put on the cover.
3. Design your calendar cover.

Talk About It

- How many animals did you have to choose from?
- Was it easy to decide which animal to put on the cover? Explain.

Present the Project

- Display your team's calendar cover. Did every team choose the same animal? Why or why not?

CHAPTER 1
SECTION
A

Reading Graphs and Facts Review

Some animals are fun to watch. Some are fun to play with. Many people work with animals every day. How can animals be helpful?

Skills Checklist

In this section, you will:

- ❏ Review Basic Addition and Subtraction Facts
- ❏ Read Pictographs, Bar Graphs, and Line Graphs
- ❏ Learn About Ordered Pairs
- ❏ Read Line Plots and Stem-and-Leaf Plots
- ❏ Solve Problems by Using a Guide
- ❏ Solve Problems by Choosing an Operation

Reading Graphs

Review addition and subtraction facts. Find each sum or difference.

1. $8 + 4$ **2.** $15 - 6$ **3.** $7 + 9$

4. $17 - 8$ **5.** $7 + 8$ **6.** $16 - 9$

7. $6 + 9$ **8.** $11 - 6$ **9.** $3 + 5$

Pictographs and Bar Graphs

You Will Learn
how to read pictographs and bar graphs

Vocabulary

pictograph
a graph that uses pictures or symbols to show data

bar graph
a graph that uses bars to show data

key
part of a pictograph that tells what quantity each symbol stands for

scale
numbers that show the units used on a graph

Did You Know?
A female sea horse lays about 200 eggs at one time. The "nest" is a pouch on the male sea horse.

Learn

Some reptiles and amphibians lay just a few eggs at one time. Others lay hundreds of eggs.

Pictographs and **bar graphs** can help you compare data.

Marbled salamander

Example

This pictograph helps you compare the numbers of eggs that some animals lay. How many eggs does a frog lay?

Eggs Laid by Animals	
Python	● ● ◐
Turtle	● ● ● ● ● ● ● ● ● ●
Frog	● ● ● ● ● ●
Salamander	● ● ● ● ● ● ◐

Each symbol stands for 10 eggs.
So, a frog lays 60 eggs.

Key 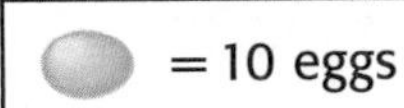 = 10 eggs

This bar graph compares the life spans of some animals. Which animal lives 40 years?

The bar for the Asian elephant reaches 40 on the **scale.** So, the Asian elephant lives 40 years.

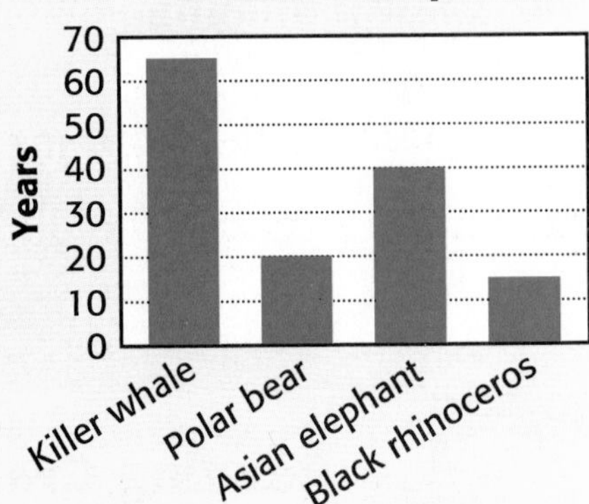

Talk About It

1. What does ◐ stand for in the pictograph?
2. How might a pictograph show the data in the graph?

Check

Use the graphs on page 10 for **1** and **2**.

1. Which animals lay more than 30 eggs?

2. Which animals live longer than 35 years?

3. Reasoning Suppose each  stands for 100 ants.

a. Draw a picture to show 200 ants.

b. Draw a picture to show 50 ants.

Practice

Skills and Reasoning

Use the bar graph of bird flight speeds for **4–6**.

Bird Flight Speeds

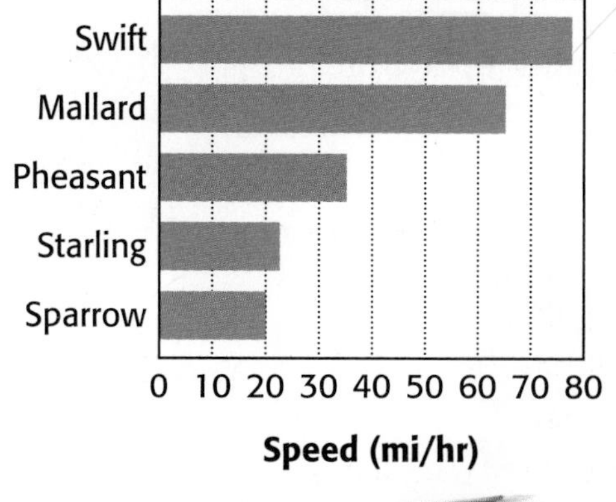

4. Which birds are faster than the pheasant?

5. How fast does the starling fly?

6. Why do you think the graph shows the birds from fastest to slowest?

Using Data Use the Data File on page 6 for **7–10.**

7. Which animals got 15 votes?

8. How many people voted?

9. How many people wanted to hold a koala?

10. How many symbols would be needed to show 25 votes?

Problem Solving and Applications

11. Using Data Use the pictograph on page 10. List the animals in order by the number of eggs laid. Start with the fewest eggs.

12. Critical Thinking Use the *Did You Know?* and pictograph on page 10. If you add the sea horse egg data to the graph, how many eggs would you draw?

13. What If You don't have the scale from the bar graph on page 10. What data could you still get from the graph?

Mixed Review: Basic Facts

STAY SHARP!

Add or subtract.

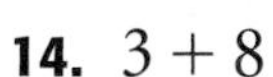

14. 3 + 8 **15.** 5 + 7 **16.** 10 − 1 **17.** 12 − 4 **18.** 6 + 7

19. 12 − 7 **20.** 5 + 9 **21.** 13 − 4 **22.** 7 + 8 **23.** 15 − 6

Chapter 1
Lesson
2

Ordered Pairs

You Will Learn
how to read points as ordered pairs on a coordinate grid

Vocabulary

coordinate grid
a graph used to locate points

ordered pair
a number pair that names a point on a coordinate grid

Learn

You can follow dinosaur tracks and find dinosaur fossils near Moab, Utah.

A **coordinate grid** helps you locate points.

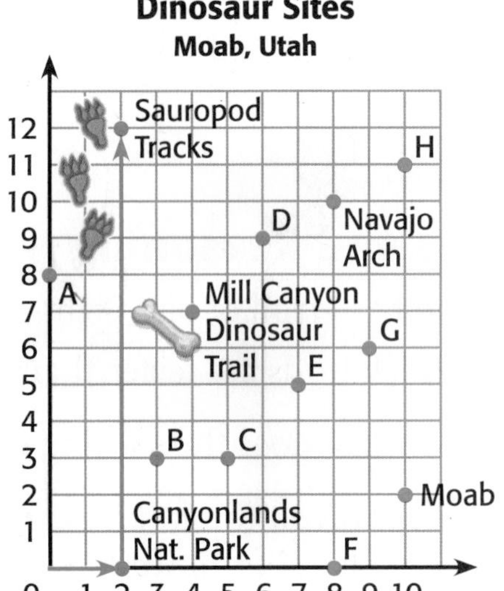

You can locate a point using an **ordered pair**.

Did You Know?
Tyrannosaurus rex, one of the largest dinosaurs, had teeth that were 7 inches long.

Example 1

What ordered pair names where the Sauropod tracks are located?

The first number in the ordered pair shows how far to the right of 0 a point is.

The second number shows how far up from 0 a point is.

So, the Sauropod tracks are located at (2,12).

You can name a point using an ordered pair.

Example 2

What point does the ordered pair (4, 7) name?

The ordered pair names the point for the Mill Canyon Dinosaur Trail.

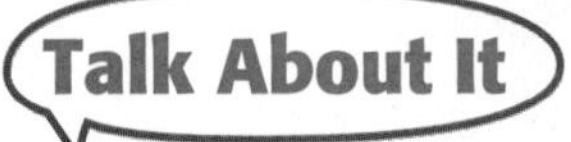

Do the ordered pairs (8, 2) and (2, 8) name the same point? Explain.

Check

Use the coordinate grid on page 12. Name the ordered pair for each point.

1. A **2.** B **3.** H **4.** E

Give the letter of the point named by each.

5. (9, 6) **6.** (5, 3) **7.** (6, 9) **8.** (8, 0)

9. Reasoning Where is the point (0, 0) located on a grid?

Practice

Skills and Reasoning

Use this coordinate grid. Name the ordered pair for each point.

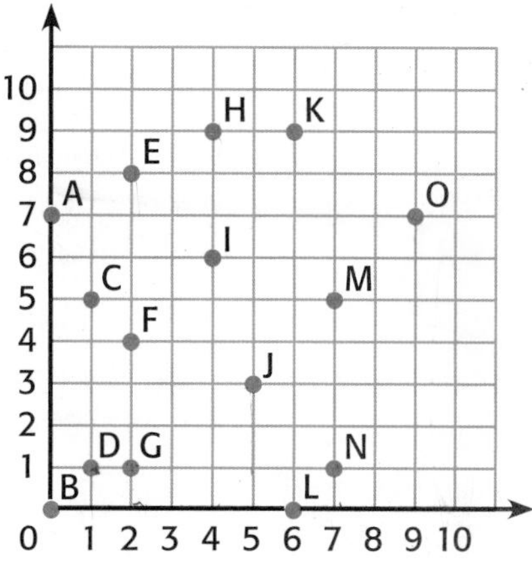

10. A **11.** H **12.** E **13.** J **14.** B

Give the letter of the point named by each.

15. (1, 5) **16.** (6, 9) **17.** (7, 1)

18. (9, 7) **19.** (2, 1) **20.** (6, 0)

21. Salina gave (1, 7) as the ordered pair for point N. What was her mistake?

22. Suppose you can locate a point on a coordinate grid by only moving up 4. What is the ordered pair for this point?

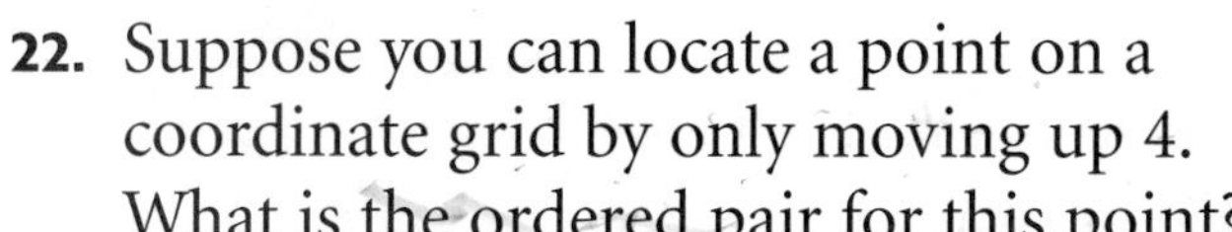

Problem Solving and Applications

23. Geometry Readiness Use grid paper to locate these points on a coordinate grid. Connect them in order: (2, 1), (2, 4), (5, 4), (5, 1), and back to (2, 1). What shape do they make?

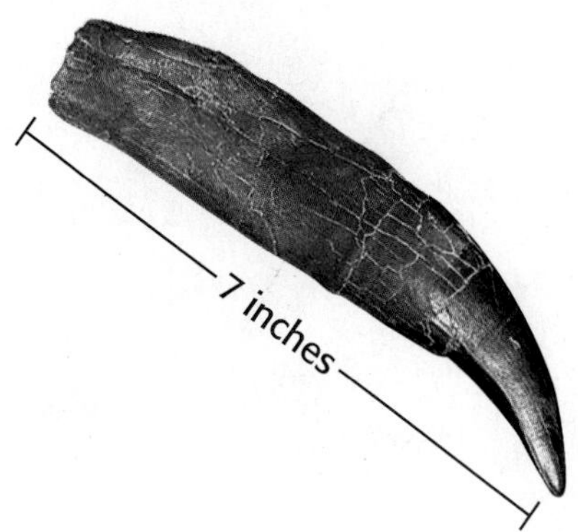

24. Using Data Use the data from the *Did You Know?* on page 12. Find something in your classroom that is about as long as a tooth of the *Tyrannosaurus rex.*

Mixed Review: Basic Facts

STAY SHARP!

Find each sum or difference.

25. $9 - 3$ **26.** $5 + 8$ **27.** $16 - 9$ **28.** $6 + 6$ **29.** $15 - 8$

30. $11 - 4$ **31.** $8 + 9$ **32.** $13 - 6$ **33.** $2 + 4$ **34.** $7 + 5$

Reading Line Graphs

You Will Learn
how to read line graphs

Vocabulary
line graph
a graph that connects points to show how data change over time

Remember
Points are named by ordered pairs.

Learn

Some people have dogs as pets. Other people use specially trained dogs, such as guide dogs, to help make their lives easier.

You can use a **line graph** to show how data changes over time.

About how many Seeing Eye® dogs were given to owners by The Seeing Eye, Inc. in 1994?

Example

Find the point on the graph that is directly above 1994.

The point is at about 280.

Its ordered pair is about (1994, 280).

So, about 280 Seeing Eye dogs were given to owners in 1994.

Dogs Given to Owners by
The Seeing Eye, Inc., Morristown, NJ

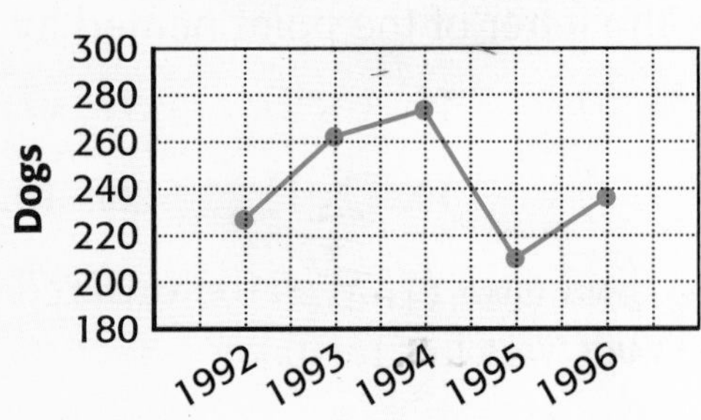

Years

Michelle Drolet and her Seeing Eye dog, Julip, live in Morristown, New Jersey.

Talk About It

Does it make sense to use the graph to predict the number of dogs that will be given to owners in the year 2000? Explain.

Check

Use the line graph above to answer **1** and **2.**

1. About how many Seeing Eye dogs were given to owners in 1996?

2. **Reasoning** What does the graph show happened between 1994 and 1995? What may have caused this change?

Practice

Skills and Reasoning

Science Use the line graph to answer **3–6.**

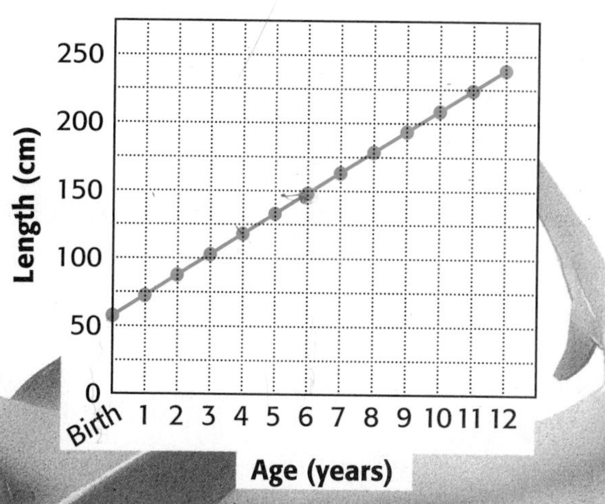

3. What is the length of a 6-year-old lemon shark?
4. Estimate the age of a 90-cm shark.
5. About how long does a lemon shark measure at birth?
6. Do you think a 24-year-old shark will be twice as long as a 12-year-old shark? Explain.

A lemon shark grows about 15 cm each year until fully grown.

Problem Solving and Applications

Using Data Use the line graph to answer **7** and **8.**

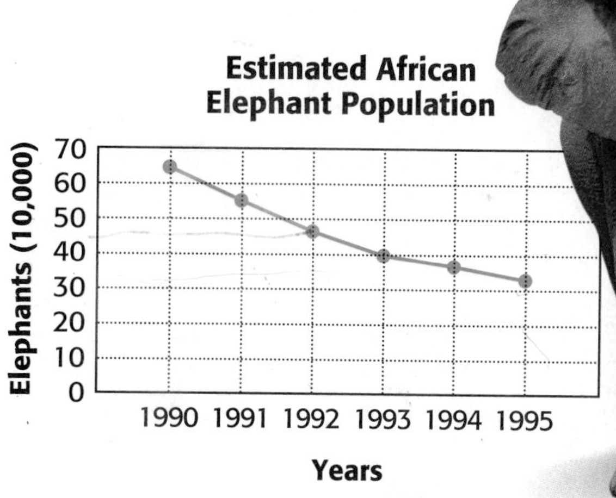

7. **Estimation** By which year was the elephant population about half as many as 1990?
8. **Reasoning** The African elephant was added to the list of protected animals in 1989. Does the graph show this protection is helping save the elephants? Explain.

9. **Journal** Explain how a line graph shows change over time.

Mixed Review: Basic Facts

Add or subtract.

10. 5 + 6	**11.** 14 − 8	**12.** 4 + 9	**13.** 16 − 7	**14.** 12 − 3
15. 8 + 8	**16.** 10 − 3	**17.** 15 − 9	**18.** 4 + 7	**19.** 16 − 9
20. 12 − 5	**21.** 9 + 9	**22.** 8 + 3	**23.** 14 − 5	**24.** 8 + 6
25. 6 − 2	**26.** 7 + 7	**27.** 5 − 4	**28.** 9 + 6	**29.** 7 − 5

Skills Practice Bank, page 559, Set 2

Reading Line Plots

You Will Learn
how to read line plots

Vocabulary

line plot
a graph that shows data along a number line

cluster
a group of data that appear often on a line plot

Learn

When is a banana not a banana? When it's a banana slug! Angela and her friends measure some slugs. Then they compare the lengths.

A **line plot** shows data along a number line. Data that appear often may form a **cluster**.

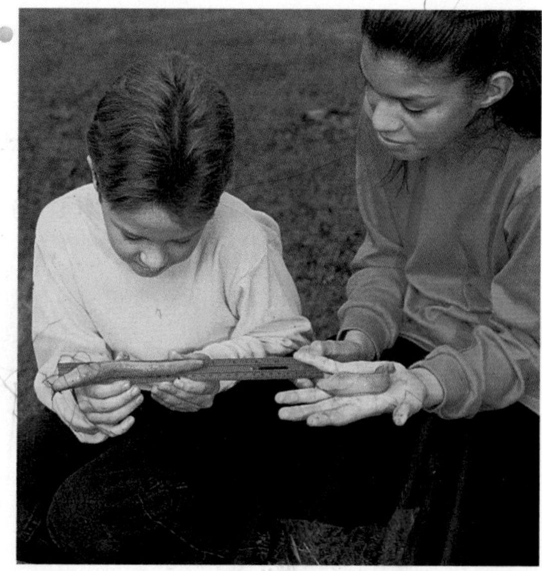

Banana slugs, found in the forests of western North America, can be very large.

Did You Know?
Banana slugs are the largest American slugs. European slugs can reach a length of 30 cm.

Example

Read the line plot.

X stands for 1 banana slug.
24 slugs were measured.

The longest banana slug is 21 cm.

The most common length for the slugs is 17 cm.

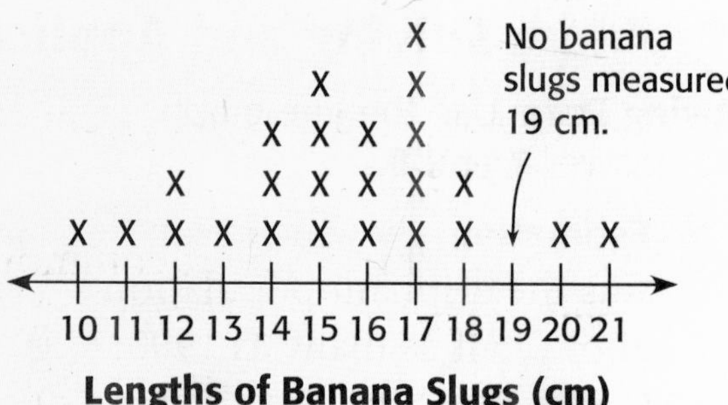

Talk About It

Do the data for lengths of banana slugs form any clusters? Explain.

Check

Use the line plot above to answer **1–3.**

1. How long is the shortest banana slug?
2. What is the difference in length between the longest and shortest banana slugs?
3. **Reasoning** Suppose you measured another banana slug. What would you expect the length to be?

Practice

Skills and Reasoning

Use the Great Gray Slug line plot for **4–8.**

4. What is the difference between the shortest and longest lengths?

5. What is the most common length?

6. Where do the data on this line plot form a cluster?

7. How many slugs measured 7 cm?

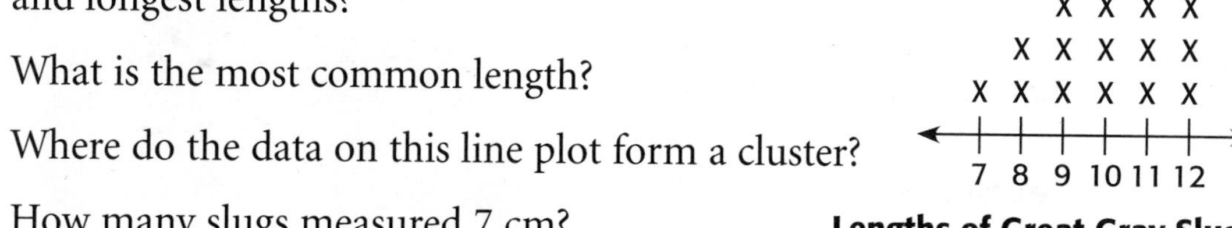

Lengths of Great Gray Slugs (cm)

8. Suppose you found a great gray slug. Would you expect the length to be less than 7 cm or more than 9 cm? Why?

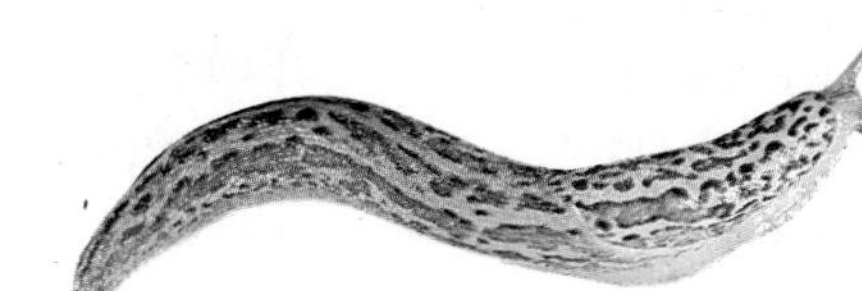

Problem Solving and Applications

Use this line plot for **9–12.**

9. How many slugs crawled 19 cm in 1 minute?

10. How many slugs crawled 11 cm in 1 minute?

11. What were the two most common lengths crawled?

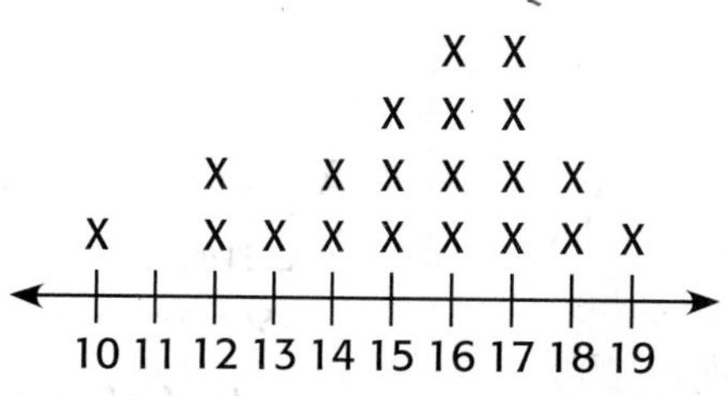

Distances Banana Slugs Crawled (cm/min)

12. Critical Thinking A great gray slug can crawl about four times as fast as a banana slug. What is the shortest distance you would expect a great gray slug to crawl in one minute?

13. Using Data Use the data from the *Did You Know?* and the line plot on page 16. About how much longer is a European slug than the longest banana slug?

Mixed Review: Basic Facts

Find each sum or difference.

14. $9 + 6$	**15.** $5 + 8$	**16.** $9 + 2$	**17.** $3 + 8$	**18.** $8 + 4$
19. $14 - 6$	**20.** $13 - 6$	**21.** $12 - 6$	**22.** $11 - 6$	**23.** $10 - 6$
24. $9 + 9$	**25.** $17 - 9$	**26.** $9 + 7$	**27.** $15 - 9$	**28.** $9 + 5$
29. $8 + 6$	**30.** $16 - 7$	**31.** $10 - 3$	**32.** $13 - 5$	**33.** $4 + 7$
34. $1 + 7$	**35.** $9 - 9$	**36.** $8 + 5$	**37.** $11 - 4$	**38.** $6 + 0$

Reading Stem-and-Leaf Plots

You Will Learn
how to read stem-and-leaf plots

Vocabulary

stem-and-leaf plot
a graph that uses place value to organize data

stem
shows the tens digit of a number

leaf
shows the ones digit of a number

Remember
A two-digit number has a tens digit and a ones digit.

Tens digit ↓ 6   Ones digit ↓ 8

Learn

Have you ever heard anyone say, "That's a whale of a fish"? Whales are very large, but they are mammals, not fish.

You can use a **stem-and-leaf plot** to organize and compare data.

How much longer is the longest whale than the shortest?

Lengths of Some Species of Whales (ft)

Stem	Leaf	
2	0	
3	3	
4		
5	0 0 8	←Shows 50, 50, and 58 ft.
6	5 2 0	←Shows 65, 62, and 60 ft.
7		
8	2	

In the stem-and-leaf plot, 82 is the greatest number, and 20 is the least.
$82 - 20 = 62$
So, the longest whale is 62 ft longer than the shortest whale.

Why are there no leaves for the stems 4 and 7?

Check

Use the stem-and-leaf plot above to answer **1** and **2.**

1. What is the length of the next-to-shortest whale?
2. **Reasoning** The shortest whale shown is a pygmy right whale. A full-size right whale is 40 ft longer. How would you show the length of a full-size right whale in the stem-and-leaf plot?

Practice

Skills and Reasoning

Science Use this stem-and-leaf plot for **3–5.**

3. What is the difference between the greatest weight of a raccoon and the least weight?

4. How many raccoons weighed less than 30 lb? More than 30 lb?

5. Why might you want to redo the leaf part of your graph and put the leaves in each row in order from least to greatest?

Raccoon Weights (lb)

Stem	Leaf
0	9 6 9
1	9 5 5 7 0
2	6 1 0 6 9
3	4 8 9 3 8 8
4	3 4 3 2 7 3 2

Problem Solving and Applications

Science A group of whales swimming together is called a *school* or *pod.* Use this stem-and-leaf plot to answer **6–9.**

Number of Whales in Schools

Stem	Leaf
1	8 9 8
2	2 5 4 2 0 1 5 5 8 9 2 0 1 4 5 9 8 7 6
3	3 4 5 3 5 3 6 2 6 1 7 8 9 0 7
4	2 5 0 2

6. Which is greater: The number of schools with fewer than 20 whales or the number of schools with 40 or more whales?

7. How many schools have 25 whales?

8. How many schools have between 23 and 33 whales?

9. What If You want to show the data about whales in a bar graph. From the stem-and-leaf plot, how can you tell which bar would be the longest? Explain.

Mixed Review: Basic Facts

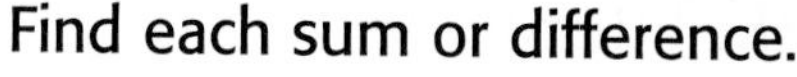

Find each sum or difference.

10. $16 - 9$ **11.** $5 + 8$ **12.** $7 + 8$ **13.** $12 - 4$ **14.** $5 + 7$

15. $9 + 8$ **16.** $18 - 9$ **17.** $17 - 8$ **18.** $16 - 7$ **19.** $8 + 3$

20. $11 - 7$ **21.** $6 + 8$ **22.** $5 + 4$ **23.** $15 - 9$ **24.** $10 - 6$

Skills Practice Bank, page 559, Set 3

Problem Solving

Analyze Word Problems: Introduction to Problem Solving Guide

You Will Learn
how using a guide can help you solve problems

Reading Tip
Read the scale along the bottom of the graph to find the years in the problem.

Learn

Be a problem solver! Using a guide can help you solve any problem.

Were there more new listings of endangered and threatened species in 1991 than in 1990?

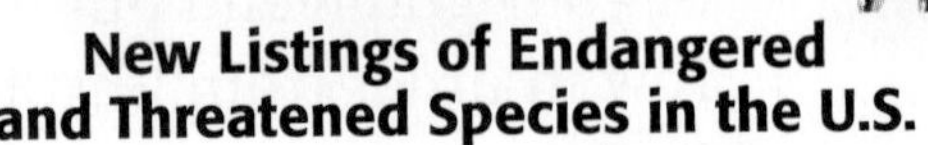

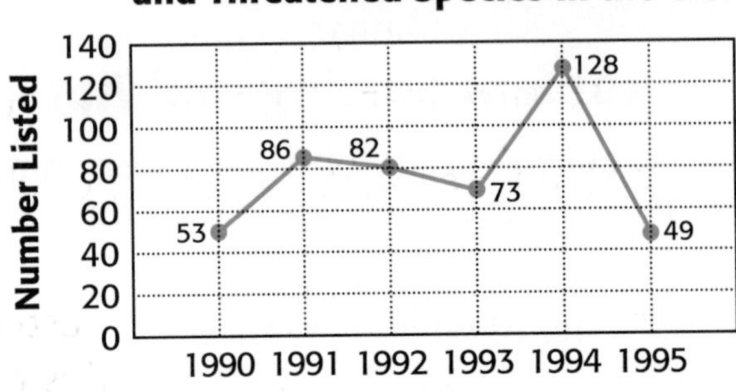

Work Together

▶ **Understand**	What do you know?	There were 53 new listings in 1990 and 86 new listings in 1991.
	What do you need to find?	Were there more new listings in 1991 than in 1990?
▶ **Plan**	Decide how you will find the answer.	You need to compare 86 to 53.
▶ **Solve**	Find the answer. Write your answer.	86 is greater than 53, so there were more new listings in 1991 than in 1990.
▶ **Look Back**	Check to see if your answer makes sense.	Look at the line graph. The point for 1991 is higher than the one for 1990.

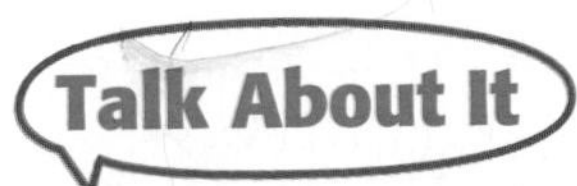

How did the steps in the guide help you solve the problem?

Check

Use the graph on page 20. Plan how you will solve the problem. Then solve.

1. **a.** Which year had the most new listings for endangered and threatened species?
   b. How many listings were in that year?

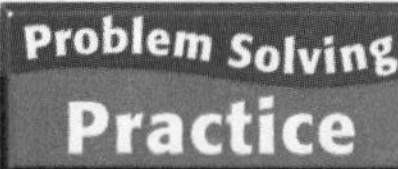

Problem Solving Practice

Problem Solving Strategies

- Use Objects/Act It Out
- Draw a Picture
- Look for a Pattern
- Guess and Check
- Use Logical Reasoning
- Make an Organized List
- Make a Table
- Solve a Simpler Problem
- Work Backward

Choose a Tool

Use the graph on page 20 for **2–4.** Plan how you will solve each problem. Then solve.

2. **a.** Which year had the fewest new listings for endangered and threatened species?
   b. How many listings were in that year?
3. Find the total number of new listings from 1990 to 1995.
4. In 1996, there were 92 new listings of endangered and threatened species. Is this more or less than the number of new listings in 1995?

Using Data Use the bar graph to answer **5** and **6.**

5. **Science** San Francisco garter snakes are an endangered species. How much longer is the San Francisco garter snake than the Florida pygmy rattlesnake?
6. What is the difference in length between the San Francisco garter snake and the Texas blind snake?

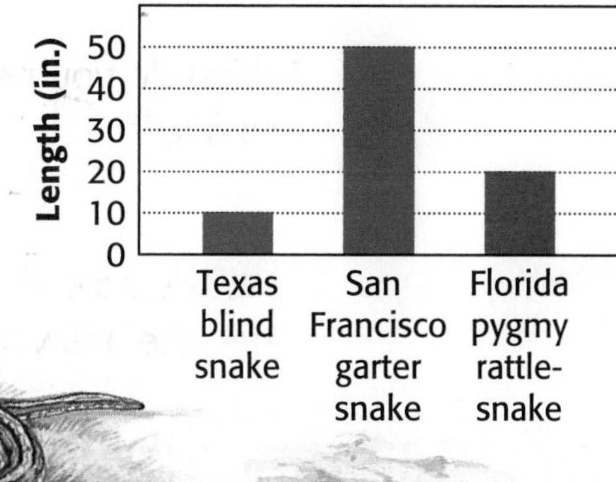

Florida pygmy rattlesnake San Francisco garter snake Texas blind snake

7. **Journal** Use data from the Data File on page 6 to write a problem about an animal. Explain the steps you might use to solve the problem.

Chapter 1 Lesson 7

Problem Solving

Analyze Word Problems: Choose an Operation

You Will Learn
how to choose the operation needed to solve a problem

Learn

The typical life span of a wild red fox is 7 years. A pet dog lives about 5 years longer. What is the typical life span of a dog?

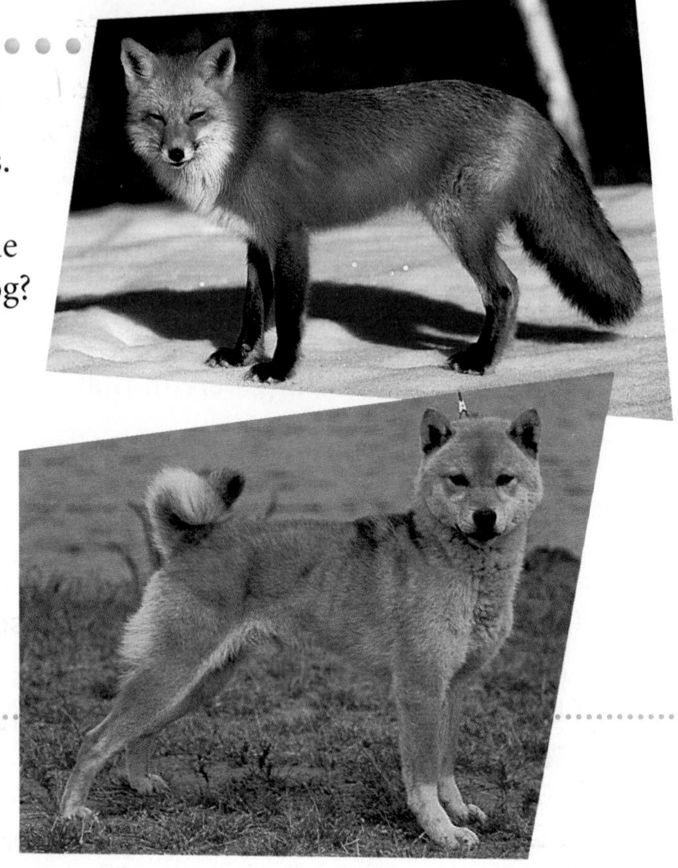

Red foxes are found in Asia, Europe, and northern North America.

A Shiba Inu dog looks like a fox.

Work Together

Understand What do you know?
What do you need to find out?

Plan Decide what operation you will use. You can add the number of years a fox lives and the number of years longer a dog lives.

Solve Write the number sentence. $7 + 5 = 12$
Find the answer. The typical life span of a dog is 12 years.

Look Back How can you check your answer?

Talk About It

How can you tell whether you need to add or subtract?

Check

Which number sentence would you use to solve? Explain.

1. The typical life span of a lion is 15 years. This is 8 years longer than the life span of a kangaroo. How long does a kangaroo usually live?

   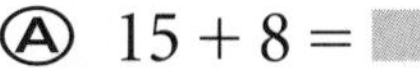

   Ⓐ $15 + 8 = \blacksquare$ Ⓑ $15 - 8 = \blacksquare$

2. **Science** A wolf is one of the largest members of the dog family. The typical weight of a wolf is about 90 pounds. A gray fox typically weighs about 10 pounds. How much more does a wolf weigh than a fox?

   Ⓐ $90 + 10 = \blacksquare$ Ⓑ $90 - 10 = \blacksquare$

Wolves live in family groups called *packs*.

PROBLEM SOLVING PRACTICE

Problem Solving Practice

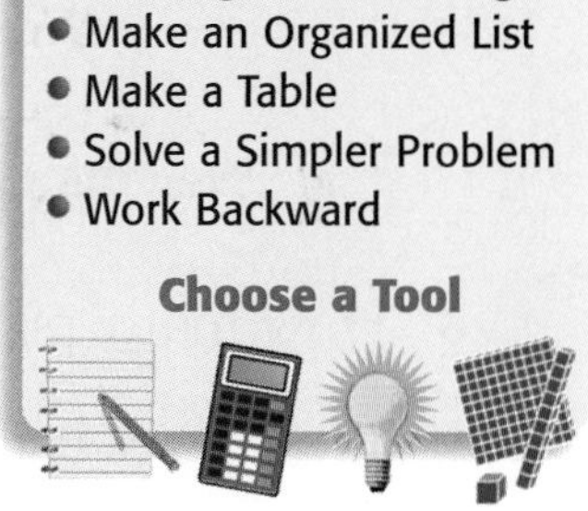

Which number sentence would you use to solve? Explain.

3. **Money** A dog show costs \$6 for adults and \$4 for children. How much will it cost for one of each?

   Ⓐ $\$6 + \$4 = \blacksquare$ Ⓑ $\$6 - \$4 = \blacksquare$

4. **Science** The gray fox is the only member of the dog family that often climbs trees. If a gray fox climbs 8 feet up a tree, and then climbs another 3 feet, how many feet has it climbed in all?

   Ⓐ $8 + 3 = \blacksquare$ Ⓑ $8 - 3 = \blacksquare$

Write which operation you would use. Then solve.

5. **Science** Fennecs, the smallest kind of foxes, are about 16 inches long. A red fox is about 25 inches long. What is the difference in length between a fennec and a red fox?

6. On Saturday, there were 15 dogs at the city animal shelter. If 9 were adopted, how many were left?

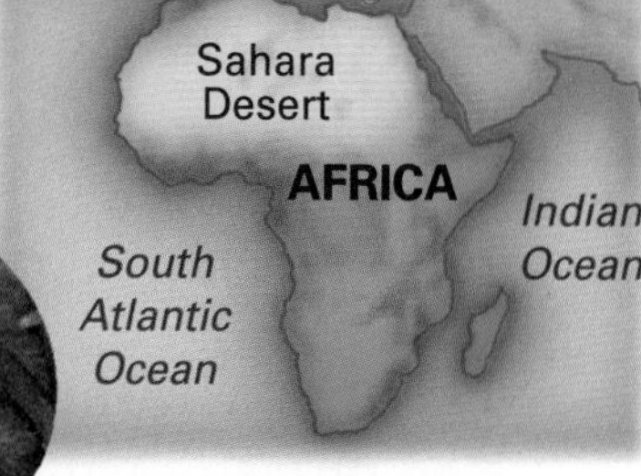

Fennecs live in the Sahara Desert in Africa.

7. **Journal** Write a problem that you could solve using $17 - 9 = 8$.

SECTION A

Review and Practice

(Lesson 1) Use the bar graph to answer **1–3.**

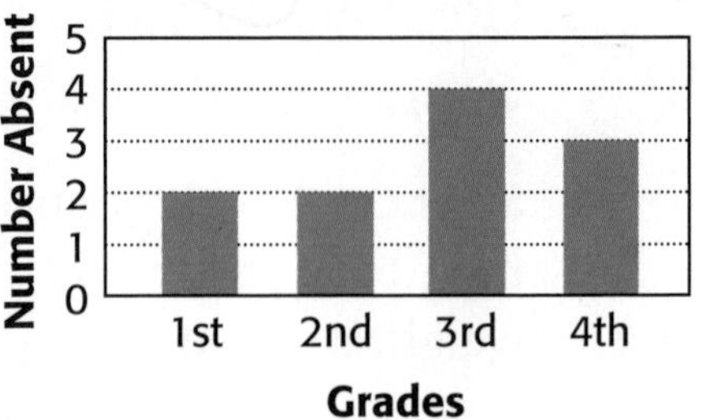

1. How many 4th graders were absent?
2. How many grades are shown in the graph?
3. Which grade had the greatest number of absent students?

(Lessons 2 and 3) Use the line graph to answer **4** and **5.**

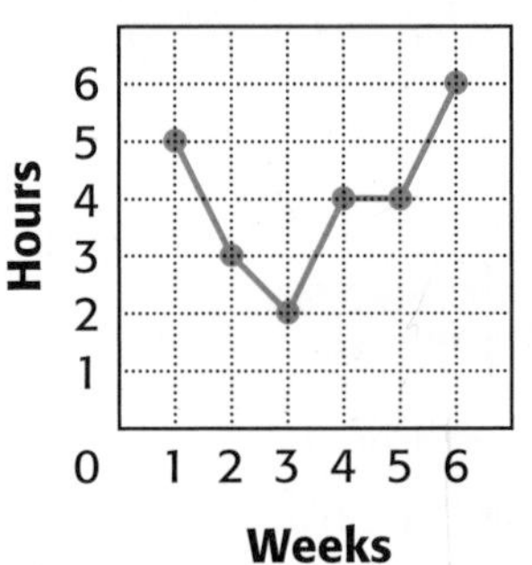

4. How many hours did Krista volunteer at the animal shelter in week 3?
5. **Reasoning** What does the ordered pair (5, 4) stand for?

(Lesson 4) Use the line plot to answer **6–8.**

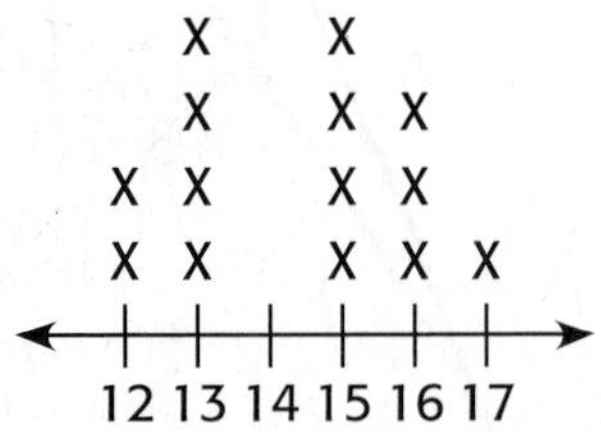

Weights of Puppies (lb)

6. How many puppies weighed 16 lb?
7. What does it mean that there is no **X** above 14?
8. What is the difference in weight between the lightest puppies and the heaviest puppy?

(Lessons 6 and 7) Write which operation you would use. Then solve.

9. If a dog eats 3 cups of dry food a day, how much does it eat in 5 days?

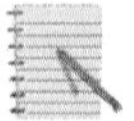

10. **Journal** Use the graphs on this page. Which graph helps you compare data? Which graph shows how data change over time? Explain.

Skills Checklist

In this section, you have:

- **Reviewed Basic Addition and Subtraction Facts**
- **Read Pictographs, Bar Graphs, and Line Graphs**
- **Learned About Ordered Pairs**
- **Read Line Plots and Stem-and-Leaf Plots**
- **Solved Problems by Using a Guide**
- **Solved Problems by Choosing an Operation**

REVIEW AND PRACTICE

CHAPTER 1

SECTION

B Making Graphs, Describing Data, and Facts Review

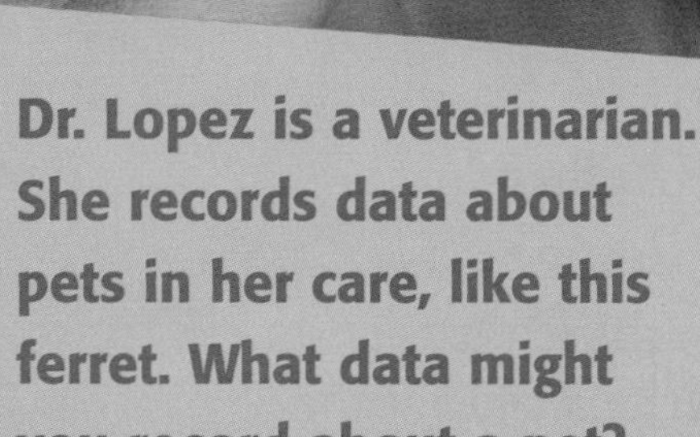

Dr. Lopez is a veterinarian. She records data about pets in her care, like this ferret. What data might you record about a pet?

Skills Checklist

In this section, you will:

- ❒ Explore Making Bar Graphs and Line Plots
- ❒ Explore Finding Range, Median, and Mode
- ❒ Explore Algebra by Finding a Rule
- ❒ Solve Problems by Guessing and Checking

GET READY!

Making Graphs

Review ordering. Write each group of numbers in order. Start with the least number.

1. 5, 3, 7, 9, 8

2. 16, 6, 5, 17, 10

3. 23, 34, 18, 29

4. 73, 49, 37, 57

5. 672, 762, 267, 600

6. 101, 99, 129, 103

Exploring Making Bar Graphs

Problem Solving Connection
- Make a Table
- Draw a Picture

Materials
grid paper

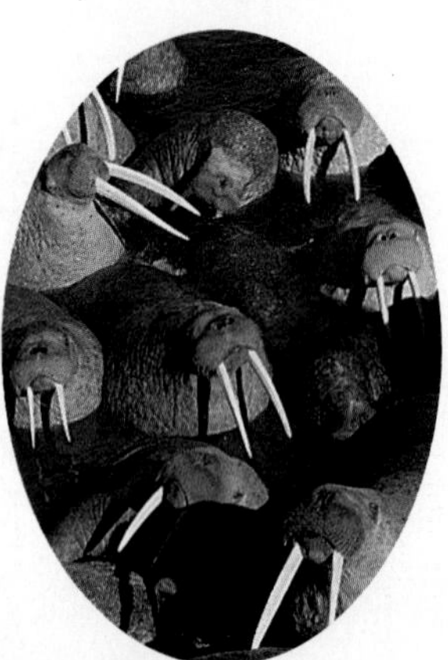

On land, a group of walruses is called a *rookery.* In water, it's called a *herd.*

Explore

You can learn a lot from teeth! The number of teeth can help classify an animal.

Work Together

Make a bar graph to compare the number of teeth for different animals. Use the data in the table.

Animal	Teeth
Dog	42
Human	32
Hyena	34
Walrus	18

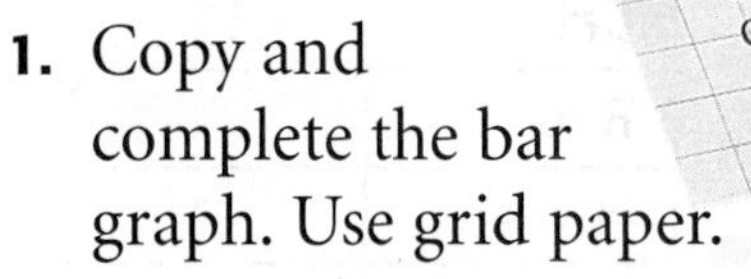

1. Copy and complete the bar graph. Use grid paper.
   a. Write a title across the top of your graph.
   b. Write a label on the left side of the graph. Write a label at the bottom for each bar.
   c. Complete the scale. Count by fives.
   d. Draw a bar for each animal. Use the scale to make each bar the correct height. Color the bars.
2. Which animal shown on the graph has the most teeth?

Problem Solving Hint
When you make a number scale for a bar graph, look at the greatest number in the data.

Talk About It

3. How did you decide on the height for each bar?
4. Crocodiles have 100 teeth. If you wanted to add crocodiles to your bar graph, how would you change your graph?

Connect

The bars on a bar graph can be horizontal or vertical.

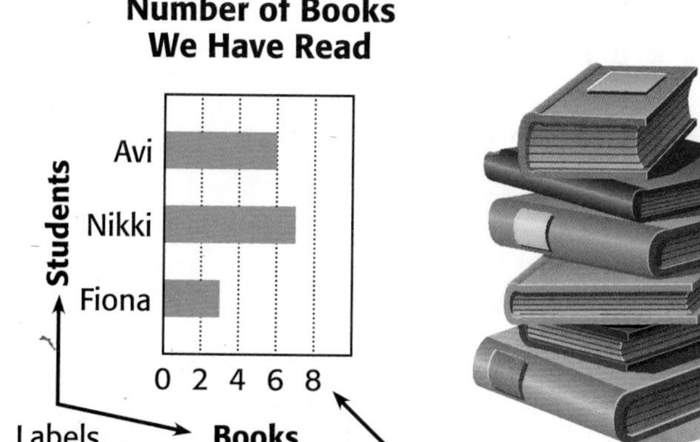

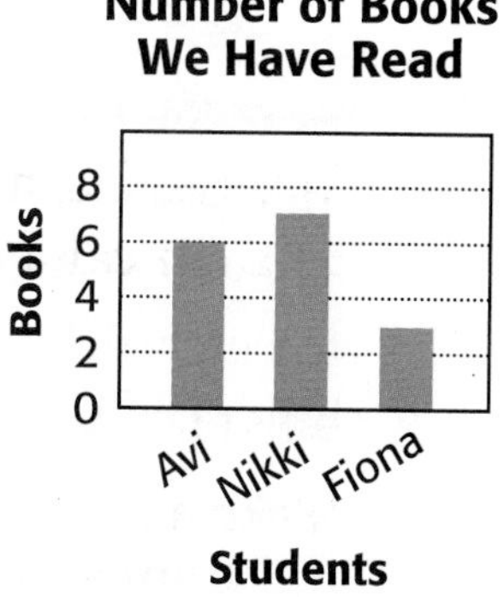

Practice

Make a bar graph to compare students' favorite animals. Use the data in the table for 1–4.

Animal	Student Votes
Cat	32
Bird	4
Hamster	13
Rabbit	14
Horse	25

1. Copy and complete the bar graph. Use grid paper.
   a. Write a title.
   b. Write labels for the bars.
   c. Complete the scale. Count by fives.
   d. Draw a bar for each animal. Use the scale to make each bar the correct height. Color the bars.
2. Which animal is most popular?
3. Are your bars vertical or horizontal?
4. If you wanted to add a different animal to your graph, how many bars would the new graph have?
5. **Journal** If you make a graph with data of 2 lb, 15 lb, 7 lb, and 10 lb, how will you decide what numbers to use for your scale?

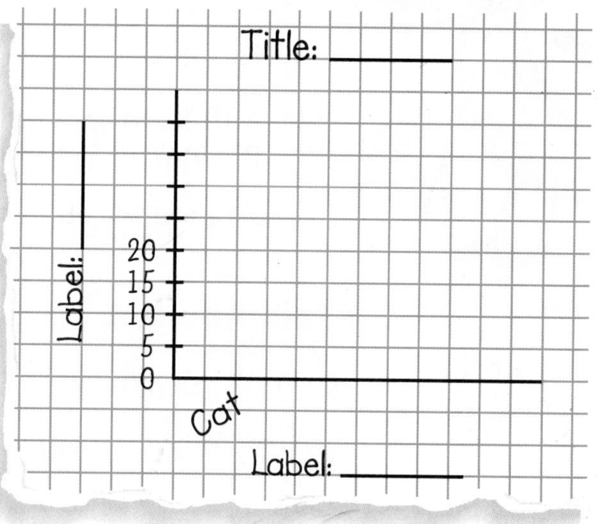

Exploring Making Line Plots

Problem Solving Connection
Draw a Picture

Explore

Pelicans are a kind of water bird. They dive down into the water to catch fish with their large bills. The white pelican is found from western Canada to southern Texas.

Work Together

The tally table shows the weights of some white pelicans. Make a line plot of the data in the table.

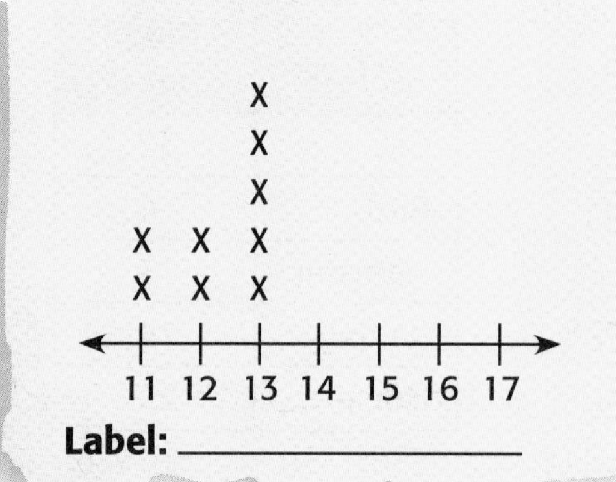

Did You Know?
The bill of the Australian pelican can be as long as $18\frac{1}{2}$ inches.

1. Copy and complete the line plot.
   a. Write a label at the bottom.
   b. Add **X**s to show the pelicans' weights. Use the data in the table.
2. What is the least weight? The greatest?

Talk About It

3. Does the data on your line plot form any clusters? Explain.
4. What is the most common weight?

Connect

Common running speeds for many animals are between 30 and 35 miles per hour.

The data from this table of animal speeds was used to make the line plot.

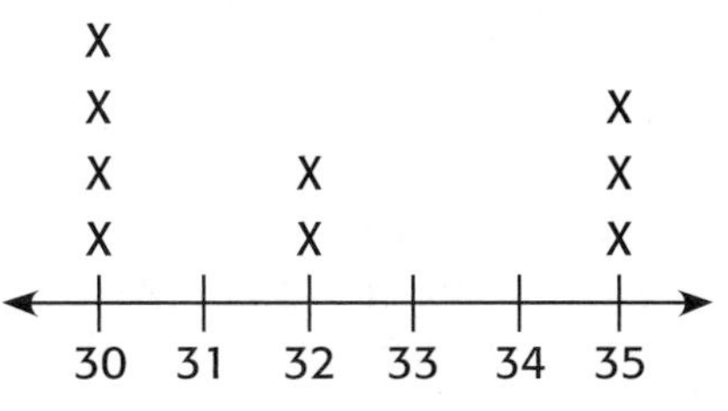

Animal	Speed (mi/hr)
Cat	30
Grizzly bear	30
Warthog	30
Deer	30
Giraffe	32
Reindeer	32
Jackal	35
Mule deer	35
Rabbit	35

30	31	32	33	34	35
X X X X		X X			X X X

Speeds of Animals (mi/hr)

Cheetahs have been clocked at 70 miles per hour! A typical freeway speed for cars is 65 miles per hour.

Practice

Using Data Use the Data File on page 7.

1. Copy and complete the line plot of distances jumped.
   - **a.** Write a label at the bottom.
   - **b.** Put **X**s on the number line to show how many kangaroos jumped each distance.
2. How many **X**s are shown for 37?
3. How many feet did most kangaroos jump?
4. How far did the winning kangaroo jump?
5. How much longer is the longest jump than the shortest jump?
6. **What If** Another kangaroo jumped 43 feet. How would you change the line plot to show this?
7. **Journal** How do you know which numbers to use on your number line?

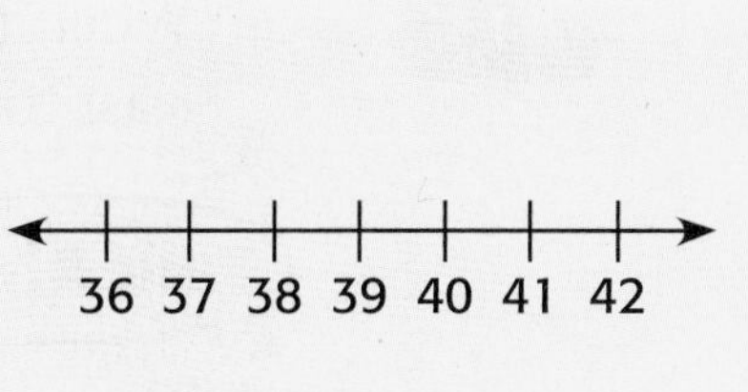

Chapter 1
Lesson
10

Exploring Range, Median, and Mode

Problem Solving Connection
Use Objects/
Act It Out

Materials
- paper
- scissors
- crayons

Vocabulary

mode
the number that occurs most often in the data

median
the middle number when the data are put in order

range
the difference between the greatest and least numbers in the data

Did You Know?
The largest domestic cat on record weighed nearly 47 pounds and was 38 inches long.

Explore

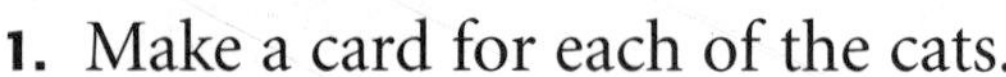

About one in three homes in the United States has a cat. Veterinarians like Dr. Maria Lopez keep a record of animals' weights. What do you think is the typical weight for a cat?

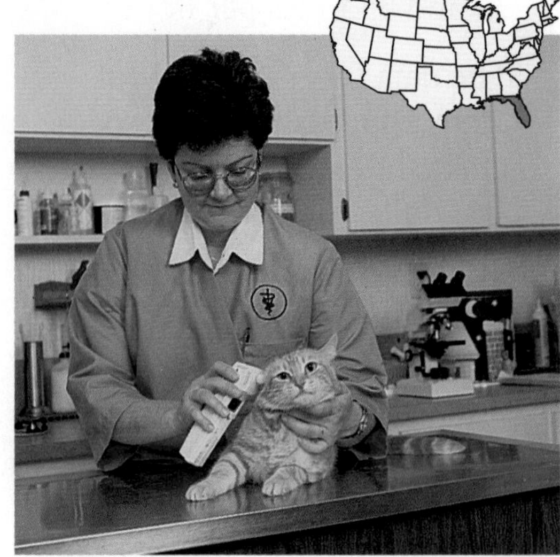

Dr. Maria Lopez cares for animals in Miami, Florida.

Work Together

Suppose these are the weights of 11 cats that Dr. Lopez saw. Organize the data to compare the cats' weights.

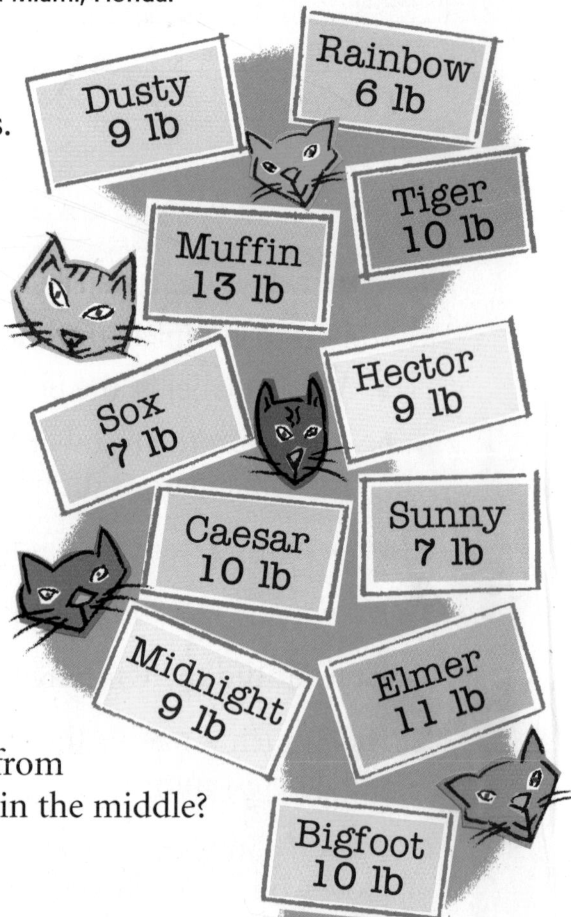

1. Make a card for each of the cats.
   a. Cut out 11 cards.
   b. Write the name and weight of a cat on each.
2. Arrange them in order. Start with the least weight.
3. What is the least weight? The greatest weight?
4. What is the difference between the greatest and least weights?
5. What weight or weights occur most often?
6. When the weights are in order from least to greatest, what weight is in the middle?

Talk About It

Which questions would be difficult to answer if you had not put the cards in order? Why?

Connect

Suppose these are the weights of 15 cats in Dr. Lopez's records.

5, 6, 6, 6, 6, 7, 9, (9), 9, 11, 11, 12, 13, 14, 15 $15 - 5 = 10$

Mode
The number that occurs most often

Median
The middle number when the data are in order

Range
The greatest value minus the least value

Math Tip
If no number in the data occurs more than once, there is no mode.

Practice

Use the data of tortoise weights for **1–4**.

1. Find the range of weights.
2. Find the median weight.
3. Find the mode of the weights.
4. **What If** A tortoise that weighs 550 lb joins the group. Now what is the range? What is the mode?
5. **Using Data** Use the data from the *Did You Know?* on page 30. Include this in the data from page 30 on the 11 cats that Dr. Lopez saw. What is the range of weights?

Use the line plot of greyhound weights for **6–9**.

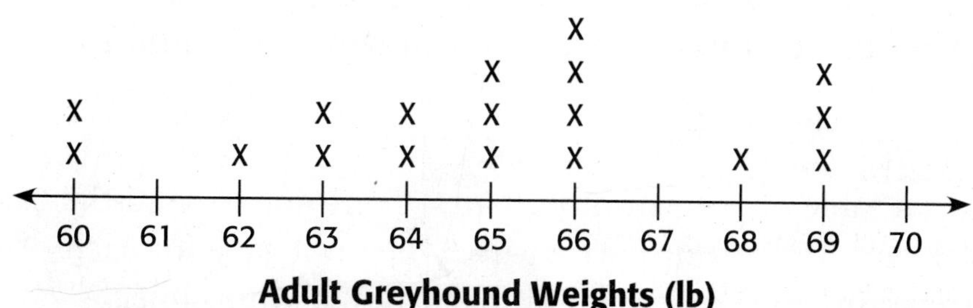

Adult Greyhound Weights (lb)

6. How many greyhounds are shown on the line plot?
7. What is the mode of the greyhound weights?
8. What is the range of weights?
9. What is the median weight?

10. **Critical Thinking** Why do you think pet owners might want to know the normal range of weights of cats?
11. **Journal** Define *range, median,* and *mode* in your own words.

Chapter 1
Lesson
11

Exploring Algebra: What's the Rule?

Problem Solving Connection
- Look for a Pattern
- Make a Table

Materials
- index cards
- 2 envelopes

Explore

A rule describes what to do to the **In** number to get the **Out** number. The rule for this table is to *subtract 2*.

In	4	5	6	7
Out	2	3	4	5

Work Together

1. Play "Guess My Rule."

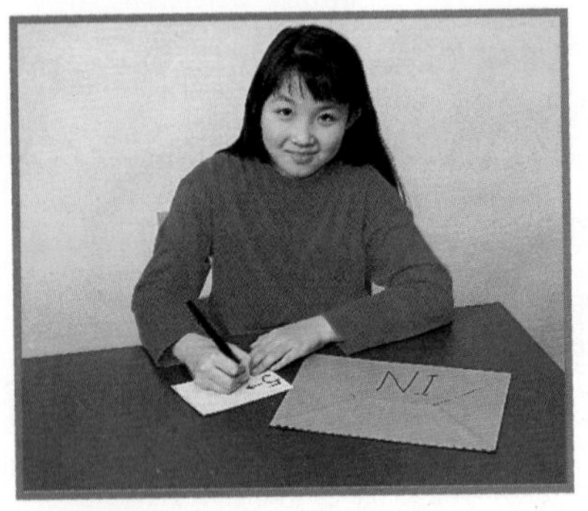

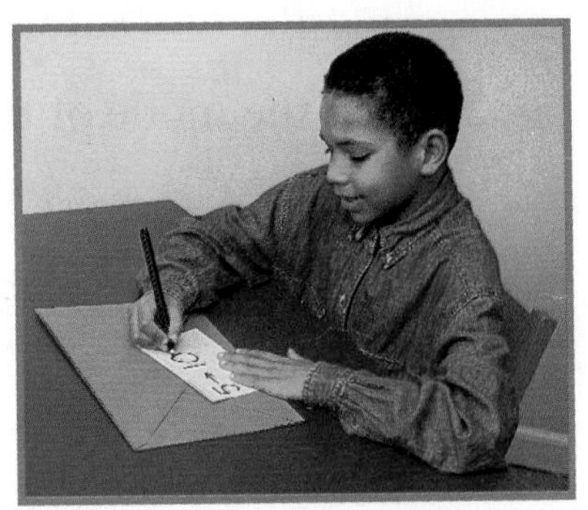

Vocabulary
variable
a letter that stands for a number or a range of numbers

a. Write a number on an index card. Draw an arrow next to it. Put it in an envelope labeled **In**. Send it to a partner.

b. Your partner thinks of a rule, uses it with your number, writes the answer on the same card, and sends it to you in an envelope labeled **Out**.

c. Start a table of your number pairs. Continue to send the cards back and forth. Your partner uses the same rule for each of your numbers. Write the number pairs in your table.

d. Continue to play until you find the rule.

e. Play again. Your partner picks a number and guesses your rule.

Problem Solving Hint
You can look for a pattern to help you find a rule.

2. Complete these tables. Give the rules for each.

In	2	3	4	5	6	7
Out	5	6	7	8		

In	19	16	12	10	8
Out	12	9	5		

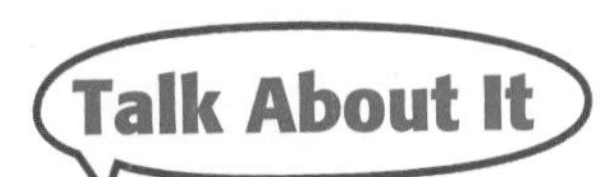

How did you find each rule?

Connect

You can use a **variable** to stand for a number or a range of numbers.

In	Earnings in Dollars	n	6	9	10	13
Out	Savings in Dollars	$n - 5$	1	4	5	

If $6 was earned, how much was saved?

$n - 5$
↓
$6 - 5 = 1$ $1 was saved.

If $13 was earned, how much was saved?

$n - 5$
↓
$13 - 5 = 8$ $8 was saved.

Practice

Copy and complete each table. Use the rule.

1.

In	n	9	4	8	5	7
Out	$n + 3$	12	7	11		

2.

In	n	9	10	11	12	13
Out	$n - 4$	5	6	7		

Copy and complete each table. Write the rule.

3.

In	n	4	5	6	7	8
Out		9	10	11		

4.

In	n	1	3	7	9	11
Out		7	9	13		

5. Danielle feeds the goldfish when her neighbors are away. Each time she is paid, she spends only $2 and saves the rest. Complete the table to show her savings.

In	Earnings	n	4	6	13	7
Out	Savings	$n - 2$				

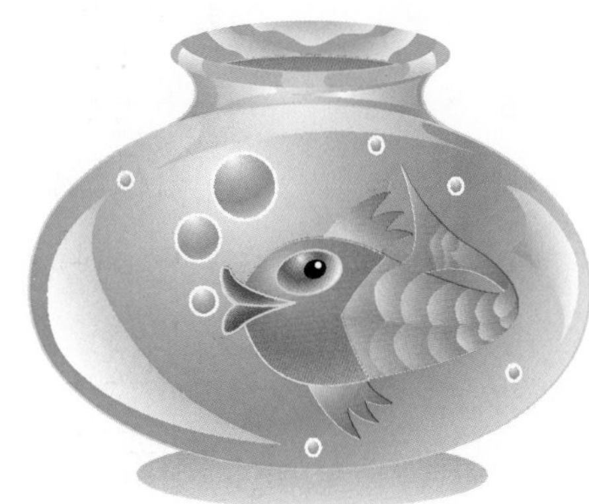

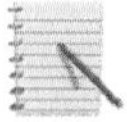

6. Journal Is it important to test a rule on all numbers in the table? Explain.

STOP and Practice

Find each sum or difference.

1. $\begin{array}{r} 3 \\ +6 \\ \hline \end{array}$	**2.** $\begin{array}{r} 5 \\ +2 \\ \hline \end{array}$	**3.** $\begin{array}{r} 8 \\ -2 \\ \hline \end{array}$	**4.** $\begin{array}{r} 9 \\ -3 \\ \hline \end{array}$	**5.** $\begin{array}{r} 16 \\ -7 \\ \hline \end{array}$
6. $\begin{array}{r} 12 \\ -5 \\ \hline \end{array}$	**7.** $\begin{array}{r} 11 \\ -6 \\ \hline \end{array}$	**8.** $\begin{array}{r} 7 \\ +7 \\ \hline \end{array}$	**9.** $\begin{array}{r} 3 \\ +4 \\ \hline \end{array}$	**10.** $\begin{array}{r} 18 \\ -9 \\ \hline \end{array}$
11. $\begin{array}{r} 8 \\ -5 \\ \hline \end{array}$	**12.** $\begin{array}{r} 17 \\ -9 \\ \hline \end{array}$	**13.** $\begin{array}{r} 9 \\ +4 \\ \hline \end{array}$	**14.** $\begin{array}{r} 2 \\ +7 \\ \hline \end{array}$	**15.** $\begin{array}{r} 15 \\ -8 \\ \hline \end{array}$
16. $\begin{array}{r} 9 \\ +9 \\ \hline \end{array}$	**17.** $\begin{array}{r} 6 \\ +2 \\ \hline \end{array}$	**18.** $\begin{array}{r} 14 \\ -6 \\ \hline \end{array}$	**19.** $\begin{array}{r} 7 \\ +8 \\ \hline \end{array}$	**20.** $\begin{array}{r} 9 \\ -7 \\ \hline \end{array}$
21. $\begin{array}{r} 7 \\ +6 \\ \hline \end{array}$	**22.** $\begin{array}{r} 15 \\ -6 \\ \hline \end{array}$	**23.** $\begin{array}{r} 5 \\ +4 \\ \hline \end{array}$	**24.** $\begin{array}{r} 10 \\ -3 \\ \hline \end{array}$	**25.** $\begin{array}{r} 6 \\ -5 \\ \hline \end{array}$
26. $\begin{array}{r} 5 \\ +7 \\ \hline \end{array}$	**27.** $\begin{array}{r} 8 \\ +3 \\ \hline \end{array}$	**28.** $\begin{array}{r} 6 \\ +6 \\ \hline \end{array}$	**29.** $\begin{array}{r} 14 \\ -8 \\ \hline \end{array}$	**30.** $\begin{array}{r} 6 \\ +4 \\ \hline \end{array}$
31. $12 - 7$	**32.** $8 - 5$	**33.** $6 + 2$	**34.** $5 - 3$	**35.** $16 - 8$
36. $9 - 5$	**37.** $11 - 8$	**38.** $6 + 6$	**39.** $1 + 5$	**40.** $13 - 8$
41. $5 + 4$	**42.** $17 - 8$	**43.** $2 + 4$	**44.** $7 + 5$	**45.** $15 - 6$
46. $5 + 5$	**47.** $8 + 8$	**48.** $13 - 6$	**49.** $8 + 5$	**50.** $6 + 8$
51. $3 + 8$	**52.** $10 - 6$	**53.** $14 - 9$	**54.** $6 + 6$	**55.** $7 - 7$
56. $14 - 6$	**57.** $7 + 9$	**58.** $6 + 5$	**59.** $8 - 3$	**60.** $3 + 9$

Error Search

Find each sum or difference that is not correct. Write it correctly and explain the error.

61. $9 + 5 = 4$ **62.** $16 - 7 = 9$ **63.** $7 + 8 = 13$ **64.** $11 - 6 = 17$ **65.** $3 + 3 = 9$

Neck and Neck!

Add or subtract to solve the riddle. Match each letter to its answer in the blank below to find out which animal has the same number of neck bones as a person. Some letters are not used.

66. 15 − 8 [F]	**67.** 8 + 5 [O]	**68.** 3 + 6 [E]	**69.** 13 − 7 [B]
70. 16 − 8 [R]	**71.** 9 − 7 [I]	**72.** 12 − 6 [M]	**73.** 9 + 2 [W]
74. 13 − 9 [A]	**75.** 4 + 8 [D]	**76.** 9 − 9 [K]	**77.** 11 − 8 [F]
78. 7 + 7 [L]	**79.** 8 − 7 [P]	**80.** 6 + 8 [H]	**81.** 14 − 9 [G]

___	___	___	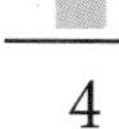 ___	___	___	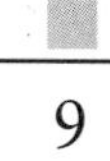 ___
5	2	8	4	7	3	9

Remember the Facts!

These activities can help you remember your basic facts.

1. **Who Knows the Fact?** Sit in a circle with three or more students. Think of an addition fact, such as 7 + 5. Clap your hands as you say each word, "Seven plus five." Then the student sitting next to you clicks his or her fingers and says, "Equals 12." Continue playing. Keep the rhythm of clapping your hands and clicking your fingers as you say the fact and give the answer.

2. **Spin Around** Use a spinner with 3, 4, 5, 6, 7, and 8 on it. Spin it twice. Use the two numbers to write an addition or subtraction fact. Repeat several times.

Problem Solving

Analyze Strategies: Guess and Check

You Will Learn
how to solve problems using the guess and check strategy

Reading Tip
Use the Glossary at the back of the book to find the meanings of *sum* and *difference.*

Learn

Jo has both a pet frog and a parrot. The frog is older than the parrot. The sum of the frog's and parrot's ages is 21 years. The difference of their ages is 5 years. How old is each animal?

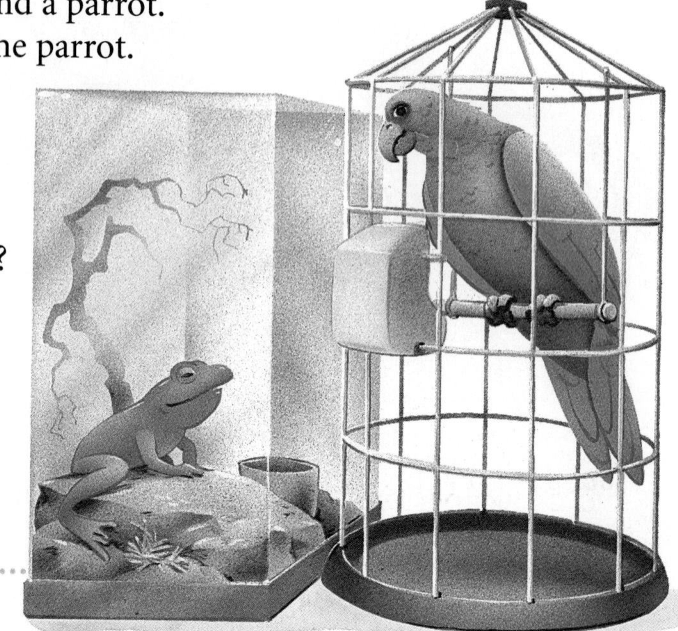

Work Together

▶ Understand

What do you know?

What do you need to find out?

▶ Plan

You may be able to solve the problem by guessing and checking.

Guess a pair of numbers.
Check if they work.

▶ Solve

Use the facts you know.

The sum of their ages is 21.

Guess 15 and 6. Check $15 + 6 = 21$.
$15 - 6 = 9$. The difference is not 5.

Guess 13 and 8. Check $13 + 8 = 21$.
$13 - 8 = 5$. That checks!

Write the answer.

The frog is 13 years old.
The parrot is 8 years old.

▶ Look Back

Check to see if your answer makes sense.

Another Example

Steven and Brian are starting an endangered species card collection. Together they have 18 cards. The difference in the number of cards they have is 4. If Steven has more cards than Brian, how many cards does each boy have?

What You Read	What You Do
They have a total of 18 cards. The difference in the number of cards they have is 4.	First guess: $10 + 8 = 18$ $10 - 8 = 2$ The difference must be 4. Second guess: $11 + 7 = 18$ $11 - 7 = 4$ That works!
Steven has more cards than Brian.	Steven has 11 cards. Brian has 7 cards.

Talk About It

1. How do you decide what your first guess will be?
2. How does your first guess help you make the second guess?

Check

Use guess and check to solve.

1. Jo walked her dog for 10 minutes more on Saturday than on Sunday. For both days she walked a total of 30 minutes. For how many minutes did she walk her dog on Sunday?

2. The record jumps for a gray kangaroo and a red kangaroo total 18 feet. The red kangaroo's record jump is 2 feet higher than the gray kangaroo's record jump.
   a. Which kangaroo jumped higher?
   b. Which numbers will you guess first?
   c. What should the difference between the two numbers be?
   d. Which two numbers have a sum of 18 and a difference of 2?
   e. What is the record jump for each kangaroo?

Red kangaroos are the most common kind of kangaroos found in Australia.

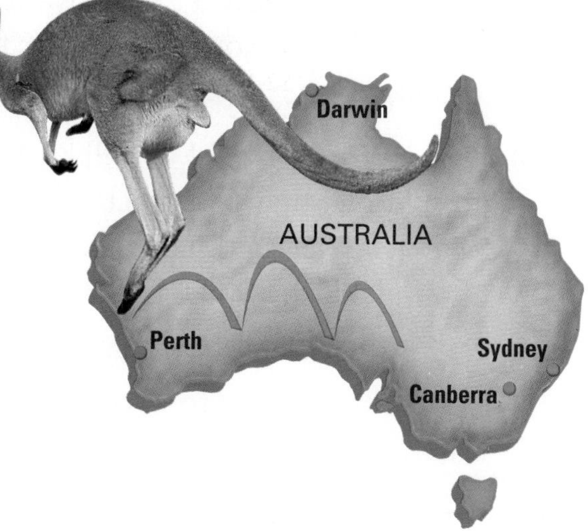

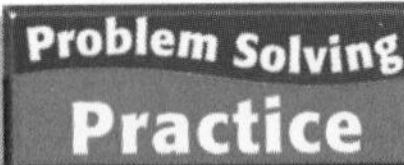

Apply the Strategy

Use guess and check to help you solve each problem.

3. Dmitri and Wayne spent a total of $12 for books. Dmitri spent $2 more than Wayne. How much did each spend?

4. Steven gave away 5 of his endangered species cards. He gave his sister 1 more card than he gave his friend. How many cards did he give his sister?

Problem Solving Strategies

- Use Objects/Act It Out
- Draw a Picture
- Look for a Pattern
- Guess and Check
- Use Logical Reasoning
- Make an Organized List
- Make a Table
- Solve a Simpler Problem
- Work Backward

Choose a Tool

Choose a Strategy

Use any strategy to solve each problem. Use the pet catalog to answer **5–9.**

5. Shalia ordered from the catalog. She spent $5 on two different items. She did not buy a bone. What did she order?

6. Stacy wanted to buy the biscuits and a bone. She had $3. What size bone could she order?

7. Rita ordered a dog dish and one other item. She paid a total of $9. What other items could Rita have ordered?

8. Kim ordered 3 bones in 3 different sizes. How much did she pay in all?

9. Suppose you have $15 and want to spend all of it. What would you order from the catalog?

10. Every morning, Jackie walks 12 blocks to school. She walks the last 9 blocks with Mai Ling. If Mai Ling walks 2 blocks farther than Jackie, how far does Mai Ling walk before meeting Jackie?

11. A bike shop has a total of 5 bicycles and tricycles to repair. There are 12 wheels. What strategy would you use to find the number of bicycles and tricycles?

Item	Price
Nylon collar	**$3.00**
Nylon leash	**$5.00**
Biscuits	**$2.00**
Bandana	**$5.00**
Rawhide bone	
small	**$1.00**
medium	**$3.00**
large	**$4.00**
Dish	**$6.00**

Problem Solving and RECREATION

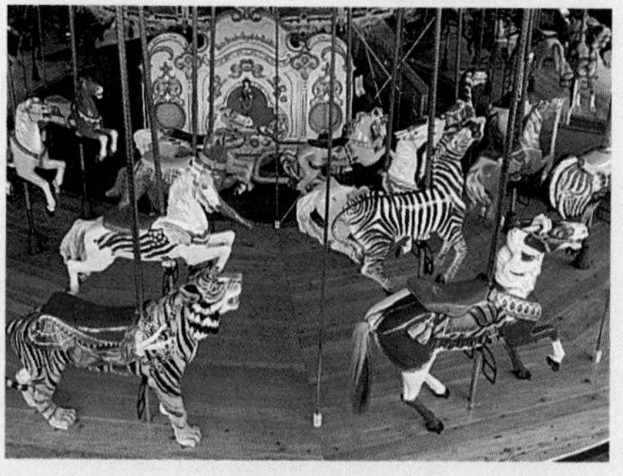

For more than 100 years, people have ridden carved animals on carousels.

Most carousels have 3 rings, with an equal number of animals on each ring. The animals on the 2 inside rings are called "jumpers." They move up and down.

12. A carousel has 36 zebras, horses, and camels.

a. How many animals are on each ring?

b. Each ring has an equal number of zebras, horses, and camels. How many of each kind of animal are on each ring?

c. How many jumpers are there?

d. A jumper has a blue or a red saddle. Six more jumpers have blue saddles than have red saddles. How many blue saddles are there?

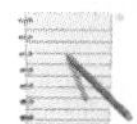

13. Journal Explain how you would use guess and check to solve problem **12d.**

Mixed Review: Basic Facts

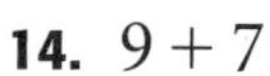

Find each sum or difference.

14. 9 + 7	**15.** 4 − 1	**16.** 4 + 3	**17.** 6 − 0	**18.** 8 + 9
19. 17 − 8	**20.** 8 + 5	**21.** 12 − 8	**22.** 15 − 8	**23.** 6 + 7
24. 9 − 0	**25.** 5 + 1	**26.** 7 + 8	**27.** 6 + 8	**28.** 7 + 9
29. 2 + 9	**30.** 5 + 7	**31.** 13 − 6	**32.** 14 − 5	**33.** 4 + 7

Skills Practice Bank, page 559, Set 6

Technology

Making Graphs

Suppose you're writing a report on sandhill cranes. You write, "Sandhill cranes laid 5 eggs in February, 55 in March, 30 in April, and 10 in May."

Which type of graph would you use to show this data?

Materials

DataWonder! or other graphing software

Work Together

Use your graphing software to select the best graph to show the data.

1. Copy the table below to create a **Simple Data Table.**

2. Click on the different graph buttons in the graph window. Select the best graph for your report.

3. Insert the table and graph into the **Report** window. Then give your graph and report a title.

Report
Show Report
Insert Graph
Insert Table

Number of Eggs		
Month		
1	February	5
2	March	55
3	April	30
4	May	10

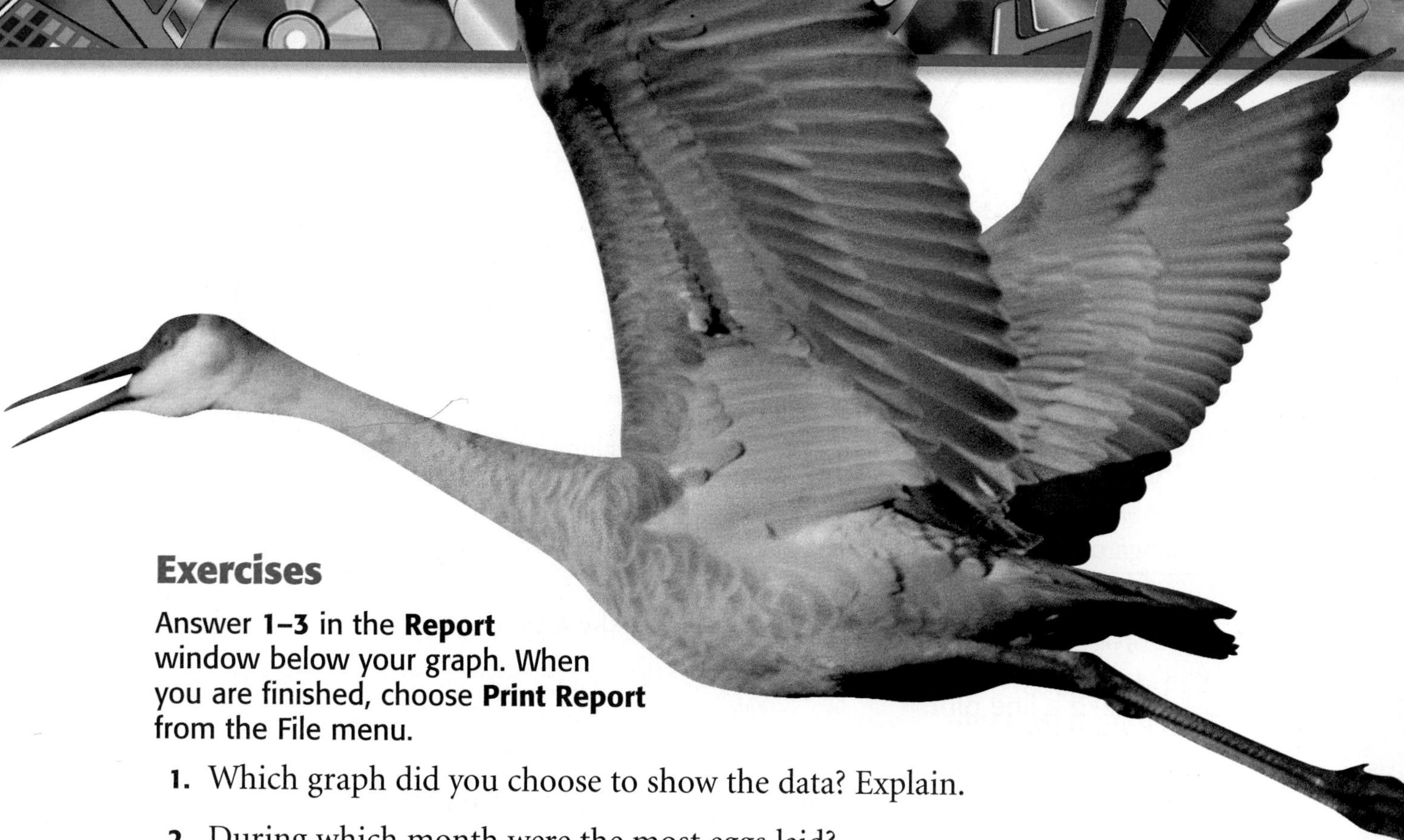

Exercises

Answer **1–3** in the **Report** window below your graph. When you are finished, choose **Print Report** from the File menu.

1. Which graph did you choose to show the data? Explain.
2. During which month were the most eggs laid?
3. How many more eggs were laid in April than in May?

Extensions

Make a **Full Data Table** graph to show the mass data in the table. Answer **4–7** in the **Report** window. Print your report when you are finished.

4. What graph did you choose to show the data? Explain.
5. What was the mass of the crane at 2 weeks? At 8 weeks?
6. How many grams did the crane gain in the first 2 weeks?

Sandhill Cranes

	Age (weeks)	Mass (grams)
1	Birth	2
2	2	287
3	4	1,145
4	6	2,035
5	8	2,754

7. Which kind of graph best shows changes over time?
8. **Write Your Own Problem** Write a problem that can be answered using your graph. Give the answer.

SECTION B
Review and Practice

(Lesson 8) Make a bar graph.

1. Use the data in the table.
   Copy and complete the bar graph.

Animal Life Spans	
Chipmunk	6 yr
Rabbit	5 yr
Kangaroo	7 yr

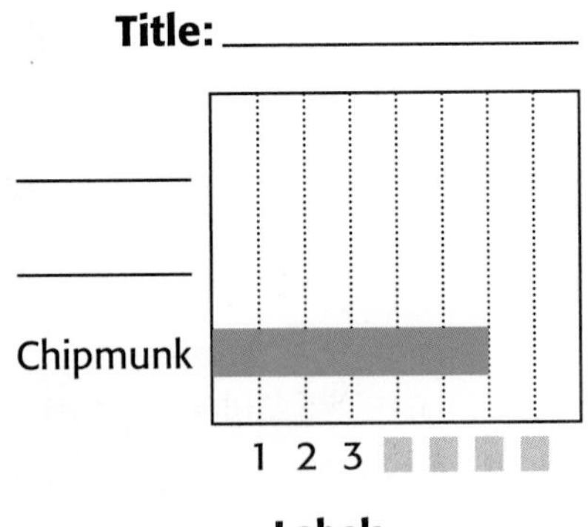

2. How could you use the life spans data to make a pictograph?

(Lesson 9) Make a line plot.

3. Use the data in the table.
   Copy and complete the line plot.

Number of Words Missed on Spelling Test	Number of Students
1	5
2	8
3	7
4	2
5	1

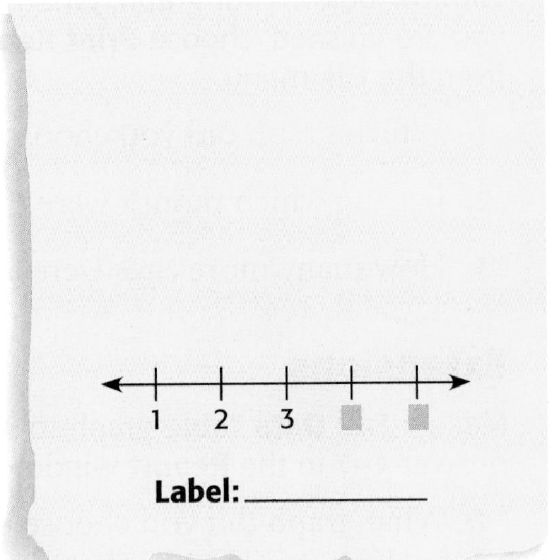

(Lesson 10) Find the range, median, and mode of each set of numbers.

4. 2, 5, 8, 4, 3, 9, 3
5. 2, 4, 6, 3, 1, 4, 4
6. 7, 3, 2, 7, 6, 7, 1

(Lesson 11) Copy and complete the table. Write the rule.

7.

In	n	10	13	8	9	12	15
Out		4	7	2			

(Lesson 12) Solve.

8. The sum of two numbers is 13, and their difference is 3. What are the two numbers?

9. **Journal** Explain how to find the range, median, and mode for 2, 9, 7, 6, 2, 4, 2.

Skills Checklist

In this section, you have:

- ☑ **Explored Making Bar Graphs and Line Plots**
- ☑ **Explored Finding Range, Median, and Mode**
- ☑ **Explored Algebra by Finding a Rule**
- ☑ **Solved Problems by Guessing and Checking**

REVIEW AND PRACTICE

Choose at least one. Use what you have learned in this chapter.

1 Range Riddle

From the seven numbers below, pick five for which the following are true.

a. Their range is 4.

b. Their mode is 5.

c. Their median is 6.

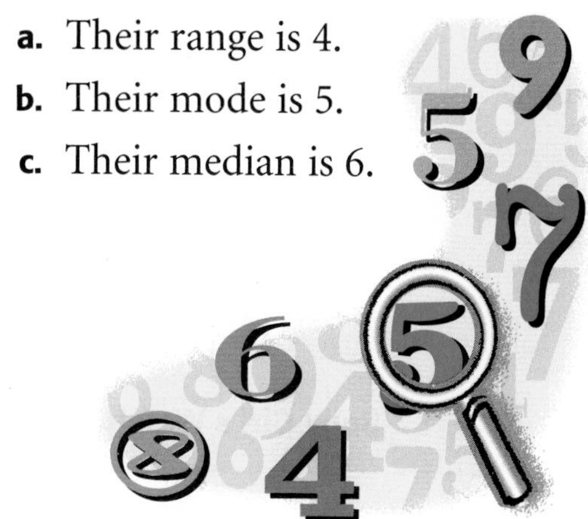

2 Picture This

Check out **www.mathsurf.com/4/ch1.** Discover how explorers today are finding treasure at archaeological sites and in sunken ships. Design a treasure hunt. Use a coordinate grid. Give clues to find your treasure by using ordered pairs.

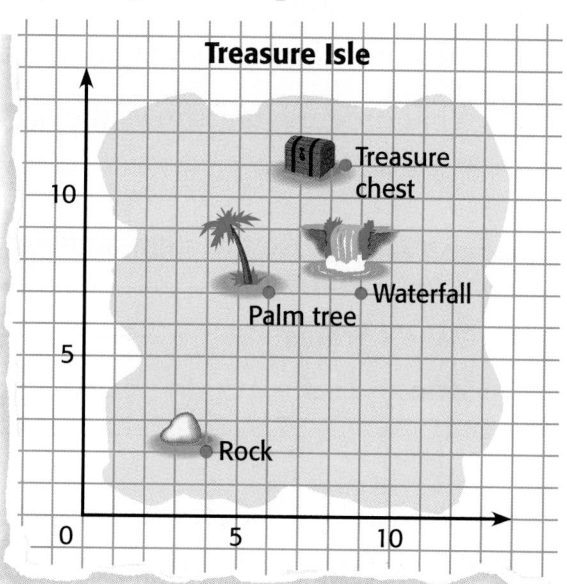

3 A Short Story

At Home Use the data displayed in this graph to write a story. Title the graph and complete the labels. Share your story with family and friends. Have them tell a different story about the graph.

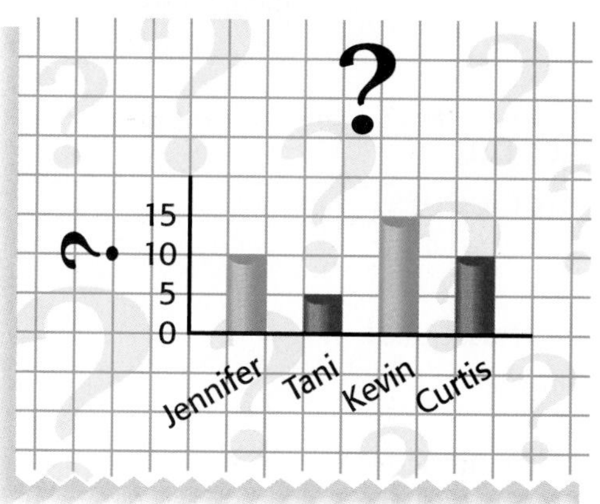

4 What's the Value of a Name?

Assign a number to each letter of your first name: A = 1, B = 2, C = 3, and so on. Add the numbers. You may use a calculator. Try to find a classmate whose name is different from yours but has the same total value.

REVIEW AND PRACTICE

CHAPTER 1

Review/Test

Vocabulary Copy and complete.

Word List
coordinate grid
stem
ordered pair

1. (2, 3) is called an _____.
2. (2, 3) can be found on a _____.
3. The _____ shows the tens digit in a stem-and-leaf plot.

(Lesson 1) Use the bar graph to answer **4** and **5**.

4. How much taller is the giraffe than the elephant?
5. Which animal is taller than the lion but shorter than the elephant?

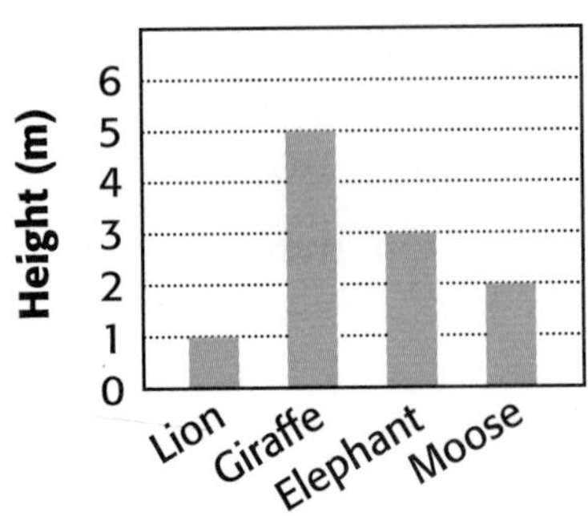

(Lessons 2 and 3) Use the line graph to answer **6** and **7.**

6. What was the baby's weight at 6 months?
7. What ordered pair shows the baby's weight at 9 months?

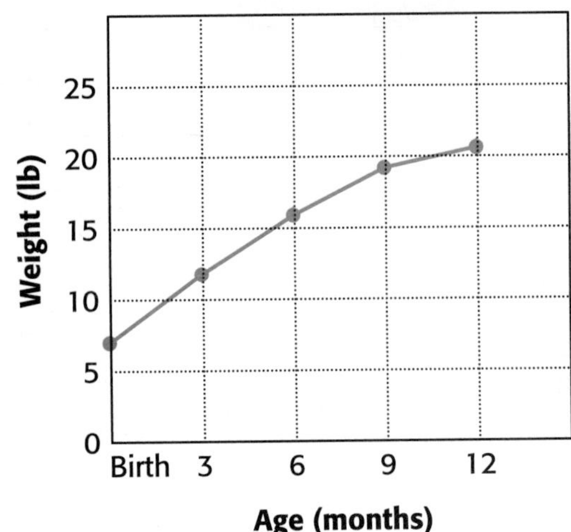

(Lessons 5 and 10) Use the stem-and-leaf plot to answer **8** and **9.**

Claire's Scores

Stem	Leaf
1	0 7 6
2	1 3 1 8
3	1 6 4

8. What is the mode of Claire's scores?
9. How many times did Claire score 21?

(Lessons 6, 7, and 12) Solve. Choose any strategy.

10. Two puppies weigh 15 lb all together. The larger puppy weighs 3 lb more than the smaller one. How much does each puppy weigh?
11. What is the difference in length between an elephant seal measuring 20 feet and a walrus measuring 12 feet?
12. **Science.** A seal can hold its breath underwater for about an hour. Can a seal swim underwater for 75 min without coming up for air? Explain.

REVIEW/TEST

CHAPTER 1

Performance Assessment

In which month are most people born? Survey several people to find out. Ask each person in what month he or she was born. Show the data on a graph.

1. **Decision Making** Decide how many people you will survey. Decide which people you will ask.

2. **Recording Data** Copy and complete the table. Include all 12 months. Record the total number of people born in each month. Then use the data you collect to make a bar graph.

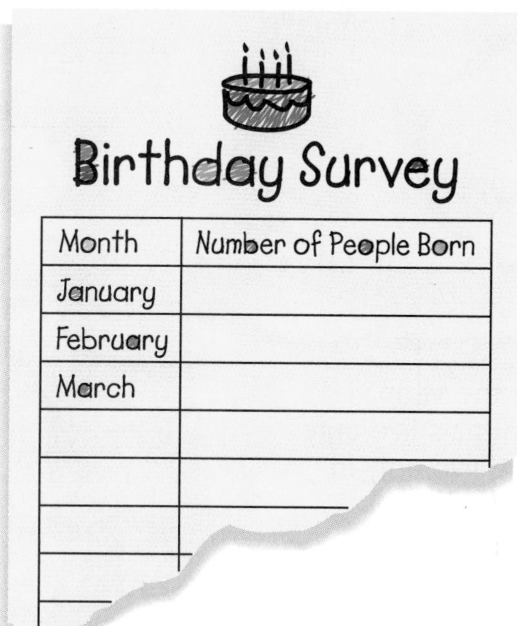

Birthday Survey

Month	Number of People Born
January	
February	
March	

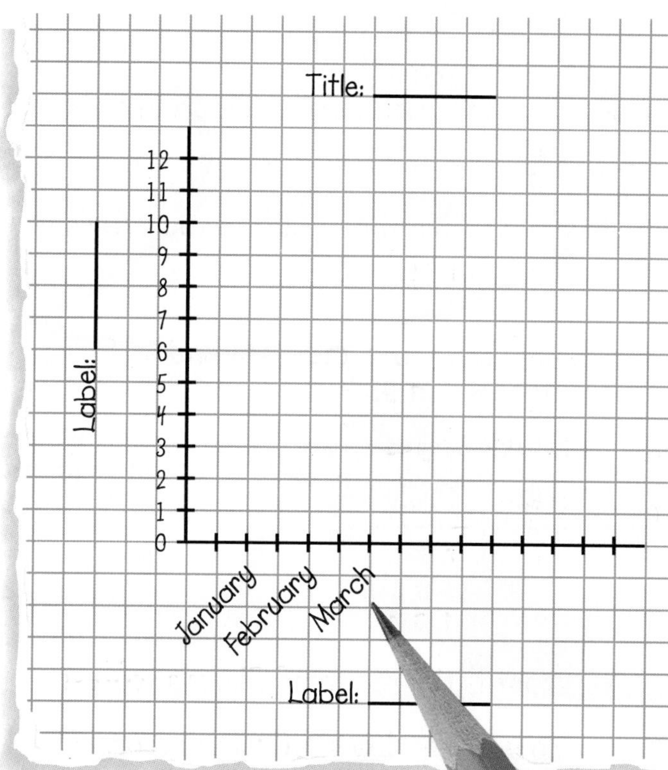

3. **Explain Your Thinking** How did you decide on the title and labels for your bar graph? Based on your bar graph, in which month are most people born? In which month are the fewest people born? Write your own question that can be answered using your graph.

4. **Critical Thinking** Would you expect to get the same results if you surveyed more people? Compare your results with those of two other students.

REVIEW/TEST

Math Magazine

Going Around in Circles

Zoologists classify animals to learn about them. If you know an animal lives in water, you can predict what type of lungs, skin covering, or behaviors the animal has. You can use Venn diagrams to organize animal data.

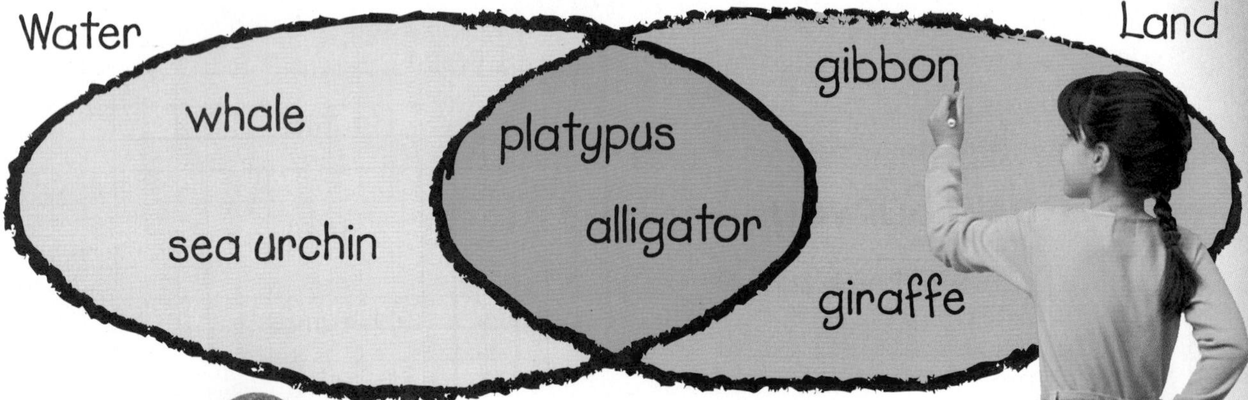

Water

Land

whale

sea urchin

platypus

alligator

gibbon

giraffe

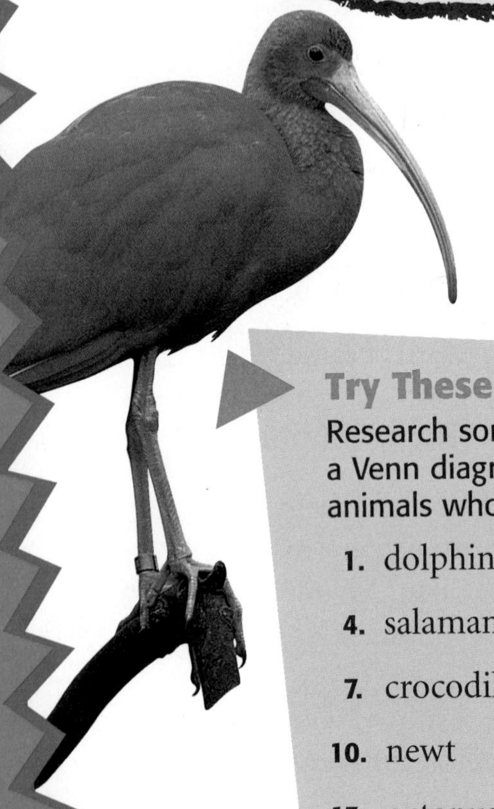

Can you tell from the Venn diagram which animals live only on land and which live only in water? Explain.

Which animals live both on land and in water? How can you tell from the Venn diagram?

Try These!

Research some of the following animals. Make a Venn diagram like the one above to classify animals who live on land, in water, or both.

1. dolphin	**2.** manatee	**3.** caribou
4. salamander	**5.** ocelot	**6.** tortoise
7. crocodile	**8.** yak	**9.** hyena
10. newt	**11.** ibis	**12.** sloth
13. octopus	**14.** otter	**15.** wildebeest

CHAPTER 1

Cumulative Review

Test Prep Strategy: Make Smart Choices

Look for patterns.

Give the next three numbers in this pattern. 1, 4, 7, 10, ■, ■, ■

Ⓐ 17, 27, 44 Ⓑ 11, 12, 13 Ⓒ 13, 16, 19 Ⓓ 14, 18, 22

Try adding 3

$1 + \mathbf{3} = 4$

$4 + \mathbf{3} = 7$

$7 + \mathbf{3} = 10$

The pattern is add 3.

So, the answer is Ⓒ.

STAY SHARP!

Write the letter of the correct answer. Look for patterns or use any strategy to help.

1. Sally baked 5 dozen chocolate chip cookies. James baked 4 dozen sugar cookies. Gretchen baked 2 dozen oatmeal cookies. How many cookies did they bake all together?

   Ⓐ 6 dozen Ⓑ 7 dozen Ⓒ 9 dozen Ⓓ 11 dozen

2. Team A scored 17 points. Team B scored 8 points. How many points ahead is team A?

   Ⓐ 8 points Ⓑ 9 points Ⓒ 25 points Ⓓ not here

3. Give the next three numbers in this pattern. 2, 6, 10, ■, ■, ■

   Ⓐ 12, 14, 16 Ⓑ 14, 18, 22 Ⓒ 1, 3, 5 Ⓓ not here

4. Which sum is the same as the difference between 14 and 6?

   Ⓐ $7 + 1$ Ⓑ $10 + 10$ Ⓒ $5 + 4$ Ⓓ $14 + 6$

5. Which sum is 1 less than the sum of 8 and 3?

   Ⓐ $8 + 3$ Ⓑ $6 + 6$ Ⓒ $5 + 6$ Ⓓ $6 + 4$

6. A tailed frog commonly lays 60 eggs. A Burmese python commonly lays 25 eggs. What operation would you use to find how many more eggs the frog lays than the python?

   Ⓐ addition Ⓑ multiplication
   Ⓒ subtraction Ⓓ division

7. A hearing guide dog worked for 7 years with one owner and 3 years with a different owner. How long did it work in all?

   Ⓐ 2 years Ⓑ 10 years Ⓒ 80 years Ⓓ 90 years

8. The largest gerbil litter was 15. If there were 8 females, how many males were there?

   Ⓐ 7 females Ⓑ 7 males Ⓒ 8 males Ⓓ 23 males

Test Prep Strategies

- Read Carefully
- Follow Directions
- Make Smart Choices
- Eliminate Choices
- Work Backward from an Answer

DATA FILE

Chapter 2

Place Value and Time

Artist Douglas Mehrens uses more crayons than anyone in the world—28,000 a year!

Understanding Place Value

51

Millions of crayons
Page 51

A little color goes a long way! What new high-tech crayon do you think might be on a time line by the year 2000?

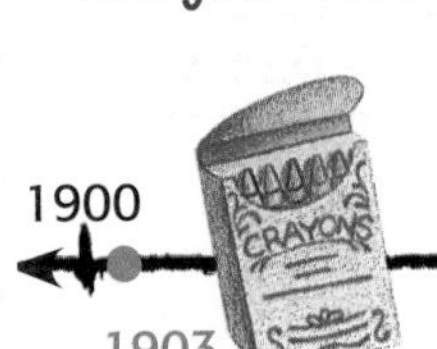

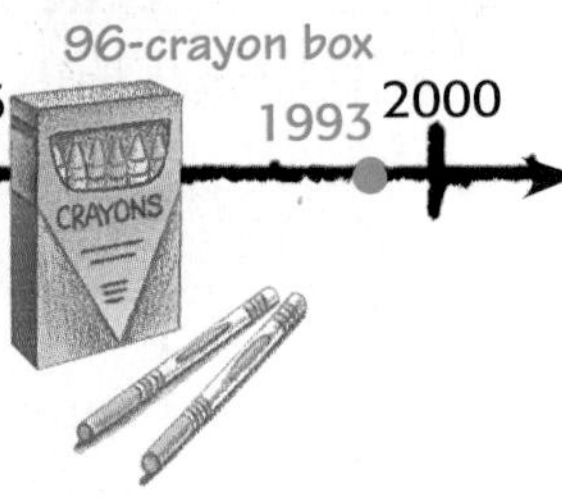

1900 — 1925 — 1950 — 1975 — 2000

1903 First box of wax crayons: black, brown, blue, red, purple, orange, yellow, green

1949 48-crayon box

1958 64-crayon box with built-in sharpener

1972 Fluorescent crayons and markers

1993 96-crayon box

Surfing the World Wide Web!

Check out **www.mathsurf.com/4/ch2** to find out about coloring and crayons.

Building Number Sense

65

In 1990, which groups had more than a million immigrants to the United States?

Asian Immigrants to U.S., 1990	
Asian Group	**Number of People in 1990**
Asian Indian	815,447
Chinese	1,645,472
Filipino	1,406,770
Japanese	847,562
Korean	798,849
Vietnamese	614,547

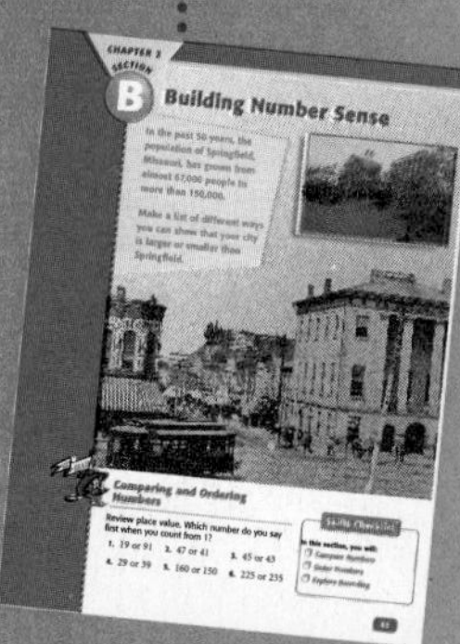

Springfield, Missouri Page 65

SECTION C

Making Sense of Time

73

Trains arrive and depart within the minute, according to this Florida schedule. What do bus, train, and plane schedules have in common?

The Silver Star Train Schedule	
City	**Arrival/Departure**
Palatka	9:06 A.M.
DeLand	9:55 A.M.
Sanford	10:15 A.M.
Orlando	11:15 A.M.
Sebring	1:17 P.M.
West Palm Beach	3:02 P.M.

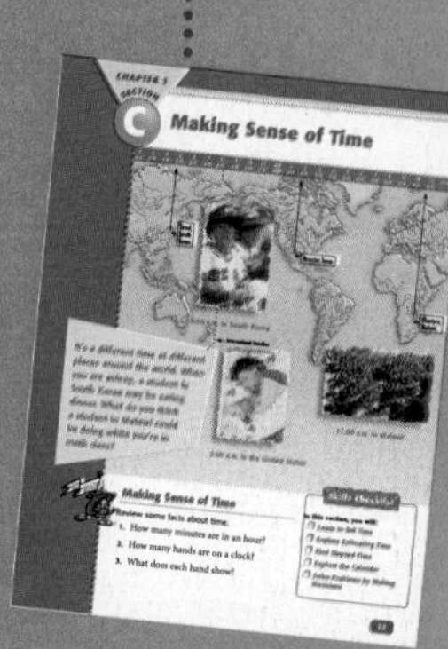

World time zones Page 73

TEAM PROJECT: It's a Matter of Fact

Materials
collection of 10 or more objects, ruler

Find your own fact about 1,000!

1,000 cheese ravioli can fill 10 baseball caps.

1,000 Chinese food take-home boxes lined up will stretch the length of a city block.

1,000 pizza boxes stacked will reach the top of a 16-story building.

Make a Plan

- Think about using a fact about 10 to help you find a fact about 1,000.
- How will your team show how big 10 is?
- How will your team show how big 1,000 is?
- How will you record and show your results?

Carry It Out

Find a fact.

1. Choose an object to show 1,000.
2. Bring 10 or more of these objects to class.
3. Measure one object. How big is 10 objects? How big is 1,000 objects?
4. Compare the measure of 1,000 objects with something in real life.

Talk About It

- How did you show how big 1,000 is?
- How did you decide what object to use?
- What do you think would happen if you used a smaller object to show how big 1,000 is?

Present the Project

- Tell the class what fact you found.
- Explain how you found that fact.

Understanding Place Value

The word *crayon* can be written in many languages.

German: *wachsmalkreide*
Spanish: *creyón*
Portuguese: *lápis de pastel*
Danish: *tegnekridt*
Cantonese: *laapbee*

How can you tell if there are between 10 and 100, or 100 and 1,000 crayons on this page?

Reading and Writing Greater Numbers

Review counting. Copy and write the missing numbers.

1. 234, 235, 236, ■, ■, ■
2. 989, ■, 991, ■, 993, ■
3. ■, 487, 486, ■, 484, ■, 482

Skills Checklist

In this section, you will:

- ❒ Learn About Place Value Through Millions
- ❒ Explore Place-Value Relationships
- ❒ Solve Problems by Making an Organized List

Chapter 2
Lesson
1

Place Value Through Thousands

You Will Learn
how to read and write numbers in the thousands

Vocabulary

place value
value given to the place a digit has in a number

digits
0, 1, 2, 3, 4, 5, 6, 7, 8, 9

period
group of 3 digits in a number, separated by a comma

Ways to Write a Number
expanded form
standard form
word name

Learn

Jigsaw puzzles can be fun but complicated to put together. It took about a week for students at Gravenvoorde School in the Netherlands to put together a giant jigsaw puzzle with 204,484 pieces!

Place value can help you understand the value of the **digits** in the number of puzzle pieces used.

Example

Thousands Period			Ones Period		
hundred thousands	ten thousands	thousands	hundreds	tens	ones
2	0	4 ,	4	8	4

Here are some ways you can write this number.

expanded form 200,000 + 4,000 + 400 + 80 + 4
standard form 204,484
word name two hundred four thousand, four hundred eighty-four

Math Tip
Use commas to separate periods when you write a number.

What is the value of each 4 in 204,484?

Check

Write the word name for each number.

1. 4,663 **2.** 23,509 **3.** 400,806 **4.** 56,803

5. Write 300,000 + 7,000 + 200 + 6 in standard form.

6. Write the value of the red digit in 31,645.

7. **Reasoning** In the number 9,026, what does the zero tell you?

Practice

Skills and Reasoning

Write the word name for each number.

8. 29,763 **9.** 78,321 **10.** 532,971 **11.** 96,673

12. Write 20,000 + 4,000 + 900 + 30 + 2 in standard form.

13. Write the value of the red digit in 54,389.

14. Write a 6-digit number with 5 in the ten-thousands place and 2 in the thousands place.

Problem Solving and Applications

15. **Geometry Readiness** Write the color of the missing jigsaw piece.

16. Wei XuChong was the winner of the world's largest musical chairs game, which was played at the Anglo-Chinese School in Singapore. The game started with 8,238 people. Write the word name for that number.

17. **Patterns** What number comes next? 548, 5,480, 54,800

Mixed Review and Test Prep

STAY SHARP!

Algebra Readiness Find each missing number.

18. $15 + 4 = n$ **19.** $18 - 4 = n$ **20.** $12 + 7 = n$ **21.** $19 - 8 = n$

22. What is the mode of the spelling test scores?
87, 85, 84, 87, 86, 87, 86, 85

Ⓐ 84 Ⓑ 85 Ⓒ 86 Ⓓ 87

Chapter 2
Lesson
2

Exploring Place-Value Relationships

Problem Solving Connection
- Draw a Picture
- Look for a Pattern

Materials
place-value blocks

Math Tip
Look for place-value patterns.

Explore

You can explore place-value patterns by using place-value blocks or by drawing pictures.

Work Together

1. Use place-value blocks or draw pictures to show your answers.
   a. How many ones are in 10?
   b. How many tens are in 100?
   c. How many tens are in 200?
   d. How many hundreds are in 300?
   e. How many hundreds are in 1,000?
2. Use patterns or draw pictures to show your answers.
   a. How many tens are in 400?
   b. How many hundreds are in 4,000?
   c. How many tens are in 1,000?
   d. How many hundreds are in 3,600?

Talk About It

3. Describe the place-value patterns you found.
4. Suppose you don't have place-value blocks or paper and pencil. How can you find the number of tens in 900?

Connect

Our place-value system is based on groups of 10.

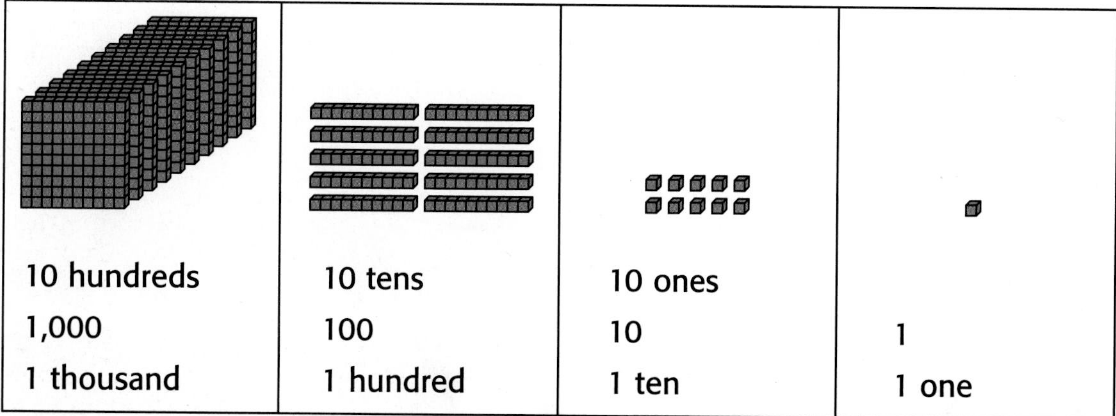

Practice

Copy and complete the table. You may use place-value blocks or draw pictures to help you.

	Number	Hundreds	Tens	Ones
1.	300	3		
2.	500			500
3.	1,800		180	
4.	2,400			

5. What is the least number of place-value blocks you need to show 5,000? The greatest?

Using Data Use the pictograph for **6–8.**

Distances Traveled to Warmer Climates	
Gray whale	● ● ● ● ● ●
White stork	● ● ● ● ● ● ● ●
Monarch butterfly	● ●
European eel	● ● ● ●

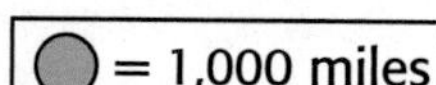

6. Which travels farther, the white stork or the gray whale?

7. How far does the European eel travel?

8. How far does the monarch butterfly fly?

9. **Journal** Suppose you had 1,200 index cards. Explain how you could stack the cards into stacks of 10, 100, and 1,000.

Chapter 2
Lesson
3

Place Value Through Millions

You Will Learn
how to read and write numbers through the hundred millions

Learn

What is the greatest number of crayons you've ever used to make a drawing? You might like to visit a crayon factory that made 145,432,279 crayons in a month!

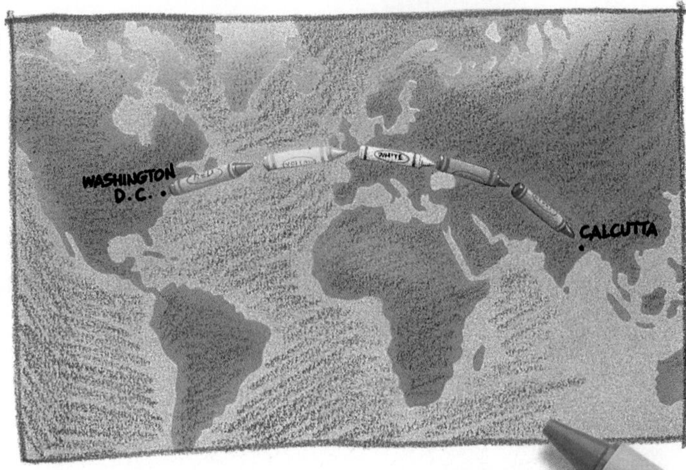

If 145,432,279 crayons were put in a row, they would almost reach from Washington, D.C., to Calcutta, India.

Place value can help you understand this number.

Millions Period			Thousands Period			Ones Period		
hundred millions	ten millions	millions	hundred thousands	ten thousands	thousands	hundreds	tens	ones
1	4	5 ,	4	3	2 ,	2	7	9

standard form 145,432,279

word name one hundred forty-five million, four hundred thirty-two thousand, two hundred seventy-nine

Math Tip
When you read a number, read the number in each period and then the period name.

Talk About It

What do the three periods—the millions, the thousands, and the ones—have in common?

Check

Write the word name for each number.

1. 36,921,438 **2.** 400,000 **3.** 8,200,000

4. Write five million, one hundred thousand in standard form.

5. Write the value of the red digit in 43,261,800.

6. **Reasoning** What is the greatest place value of an 8-digit number?

Practice

Skills and Reasoning

Write the word name for each number.

7. 9,253,074 8. 10,634,000 9. 23,046,116 10. 15,306,108

Write the standard form for each number.

11. four million, seven hundred thousand, nine hundred fifty
12. five million, three hundred ninety thousand, seven
13. Write the value of the red digit in 10,100,110.
14. Write a 7-digit number with 4 in the ten-thousands place and 4 in the thousands place.
15. In the number 12,345,678, which digit has the greatest value?

Problem Solving and Applications

16. **Using Data** Use the Data File on page 48. Write the word name for the number of crayons Douglas Mehrens uses.

Patterns Look for a pattern. Write the number that comes next.

17. 429, 4,290, 42,900 18. 5,625,000, 562,500, 56,250

19. **Collecting Data** Find a fact that uses a number in the millions. Write the standard form or the word name for the number.
20. **Critical Thinking** A certain number has six digits. Can the number be in the millions? Explain.

Mixed Review and Test Prep

STAY SHARP!

Find each answer.

21. $3 + 8 = n$
22. $18 - 8 = n$
23. Find the median weight of the soccer players.
    Ⓐ 72 lb
    Ⓑ 70 lb
    Ⓒ 63 lb
    Ⓓ 61 lb

Chapter 2
Lesson
4

Problem Solving

Analyze Strategies: Make an Organized List

You Will Learn
how making an organized list can help you solve problems

Learn

Do you enjoy doodling? If you are 10 years old, you probably have already worn down about 730 crayons.

How many two-color combinations of doodles can you make with green, blue, purple and yellow crayons?

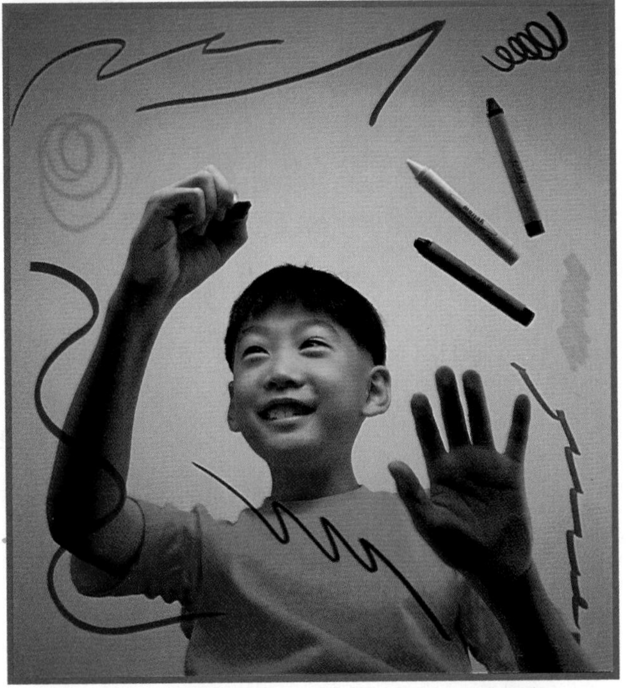

Work Together

▶ Understand

What do you know?

What do you need to find out?

▶ Plan

Decide how to organize your list.

Make an organized list of all two-color combinations.

Use an abbreviation like P-Y for a purple-yellow combination.

 is the same as 

▶ Solve

Start your list using green. Repeat for each color.

List all the possible combinations.

G-B	B-P	P-Y
G-P	B-Y	
G-Y		

Use a pattern to organize your list.

$3 + 2 + 1 = 6$

What's the answer?

There are 6 different combinations.

Problem Solving Hint
Combine each color with all the other colors.

▶ Look Back

How can you check your answer?

Another Example

Here's another chance to be an artist. Shirts come in red, white, or blue. Letters on the shirts can be purple or green. Can you design 7 different two-color shirts?

What You Read	What You Do
a. Shirts come in red, white, or blue. Lettering can be purple or green.	Make a list. RP WP BP RG WG BG
b. Can you design 7 different two-color shirts?	Count the entries
No, you can only make 6 different shirts.	There are 6 entries.

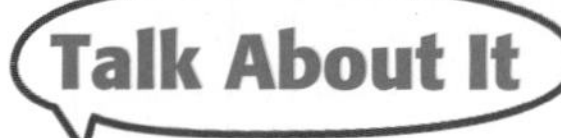

Why is making an organized list a good strategy to use to solve the problems in the Examples?

Check

Use an organized list to help solve each problem.

1. How many two-color combinations can you make with one primary and one secondary color?

   a. To start your list, pick a primary color.
   b. Combine that color with each secondary color. Then for each other primary color, write its combinations with each secondary color.
   c. How many different ways did you find?
   d. Did you find them all?

2. At Picasso's Art Shop, paint brushes are packed in boxes of 10, 100, or 1,000 brushes. There is an order for 1,150 paint brushes.
   a. Find three different ways to fill the order.
   b. What is the fewest number of boxes needed to fill the order?
   c. What is the greatest number of boxes needed to fill the order?

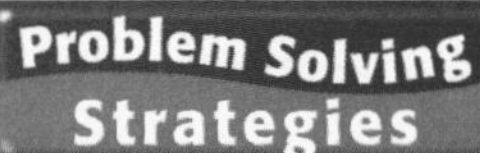

- Use Objects/Act It Out
- Draw a Picture
- Look for a Pattern
- Guess and Check
- Use Logical Reasoning
- Make an Organized List
- Make a Table
- Solve a Simpler Problem
- Work Backward

Choose a Tool

Apply the Strategy

Make an organized list to solve each problem.

3. Suppose you have 5 neon markers: green, purple, blue, yellow, and pink. You choose 2 markers to make a drawing.

a. How many different choices do you have?

b. If one color must be green, how many choices do you have?

c. If someone gave you an orange marker so you had 6 markers in all, how many choices do you have?

4. At the store, paper is packed in boxes of 10, 100, or 1,000 sheets. Suppose a customer orders 2,250 sheets.

a. Find three ways the order can be filled.

b. What is the fewest boxes needed to fill the order?

c. What is the most boxes needed to fill the order?

Choose the Strategy

Make an organized list or use any strategy to solve each problem.

5. **Fine Arts** How many different faces can you make?

Pairs of eyes: 

Noses: 

Mouth:

Explain the strategy you used.

6. Mike and Nadi have a total of 15 markers. Nadi has 3 less than Mike. How many markers do each have?

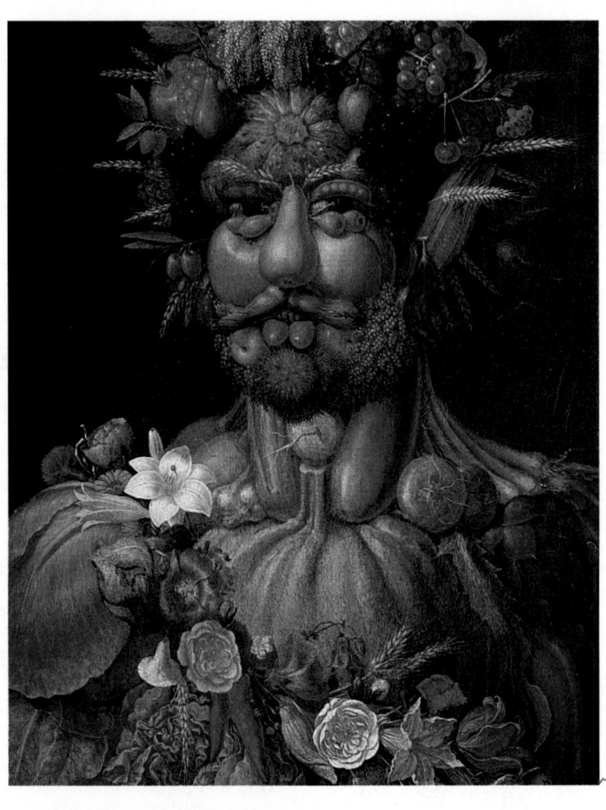

Painting by Italian artist Giuseppe Arcimboldo (1527–1593)

Problem Solving and GEOGRAPHY

When maps are drawn, areas that touch are given different colors. To fill in any map, you need at most four different colors.

7. How many four-color combinations are possible with 5 crayons?

8. Delaware has 20 counties fewer than Wyoming. How many counties does Delaware have?

9. **Collecting Data** What states border Wyoming?

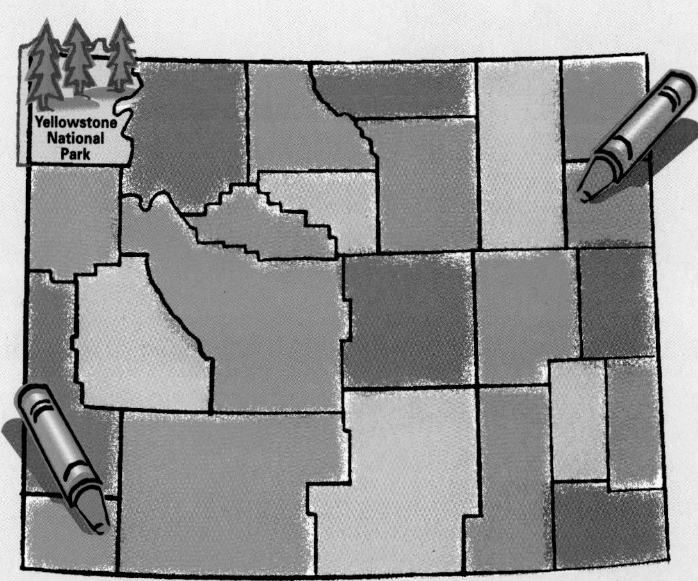

The state of Wyoming has 23 counties, which are shown here.

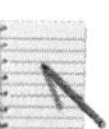

10. **Journal** Use the art supplies to write a problem that can be solved by making an organized list.

Art Supplies
Crayon
Paint
Chalk
Chart paper
Poster board

Mixed Review and Test Prep

Algebra Readiness Find each sum or difference.

11. $9 + 3 = n$
12. $14 - 9 = n$
13. $8 + 4 = n$
14. $17 - 6 = n$
15. $8 + 7 = n$
16. $17 - 8 = n$
17. $6 + 8 = n$
18. $18 - 9 = n$

Using Data Use the bar graph to answer **19–21.**

19. Which is the most popular color?

20. Which color had 2 more votes than violet?

21. How many students were asked which was their favorite color?

Ⓐ 12 Ⓑ 22

Ⓒ 32 Ⓓ 42

Our Favorite Colors

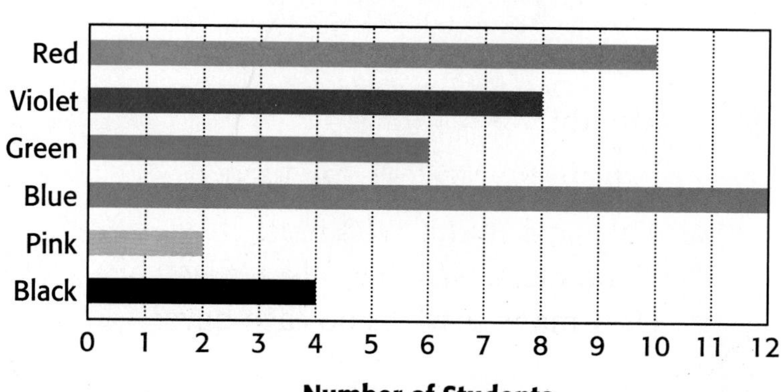

The TEN GRAND Game

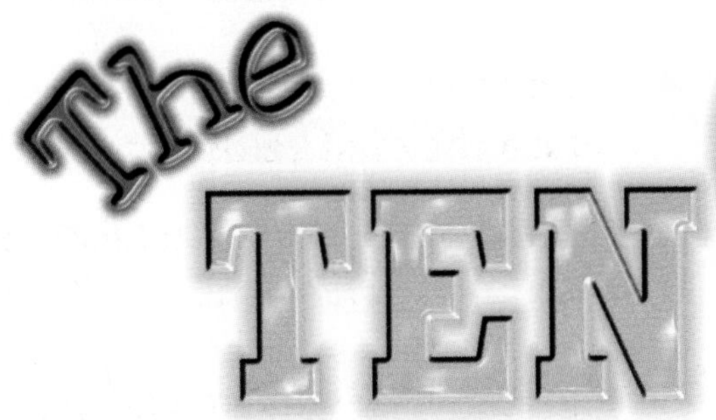

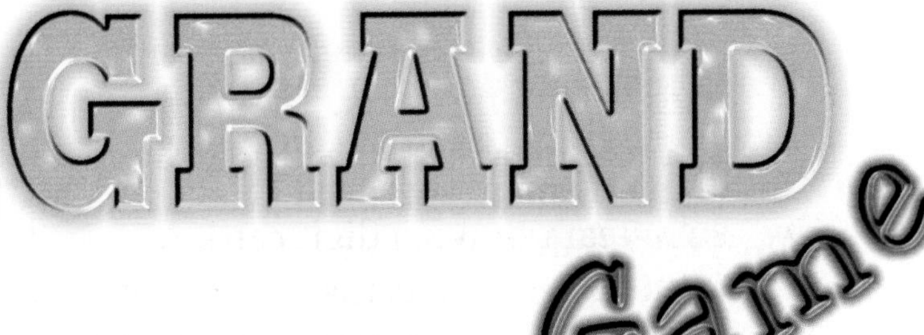

Players
2 teams

Materials

- calculator

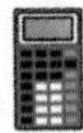

- gameboard
- 2 markers
- set of digit cards

1 2 3 4

5 6 7 8 9

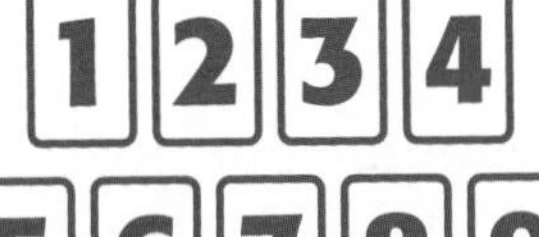

Object
The object of the game is to get a total score of exactly "ten grand," or 10,000.

How to Play

1. Each team places a marker on any square on the gameboard.

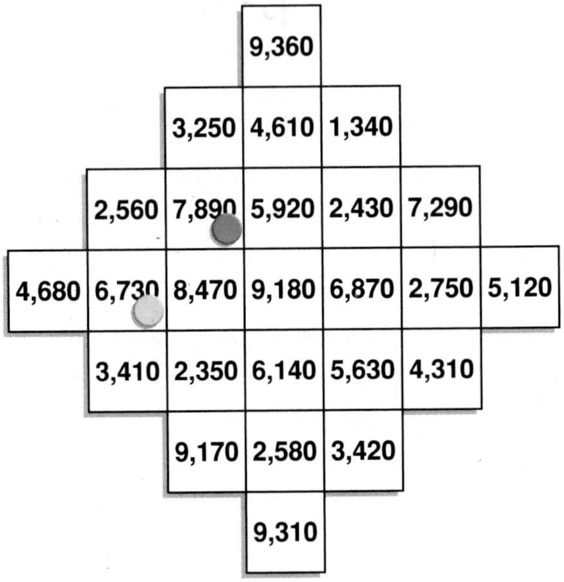
9,360
3,250 4,610 1,340
2,560 7,890 5,920 2,430 7,290
4,680 6,730 8,470 9,180 6,870 2,750 5,120
3,410 2,350 6,140 5,630 4,310
9,170 2,580 3,420
9,310

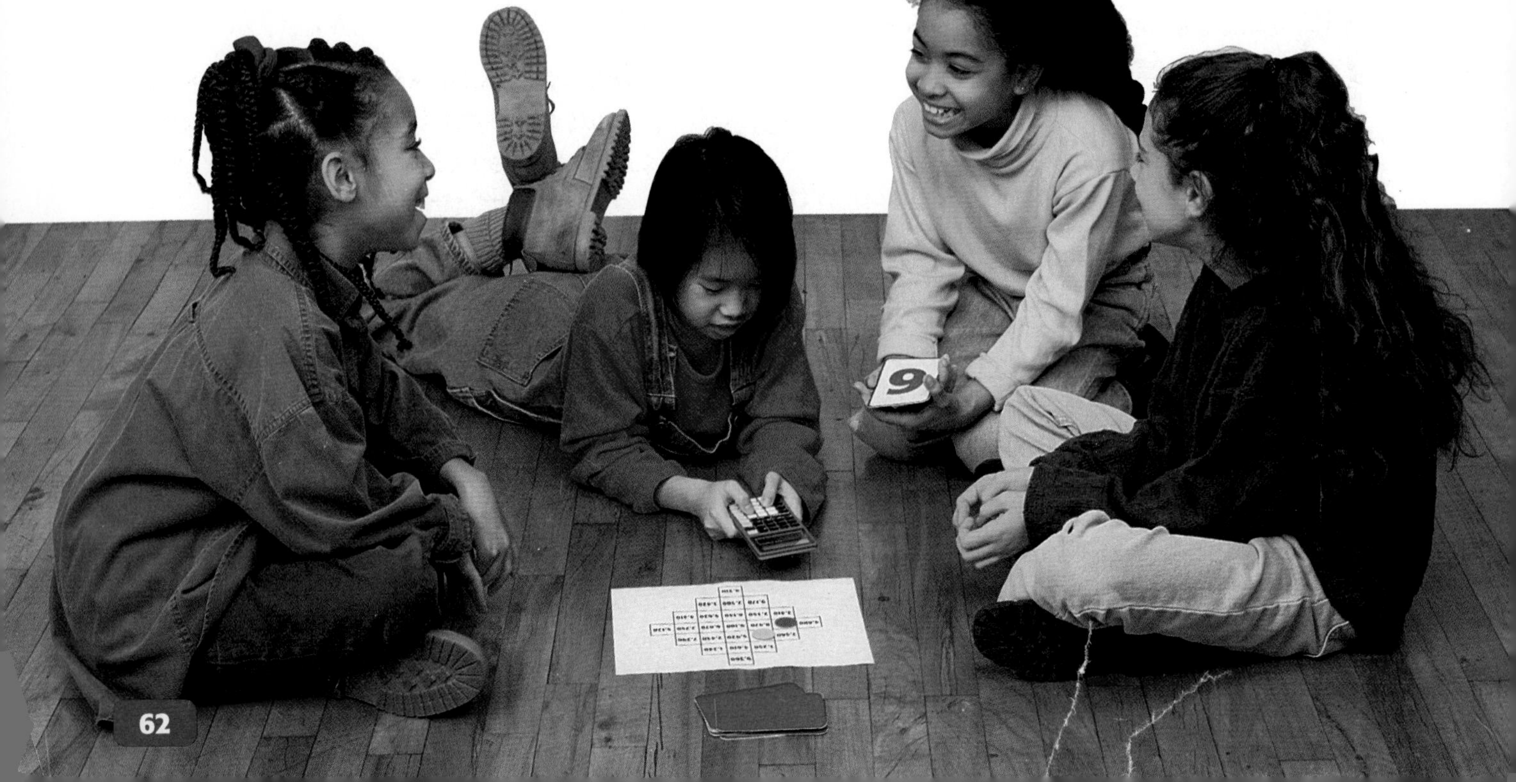
9

2 Each team draws a digit card and returns it to the stack. The team with the greater number goes first.

3 Each team draws a digit card. A team may move its marker to any "touching" square with a matching digit. The marker may be moved up, down, left, right, or diagonally.

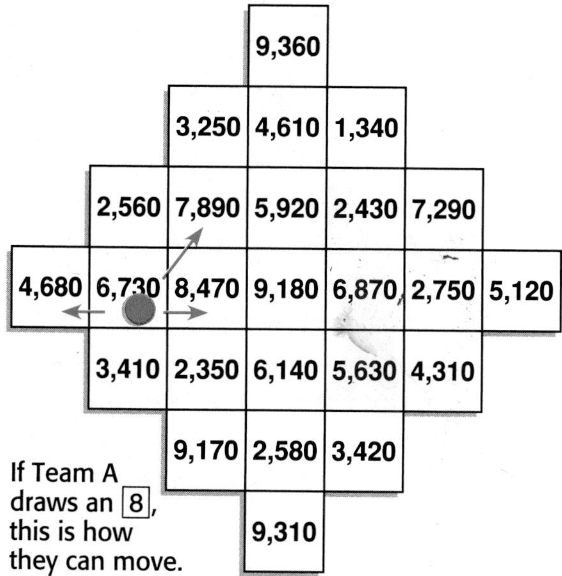

4 If no "touching" square has the digit, the team loses a turn.

5 Each team scores the place value of the matching digit.

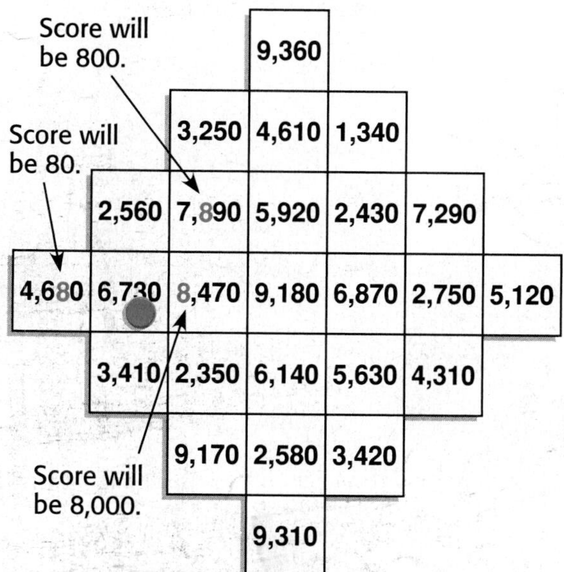

6 Both teams record their scores and return the digit cards to the stack.

7 Both teams continue to take turns. Each team adds its scores. The first team to score exactly 10,000 wins. If a team goes over 10,000, it loses.

Talk About It

1. Did you always choose to move to the greatest number? Explain.
2. What strategies did you use to get to 10,000 without "going over"?

More Ways to Play

- Play again. Make a 0 digit card for the stack.
- Play again. Change your goal from 10,000 to 20,000.
- Make your own gameboard by copying the grid and putting your own 4-digit numbers in the squares.

Reasoning

1. Suppose your score was 8,000 and your digit card was 2. Would 2,560 or 3,420 be a better choice for your move? Explain.
2. Suppose your score was 8,000 and your digit card was 3. Would 3,420 or 9,310 be a better choice for your move? Explain.
3. If your score was 6,800, what numbers would you need to win in two moves? In three moves?

SECTION A

Review and Practice

Vocabulary Match each with its example.

1. number with three periods
2. standard form
3. expanded form
4. word name

a. twenty-five thousand, one hundred eleven
b. 2,154
c. 100,000,000
d. 50,000 + 2,000 + 600 + 40 + 3

(Lesson 1) Write the word name for each number.

5. 14,913 6. 892,211 7. 3,479 8. 555,000 9. 5,006,390

(Lesson 2) Copy and complete the table.

	Number	Hundreds	Tens	Ones
10.	4,000			4,000
11.	2,900			

(Lesson 3) Write the value of each red digit.

12. 86,987,002 13. 72,989,920 14. 900,900,020 15. 362,481

16. **Science** Earth is about 93,000,000 miles from the sun. Mercury is about 36,000,000 miles from the sun and is the planet closest to the sun. Write the value of the digit 3 in each number.

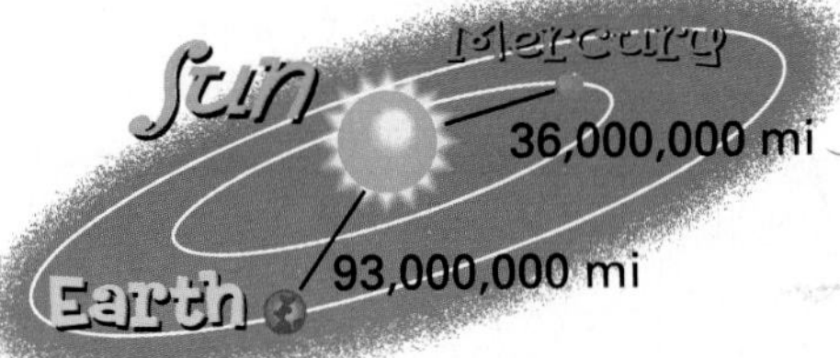

(Lesson 4) Make an organized list or use any strategy to solve.

17. Cards are packed in boxes of 10, 100, or 1,000 cards.
    a. Find three different ways to fill an order for 1,750 cards.
    b. What is the fewest number of boxes needed to fill the order?
    c. What is the greatest number of boxes needed to fill the order?

18. **Journal** How would you explain to a friend what place value means? What tools or pictures would you use?

Skills Checklist

In this section, you have:

- ☑ Learned About Place Value Through Millions
- ☑ Explored Place-Value Relationships
- ☑ Solved Problems by Making an Organized List

REVIEW AND PRACTICE

CHAPTER 2

SECTION

B Building Number Sense

In the past 50 years, the population of Springfield, Missouri, has grown from almost 67,000 people to more than 150,000.

Make a list of different ways you can show that your city is larger or smaller than Springfield.

GET READY!

Comparing and Ordering Numbers

Review place value. Which number do you say first when you count from 1?

1. 19 or 91 **2.** 47 or 41 **3.** 45 or 43

4. 29 or 39 **5.** 160 or 150 **6.** 225 or 235

Skills Checklist

In this section, you will:

- ❒ Compare Numbers
- ❒ Order Numbers
- ❒ Explore Rounding

Chapter 2
Lesson
5

Comparing Numbers

You Will Learn
how to compare numbers to find which is greater

Vocabulary
compare
to decide which of two numbers is greater

Learn

On which day of the week were you born?

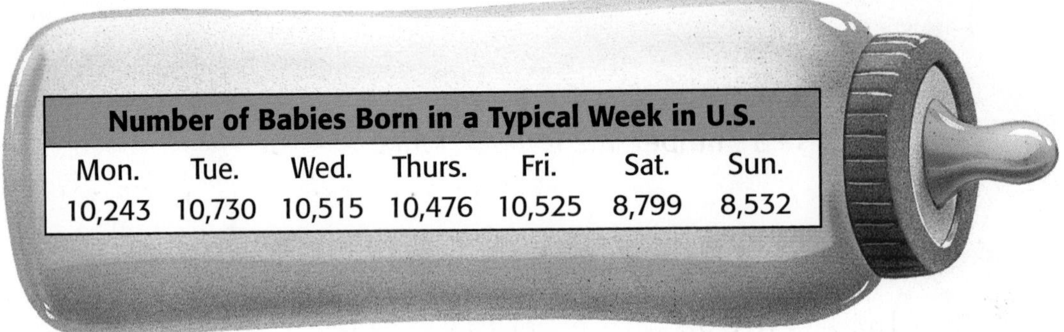

Number of Babies Born in a Typical Week in U.S.						
Mon.	Tue.	Wed.	Thurs.	Fri.	Sat.	Sun.
10,243	10,730	10,515	10,476	10,525	8,799	8,532

You can use a number line to **compare** numbers.

Math Tip
> means "is greater than"
< means "is less than"

Example 1

Were there more babies born on Wednesday than on Friday?

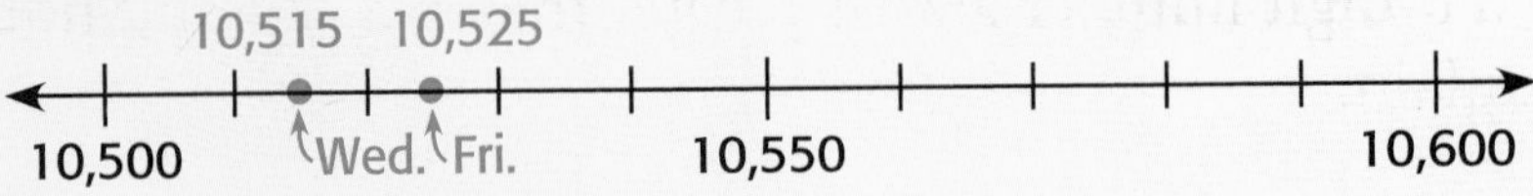

10,525 > 10,515 More babies were born on Friday than on Wednesday.

You can also use place value to compare numbers.

Example 2

Compare 41,572 and 43,245.

Step 1

Begin at the left. Compare.
41,572
43,245
Both numbers have 4 ten thousands or 40,000.

Step 2

Find the first place where the digits are different. Compare.
41,572
43,245
1 thousand < 3 thousands

So, 41,572 < 43,245 or 43,245 > 41,572

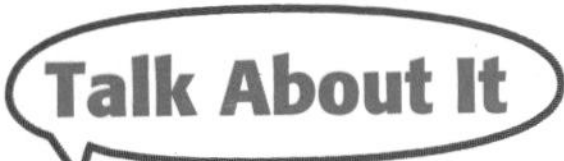

Why do you begin at the left to compare digits?

Check

Compare. Use a number line to help. Write >, <, or =.

1. 9,110 ● 9,190 **2.** 8,950 ● 9,220 **3.** 9,210 ● 9,190 **4.** 35,952 ● 53,952

5. Reasoning Write a 5-digit number greater than 12,247 and less than 12,427.

Practice

Skills and Reasoning

Compare. Use a number line to help. Write >, <, or =.

6. 455 ● 426 **7.** 32,111 ● 31,222 **8.** 75,491 ● 83,491

9. 67,094 ● 63,215 **10.** 30,034 ● 30,035 **11.** 9,999 ● 10,000

12. 81,032 ● 81,132 **13.** 94,738 ● 94,638 **14.** 6,514 ● 6,514

15. 32,334 ● 32,443 **16.** 1,468,092 ● 9,579 **17.** 4,237 ● 42,370

Using Data Use the baby data on page 66 for **18** and **19**.

18. List numbers less than 10,000. **19.** List numbers greater than 10,520.

20. Is a 6-digit number always greater than a 5-digit number? Explain.

Problem Solving and Applications

Using Data Use the table for **21** and **22**.

21. Do more people have the name Rivera or Long?

22. Do more people have the name López or Cox?

23. Collecting Data Ask your classmates on which days of the week they were born. Make a bar graph. Compare it with the data on page 66.

Number of People in U.S. with the Same Last Names	
Last Name	**Number**
Long	229,615
López	254,535
Rivera	238,457
Cox	256,842

Mixed Review and Test Prep

Algebra Readiness Copy and complete.

24. $12 + 5 = n$ **25.** $16 - n = 11$ **26.** $n - 4 = 12$ **27.** $n + 9 = 16$

28. Which number has 4 in the thousands place and 3 in the tens place?

Ⓐ 13,542 Ⓑ 34,215 Ⓒ 24,531 Ⓓ 43,152

PRACTICE AND APPLY

Chapter 2
Lesson
6

Ordering Numbers

You Will Learn
how to order a group of numbers

Vocabulary
order
to place numbers from least to greatest or greatest to least

Learn

In her diary, Laura Ingalls Wilder wrote, "As we climbed the hills this side of Springfield, the air grew fresher."

Which Springfield was she talking about? When you put the population numbers in order, it is next to the greatest number.

City and State	Population, 1990
Springfield, Missouri	140,494
Springfield, Illinois	105,227
Springfield, Massachusetts	156,983
Springfield, Ohio	70,487
Springfield, New Jersey	13,420

You can use place value to **order** the numbers.

Example

Step 1
Compare the numbers two at a time to find the greatest number.
140,494 > 105,227
156,983 > 140,494
156,983 > 70,487
156,983 > 13,420

Step 2
Continue comparing the other numbers.
140,494 > 105,227
105,227 > 70,487
70,487 > 13,420

Step 3
Then order the numbers from greatest to least.
156,983
140,494
105,227
70,487
13,420

If 156,983 is the greatest number, 140,494 is the next greatest number.
So, Wilder wrote about Springfield, Missouri!

Did You Know?
There are more than 20 places named Springfield in the United States!

Talk About It

Why did you begin by comparing two numbers at a time?

Check

1. Order the numbers from least to greatest.
524,500, 524,050, 524,505, 524,550

2. Write three numbers that are more than 80,000 but less than 81,000.

Practice

Skills and Reasoning

Order the numbers from least to greatest.

3. 70,000, 70,700, 77,000, 70,770 **4.** 41,253, 714,253, 542,708, 312,649

Order the numbers from greatest to least.

5. 40,000, 44,000, 40,400, 40,440

6. 343,343, 334,434, 334,343, 343,433

7. Write a number between 14,250 and 14,750.

8. These numbers are ordered from greatest to least: 147,211, 144,936, 141,587, 139,894. Between which two numbers is 143,768?

Problem Solving and Applications

9. Logic Use the digits 7, 7, 5, and 5. Create as many 4-digit numbers as you can. Order them from greatest to least.

Using Data Use the table for **10–12.**

State	Number of People	Area (square miles)
Alaska	603,617	570,374
Delaware	717,197	1,982
North Dakota	641,367	68,994
Utah	1,951,408	82,168
Wyoming	480,184	97,105

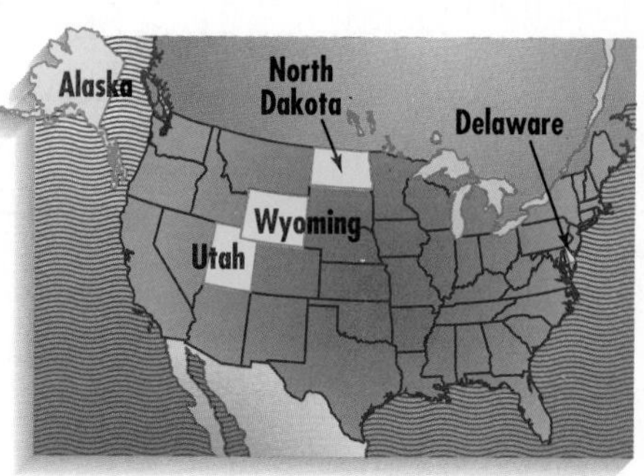

10. Name the states in order from fewest people to most people.

11. Name the states in order from least area to greatest area.

12. Critical Thinking Do the states with the fewest people also have the least area? Explain.

Mixed Review and Test Prep

Algebra Readiness Find each answer.

13. $17 - 6 = n$ **14.** $15 - 8 = n$ **15.** $8 + 3 + 4 = n$ **16.** $2 + 7 + 5 = n$

17. Name the period shown by the red digits in 413,296,083.

Ⓐ ones Ⓑ thousands Ⓒ millions Ⓓ not here

Exploring Rounding

Problem Solving Connection
- Draw a Picture
- Use Logical Reasoning

Materials
ruler

Vocabulary
estimate
to find a number that is close to the exact number

rounding
replacing a number with a number that tells about how many or how much

Explore

Don't let it bug you, but new insects are discovered all the time. Scientists discover about 7,000 new kinds of insects every year!

In this case, the number 7,000 is not an exact number. It is an **estimate**.

Rounding is one way to estimate.

Work Together

1. Copy each number line. Show what number is halfway between the two given numbers.

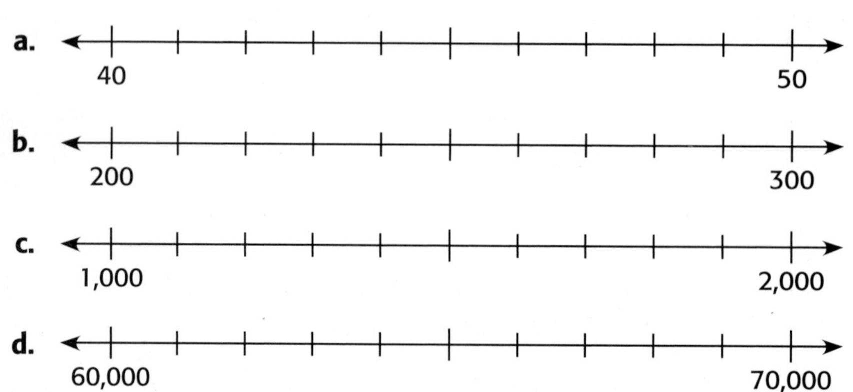

2. Use your number lines to help answer each.
   - a. Is 48 closer to 40 or 50?
   - b. Is 241 closer to 200 or 300?
   - c. Is 1,392 closer to 1,000 or 2,000?
   - d. Is 65,017 closer to 60,000 or 70,000?

Did You Know?
You can hear the "tsh-ee-EEEE-e-ou" sound of the male cicada from about 450 yards away.

Talk About It

3. How did you find each halfway number?
4. Explain how you decide if 2,493 is closer to 2,000 or 3,000.

Connect

Here is a method for rounding.

Example

Round the number to the nearest hundred.

Step 1	Step 2
Find the digit in the place to which you are rounding. 635 ↑ Round to the nearest hundred.	Look at the digit to the right. 635 ↑ Round down, if the number is less than 5. or Round up, if the number is 5 or greater. 3 < 5 So, 6 stays the same.

635 rounds to 600.

Practice

Round each number to the nearest hundred.

1. 276 **2.** 552 **3.** 385 **4.** 197 **5.** 545

Round each number to the nearest thousand.

6. 4,000 **7.** 8,045 **8.** 4,984 **9.** 5,409 **10.** 5,555

11. 6,514 **12.** 3,251 **13.** 6,189 **14.** 8,073 **15.** 6,438

16. Is 56,053 closer to 50,000 or 60,000? Explain.

17. Is 213,900 closer to 210,000 or 220,000? Explain.

18. Reasoning Write five numbers that round to 200 when rounded to the nearest hundred.

19. Science There are 136,800 kinds of butterflies and crickets.

a. Round this number to the nearest ten thousand.

b. Round this number to the nearest hundred thousand.

20. Critical Thinking I am a 3-digit number. Use the clues to find me.

- I am greater than 700.
- I am less than 757.
- My ones digit is a 3.
- I am 800 when rounded to the nearest hundred.

21. Journal You want to round 462 to the nearest hundred. How does it help to know what number is halfway between 400 and 500?

Skills Practice Bank, page 560, Set 3

SECTION B

Review and Practice

Vocabulary Choose the best word to complete each exercise.

Word List
order rounds compare

1. 4,932 ____ to 5,000
2. You can ____ 4,932, 4,923, and 4,329 to find which number is greatest. Then you can put them in ____ from greatest to least.

(Lesson 5) Compare. Write >, <, or =.

3. 80,001 ● 80,100
4. 4,990 ● 4,929
5. 7,332,878 ● 7,323,878
6. 455,311 ● 455,331
7. 2,999 ● 3,001
8. 629,348 ● 629,348
9. Write the greatest number using the digits 1, 7, 9, 3, and 2.
10. Write the least number using the digits 8, 4, 6, 1, 9, and 7.

(Lesson 6) Order each set of numbers from least to greatest.

11. 880,000, 80,000, 800,000
12. 314,500, 632,070, 504,707
13. **Logic** Use the digits 6, 9, 5. Create as many 3-digit numbers as you can. Order the numbers from greatest to least.

(Lesson 7) Round each number to the nearest hundred.

14. 529
15. 879
16. 497
17. 634
18. 821

Round each number to the nearest thousand in **19–21.**

19. The largest teddy bear picnic was attended by 18,116 bears.
20. The largest balloon sculpture had 25,344 colored balloons.
21. **History** At a New Year's Day Celebration in 1907, President Roosevelt shook hands with 8,513 people.
22. **Reasoning** Write four numbers that when rounded to the nearest thousand would be 3,000.
23. **Using Data** Use the Data File on page 49. Which group had the greatest number of people coming to the United States in 1990? The least number of people?
24. **Journal** Describe how you can compare two 4-digit numbers.

Skills Checklist

In this section, you have:

- ☑ Compared Numbers
- ☑ Ordered Numbers
- ☑ Explored Rounding

CHAPTER 2

SECTION

C Making Sense of Time

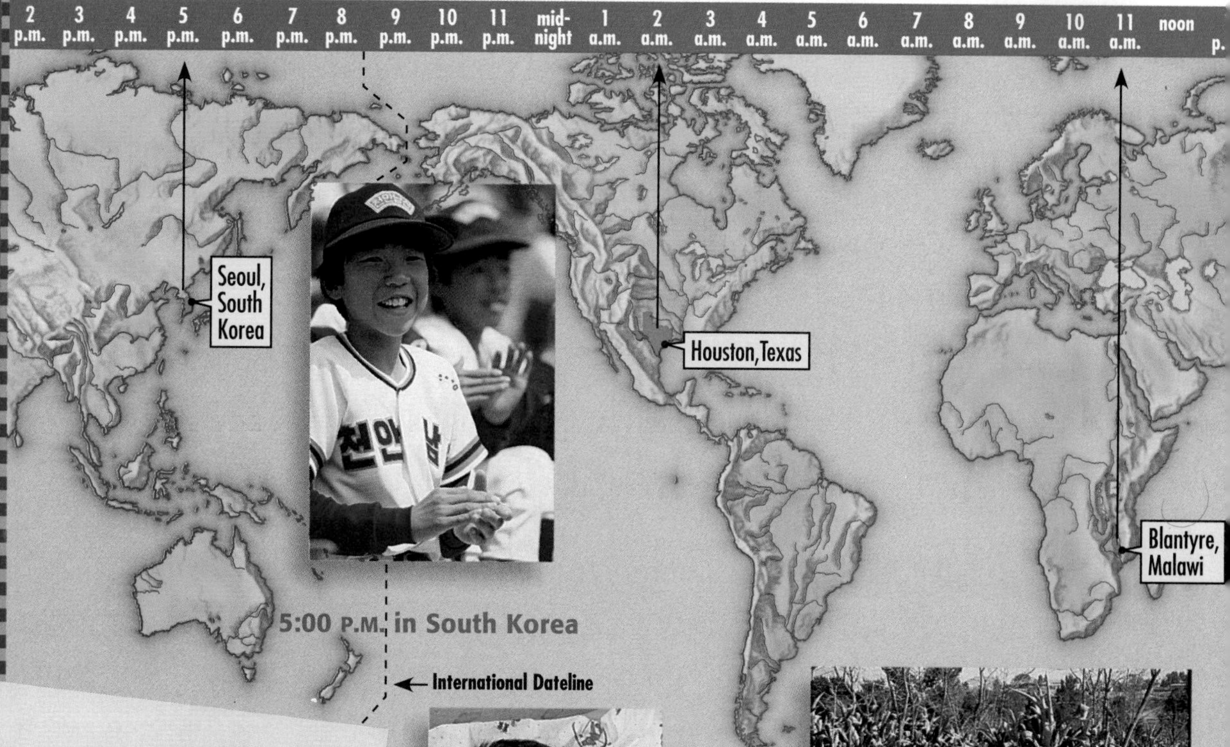

2 p.m. 3 p.m. 4 p.m. 5 p.m. 6 p.m. 7 p.m. 8 p.m. 9 p.m. 10 p.m. 11 p.m. mid-night 1 a.m. 2 a.m. 3 a.m. 4 a.m. 5 a.m. 6 a.m. 7 a.m. 8 a.m. 9 a.m. 10 a.m. 11 a.m. noon

Seoul, South Korea

Houston, Texas

Blantyre, Malawi

International Dateline

5:00 P.M. in South Korea

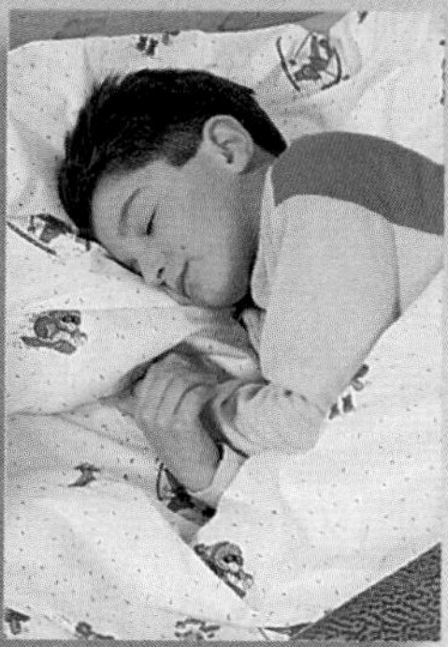

2:00 A.M. in the United States

11:00 A.M. in Malawi

It's a different time at different places around the world. When you are asleep, a student in South Korea may be eating dinner. What do you think a student in Malawi could be doing while you're in math class?

Making Sense of Time

Review some facts about time.

1. How many minutes are in an hour?
2. How many hands are on a clock?
3. What does each hand show?

Skills Checklist

In this section, you will:

- ❐ Learn to Tell Time
- ❐ Explore Estimating Time
- ❐ Find Elapsed Time
- ❐ Explore the Calendar
- ❐ Solve Problems by Making Decisions

Chapter 2
Lesson
8

Telling Time

You Will Learn
how to tell time to the minute and identify A.M. and P.M.

Vocabulary

analog clock
a clock with hands

digital clock
a clock that displays just numbers

A.M.
times from midnight to noon

P.M.
times from noon to midnight

Learn

You can show and read time in different ways.

Analog clock

Digital clock

You can read or write the time as 2:40 or as 20 minutes to 3.

Danielle will get out of school at 2:40. Is that A.M. or P.M.?

She gets out of school in the afternoon. So, it is 2:40 P.M.

Talk About It

What might Danielle be doing at 4:30 A.M.?

Check

Write each time two ways.

1.

2.

3. **Reasoning** What is the greatest number of minutes a digital clock can show?

Practice

Skills and Reasoning

Write each time two ways.

4. 

5. 

Write a reasonable time for each. Use A.M. or P.M.

6. Eat lunch
7. Start school
8. Play outside
9. Do homework
10. Have recess
11. Look at the moon

Draw an analog clock and a digital clock for each time.

12. quarter to four
13. half past midnight
14. eleven twenty
15. How many times in one day will a clock show the time 3:48?
16. What time is 1 minute earlier than 3 o'clock?

Problem Solving and Applications

17. **Patterns** Danielle hears the weather forecast at 8:08 A.M., 8:18 A.M., and 8:28 A.M. When will the next forecast be?
18. Danielle and Lorenzo met for lunch. Danielle arrived at 15 min before 1 P.M. Lorenzo arrived at 12:43 P.M. Who got there first?
19. **History** Among the oldest working clocks in Europe are the Salisbury Cathedral clock built in 1386, and the Wells Cathedral clock built in 1392. Which clock is older?

Wells Cathedral clock

Mixed Review and Test Prep

STAY SHARP!

 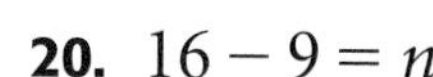 Find each missing number.

20. $16 - 9 = n$
21. $14 - 8 = n$
22. $15 - 4 = n$
23. $18 - 5 = n$
24. **Health** In which country do people eat the most calories daily?

Ⓐ Bulgaria

Ⓑ United States

Ⓒ Ireland

Ⓓ Greece

Country	Daily Calories (per person)
Bulgaria	3,634
United States	3,642
Ireland	3,692
Greece	3,688

Skills Practice Bank, page 560, Set 4

Exploring Time: Exact or Estimate?

Problem Solving Connection
- Look for a Pattern
- Use Logical Reasoning

Remember
The units of time are seconds, minutes, hours, days, weeks, months, and years.

Work Together

1. Read the paragraph. Write the most reasonable unit of time for each activity.

Spot's Diary, June 15

6:00: Woke up. Yawned and stretched for 15 __a.__. Scratched my ears for 2 or 3 __b.__. 6:05: Went to find Louie. Barked for 30 __c.__ until Louie took me out. 6:30: Tired. Went back to sleep for 2 __d.__. 8:30: Yawned. Tired. Went back to sleep for 45 __e.__. 9:15: Stared at food bowl for 15 __f.__ until Louie fed me. 9:30: Ate. Took about 90 __g.__. Went back to sleep. 11:10: Chewed on a bone. After 6 __h.__ of chewing, it's pretty slimy. 12:00: Took long walk with Louie for about 2 __i.__. Chased a little kid. I'm still a puppy, but I am almost 6 __j.__ old in human years. I sat and thought about that for a __k.__, and decided it's a dog's life.

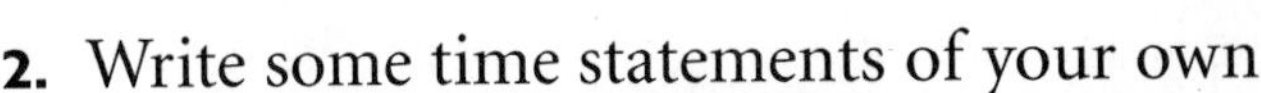

2. Write some time statements of your own.
   a. Think of events that take you different times to do.
   b. Make a list of the events. Leave a blank for the unit of time.
   c. Trade lists with a partner. Fill in the blanks.

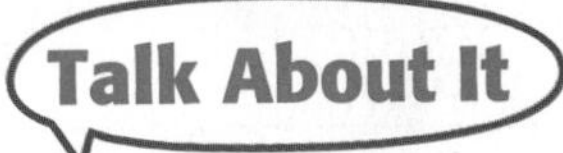

For which events on your partner's list was it reasonable to have different units of time? Why?

Connect

Time is measured in different units.

1 minute (min) = 60 seconds (sec)
1 hour (hr) = 60 minutes
1 day (d) = 24 hours
1 week (wk) = 7 days
1 month (mo) = about 4 weeks
1 year (yr) = 12 months
1 year = 365 days
1 leap year = 366 days
1 decade = 10 years
1 century = 100 years

Practice

Compare. Write <, >, or =.

1. half hour ● 20 minutes
2. 9 days ● 1 week
3. 95 minutes ● 2 hours
4. 14 months ● 1 year
5. 2 years ● 100 weeks
6. 2 months ● 12 weeks
7. Wilma likes to use big numbers. She has recorded all of her times in seconds. What unit would be more reasonable for measuring each event?
   a. "Last night I bowled for 5,260 seconds."
   b. "Washing the dinner dishes took me 1,220 seconds."
   c. "I missed about 100,000 seconds of school last year."
   d. "Our vacation in Nova Scotia lasted for 1,244,200 seconds."

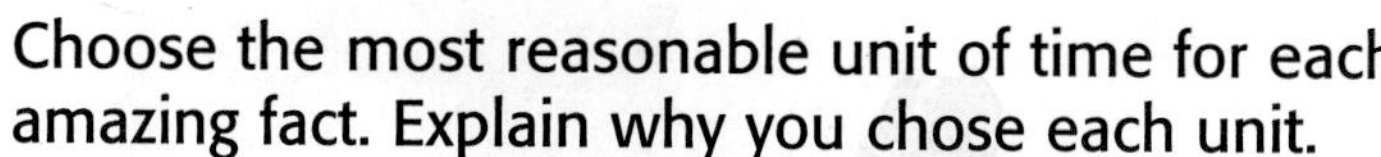

Choose the most reasonable unit of time for each amazing fact. Explain why you chose each unit.

8. The average person spends about 20 _____ of her or his life asleep.
9. **Science** The Venus flytrap plant is fast. Its leaves shut on an insect in less than one-half of a _____.
10. **Health** The bacteria droplets from a sneeze can float in the air for 40 _____. That's almost the same length of time as a math class.
11. With a single push, Klaus Friedrich knocked down a chain of 281,581 dominoes. It took the dominoes almost 13 _____ to fall.
12. **Journal** Describe things you do that take you about 1 second, 1 minute, 1 hour, 1 week, and 1 month.

Chapter 2
Lesson
10

Elapsed Time

You Will Learn
how to find elapsed time

Vocabulary
elapsed time
the difference between two times

Learn

Arrival/Departure Times	
Orlando	11:15 A.M.
Winter Haven	12:37 P.M.
West Palm Beach	3:02 P.M.
Fort Lauderdale	3:55 P.M.
Miami	4:44 P.M.

Here's a man who loved to read train schedules. Never traveling on the same track, John E. Ballenger of Florida traveled 76,485 miles by train.

When you read train schedules, it is useful to know how to find **elapsed time**.

Example

Find the time it takes to travel between Orlando and Miami starting at 11:15 A.M.

Step 1

Count the full hours.

11:15 → 4:15

Step 2

Count the minutes.

4:15 → 4:44

Step 3

Write the elapsed time.

5 hours 29 minutes

A trip from Orlando to Miami takes 5 hours and 29 minutes.

Math Tip
You can skip count by fives to help you count the number of minutes on a clock.

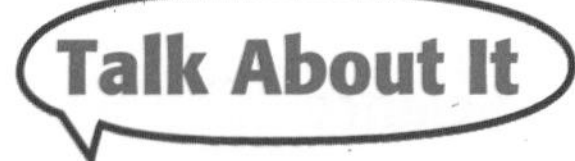

Describe how you could find the elapsed time from 11:15 A.M. to 4:05 P.M.

Check

Find each elapsed time.

1. 3:15 P.M. to 5:54 P.M.
2. 6:30 A.M. to 2:05 P.M.
3. **Reasoning** Explain how you counted the minutes between 6:30 A.M. and 2:05 P.M.

Practice

Skills and Reasoning

Find each elapsed time.

4. 7:44 A.M. to 10:50 A.M. **5.** 1:25 P.M. to 6:15 P.M.

6. 5:03 A.M. to 1:56 P.M. **7.** 8:10 P.M. to 2:08 A.M.

Mental Math Find each elapsed time.

8. 4:00 P.M. to 5:30 P.M. **9.** 4:15 P.M. to 9:15 P.M.

10. Explain why it was easy to find the elapsed times in **8** and **9** mentally.

Copy and complete.

	Start Time	End Time	Elapsed Time
11.	8:22 P.M.		3 hr 33 min
12.		9:00 P.M.	5 hr 54 min

Problem Solving and Applications

13. Health Doctors recommend at least 20 minutes of aerobic exercise a day. Phil starts jogging at 8:52 A.M. and jogs until 9:15 A.M. Has he met the 20-minute aerobic exercise requirement for that day? Explain.

14. Jed rides a unicycle. Suppose he starts riding at 10:20 A.M. and rides for 6 hr and 32 min. When will he stop?

Using Data Use the Data File on page 49 for **15** and **16.**

15. Estimation If you get on the *Silver Star* in Sanford and get off the train in Sebring, about how long are you on the train?

16. If you get on the train in Palatka and get off 2 hours and 10 minutes later, where will you be?

Mixed Review and Test Prep

Find each sum.

17. $8 + 4 + 3$ **18.** $7 + 2 + 4$ **19.** $5 + 7 + 6$ **20.** $2 + 6 + 9$

21. Patterns What is the missing number in the number pattern?

58, 49, 40, ■, 22, 13, …

Ⓐ 29 Ⓑ 31 Ⓒ 39 Ⓓ 42

PRACTICE AND APPLY

Chapter 2
Lesson
11

Exploring the Calendar

Problem Solving Connection

- Look for Patterns
- Use Logical Reasoning

Materials

calendar

Vocabulary

ordinal number
a number used to tell order—for example, second or third

Did You Know?

During a leap year, February has 29 days.

Explore

We use a calendar created under Julius Caesar in 46 B.C. Every fourth year is usually a leap year and has an extra day. Years ending in 00, however, are not leap years unless they can be divided by 400.

SUNDAY	MONDAY	TUESDAY	WEDNESDAY	THURSDAY	FRIDAY	SATURDAY
					1	2
3	4	5	6	7	8	9
10	11	12	13	14	15	16
17	18	19	20	21	22	23
24	25	26	27	28	29	30

September 2000

1600 and 2000 are leap years. 1700 is not.

When you read a calendar, you use **ordinal numbers**, such as first, fifth, and twentieth, to read the dates.

Felt Hat Day is on the fifteenth of September. September is the ninth month of the year.

Work Together

Use the calendar in your classroom.

1. Which day of the week occurs most often in December?
2. Which month is the seventh month of the year?
3. Thanksgiving always falls on the fourth Thursday of November. What is Thanksgiving's date?
4. Which months have five Sundays?
5. Is this year a leap year? Explain.
6. If September 5 falls on a Wednesday, what is the date two weeks later?

Talk About It

What do you notice about the first and last days of this year? Is this true for all years? Explain.

Connect

Here are two ways to remember the number of days in each month.

Some people use an old rhyme.

Thirty days hath
September, April,
June, and November;
All the rest have
thirty-one,
Excepting February
alone, Which hath but
twenty-eight, in fine,
Till leap year gives it
twenty-nine.

Some people count on their knuckles.

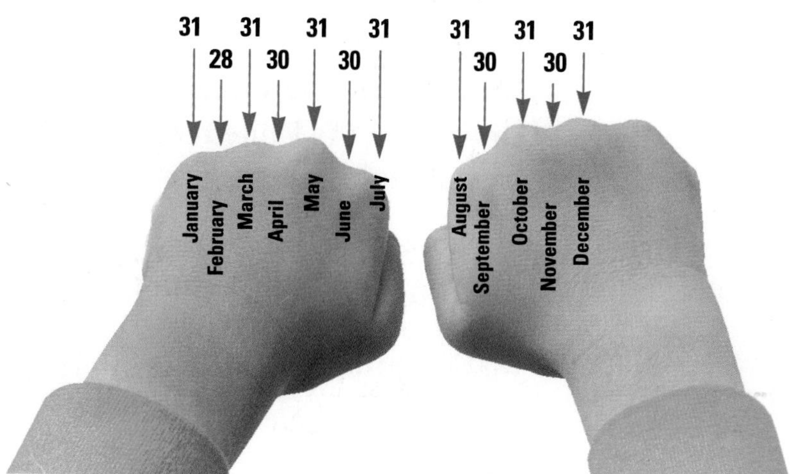

Practice

Use the calendar in your classroom.

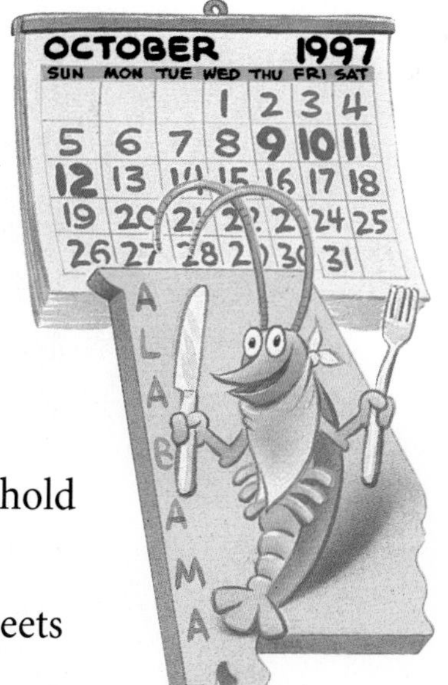

1. How many days are in a leap year?
2. Use ordinal numbers to name the months of the year that do *not* have 31 days.
3. Benjamin was born in 1988. He jokingly says that he has a birthday only every four years. On which day do you think Benjamin was born?
4. In 1997, the National Shrimp Festival in Gulf Shores, Alabama, was October 9–12. A nearby town wanted to hold a festival 4 weeks later. When would their festival start?
5. Suppose you take your puppy to a training class that meets every other week on Wednesdays. If the first class is on March 15th, what are the dates of the next three classes?
6. If July 4 falls on a weekend, workers are often given Friday or Monday off. Did it happen this year? Explain.
7. December, January, and February are winter months. Which are the months in spring? In summer? In fall?
8. **Journal** Explain how you can find the elapsed time from the last day of third grade until the first day of fourth grade.

Chapter 2 Lesson 12

Problem Solving

Decision Making: Scheduling Time

You Will Learn
how creating a schedule can help you make decisions

Explore

Abwenzi African Studies helps students in the United States become friends with students in Africa.

Suppose your class decides to join this exciting project by sending an audio tape to a class in Malawi. You want to make a 30-minute tape of information about your class.

Did You Know?
Abwenzi is the word for "friends" in the Chichewa language of Malawi, Africa.

Decide how you will introduce yourselves. What is important to tell about your class? How will you schedule your time so that your tape is about 30 minutes long?

Here's a sample schedule:

Event	Time (min)	Total Time (min)
Class song	3	3
Hello speech	5	8
Classroom tour	5	13

Work Together

Understand

1. What do you know?
2. What do you need to decide?
3. What information will you need to help you make a decision?

Plan and Solve

4. What are some things about yourselves that you would like to tell the class in Malawi?
5. Make a list of the speakers and what they will do.
6. How can counting the minutes of each speaker help you plan your tape?
7. One student has an idea. "I think each of us should just get 5 minutes." If your class follows this idea, how long will your tape be?
8. Another student has an idea. "Let's talk on one side of the tape and put our favorite songs on the other side." If your class follows this idea, will you have enough tape to include 10 songs? Explain.
9. Should you include extra time in your schedule? Why or why not?

Make a Decision

10. Write a final list of the order of the speakers.
11. Make a schedule to help guide your taping.

Present Your Decision

12. Show your schedule to the class.
13. Does your schedule allow enough time to tell about your class?
14. Compare the different group schedules. What was the longest tape time? The shortest?

15. Check out **www.mathsurf.com/4/ch2** to find out more about Malawi and other African countries.

PROBLEM SOLVING PRACTICE

SECTION C

Review and Practice

Vocabulary Match each with its example.

1. analog clock

2. digital clock

3. elapsed time

a. 

b. 

c. time from 8:20 A.M. to 2:30 P.M.

(Lesson 8) Write each time two different ways.

4. 

5. 

(Lesson 9) Compare. Write >, <, or =.

6. 1 hour ● 71 minutes
7. 48 hours ● 3 days
8. 380 days ● 1 year
9. 3 years ● 100 weeks

(Lesson 10) Find each elapsed time.

10. 6:00 A.M. to 6:00 P.M.
11. 12:20 P.M. to 2:30 P.M.

JANUARY

S	M	T	W	T	F	S
					1	2
3	4	5	6	7	8	9
10	11	12	13	14	15	16
17	18	19	20	21	22	23
24	25	26	27	28	29	30
31						

(Lesson 11) Use the January calendar for **12–14**.

12. How many Sundays are there between January 1st and January 31st?
13. If you go to school every weekday in January, how many days do you go to school?
14. Jodi's birthday is Jan. 25. Her sister's birthday is 8 days earlier. What is the date of her birthday?
15. **Journal** Tell a story about a fun day you had with your family or friends. Include as many statements about time as you can.

Skills Checklist

In this section, you have:

- **Learned to Tell Time**
- **Explored Estimating Time**
- **Found Elapsed Time**
- **Explored the Calendar**
- **Solved Problems by Making Decisions**

REVIEW AND PRACTICE

Choose at least one. Use what you have learned in this chapter.

1 Math Big-tionary

Make your own number dictionary. Make a page for each place value, including the hundred millions. For each place give an example or two. Your examples can be pictures, stories, or amazing facts.

2 Number Round-Up

Challenge a partner to think of a situation where a number rounds to a chosen number. For example, if you choose 300: "There are 275 baseball cards in my collection!" Then switch roles.

3 Number Cube

Use the digits 1, 2, 3. Use each digit only once. Find the missing numbers for the other sides of the cube. Then make your own number cube, using different digits.

4 Calendar Clues

At Home Pick one day of the year (don't tell). Give clues to help someone guess the day.

- in a month that begins with J
- 2-digit date
- not a week-end day … (and so on)

Challenge a friend or family member to guess your day.

5 Cyber Search

Look at **www.mathsurf.com/4/ch2** for sites with big numbers. The sites might show population, world records, or distances in outer space. Order the numbers. Put the ordered numbers in a table. Give your table a title.

CHAPTER 2

Review/Test

Vocabulary Match each with its meaning.

1. standard form	**a.** a group of three digits in a number, separated by a comma
2. digital clock	**b.** shows the time with digits
3. period	**c.** a way to write a number

(Lessons 1, 2, and 3) Give the value of each red digit.

4. 2,556 **5.** 1,812 **6.** 7,985 **7.** 10,031 **8.** 7,301,299

(Lesson 4) Solve. Use any strategy.

9. How many combinations of pants and shirts can you make? Write the combinations. Use the table.

Clothes Choices	
Pants	**Shirts**
Jeans	Red
Shorts	Checked

(Lesson 5) Compare. Write >, <, or =.

10. 2,003 ● 2,005 **11.** 65,656 ● 65,565 **12.** 933,771 ● 1,399,771

(Lesson 6) Order the numbers from least to greatest.

13. 6,161, 6,661, 6,116 **14.** 42,887, 41,987, 42,779

(Lesson 7) Round each number to the nearest thousand.

15. 9,226 **16.** 5,811 **17.** 3,600 **18.** 1,846 **19.** 2,376

(Lessons 8 and 9) Compare. Write >, <, or =.

20. 72 hours ● 4 days **21.** 28 minutes ● half hour **22.** 359 days ● 1 year

(Lesson 10) Find each elapsed time for **23** and **24.**

23. 10:30 A.M. to 12:30 P.M.

24. Belva went to a square dance that started at 2:15 P.M. and ended at 5:00 P.M. How long was she at the dance?

25. **(Lesson 11)** **Reasoning** If a month starts on a Monday, how many Mondays are in the month?

CHAPTER 2

Performance Assessment

A Place Value

Read the story about Handley School. Use numbers in the clouds to fill in each blank. One number will not be used.

At Handley School, there are just under 500 students. The school gives the __a.__ students 2 pencils a year, or __b.__ pencils.
The teachers use __c.__ pieces of chalk, a little more than the number of pencils used by the students.
Each year the school serves almost 100,000 pints of milk and 50,000 lunches.
That's __d.__ pints of milk and __e.__ lunches.

1. **Explain Your Thinking** How did you choose the numbers to put in the blanks?

2. **Decision Making** Write a story with numbers in the hundreds, thousands, and millions. Leave blanks for each number. Exchange stories with a partner and fill in the best number for each blank.

3. **Critical Thinking** Suppose there were twice as many students at Handley School. How would you rewrite the story?

B Time

Make a schedule of your activities on a Saturday. Write the start and end time for each activity. Include at least 5 events.

4. **Decision Making** Decide which activities to include. When does the activity begin? When does it end? How long is each activity?

5. **Explain Your Thinking** Explain how you find the elapsed time for each activity.

6. **Critical Thinking** How long do you play outside in a day? In a week?

Math Magazine

No Place for Zeros **Ancient Romans used a number system that used these symbols:**

I	V	X	L	C	D	M
1	5	10	50	100	500	1,000

From these symbols, you can make other numbers, but the system does not use place value or zeros.

When in Rome, do as the Romans did! Read and write Roman numerals. When a symbol meaning less is to the right, add.

III = 3 1 + 1 + 1 Add to get 3.	XXI = 21 10 + 10 + 1 Add to get 21.	CCLXI = 261 100 + 100 + 50 + 10 + 1 Add to get 261.	DCCC = 800 500 + 100 + 100 + 100 Add to get 800.

When a symbol meaning less is to the left, subtract.

IX = 9 10 − 1 Subtract to get 9.	XL = 40 50 − 10 Subtract to get 40.	CD = 400 500 − 100 Subtract to get 400.	CM = 900 1,000 − 100 Subtract to get 900.

Try These!

Write the standard number for the Roman numerals.

1. IV **2.** CCXL **3.** MDL **4.** LXII **5.** DCIX

6. Use an encyclopedia to find symbols that represent numbers. Share them with the class.

7. Make up your own number system for numbers 1 through 4. Then tell how it works.

CHAPTERS 1–2

Cumulative Review

Test Prep Strategy: Follow Directions!

Watch for words like *not*.
Write a number that is not between 42,931 and 42,941.

Ⓐ 42,930 Ⓑ 42,940 Ⓒ 42,939 Ⓓ 42,932

Choices Ⓑ, Ⓒ, and Ⓓ are between 42,931 and 42,941. Ⓐ is *not* between 42,931 and 42,941. The answer is Ⓐ.

STAY SHARP!

Test Prep Strategies

- Read Carefully
- Follow Directions
- Make Smart Choices
- Eliminate Choices
- Work Backward from an Answer

Write the letter of the correct answer. Use any strategy.

1. Which number is not less than 2,555,999?

   Ⓐ 2,499,999 Ⓑ 2,556,005
   Ⓒ 2,554,999 Ⓓ 2,500,005

2. Which number rounded to the nearest thousand is greater than 3,000?

   Ⓐ 3,334 Ⓑ 3,198 Ⓒ 3,502 Ⓓ 3,099

3. How many hours are there in 3 days?

   Ⓐ 48 Ⓑ 72
   Ⓒ 720 Ⓓ 180

Use the pictograph to answer **4–7.**

Diskette Collection	
Eric	💾 💾 💾 💾 💾
Salima	💾 💾 💾
Steve	💾
Martin	💾 💾
Leah	💾 💾
Bobby	💾 💾 💾
Aviva	💾 💾 💾 💾
Luis	💾 💾 💾

💾 = 10 disks

4. Who did not collect twenty or more diskettes?

   Ⓐ Martin Ⓑ Eric
   Ⓒ Steve Ⓓ Salima

5. Who collected the same number of diskettes as Martin?

   Ⓐ Eric Ⓑ Bobby
   Ⓒ Salima Ⓓ Leah

6. How many diskettes did Eric and Salima collect combined?

   Ⓐ 80 Ⓑ 90
   Ⓒ 70 Ⓓ 60

7. What was the mode of the diskettes collected?

   Ⓐ 40 Ⓑ 30 Ⓒ 20 Ⓓ 10

REVIEW AND PRACTICE

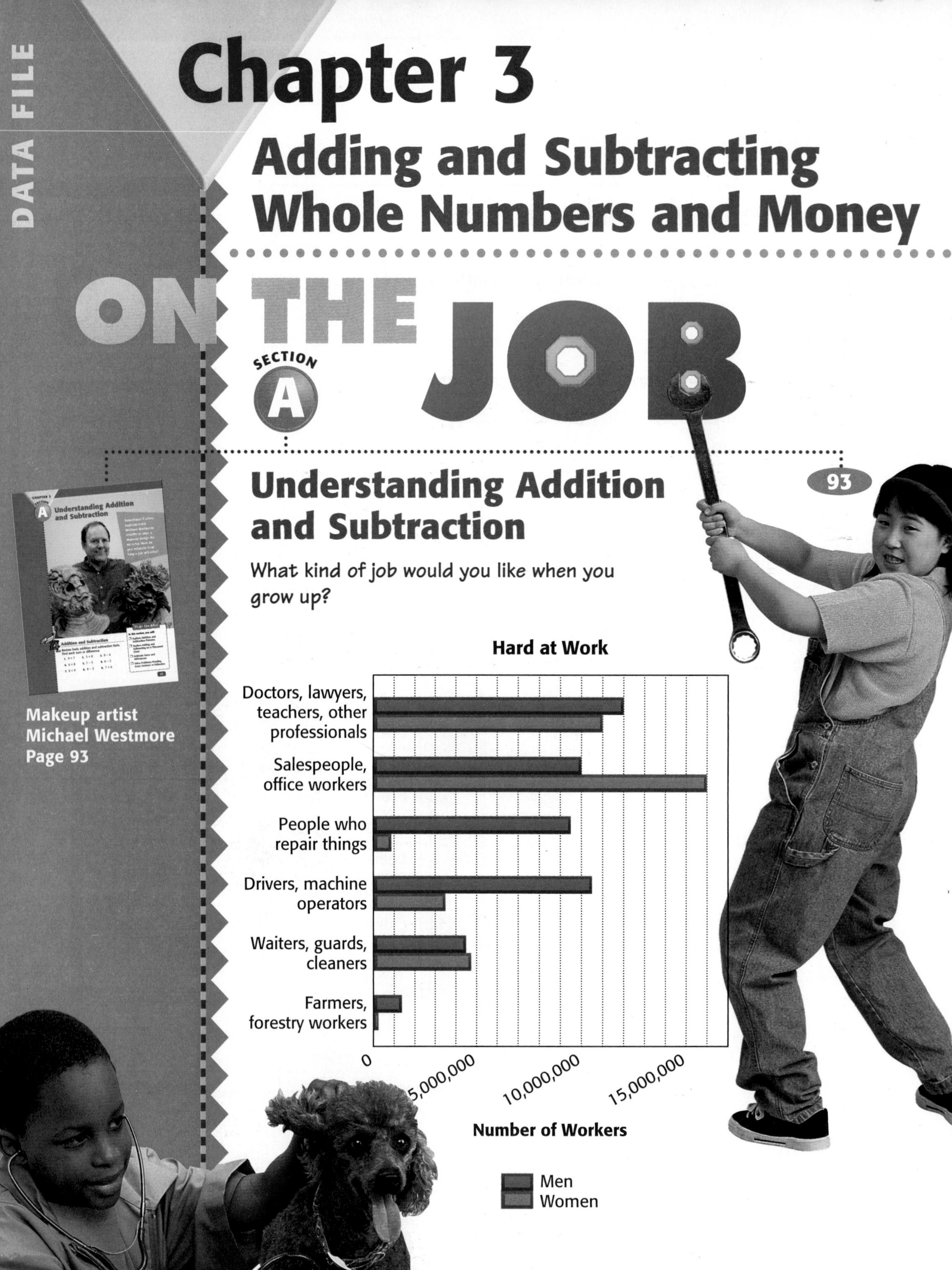
DATA FILE
Chapter 3
Adding and Subtracting Whole Numbers and Money
ON THE JOB
SECTION A
Understanding Addition and Subtraction
93
What kind of job would you like when you grow up?
Makeup artist Michael Westmore Page 93
Hard at Work
Doctors, lawyers, teachers, other professionals
Salespeople, office workers
People who repair things
Drivers, machine operators
Waiters, guards, cleaners
Farmers, forestry workers
0
5,000,000
10,000,000
15,000,000
Number of Workers
Men
Women

Adding and Subtracting

103

Americans celebrate Take Our Daughters to Work® day in April. How popular is the program? How can you tell? How popular would such a program be for sons?

After the 1995 Take Our Daughters to Work day, a poll showed that:

- 140 million Americans were familiar with the program.
- 129 million Americans thought the program was a good idea.
- 9 million Americans took their daughters to work.
- 125 million Americans wanted to take their sons to work, too.

Surfing the World Wide Web!

Have you ever visited the workplace of your parents or another adult? Want to learn more about jobs? Check out **www.mathsurf.com/4/ch3** to find out more.

SECTION C

Using Money

125

How has the average hourly wage changed in the United States? Predict how it will change in the future.

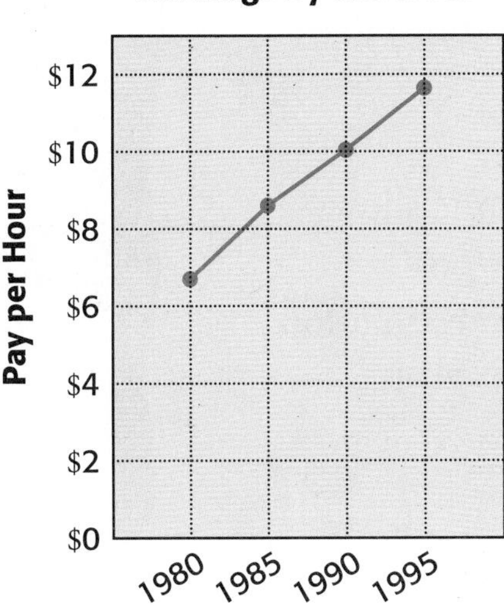

Business owner Helen Chavez-Hansen Page 103

Importer of African goods Philomena Okigbo Page 125

Materials
paper, markers or colored pencils

Do you enjoy reading comics? Make your own funny drawings to show when you might estimate.

You might estimate when:

- **You aren't able to use a calculator**
- **A "rough" answer is good enough**
- **You need an answer quickly**

Make a Plan

- How will your team make a funny comic that shows estimation?
- How will you share the writing and the drawing?

Will there be time to buy popcorn before the movie starts?

Carry It Out

1. Discuss your ideas.
2. Decide on an estimating situation.
3. Decide how you can make the situation funny.
4. Draw a comic. Write a caption.

Talk About It

- How does your comic show an estimating situation?
- Have you ever used estimation in a similar way? Explain.

How many stars are in the sky?

Present the Project

- Share your estimation situation with the class.

Understanding Addition and Subtraction

Sometimes it takes makeup artist Michael Westmore months to plan a makeup design for an actor. How do you estimate how long a job will take?

GET READY!

Addition and Subtraction

Review basic addition and subtraction facts. Find each sum or difference.

1. $9 + 7$ **2.** $5 + 8$ **3.** $9 - 4$

4. $6 + 8$ **5.** $7 - 5$ **6.** $6 - 2$

7. $8 + 9$ **8.** $8 - 3$ **9.** $7 + 6$

Skills Checklist

In this section, you will:

- ❐ Explore Addition and Subtraction Patterns
- ❐ Explore Adding and Subtracting on a Thousand Chart
- ❐ Estimate Sums and Differences
- ❐ Solve Problems Needing Exact Answers or Estimates

Chapter 3
Lesson
1

Exploring Addition and Subtraction Patterns

Problem Solving Connection
Look for a Pattern

Materials
calculator

Vocabulary

sum
the number obtained by adding numbers

difference
the number obtained by subtracting one number from another

Remember
Think about using basic facts.

Explore

How can you use patterns to add and subtract tens, hundreds, and thousands mentally?

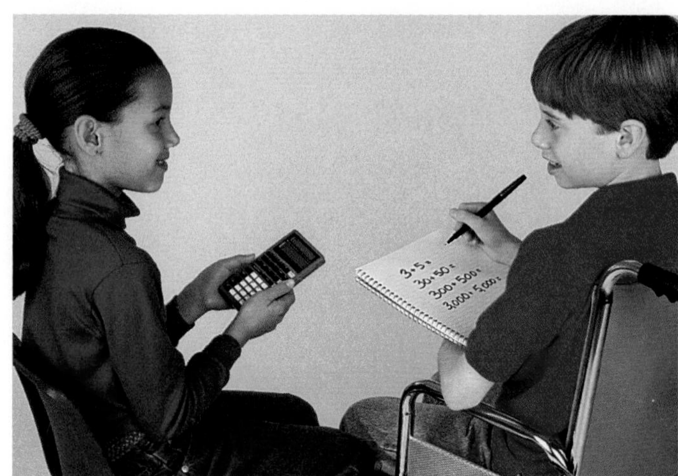

Work Together

1. Use a calculator to find each sum or difference. Look for patterns.

a.	**b.**	**c.**
$3 + 5 = n$	$8 + 7 = n$	$8 - 4 = n$
$30 + 50 = n$	$80 + 70 = n$	$80 - 40 = n$
$300 + 500 = n$	$800 + 700 = n$	$800 - 400 = n$
$3{,}000 + 5{,}000 = n$	$8{,}000 + 7{,}000 = n$	$8{,}000 - 4{,}000 = n$

2. Look for patterns to help you find each sum or difference. Use a calculator to check your answers.

a.	**b.**	**c.**
$10 - 8 = n$	$14 + 4 = n$	$9 - 3 = n$
$100 - 80 = n$	$140 + 40 = n$	$90 - 30 = n$
$1{,}000 - 800 = n$	$1{,}400 + 400 = n$	$900 - 300 = n$
$10{,}000 - 8{,}000 = n$	$14{,}000 + 4{,}000 = n$	$9{,}000 - 3{,}000 = n$

Talk About It

3. What patterns did you find?

4. Explain how to add 7,000 + 8,000 mentally.

5. If you know the difference between 9 and 5, how can you find the difference between 9,000 and 5,000?

Connect

You can use mental math to add and subtract.

Find the **sum** of 200 and 500.

$200 + 500 = n$

Think: $2 + 5 = 7$.

So, $200 + 500 = 700$.

Find the **difference** between 6,000 and 4,000.

$6{,}000 - 4{,}000 = n$

Think: $6 - 4 = 2$.

So, $6{,}000 - 4{,}000 = 2{,}000$.

Practice

Copy and complete.

1. $70 + 10 = n$
$700 + 100 = n$
$7{,}000 + 1{,}000 = n$
2. $n + 40 = 90$
$n + 400 = 900$
$n + 4{,}000 = 9{,}000$
3. $90 + n = 170$
$900 + n = 1{,}700$
$9{,}000 + n = 17{,}000$

Find each sum or difference.

4. $5{,}000 + 5{,}000$
5. $8{,}000 + 1{,}000$
6. $6{,}000 + 2{,}000$
7. $3{,}000 + 9{,}000$
8. $9{,}000 - 7{,}000$
9. $5{,}000 - 3{,}000$
10. $80{,}000 - 40{,}000$
11. $50{,}000 - 30{,}000$
12. $30{,}000 + 60{,}000$

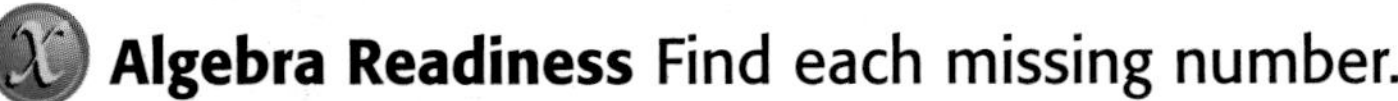

Algebra Readiness Find each missing number.

13. $90 - n = 80$
$900 - n = 800$
$9{,}000 - 1{,}000 = n$
14. $n - 20 = 50$
$700 - 200 = n$
$7{,}000 - n = 5{,}000$
15. $90 - n = 30$
$900 - 600 = n$
$n - 6{,}000 = 3{,}000$
16. **Money** A new CD player costs \$90. Three CDs cost \$40 all together. How much will the CD player and the three CDs cost in all?

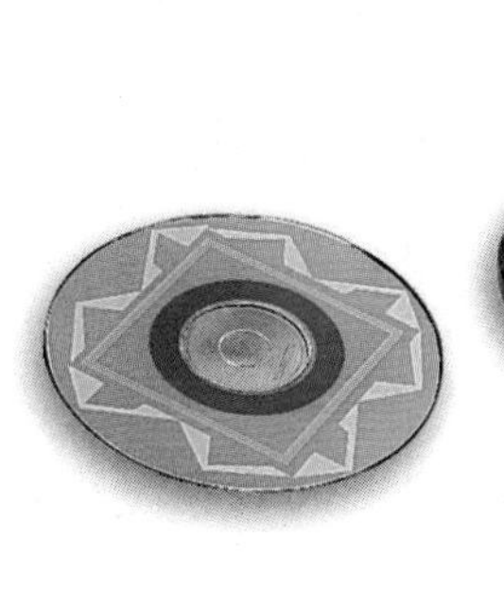

17. **Critical Thinking** What do you notice about the sums for the following pairs: $500 + 600$ and $600 + 500$?

18. **Geometry Readiness** Copy and complete the pattern.

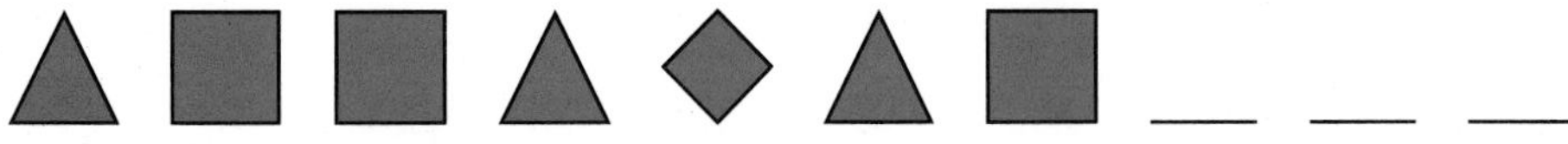

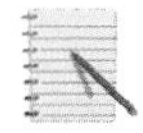

19. **Journal** Use patterns and place value to explain how adding $7{,}000 + 4{,}000$ is like adding $70{,}000 + 40{,}000$. How is it different?

Chapter 3
Lesson
2

Exploring Adding and Subtracting on a Thousand Chart

Problem Solving Connection
- Use Objects/ Act It Out
- Look for a Pattern

Materials
- thousand chart
- counters

Explore

You can use a thousand chart to help find sums and differences.

Work Together

1. Use a thousand chart to find each sum or difference. Record your answers.

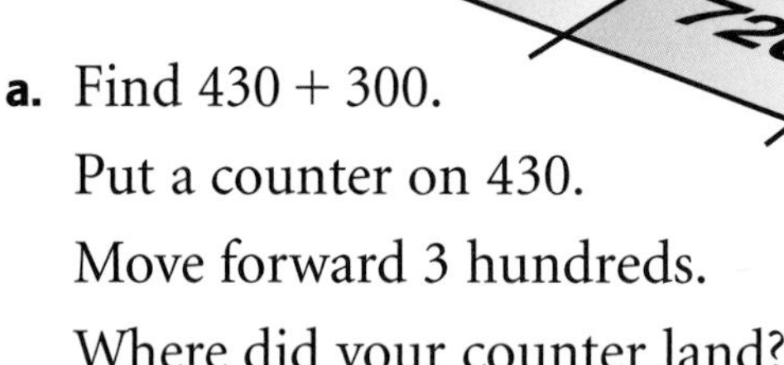

Math Tip
Think about counting by tens and hundreds.

   a. Find 430 + 300.
   Put a counter on 430.
   Move forward 3 hundreds.
   Where did your counter land?

   b. Find 680 − 240.
   Put a counter on 680.
   Move back 2 hundreds.
   Then move back 4 tens.
   What square did you land on?

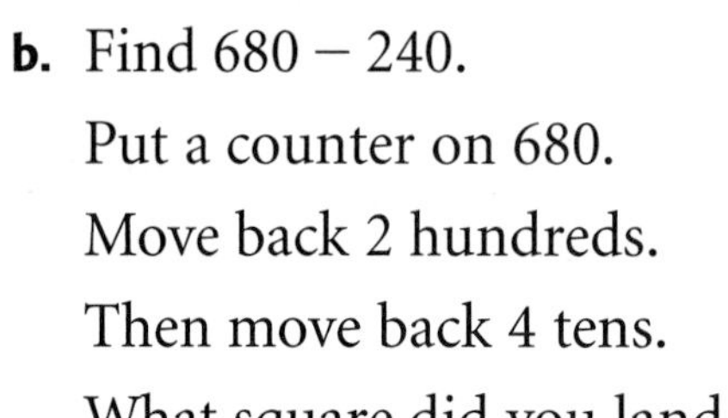

440	450	460	470	480	490	500
540	550	560	570	580	590	600
640	650	660	670	680	690	700

2. Use a thousand chart to find each sum or difference.

   a. 230 + 180 **b.** 370 + 130 **c.** 600 − 120 **d.** 720 − 190
   e. 160 + 470 **f.** 430 − 190 **g.** 300 − 180 **h.** 410 + 410

3. Place a counter on a number that has a 5 in the hundreds place. Place another counter on a number that has a 5 in the tens place. What is the difference between the two numbers?

Talk About It

4. How would you use a thousand chart to show 470 + 120?

5. Explain two ways to find 340 + 280 on a thousand chart.

Connect

Here are two different ways to subtract numbers.

Find 540 – 130.

You can use mental math.

540 minus 100 is 440.

Subtract 30 more.

440 – 30 = 410

You can use a thousand chart.

Start at 540 and move back 1 hundred to 440. Then move back 3 tens to 410.

310	320	330	340	350
410	420	430	440	450
510	520	530	540	550

Practice

Find each sum or difference. Use a thousand chart or mental math.

1. 160 + 300 **2.** 970 – 220 **3.** 600 – 430 **4.** 560 + 150

5. 720 + 190 **6.** 650 – 560 **7.** 470 – 280 **8.** 760 – 390

9. 800 + 140 **10.** 610 + 240 **11.** 630 – 370 **12.** 590 + 310

13. Find the difference between 540 and 370.

14. Logic Jan places two counters on her chart. The counters are apart by 240. One of them is on 720. Where is the other counter?

15. Critical Thinking What number is equally far from 630 and 410? Explain how you can use a thousand chart to find the number.

16. Write Your Own Problem Write a set of clues that will help a partner guess where a counter is on your thousand chart.

17. Fine Arts "The Great Wall" in Los Angeles is the longest mural in the world. It is 2,500 feet long. It took 250 teenagers and 50 adults 10 years to finish painting this wall.

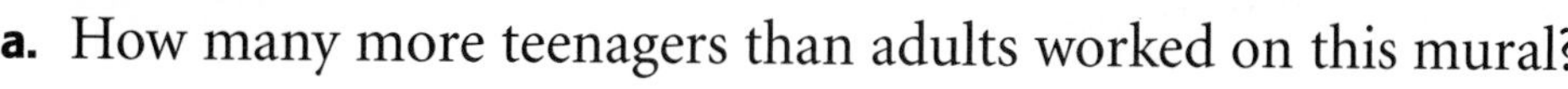

a. How many more teenagers than adults worked on this mural?

b. If some teenagers were 13 years old when the painting began, how old were they when the mural was finished?

18. Journal Explain how you can use a thousand chart or mental math to find 440 + 460 and 830 – 150.

Estimating Sums and Differences

You Will Learn
how to estimate sums and differences using rounding

Vocabulary
estimate
to find a number close to an exact answer

Learn

Let the cameras roll! First, makeup artists have to plan ahead. They can **estimate** about how many people will need special makeup for a big movie scene.

Makeup artist Michael Westmore creates alien faces for actors in his studio in Hollywood, California.

You can round to estimate sums.

Remember
You can use a number line to help you round numbers.

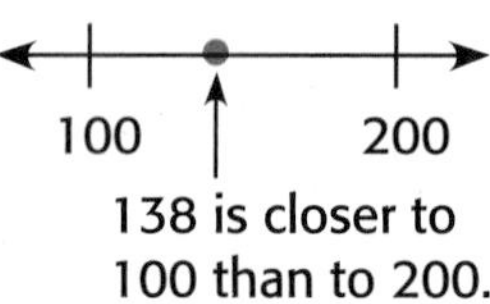

138 is closer to 100 than to 200.

Example 1

About how many actors will need special makeup for the crowd scene?

Estimate 138 + 224 by rounding to the nearest hundred.

$$\begin{array}{r} 138 \\ +224 \\ \hline \end{array} \longrightarrow \begin{array}{r} 100 \\ +200 \\ \hline 300 \end{array}$$

About 300 actors will need makeup.

EXTRAS NEEDED
For Alien Crowd Scene

Actors	Number Signed Up
Scaly aliens	138
Hairy aliens	224

You can also use rounding to estimate differences.

Other Examples

A. Estimate 1,252 − 564.
Round to the nearest hundred.

$$\begin{array}{r} 1,252 \\ -\ 564 \\ \hline \end{array} \longrightarrow \begin{array}{r} 1,300 \\ -\ 600 \\ \hline 700 \end{array}$$

B. Estimate 2,975 − 1,778.
Round to the nearest thousand.

$$\begin{array}{r} 2,975 \\ -1,778 \\ \hline \end{array} \longrightarrow \begin{array}{r} 3,000 \\ -2,000 \\ \hline 1,000 \end{array}$$

Talk About It

Is the total number of actors for the crowd scene greater than or less than 300? Explain.

Check

Estimate each sum or difference. Round to the nearest hundred.

1. 385 + 224 **2.** 585 − 157 **3.** 721 + 137 **4.** 915 − 228

Estimate each sum or difference. Round to the nearest thousand.

5. 4,424 − 2,788 **6.** 7,881 + 1,589 **7.** 3,580 − 1,625 **8.** 4,292 + 1,114

9. **Reasoning** Estimate the sum of 551 and 475. Will the exact answer be less than or greater than your estimate? Explain.

Practice

Skills and Reasoning

Estimate each sum or difference. Round to the nearest hundred.

10. 567 + 241 **11.** 842 − 390 **12.** 410 + 710 **13.** 674 − 221

Estimate each sum or difference. Round to the nearest thousand.

14. 3,387 + 4,835 **15.** 9,394 − 6,240 **16.** 2,111 + 1,753 **17.** 8,887 − 3,721

18. Estimate the difference between 821 and 379 to the nearest hundred.

19. Estimate the sum of 3,921 and 4,693 to the nearest thousand.

20. Is the sum of 327 and 215 greater than or less than 500? Explain.

Problem Solving and Applications

21. **Using Data** Use the Data File on page 90. Which job group has almost the same number of women as men?

22. **Time** Makeup artists often start work at 4:00 A.M., so the actors will be ready for filming at 10:00 A.M. How much time do the artists spend at work before filming begins?

23. **Logic** The yellow alien held its ears and said nothing when the green alien screeched, "No!" in response to the blue alien. Then the red alien yelled, "Yes!" Which alien spoke first?

Mixed Review and Test Prep

Compare. Write >, <, or =.

24. 8,919 ● 8,199 **25.** 9,770 ● 9,070 **26.** 7,500 ● 9,509

27. Which number is between 198,247 and 199,274?

Ⓐ 197,472 Ⓑ 198,742 Ⓒ 199,742 Ⓓ not here

Chapter 3
Lesson
4

Problem Solving

Analyze Word Problems: Exact or Estimate?

You Will Learn
how to decide if you need an exact answer or an estimate

Learn

School cafeteria workers know what most students like to eat: chicken nuggets!

The cafeteria workers keep track of how many lunches they serve each day. How many chicken nugget lunches should they plan for next week?

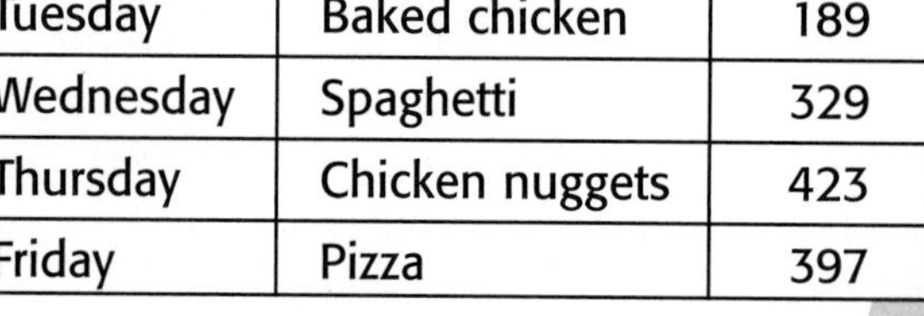

Day	Lunch	Number Served
Monday	Hamburgers	285
Tuesday	Baked chicken	189
Wednesday	Spaghetti	329
Thursday	Chicken nuggets	423
Friday	Pizza	397

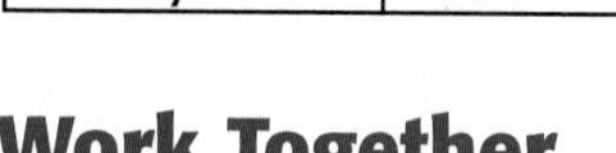

Work Together

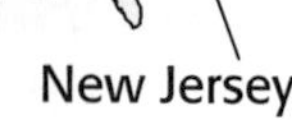

Patricia Scro serves school lunches in Jefferson Township, New Jersey.

▶ **Understand**

What do you know?

What do you need to find out?

▶ **Plan**

Do you need an exact answer or will an estimate do?

Estimate. You don't know exactly how many students will eat lunch.

▶ **Solve**

Decide if your estimate should be greater than or less than the number served last week. What's the answer?

To be sure enough chicken nugget meals are available, the estimate should be greater than 423. Workers should plan 430 lunches.

▶ **Look Back**

Is your answer reasonable?

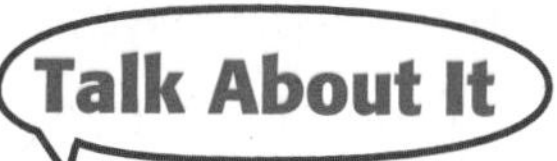

Talk About It

How could cafeteria workers plan for the exact number of lunches?

Check

Decide if you need an exact answer or an estimate. Solve.

1. If 10 pizzas serve 80 students, how many students will 20 pizzas serve?
2. Use the table on page 100. The cafeteria serves salad with each spaghetti lunch. How many salads were served last week?
3. Use the table on page 100. If the cafeteria plans to serve baked chicken next week, about how many such lunches should the cooks plan for?

Problem Solving Practice

Problem Solving Strategies

- Use Objects/Act It Out
- Draw a Picture
- Look for a Pattern
- Guess and Check
- Use Logical Reasoning
- Make an Organized List
- Make a Table
- Solve a Simpler Problem
- Work Backward

Choose a Tool

Using Data Use the table on page 100 for **4** and **5**.

4. The cafeteria served 22 fewer chicken nuggets lunches two weeks ago than it did last week. How many were served that week?
5. The cafeteria provides milk with each meal. It also sells milk to students who bring bag lunches. Last Wednesday, 20 students bought milk. How many cartons of milk did the cafeteria need that day?
6. **Health** There are 11,000 international units (I.U.) of vitamin A in a carrot. A sweet potato has about 9,000. About how much more vitamin A does a carrot have than a sweet potato?
7. **History** Sweet potatoes were first grown in southern Mexico and Central America. Spanish explorers of the 1500s introduced them to other parts of the world. About how long ago was that?

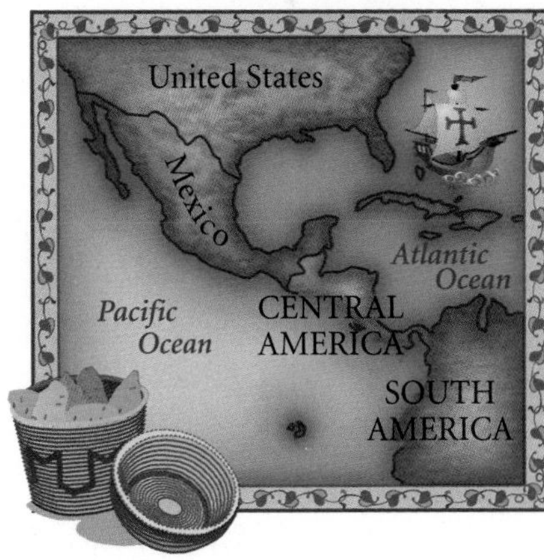

8. **Collecting Data** Make a chart of cafeteria lunches at your school. Log the number of lunches served each day for a week. Find the most and least popular meals.
9. Jackson stands between Ko and Sita in the hot lunch line. Jackson is ahead of Ko. Which of these three students is third in line? What strategy did you use?
10. **Journal** Write about a problem you solved using estimates. Tell why you used estimates. Then tell how you solved the problem.

Skills Practice Bank, page 561, Set 6

SECTION A

Review and Practice

Vocabulary Match each word with its meaning.

1.	estimate	**a.**	number obtained by adding
2.	sum	**b.**	number obtained by subtracting
3.	difference	**c.**	to find a number close to an exact answer

(Lesson 1) Copy and complete each number sentence.

4. $2 + 1 = n$
$20 + 10 = n$
$200 + 100 = n$
$2{,}000 + 1{,}000 = n$

5. $9 - 7 = n$
$90 - 70 = n$
$900 - 700 = n$
$9{,}000 - 7{,}000 = n$

6. $3 + 2 = n$
$30 + 20 = n$
$300 + 200 = n$
$3{,}000 + 2{,}000 = n$

(Lesson 2) Mental Math Find each sum or difference.

7. 120 + 200	**8.** 330 − 100	**9.** 840 − 110	**10.** 460 + 250
11. 770 − 220	**12.** 580 + 120	**13.** 490 − 130	**14.** 550 + 310
15. 320 + 210	**16.** 640 − 200	**17.** 270 + 120	**18.** 930 − 520

19. Science In three months, a dolphin at the Dolphin Research Center ate about 120 pounds of butter fish and 480 pounds of herring. How many pounds of fish did the dolphin eat in all?

(Lesson 3) Estimate each sum or difference. Round to the nearest thousand.

20. 2,663 + 1,422	**21.** 1,585 − 1,400	**22.** 2,357 + 3,042	**23.** 3,310 − 697

(Lesson 4) Decide if an exact answer or an estimate is needed. Explain.

24. You want to buy a sandwich, milk, and an apple. You need to know quickly if you have enough money.

25. You time yourself to find how long it takes to run 100 yards. You want to see if you can better your time, so you run 100 yards again.

26. Journal Describe a situation in which you might estimate.

Skills Checklist

In this section, you have:

- ☑ **Explored Addition and Subtraction Patterns**
- ☑ **Explored Adding and Subtracting on a Thousand Chart**
- ☑ **Estimated Sums and Differences**
- ☑ **Solved Problems Needing Exact Answers or Estimates**

REVIEW AND PRACTICE

CHAPTER 3

SECTION

B Adding and Subtracting

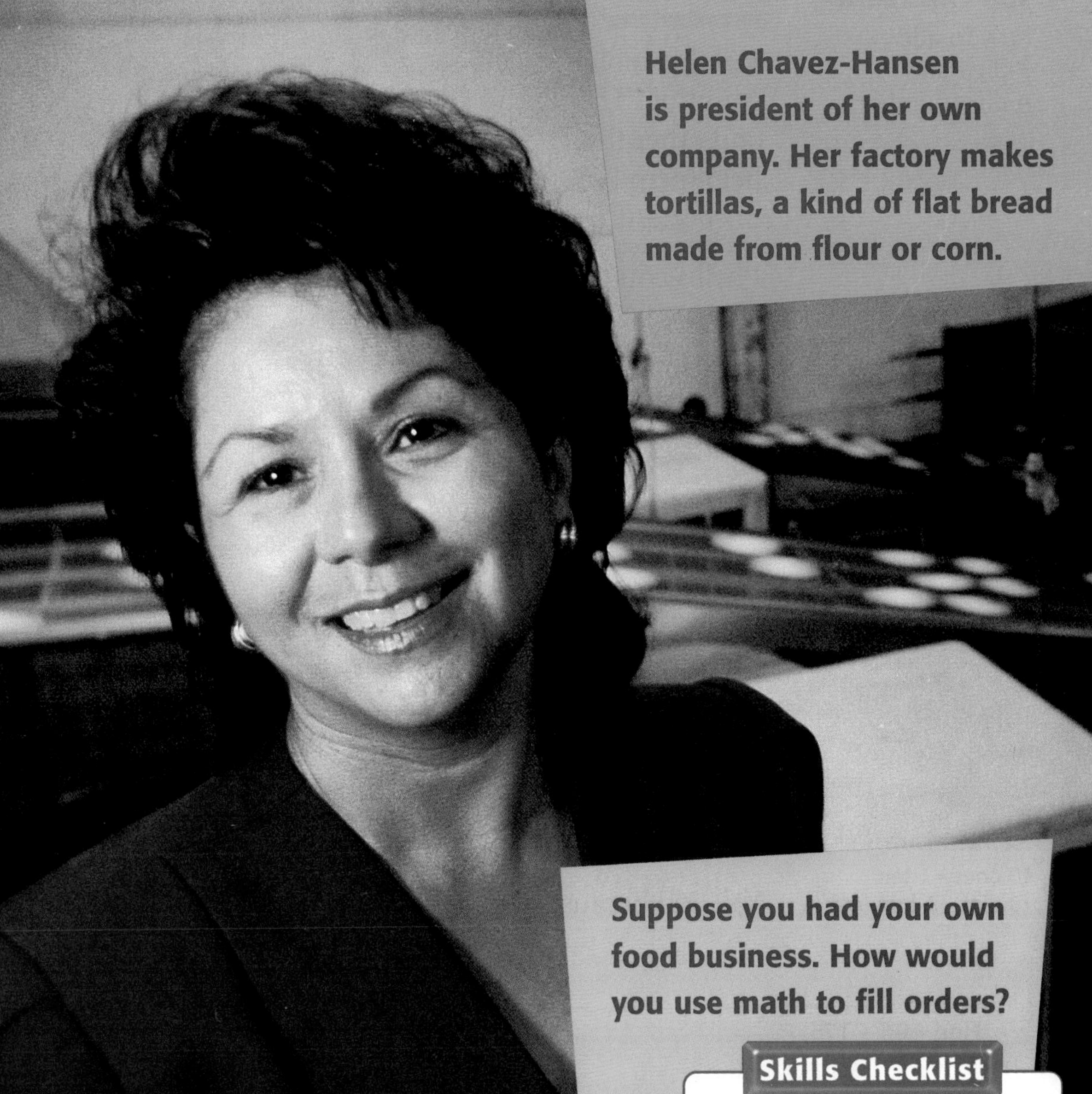

Helen Chavez-Hansen is president of her own company. Her factory makes tortillas, a kind of flat bread made from flour or corn.

Suppose you had your own food business. How would you use math to fill orders?

GET READY!

Addition with Greater Numbers

Review regrouping. Copy and complete.

1. 8 ones + 3 ones = ▒ tens, ▒ ones
2. 7 ones + 6 ones = ▒ tens, ▒ ones
3. 8 tens + 3 tens = ▒ hundreds, ▒ tens
4. 7 tens + 6 tens = ▒ hundreds, ▒ tens

Skills Checklist

In this section, you will:

- ❒ Add and Subtract Greater Numbers
- ❒ Subtract with Middle Zeros
- ❒ Solve Multiple-Step Word Problems
- ❒ Add and Subtract Mentally
- ❒ Choose a Calculation Method

Chapter 3
Lesson
5

Adding

You Will Learn
how to add 3-digit and 4-digit numbers

Learn

Wildlife biologists can spend all day counting. They count birds, fish, trees, and other things. Why? The counts help them keep track of populations of species from year to year.

Phyllis counts nests for two kinds of albatrosses, which are sea birds. In one area, she counts 696 Laysan albatross nests and 175 black-footed albatross nests. How can you find out how many nests she counts in all?

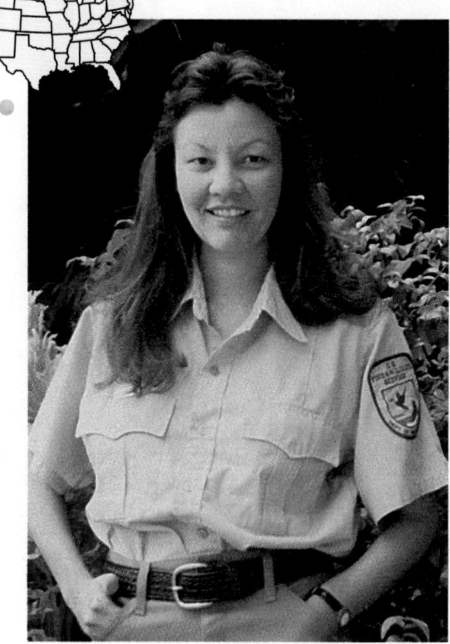

Phyllis Ha works for the U.S. Fish and Wildlife Service in Honolulu, Hawaii.

Remember
10 ones = 1 ten
10 tens = 1 hundred

You add because you need to put together amounts to find the total.

Example 1

Find 696 + 175.

Step 1	Step 2	Step 3
Add the ones. Regroup as needed.	Add the tens. Regroup as needed.	Add the hundreds.
$\begin{array}{r} ^{1} \\ 696 \\ +175 \\ \hline 1 \end{array}$ 6 ones + 5 ones = 1 ten, 1 one	$\begin{array}{r} ^{1\,1} \\ 696 \\ +175 \\ \hline 71 \end{array}$ 1 ten + 9 tens + 7 tens = 1 hundred, 7 tens	$\begin{array}{r} ^{1\,1} \\ 696 \\ +175 \\ \hline 871 \end{array}$ 1 hundred + 6 hundreds + 1 hundred = 8 hundreds

696 + 175 = 871

Estimate to check. 700 + 200 = 900
Since 871 is close to 900, the answer is reasonable.

So, Phyllis counted 871 nests in all.

Other Examples

You can also add greater numbers the same way.

A.
$$\begin{array}{r} \scriptstyle 1\ 1 \\ 9{,}864 \\ +\ \ 383 \\ \hline 10{,}247 \end{array}$$

B.
$$\begin{array}{r} \scriptstyle 1\ 11 \\ 2{,}255 \\ +2{,}867 \\ \hline 5{,}122 \end{array}$$

C.
$$\begin{array}{r} \scriptstyle 1\ 11 \\ 3{,}752 \\ +5{,}489 \\ \hline 9{,}241 \end{array}$$

Talk About It

1. How did you use regrouping in Example B?
2. When do you have to regroup?
3. How can you check to see if a sum is correct?

Laysan albatross

Check

Copy and complete.

1.
$$\begin{array}{r} 4\ 1 \\ +\ 2\ 6 \\ \hline \blacksquare\ 7 \end{array}$$

2.
$$\begin{array}{r} \scriptstyle 1 \\ 5\ 0\ 7 \\ +\ \ \ 2\ 8 \\ \hline \blacksquare\blacksquare\ 5 \end{array}$$

3.
$$\begin{array}{r} \scriptstyle 1 \\ 6\ 7\ 3 \\ +4\ 9\ 1 \\ \hline \blacksquare,\blacksquare\blacksquare\ 4 \end{array}$$

4.
$$\begin{array}{r} 9\ 5\ 2 \\ +5\ 2\ 3 \\ \hline \blacksquare,\blacksquare\blacksquare\ 5 \end{array}$$

5.
$$\begin{array}{r} \scriptstyle 1\ \ 1 \\ 1{,}7\ 6\ 8 \\ +\ \ \ 3\ 5\ 1 \\ \hline \blacksquare,\blacksquare\blacksquare\ 9 \end{array}$$

Find each sum. Estimate to check.

6.
$$\begin{array}{r} 357 \\ +193 \\ \hline \end{array}$$

7.
$$\begin{array}{r} 1{,}892 \\ +2{,}751 \\ \hline \end{array}$$

8.
$$\begin{array}{r} 471 \\ +\ 82 \\ \hline \end{array}$$

9.
$$\begin{array}{r} 3{,}576 \\ +\ \ 763 \\ \hline \end{array}$$

10.
$$\begin{array}{r} 7{,}145 \\ +9{,}374 \\ \hline \end{array}$$

11. $324 + 452$ **12.** $518 + 276$ **13.** $793 + 189$ **14.** $437 + 825$

15. $1{,}482 + 4{,}209$ **16.** $6{,}429 + 2{,}538$ **17.** $8{,}598 + 5{,}305$ **18.** $4{,}592 + 7{,}009$

19. Find the sum of 758 and 195. **20.** Add 2,937 and 5,494.

21. **Reasoning** Copy and complete. Write 1, 2, or 3 in each box. Use all three digits in each number. $\blacksquare\blacksquare\blacksquare + \blacksquare\blacksquare\blacksquare = n$

a. Write one number sentence that has the greatest possible sum.

b. Write one number sentence that has the least possible sum.

Practice

Skills and Reasoning

Find each sum.

22. $\begin{array}{r} 84 \\ +\ 31 \\ \hline ■■5 \end{array}$

23. $\begin{array}{r} {}^{1\,1} \\ 986 \\ +\ 85 \\ \hline ■,■■1 \end{array}$

24. $\begin{array}{r} 402 \\ +\ 290 \\ \hline ■■2 \end{array}$

25. $\begin{array}{r} {}^{1\,1} \\ 179 \\ +\ 444 \\ \hline ■■3 \end{array}$

26. $\begin{array}{r} {}^{1} \\ 3,490 \\ +\ 322 \\ \hline ■,■■2 \end{array}$

27. $\begin{array}{r} 3,094 \\ +\ 8,371 \\ \hline \end{array}$

28. $\begin{array}{r} 390 \\ +\ 611 \\ \hline \end{array}$

29. $\begin{array}{r} 4,218 \\ +\ 303 \\ \hline \end{array}$

30. $\begin{array}{r} 650 \\ +\ 772 \\ \hline \end{array}$

31. $\begin{array}{r} 6,598 \\ +\ 2,602 \\ \hline \end{array}$

32. $\begin{array}{r} 499 \\ +\ 517 \\ \hline \end{array}$

33. $\begin{array}{r} 7,821 \\ +\ 699 \\ \hline \end{array}$

34. $\begin{array}{r} 989 \\ +\ 555 \\ \hline \end{array}$

35. $\begin{array}{r} 3,271 \\ +\ 3,185 \\ \hline \end{array}$

36. $\begin{array}{r} 2,203 \\ +\ 9,034 \\ \hline \end{array}$

37. 571 + 225
38. 842 + 398
39. 384 + 295
40. 245 + 83
41. 948 + 575
42. 4,921 + 3,038
43. 8,480 + 1,842
44. 4,421 + 355
45. 7,565 + 7,565
46. 2,549 + 9,805
47. 3,821 + 5,096
48. 6,002 + 7,777
49. Find the sum of 356 and 489.
50. Add 1,827 and 945.
51. Copy and complete. Write 4, 5, 6, 7, 8, or 9 in each box. Use each digit only once. ■■■ + ■■■ = n
    a. Write a number sentence that has the greatest sum.
    b. Write a number sentence that has the least sum.

Problem Solving and Applications

Mental Math Write <, >, or =.

52. 453 + 198 ● 453 + 199
53. 453 + 200 ● 200 + 453

54. Phyllis and her partner count fish at the mouth of a river in Hawaii. They count 217 silversides and 158 mullet. How many fish is this?

55. Phyllis counts 1,392 Laysan albatross and 350 black-footed albatross. How many albatrosses is this?

Using Data Use the table for **56** and **57.**

56. **Mental Math** How many clams did the biologists count?

57. How many more clams did they count at Site 2 than at Site 1?

Wildlife Refuge Population Counts for Giant Clams

Site	Number of Giant Clams
Site 1	200
Site 2	300
Site 3	150

Problem Solving and SOCIAL STUDIES

One February morning in 1943, a farmer in Mexico noticed a volcano forming in his field. The next morning it had grown another 10 meters. After a week, it was 150 meters high. It grew another 290 meters in the first year. By 1952, it had stopped growing.

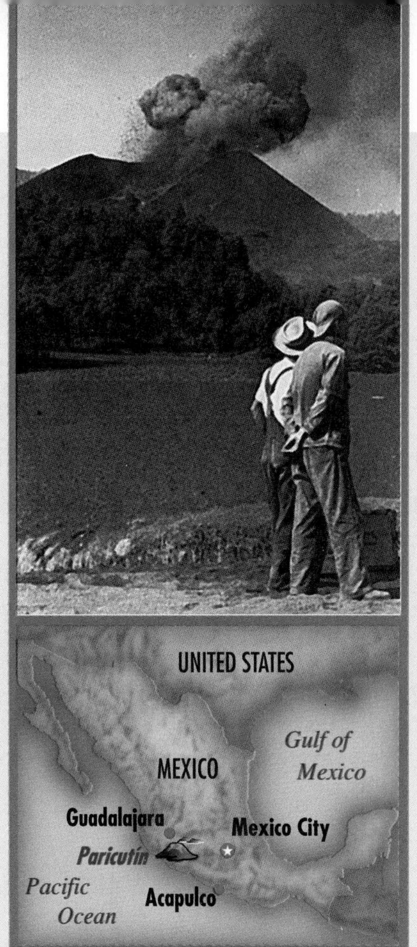

The Paricutín (pah ree koo TEEN) volcano in Mexico is one of the youngest volcanoes on Earth.

58. How high was the volcano after the first year?

59. Paricutín continued to grow another 77 meters until it stopped in 1952. How tall is it now?

60. Geography Use the map. Is Paricutín closer to Mexico City or Guadalajara?

61. Geometry Readiness What geometric shape do you think the volcano most looks like—a pyramid, a cone, or a rectangular prism?

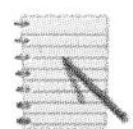

62. Journal Explain how you use regrouping to add 587 and 624.

Mixed Review and Test Prep

63. Use the numbers in the box.

a. List the numbers that are greater than 4,560.

b. List the numbers that are less than 5,250.

5,254	3,425
4,542	5,450
5,245	5,054

Using Data Use the pictograph for **64** and **65**.

64. How many snow globes and wind-up toys did the shop sell?

65. How many more buttons than cookie cutters did the shop sell?

Sales at the Old Treasure Shop	
Cookie cutters	🎁🎁🎁🎁
Snow globes	🎁🎁🎁🎁🎁🎁🎁🎁
Fancy buttons	🎁🎁🎁🎁🎁🎁
Wind-up toys	🎁🎁🎁🎁🎁

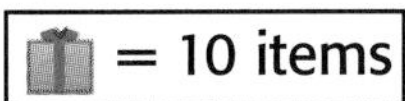

66. Which is a 7-digit number with a 4 in the hundred thousands place and a 0 in the hundreds place?

Ⓐ 3,467,074 Ⓑ 3,764,047

Ⓒ 437,604 Ⓓ 3,067,474

Chapter 3 Lesson 6

Column Addition

You Will Learn
how to add 3 or 4 addends

Vocabulary

addends
numbers that are added together to make a sum

front-end estimation
a way to estimate by first looking at the leading digits

Learn

"Don't get in over your head," reads Jonathan's ad. His ad reaches many people who don't know how to use computers. Jonathan prints 442 flyers, 339 brochures, and 628 bookmarks. How many items does he print in all?

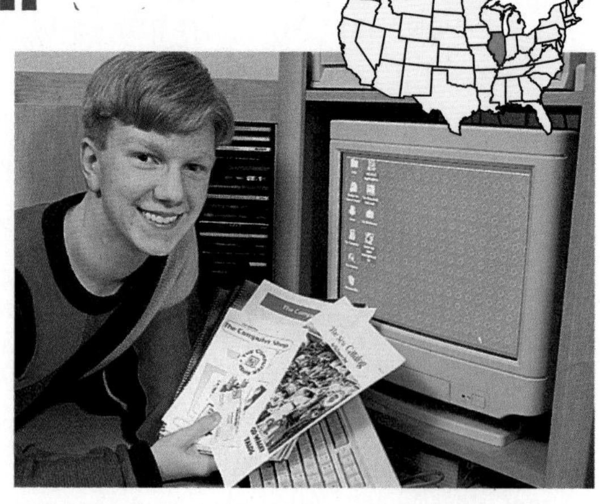

Jonathan runs a desktop publishing business in Farmersville, Illinois.

You can add three **addends** to find the total number of items. Use **front-end estimation** to check.

Example

Find 442 + 339 + 628.

Step 1	Step 2	Step 3
Add the ones. Regroup as needed.	Add the tens. Regroup as needed.	Add the hundreds.
$\begin{array}{r} {}^{1} \\ 442 \\ 339 \\ +\ 628 \\ \hline 9 \end{array}$	$\begin{array}{r} {}^{1\,1} \\ 442 \\ 339 \\ +\ 628 \\ \hline 09 \end{array}$	$\begin{array}{r} {}^{1\,1} \\ 442 \\ 339 \\ +\ 628 \\ \hline 1{,}409 \end{array}$

Round to the front-end, or leading, digits.

$$\begin{array}{rcr} 442 & \longrightarrow & 400 \\ 339 & \longrightarrow & 300 \\ +\ 628 & \longrightarrow & +\ 600 \\ \hline & & 1{,}300 \end{array}$$

Adjust your estimate.

$$\begin{array}{rcr} 442 & \longrightarrow & 40 \\ 339 & \longrightarrow & 40 \\ +\ 628 & \longrightarrow & +\ 30 \\ \hline & & 110 \end{array}$$

1,300 + 110 = 1,410

Since 1,409 is close to 1,410, the answer is reasonable.

Jonathan needs to print 1,409 items.

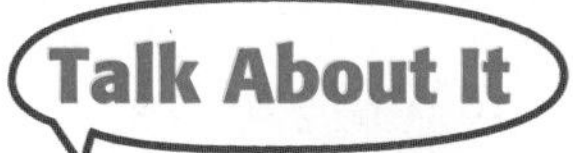

Talk About It

Why do you line up the ones, tens, and hundreds before you add?

Check

Find each sum. Estimate to check.

1. $\begin{array}{r} 32 \\ 41 \\ +\ 26 \\ \hline \end{array}$ **2.** $\begin{array}{r} 472 \\ 208 \\ +\ 325 \\ \hline \end{array}$ **3.** $\begin{array}{r} 984 \\ 27 \\ +\ 3,845 \\ \hline \end{array}$ **4.** $\begin{array}{r} 75 \\ 348 \\ +\ 590 \\ \hline \end{array}$ **5.** $\begin{array}{r} 3,004 \\ 12 \\ +\ 8,984 \\ \hline \end{array}$

6. Reasoning When you add three or more addends, does it matter if you change the order of the addends? Explain.

Practice

Skills and Reasoning

Find each sum. Estimate to check.

7. $\begin{array}{r} 51 \\ 41 \\ +\ 85 \\ \hline \end{array}$ **8.** $\begin{array}{r} 487 \\ 564 \\ +\ 812 \\ \hline \end{array}$ **9.** $\begin{array}{r} 280 \\ 85 \\ +\ 946 \\ \hline \end{array}$ **10.** $\begin{array}{r} 3,298 \\ 2,408 \\ +\ 6,091 \\ \hline \end{array}$ **11.** $\begin{array}{r} 7,855 \\ 4,080 \\ +\ \ \ 28 \\ \hline \end{array}$

12. 43 + 27 + 74 **13.** 205 + 398 + 190 **14.** 147 + 2,490 + 3,580

15. Find the sum of 2,220 and 540 and 217.

16. Write this number sentence in another way so it has the same sum. 245 + 678 + 2,503 = 3,426

Mental Math Write >, <, or =. Decide without finding the sum.

17. 59 + 34 + 82 ● 49 + 24 + 72 **18.** 422 + 659 + 394 ● 427 + 664 + 402

Problem Solving and Applications

19. Suppose Jonathan prints 35 forms, 148 brochures, and 268 flyers. How many items does he print?

20. Money Jonathan charged $25 for flyers, $18 for charts, and $22 for banners. What was the total?

21. Logic If you use one sheet of paper in an envelope, how many different color combinations can you make?

Mixed Review and Test Prep

STAY SHARP!

Mental Math Find each sum or difference.

22. 6,000 + 5,000 **23.** 20,000 − 10,000 **24.** 70,000 − 20,000

25. Find the number that means 3 hundreds, 8 tens, and 6 ones.

Ⓐ 3,086 Ⓑ 317 Ⓒ 386 Ⓓ not here

Chapter 3
Lesson
7

Subtracting

You Will Learn
how to subtract 3-digit and 4-digit numbers

Learn

Ernest Johnson's classes make a splash! He teaches swimming and works as a lifeguard. In 1996, 358 children signed up for swim classes at Ernest's club. In 1995, 189 children signed up. How many more children signed up in 1996?

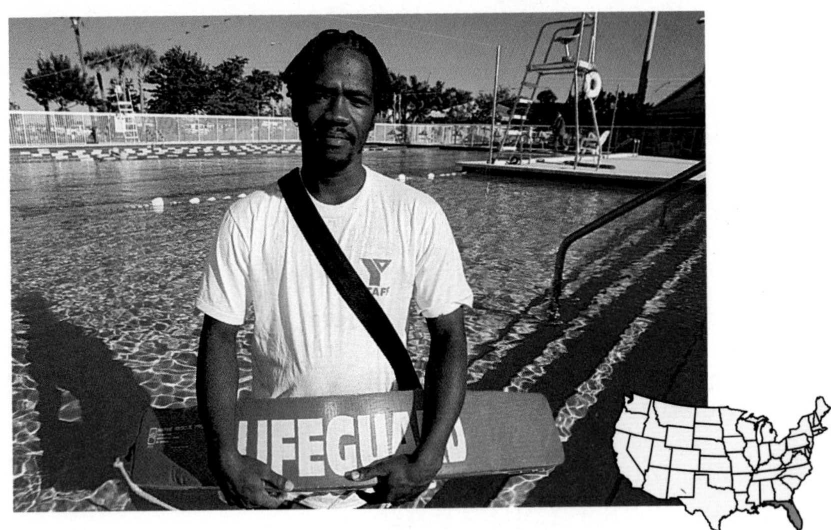

Lifeguard Ernest Johnson lives in Homestead, Florida.

Remember
18 ones is the same as 1 ten, 8 ones.

Subtract to compare the number of swimmers.

Example 1

Find 358 − 189.

Step 1	Step 2	Step 3
Subtract the ones. Regroup as needed.	Subtract the tens. Regroup as needed.	Subtract the hundreds.
$\begin{array}{r} {\scriptstyle 4\,18} \\ 3\not{5}\not{8} \\ -\,189 \\ \hline 9 \end{array}$ Regroup 5 tens as 4 tens, 10 ones.	$\begin{array}{r} {\scriptstyle 14} \\ {\scriptstyle 2\,\not{4}\,18} \\ \not{3}\not{5}\not{8} \\ -\,189 \\ \hline 69 \end{array}$ Regroup 3 hundreds as 2 hundreds, 10 tens.	$\begin{array}{r} {\scriptstyle 14} \\ {\scriptstyle 2\,\not{4}\,18} \\ \not{3}\not{5}\not{8} \\ -\,189 \\ \hline 169 \end{array}$

358 − 189 = 169

Estimate to check.

358 − 189 = 169 is about 400 − 200 = 200

Since 169 is close to 200, the answer is reasonable.

In 1996, 169 more swimmers signed up than in 1995.

Example 2

You can subtract greater numbers using the same steps.

Find 4,925 − 1,862.

Step 1	Step 2	Step 3	Step 4
Subtract ones. Regroup as needed.	Subtract tens. Regroup as needed.	Subtract hundreds. Regroup as needed.	Subtract thousands.
4,925 − 1,862 3	8 12 4,~~9~~~~2~~5 − 1,862 63	8 12 4,~~9~~~~2~~5 − 1,862 063	8 12 4,~~9~~~~2~~5 − 1,862 3,063

4,925 − 1,862 = 3,063   You can use addition to check.

$$\begin{array}{r} 3{,}063 \\ +\ 1{,}862 \\ \hline 4{,}925 \end{array}$$

Talk About It

1. How is subtracting 4-digit numbers like subtracting 3-digit numbers? How is it different?
2. How would you check Example 2 using estimation?
3. Why don't you regroup ones and thousands in Example 2?

Check

Copy and complete.

1. 5 15 / ~~6~~~~5~~ − 39 = ■6
2. 5 17 / ~~6~~~~7~~4 − 381 = ■■3
3. 12 / 8 ~~2~~ 11 / ~~9~~~~3~~~~1~~ − 683 = ■■8
4. 12 / 3 ~~2~~ 12 / ~~4~~~~3~~~~2~~ − 69 = ■■3
5. 8 11 / 2,3~~9~~~~1~~ − 2,056 = ■■5

Subtract.

6. 3,386 − 1,243
7. 8,425 − 2,511
8. 5,257 − 3,685
9. 3,984 − 588
10. 9,145 − 404

11. 772 − 594
12. 972 − 87
13. 4,298 − 3,575
14. 8,552 − 915
15. Find the difference between 459 and 290.
16. Subtract 655 from 9,249.
17. **Reasoning** How would you use regrouping to find 645 − 151?
18. **Reasoning** How would you use regrouping to find 9,195 − 2,487?

Practice

Skills and Reasoning

Subtract.

19. $\begin{array}{r} {}^{6\ 12} \\ 5\cancel{7}\cancel{2} \\ -\ \ 56 \\ \hline \blacksquare\blacksquare 6 \end{array}$ **20.** $\begin{array}{r} {}^{7\ 13} \\ \cancel{8}\cancel{3}8 \\ -155 \\ \hline \blacksquare\blacksquare 3 \end{array}$ **21.** $\begin{array}{r} {}^{13} \\ {}^{7\ \cancel{3}\ 11} \\ \cancel{8}\cancel{4}\cancel{1} \\ -642 \\ \hline \blacksquare\blacksquare 9 \end{array}$ **22.** $\begin{array}{r} {}^{15} \\ {}^{\cancel{5}\ 13} \\ \cancel{1},\cancel{6}\cancel{3}4 \\ -\ \ 943 \\ \hline \blacksquare\blacksquare 1 \end{array}$ **23.** $\begin{array}{r} {}^{11\ 14} \\ {}^{7\ \cancel{1}\ \cancel{4}\ 14} \\ \cancel{8},\cancel{2}\cancel{5}\cancel{4} \\ -6,365 \\ \hline \blacksquare,\blacksquare\blacksquare 9 \end{array}$

24. $\begin{array}{r} 285 \\ -162 \\ \hline \end{array}$ **25.** $\begin{array}{r} 478 \\ -259 \\ \hline \end{array}$ **26.** $\begin{array}{r} 851 \\ -587 \\ \hline \end{array}$ **27.** $\begin{array}{r} 119 \\ -\ \ 54 \\ \hline \end{array}$ **28.** $\begin{array}{r} 633 \\ -\ \ 49 \\ \hline \end{array}$

29. $\begin{array}{r} 6,295 \\ -2,174 \\ \hline \end{array}$ **30.** $\begin{array}{r} 7,221 \\ -5,321 \\ \hline \end{array}$ **31.** $\begin{array}{r} 3,936 \\ -2,878 \\ \hline \end{array}$ **32.** $\begin{array}{r} 1,111 \\ -\ \ 674 \\ \hline \end{array}$ **33.** $\begin{array}{r} 7,462 \\ -\ \ 189 \\ \hline \end{array}$

34. 852 − 451 **35.** 579 − 498 **36.** 265 − 77 **37.** 7,839 − 2,842

38. 523 − 56 **39.** 7,359 − 367 **40.** 4,138 − 197 **41.** 8,347 − 1,358

42. 931 − 78 **43.** 532 − 69 **44.** 1,634 − 943 **45.** 4,254 − 2,965

46. Find the difference between 4,148 and 2,891.

47. How would you regroup 3 tens to find the difference between 232 and 128?

48. Algebra Readiness Find the rule. Complete the table.

In	470	550	630	710
Out	490	570		

Patterns Copy and complete.

49. 287, 278, 269, ■, ■, ■

50. 1,092, 1,097, 1,102, ■, ■, ■

Problem Solving and Applications

Using Data Use the table for **51–53**.

51. In which year did the lifeguards make the fewest rescues at this Florida beach?

52. Mental Math What is the difference between the number of rescues in 1992 and the number in 1993?

53. Calculator In the four-year period, how many people were rescued at this Florida beach?

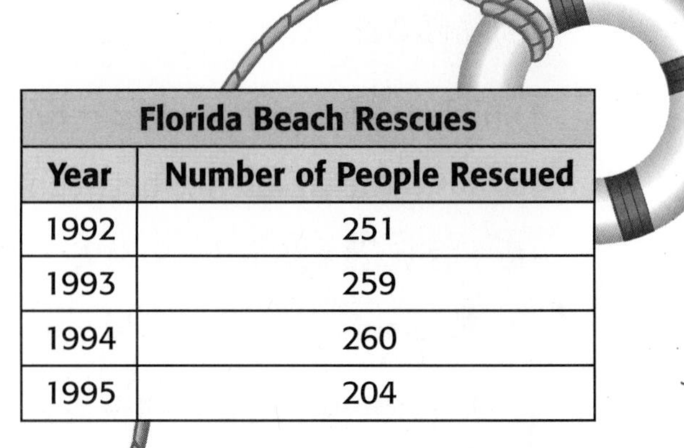

Florida Beach Rescues

Year	Number of People Rescued
1992	251
1993	259
1994	260
1995	204

Problem Solving and SCIENCE

Marine animals get a seal of approval for helping in underwater rescues! Seals, whales, and other marine animals can dive deep into the ocean.

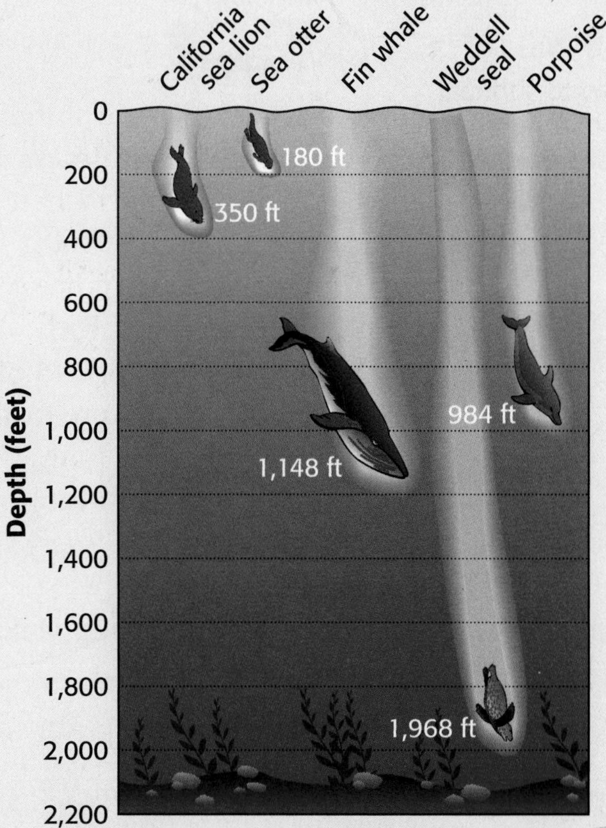

Using Data Use the graph for **54–58.**

54. Which dives deeper, a porpoise or a California sea lion? How much deeper can it dive?

55. **a.** Which animal can dive to the greatest depth? The least depth?

b. Find the difference between these two diving depths.

56. How much deeper can a fin whale dive than a porpoise?

57. How much deeper can a porpoise dive than a sea otter?

58. **Critical Thinking** Suppose a boat loses its anchor. The ocean floor is about 1,500 feet below the boat. Which animals might the crew use to get the anchor? How can you tell?

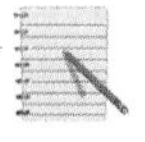

59. **Journal** Use the table on page 112. Explain how you would find the difference in the number of rescues between any two years. How would you check your answer?

Mixed Review and Test Prep

STAY SHARP!

Add or subtract.

60. 254 + 68 + 543 **61.** 1,843 − 1,575 **62.** 846 + 3,257 + 2,182

Write each number in standard form.

63. nine thousand, three hundred eight **64.** seventy thousand, two hundred

65. Over 7 years, the annual rescues at a beach were 191, 203, 410, 203, 198, 325, and 273. What is the mode?

Ⓐ 273 Ⓑ 203 Ⓒ 258 Ⓓ not here

Skills Practice Bank, page 561, Set 2

Chapter 3
Lesson
8

Subtracting with Middle Zeros

You Will Learn
how to subtract from a number that has zeros

Learn

Teachers rise and shine in harmony with their students at Interlochen Arts Camp. In 1996, music, art, and dance teachers worked with 2,001 students. If 148 of these students were from other countries, how many came from the United States?

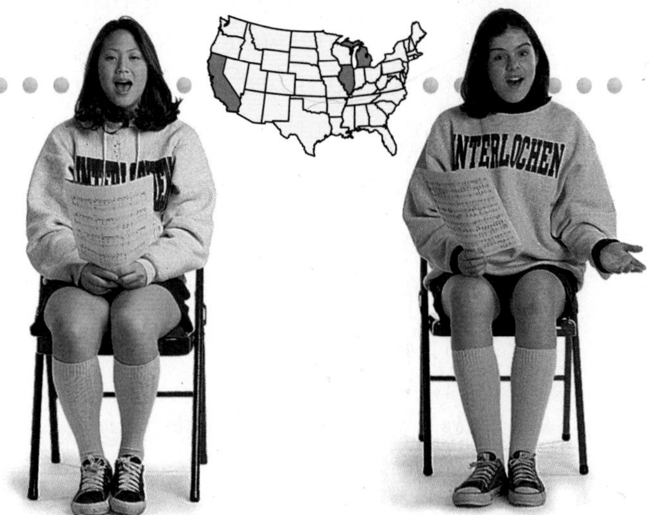

Jennifer is from Madera, California. Philippa is from Champaign, Illinois. Both studied singing at Interlochen Arts Camp in Michigan.

Math Tip
2,000 is the same as 199 tens, 1 ten.

Jennifer and Philippa solved the problem in different ways.

Jennifer's Way

```
      9  9
   1 10 10 11
   2, 0  0  1
 −    1  4  8
   1, 8  5  3
```

Not enough ones, tens, or hundreds.

Regroup thousands.

1,000 is 10 hundreds.

100 is 10 tens.

Philippa's Way

```
   199  11
   2,0 0 1
 −   1 4 8
   1,8 5 3
```

Regroup.

2,000 is 200 tens.

200 tens is 199 tens, 1 ten.

2,001 is 199 tens, 11 ones.

1,853 students were from the United States.

Other Examples

```
A.    9            B.   9 11          C.      9           D.      9  9
    4 10 14           2   10  1 11          3   10 10           5   10 10 17
    5  0  4           3 , 0  2  1           4 , 0  0  6         6 , 0  0  7
  − 1  8  7         − 2 , 4  3  2         − 1 , 2  4  4       − 2 , 7  5  8
    3  1  7                5  8  9          2 , 7  6  2         3 , 2  4  9
```

Talk About It

How did Jennifer and Philippa regroup differently?

Check

Find each difference.

1. 700 − 382
2. 2,000 − 1,248
3. 805 − 622
4. 4,049 − 1,917
5. 3,003 − 430

6. **Reasoning** How would you regroup to find 602 − 143? Solve.

Practice

Skills and Reasoning

Find each difference.

7. 600 − 418
8. 8,000 − 3,857
9. 409 − 137
10. 3,051 − 1,541
11. 7,004 − 373

12. 2,100 − 1,698
13. 4,800 − 779
14. 6,008 − 338
15. 5,000 − 3,553
16. 804 − 358
17. 4,006 − 3,329
18. 7,060 − 785
19. 4,900 − 3,250
20. What number is 424 less than 1,000?
21. How could thinking about 300 tens help you find 3,005 − 1,827?

Problem Solving and Applications

Using Data Use the bar graph for **22–24.**

22. From which state did most students come?
23. How many more students came from Michigan than Indiana?
24. **Write Your Own Problem** Use the data to write your own problem.
25. **Science** Mockingbirds can sing about 200 songs. That's about 195 more songs than other birds sing. About how many songs do other birds sing?

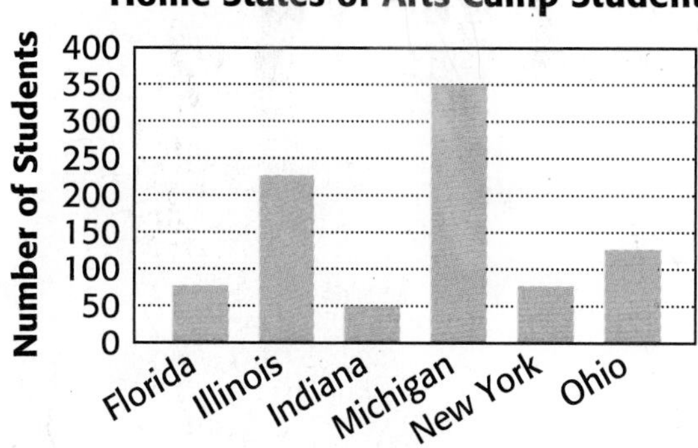

Mixed Review and Test Prep

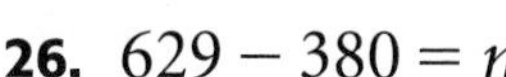

Algebra Readiness Find each missing number.

26. $629 - 380 = n$
27. $141 - 37 = n$
28. $1{,}588 - 1{,}003 = n$
29. Two hundred thousand, four is the word name for what number?
   Ⓐ 200,400,000 Ⓑ 20,000,004 Ⓒ 200,004 Ⓓ 2,004

Zeroing in on Addition and Subtraction

Players

2 or more players

Materials

2 sets of digit cards

Object

The object of the game is to estimate a sum as close to the exact answer as possible.

How to Play

1. Each player draws an addition grid like this.

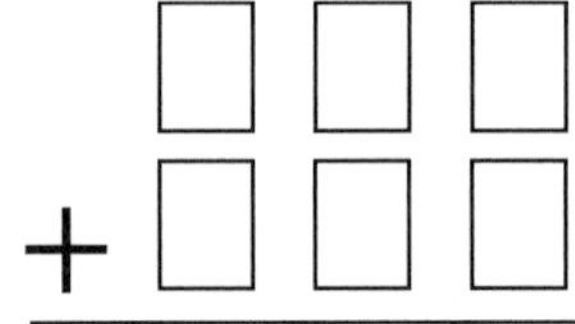

2. Each player shuffles a set of digit cards and places them face down. Each player then takes three cards, puts them in a row to make a three-digit number, and records the number on the grid.

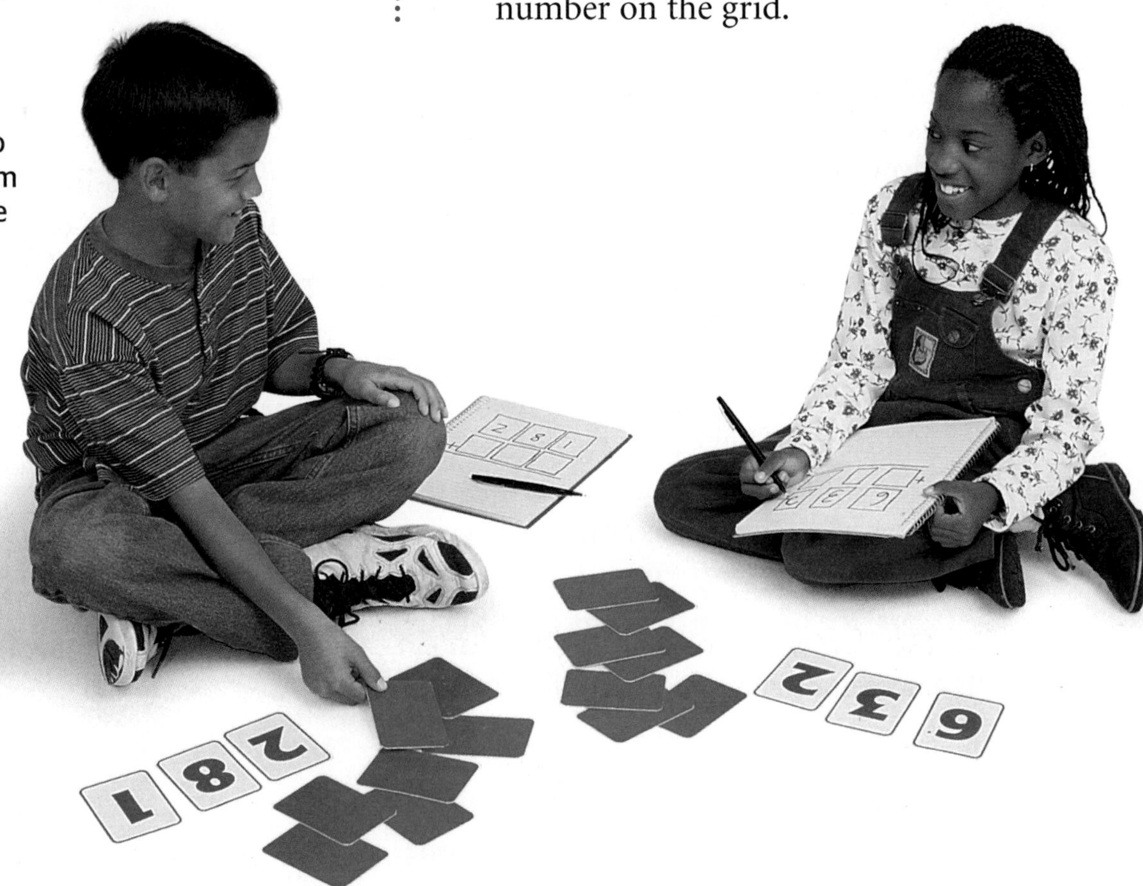

3 Each player draws three more cards, makes a three-digit number in the second row, and records it on the grid.

4 Players estimate the sum to the nearest hundred. Then they find the actual sum.

5 Now players find the difference between the estimate and the sum.

Chad's Cards

Estimate: 300   2 8 1
+ 300   + 3 4 9
600   6 3 0

6 Each player records the difference as his or her score. The player with the lowest score wins.

630 Sum
− 600 Estimate
30 Difference

7 Play five or more games. Look for winning strategies.

Talk About It

1. What winning strategies did you find?
2. Suppose you have 247 in the first row and then pick 6, 3, and 1. What number can you make to get the lowest score? Explain.

More Ways to Play

- Play the game using subtraction. Each player takes six cards and places them anywhere in a subtraction grid.
- Play again. Use a grid like this.

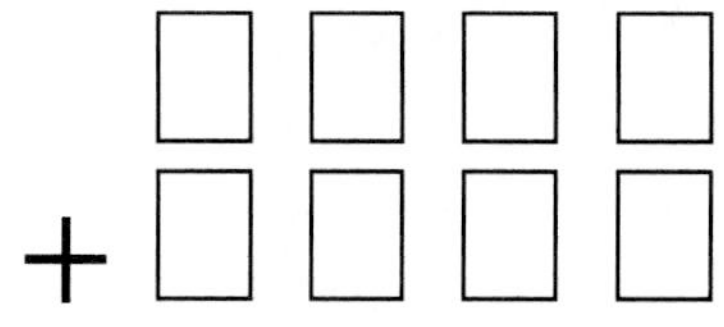

Reasoning

1. Suppose the number in the top row of an addition grid is 207. The cards you draw for the second row are 3, 9, and 4. What number should you make? Explain.
2. Suppose your grid looks like this. Which cards would be best to get? Explain.

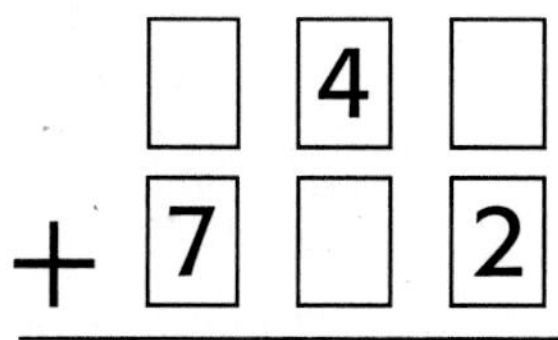

Chapter 3
Lesson
9

Problem Solving

Analyze Word Problems: Multiple-Step Problems

You Will Learn
how to solve problems that have more than one step

Learn

Young writers can publish their stories on the World Wide Web. Look at the number of hits on this publishing website. How many more hits came from North America than Australia?

Solve this problem one step at a time.

Publishing Website	
Hits from North America	
Canada	2,485
Mexico	10
United States	1,199
Hits from Oceania	
Australia	2,465
New Zealand	464

Work Together

▶ Understand What do you know?

What do you need to find out?

▶ Plan How can you find out? Find the total hits from North America.

What's the next step? Compare the total to hits from Australia.

▶ Solve

Step 1: Add to find the number of hits from North America.

Canada	2,485
Mexico	10
United States	+ 1,199
	3,694

Step 2: Subtract to compare the hits from North America and Australia.

North America	3,694
Australia	− 2,465
	1,229

What's the answer? The difference is 1,229 hits.

Math Tip
A *hit* is a visit to a website.

▶ Look Back Does your answer make sense?

How do you know?

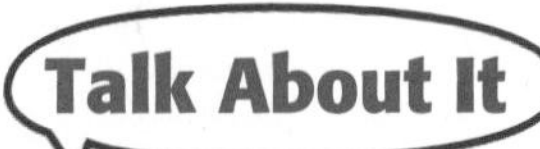

Why did this problem have to be solved in two steps?

Check

1. Gayle's first draft of a story had 212 words. When she edited the story, she crossed out 24 words and added 47 new ones.
   a. How long was the story after she crossed out words?
   b. How long was the story when she added new words?
2. The publishing website got 795 hits from England. How many more hits came from Oceania than England?

Problem Solving Practice

Problem Solving Strategies

- Use Objects/Act It Out
- Draw a Picture
- Look for a Pattern
- Guess and Check
- Use Logical Reasoning
- Make an Organized List
- Make a Table
- Solve a Simpler Problem
- Work Backward

Choose a Tool

3. Kyle's first published story is 117 words long. His second story is 42 words longer. His third story is 56 words shorter than his second story. How long is his third story?
4. Emil uses a computer for 1 hour. He spends 26 minutes writing a story and 21 minutes correcting it. How much time does he have left?
5. It takes Maurice 87 seconds to log on, 24 seconds to find an e-mail note, and 92 seconds to read it. Does this take more than 3 minutes? Explain.

Using Data Use the table for **6–8.**

6. How much more time is spent watching TV than reading books?
7. How much less time do people spend reading in general than watching TV?
8. **What If** You are a journalist. Would you have a greater audience if you worked for cable TV or for newspapers and magazines? Explain.
9. **Collecting Data** Keep a log to find out how much time you spend with different media in a week. Share your data. Make a bar graph of class data.

Annual Media Use

Media	Hours Per Person
Network TV	925
Independent TV	149
Cable TV	451
Recorded music	274
Newspapers	166
Magazines	84
Books	100

10. **Time** Suppose you sign up for a one-day World Wide Web class. The class includes three lessons, each 1 hour long. There is a 2-hour practice session, after a 30-minute lunch break. The class ends at 3:30 P.M.
    a. What time did the class begin?
    b. What strategies did you use to solve this problem?

PROBLEM SOLVING PRACTICE

Chapter 3
Lesson
10

Using Mental Math

You Will Learn
how to add and subtract numbers mentally

Did You Know?
Children in the United States laugh about 400 times a day. Adults laugh about 15 times a day.

Learn

Laughter is everybody's business at the Belfast Circus School. Students practice juggling, tumbling, unicycle riding, and clowning around.

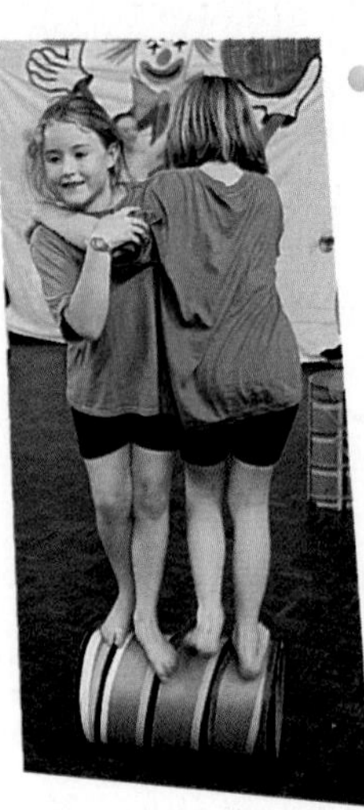

The Belfast Circus School in Northern Ireland

Suppose the students make 500 fliers to advertise their shows. If they post 197 fliers, how many do they have left?

There are many ways to add and subtract mentally. You can invent your own ways, too.

Here is how Deeva and Kevin find 500 – 197 mentally.

Deeva's Way

I know that 500 – 200 = 300.

I took away 3 too many, so I'll add back 3.
The answer is 303.

Kevin's Way

I'll add 3 to each number.

$$\begin{array}{rcr} 500 + 3 & \longrightarrow & 503 \\ -\ 197 + 3 & \longrightarrow & -\ 200 \\ \hline & & 303 \end{array}$$

Talk About It

1. Why did Kevin add 3 to each number before subtracting?
2. Explain how you would add 195 and 49 mentally.

Check

Add or subtract mentally. Choose any method.

1. 99 + 67 **2.** 98 + 53 **3.** 403 + 87 **4.** 695 + 125 **5.** 258 + 111

6. 200 – 99 **7.** 800 – 195 **8.** 805 – 150 **9.** 275 – 125 **10.** 355 – 225

11. Reasoning Explain two ways to find 300 – 198.

Practice

Skills and Reasoning

Mental Math Add or subtract mentally. Choose any method.

12. 99 + 73 **13.** 95 + 305 **14.** 600 − 99 **15.** 300 − 48

16. 568 + 195 **17.** 4,768 − 599 **18.** 125 + 68 + 875 **19.** 133 + 550 + 450

20. Find the sum of 406 and 394. **21.** Find the difference between 702 and 498.

Copy and complete. Write >, <, or =.

22. 453 + 198 ● 353 + 299 **23.** 536 − 198 ● 536 − 199

24. 748 + 12 ● 748 − 12 **25.** 807 − 200 ● 507 + 100

26. Algebra Readiness Find the rule. Complete the table.

In	500	700	900	1,100	1,300
Out	425	625	825		

Problem Solving and Applications

27. The Belfast Circus School performers give two shows in town. A total of 398 people go to the shows. If 202 people are at the first show, how many are at the second show?

28. Science For humans, smiling uses 17 muscles in the face. Frowning uses 43 muscles. How many more muscles does it take to frown?

29. Measurement Spotted hyenas are noisy animals. They cackle, screech, and sometimes laugh. A typical female spotted hyena weighs 173 pounds. A male weighs about 121 pounds. What is the difference in their weights?

30. Collecting Data Make a tally chart of the number of times you see someone laugh during lunchtime. Record data separately for adults and children. Then compare it with the data in *Did You Know?* on page 120.

Mixed Review and Test Prep

Add.

31. 564 + 221 **32.** 329 + 504 **33.** 781 + 178 **34.** 206 + 206

35. Which set of numbers is ordered from greatest to least?

Ⓐ 378, 738, 873 Ⓑ 873, 783, 378 Ⓒ 873, 837, 883

Chapter 3
Lesson
11

Choosing a Calculation Method

You Will Learn
how to choose a calculation method

Learn

Warm them, roll them, fill them! However you eat them, tortillas are a well-rounded meal.

In a typical week, a tortilla factory produces 98,448 packages of corn tortillas and 85,178 packages of flour tortillas. How many packages does it make in all?

Helen Chavez-Hansen bakes traditional and fruit tortillas in her factory in Fresno, California.

Did You Know?
Machines can make about 66,000 corn tortillas (tor-TEE-yah) and about 28,800 flour tortillas in an hour.

You can use different calculation methods to find 98,448 + 85,178.

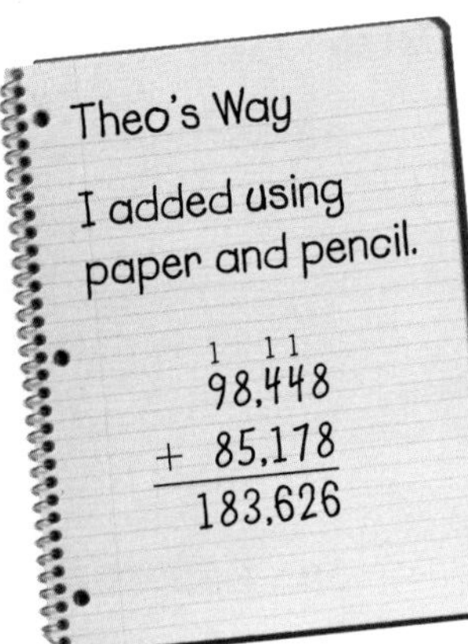

Carly's Way

I knew there would be a lot of regrouping, so I used a calculator.

I keyed in the addition.
98,448 [+] 85,178 [=]

183626

In a typical week, a factory might make 183,626 packages of tortillas.

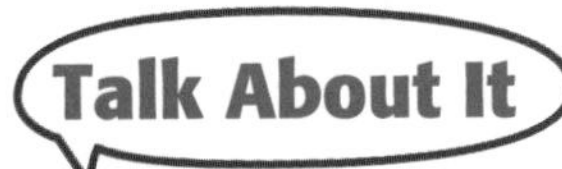

When might it be better to use a calculator?

Check

Find each sum or difference. Choose any method.

1. 27,400 − 12,650

2. 58,000 + 30,000

3. 27,650 + 12,400

4. 36,000 − 16,000

5. Reasoning Which calculation method would you use to find the difference between 12,825 and 9,948? Explain.

Practice

Skills and Reasoning

Find each sum or difference. Choose any method.

6. 44,200 − 22,100

7. 36,584 − 6,798

8. 28,500 + 28,500

9. 76,345 − 46,345

10. 32,008 − 11,003

11. 91,100 − 80,000

12. 21,339 + 66,783

13. 38,911 − 29,745

14. Find the sum of 3,700 and 54,200.

15. Subtract 59,000 from 89,000.

16. What is the greatest possible sum of two 5-digit numbers?

Problem Solving and Applications

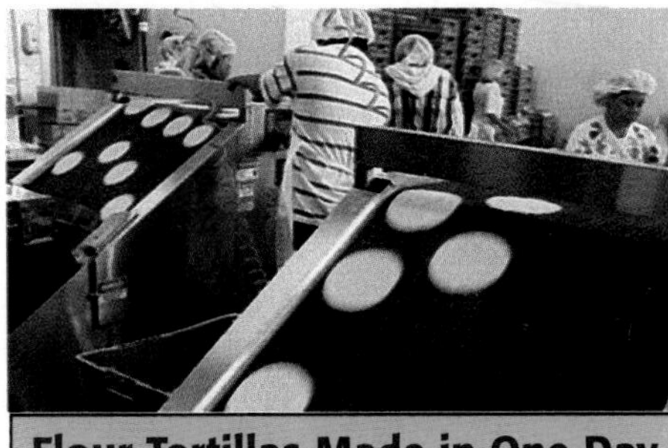

17. Using Data Use the facts from *Did You Know?* on page 122. About how many more corn tortillas than flour tortillas can a factory make in an hour?

Using Data Use the table for **18** and **19.**

Flour Tortillas Made in One Day	
Size	**Number of Packages**
7 inch	497
8 inch	1,591
10 inch	354
12 inch	1,669
14 inch	17

18. How many packages of the two most popular sizes of flour tortillas were made that day?

19. How many packages of flour tortillas were made that day?

20. Geometry Readiness Draw a picture of a tortilla folded in half. What shape is it?

21. Using Data Use the Data File on page 91. Of the people who knew about the "Take Our Daughters to Work" program, how many did *not* take a daughter to work?

Mixed Review and Test Prep

Compare each pair of numbers. Write > or <.

22. 699 ● 669

23. 1,220 ● 1,720

24. 1,652 ● 1,662

25. 2,812 ● 1,282

26. 12,695 ● 16,692

27. 3,796 ● 3,794

28. Patterns Which pair of numbers continues the pattern?
500, 1,000, 1,500, ■, ■

Ⓐ 1,600, 1,700 Ⓑ 2,000, 2,500 Ⓒ 1,000, 500 Ⓓ not here

SECTION B

Review and Practice

Vocabulary Match each word with its meaning.

1. front-end estimation
2. addends

a. numbers added together to make a sum
b. a way to estimate using leading digits

(Lessons 5 and 6) Find each sum. Estimate to check.

3. $781 + 112$ **4.** $853 + 250$ **5.** $823 + 415$ **6.** $646 + 789$

7. $227 + 240 + 352$ **8.** $2{,}425 + 55 + 436$ **9.** $689 + 99 + 8{,}324$ **10.** $810 + 436 + 3{,}352$ **11.** $1{,}915 + 6{,}485 + 9{,}399$

12. Science Mauna Loa volcano, in Hawaii, rises 4,170 meters above sea level. About 6,000 meters more of the volcano are underwater. How tall is the volcano in all?

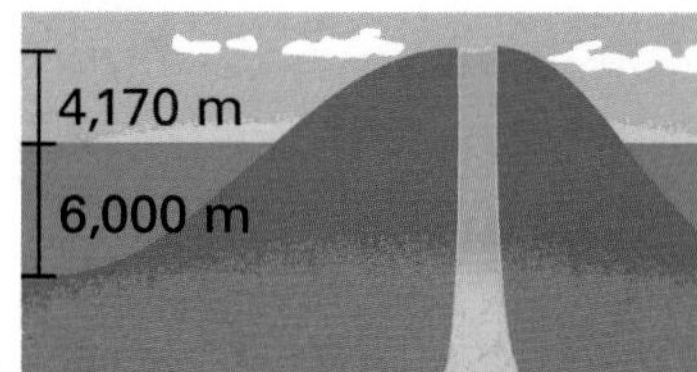

(Lessons 7 and 8) Subtract.

13. $632 - 110$ **14.** $463 - 253$ **15.** $1{,}289 - 975$ **16.** $2{,}498 - 1{,}178$

17. $203 - 51$ **18.** $700 - 525$ **19.** $6{,}001 - 3{,}210$ **20.** $2{,}000 - 323$ **21.** $8{,}100 - 7{,}321$

(Lesson 9) Solve.

22. Music At Interlochen, 47 students play in the orchestra, 36 students play in the band, and 86 students sing in the chorus. How many more students sing than play musical instruments?

(Lessons 10) **Mental Math** Add or subtract mentally.

23. $749 - 201$ **24.** $99 + 75$ **25.** $1{,}435 - 405$

(Lesson 11) Find each sum or difference.

26. $5{,}003 + 4{,}210$ **27.** $6{,}314 - 2{,}831$ **28.** $92{,}131 + 12{,}476$

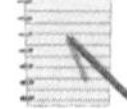

29. Journal Explain how you would compare the number of classmates who want to become scientists or musicians with the total number of classmates.

Skills Checklist

In this section, you have:

- ☑ Added and Subtracted Greater Numbers
- ☑ Subtracted with Middle Zeros
- ☑ Solved Multiple-Step Word Problems
- ☑ Added and Subtracted Mentally
- ☑ Chosen a Calculation Method

CHAPTER 3

SECTION C

Using Money

Philomena Okigbo imports arts and crafts from Africa to sell in the United States. Her work gives her a chance to teach people about African culture.

When you buy things, how can you tell that you'll have enough money? How do you know how much change you'll get back?

GET READY!

Adding and Subtracting Money

Review money. Copy and complete.

1. $0.10 = ■ pennies
2. $1.00 = ■ quarters
3. $0.25 = ■ nickels
4. $0.80 = ■ dimes

Skills Checklist

In this section, you will:

- ❒ Count Money
- ❒ Add and Subtract Money
- ❒ Explore Making Change
- ❒ Explore Algebra by Balancing Number Sentences
- ❒ Solve Problems by Looking for Patterns

Counting Money

You Will Learn
how to count and compare money

Vocabulary
decimal point
a symbol (.) that separates dollar and cent amounts

Philomena Okigbo sells clothing, arts, and crafts from Africa.

Suppose you have some bills and coins. Do you have enough money to buy this cowrie necklace?

$8.75

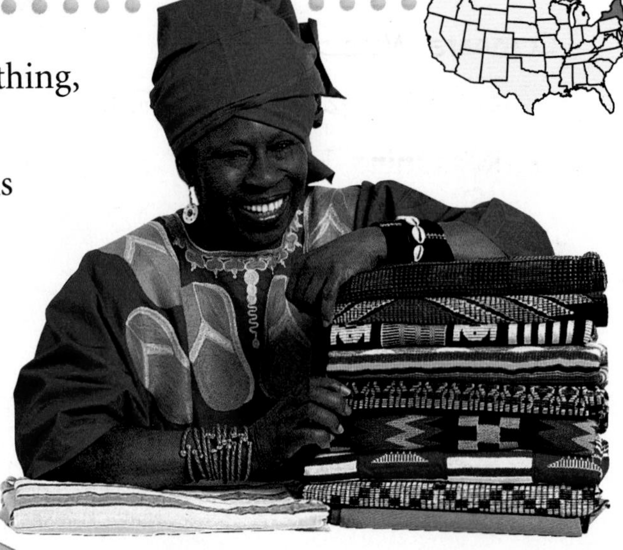

Philomena Okigbo came from Nigeria, in western Africa. Now she works in Ithaca, New York.

Did You Know?
The average life of a $1 bill is 18 months, and that of a $10 bill is 3 years.

Example

You can count dollar and coin amounts to compare money.

Step 1

Count the dollars.
You count: 5, 6, 7, 8 dollars.

Step 2

Count the coin amounts.
You count: 25, 50, 75 … 85, 90, 91, 92 cents.

You have: $8.92.
You need: $8.75.

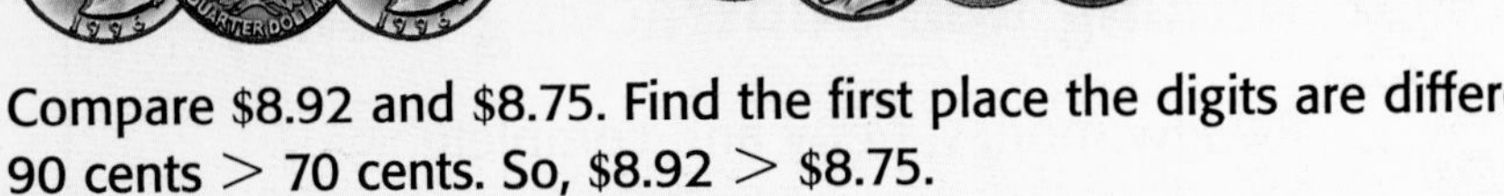

Compare $8.92 and $8.75. Find the first place the digits are different.
90 cents > 70 cents. So, $8.92 > $8.75.
You have enough money to buy the necklace.

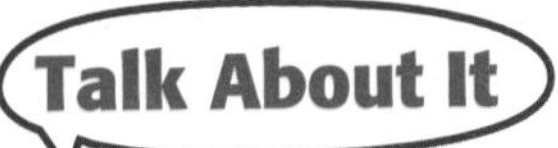

How is comparing money different from comparing whole numbers?

Check

Count the money. Write each amount with dollar sign and decimal point.

1. 3 dollars, 2 quarters, 3 pennies
2. one $20.00 bill, 2 $10.00 bills, 4 dimes, 1 nickel

Compare. Write >, <, or =.

3. $25.94 ● $25.49
4. $94.06 ● $94.01
5. $0.38 ● $1.37
6. $42.40 ● $4.24
7. **Reasoning** How could you make $37.95 with the fewest bills and coins?

Practice

Skills and Reasoning

Count the money. Write each amount with dollar sign and decimal point.

8. one $10.00 bill, 1 dollar, 1 quarter, 1 nickel
9. 4 dollars, 2 quarters, 1 dime, 3 pennies

Compare. Write >, <, or =.

10. $0.77 ● $67.00
11. $75.57 ● $57.75
12. $245.00 ● $254.00
13. 3 dollars, 5 quarters, 2 nickels ● $4.35
14. $7.34 ● 1 $5.00 bill, 2 dollars, 3 dimes, 4 nickels
15. How could you make $55.28 with only 4 bills and 4 coins?

Problem Solving and Applications

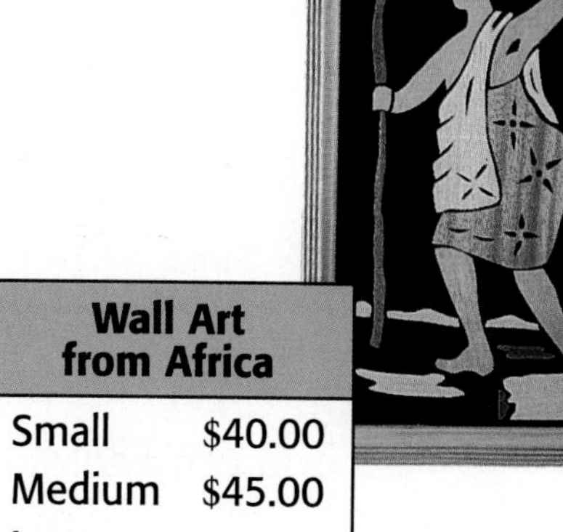

Wall Art from Africa	
Small	$40.00
Medium	$45.00
Large	$50.00

16. What is the greatest number of five-dollar bills you would need to buy the medium wall art?
17. Suppose you have 1 twenty-dollar bill, 1 ten-dollar bill, 2 five-dollar bills, 10 quarters, 7 dimes. What is the largest wall art you could buy? Write the amount you have.

Mixed Review and Test Prep

STAY SHARP!

Patterns Copy and complete each pattern.

18. 3, 6, 9, 12, ■, ■, ■
19. 70, 60, 50, 40, ■, ■, ■
20. **Time** Which is the fifth month of the year?

Ⓐ March Ⓑ September Ⓒ May Ⓓ April

Chapter 3
Lesson
13

Adding and Subtracting Money

You Will Learn
how to add and subtract money amounts

Did You Know?
There are at least 50 million dog owners and 58 million cat owners in the United States.

Learn

"The secret is patience," says Ryan's mom. "Just keep trying till the puppies learn to follow your lead!"

Ryan and Aubrey help their mom with her dog training business in Royal Oak, Michigan.

A leather dog collar costs $12.69. A cloth one costs $7.95. How much more does the leather one cost?

Subtract to compare the two amounts.

Example 1

Find $12.69 – $7.95.

Step 1	Step 2	Step 3
Line up the decimals.	Subtract as you would with whole numbers.	Write the decimal point and dollar sign in the difference.
$12.69 – 7.95	11 (regrouped: 1̸ 16) $1̸2̸.6̸9 – 7.95 474	11 (regrouped: 1̸ 16) $1̸2̸.6̸9 – 7.95 $4.74

Estimate to check. $13.00 – $8.00 = $5.00
Since $4.74 is close to $5.00, the answer is reasonable.
The leather collar costs $4.74 more.

You can add dollar amounts in the same way.

Other Examples

A.	B.	C.
1 $9.29 + 4.68 $13.97	1 1 1 $49.79 + 7.34 $57.13	1 $98.00 + 27.95 $125.95

Why do you need to line up the decimal points?

Check

Add or subtract. Estimate to check.

1. $\begin{array}{r} \$2.25 \\ +\ 1.10 \\ \hline \end{array}$ **2.** $\begin{array}{r} \$9.94 \\ -\ 2.10 \\ \hline \end{array}$ **3.** $\begin{array}{r} \$10.59 \\ -\ 2.35 \\ \hline \end{array}$ **4.** $\begin{array}{r} \$15.38 \\ +\ 22.95 \\ \hline \end{array}$ **5.** $\begin{array}{r} \$24.66 \\ +\ 0.76 \\ \hline \end{array}$

6. $6.42 + $13.16 **7.** $32.20 − $11.12 **8.** $47.12 − $13.98

9. Reasoning Suppose you added $15.11, $32, and $0.38 and got $15.81. Explain why this sum is incorrect.

PRACTICE AND APPLY

Practice

Skills and Reasoning

Add or subtract. Estimate to check.

10. $\begin{array}{r} \$3.06 \\ +\ 6.20 \\ \hline \end{array}$ **11.** $\begin{array}{r} \$9.98 \\ -\ 2.11 \\ \hline \end{array}$ **12.** $\begin{array}{r} \$7.59 \\ -\ 2.32 \\ \hline \end{array}$ **13.** $\begin{array}{r} \$11.22 \\ +\ 7.88 \\ \hline \end{array}$ **14.** $\begin{array}{r} \$20.35 \\ +\ 9.63 \\ \hline \end{array}$

15. $\begin{array}{r} \$23.06 \\ +\ 1.10 \\ \hline \end{array}$ **16.** $\begin{array}{r} \$8.56 \\ -\ 0.92 \\ \hline \end{array}$ **17.** $\begin{array}{r} \$18.60 \\ -\ 11.49 \\ \hline \end{array}$ **18.** $\begin{array}{r} \$21.88 \\ -\ 20.81 \\ \hline \end{array}$ **19.** $\begin{array}{r} \$14.31 \\ +\ 5.39 \\ \hline \end{array}$

20. $41.41 + $15.50 **21.** $0.87 + $145.45 **22.** $60.10 − $16.38

23. Find the difference between $35.60 and $17.99.

24. Find the sum of $856 and $1,296.

25. Estimate to decide if the sum of $24.73 and $24.28 is greater than $50.00. Explain.

Problem Solving and Applications

26. Suppose Ryan and Aubrey buy a new dog brush for $6.99. How much change will they get back from a $10 bill?

27. Ryan and Aubrey's mom charges $5.50 per night for a dog to sleep over. Food is $2.35 more. What is the total cost per night?

28. Using Data Use the Data File on page 91. About how much did the average hourly wage go up from 1980 to 1995?

Mixed Review and Test Prep

Patterns Copy and complete each pattern.

29. 75, 85, 95, ■, ■

30. 20, 300, 4,000, ■, ■

31. In the number 2,374,285, what is the value of the digit 7?

Ⓐ 7 thousands Ⓑ 70 thousands Ⓒ 7 hundreds Ⓓ not here

Chapter 3 Lesson 14

Exploring Making Change

Problem Solving Connection
Use Objects/ Act It Out

Materials
play money: coins and bills

Explore

You reeled in a job at Buddy's Bait Stand! That's where anglers pick up their fishing supplies.

Work Together

Work with play money, or draw pictures.

1. A customer buys a box of worms.
   a. The customer pays with a $5 bill. The cash drawer doesn't have any quarters. What change will you give?
   b. Suppose the customer pays with a $10 bill. You just got some quarters to put in the cash drawer. How would you count on to $10.00?

Remember
$10.00 is the same as $10.

2. A customer buys a box of slugs and pays with a $20 bill.
   a. How much is the change?
   b. What is one combination of coins and bills that you could give as change?
   c. Suppose there are no dollar bills in the cash drawer. How would you give change?

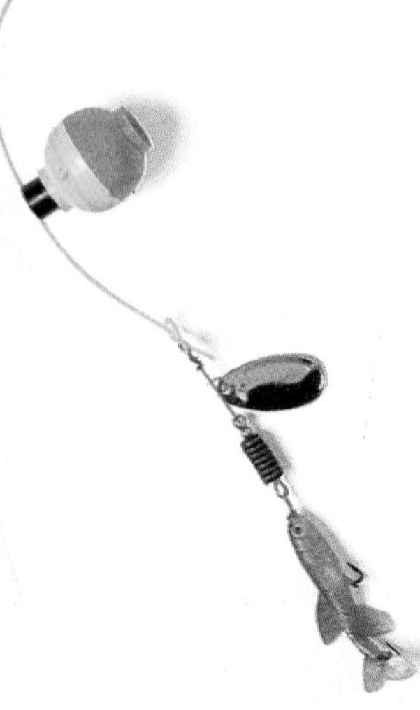

BUDDY'S BAIT STAND

Bait and Supplies	Price
Worms	$2.25 per box
Grasshoppers	$1.79 per box
Slugs	$3.75 per box
Fishing line	$14.99 each
Floating fly	$9.49 each
Minnow float	$6.99 each
Shrimp fly	$4.50 each

Talk About It

3. When is counting on a helpful way to give change?
4. When counting on, why might you start with pennies and work your way up to quarters?

Connect

Bob and Mike also work at Buddy's. Each one serves a customer who buys a box of grasshoppers and pays with a $10 bill. Here is how Bob and Mike make change.

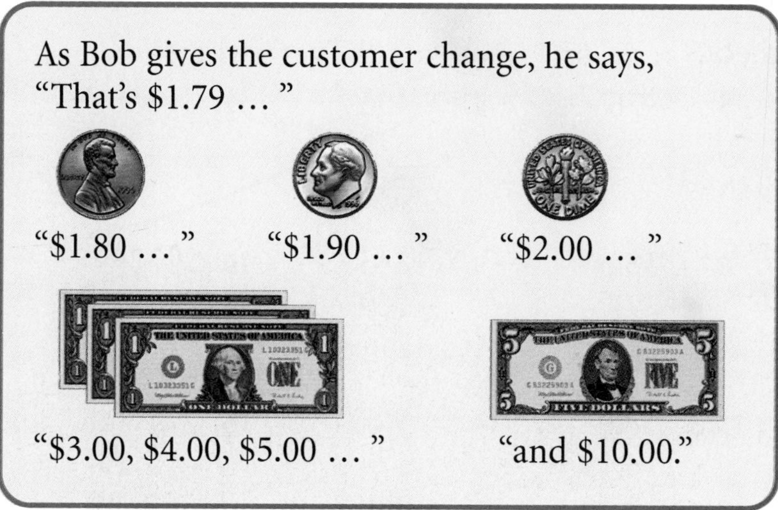

As Bob gives the customer change, he says, "That's $1.79 ... "

"$1.80 ... " "$1.90 ... " "$2.00 ... "

"$3.00, $4.00, $5.00 ... " "and $10.00."

Before Mike gives his customer change, he subtracts.

```
     9   9
    10  10 10
$ 1  0 . 0  0
-      1 . 7  9
$      8 . 2  1
```

Bob and Mike both give $8.21 change.

Practice

Using Data Use the data on page 130 for **1–3.** Write the change for each purchase.

1. A customer buys a floating fly and a box of grasshoppers and pays with a $20 bill.
2. A friend buys 3 shrimp flies and pays with $15.
3. A family buys fishing line, a minnow float, a shrimp fly, and a box of worms. The family pays with two $20 bills.
4. Copy and complete the table. Write each amount of change.

Cost	$0.32	$12.39	$3.44	$29.80	$17.36
Amount Given	$5.00	$13.00	$20.00	$50.00	$17.50
Change					

5. Suppose you have this money in your pocket. List three ways you could pay for a minnow float.
6. **Critical Thinking** Why might you give a clerk $5.06 to pay for a $3.06 item?

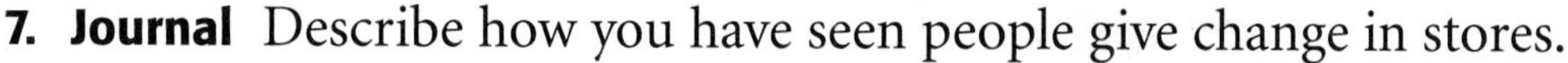

7. **Journal** Describe how you have seen people give change in stores.

STOP and Practice

Add or subtract. Estimate to check.

1. 245 − 234	**2.** 467 + 897	**3.** 976 − 86	**4.** 456 + 342	**5.** 308 − 175
6. 233 + 741	**7.** 808 − 256	**8.** 584 + 77	**9.** 845 − 209	**10.** 729 − 64
11. 28 43 + 62	**12.** 473 67 + 539	**13.** \$8.95 4.13 + 2.68	**14.** 9,634 903 + 1,823	**15.** 846 3,237 + 2,184

16. \$15.12 − \$9.35 **17.** \$8.95 + \$8.57 **18.** \$29.49 − \$15.95

19. \$77.89 − \$14.36 **20.** \$12.45 + \$18.96 **21.** \$39.49 + \$10.23

22. \$65.18 + 55.10	**23.** \$98.01 − 10.99	**24.** \$76.83 + 12.83	**25.** \$22.90 + 7.95
26. 9,876 + 2,134	**27.** 7,919 − 3,912	**28.** 4,817 − 2,111	**29.** 6,789 + 5,217

30. 275 − 150 **31.** 899 + 100 **32.** 230 − 149

33. 1,500 + 150 + 200 **34.** 665 + 195 + 489 **35.** 1,300 + 25 + 275

36. 422 + 59 + 305 **37.** 781 + 201 + 35 **38.** 1,469 + 23 + 140

Error Search

Find each sum or difference that is not correct. Write it correctly and explain the error.

39. \$18.65 − 7.49 \$1,116	**40.** 1,189 − 1,054 2,243	**41.** \$12.00 + 22.00 \$340.00	**42.** 1,022 − 889 133

Hog Wild!

Add or subtract. Match each letter with its answer below to solve the riddle. Some letters are not used.

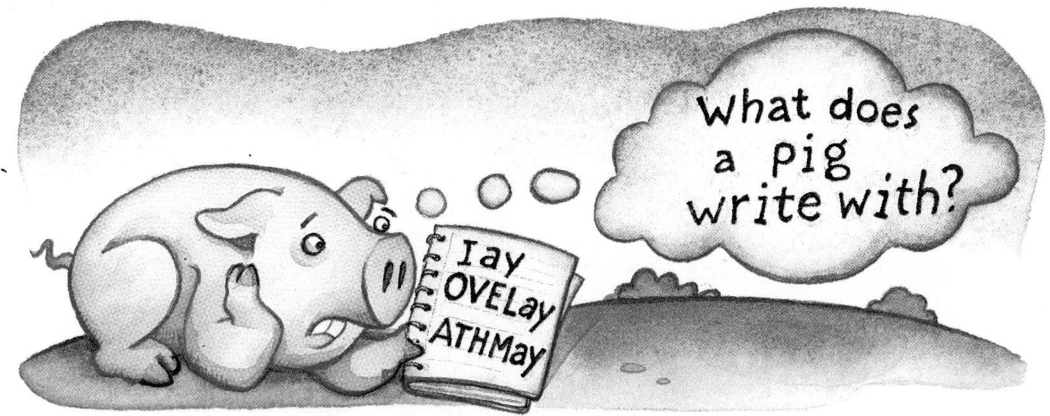

43. 854 − 76 [G]

44. 352 + 276 [A]

45. 509 − 234 [C]

46. 431 + 592 [P]

47. 257 + 936 [B]

48. 454 − 323 [P]

49. 672 + 44 [I]

50. 707 − 342 [M]

51. 475 + 150 [D]

52. 692 − 88 [E]

53. 563 + 57 [O]

54. 340 − 139 [N]

___	___	___	___	___	___	___
628	1,023	716	778	131	604	201

Number Sense Reasoning

Write whether each statement is true or false. Explain your answer.

55. \$5.50 + \$10.95 > \$55.50 + \$10.95

56. \$75.03 − \$1.00 > \$75.30 − \$1.00

57. \$5.55 + \$7.89 = \$7.89 − \$5.55

58. \$78.90 − \$78.09 > \$4.99 − \$2.99

59. \$1.89 + \$4.98 + \$3.95 < \$11.23 + \$2.05

60. \$10.00 + \$20.00 + \$3.00 < \$1.00 + \$20.00 + \$30.00

61. \$0.73 + \$3.50 = \$3.50 + \$0.73

Exploring Algebra: Balancing Number Sentences

Problem Solving Connection
Use Objects/
Act It Out

Materials
- counters
- small envelope
- piece of paper

Explore

A number sentence balances when the value of the left side equals the value of the right side. You can use a number sentence workmat and counters to show the values.

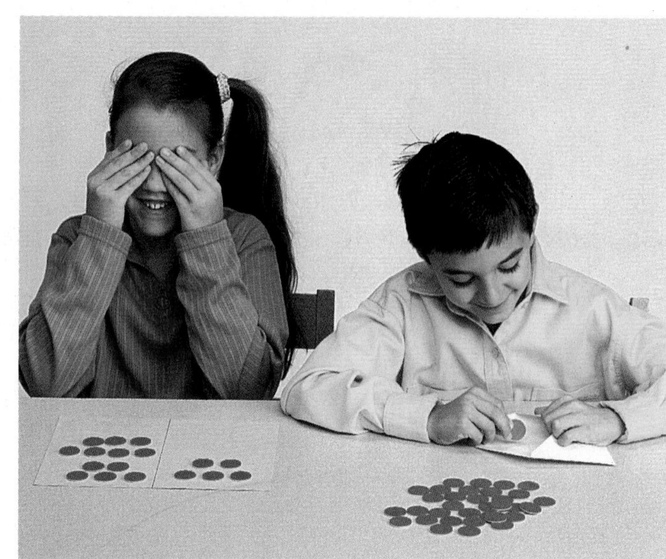

Work Together

1. Make a number sentence workmat.
2. Work with your partner to show $5 + n = 12$.
   a. One person places counters on the right side of the mat. That person places the same number of counters on the left side, hiding some of the counters in an envelope.
   b. The partner guesses how many counters are in the envelope.

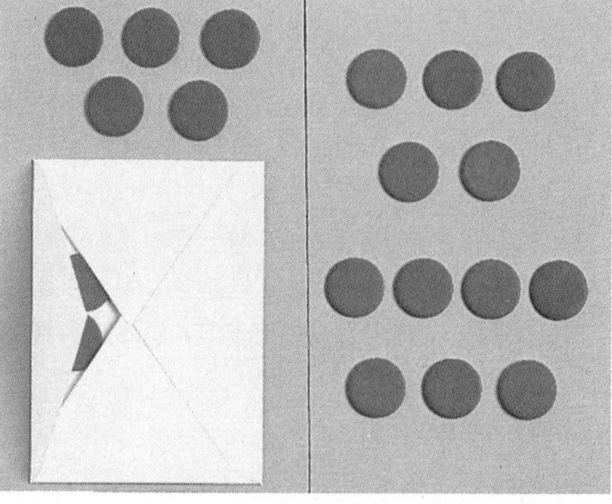

3. Take turns finding the value for n in the following number sentences. Keep a record of your work.

a. $8 + n = 12$	**b.** $3 + n = 11$	**c.** $5 + n = 14$
d. $15 + n = 21$	**e.** $19 + n = 27$	**f.** $9 + n = 12$

Remember
A variable n can be used in place of a number.

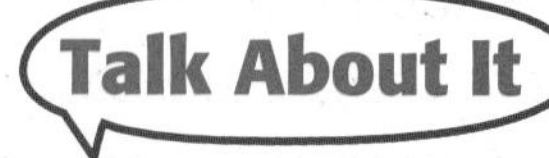

What strategy did you use to find the value for n?

Connect

The variable n may appear on either side of a number sentence.

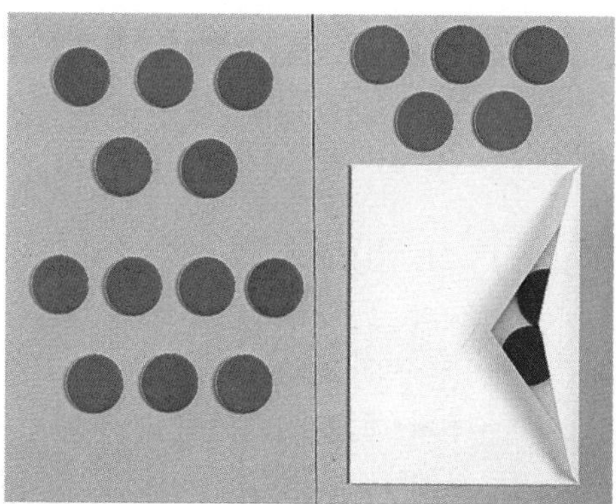

These number sentences have the same meaning:

$5 + n = 12$ $\qquad 12 = 5 + n$

$n + 5 = 12$ $\qquad 12 = n + 5$

Problem Solving Hint
To find the value for n, look at the numbers or amounts on both sides of the number sentence.

Practice

Find the value for n in each of the following number sentences. You may use counters to help.

1. $n + 6 = 11$ **2.** $12 + n = 18$ **3.** $17 = 9 + n$ **4.** $13 = n + 4$

5. $8 + n = 15$ **6.** $n + 9 = 22$ **7.** $20 = n + 5$ **8.** $23 = 7 + n$

9. Patterns Use number patterns to find the value for each n.

a. $n + 17 = 28$ **b.** $n + 17 = 38$ **c.** $n + 17 = 48$ **d.** $n + 17 = 58$

10. Critical Thinking Explain how to find the value for n in this number sentence. $n + n = 18$

Calculator Find the value for n in each of the following.

11. $955 + n = 994$ **12.** $4{,}312 = n + 1{,}096$ **13.** $372 + n = 2{,}007$

14. $709 = n + 42$ **15.** $953 + n = 1{,}035$ **16.** $n + 687 = 741$

Mental Math Find the value for n in each of the following.

17. $n + 100 = 125$ **18.** $500 + n = 800$ **19.** $7{,}000 = n + 4{,}000$

20. $600 + n = 660$ **21.** $n + 75 = 575$ **22.** $900 = 200 + n$

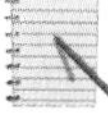

23. Journal Compare the number sentences $n + 12 = 21$ and $21 = n + 12$. Explain why the value for n stays the same even when the number sentence is written in a different way. Explain how n can appear in any position in a number sentence.

Chapter 3
Lesson
16

Problem Solving

Analyze Strategies: Look for a Pattern

You Will Learn
how to solve problems by looking for a pattern.

Learn

Fabric and wallpaper designers, architects, and biologists all work with patterns.

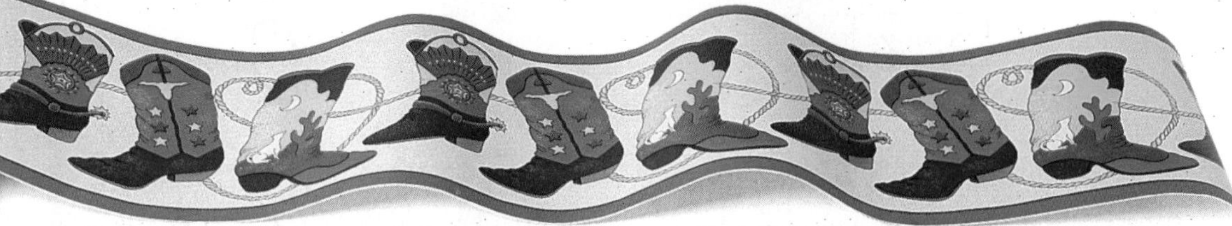

Look at the table. The patterns in a row follow the same rule. Each row has a different rule. Find the rule for each row.

	Number Pattern	Figure Pattern	Letter Pattern
Row 1	134 137 140 143 ...		A D G J M ...
Row 2	156 154 152 150 ...		M K I G E ...
Row 3	178 180 175 177 ...		T V Q S N ...

Work Together

Understand
What do you know?
What do you need to find out?

Plan
Identify the pattern in each row.
Look at the relationship between each number, figure, or letter and the item that comes next.

Solve
Find a rule that describes the pattern in each row.
Row 1: Add 3.
Row 2: Subtract 2.
Row 3: Add 2, subtract 5.

Look Back
Do the patterns in a row follow the same rule?

What other kinds of patterns can you make?

Check

Find the rule for each pattern. Describe it.

1.

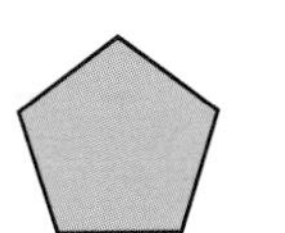
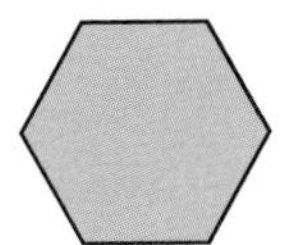

2.

x	x				
x	x	x	x	x	x
x	x	x			
x	x	x	x	x	x
x	x	x	x		
x	x	x	x	x	x
x	x	x	x	x	
x	x	x	x	x	x

3.

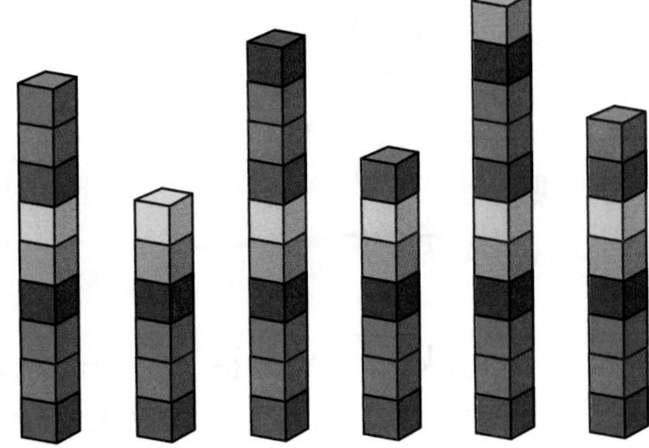

Copy and continue each pattern. Describe the rule.

4. 7, 17, 27, 37, 47, ■, ■, ■

5. A, C, B, D, ■, ■, ■

Problem Solving Practice

Copy and continue each pattern. Describe the rule.

6. 2,001, 1,901, 1,811, 1,731, 1,661, ■, ■, ■

7. 4,015, 4,025, 3,975, 3,985, 3,935, ■, ■, ■

8. 4,321 → 4,432 → 4,210 → 4,321 → ■ → ■

9. **Careers** A mason works with brick and tile. How would a mason describe the pattern in this brick walkway?

10. Describe the rule for the pattern in the wallpaper border on page 136.

11. Dale and three friends sat at a round table. Adam sat across from Ben. Carlos sat at Adam's right. Who sat at Ben's right? What strategy did you use to solve the problem?

Problem Solving Strategies

- Use Objects/Act It Out
- Draw a Picture
- Look for a Pattern
- Guess and Check
- Use Logical Reasoning
- Make an Organized List
- Make a Table
- Solve a Simpler Problem
- Work Backward

Choose a Tool

SECTION C

Review and Practice

(Lesson 12) Count the money. Write each amount with dollar sign and decimal point.

1. 2 \$20 bills, 1 \$10 bill, 3 \$5 bills, 2 quarters, 1 dime, 1 nickel
2. 5 \$10 bills, 1 \$5 bill, 2 \$1 bills, 6 dimes, 5 nickels

Compare. Write >, <, or =.

3. \$0.27 ● \$26.00
4. \$723 ● \$732
5. \$321.10 ● \$321.01
6. **Reasoning** Suppose you have just five coins in your pocket. They add up to 51 cents. What coins are they?

(Lesson 13) Add or subtract. Estimate to check.

7. \$10.26 + \$32.02
8. \$124.33 + \$73.20
9. \$6.76 + \$3.14 + \$10.45
10. \$60.11 − \$44.45
11. \$7.95 − \$6.10
12. \$25.49 − \$10.99
13. \$8.63 + \$9.95
14. \$20.64 + \$110.92
15. \$125.43 − \$72.95

(Lesson 14) Using Data Use data from the table for **16–18.**

Movie Theater Snacks	
Popcorn	\$2.50
Soda	\$1.75
Fruit drops	\$2.00

16. Marcus bought soda and fruit drops. He gave the clerk a \$10 bill. What was his change?
17. Carol bought 2 bags of popcorn. She gave the clerk a \$5.00 bill. Did she get any change? Explain.
18. **Reasoning** Nikira spent \$8.00. What did she buy?

(Lesson 15) Algebra Readiness Find the value for n in each of the following.

19. $n + 100 = 200$
20. $n + 37 = 87$
21. $923 = 902 + n$
22. $n + 77 = 100$
23. $785 = 734 + n$
24. $307 = 290 + n$

(Lesson 16) Patterns Continue each pattern. Describe the pattern.

25. 510, 51, 610, 61, ■, ■, ■
26. 10, 17, 16, 23, 22, ■, ■, ■
27. 25, 30, 28, 33, 31, ■, ■, ■

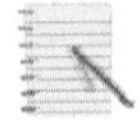

28. **Journal** Suppose you sell something for \$6.25. The customer gives you a \$10 bill. Explain the different ways you could give change.

Skills Checklist

In this section, you have:

- ☑ Counted Money
- ☑ Added and Subtracted Money
- ☑ Explored Making Change
- ☑ Explored Algebra by Balancing Number Sentences
- ☑ Solved Problems by Looking for a Pattern

Choose at least one. Use what you have learned in this chapter.

1 Number Trick!

At Home Ask a family member or a friend to enter any 3-digit number on a calculator. Have that person:

- add 242
- subtract 38
- add 96

Then ask for the answer. Subtract 300 from the answer. Tell the person the starting number. How does the trick work? Make up your own tricks!

2 Teach It

Your teacher announces that she is going to be absent tomorrow. She needs a volunteer to teach the math lesson.

Make a poster explaining how to add and subtract 3-digit numbers with and without regrouping.

3 Puzzlemania

Make a crossword puzzle for your class using numbers on grid paper. Use addition and subtraction. Write at least ten math problems for each of the Across and Down sections. Make a key to show all of the correct answers.

Ⓐ 6	4	9	■	Ⓑ 1	1	1	■	Ⓒ
2	■	■	■	2	■	■	■	
Ⓓ 1		■	Ⓔ	5	■	Ⓕ		

Across	Down
Ⓐ 324 + 325	Ⓐ 514 + 107
Ⓑ 921 − 810	Ⓑ 623 − 498

4 Dream Vacation

Work in a small group. Choose a place you'd like to visit. Start your group's tour at **www.mathsurf.com/4/ch3.** Find the cost of:

- plane or train tickets
- hotels or camping
- food
- tours

How much will your "dream vacation" cost? Design a brochure to advertise your vacation spot.

CHAPTER 3

Review/Test

Vocabulary Match each word with its meaning.

1. addends — a. the number obtained by subtracting
2. sum — b. numbers that are added together to make a sum
3. difference — c. the number obtained by adding

(Lessons 1 and 2) **Mental Math** Find each sum or difference.

4. $320 + 400$ 5. $550 - 110$ 6. $770 - 130$ 7. $560 + 240$

(Lesson 3) Estimate each sum or difference. Round to the nearest hundred.

8. $591 - 320$ 9. $419 + 333$ 10. $775 - 662$ 11. $314 + 106$

(Lessons 5 and 6) Find each sum. Estimate to check.

12. $486 + 40 + 981$
13. $165 + 895 + 3{,}420$
14. $691 + 299 + 2{,}789$
15. $1{,}035 + 4{,}503 + 1{,}290$
16. $2{,}395 + 7{,}593 + 8{,}392$

(Lessons 7 and 8) Subtract. Add or estimate to check.

17. $753 - 458$ 18. $460 - 182$ 19. $3{,}204 - 2{,}999$ 20. $4{,}001 - 2{,}432$

(Lessons 10 and 11) Find each sum or difference. Choose any calculation method.

21. $1{,}355 + 2{,}143$ 22. $1{,}352 + 2{,}002$ 23. $7{,}640 - 6{,}000$

(Lesson 12) Compare. Write >, <, or =.

24. \$128.00 ● \$12.80 25. \$6.70 ● \$11.99 26. \$55.02 ● \$52.05

(Lessons 13 and 14) Add or subtract. Estimate to check.

27. \$42.78 + \$15.37 28. \$67.00 − \$43.19 29. \$25.25 + \$25.50 + \$25.75

(Lesson 15) **Algebra Readiness** Find the value for each *n*.

30. $n + 17 = 58$ 31. $n + n = 80$ 32. $400 + n = 600$

(Lesson 16) Use any strategy to solve.

33. Ernest posted the photos of the swim team on the notice board. He put 6 in the top row, 9 in the second row, 12 in the third row, and so on. How many photos did he put in the fifth row?

CHAPTER 3

Performance Assessment

Suppose you've been saving up for a new mountain bike and need $75 more. You decide to earn the money. What jobs would you do to earn $75?

1. **Decision Making** Decide which jobs you might want to do. Estimate how much time you would have to spend at each job to earn $75.

2. **Recording Data** Copy and fill out the table below. Remember you must earn at least $75.

Job	Pay	Customers or Time Needed	Total Earnings
		Total	

3. **Explain Your Thinking** How did you decide on which jobs to do?

4. **Critical Thinking** Which job has the greatest range in how much money you could earn in a day? Why? How would a "slow" day affect your earnings with that job?

Math Magazine

Fair Exchange **What if the next time you went to the store you bought your purchases using beads, camels, or yams? Throughout history, people have used objects in place of money.**

All of the following items were once used as money.

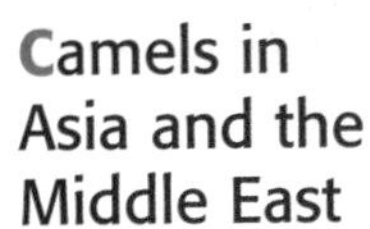

Camels in Asia and the Middle East

Yams in Africa and the Pacific Islands

Salt in the Middle East

Trading beads in Africa

Try These!

1. If 500 trading beads bought a goat, how many beads would you need to buy 4 goats?

2. Suppose you want to trade some modern goods for a pair of inline skates. What goods might you exchange?

3. Today most people use coins and paper money. Check out **www.mathsurf.com/4/ch3** to find out about money from different countries.

CHAPTERS 1–3

Cumulative Review

Test Prep Strategy: Make Smart Choices

Use mental math.

The Radical Reptiles pet store had a sale on iguanas. The store sold 12 iguanas on Monday, 23 on Tuesday, 14 on Wednesday, and 25 on Thursday. How many iguanas did it sell over four days?

Ⓐ 77 Ⓑ 74 Ⓒ 48 Ⓓ 40

Start by adding the two greatest numbers mentally.
23 + 25 = 48. Add 12 more to get 60 and add 14 more to get 74. The answer is Ⓑ.

Test Prep Strategies

- Read Carefully
- Follow Directions
- Make Smart Choices
- Eliminate Choices
- Work Backward from an Answer

Write the letter of the correct answer.

1. What are the coordinates for the point on the graph?

Ⓐ (1, 2)

Ⓑ (4, 3)

Ⓒ (3, 5)

Ⓓ (3, 4)

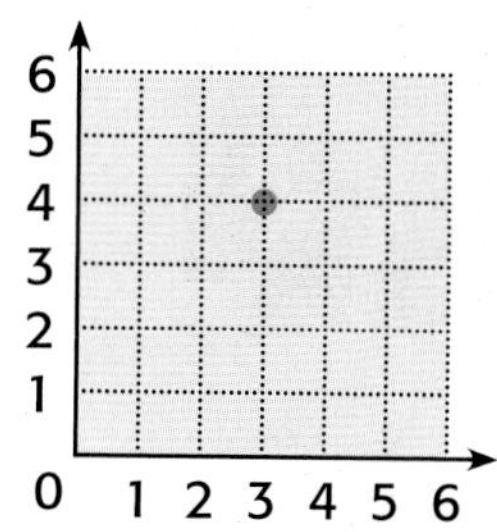

2. In the number 7,389,052, what is the value of the digit 9?

Ⓐ 9 Ⓑ 9,000 Ⓒ 90,000 Ⓓ not here

3. Which numbers are in order from least to greatest?

Ⓐ 2,209, 30,098, 3,001 Ⓑ 999, 1,001, 20,098

Ⓒ 3,001, 398, 3,998 Ⓓ 573, 537, 5,730

4. Read the clock. What time does it show?

Ⓐ 6:30 Ⓑ 6:35

Ⓒ 6:38 Ⓓ 7:38

5. The fourth grade made \$1,293 selling wrapping paper. The fifth grade made \$905. How much more did the fourth grade make?

Ⓐ \$388 Ⓑ \$492 Ⓒ \$2,198 Ⓓ \$298

6. What is the value for n in the number sentence $5 + n = 16$?

Ⓐ 21 Ⓑ 9 Ⓒ 11 Ⓓ 16

Chapter 4
Multiplication and Division Concepts and Facts

SECTION A

Understanding Multiplication

147

Ashrita Furman of New York has broken many world records! Here are some of the 47 records he holds.

- Balancing 55 glasses on his chin for 10 seconds
- Bouncing 16 miles on a pogo stick
- Performing 8,341 somersaults in 10 hours, 30 minutes
- Dribbling a basketball 83 miles in 24 hours

In the swim
Page 147

If you dribble a basketball around the outside of a basketball court 20 times, the distance will be about 1 mile. How can you find how many times you would have to travel around the outside of the court to equal Ashrita's record?

Surfing the World Wide Web!

How do you keep fit? Go to **www.mathsurf.com/4/ch4** to find out how your favorite fitness activities compare with those of other students in your grade. Share the data you find with your classmates.

SECTION B

Understanding Division

165

This table shows the goals scored in a soccer game between the Cleveland Crunch and the Baltimore Spirit. By how many points did the Crunch beat the Spirit?

Team	Period 1	Period 2	Period 3	Period 4
Crunch	2	0	8	4
Spirit	0	4	4	0

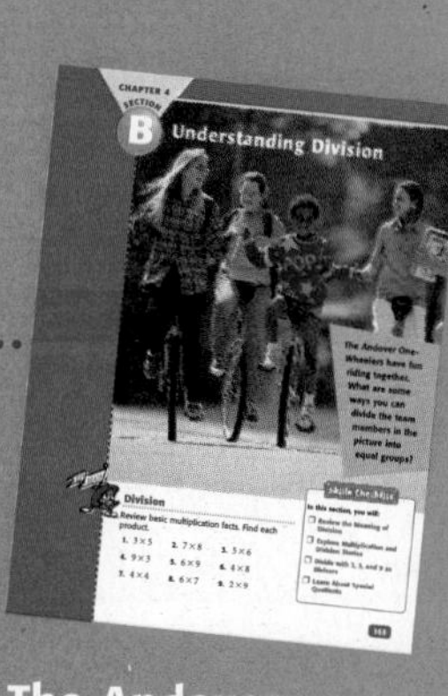

The Andover One-Wheelers
Page 165

SECTION C

Extending Multiplication and Division

175

The number of players on a team is an important part of the rules of a game. In an official volleyball game, how many players should be on the court?

Official Number of Players per Team	
Basketball	👕 👕 ½👕
Soccer	👕 👕 👕 👕 👕 ½👕
Volleyball	👕 👕 👕
Baseball	👕 👕 👕 👕 ½👕
Field Hockey	👕 👕 👕 👕 👕 ½👕
Men's Lacrosse	👕 👕 👕 👕 👕
Ice Hockey	👕 👕 👕
Women's Lacrosse	👕 👕 👕 👕 👕 👕

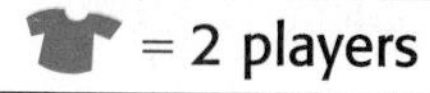

👕 = 2 players

A good skate
Page 175

Materials
butcher paper, markers, ball

Play a recess game with a multiplication twist.

Four Square Rules

- **A player wearing a number stands outside each square. The other players wait in line.**
- **A player bounces the ball into another square. The player outside that square catches it and says out loud the product of the tosser's number and his or her own number.**
- **If the player misses the ball or says an incorrect answer, he or she goes to the end of the line. A new player stands outside the square.**

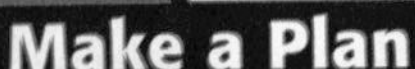

Make a Plan

- Make sure everyone in your group knows how to play Four Square.

Carry It Out

1. On butcher paper or on the playground, draw 4 equal squares about 3 feet by 3 feet each.
2. Choose a number between 1 and 9. Write the number on paper and tape it to your shirt.
3. Play the game. Remember to say the product out loud.

Talk About It

- Did you find it hard to multiply some numbers? Explain.
- Was it harder or easier to multiply numbers as the game got faster? Explain.

Present the Project

- Tell how your team played the game.
- Discuss how other recess games, such as jacks or jumping rope, involve math.

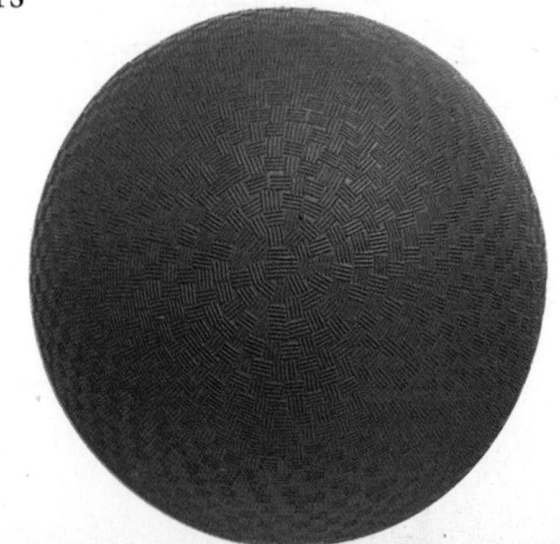

CHAPTER 4

SECTION

A Understanding Multiplication

Allie keeps fit by swimming. If she trains an equal number of hours each day, how could you find how many hours she trains in 3 days?

GET READY!

Multiplication

Review addition. Find each sum.

1. $3 + 3 + 3$
2. $4 + 4 + 4 + 4 + 4$
3. $6 + 6 + 6$
4. $\$9 + \$9 + \$9 + \$9$
5. $8 + 8 + 8 + 8$
6. $2 + 2 + 2 + 2 + 2$
7. $5 + 5 + 5$
8. $\$7 + \$7 + \$7 + \$7$

Skills Checklist

In this section, you will:

- ❒ Review the Meaning of Multiplication
- ❒ Explore Patterns in Multiplying by 0, 1, 2, 5, and 9
- ❒ Multiply with 3, 4, 6, 7, and 8 as Factors
- ❒ Explore Patterns in Multiples of 10, 11, and 12
- ❒ Solve Problems by Making Decisions

Reviewing the Meaning of Multiplication

You Will Learn
ways to think about multiplying

Vocabulary

array
objects arranged in rows and columns

factors
numbers multiplied together to obtain a product

product
the number obtained after multiplying

Learn

Eric plays baseball every day after school. That's 5 games a week! How many games does he play in 4 weeks?

Eric lives in New York City. He loves to play baseball.

You can show multiplication using equal groups, or **arrays**.

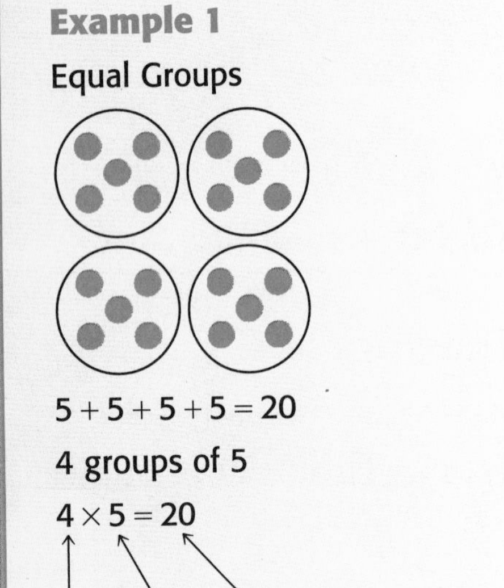

Example 1

Equal Groups

$5 + 5 + 5 + 5 = 20$

4 groups of 5

$4 \times 5 = 20$

factor factor product

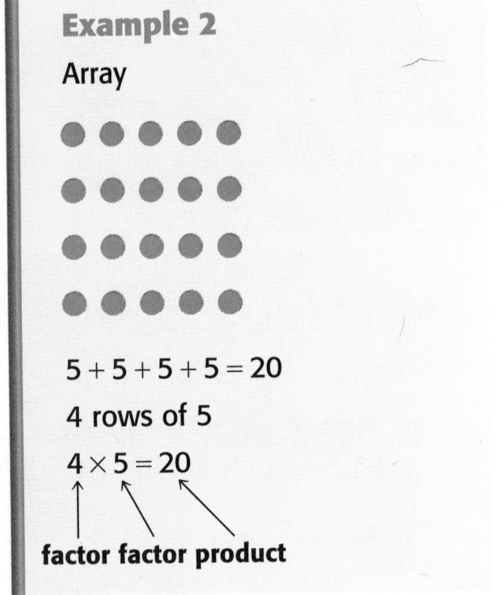

Example 2

Array

$5 + 5 + 5 + 5 = 20$

4 rows of 5

$4 \times 5 = 20$

factor factor product

Math Tip
When you put together *equal* groups you can add *or* multiply.

So, Eric plays 20 games in 4 weeks.

Talk About It

1. Give an example of an addition sentence that can be written as a multiplication sentence.
2. Give an example of an addition sentence that **cannot** be written as a multiplication sentence.

Check

Copy and complete each number sentence.

1. 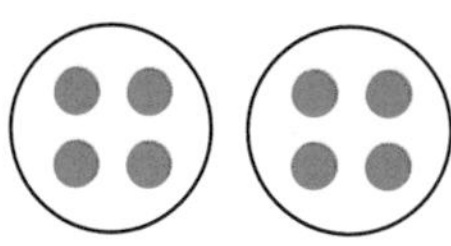

   a. ■ + ■ = ■

   b. ■ × ■ = ■

2. a. ■ + ■ + ■ = ■

   b. ■ × ■ = ■

3. **Reasoning** How could you use multiplication to find 6 + 6 + 6?

Practice

Skills and Reasoning

Copy and complete each number sentence.

4. 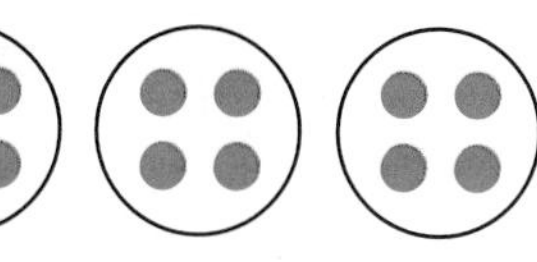

   a. ■ + ■ + ■ = ■

   b. ■ × ■ = ■

5. 

   a. ■ + ■ + ■ = ■

   b. ■ × ■ = ■

6. Draw two different pictures to show 3 × 6.

7. Can you use multiplication to find 10 + 10 + 10? Explain.

Problem Solving and Applications

Write an addition and a multiplication sentence for each. Solve.

8. **Money** Suppose it costs $2 each to watch a baseball game. How much will a family of 5 pay?

9. **What If** Eric practices batting 3 hours a day at baseball camp. How many hours will he practice in 6 days?

Mixed Review and Test Prep

STAY SHARP!

Algebra Readiness Find each sum or difference.

10. 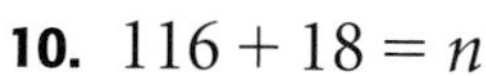 $116 + 18 = n$
11. 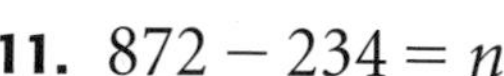 $872 - 234 = n$
12. $202 + 343 = n$
13. $409 - 24 = n$

14. **Money** How much change would you get from a $10 bill, if you bought a baseball for $7.79?

    Ⓐ $17.79　Ⓑ $3.79 　Ⓒ $3.21　Ⓓ $2.21

Exploring Patterns in Multiplying by 0, 1, 2, 5, and 9

Problem Solving Connection
Look for a Pattern

Materials
- hundred chart
- yellow, blue, and red pencils

Vocabulary
multiple
the product of a given whole number and any other whole number

Explore

Patterns can help you remember multiplication facts.

Work Together

1. Use a hundred chart. Look for patterns as you shade in numbers.
   a. Skip count by 2s. Shade each **multiple** of 2 yellow.
   b. Skip count by 5s. Shade each multiple of 5 blue.
   c. Skip count by 9s. Shade each multiple of 9 red.
2. What patterns do you see in the multiples of 2? Of 5? Of 9?

Math Tip
Look for patterns to help you find the multiples more quickly!

Talk About It

3. Which multiples do 2 and 5 have in common on the hundred chart?
4. Which multiples do 5 and 9 have in common on the hundred chart?

Connect

Look for patterns to help you remember multiples of 2, 5, and 9.

Multiples of 2	Multiples of 5	Multiples of 9
$2 \times 0 = 0$ $2 \times 1 = 2$ $2 \times 2 = 4$ $2 \times 3 = 6$ $2 \times 4 = 8$ $2 \times 5 = 10$ $2 \times 6 = 12$ $2 \times 7 = 14$ $2 \times 8 = 16$ $2 \times 9 = 18$	$5 \times 0 = 0$ $5 \times 1 = 5$ $5 \times 2 = 10$ $5 \times 3 = 15$ $5 \times 4 = 20$ $5 \times 5 = 25$ $5 \times 6 = 30$ $5 \times 7 = 35$ $5 \times 8 = 40$ $5 \times 9 = 45$	$9 \times 0 = 0$ $9 \times 1 = 9$ $9 \times 2 = 18$ $9 \times 3 = 27$ $9 \times 4 = 36$ $9 \times 5 = 45$ $9 \times 6 = 54$ $9 \times 7 = 63$ $9 \times 8 = 72$ $9 \times 9 = 81$
Multiples of 2 end in 0, 2, 4, 6, 8.	Multiples of 5 end in 0 or 5.	Multiples of 9: The tens digit is 1 less than the other factor. The sum of the digits is 9.

Learning multiplication properties can also help you remember basic facts.

Order Property
Two numbers can be multiplied in any order.
$5 \times 4 = 4 \times 5$

One Property
The product of a number and 1 is that number.
$5 \times 1 = 5$

Zero Property
The product of a number and 0 is 0.
$5 \times 0 = 0$

Practice

Find each product.

1. 2×6 **2.** 2×9 **3.** 9×1 **4.** 2×8 **5.** 9×6

6. 3×9 **7.** 5×5 **8.** 9×8 **9.** 2×5 **10.** 0×2

11. 5×9 **12.** 2×7 **13.** 5×8 **14.** 9×0 **15.** 1×2

16. 5×7 **17.** 9×9 **18.** 2×3 **19.** 5×4 **20.** 9×4

21. Find the product of 9 and 7. **22.** Find the product of 2 and 4.

23. Critical Thinking 10 is a multiple of 2 and 5. Is the product of any number and 10 also a multiple of 2 and 5? Explain.

24. Journal Describe the number patterns that could help you remember multiples of 2, 5, and 9.

Chapter 4
Lesson
3

Multiplying with 3 and 4 as Factors

You Will Learn
how to use known facts to multiply with 3 or 4 as a factor

Math Tip
4×7 is the same as 2×7 plus 2×7. It's a "double double."

Learn

Watch out for Dylan! He's speedy on his inline skates. He often plays roller hockey with friends in his neighborhood.

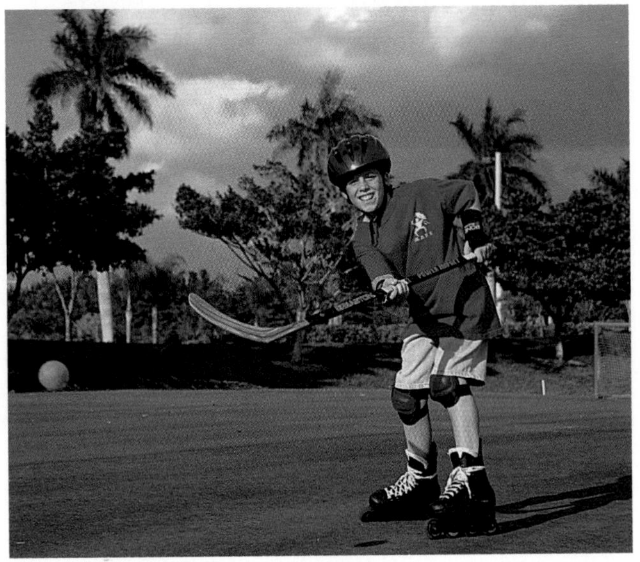

Dylan lives in Cooper City, Florida.
He gets a lot of exercise by inline skating.

Example 1

Suppose Dylan plays 6 games of roller hockey each week for 3 weeks. How many games will he play?

Use 2s facts to find 3×6.

●●●●●●
●●●●●● $2 \times 6 = 12$

●●●●●● $1 \times 6 = 6$

$12 + 6 = 18$

$3 \times 6 = 18$

So, Dylan will play 18 games.

Example 2

Suppose 7 friends each wore 4 guards—2 wrist guards and 2 knee guards. How many guards were worn in all?

Use 2s facts to find 4×7.

●●●●●●●
●●●●●●● $2 \times 7 = 14$

●●●●●●●
●●●●●●● $2 \times 7 = 14$

$14 + 14 = 28$

$4 \times 7 = 28$

So, there were 28 wrist and knee guards.

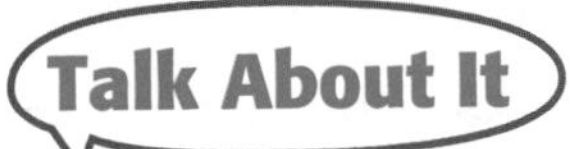

Talk About It

How can you use 2×9 to find 3×9?

Check

Find each product.

1. 3×5 **2.** 4×9 **3.** 4×8 **4.** 3×7 **5.** 3×9

6. Reasoning How can you use 2×6 to find 4×6?

Practice

Skills and Reasoning

Find each product.

7. $\begin{array}{r} 2 \\ \times 3 \\ \hline \end{array}$	**8.** $\begin{array}{r} 5 \\ \times 4 \\ \hline \end{array}$	**9.** $\begin{array}{r} 3 \\ \times 4 \\ \hline \end{array}$	**10.** $\begin{array}{r} 2 \\ \times 5 \\ \hline \end{array}$	**11.** $\begin{array}{r} 3 \\ \times 8 \\ \hline \end{array}$
12. $\begin{array}{r} 4 \\ \times 4 \\ \hline \end{array}$	**13.** $\begin{array}{r} 3 \\ \times 3 \\ \hline \end{array}$	**14.** $\begin{array}{r} 4 \\ \times 3 \\ \hline \end{array}$	**15.** $\begin{array}{r} 9 \\ \times 4 \\ \hline \end{array}$	**16.** $\begin{array}{r} 8 \\ \times 3 \\ \hline \end{array}$
17. 3×7	**18.** 5×5	**19.** 0×8	**20.** 4×7	**21.** 4×2
22. 2×9	**23.** 5×6	**24.** 4×5	**25.** 3×6	**26.** 5×7

27. Find the product of 4 and 6. **28.** Find the product of 3 and 7.

29. To multiply 7 by 3 you can find the product of 2 and 7 and the product of 1 and 7 and _____ them.

Problem Solving and Applications

30. Health You can burn about 285 calories during a 30-minute skate. If you skate for an hour, about how many calories will you burn?

31. History J. L. Plimpton invented a four-wheel roller-skate design in 1863. How many wheels did he need to make the first four pairs of skates?

 **Algebra Readiness** Copy and complete.

32. Find 4×6.
■ $\times 6 = 12$
$12 + 12 =$ ■

33. Find 3×5.
■ $\times 5 = 10$
$10 + 5 =$ ■

34. Find 4×9.
■ $\times 9 = 18$
$18 + 18 =$ ■

Mixed Review and Test Prep

STAY SHARP!

Mental Math Use mental math to find each answer.

35. $22 + 23$ **36.** $29 - 7$ **37.** $33 + 35$ **38.** $55 - 25$ **39.** $95 - 20$

40. Which of the following shows the Order Property for addition?

Ⓐ $5 + 0 = 5$ Ⓑ $5 + 4 = 4 + 5$ Ⓒ $0 + 3 = 3$ Ⓓ $0 \times 1 = 0 \times 1$

Multiplying with 6, 7, and 8 as Factors

You Will Learn
how to use known facts to multiply with 6, 7, or 8 as a factor

Vocabulary
square number
the product when both factors are the same

Learn

Allie and her friends swim on a team. They practice 5 days a week and go to swim meets on weekends. Allie sets the same goal for every race—to go faster than in her previous race.

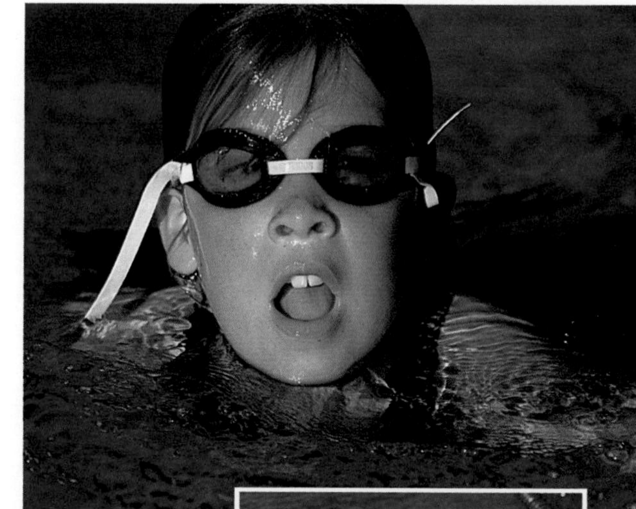

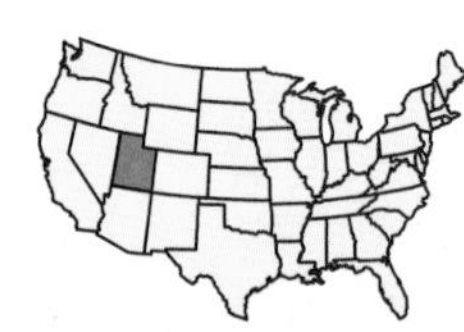

Allie, from Salt Lake City, Utah, was one of five American finalists for an Arete Award. This award is given to athletes who overcome difficult challenges.

Example 1

Suppose Allie swims 7 laps, then rests. She does this 6 times. How many laps will she swim in all?

Use 3s facts to find 6×7.

$3 \times 7 = 21$

$3 \times 7 = 21$

$21 + 21 = 42$

$6 \times 7 = 42$

So, Allie will swim a total of 42 laps.

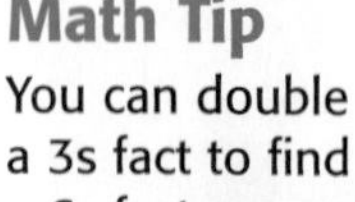

Math Tip
You can double a 3s fact to find a 6s fact.

Example 2

Suppose Allie takes 8 breaths in each lap across the pool. If she swims 7 laps, how many breaths will she take?

Use 5s and 2s facts to find 7×8.

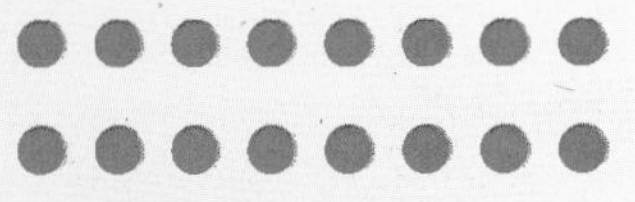

$5 \times 8 = 40$

$2 \times 8 = 16$

$40 + 16 = 56$

$7 \times 8 = 56$

So, she will take 56 breaths.

Example 3

Suppose there are 8 lanes in a swimming pool. Each lane has 8 swimmers. How many swimmers are in the pool?

Use 4s facts to find 8×8.

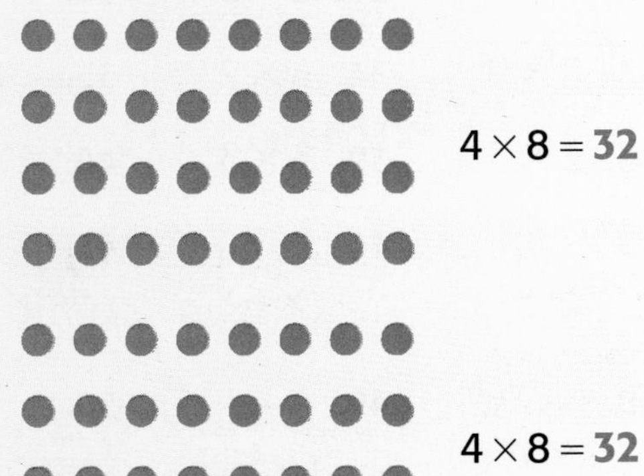

$4 \times 8 = 32$

$4 \times 8 = 32$

$32 + 32 = 64$

$8 \times 8 = 64$

So, there are 64 swimmers in the pool.

The product when both factors are the same is a **square number**. The product of 8×8 is a square number. So, 64 is a square number.

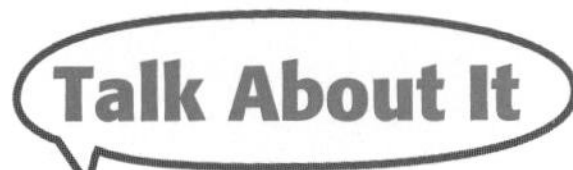

Talk About It

1. What is another way you could use facts you know to find 6×7?
2. How can you use doubling to find 8×5?

Check

Find each product.

1. 8×6	**2.** 6×9	**3.** 6×6	**4.** 7×9	**5.** 7×7
6. 6×4	**7.** 8×2	**8.** 7×6	**9.** 8×5	**10.** 7×3
11. 4×8	**12.** 9×9	**13.** 6×5	**14.** 8×7	**15.** 7×2
16. 6×2	**17.** 7×4	**18.** 3×6	**19.** 7×5	**20.** 8×3

21. Reasoning How could you use the product of 3×4 to find 6×4?

22. Reasoning Seven multiplied by a number is a square number. What are the two factors? What is the square number?

Practice

Skills and Reasoning

Find each product.

23. 8×3 **24.** 6×9 **25.** 5×6 **26.** 7×8 **27.** 6×7

28. 6×3 **29.** 2×8 **30.** 7×4 **31.** 3×8 **32.** 8×4

33. 8×9 **34.** 6×2 **35.** 7×5 **36.** 6×6 **37.** 9×7

38. 2×5 **39.** 3×3 **40.** 4×7 **41.** 3×6 **42.** 5×8

43. $\begin{array}{r} 8 \\ \times 8 \\ \hline \end{array}$ **44.** $\begin{array}{r} 7 \\ \times 6 \\ \hline \end{array}$ **45.** $\begin{array}{r} 9 \\ \times 8 \\ \hline \end{array}$ **46.** $\begin{array}{r} 1 \\ \times 8 \\ \hline \end{array}$ **47.** $\begin{array}{r} 7 \\ \times 5 \\ \hline \end{array}$

48. $\begin{array}{r} 7 \\ \times 7 \\ \hline \end{array}$ **49.** $\begin{array}{r} 6 \\ \times 4 \\ \hline \end{array}$ **50.** $\begin{array}{r} 6 \\ \times 8 \\ \hline \end{array}$ **51.** $\begin{array}{r} 5 \\ \times 3 \\ \hline \end{array}$ **52.** $\begin{array}{r} 4 \\ \times 4 \\ \hline \end{array}$

53. $\begin{array}{r} 4 \\ \times 5 \\ \hline \end{array}$ **54.** $\begin{array}{r} 9 \\ \times 3 \\ \hline \end{array}$ **55.** $\begin{array}{r} 7 \\ \times 2 \\ \hline \end{array}$ **56.** $\begin{array}{r} 7 \\ \times 8 \\ \hline \end{array}$ **57.** $\begin{array}{r} 9 \\ \times 4 \\ \hline \end{array}$

58. $\begin{array}{r} 5 \\ \times 0 \\ \hline \end{array}$ **59.** $\begin{array}{r} 3 \\ \times 7 \\ \hline \end{array}$ **60.** $\begin{array}{r} 4 \\ \times 3 \\ \hline \end{array}$ **61.** $\begin{array}{r} 8 \\ \times 9 \\ \hline \end{array}$ **62.** $\begin{array}{r} 9 \\ \times 6 \\ \hline \end{array}$

63. Draw an array for $5 \times 5 = 25$. Explain why it makes sense to call 25 a square number.

64. Jair says that after he multiplied 7×9, he knew the answer to 9×7 as well. What does he mean?

Problem Solving and Applications

65. Algebra Readiness Ramón multiplied two numbers. The product was 24. One factor was 6. What was the other factor?

66. Money Tickets to the fair cost $6 each. How much money would you need to buy 8 tickets?

67. History In 1875, Matthew Webb became the first person to swim the English Channel. His time was 21 hours and 45 minutes. In 1994, Chad Hundeby swam the English Channel in 7 hours and 17 minutes.

a. What is the difference in swimming times between the two records?

b. How many years were there between the two records?

Problem Solving and SOCIAL STUDIES

Children and adults in Barbados, a Caribbean Island, play a game from England called cricket. Cricket matches can last as long as 5 days!

Cricket Rules

- A batter must run to a marker called a "wicket" to score a run.
- If a ball is hit to the boundary, it scores 4 runs.
- If a ball is hit to the boundary without a bounce, it scores 6 runs.

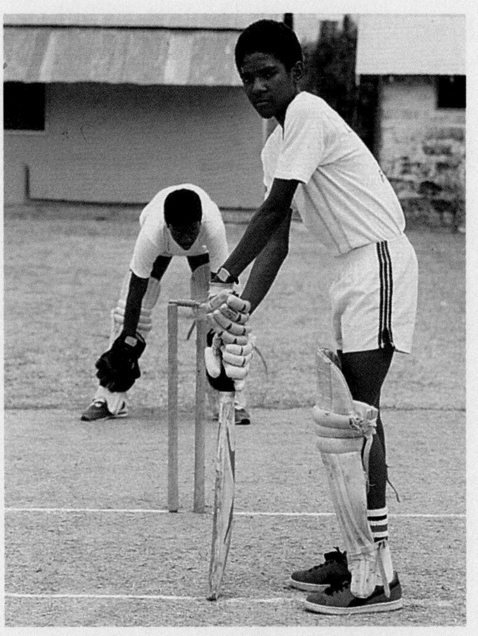

In cricket, teams take turn to bat and field. There are two batters on the field at one time.

68. If 5 balls are batted to the boundary with bounces, how many runs are scored?

69. If 5 balls are batted to the boundary without bounces, how many runs are scored?

70. If there are 10 fielders, 1 bowler, 2 batters, and 2 umpires on the cricket field, how many people are on the field?

71. **Write Your Own Problem** Use multiplication facts to write a problem about a cricket game.

72. **Journal** Write two ways to solve 9×6 using facts you know.

Mixed Review and Test Prep

Find each sum or difference.

73. $45 + 98$ **74.** $759 + 549$ **75.** $720 + 318$ **76.** $673 + 1{,}287$

77. $354 - 89$ **78.** $709 - 465$ **79.** $3{,}009 - 2{,}978$ **80.** $8{,}090 - 1{,}272$

Algebra Readiness Copy and complete each table. Then write the rule.

81.

In	2	3	4	5	7	9
Out	18	27	36			

82.

In	5	6	4	2	8	3
Out	35	42	28			

83. **Patterns** Which of the following completes the pattern?
18, 21, 24, ▢, ▢

Ⓐ 25, 26 Ⓑ 27, 30 Ⓒ 26, 28 Ⓓ 34, 44

Exploring Patterns in Multiples of 10, 11, and 12

Problem Solving Connection
- Look for a Pattern
- Make a Table

Materials
fact table

Explore

You can use patterns to fill in a multiplication table.

Work Together

Copy and complete the table.

X	0	1	2	3	4	5	6	7	8	9	10	11	12
0											0		
1											10		
2											20		
3											30		
4											40		
5											50		
6											60		
7													
8													
9													
10	0	10	20	30	40	50							
11													
12													

Remember
A multiple is the product of a whole number and any whole number.

Talk About It

1. What patterns can you find in the table?
2. Which numbers on the chart are multiples of both 10 and 12?

Connect

Here are some patterns in the multiples of 10, 11, and 12.

Multiples of 10	Multiples of 11	Multiples of 12
$10 \times 0 = 0$	$11 \times 0 = 0$	$12 \times 0 = 0$
$10 \times 1 = 10$	$11 \times 1 = 11$	$12 \times 1 = 12$
$10 \times 2 = 20$	$11 \times 2 = 22$	$12 \times 2 = 24$
$10 \times 3 = 30$	$11 \times 3 = 33$	$12 \times 3 = 36$
$10 \times 4 = 40$	$11 \times 4 = 44$	$12 \times 4 = 48$
$10 \times 5 = 50$	$11 \times 5 = 55$	$12 \times 5 = 60$
$10 \times 6 = 60$	$11 \times 6 = 66$	$12 \times 6 = 72$
$10 \times 7 = 70$	$11 \times 7 = 77$	$12 \times 7 = 84$
$10 \times 8 = 80$	$11 \times 8 = 88$	$12 \times 8 = 96$
$10 \times 9 = 90$	$11 \times 9 = 99$	$12 \times 9 = 108$
$10 \times 10 = 100$	$11 \times 10 = 110$	$12 \times 10 = 120$
$10 \times 11 = 110$	$11 \times 11 = 121$	$12 \times 11 = 132$
$10 \times 12 = 120$	$11 \times 12 = 132$	$12 \times 12 = 144$
Zero is in the ones place.	Ones digit increases by 1 each time.	Ones digit increases by 2 each time.

Practice

Find each product.

1. 12×8 **2.** 11×9 **3.** 7×10 **4.** 6×12 **5.** 11×5

6. 4×12 **7.** 12×9 **8.** 10×8 **9.** 3×11 **10.** 12×5

11. 10×6 **12.** 7×11 **13.** 12×2 **14.** 10×10 **15.** 12×12

16. 11×6 **17.** 10×12 **18.** 11×11 **19.** 5×10 **20.** 3×12

21. How can you use the fact $5 \times 12 = 60$ to solve 7×12?

22. **Measurement** The recipe for the world's largest pancake calls for 7 cartons of eggs. Each carton contains 1 dozen eggs. How many eggs does the recipe call for in all?

23. **Using Data** Use the Data File on page 144. Write a multiplication sentence using the number 11 and the number of glasses that Ashrita Furman balanced on his chin.

24. **Journal** Describe patterns for multiples of 10, 11, and 12.

and Practice

Find each product.

1. $\begin{array}{r} 3 \\ \times 4 \\ \hline \end{array}$	**2.** $\begin{array}{r} 7 \\ \times 0 \\ \hline \end{array}$	**3.** $\begin{array}{r} 6 \\ \times 4 \\ \hline \end{array}$	**4.** $\begin{array}{r} 2 \\ \times 8 \\ \hline \end{array}$	**5.** $\begin{array}{r} 7 \\ \times 3 \\ \hline \end{array}$
6. $\begin{array}{r} 7 \\ \times 4 \\ \hline \end{array}$	**7.** $\begin{array}{r} 5 \\ \times 6 \\ \hline \end{array}$	**8.** $\begin{array}{r} 3 \\ \times 8 \\ \hline \end{array}$	**9.** $\begin{array}{r} 5 \\ \times 7 \\ \hline \end{array}$	**10.** $\begin{array}{r} 9 \\ \times 3 \\ \hline \end{array}$
11. $\begin{array}{r} 8 \\ \times 4 \\ \hline \end{array}$	**12.** $\begin{array}{r} 7 \\ \times 1 \\ \hline \end{array}$	**13.** $\begin{array}{r} 11 \\ \times 8 \\ \hline \end{array}$	**14.** $\begin{array}{r} 6 \\ \times 7 \\ \hline \end{array}$	**15.** $\begin{array}{r} 8 \\ \times 3 \\ \hline \end{array}$
16. $\begin{array}{r} 9 \\ \times 4 \\ \hline \end{array}$	**17.** $\begin{array}{r} 8 \\ \times 5 \\ \hline \end{array}$	**18.** $\begin{array}{r} 6 \\ \times 0 \\ \hline \end{array}$	**19.** $\begin{array}{r} 8 \\ \times 8 \\ \hline \end{array}$	**20.** $\begin{array}{r} 7 \\ \times 7 \\ \hline \end{array}$
21. $\begin{array}{r} 7 \\ \times 10 \\ \hline \end{array}$	**22.** $\begin{array}{r} 6 \\ \times 9 \\ \hline \end{array}$	**23.** $\begin{array}{r} 7 \\ \times 8 \\ \hline \end{array}$	**24.** $\begin{array}{r} 9 \\ \times 8 \\ \hline \end{array}$	**25.** $\begin{array}{r} 9 \\ \times 9 \\ \hline \end{array}$
26. $\begin{array}{r} 11 \\ \times 3 \\ \hline \end{array}$	**27.** $\begin{array}{r} 6 \\ \times 6 \\ \hline \end{array}$	**28.** $\begin{array}{r} 4 \\ \times 9 \\ \hline \end{array}$	**29.** $\begin{array}{r} 9 \\ \times 6 \\ \hline \end{array}$	**30.** $\begin{array}{r} 8 \\ \times 7 \\ \hline \end{array}$
31. 10×5	**32.** 3×3	**33.** 2×12	**34.** 10×8	**35.** 10×2
36. 10×10	**37.** 7×5	**38.** 4×9	**39.** 7×6	**40.** 12×1
41. 10×0	**42.** 2×9	**43.** 0×12	**44.** 10×4	**45.** 8×9
46. 6×8	**47.** 4×7	**48.** 5×11	**49.** 8×6	**50.** 3×9

Error Search

Find each sentence that is not correct. Write it correctly. Explain the error.

51. 42 is a multiple of 8.

52. The product of 6 and 0 is 6.

53. 5×9 equals 9×5.

54. 11 multiplied by 2 is 33.

55. The product of 9 and 1 is 1.

56. The product of 8×9 is equal to the product of 4×9 doubled.

Underwater Riddle!

What do you call a hockey game that is played on the floor of a swimming pool? Multiply to solve the riddle. Match each letter to its answer in the blank below. Some letters are not used.

57. 12×5 [A]	**58.** 4×6 [T]	**59.** 3×1 [W]	**60.** 9×3 [H]
61. 4×3 [B]	**62.** 11×7 [C]	**63.** 12×4 [E]	**64.** 2×5 [L]
65. 9×2 [O]	**66.** 7×9 [U]	**67.** 10×10 [D]	**68.** 5×8 [P]
69. 3×11 [M]	**70.** 5×5 [K]	**71.** 8×2 [S]	**72.** 9×5 [O]

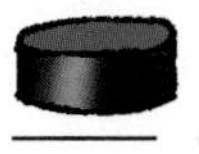		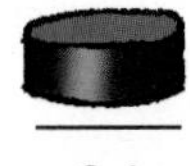		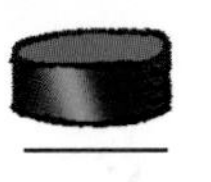		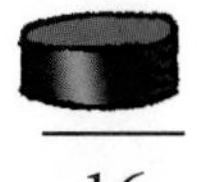	
___	___	___	___	___	___	___	___
45	77	24	18	40	63	16	27

Remember the Facts!

Use these activities anytime to help you remember your multiplication facts.

1. **Spinner Game** Make a spinner numbered 1 through 12. With a partner, spin the spinner twice. Take turns telling the product of the numbers.

2. **Multiplication Jingles** Make up rhymes to match each multiplication fact. For example:

6×7 is 42. I'll say that when I tie my shoe.	7×8 is 56. That's 5, 6, 7, 8. What a mix!

Chapter 4
Lesson
6

Problem Solving

Decision Making: Raising Money for Sneakers

You Will Learn
how to use facts to make a decision

Explore

"Practice! Practice! Practice! We have two months until our first game," said the coach. The basketball team plans to buy new sneakers before the season starts. Sneakers cost about $60 per pair, so they will need to raise about $600. How can the team raise the money?

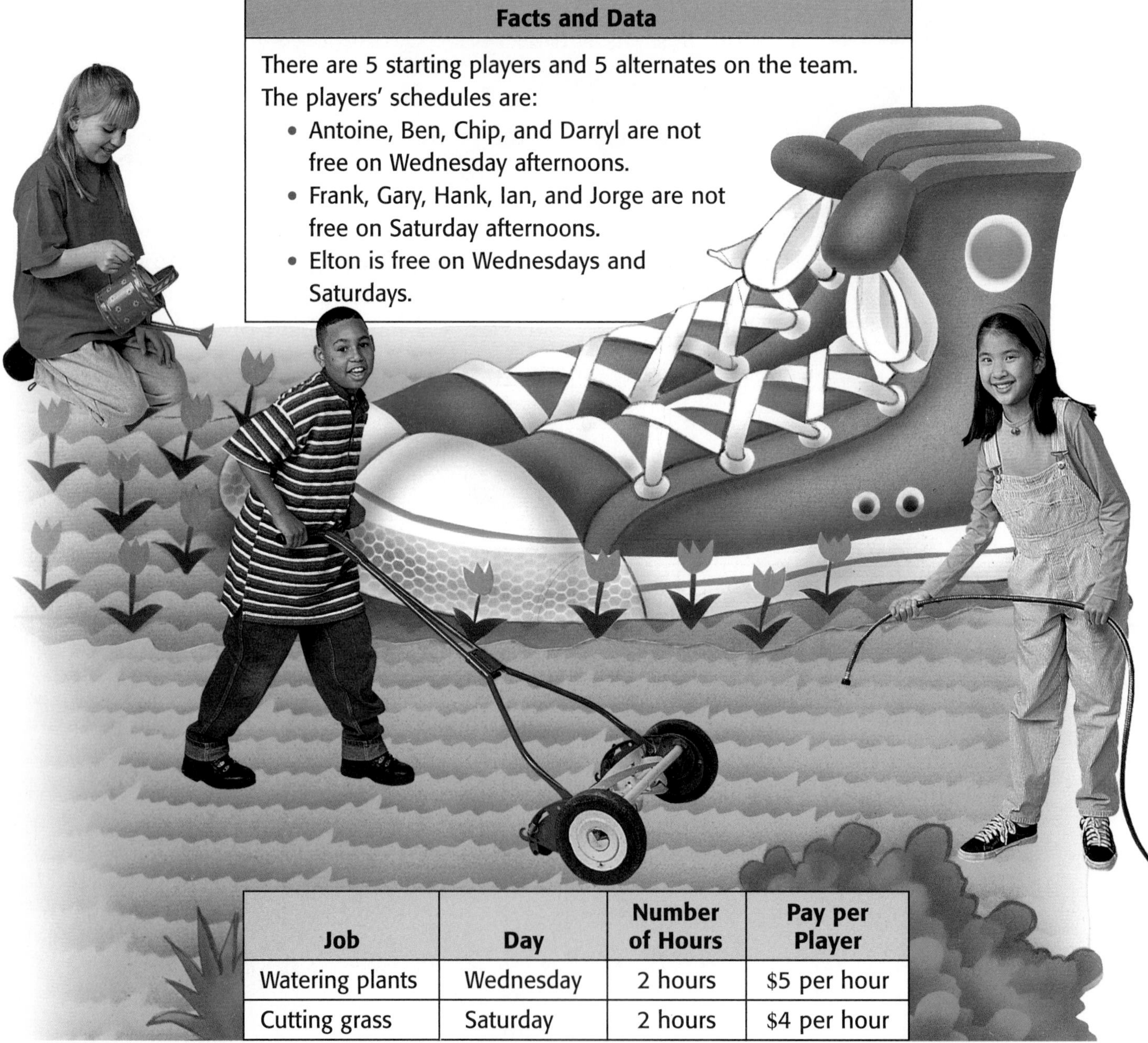

Facts and Data

There are 5 starting players and 5 alternates on the team.
The players' schedules are:

- Antoine, Ben, Chip, and Darryl are not free on Wednesday afternoons.
- Frank, Gary, Hank, Ian, and Jorge are not free on Saturday afternoons.
- Elton is free on Wednesdays and Saturdays.

Job	Day	Number of Hours	Pay per Player
Watering plants	Wednesday	2 hours	$5 per hour
Cutting grass	Saturday	2 hours	$4 per hour

Work Together

Understand

1. What do you know?
2. What do you need to find out?
3. What is the main decision you are being asked to make?

Plan and Solve

4. How much money can the team earn in a week watering plants?
5. How much money can the team earn in a week cutting grass?
6. How many weeks will it take to earn $600 watering plants? Cutting grass?
7. a. **What If** The players work at both jobs each week. How much can they earn in one week?
   b. About how many weeks would it take to earn $600?

Make a Decision

8. How can the team earn the money?

Present Your Decision

9. Make a table to show the number of weeks it will take to earn the money. Explain your decision on how to raise $600.

Money Earned			
	1st Week	2nd Week	3rd Week
Wednesday			
Saturday			
Wednesday and Saturday			

10. Find out how schools raise money for sports equipment, or other items they need. Check out **www.mathsurf.com/4/ch4.** Did you get any ideas for your school?

SECTION A

Review and Practice

Vocabulary Match each with its example.

1.	array	**a.**	66
2.	multiple of 11	**b.**	6 and 7
3.	product of 5×5	**c.**	square number
4.	factors of 42	**d.**	● ● ● ● ● ●

(Lesson 1) Copy and complete each number sentence.

5.

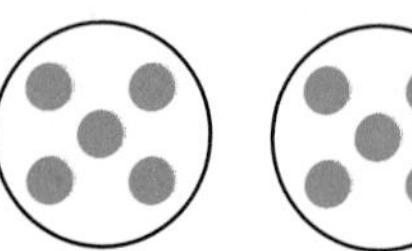

a. ■ + ■ + ■ = ■

b. ■ × ■ = ■

6.

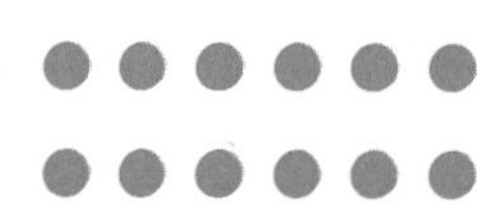

a. ■ + ■ = ■

b. ■ × ■ = ■

(Lesson 2) Copy and complete.

7. The product of 0 and any number is ■.

8. $1 \times 3 =$ ■

9. 0, 2, 4, 6, and 8 are the first five multiples of ■.

10. 0, 9, 18, 27, and 36 are the first five multiples of ■.

(Lessons 3–5) Find each product.

11. 3×5	**12.** 3×7	**13.** 4×4
14. 6×8	**15.** 7×9	**16.** 8×4
17. 4×10	**18.** 8×9	**19.** 8×11
20. 2×2	**21.** 3×2	**22.** 2×5

23. Reasoning How can you use the product of 4×7 to find 8×7?

(Lesson 6) Solve.

24. Time Keith drinks 3 glasses of milk each day. How many glasses of milk does he drink in a week?

25. Journal Use words or pictures to find 7×9.

Skills Checklist

In this section, you have:

- ☑ **Reviewed the Meaning of Multiplication**
- ☑ **Explored Patterns in Multiplying by 0, 1, 2, 5, and 9**
- ☑ **Multiplied with 3, 4, 6, 7, and 8 as Factors**
- ☑ **Explored Patterns in Multiples of 10, 11, and 12**
- ☑ **Solved Problems by Making Decisions**

CHAPTER 4

SECTION

B Understanding Division

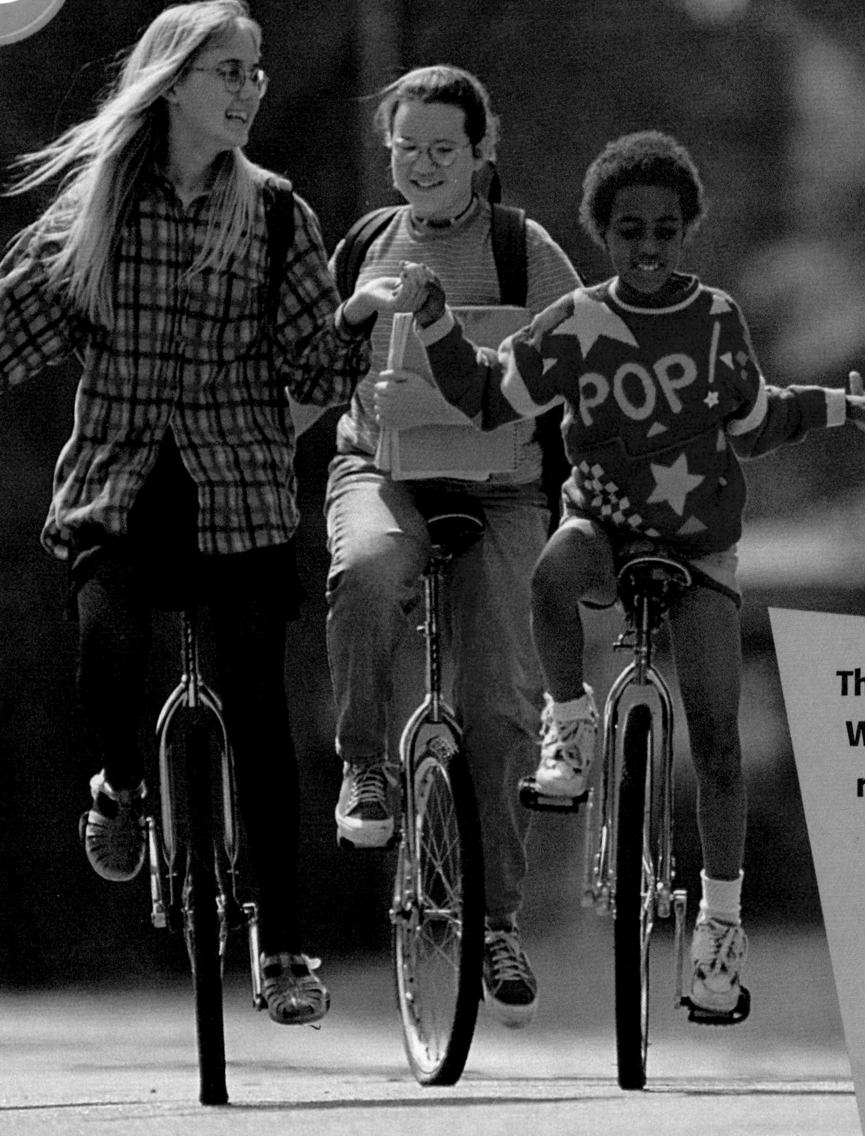

The Andover One-Wheelers have fun riding together. What are some ways you can divide the team members in the picture into equal groups?

GET READY!

Division

Review basic multiplication facts. Find each product.

1. 3×5
2. 7×8
3. 5×6
4. 9×3
5. 6×9
6. 4×8
7. 4×4
8. 6×7
9. 2×9

Skills Checklist

In this section, you will:

- ❐ Review the Meaning of Division
- ❐ Explore Multiplication and Division Stories
- ❐ Divide with 2, 5, and 9 as Divisors
- ❐ Learn About Special Quotients

Chapter 4
Lesson
7

Reviewing the Meaning of Division

You Will Learn
three ways to think about division

Learn

Could you ride a bike with no brakes, no handlebars, and only one wheel? The Andover One-Wheelers do it all the time! It's a club for unicycle riders.

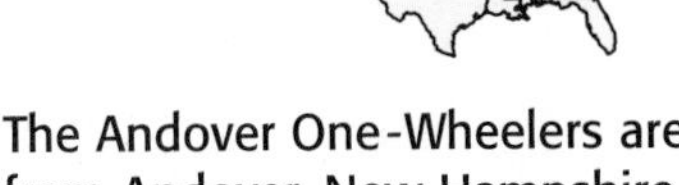

The Andover One-Wheelers are from Andover, New Hampshire.

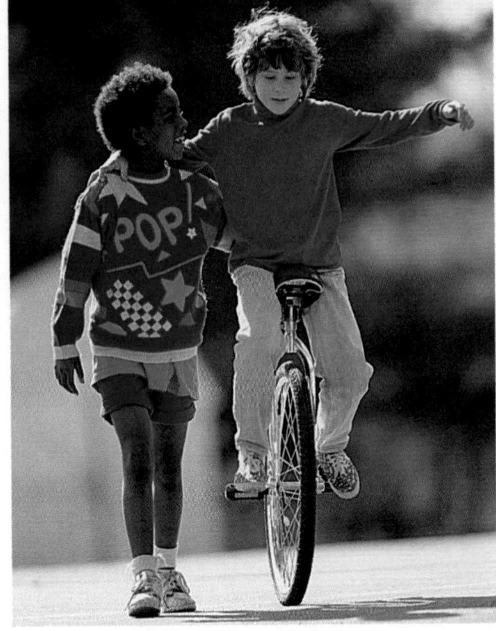

Example 1

You can think of division as sharing.

Suppose 24 riders form 3 circles. How many riders are in each circle?

Find $24 \div 3$.

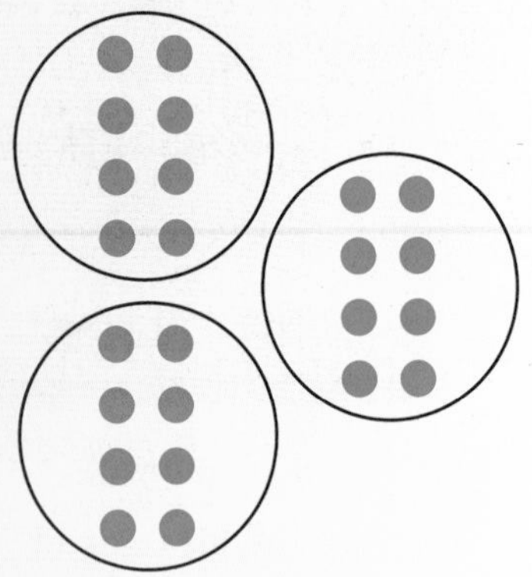

8 riders are in each circle.

Example 2

You can think of division as repeated subtraction.

If 24 riders form circles with 6 riders in each circle, how many circles are there?

Find $24 \div 6$.

Subtract 6 from 24 until you have 0. Count how many times you subtracted.

$24 - \mathbf{6} = 18$
$18 - \mathbf{6} = 12$
$12 - \mathbf{6} = 6$
$6 - \mathbf{6} = 0$

$24 \div 6 = 4$
There are 4 circles.

Example 3

You can think of division as the opposite of multiplication.

Suppose 24 riders form 2 rows with an equal number of riders in each row. How many riders are in each row?

$24 \div 2 = ?$
$2 \times ? = 24$
$2 \times 12 = 24$
$24 \div 2 = 12$

So, there are 12 riders in each row.

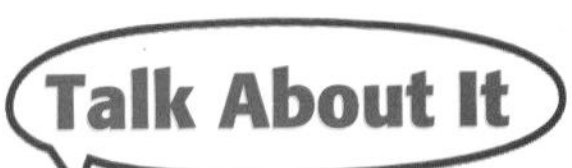

Talk About It

What multiplication fact can help you find $36 \div 4$?

Check

Divide.

1. 12 ÷ 3 2. 10 ÷ 2 3. 14 ÷ 7 4. 20 ÷ 4 5. 72 ÷ 8

6. 16 ÷ 4 7. 15 ÷ 5 8. 35 ÷ 7 9. 36 ÷ 9 10. 36 ÷ 6

11. **Reasoning** How can you use repeated subtraction to find 54 ÷ 9?

Practice

Skills and Reasoning

Divide.

12. 21 ÷ 3 13. 24 ÷ 6 14. 32 ÷ 4 15. 27 ÷ 3 16. 4 ÷ 2

17. 42 ÷ 7 18. 48 ÷ 8 19. 81 ÷ 9 20. 32 ÷ 4 21. 56 ÷ 7

22. 25 ÷ 5 23. 30 ÷ 6 24. 27 ÷ 3 25. 16 ÷ 2 26. 30 ÷ 5

27. By what number do you divide 10 to get 5?

28. What multiplication fact can help you find 56 ÷ 7?

Problem Solving and Applications

29. Suppose 12 players make 2 teams with an equal number of players on each team. How many players are on each team?

30. If 3 players each scored 4 goals, how many goals were scored all together?

31. **Sports** At the end of the first quarter, the basketball team scored 18 points. How many baskets did they make, if each basket was worth 2 points?

32. **What If** The Andover One-Wheelers practice for 2 hours each week. How many weeks will it take them to practice 10 hours?

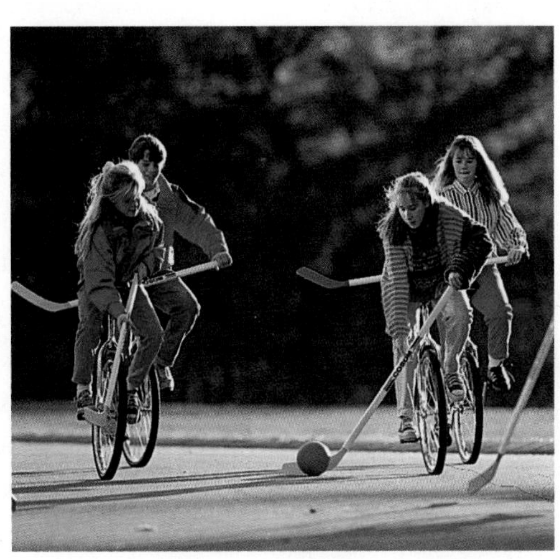

The One-Wheelers have fun playing hockey, tag, and basketball.

Mixed Review and Test Prep

STAY SHARP!

Find each product.

33. 2 × 3 34. 5 × 7 35. 9 × 9 36. 12 × 0 37. 7 × 8

38. Find the sum of 409 and 389.

Ⓐ 889 Ⓑ 788 Ⓒ 898 Ⓓ 798

Chapter 4
Lesson
8

Exploring Multiplication and Division Stories

Problem Solving Connection
Work Backward

Vocabulary
fact family
a group of related facts using the same set of numbers

Math Tip
Don't forget to end your story with a question!

Explore

Write multiplication and division stories about yourself.

42 ÷ 7
I love soccer! I can't wait for the season to start. We still have 42 days before the first game. I figured out how many weeks that is. Can you?

6 x 7
Our first soccer game is in 6 weeks, against the Raging Rapids team. How many days until we play them?

Work Together

1. Write your own multiplication and division stories for $42 \div 7$ and 6×7. Then solve them.

2. Write multiplication and division stories for each. Solve.

   a. 7×8 **b.** 5×7 **c.** $56 \div 7$ **d.** $35 \div 5$

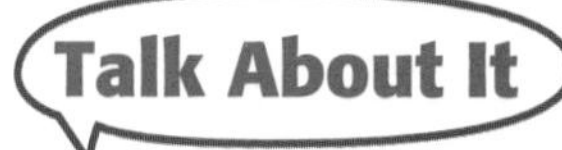

Talk About It

How does 8×9 help you find $72 \div 8$?

Connect

You can think about **fact families** to connect multiplication and division.

Fact Family

$7 \times 8 = 56$ $56 \div 7 = 8$

$8 \times 7 = 56$ $56 \div 8 = 7$

PRACTICE AND APPLY

Practice

Copy and complete each fact family.

1. 6, 8, 48
■ × ■ = 48
■ × ■ = 48
48 ÷ ■ = ■
48 ÷ ■ = ■

2. 36, 6, 6
■ × ■ = 36
■ ÷ ■ = 6

3. 3, 27, 9
■ × ■ = 27
27 ÷ ■ = ■
■ × ■ = 27
27 ÷ ■ = ■

4. 81, 9, 9
■ × ■ = 81
■ ÷ ■ = 9

5. 20, 5, 4
■ × ■ = 20
20 ÷ ■ = ■
■ × ■ = 20
20 ÷ ■ = ■

6. 32, 8, 4
■ × ■ = 32
■ ÷ ■ = 8
■ × 8 = ■
■ ÷ ■ = 4

7. 28, 7, 4
■ ÷ 7 = ■
■ × ■ = 28
4 × ■ = ■
28 ÷ ■ = ■

8. 8, 2, 16
2 × ■ = 16
■ ÷ ■ = 8
■ × ■ = 16
16 ÷ ■ = 2

Write a fact family for each set of numbers.

9. 54, 6, 9 **10.** 36, 9, 4 **11.** 25, 5, 5

12. 21, 3, 7 **13.** 40, 5, 8 **14.** 72, 9, 8

15. **Reasoning** The fact family for 49, 7, and 7 has only two number sentences. What is another fact family that has only two sentences?

Write a question to finish **16** and **17.** Then solve each.

16. "I picked 16 daisies and put them into 2 bunches."

17. "I have 2 bunches with 8 daisies in each bunch."

18. At soccer practice, Byron saved 7 goals and Jim saved 5 goals. How many goals did they save all together?

19. **Journal** Describe a situation at school or at home where you have used multiplication or division facts.

Chapter 4
Lesson
9

Dividing with 2, 5, and 9

You Will Learn
how multiplication can help you divide by 2, 5, and 9

Vocabulary

quotient
the answer to a division problem

dividend
the number to be divided in a division number sentence

divisor
the number by which a dividend is divided

Learn

Chamear likes to exercise regularly. She rode her bike for 25 hours over 5 weeks. If she rode the same number of hours each week, how many hours a week did she ride?

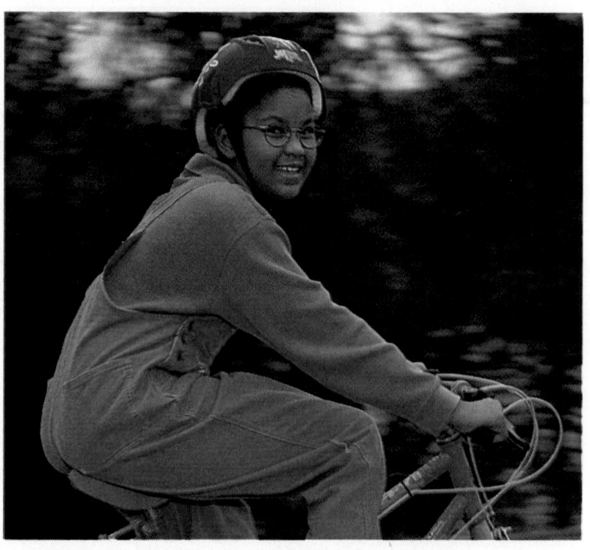

Chamear lives in Charleston, West Virginia. She enjoys riding her bike.

Since you are separating 25 into 5 equal groups, you can divide.

Find 25 ÷ 5.

Think: 5 times what number equals 25?

$5 \times 5 = 25$

So, 25 ÷   = **5**

Chamear rode her bike for 5 hours each week.

Did You Know?
Bicycle racing began in France in 1869.

You can write a division number sentence in two ways.

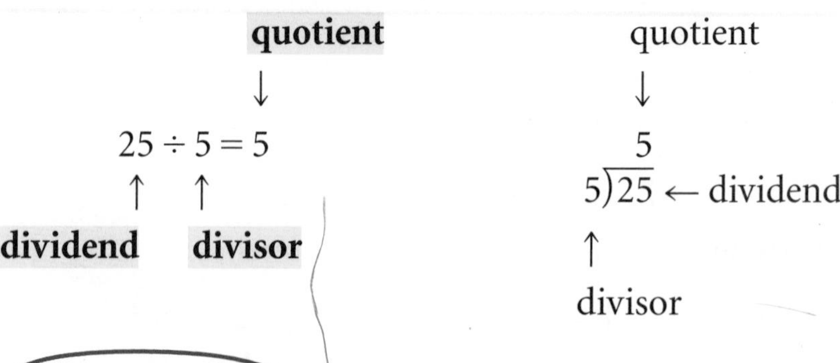

1. What multiplication fact can help you find 54 ÷ 9?
2. What multiplication fact can help you find 35 ÷ 5?

Check

Find each quotient.

1. 45 ÷ 5 2. 54 ÷ 6 3. 14 ÷ 2 4. 72 ÷ 9 5. 30 ÷ 5

6. $2\overline{)12}$ 7. $5\overline{)15}$ 8. $2\overline{)8}$ 9. $9\overline{)81}$ 10. $5\overline{)40}$

11. **Reasoning** If 45 ÷ 9 = 5, what does 45 ÷ 5 equal? Explain.

Practice

Skills and Reasoning

Find each quotient.

12. 10 ÷ 2 13. 27 ÷ 9 14. 10 ÷ 5 15. 18 ÷ 9 16. 45 ÷ 5

17. 15 ÷ 3 18. 81 ÷ 9 19. 36 ÷ 9 20. 35 ÷ 7 21. 30 ÷ 5

22. $2\overline{)18}$ 23. $9\overline{)63}$ 24. $9\overline{)72}$ 25. $5\overline{)45}$ 26. $2\overline{)6}$

27. $3\overline{)27}$ 28. $5\overline{)20}$ 29. $8\overline{)72}$ 30. $6\overline{)54}$ 31. $2\overline{)16}$

32. 5 is the divisor. 35 is the dividend. What is the quotient?

33. 63 is the dividend. 9 is the divisor. What is the quotient?

Problem Solving and Applications

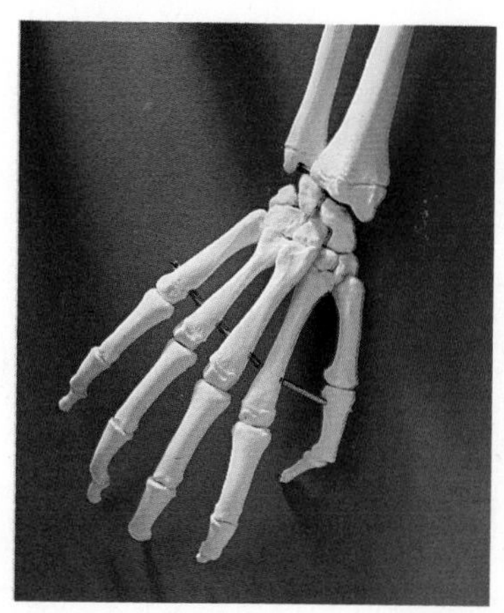

34. **Time** Kerry rode her bike a total of 35 miles in a week. If she rode the same number of miles each day, how many miles did she ride each day?

35. **Money** If Chamear rents a bike for 2 hours at $11 an hour, how much does she pay?

36. **Using Data** How many years ago did people begin racing bikes? Use the *Did You Know?* on page 170.

37. **Science** There are 3 bones in each finger and 2 bones in each thumb. How many bones are in all your fingers and thumbs?

Mixed Review and Test Prep

STAY SHARP!

Mental Math Use mental math to find each sum.

38. 450 + 50 39. 825 + 150 40. 330 + 160 41. 540 + 222

42. Find the number that means 5 thousands, 8 tens, 6 ones.

Ⓐ 586 Ⓑ 5,806 Ⓒ 5,068 Ⓓ 5,086

Skills Practice Bank, page 563, Set 5

Chapter 4
Lesson
10

Special Quotients

You Will Learn
how to divide with 0 and 1

Learn

Look what happened to the calculator display when Jeremy tried to divide 2 by 0. Division rules with 0 and 1 can help you divide.

Example 1

Division rules with 0.

$0 \div 2 = n$

Think: $2 \times 0 = 0$

Divide. $0 \div 2 = 0$

0 divided by any number (except 0) is 0.

$2 \div 0 = n$

Think: $0 \times \square = 2$

No numbers work.

You cannot divide by 0.

Here are rules to remember when you divide by 1.

Example 2

Division rules with 1.

$6 \div 1 = n$

Think: $1 \times 6 = 6$

Divide. $6 \div 1 = 6$

Any number divided by 1 is that number.

$6 \div 6 = n$

Think: $6 \times 1 = 6$

Divide. $6 \div 6 = 1$

Any number divided by itself (except 0) is 1.

Talk About It

What is the fact family for 5, 5, and 1?

Remember
Think about multiplication to help you divide.

Check

Find each quotient.

1. $8 \div 1$ **2.** $0 \div 7$ **3.** $0 \div 8$ **4.** $9 \div 3$ **5.** $9 \div 9$

6. $4 \div 4$ **7.** $3\overline{)0}$ **8.** $4 \div 1$ **9.** $2\overline{)12}$ **10.** $1\overline{)3}$

11. Reasoning Can you divide 0 by 0? Explain.

Practice

Skills and Reasoning

Find each quotient.

12. $12 \div 1$ **13.** $0 \div 3$ **14.** $8 \div 8$ **15.** $9 \div 1$ **16.** $35 \div 5$

17. $5\overline{)0}$ **18.** $2\overline{)2}$ **19.** $7\overline{)0}$ **20.** $1\overline{)6}$ **21.** $9\overline{)0}$

22. $18 \div 6$ **23.** $24 \div 6$ **24.** $7 \div 7$ **25.** $12 \div 3$ **26.** $6 \div 6$

27. $1\overline{)2}$ **28.** $4\overline{)0}$ **29.** $3\overline{)15}$ **30.** $5\overline{)5}$ **31.** $2\overline{)14}$

32. Find the quotient of 8 divided by 8. **33.** Divide 0 by 5.

34. Explain which rule you would use to help you find $24 \div 24$.

35. Write a fact family for this set of numbers: 8, 8, 1.

Problem Solving and Applications

Using Data Use the Data File on page 145 to answer **36** and **37.**

36. In the second period, 4 Spirit players scored goals. How many goals did each player score?

37. In the fourth period, how many more goals did the Crunch score than the Spirit?

Algebra Readiness Copy and complete each table. Then write the rule.

38.

In	8	4		2	5
Out	40	20	35		

39.

In	18	36	45	63	81
Out	2	4			

40. Health A typical eye blinks once every 5 seconds. How many times would a typical eye blink in 30 seconds?

41. Critical Thinking If the quotient is 0, what do you know about the dividend?

Mixed Review and Test Prep

Find each difference.

42. 2,008 − 1,214 **43.** 3,090 − 2,913 **44.** 5,004 − 3,883

45. Time Romunda started her homework at 4:30 P.M. She worked for 35 minutes. Then she took a 15 minute break. It took her another 20 minutes to finish all her homework. What time did she finish?

Ⓐ 6:40 P.M. Ⓑ 5:20 P.M. Ⓒ 5:25 P.M. Ⓓ 5:40 P.M.

SECTION B

Review and Practice

(Lesson 7) Divide.

1. $20 \div 4$ **2.** $12 \div 6$ **3.** $32 \div 4$ **4.** $18 \div 3$ **5.** $15 \div 3$

6. Reasoning Which multiplication fact will help you find $64 \div 8$?

7. There were 48 cyclists in a parade, with 6 cyclists in each row. How many rows were there?

(Lesson 8) Copy and complete each fact family.

8. 42, 7, 6
$6 \times \blacksquare = 42$
$\blacksquare \times \blacksquare = 42$
$\blacksquare \div 7 = \blacksquare$
$\blacksquare \div \blacksquare = 7$

9. 49, 7, 7
$\blacksquare \times \blacksquare = 49$
$\blacksquare \div 7 = \blacksquare$

10. 63, 9, 7
$\blacksquare \times 9 = 63$
$\blacksquare \times 7 = 63$
$63 \div \blacksquare = \blacksquare$
$\blacksquare \div 7 = \blacksquare$

11. 16, 4, 4
$\blacksquare \div 4 = \blacksquare$
$\blacksquare \times \blacksquare = 16$

Write a fact family for each set of numbers.

12. 35, 5, 7 **13.** 8, 1, 8 **14.** 18, 6, 3 **15.** 63, 9, 7

16. Write a question to finish the problem. "I have a dozen pieces of licorice. I'll share them equally with my 3 friends."

(Lessons 9 and 10) Find each quotient.

17. $2\overline{)14}$ **18.** $5\overline{)35}$ **19.** $9\overline{)27}$ **20.** $2\overline{)10}$ **21.** $9\overline{)63}$

22. $10 \div 2$ **23.** $27 \div 9$ **24.** $15 \div 5$ **25.** $18 \div 9$ **26.** $45 \div 5$

27. $7 \div 7$ **28.** $0 \div 3$ **29.** $4 \div 4$ **30.** $16 \div 1$ **31.** $0 \div 9$

32. $40 \div 5$ **33.** $9 \div 9$ **34.** $9\overline{)81}$ **35.** $30 \div 5$ **36.** $16 \div 2$

37. $0 \div 4$ **38.** $5 \div 5$ **39.** $6 \div 1$

40. Reasoning 72 is the dividend. 9 is the divisor. What is the quotient?

41. Health The outer skin on the human body is replaced about once a month. How many times is it replaced in a year?

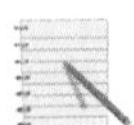

42. Journal Explain how multiplication facts help you divide.

Skills Checklist

In this section, you have:

- ☑ Reviewed the Meaning of Division
- ☑ Explored Multiplication and Division Stories
- ☑ Divided with 2, 5, and 9 as Divisors
- ☑ Learned About Special Quotients

CHAPTER 4

SECTION

C Extending Multiplication and Division

Once a month, Brittany and her classmates go to skating nights from 6:00 P.M. to 8:00 P.M. During the school year, how many total hours do they skate on these nights?

GET READY!

Extending Multiplication and Division

Review basic facts. Find each product.

1. 7×9 **2.** 8×4 **3.** 6×8

4. 7×4 **5.** 9×3 **6.** 8×8

7. 6×5 **8.** 2×7 **9.** 3×5

Skills Checklist

In this section, you will:

- ❒ Divide with 3, 4, 6, 7, and 8 as Divisors
- ❒ Explore Even and Odd Numbers
- ❒ Explore Factors
- ❒ Solve Problems with Too Much or Too Little Information
- ❒ Solve Problems by Comparing Strategies: Guess and Check/Draw a Picture

Chapter 4
Lesson
11

Dividing with 3 and 4

You Will Learn
how multiplication can help you divide with 3 and 4

Learn

In 1994, Krissy was voted best baseball player in the Little League World Series. She was the only girl playing!

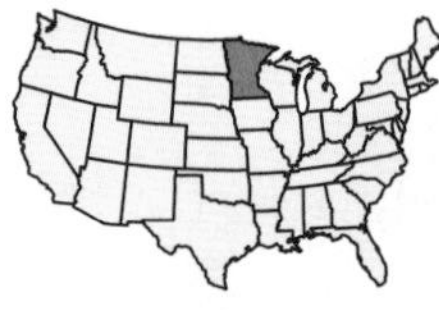

Krissy, from Brooklyn Center, Minnesota, is a star player on more than one sports team.

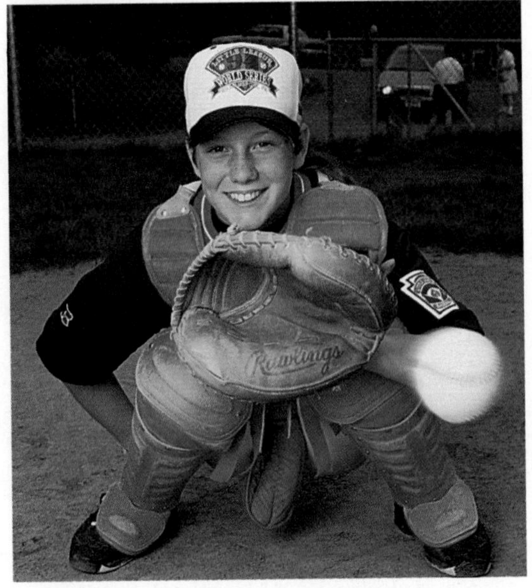

Example 1

Suppose the pitcher on Krissy's team pitched 27 balls at practice. He pitched 3 balls to each batter. How many batters were there?

Find $27 \div 3$.

Think: 3 times what number equals 27?

$3 \times 9 = 27$

$27 \div 3 = 9$ $\qquad 3\overline{)27}$ with quotient 9

So, there were 9 batters.

Example 2

Krissy also plays tennis. In doubles tennis, 4 players play on a court. If 32 players are in a tournament, how many courts are needed for all players to play at one time?

Find $32 \div 4$.

Think: 4 times what number equals 32?

$4 \times 8 = 32$

$32 \div 4 = 8$ $\qquad 4\overline{)32}$ with quotient 8

So, 8 courts are needed.

Talk About It

What multiplication fact can you use to find $21 \div 3$?

Remember
Think about multiplication to divide!

Check

Find each quotient.

1. $24 \div 3$ **2.** $16 \div 4$ **3.** $15 \div 3$ **4.** $28 \div 4$ **5.** $18 \div 3$

6. Reasoning How do multiplication facts of 3 and 4 help you divide by 3 and 4?

Practice

Skills and Reasoning

Find each quotient.

7. $3\overline{)18}$ **8.** $9\overline{)36}$ **9.** $4\overline{)20}$ **10.** $3\overline{)27}$ **11.** $3\overline{)6}$

12. $28 \div 4$ **13.** $27 \div 9$ **14.** $12 \div 3$ **15.** $15 \div 3$ **16.** $32 \div 8$

17. $9 \div 3$ **18.** $24 \div 3$ **19.** $0 \div 5$ **20.** $21 \div 3$ **21.** $16 \div 4$

22. $4\overline{)36}$ **23.** $3\overline{)3}$ **24.** $4\overline{)32}$ **25.** $4\overline{)24}$ **26.** $3\overline{)0}$

27. $12 \div 4$ **28.** $4 \div 4$ **29.** $15 \div 5$ **30.** $8 \div 4$ **31.** $0 \div 4$

32. Divide 36 by 4. **33.** Divide 21 by 3.

34. What multiplication fact can help you find $24 \div 3$?

Problem Solving and Applications

35. Krissy played 24 innings in 3 baseball games.

a. If she played the same number of innings in each game, how many innings did she play in each?

b. If each game had 9 innings, for how many innings was Krissy on the bench?

36. **Measurement** Wooden baseball bats usually weigh 2 or 3 ounces less than the number of inches in their length. If a wooden bat is 28 inches long, how much will it weigh?

37. **History** Baseball gloves were not used until 1875. That was 25 years after baseball was invented. When was baseball invented?

Algebra Readiness Copy and complete the table. Then write the rule.

38.

In	12	21	27	18	9
Out	4	7			

39.

In	16	20	36		8
Out	4	5		6	

Mixed Review and Test Prep

STAY SHARP!

Find each sum or difference.

40. \$297 + \$189 **41.** \$507 − \$312 **42.** \$1,251 + \$912

43. **Science** A newborn baby's body has 350 bones. An adult's body has 206 bones. How many more bones does a newborn have?

Ⓐ 556 Ⓑ 146 Ⓒ 144 Ⓓ not here

Chapter 4
Lesson
12

Dividing with 6, 7, and 8

You Will Learn
how multiplication can help you divide with 6, 7, and 8

Learn

"All skaters! Please turn around and skate in the opposite direction now. Remember to stay in your groups!"

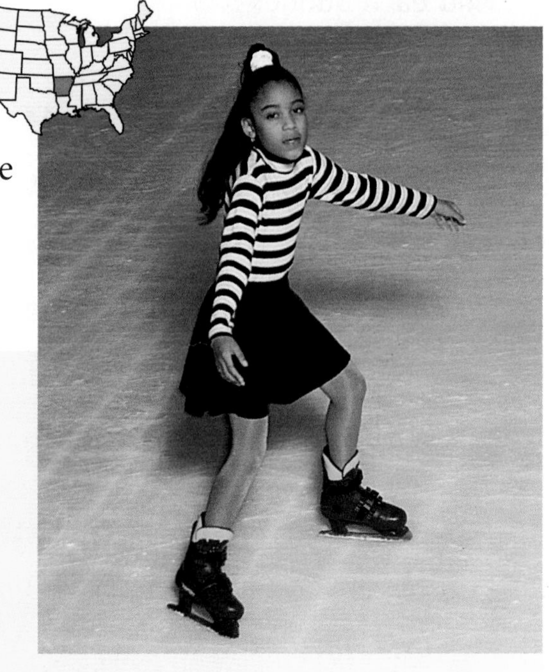

Brittany of Sherwood, Arkansas, keeps fit by ice skating.

Example

Suppose 30 classmates skated in groups of 6. How many groups went skating?

Find 30 ÷ 6.

Think: 6 times what number equals 30?

$6 \times \mathbf{5} = 30$

$30 \div 6 = \mathbf{5}$ $\qquad 6\overline{)30}$ with quotient **5**

So, 5 groups went skating.

Use multiplication facts of 7 and 8 to help you divide.

Other Examples

A. Find 48 ÷ 8.

Think: 8 times what number equals 48?

$8 \times \mathbf{6} = 48$

$48 \div 8 = \mathbf{6}$ $\qquad 8\overline{)48}$ with quotient **6**

B. Find 56 ÷ 7.

Think: 7 times what number equals 56?

$7 \times \mathbf{8} = 56$

$56 \div 7 = \mathbf{8}$ $\qquad 7\overline{)56}$ with quotient **8**

Which multiplication fact can help you find 42 ÷ 7?

Check

Find each quotient. Use multiplication facts to help.

1. 18 ÷ 6 **2.** 24 ÷ 8 **3.** $7\overline{)14}$ **4.** 54 ÷ 6 **5.** $7\overline{)28}$

6. Reasoning Is the quotient of 63 ÷ 7 greater than or less than the quotient of 64 ÷ 8? Explain.

Practice

Skills and Reasoning

Find each quotient.

7. $64 \div 8$ **8.** $7 \div 7$ **9.** $40 \div 8$ **10.** $42 \div 7$ **11.** $32 \div 8$

12. $30 \div 6$ **13.** $28 \div 7$ **14.** $32 \div 4$ **15.** $35 \div 7$ **16.** $49 \div 7$

17. $6\overline{)42}$ **18.** $7\overline{)21}$ **19.** $8\overline{)56}$ **20.** $8\overline{)72}$ **21.** $6\overline{)36}$

22. $8\overline{)16}$ **23.** $7\overline{)56}$ **24.** $7\overline{)63}$ **25.** $8\overline{)8}$ **26.** $6\overline{)48}$

27. Divide 0 by 8. **28.** Divide 42 by 6.

29. If you divide a number by 4, will the quotient be greater than or less than the quotient of the same number divided by 8? Explain.

Problem Solving and Applications

30. Time Corie practices ice skating 14 hours a week. If she practices the same number of hours each day, how many hours does she practice a day?

31. In an ice show, 24 skaters entered the ice rink in equal rows. If there were 8 skaters in each row, how many rows were there?

32. Sports In the 1984 Olympics, Jane Torvill and Christopher Dean were the first skaters to score nine perfect sixes. What was their total score?

Jane Torvill and Christopher Dean

Using Data Use the Data File on page 145 to solve **33** and **34.**

33. If there are 72 baseball players, how many official teams can be formed?

34. How many field hockey players do you need to make 4 teams?

Mixed Review and Test Prep

STAY SHARP!

Find each difference.

35. $270 - 49$ **36.** $103 - 58$ **37.** $4{,}039 - 322$ **38.** $4{,}007 - 399$

39. Money If you buy a ticket to an ice-skating rink for \$2.79 and pay with a \$5 bill, how much change will you get?

Ⓐ \$7.79 Ⓑ \$3.21 Ⓒ \$3.20 Ⓓ \$2.21

Skills Practice Bank, page 563, Set 6

Chapter 4
Lesson
13

Exploring Even and Odd Numbers

Problem Solving Connection
- Use Objects/ Act It Out
- Look for a Pattern

Materials
counters

Vocabulary

even number
a whole number that has 0, 2, 4, 6, or 8 in the ones place

odd number
a whole number that has 1, 3, 5, 7, or 9 in the ones place

Problem Solving Hint
Look for a pattern in the digits in the ones place.

Explore

You can divide to decide if a number is even or odd.

An **even number** can be divided into two equal groups.

An **odd number** has one left over when it is divided into two equal groups.

Work Together

Use counters or draw pictures.

1. Try to divide each number from 2 through 18 into two equal groups.

a. Which numbers can be divided into two equal groups?

b. Which numbers have one left over?

c. Which of the numbers are even numbers? Which are odd numbers?

2. Copy and complete the table. Write if each sum or product will be even or odd. Give four examples for each case.

Numbers	Sum	Product
2 even numbers	even	
2 odd numbers		
1 even number, 1 odd number		

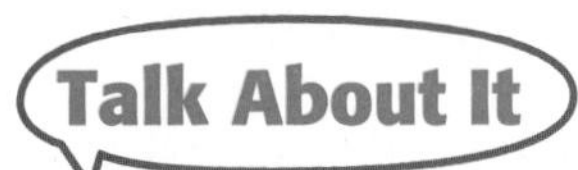

Can a number be both even and odd? Explain.

Connect

An even number can be divided by 2 with no leftovers. An odd number has one left over when it is divided by 2.

You can find patterns in even and odd numbers.

Even numbers have a 0, 2, 4, 6, or 8 in the ones place.

Odd numbers have a 1, 3, 5, 7, or 9 in the ones place.

1	2	3	4	5	6	7	8	9	10
11	12	13	14	15	16	17	18	19	20
21	22	23	24	25	26	27	28	29	30
31	32	33	34	35	36	37	38	39	40
41	42	43	44	45	46	47	48	49	50
51	52	53	54	55	56	57	58	59	60
61	62	63	64	65	66	67	68	69	70
71	72	73	74	75	76	77	78	79	80
81	82	83	84	85	86	87	88	89	90
91	92	93	94	95	96	97	98	99	100

PRACTICE AND APPLY

Practice

Write *odd* or *even* for each. You may use counters or draw pictures.

1. ● ● ● ● ● ● ●
● ● ● ● ● ● ●

2. ● ● ● ● ● ●
● ● ● ● ● ● ●

3. 33 **4.** 66 **5.** 35 **6.** 71 **7.** 24

8. 60 **9.** 19 **10.** 25 **11.** 100 **12.** 289

13. Start with 12 and name the next 4 even numbers. Explain how you know which numbers are even.

14. **Reasoning** Choose at least two questions to answer. Give three examples to explain your answers.

a. If you add three odd numbers, will the sum be odd or even?

b. If you add three even numbers, will the sum be odd or even?

c. If you add two even numbers and an odd number, will the sum be odd or even?

d. If you add two odd numbers and an even number, will the sum be odd or even?

Patterns Copy and complete the pattern. Then write *odd* or *even* for each group of numbers.

15. 234, 236, 238, ■, ■, ■ **16.** 2,555, 2,553, 2,551, ■, ■, ■

17. **Collecting Data** Find at least five numbers in the sports section of a newspaper or magazine. Copy the numbers and write if each is even or odd.

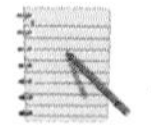

18. **Journal** Describe the patterns you see in even numbers. Describe the patterns you see in odd numbers.

and Practice

Find each product.

1. $\begin{array}{r} 6 \\ \times 2 \\ \hline \end{array}$	**2.** $\begin{array}{r} 5 \\ \times 0 \\ \hline \end{array}$	**3.** $\begin{array}{r} 6 \\ \times 4 \\ \hline \end{array}$	**4.** $\begin{array}{r} 2 \\ \times 8 \\ \hline \end{array}$	**5.** $\begin{array}{r} 7 \\ \times 3 \\ \hline \end{array}$
6. $\begin{array}{r} 3 \\ \times 5 \\ \hline \end{array}$	**7.** $\begin{array}{r} 8 \\ \times 9 \\ \hline \end{array}$	**8.** $\begin{array}{r} 4 \\ \times 4 \\ \hline \end{array}$	**9.** $\begin{array}{r} 3 \\ \times 9 \\ \hline \end{array}$	**10.** $\begin{array}{r} 4 \\ \times 9 \\ \hline \end{array}$
11. 6×8	**12.** 7×9	**13.** 8×4	**14.** 9×5	**15.** 7×7
16. 4×10	**17.** 12×9	**18.** 9×11	**19.** 12×8	**20.** 11×6
21. 6×1	**22.** 7×8	**23.** 11×4	**24.** 9×0	**25.** 7×10

Find each quotient.

26. $14 \div 2$	**27.** $27 \div 9$	**28.** $15 \div 5$	**29.** $18 \div 2$	**30.** $45 \div 5$
31. $4\overline{)20}$	**32.** $6\overline{)42}$	**33.** $3\overline{)24}$	**34.** $3\overline{)9}$	**35.** $9\overline{)9}$
36. $20 \div 5$	**37.** $0 \div 3$	**38.** $2 \div 2$	**39.** $28 \div 4$	**40.** $64 \div 8$
41. $2\overline{)16}$	**42.** $5\overline{)35}$	**43.** $9\overline{)81}$	**44.** $2\overline{)10}$	**45.** $9\overline{)72}$
46. $8\overline{)48}$	**47.** $6\overline{)54}$	**48.** $9\overline{)36}$	**49.** $8\overline{)72}$	**50.** $9\overline{)63}$

Error Search

Find each sentence that is not correct. Write it correctly and explain the error.

51. 56 is a multiple of 9.

52. The quotient of 0 divided by 4 is 4.

53. $45 \div 9$ equals $35 \div 7$.

54. The quotient of $9 \div 9$ is 0.

55. The quotient of $12 \div 6$ is greater than $12 \div 4$.

56. 100 is a multiple of 10.

Goal!

The world's largest soccer stadium is in Rio de Janeiro, Brazil. It holds 165,000 people. What is its name? Multiply or divide to find the answer. Match each letter to its answer in the blank. Some letters are not used.

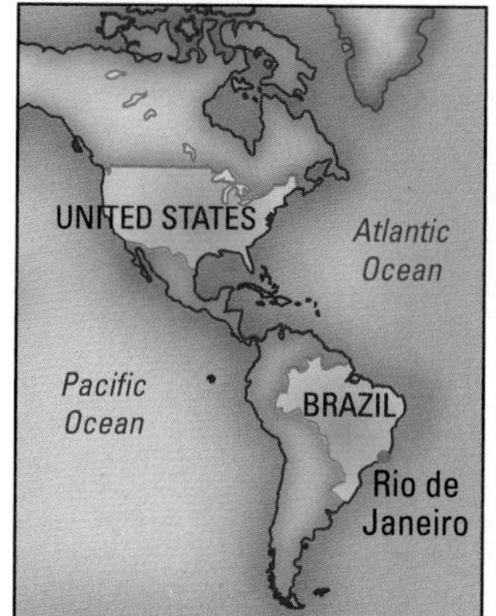

57. $81 \div 9$ [A] **58.** $56 \div 7$ [I] **59.** $8 \div 8$ [A] **60.** $18 \div 9$ [A]

61. 3×7 [N] **62.** 8×8 [W] **63.** 11×5 [R] **64.** 5×7 [B]

65. $42 \div 6$ [D] **66.** $40 \div 8$ [G] **67.** $0 \div 6$ [V] **68.** $15 \div 5$ [T]

69. 4×8 [M] **70.** 9×7 [S] **71.** 4×6 [A] **72.** 7×8 [E]

73. $24 \div 4$ [A] **74.** 5×8 [F] **75.** $16 \div 4$ [O] **76.** 8×9 [C]

___ ___ ___ ___ ___ ___ ___
56 63 3 9 7 8 4

___ ___ ___ ___ ___ ___ ___ ___
32 6 55 1 72 2 21 24

Remember the Facts!

Use this activity any time to help you remember your multiplication and division facts.

Be a Writer! Make your own multiplication and division book. Choose 10 difficult facts you want to remember. Draw a picture and write a number sentence for each.

Chapter 4
Lesson
14

Exploring Factors

Problem Solving Connection
- Use Objects/ Act It Out
- Make an Organized List

Materials
grid paper

Vocabulary
prime number
a whole number greater than 1 that has only two factors, itself and 1

composite number
a whole number greater than 1 with more than two factors

Explore

You can use rectangles to find factors.
These rectangles show the factors of 12.

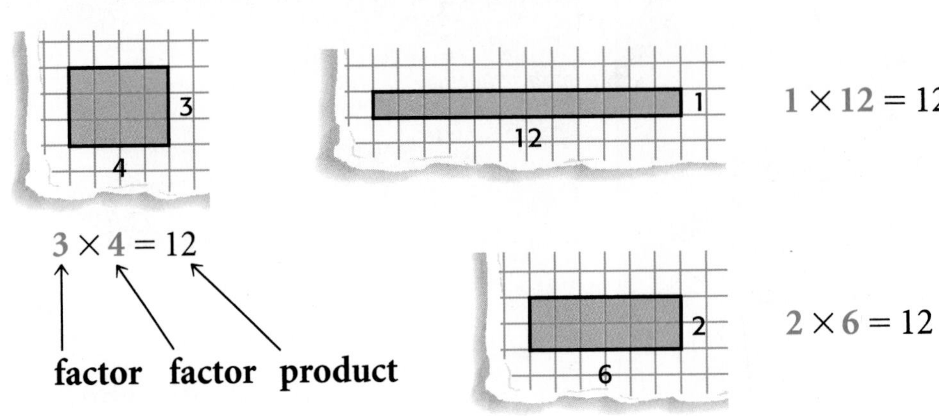

$1 \times 12 = 12$

$3 \times 4 = 12$
factor factor product

$2 \times 6 = 12$

Factors of 12: 1, 2, 3, 4, 6, 12

Work Together

Use grid paper to find different factors of a number.

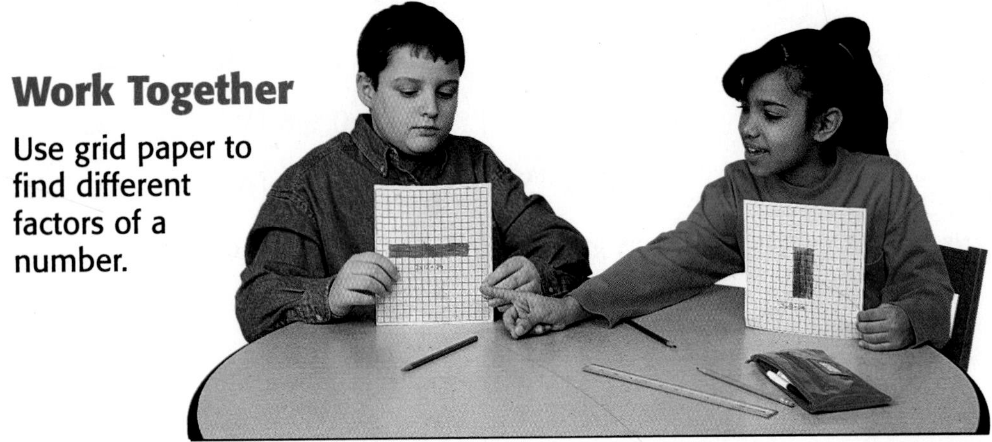

Remember
A square is also a rectangle.

1. **a.** Draw rectangles that have a total of 24 squares.
   b. For each rectangle write a multiplication sentence: ■ × ■ = 24.
2. **a.** Draw rectangles that have a total of 36 squares.
   b. For each rectangle write a multiplication sentence: ■ × ■ = 36.
3. Use rectangles to find all the factors of 11. List all the factors.

Talk About It

4. What are all of the factors of 24? Of 36?
5. What factors do 24 and 36 have in common?

Connect

A **prime number** has exactly two factors, 1 and itself.

You can draw only one rectangle to show a prime number.

Factors of 7: 1, 7

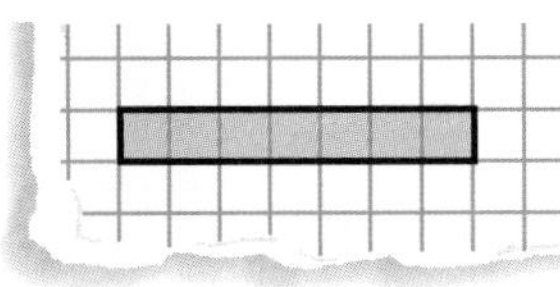

7 is a prime number.

$1 \times 7 = 7$

A **composite number** has more than two factors.

You can draw more than one rectangle to show a composite number.

Factors of 8: 1, 2, 4, 8

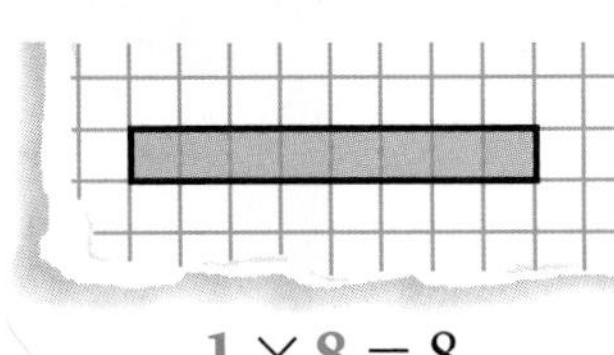

$1 \times 8 = 8$

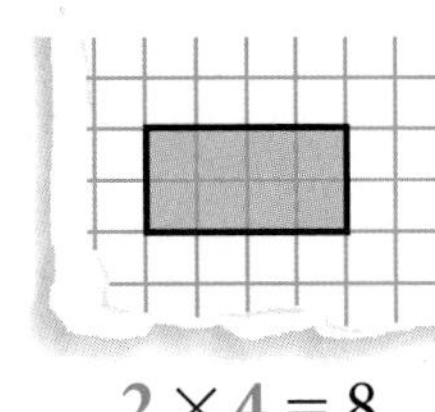

$2 \times 4 = 8$

8 is a composite number.

The number 1 is neither prime nor composite.

Practice

Copy and complete. Then list all the factors for each number.

1. $1 \times ■ = 9$; $■ \times 3 = 9$ **2.** $■ \times ■ = 5$ **3.** $1 \times ■ = 15$; $■ \times 5 = 15$ **4.** $■ \times ■ = 13$

List the factors for each number. You may draw rectangles to help you.

5. 20 **6.** 14 **7.** 17 **8.** 12 **9.** 19 **10.** 3 **11.** 22

Write whether each number is prime or composite.

12. 18 **13.** 11 **14.** 15 **15.** 3 **16.** 10 **17.** 4 **18.** 17

Copy and complete each list of prime numbers.

19. 3, 5, 7, ■, ■ **20.** 13, 17, 19, ■, ■

Copy and complete each list of composite numbers.

21. 12, 14, 15, ■, ■ **22.** 24, 25, 26, ■, ■

23. Reasoning What is the only even prime number? Explain.

24. Journal How do you decide if a number is prime or composite?

Chapter 4
Lesson
15

Problem Solving

Analyze Word Problems: Too Much or Too Little Information

You Will Learn
how to solve problems with too much or too little information

Learn

Sometimes when you solve problems, you may have more information than you need. Or, you may not have enough.

Jared's coach bought a baseball and a bat. He also bought a $10 football and a $25 football helmet. He spent $57. How much did the baseball cost?

Item	Cost
Football	$10
Helmet	$25
Bat	?

Work Together

▶ Understand

What do you know?

What do you need to find out?

▶ Plan

To find the cost of the baseball, add the cost of all the items except the baseball. Then subtract that total from $57.

▶ Solve

Add the cost of the football, helmet, and bat.

You cannot add in the cost of the bat because it is not known.

▶ Look Back

Can you get an answer? Explain.

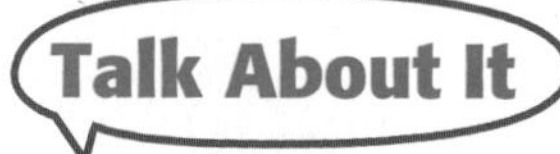

Can you solve problems with too little information? Too much? Explain.

Check

Decide if the problem has too much or too little information. Then solve, if possible.

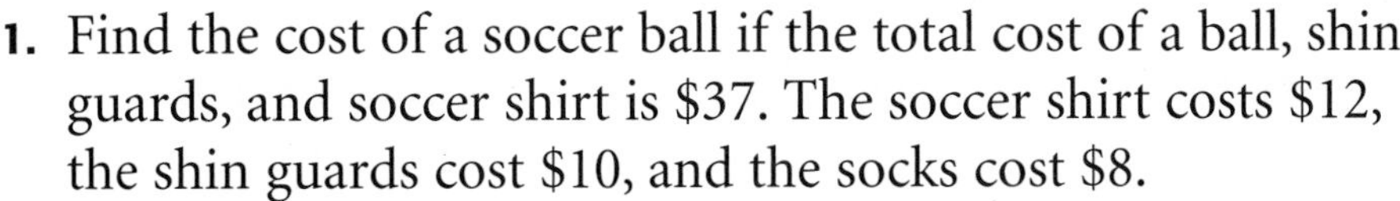

1. Find the cost of a soccer ball if the total cost of a ball, shin guards, and soccer shirt is $37. The soccer shirt costs $12, the shin guards cost $10, and the socks cost $8.

2. Find the cost of two soccer balls, shin guards, socks, and a shirt. The two soccer balls cost $40, and the shirt costs $12.

Problem Solving Practice

Problem Solving Strategies

- Use Objects/Act It Out
- Draw a Picture
- Look for a Pattern
- Guess and Check
- Use Logical Reasoning
- Make an Organized List
- Make a Table
- Solve a Simpler Problem
- Work Backward

Choose a Tool

Decide if the problem has too much or too little information. Then solve, if possible.

3. In a soccer game, Jon scored 1 goal and Jason scored 3 goals. If Ron also scored 1 goal, how many goals did Azzam score?

4. Sue, Leanne, and Ash made a total of 10 goals. Sue made 4 goals and Leanne made 2. Ash made twice as many goals as Leanne. How many goals did Ash make?

5. **Social Studies** In Missouri, about 15,000 people live in Warrensburg. About 140,000 people live in Springfield, and about 430,000 live in Kansas City. About how many more people live in Kansas City than in Springfield?

6. David's father works for a baseball team. He gave David some $5 tickets to a game to give to 6 of his friends. Each friend got 2 tickets. How many tickets did David's father give him?

Using Data Use the bar graph to answer **7–9**.

7. About how many more hours of sleep per day does a 40 year old need than a 70 year old?

8. About how many more hours of sleep does a newborn baby need than a 4 year old?

9. Kim is 10 years old. If she went to sleep at 8:15 P.M. and woke up at about 7:30 A.M., did she get enough sleep? Explain.

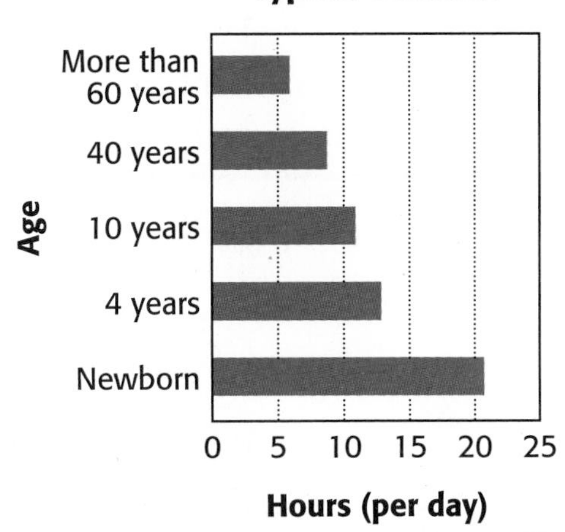

PROBLEM SOLVING PRACTICE

Chapter 4
Lesson
16

Problem Solving

Compare Strategies: Guess and Check/Draw a Picture

You Will Learn
how to solve problems using Guess and Check and Draw a Picture

Learn

Together, Toby and Warren brought 16 oranges for their field hockey team to eat at halftime. Toby brought 2 more oranges than Warren did. How many did they each bring?

Here are two ways to solve the problem.

One Way

Use guess and check to find the answer.

First, guess Toby brought 10 oranges and Warren brought 6.

Then, check:
$10 + 6 = 16$
$10 - 6 = 4$ Too much

Now, guess 9 and 7.
$9 + 7 = 16$
$9 - 7 = 2$ That checks!

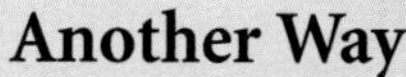

Another Way

Draw a picture.

First, divide 16 by 2 to find how many they each brought if they each brought the same amount.

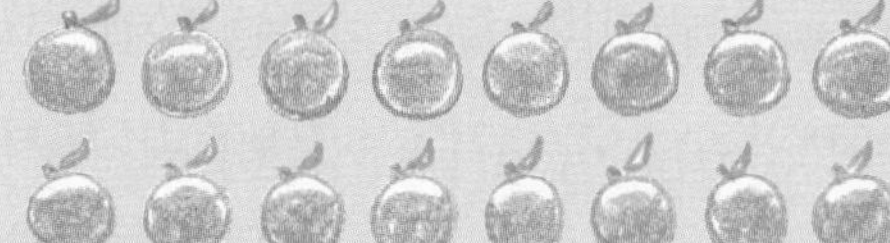

Then, erase 1 orange from the first row and add it to the second row.

So, Toby brought 9 oranges. Warren brought 7.

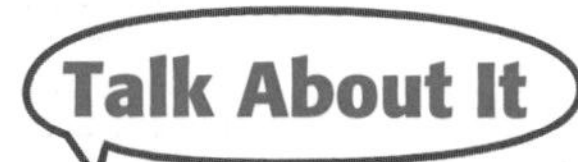

Which strategy would you use to solve this problem? Explain.

Check

Use Guess and Check, Draw a Picture, or any other strategy to solve the problem.

1. Sam has eight loose sports socks in a drawer. Four of them have green stripes and four have red stripes. He wants a matching pair of socks, but it is too dark to see. What is the least number of socks he can take out to be sure of having a matching pair? Explain.

Problem Solving Practice

Use any strategy to solve each problem.

2. The field hockey coach asked Mariel's mom to bring oranges for the 11 players to eat at halftime. Each player needs $1\frac{1}{2}$ oranges. How many oranges should Mariel's mom bring?

3. The coach wants to bring string cheese sticks for the team. He needs 12 sticks. How many bags should he buy, if each bag contains 4 sticks?

4. The Taneytown Cyclers put on a show. They used tricycles and bicycles. There were 12 tricycles and bicycles with a total of 27 wheels in the show. How many bicycles were there?

5. **Health** A typical young child has these teeth in each jaw: 4 incisors, 2 canines, and 4 molars.
   a. How many teeth are in both jaws of a typical young child?
   b. A typical adult has 32 permanent teeth. Typically, how many more teeth does an adult have than a young child?

Using Data Use the table to answer **6–8.**

6. How much will two mouth guards cost?

7. What is the difference in price between a hockey stick and a hockey ball?

8. How many shin guards can you buy with $45?

Problem Solving Strategies

- Use Objects/Act It Out
- Draw a Picture
- Look for a Pattern
- Guess and Check
- Use Logical Reasoning
- Make an Organized List
- Make a Table
- Solve a Simpler Problem
- Work Backward

Choose a Tool

Field Hockey Equipment	
Hockey stick	$37.50
Shin guard	$15.25
Mouth guard	$2.95
Hockey ball	$5.75

PROBLEM SOLVING PRACTICE

SECTION C

Review and Practice

Vocabulary Match each word with its meaning.

1. composite number
2. prime number
3. even
4. odd

a. a number that has only two factors, itself and 1

b. a number that has more than two factors

c. a number that cannot be divided into two equal groups

d. a number that can be divided into two equal groups

(Lessons 11 and 12) Find each quotient.

5. $4\overline{)24}$	**6.** $3\overline{)12}$	**7.** $9\overline{)27}$	**8.** $6\overline{)18}$	**9.** $7\overline{)63}$
10. $8\overline{)24}$	**11.** $7\overline{)35}$	**12.** $6\overline{)36}$	**13.** $4\overline{)32}$	**14.** $3\overline{)21}$
15. $12 \div 6$	**16.** $28 \div 4$	**17.** $0 \div 6$	**18.** $81 \div 9$	**19.** $24 \div 4$
20. $45 \div 5$	**21.** $54 \div 9$	**22.** $14 \div 7$	**23.** $72 \div 8$	**24.** $48 \div 6$

(Lesson 13) Write *even* or *odd* for each.

25. 32	**26.** 19	**27.** 15	**28.** 16	**29.** 57
30. 159	**31.** 400	**32.** 921	**33.** 1,024	**34.** 1,185

(Lesson 14) Copy and complete. Then list all the factors of each number.

35. $1 \times \blacksquare = 12$
$2 \times \blacksquare = 12$
$3 \times \blacksquare = 12$

36. $1 \times \blacksquare = 18$
$2 \times \blacksquare = 18$
$3 \times \blacksquare = 18$

37. $\blacksquare \times \blacksquare = 11$

Write whether each number is prime or composite.

38. 7 **39.** 28 **40.** 17 **41.** 39

(Lesson 15) Use any strategy to solve.

42. History In the 1940s, soccer shoes weighed about 1 lb each. Today soccer shoes weigh about 8 oz each and have 6 studs on the soles. Today, what is the weight of a pair of soccer shoes?

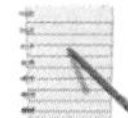

43. Journal What multiplication fact would you use to find $63 \div 7$? Explain.

Skills Checklist

In this section, you have:

- ☑ **Divided with 3, 4, 6, 7, and 8 as Divisors**
- ☑ **Explored Even and Odd Numbers**
- ☑ **Explored Factors**
- ☑ **Solved Problems with Too Much or Too Little Information**
- ☑ **Solved Problems by Comparing Strategies: Guess and Check/Draw a Picture**

Choose at least one. Use what you have learned in this chapter.

1 Let the Good Times Roll

Think of a favorite song. Rewrite it using words about multiplying or dividing. Make it silly, dramatic, or serious! When you are done, share it with your classmates.

2 The Daily Times

At Home Work with a family member or friend. Think about shopping, traveling, or cooking. Find at least three ways you use multiplication. Write multiplication stories and number sentences for these ways.

3 Follow the Map

Complete each fact. Then add the answers to find the shortest way from home to the park.

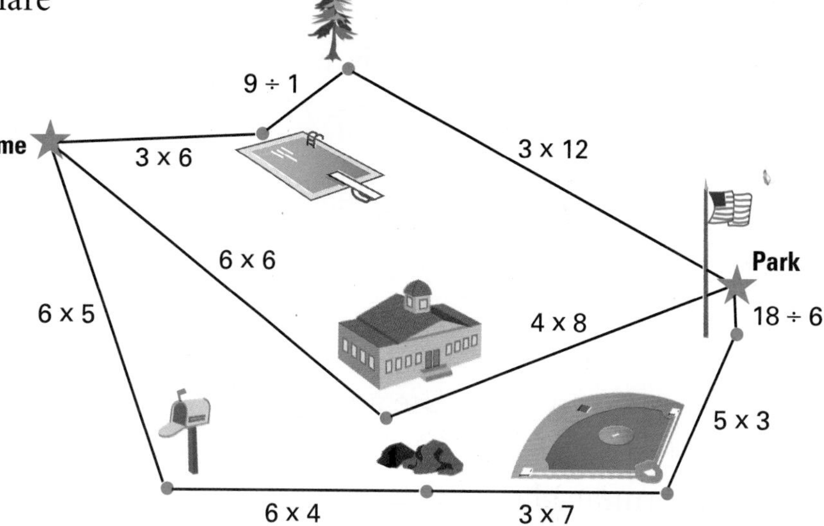

4 Beans on the Table

Share jelly beans with 3 friends. Make a table that shows how many jelly beans you will each get from 1 dozen jelly beans, 2 dozen jelly beans, 3 dozen jelly beans, and 4 dozen jelly beans. You can use a calculator to help you.

	Number of Jelly Beans	Each Person's Share
1 dozen	12	3
2 dozen		
3 dozen		
4 dozen		

REVIEW AND PRACTICE

CHAPTER 4

Review/Test

Vocabulary Complete each sentence with the correct word.

Word List
product
fact family
multiple
divisor
dividend
quotient

1. 28 is a _____ of 2.
2. The _____ is the answer to a division problem.
3. The _____ is the answer to a multiplication problem.
4. The number by which another number is to be divided is the _____.
5. The number that is to be divided is the _____.
6. $9 \times 5 = 45$ and $45 \div 9 = 5$ are in the same _____.

(Lessons 1–5) Find each product.

7. 3×3
8. 6×4
9. 12×7
10. 7×6
11. 0×11
12. 6×9
13. 5×11
14. 7×4
15. 4×8
16. 1×9

(Lesson 8) Write a story for each number sentence.

17. $6 \times 8 = 48$
18. $21 \div 3 = 7$
19. $5 \times 4 = 20$
20. $36 \div 9 = 4$

(Lessons 7, 9–12) Find each quotient.

21. $18 \div 3$
22. $81 \div 9$
23. $24 \div 4$
24. $48 \div 8$
25. $0 \div 5$
26. $9\overline{)9}$
27. $7\overline{)63}$
28. $8\overline{)72}$
29. $6\overline{)36}$
30. $2\overline{)14}$

(Lessons 15 and 16) Solve. Use any strategy.

31. Becky ran 5 miles every day after school. How many miles did she run in all?
32. Jonah and Robyn scored 24 runs together during the baseball season. Jonah scored 4 runs fewer than Robyn. How many runs did Robyn score?
33. Sometimes Anna takes a bus to school. It costs 25¢ and the ride takes 4 minutes. How long does it take Anna to go to school and back home again?

REVIEW/TEST

CHAPTER 4

Performance Assessment

After the first month of the Little League baseball season, the Huntsville Tigers compared their hitting records. Here's how they looked:

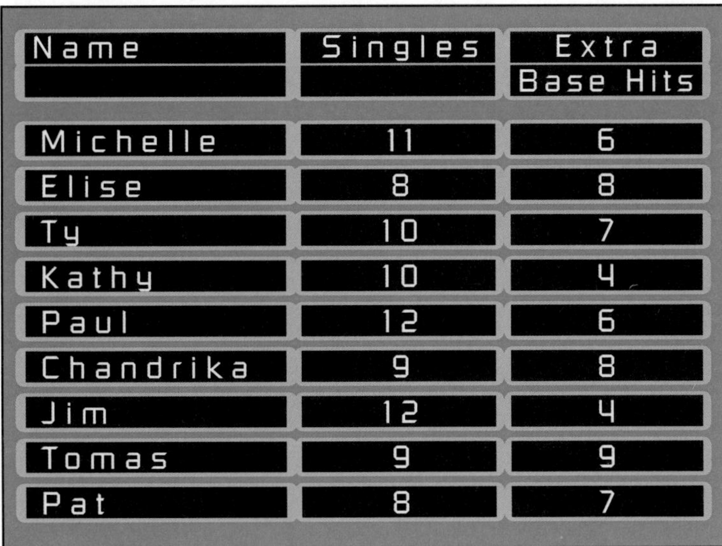

Name	Singles	Extra Base Hits
Michelle	11	6
Elise	8	8
Ty	10	7
Kathy	10	4
Paul	12	6
Chandrika	9	8
Jim	12	4
Tomas	9	9
Pat	8	7

Match the name of the player with the position he or she plays. Use the facts to help.

- The sum of the pitcher's hits is 15 and the product is 56.
- The sum of the catcher's hits is 16 and the quotient is 3.
- The sum of the shortstop's hits is 16 and the quotient is 1.
- The sum of the first baseman's hits is 14 and the product is 40.
- The sum of the center fielder's hits is 17 and the product is 70.
- The sum of the left fielder's hits is 17 and the product is 72.

1. **Decision Making** Decide how your group will match six of the players with the position he or she plays.

2. **Recording Data** Make a list or table to show your solution.

3. **Critical Thinking** Write your own riddles to match the remaining players with these positions: right field, third base, and second base.

4. **Explain Your Thinking** How did your group divide the work? How did you figure out each player's position? How can you change the lineup by using different sum, product, and quotient riddles?

REVIEW/TEST

Math Magazine

Prime Time: The Sieve of Eratosthenes

An ancient Greek named Eratosthenes (ER-uh-TAHS-thuh-neez) invented a way to find prime numbers quickly. Mathematicians still use his method today. It is called the sieve of Eratosthenes.

Remember

A prime number is a whole number greater than 1 that has only two factors, itself and 1.

Materials

- hundred chart
- calculator

Try These!

To make your own sieve of Eratosthenes, use a hundred chart.

1. Shade 2 red. Then cross off all other multiples of 2.

1	2	3	4	5	6	7	8	9	10
11	12	13	14	15	16	17	18	19	20
21	22	23	24	25	26	27	28	29	30
31									

2. Shade 3 red. Cross off all other multiples of 3.
3. Shade 5 red. Cross off all other multiples of 5.
4. Shade 7 red. Cross off all other multiples of 7.
5. Shade 11 red. Cross off all other multiples of 11.
6. Shade all the remaining numbers red.
7. Check if all the numbers shaded in red are prime numbers. List the prime numbers you found.

CHAPTERS 1–4

Cumulative Review

Test Prep Strategy: Make Smart Choices

Use logical reasoning.

Find the set of numbers that is in order from greatest to least.

Ⓐ 10, 1,000, 100 Ⓑ 100, 1,000, 10
Ⓒ 1,000, 100, 10 Ⓓ 10, 100, 1,000

STAY SHARP! The numbers are in order in Ⓒ and Ⓓ. In Ⓒ, the numbers are in order from *greatest to least.* The answer is Ⓒ!

Test Prep Strategies

- Read Carefully
- Follow Directions
- Make Smart Choices
- Eliminate Choices
- Work Backward from an Answer

Write the letter of the correct answer. Make smart choices or use any strategy to help.

1. Which number is greater than 11,000?
   Ⓐ 1,100 Ⓑ 10,100 Ⓒ 1,000 Ⓓ 11,100

2. Kyle looked at his watch at 3:05 P.M. What was the time 15 minutes later?
   Ⓐ 3:20 P.M. Ⓑ 3:25 P.M. Ⓒ 3:00 P.M. Ⓓ 3:30 P.M.

3. Janita's class has 7 rows with 3 students in each row. How many students are in Janita's class?
   Ⓐ 10 Ⓑ 14 Ⓒ 20 Ⓓ 21

4. What is the quotient of 48 divided by 6?
   Ⓐ 7 Ⓑ 36 Ⓒ 48 Ⓓ 8

Use the bar graph to answer **5-7.**

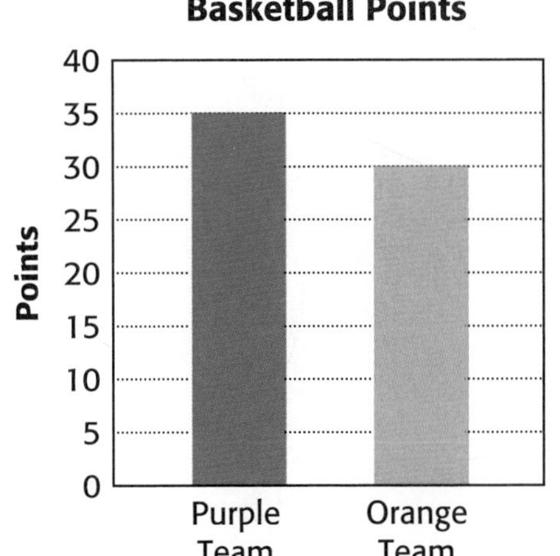

5. How many more points did the Purple Team score than the Orange Team?
   Ⓐ 5 Ⓑ 30
   Ⓒ 35 Ⓓ 65

6. How many points did the two teams score in all?
   Ⓐ 30 Ⓑ 35
   Ⓒ 55 Ⓓ 65

7. Five players on the Orange Team scored all the team's points. If each player scored equal points, how many points did each score?
   Ⓐ 6 Ⓑ 5
   Ⓒ 7 Ⓓ 4

REVIEW AND PRACTICE

Chapter 5
Multiplying by 1-Digit Factors

TIME OUT FROM School

SECTION

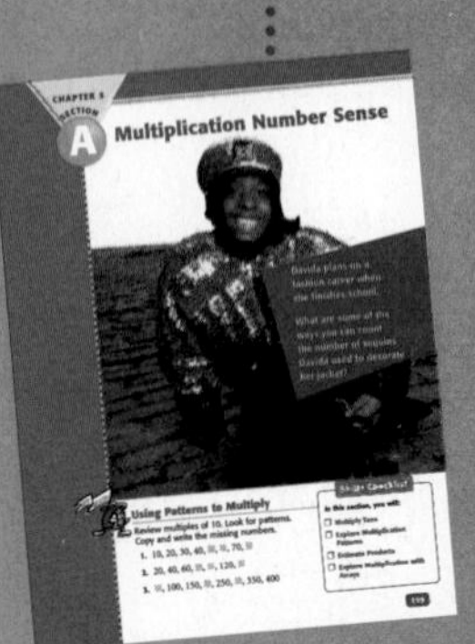

Davida, fashion designer
Page 199

Multiplication Number Sense 199

Stringing beads is a colorful pastime. It was so popular in Ghana that tons of beads were imported there until the 1970s! Just where did all the beads come from? Take a look.

Shipments of Beads to Ghana, West Africa

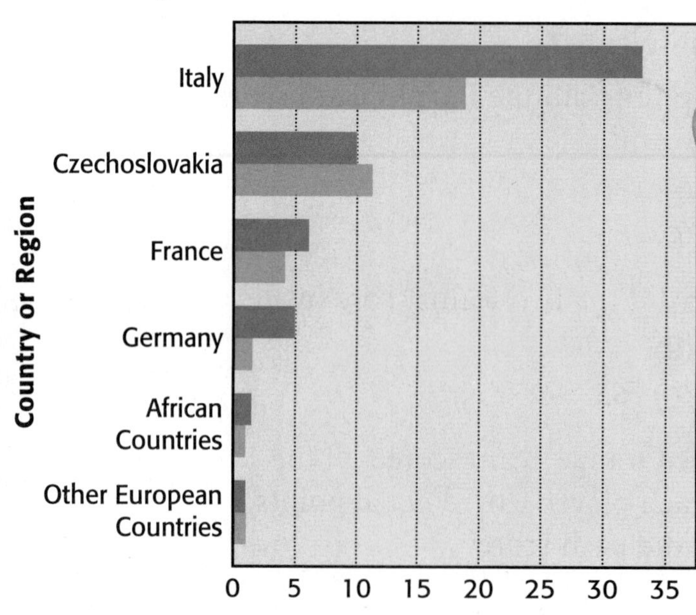

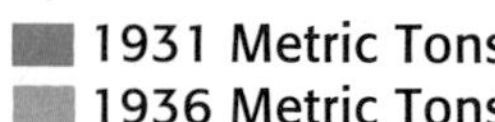

Multiplying

209

Is jumping rope for 10 minutes as good for you as jogging for 10 minutes or skiing for 30 minutes? Explain.

Health Ratings for Various Activities		
Activity	**Time**	**Health Rating**
Jumping rope	10 minutes	★★★
Jogging (1 mile)	10 minutes	★★★
Tennis, singles	20-minute set	★½
Swimming (300 yards)	10 minutes	★
Bicycling (2 miles)	8–10 minutes	★
Skiing, water or snow	30 minutes	★★★
Square dancing	30 minutes	★★½

Surfing the World Wide Web!

Do you have a favorite sports activity? Find out how your choice compares with those of other students around the country. Walk, jog, swim, or ski over to **www.mathsurf.com/4/ch5.**

Use the data you find to report the top three sports activities preferred by other students in your grade.

Jump rope champions
Page 209

SECTION C

Extending Multiplication

223

Some students cook up a storm when school gets out. Here's a recipe for a high-energy snack. How many friends could you serve if you made 3 times the recipe amount?

Meatless Pemmican
(Serves 12)

8 tbsp raisins
8 tbsp peanuts
8 tbsp hickory nuts
8 tbsp dried apples
8 tbsp dried pumpkin
8 tbsp dry cornmeal
6 tbsp honey

Chop up the raisins, nuts, dried apples, and dried pumpkin. Combine all of these ingredients in a bowl. Stir in the cornmeal. Add the honey, and blend completely. Press a large spoonful of the mixture to form a small cake. Repeat until you have used all of the mixture.

Musical instruments around the world
Page 223

Materials

10-inch-square piece of paper, scissors, ruler, markers or crayons, clock or watch to measure seconds, pencil, thumbtack

Windmills can use wind energy to grind grain, pull water, or make electricity. The greater the wind energy, the faster the windmill turns. We can measure the speed in revolutions (turns) per minute (RPMs).

How can you count the RPMs of a pinwheel? Would you have to count for a whole minute?

Make a Plan

- How will your team work together to make the pinwheel and count the revolutions?
- How will you record your data?

Carry It Out

1. Make the pinwheel.

   a. Draw two straight lines. Color one corner.

   b. Cut along the lines to 1 inch from the center.

   c. Fold the corners to the center and attach with the thumbtack.

2. Blow steadily on the pinwheel to make it turn. Find the number of RPMs.

Talk About It

- What makes it difficult to count the RPMs?
- How did you overcome these problems?

Present the Project

- Collect the class data.
- Decide what number best represents the RPMs of a pinwheel powered by a person blowing on it.
- Tell how you used math to complete the project.

CHAPTER 5

SECTION

A Multiplication Number Sense

Davida plans on a fashion career when she finishes school.

What are some of the ways you can count the number of sequins Davida used to decorate her jacket?

GET READY!

Using Patterns to Multiply

Review multiples of 10. Look for patterns. Copy and write the missing numbers.

1. 10, 20, 30, 40, ■, ■, 70, ■
2. 20, 40, 60, ■, ■, 120, ■
3. ■, 100, 150, ■, 250, ■, 350, 400

Skills Checklist

In this section, you will:

- ❒ Multiply Tens
- ❒ Explore Multiplication Patterns
- ❒ Estimate Products
- ❒ Explore Multiplication with Arrays

Multiplying Tens

You Will Learn
how to multiply by multiples of ten

Learn

The principal announced, "If the school collects enough labels for a new computer, I'll kiss a frog!"

Julie and some friends formed a team to collect soup labels. How many labels did her team collect?

Remember
10, 20, 30, 40, and 50 are multiples of ten.

Here is one way Julie can count the labels her team collected.

Julie stacks her labels in 5 groups of 20.

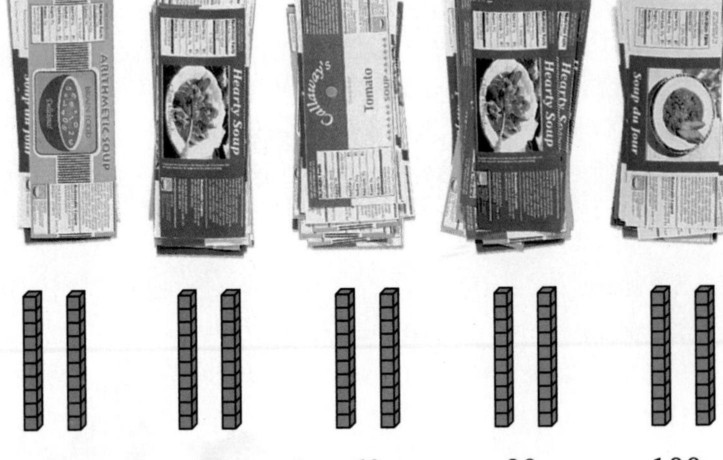

She counts: 20 40 60 80 100

5 groups of 20 labels
5×2 tens $= 10$ tens
$5 \times 20 = 100$

So, Julie's team has collected 100 labels.

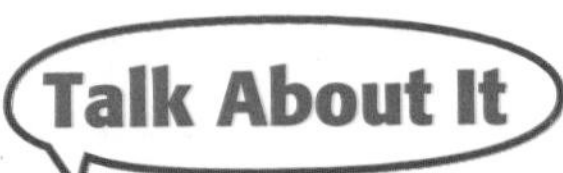

Why is it helpful to put things into equal groups of 20?

Check

Use a multiplication fact to help you find each product.

1. 4×2 tens = ▇ tens
   4×20 = ▇
2. 5×3 tens = ▇ tens
   5×30 = ▇
3. 5×4 tens = ▇ tens
   5×40 = ▇
4. **Reasoning** How are your answers to **1–3** alike?

Practice

Skills and Reasoning

Use a multiplication fact to help you find each product.

5. 3×1 ten = ▇ tens
   3×10 = ▇
6. 3×5 tens = ▇ tens
   3×50 = ▇
7. 4×9 tens = ▇ tens
   4×90 = ▇

8. 2×30
9. 7×10
10. 4×80
11. 7×50
12. 5×60
13. 5×20
14. 8×20
15. 6×60
16. 9×50
17. 4×70
18. Can you use the same multiplication fact to find 6×40 and 4×60? Explain.

Problem Solving and Applications

19. One team collected 4 stacks of 10 labels each. Another team collected 8 stacks of 50 labels each. Julie's team collected 120 labels. In all, how many labels did these three teams collect?
20. **Recreation** Cricket is a popular ball game in England. If Eric's team scored 60 runs on each day of a 3-day cricket match, how many runs did his team score in all?
21. **Science** Tadpoles hatch from frogs' eggs. It takes a tadpole about 12 weeks to become a frog and leave the water. About how many days does it take for the tadpole to become a frog?

22. **Journal** Explain why 10 is a multiple of 10.

Mixed Review and Test Prep

STAY SHARP!

Find each sum or difference.

23. $52 + 14$
24. $67 + 39$
25. $131 + 92$
26. $209 + 71$
27. $1{,}423 + 384$
28. $37 - 19$
29. $58 - 39$
30. $112 - 23$
31. $75 - 48$
32. $317 - 154$
33. Find $7{,}008 - 4{,}319$.

   Ⓐ 2,391 Ⓑ 11,327 Ⓒ 3,317 Ⓓ not here

Chapter 5
Lesson
2

Exploring Multiplication Patterns

Problem Solving Connection

Look for a Pattern

Materials

calculator

Explore

Place value and patterns can help you multiply.

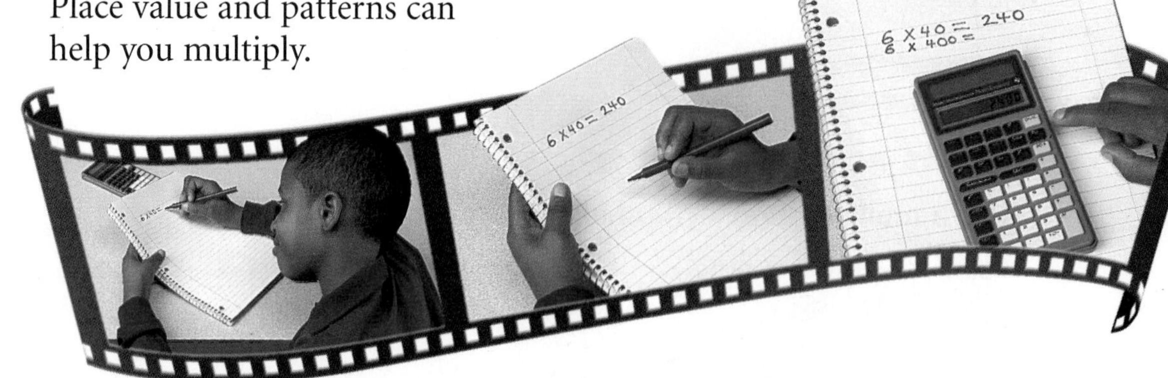

Work Together

1. Use a calculator to find each product. Look for patterns.

   a. $6 \times 40 = n$
   $6 \times 400 = n$
   $6 \times 4{,}000 = n$

   b. $5 \times 30 = n$
   $5 \times 300 = n$
   $5 \times 3{,}000 = n$

   c. $2 \times 70 = n$
   $2 \times 700 = n$
   $2 \times 7{,}000 = n$

Math Tip
Think about using basic facts.

2. Use patterns to find each product. Then check your answers with a calculator.

   a. $5 \times 60 = n$
   $5 \times 600 = n$
   $5 \times 6{,}000 = n$

   b. $2 \times 50 = n$
   $2 \times 500 = n$
   $2 \times 5{,}000 = n$

   c. $8 \times 700 = n$
   $8 \times 7{,}000 = n$
   $8 \times 70{,}000 = n$

   d. $4 \times 80 = n$
   $4 \times 800 = n$
   $4 \times 8{,}000 = n$
   $4 \times 80{,}000 = n$

   e. $7 \times 60 = n$
   $7 \times 600 = n$
   $7 \times 6{,}000 = n$
   $7 \times 60{,}000 = n$

   f. $3 \times 90 = n$
   $3 \times 900 = n$
   $3 \times 9{,}000 = n$
   $3 \times 90{,}000 = n$

Talk About It

3. Describe the patterns you found.

4. Explain how you can find 5×400 mentally.

5. If you know the product of 7×6, how can you find the product of 7 and 6,000?

Connect

Place-value patterns and mental math can help you find $3 \times 4{,}000$.

3×4 ones $= 12$ ones
$3 \times 4 = 12$

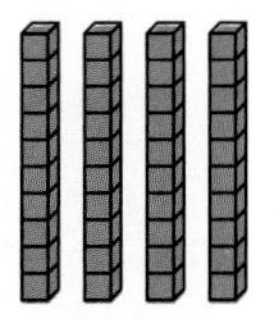
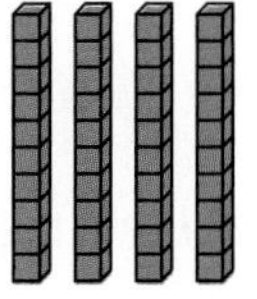
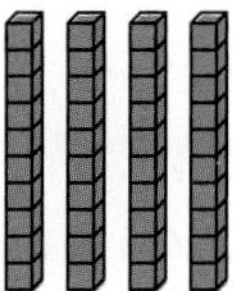

3×4 tens $= 12$ tens
$3 \times 40 = 120$

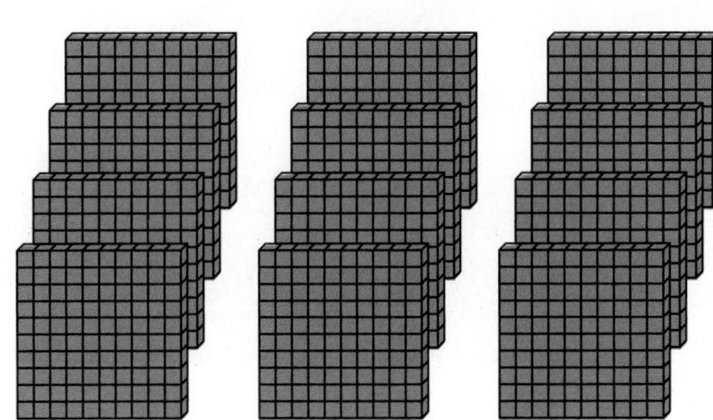

3×4 hundreds $= 12$ hundreds
$3 \times 400 = 1{,}200$

3×4 thousands $= 12$ thousands
$3 \times 4{,}000 = 12{,}000$

Practice

Use patterns to find each product. Check your answers.

1. $4 \times 7 = n$
$4 \times 70 = n$
$4 \times 700 = n$

2. $6 \times 3 = n$
$6 \times 30 = n$
$6 \times 300 = n$

3. $5 \times 8 = n$
$5 \times 80 = n$
$5 \times 800 = n$

4. $9 \times 6 = n$
$9 \times 60 = n$
$9 \times 600 = n$

Mental Math Find each product.

5. 5×90 **6.** 7×600 **7.** $3 \times 4{,}000$ **8.** 90×2 **9.** 8×30

10. 4×500 **11.** $6 \times 8{,}000$ **12.** 2×200 **13.** 7×700 **14.** $5{,}000 \times 6$

15. $3 \times 2{,}000$ **16.** 400×4 **17.** $5 \times 60{,}000$ **18.** 40×9 **19.** $2 \times 7{,}000$

20. Amy's team collects soup labels for the school contest. If the team collects 400 labels a week for 3 weeks, will it reach the goal of 1,200? Explain.

21. Critical Thinking What pattern do you notice about the products for pairs like 9×300 and 300×9, and 4×500 and 500×4?

22. Journal Explain how to find 800×4 using place value and patterns. Then explain how to find 500×2.

Skills Practice Bank, page 564, Set 1

Chapter 5 Lesson 3

Estimating Products

You Will Learn
how to estimate products

Learn

Davida had a sparkling idea! Instead of paying for decorated clothes, she decided to make them herself. Now Davida sells her creations and saves the money for college.

Davida is a young fashion designer in Philadelphia, Pennsylvania.

Example 1

Davida needs about 600 beads to decorate a jacket. She takes 8 scoops. Each scoop holds about 78 beads. Will she have enough beads for the jacket?

Number of scoops ↓ Number of beads in one scoop ↓

8×78

Round 78 to the nearest 10.

$8 \times 80 = 640$

There are about 640 beads in 8 scoops. So, Davida will have enough beads.

Example 2

A bag holds 625 sequins. Will 7 bags be enough for Davida to decorate a hat with about 4,000 sequins?

Number of bags ↓ Number of sequins in one bag ↓

7×625

Round 625 to the nearest 100.

$7 \times 600 = 4{,}200$

Davida will have about 4,200 sequins. So, 7 bags will be enough.

Math Tip
When you don't need an exact amount, an estimate is good enough.

Talk About It

Does Davida need to know the exact number of beads in a scoop? Explain.

Check

Estimate each product.

1. 5×81 **2.** 54×3 **3.** 98×3 **4.** 43×6 **5.** 7×79

6. 5×224 **7.** 557×4 **8.** 2×312 **9.** 3×697 **10.** 493×8

11. Reasoning Estimate to decide how many digits are in the product of 2 and 62.

Practice

Skills and Reasoning

Estimate each product.

12. 6×34 **13.** 7×284 **14.** 9×53 **15.** 5×636 **16.** 2×76

17. 36×4 **18.** 8×395 **19.** 3×825 **20.** 7×79 **21.** 37×9

22. 5×299 **23.** 9×889 **24.** 58×3 **25.** 42×7 **26.** 23×8

27. Estimate the product of 6 and 98.

28. Estimate the product of 4 and 613.

29. Estimate to decide if the product of 6 and 79 will be less than or greater than 480. Explain.

30. Estimate to decide if the product of 6 and 435 will be less than or greater than 2,400. Explain.

Problem Solving and Applications

31. Money Each Bike-a-Thon rider who earns at least $30 will win a T-shirt decorated by Davida. Geri earns $2 for each mile she rides. If she rides for 19 miles, will she win a T-shirt? Explain.

32. Probability One in ten bicyclists at the Bike-a-Thon is likely to earn at least $30. If there are 78 riders, about how many of them might earn $30?

Using Data Use the Data File on page 196 to solve **33** and **34**.

33. Which country shipped more beads to Ghana in 1936 than in 1931?

34. Which regions shipped at least twice as many beads to Ghana in 1931 than in 1936?

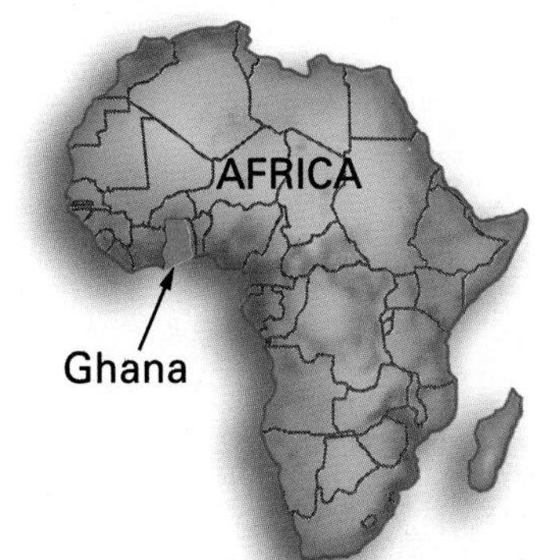

Mixed Review and Test Prep

STAY SHARP!

Find each sum or difference.

35. $518 + 397$

36. $407 - 169$

37. $1{,}548 + 9{,}252$

38. $2{,}004 - 1{,}653$

39. $4{,}081 - 3{,}294$

Algebra Readiness Find each missing number.

40. $407 + n = 943$ **41.** $n + 127 = 682$ **42.** $554 + n = 813$

43. Find the difference between $6.02 and $0.69.

Ⓐ $6.08 Ⓑ $5.33 Ⓒ $12.92 Ⓓ not here

Chapter 5
Lesson
4

Exploring Multiplication with Arrays

Problem Solving Connection
- Use Objects/Act It Out
- Solve a Simpler Problem

Materials
place-value blocks

Vocabulary
array
data arranged in rows and columns

Explore

School's out! Where's Caleb? He's on another egg hunt! Caleb raises Rhode Island Red chickens. Every day he collects eggs to sell to his neighbors and friends.

Two of Caleb's cartons hold 5 rows of 12 eggs each. How many eggs are in Caleb's cartons?

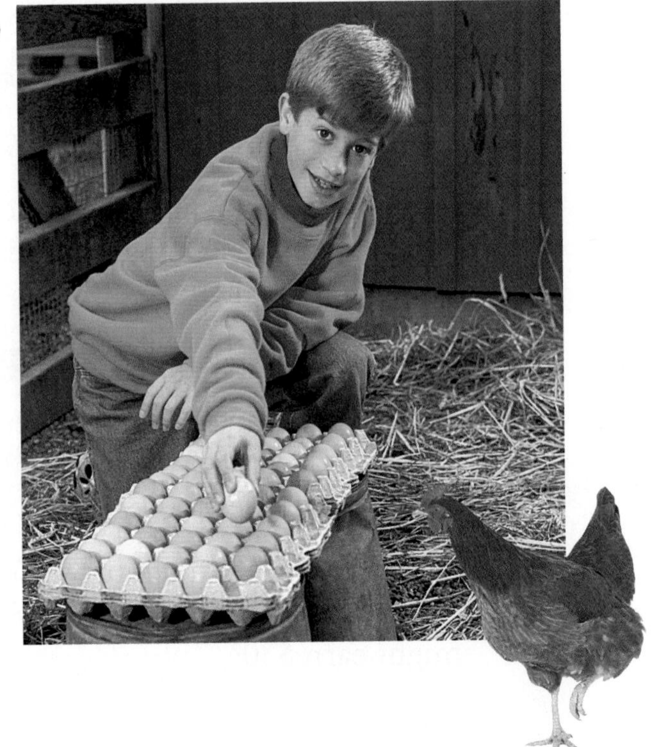

Work Together

1. Use place-value blocks to show an **array**. Find 5×12.
   a. Show 1 ten and 2 ones in a row. This shows 1×12.
   b. Make 4 more rows of 12. Now this shows 5×12.
   c. How many tens are there? How many ones?
   d. What is the product for 5×12?
2. Use the place-value blocks to show 3×16 and 4×13. Draw pictures to show what you did with the place-value blocks. Write the product for each.

Did You Know?
A typical chicken lays about 18 eggs a month.

Talk About It

3. Describe the array you made to show 3×16.
4. Explain how multiplying with place-value blocks is like solving two simpler problems.

Connect

You can use what you know about arrays to multiply. Find 4×13.

What You See

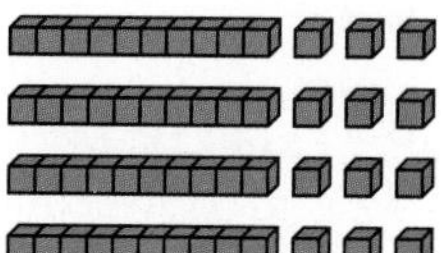

$4 \times 10 = 40$ $4 \times 3 = 12$

$40 + 12 = 52$

What You Write

$$\begin{array}{rl} 13 & \\ \times\ 4 & \\ \hline 12 & 4 \times 3 \text{ ones} \\ +40 & 4 \times 1 \text{ ten} \\ \hline 52 & \end{array}$$

Practice

Copy and complete to find each product. You may use place-value blocks to help.

1. $\begin{array}{r} 24 \\ \times\ 3 \\ \hline 12 \\ 60 \\ \hline \square\square \end{array}$

$3 \times 20 = 60$ $3 \times 4 = 12$

2. $\begin{array}{r} 18 \\ \times\ 7 \\ \hline 56 \\ \square\square \\ \hline \square\square\square \end{array}$

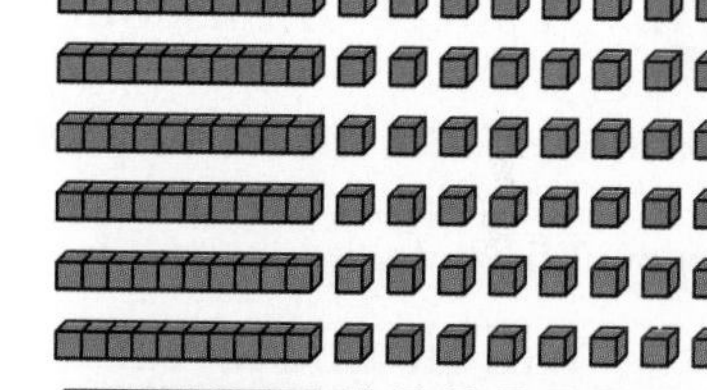

$7 \times 10 = n$ $7 \times 8 = 56$

Find each product. Draw pictures to help.

3. $\begin{array}{r} 37 \\ \times\ 4 \\ \hline 28 \\ 120 \\ \hline \square\square\square \end{array}$ **4.** $\begin{array}{r} 62 \\ \times\ 7 \\ \hline \square\square \\ \square\square\square \\ \hline \square\square\square \end{array}$ **5.** $\begin{array}{r} 72 \\ \times\ 8 \\ \hline \square\square \\ \square\square\square \\ \hline \square\square\square \end{array}$ **6.** $\begin{array}{r} 49 \\ \times\ 5 \\ \hline \square\square \\ \square\square\square \\ \hline \square\square\square \end{array}$ **7.** $\begin{array}{r} 58 \\ \times\ 6 \\ \hline \square\square \\ \square\square\square \\ \hline \square\square\square \end{array}$

8. $\begin{array}{r} 23 \\ \times\ 5 \\ \hline \end{array}$ **9.** $\begin{array}{r} 45 \\ \times\ 2 \\ \hline \end{array}$ **10.** $\begin{array}{r} 34 \\ \times\ 3 \\ \hline \end{array}$ **11.** $\begin{array}{r} 28 \\ \times\ 8 \\ \hline \end{array}$ **12.** $\begin{array}{r} 39 \\ \times\ 4 \\ \hline \end{array}$

13. Is 3×28 the same as 3×8 plus 3×20? Explain.

14. Critical Thinking A typical large egg has a mass of 56 grams. The egg that has the greatest mass on record is 8 times as much as that of a typical egg. How many grams is that?

15. Using Data Caleb has 8 chickens. About how many eggs will Caleb collect each month? Use the fact from *Did You Know?* on page 206 to help answer the question.

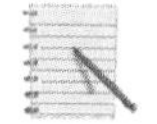

16. Journal Explain how to find 5×18 by breaking it into two simpler problems.

SECTION A

Review and Practice

(Lesson 1) Use a multiplication fact to help you find each product.

1. 4×30 **2.** 2×70 **3.** 7×50 **4.** 8×60 **5.** 5×80

(Lesson 2) Use patterns to find each product.

6. $7 \times 9 = n$ **7.** $8 \times 3 = n$ **8.** $4 \times 7 = n$

$7 \times 90 = n$ $8 \times 30 = n$ $4 \times 70 = n$

$7 \times 900 = n$ $8 \times 300 = n$ $4 \times 700 = n$

Mental Math Find each product.

9. 8×400 **10.** $6 \times 3{,}000$ **11.** 5×60 **12.** $6 \times 2{,}000$

13. A sheet of baseball cards has 100 cards. How many cards are there in 5 sheets?

Using Data Use the pictograph for **14** and **15.**

14. How many people will fit in the Tampa Thunderdome?

15. How many people will fit in the Calgary Saddledome?

Capacity of Hockey Stadiums	
Madison Square Garden	
Tampa Thunderdome	
Calgary Olympic Saddledome	

= 4,000 people

(Lesson 3) Estimate each product.

16. 6×64 **17.** 5×914 **18.** 8×47 **19.** 7×23 **20.** 5×91

21. 9×58 **22.** 4×573 **23.** 3×285 **24.** 5×143 **25.** 9×362

(Lesson 4) Find the product. Use the array to help.

26. $\begin{array}{r} 17 \\ \times\ 6 \\ \hline \end{array}$

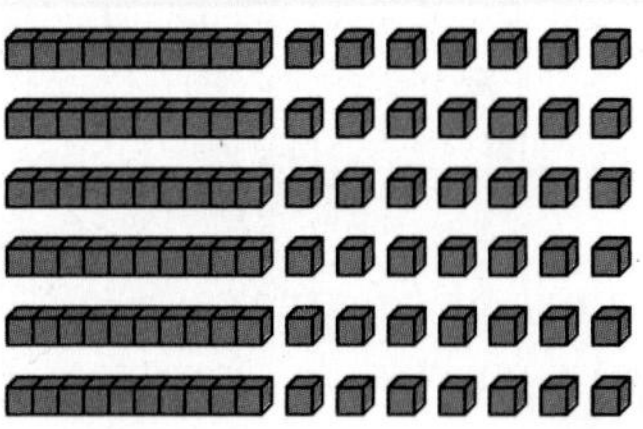

$6 \times 10 = n$ $6 \times 7 = 42$

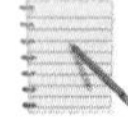

27. Journal Explain what you have learned about multiplication. Use any of the following words: multiple, array, factor, or product.

Skills Checklist

In this section, you have:

- **Multiplied Tens**
- **Explored Multiplication Patterns**
- **Estimated Products**
- **Explored Multiplication with Arrays**

CHAPTER 5

SECTION

B Multiplying

When the Happy Hoppers of Dayton, Ohio, compete, the team scores high. Each jump scores a specific number of points. How do you think the team keeps track of its scores?

Multiplying Greater Numbers

Review multiplication facts. Find each product.

1. 4×6	**2.** 5×8	**3.** 3×4
4. 7×2	**5.** 9×4	**6.** 5×7
7. 3×9	**8.** 6×6	**9.** 8×7
10. 4×4	**11.** 9×5	**12.** 8×8

Skills Checklist

In this section, you will:

- ❐ Multiply 2-Digit Numbers
- ❐ Multiply 3-Digit Numbers
- ❐ Solve Problems by Making Decisions
- ❐ Choose a Calculation Method

Chapter 5
Lesson
5

Multiplying 2-Digit Numbers

You Will Learn
how to multiply without using place-value blocks

Learn

After school, Jerry did one of the exercises his sister Pam had for homework. He was surprised by the result.

Remember
18 ones is the same as 1 ten and 8 ones.

How are Pam's and Jerry's ways alike? How are they different?

Another Example

Use Pam's method to find 4×28.

Step 1

Multiply the ones.
Regroup.

$$\begin{array}{r} \overset{3}{2}8 \\ \times\ 4 \\ \hline 2 \end{array}$$

4×8 ones = 32 ones

Regroup 32 ones as 3 tens, 2 ones

Step 2

Multiply the tens.
Add the extra tens.

$$\begin{array}{r} \overset{3}{2}8 \\ \times\ 4 \\ \hline 112 \end{array}$$

4×2 tens = 8 tens

8 tens + 3 tens = 11 tens

$4 \times 28 = 112$

Estimate to check.
4×28 is close to 4×30.
$4 \times 30 = 120$
Because 112 is close to 120, the answer is reasonable.

Talk About It

1. What does the small 3 above the 2 in the tens place mean?
2. Do you need to regroup to find 2×34? Explain.

Check

Copy and complete.

1. $\begin{array}{r} 12 \\ \times\ 3 \\ \hline \blacksquare 6 \end{array}$
2. $\begin{array}{r} 32 \\ \times\ 4 \\ \hline \blacksquare\blacksquare 8 \end{array}$
3. $\begin{array}{r} 51 \\ \times\ 9 \\ \hline \blacksquare\blacksquare 9 \end{array}$
4. $\begin{array}{r} \overset{4}{4}8 \\ \times\ 5 \\ \hline \blacksquare\blacksquare 0 \end{array}$
5. $\begin{array}{r} \overset{1}{6}5 \\ \times\ 2 \\ \hline \blacksquare\blacksquare 0 \end{array}$

Find each product. Estimate to check.

6. $\begin{array}{r} 12 \\ \times\ 6 \\ \hline \end{array}$
7. $\begin{array}{r} 18 \\ \times\ 7 \\ \hline \end{array}$
8. $\begin{array}{r} 72 \\ \times\ 5 \\ \hline \end{array}$
9. $\begin{array}{r} 49 \\ \times\ 8 \\ \hline \end{array}$
10. $\begin{array}{r} 63 \\ \times\ 3 \\ \hline \end{array}$
11. $\begin{array}{r} 15 \\ \times\ 5 \\ \hline \end{array}$
12. $\begin{array}{r} 14 \\ \times\ 6 \\ \hline \end{array}$
13. $\begin{array}{r} 28 \\ \times\ 3 \\ \hline \end{array}$
14. $\begin{array}{r} 34 \\ \times\ 7 \\ \hline \end{array}$
15. $\begin{array}{r} 43 \\ \times\ 4 \\ \hline \end{array}$
16. 4×42
17. 6×75
18. 5×47
19. 3×92
20. 7×29
21. Find the product of 4 and 72.
22. How many days are in 16 weeks?
23. **Reasoning** How would you use regrouping to find 8 times 17?
24. **Reasoning** If you wanted to find the product of 38 and 8, how would you estimate to check your answer?

Practice

Skills and Reasoning

Find each product. Estimate to check.

25. $\begin{array}{r} 26 \\ \times\ 5 \\ \hline \end{array}$ **26.** $\begin{array}{r} 71 \\ \times\ 8 \\ \hline \end{array}$ **27.** $\begin{array}{r} 48 \\ \times\ 9 \\ \hline \end{array}$ **28.** $\begin{array}{r} 33 \\ \times\ 6 \\ \hline \end{array}$ **29.** $\begin{array}{r} 91 \\ \times\ 7 \\ \hline \end{array}$

30. $\begin{array}{r} 96 \\ \times\ 4 \\ \hline \end{array}$ **31.** $\begin{array}{r} 74 \\ \times\ 7 \\ \hline \end{array}$ **32.** $\begin{array}{r} 59 \\ \times\ 8 \\ \hline \end{array}$ **33.** $\begin{array}{r} 65 \\ \times\ 3 \\ \hline \end{array}$ **34.** $\begin{array}{r} 88 \\ \times\ 6 \\ \hline \end{array}$

35. $\begin{array}{r} 27 \\ \times\ 8 \\ \hline \end{array}$ **36.** $\begin{array}{r} 93 \\ \times\ 4 \\ \hline \end{array}$ **37.** $\begin{array}{r} 52 \\ \times\ 5 \\ \hline \end{array}$ **38.** $\begin{array}{r} 47 \\ \times\ 8 \\ \hline \end{array}$ **39.** $\begin{array}{r} 46 \\ \times\ 3 \\ \hline \end{array}$

40. 9×24 **41.** 5×43 **42.** 7×55 **43.** 4×61 **44.** 7×68

45. Find the product of 3 and 42.

46. Find the product of 67 and 9.

47. How would you use regrouping to find the product of 23 and 9?

48. **Estimation** Use estimation to find the greater product: 906×3 or 806×4?

Problem Solving and Applications

49. **Time** Jerry has to read a book that has 157 pages. If he reads 15 pages a night, will he finish the book in a week? Explain.

Using Data Use the double-bar graph for **50–53.**

50. On which day did Jerry spend more time doing homework than Pam?

51. About how many hours did Jerry spend doing homework that week?

52. How much more time did Pam spend than Jerry doing homework that week?

53. **Write Your Own Problem** Write a question that can be answered using the bar graph. Ask a friend to solve it.

54. **Collecting Data** Work with a partner to keep track of the time you spend doing homework each day for a week. Make a double-bar graph of your data.

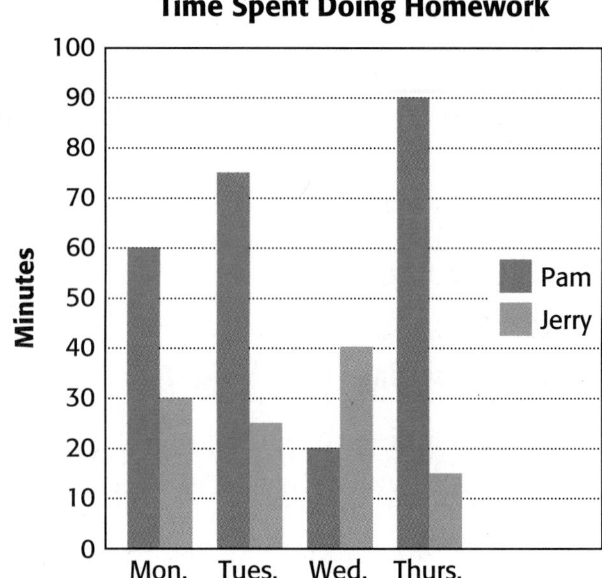

Problem Solving and SCIENCE

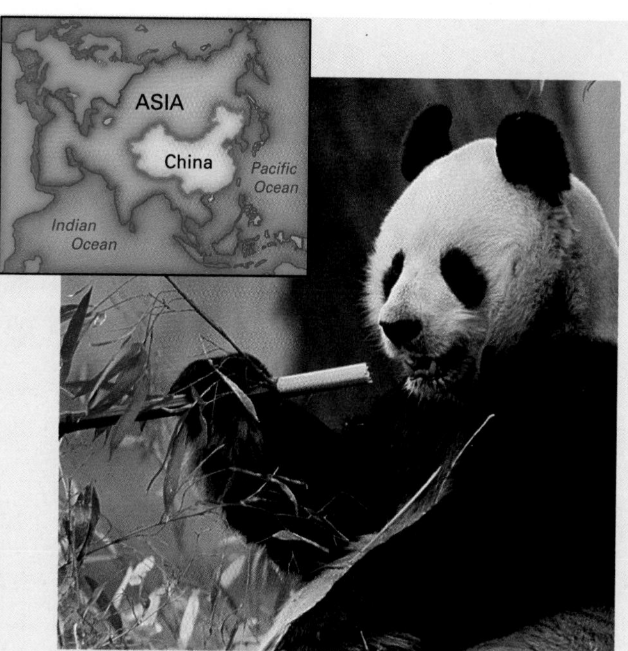

China is the home of the giant panda. Its Chinese name, Xiong Mao (shee-ung mow), means "giant cat bear." A giant panda eats about 32 pounds of bamboo leaves and stems each day. Giant pandas grow to 5 ft tall and weigh about 330 pounds.

55. About how many pounds of bamboo leaves and stems does a giant panda eat in a week?

56. A giant panda spends about 14 hours each day eating. How many hours in a week does a panda spend eating?

57. A giant panda eats about 84 pounds of bamboo shoots each day. About how many pounds does it eat in 5 days?

58. A zoo needs to transport 2 pandas to another zoo. The zoo has a medium-size truck that can hold 1,000 pounds. Will the truck be able to hold both pandas at the same time? Explain.

59. **Write Your Own Problem** Use the data about pandas. Write a question that can be answered using multiplication.

60. **Geography** The world's tallest mountain peak, Mt. Everest, is on the border of China and Nepal. It is almost 9,000 ft taller than Mt. McKinley. At 20,320 ft, Mt. McKinley is the tallest U.S. mountain. About how tall is Mt. Everest?

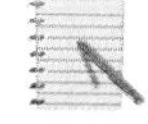

61. **Journal** How do you use place value to help you find 3×34?

Mixed Review and Test Prep

Algebra Readiness Find each missing number.

62. $4 \times n = 2{,}400$ **63.** $n \times 30 = 90$ **64.** $n \times 700 = 5{,}600$ **65.** $5 \times 200 = n$

66. $6 \times n = 36$ **67.** $n \times 4 = 36$ **68.** $18 \div n = 9$ **69.** $n \div 3 = 6$

70. **Estimation** A package of cookies contains 18 cookies. About how many cookies are in 4 packages?

Ⓐ 40 cookies Ⓑ 50 cookies Ⓒ 80 cookies Ⓓ not here

Skills Practice Bank, page 564, Set 2

Multiplying 3-Digit Numbers

You Will Learn
how to multiply a 3-digit number by a 1-digit number

Learn

Taz cares for worms that recycle garbage into rich soil. A start-up worm kit has 125 red worms.

Example 1

How many red worms are needed for 6 kits? Find 6×125.

Step 1	Step 2	Step 3
Multiply the ones. Regroup as needed.	Multiply the tens. Add any extra tens. Regroup as needed.	Multiply the hundreds. Add any extra hundreds.
$\begin{array}{r} \scriptstyle 3 \\ 125 \\ \times \quad 6 \\ \hline 0 \end{array}$	$\begin{array}{r} \scriptstyle 1\,3 \\ 125 \\ \times \quad 6 \\ \hline 50 \end{array}$	$\begin{array}{r} \scriptstyle 1\,3 \\ 125 \\ \times \quad 6 \\ \hline 750 \end{array}$

$6 \times 125 = 750$ So, 750 worms are needed for 6 kits.

Here's how to multiply when there's a zero in a 3-digit number.

Example 2

Find 8×208.

Step 1	Step 2	Step 3
Multiply the ones. Regroup as needed.	Multiply the tens. Add any extra tens. Regroup as needed.	Multiply the hundreds. Add any extra hundreds.
$\begin{array}{r} \scriptstyle 6 \\ 208 \\ \times \quad 8 \\ \hline 4 \end{array}$	$\begin{array}{r} \scriptstyle 6 \\ 208 \\ \times \quad 8 \\ \hline 64 \end{array}$	$\begin{array}{r} \scriptstyle 6 \\ 208 \\ \times \quad 8 \\ \hline 1{,}664 \end{array}$

$8 \times 208 = 1{,}664$

Remember
You can multiply this way, too.

$$\begin{array}{r} 208 \\ \times \quad 8 \\ \hline 64 \\ 0 \\ 1{,}600 \\ \hline 1{,}664 \end{array}$$

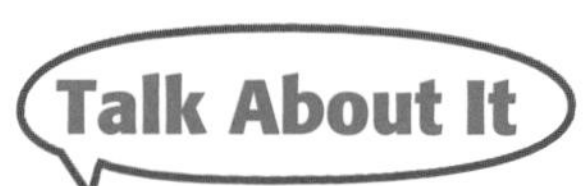

How can you estimate each product in the Examples?

Check

Multiply. Estimate to check.

1. $\begin{array}{r} 234 \\ \times \ 3 \\ \hline \end{array}$
2. $\begin{array}{r} 903 \\ \times \ 5 \\ \hline \end{array}$
3. $\begin{array}{r} 829 \\ \times \ 6 \\ \hline \end{array}$
4. $\begin{array}{r} 706 \\ \times \ 4 \\ \hline \end{array}$
5. $\begin{array}{r} 617 \\ \times \ 8 \\ \hline \end{array}$

6. **Reasoning** How could you use the product of 104 and 6 to find the product of 208 and 6?

Practice

Skills and Reasoning

Multiply. Estimate to check.

7. $\begin{array}{r} 301 \\ \times \ 8 \\ \hline \end{array}$
8. $\begin{array}{r} 562 \\ \times \ 6 \\ \hline \end{array}$
9. $\begin{array}{r} 408 \\ \times \ 3 \\ \hline \end{array}$
10. $\begin{array}{r} 346 \\ \times \ 5 \\ \hline \end{array}$
11. $\begin{array}{r} 608 \\ \times \ 7 \\ \hline \end{array}$
12. $\begin{array}{r} 613 \\ \times \ 4 \\ \hline \end{array}$
13. $\begin{array}{r} 204 \\ \times \ 8 \\ \hline \end{array}$
14. $\begin{array}{r} 647 \\ \times \ 4 \\ \hline \end{array}$
15. $\begin{array}{r} 302 \\ \times \ 7 \\ \hline \end{array}$
16. $\begin{array}{r} 404 \\ \times \ 9 \\ \hline \end{array}$

17. 783×9
18. 7×553
19. 5×641
20. 3×842

21. Find the product of 9 and 206.
22. Multiply 3 and 108.

Problem Solving and Applications

Using Data Taz measured some red worms. Use the table to answer **23** and **24**.

Worm Number	1	2	3	4	5	6	7
Length (mm)	63	100	123	55	71	86	128

23. Which two worms are about 2 times as long as worm 1?

24. **Science** An Australian worm is 8 times as long as worm 3. What is its length?

25. **Critical Thinking** Would 500 worms fill 4 start-up kits? Explain.

Mixed Review and Test Prep

Find each sum.

26. $78 + 53$
27. $43 + 29$
28. $472 + 309$
29. $298 + 379$

30. **Patterns** Complete the pattern. 600, 1,200, ■, 2,400

Ⓐ 1,500 Ⓑ 1,600 Ⓒ 1,800 Ⓓ 2,100

Skills Practice Bank, page 564, Set 3

Chapter 5
Lesson
7

Problem Solving

Decision Making: What's Cooking?

You Will Learn
how to solve problems by making decisions

Explore

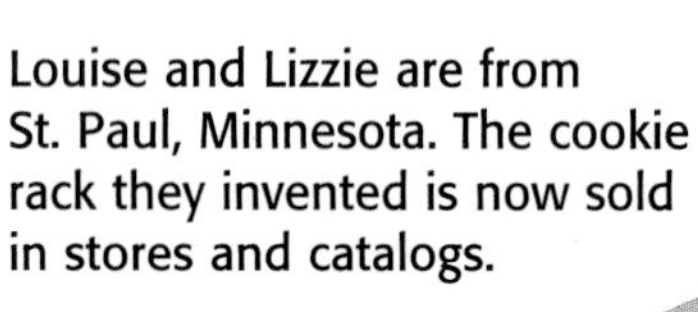

Louise and Lizzie invented a rack that holds 3 cookie sheets. Each cookie sheet holds 16 cookies. Your group has offered to bake cookies for Family Night at school. Plan to use one of Louise and Lizzie's racks. What kinds of cookies will you make? How many cookies will you make of each kind?

Louise and Lizzie are from St. Paul, Minnesota. The cookie rack they invented is now sold in stores and catalogs.

Facts and Data

You need to make at least 20 dozen cookies for Family Night.

You want to make at least three different kinds of cookies.

You have only two hours to bake the cookies.

The baking times and temperatures of some kinds of cookies are different.

Kind of Cookie	Quantity in Recipe	Number per Cookie Sheet	Baking Time	Temperature
Chocolate chip	3 dozen	12 cookies	20 min	350°F
Peanut butter	6 dozen	16 cookies	15 min	375°F
Almond	5 dozen	16 cookies	12 min	350°F
Gingersnaps	5 dozen	16 cookies	10 min	350°F
Cinnamon	4 dozen	16 cookies	12 min	375°F
Sugar	4 dozen	12 cookies	10 min	375°F

Work Together

Understand

1. What do you know?
2. What are you asked to do?
3. What is the main decision you have to make?

Plan and Solve

4. Which cookie recipe provides the greatest quantities?
5. Which kinds of cookies let you bake the most on a cookie sheet at one time?
6. Which cookies bake at the same temperature?
7. Which cookies do you want to make?
8. Find out how many of each kind of cookie you can bake at one time.

Problem Solving Tip

Estimate to help you make decisions.

Make a Decision

9. Write a list of the cookies that you plan to make.
10. How many cookies of each kind will you make?
11. What is the total amount of time you will spend baking cookies?

Present Your Decision

12. Tell how you arrived at your plan.
13. What activities related to making cookies does the table on page 216 not include?
14. Do you think you would still be able to make at least 20 dozen cookies within 2 hours?
15. How did you use multiplication to make decisions?
16. Check out **www.mathsurf.com/4/ch5** to look for cookie recipes. Then try a recipe to bake cookies for your friends.

Chapter 5
Lesson
8

Choosing a Calculation Method

You Will Learn
how to multiply using different methods

Learn

Jumping rope is no longer just a backyard sport. In one contest, the Happy Hoppers jump-rope team earned 3 points for each jump. How many points did the Happy Hoppers earn if the team jumped a total of 1,094 times?

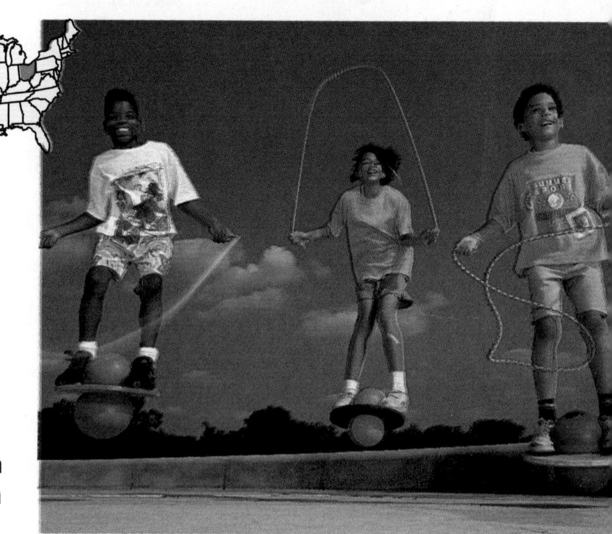

The Happy Hoppers, from Dayton, Ohio, compete in jump-rope contests.

Did You Know?
In 1988, 90 teenagers in Japan used a single jump rope to make 163 jumps in a row—all together.

John, Shauna, and Albert used different ways to find $3 \times 1{,}094$.

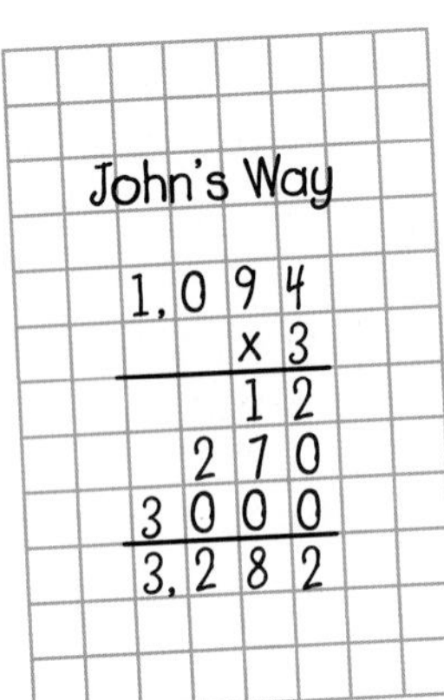

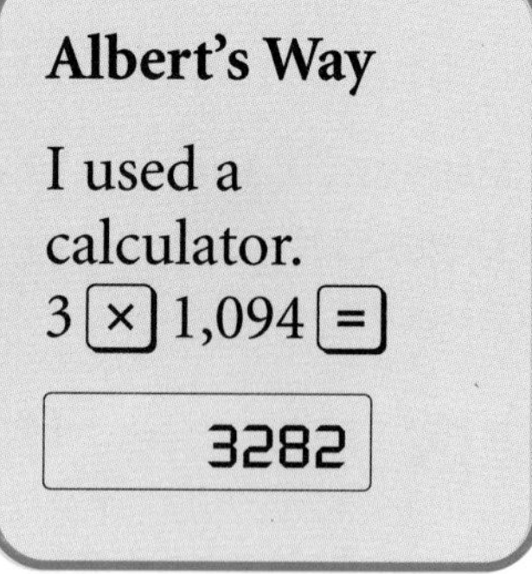

The Happy Hoppers earned 3,282 points.

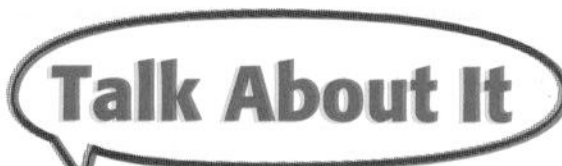

When might using a calculator be a good method for multiplying?

Check

Multiply.

1. $\begin{array}{r} 3{,}041 \\ \times \quad 6 \\ \hline \end{array}$ **2.** $\begin{array}{r} 1{,}907 \\ \times \quad 6 \\ \hline \end{array}$ **3.** $\begin{array}{r} 2{,}930 \\ \times \quad 4 \\ \hline \end{array}$ **4.** $\begin{array}{r} 4{,}221 \\ \times \quad 5 \\ \hline \end{array}$

5. Reasoning How would you find $3 \times 4{,}000$? Explain.

Practice

Skills and Reasoning

Multiply.

6. $2{,}567 \times 4$ 7. $4{,}623 \times 6$ 8. $8{,}061 \times 5$ 9. $6{,}000 \times 3$ 10. $8{,}513 \times 8$

11. $4{,}010 \times 3$ 12. $3{,}728 \times 4$ 13. $5{,}000 \times 3$ 14. $7{,}842 \times 9$ 15. $4{,}874 \times 7$

16. $8{,}009 \times 4$ 17. $9{,}000 \times 6$ 18. $9{,}726 \times 9$ 19. $6{,}736 \times 8$ 20. $7{,}309 \times 7$

21. **Mental Math** How would you use mental math to find $3{,}100 \times 2$?

22. Find the product of 8 and 7,009.

23. Multiply 6 and 5,437.

24. **Estimation** Is $4 \times 3{,}918$ greater than 15,000? Explain.

Problem Solving and Applications

25. In the game of "Bounce Off," you get 9 points if you jump rope and bounce a ball at the same time. The Happy Hoppers made 1,043 jumps and bounces. How many points did they get?

26. **Science** There are about 7,688 giant redwood seeds in 1 oz of seeds. About how many seeds are there in half a pound?

Remember
16 ounces (oz) = 1 pound (lb)

27. **Using Data** Use the Data File on page 197. Which activities have the same health rating as jumping rope?

Mixed Review and Test Prep

Find each quotient.

28. $18 \div 9$ 29. $54 \div 6$ 30. $63 \div 9$ 31. $21 \div 3$

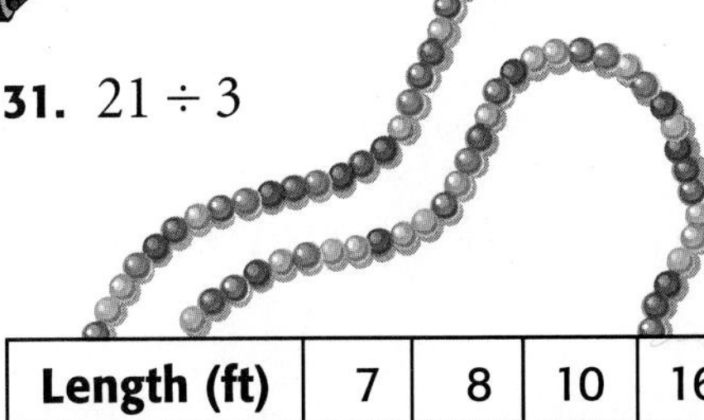

32. **Using Data** Use the table to answer. Ms. Owens ordered eight 10-ft jump ropes, eight 8-ft jump ropes, and two 16-ft jump ropes for her P.E. class. How much did the order cost?

Ⓐ \$176 Ⓑ \$106

Ⓒ \$84 Ⓓ \$66

Length (ft)	7	8	10	16
Price	\$4	\$5	\$6	\$9

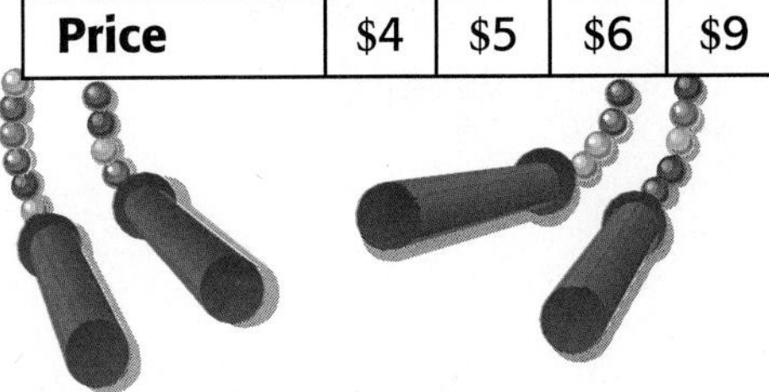

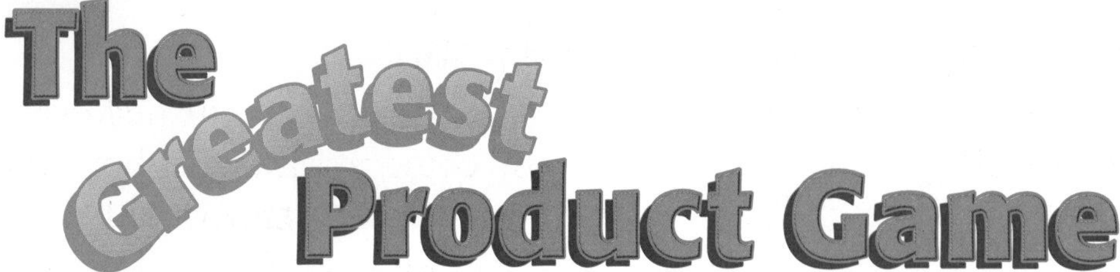

The Greatest Product Game

Players
2 or more

Materials
set of digit cards

0	1	2	3	4
5	6	7	8	9

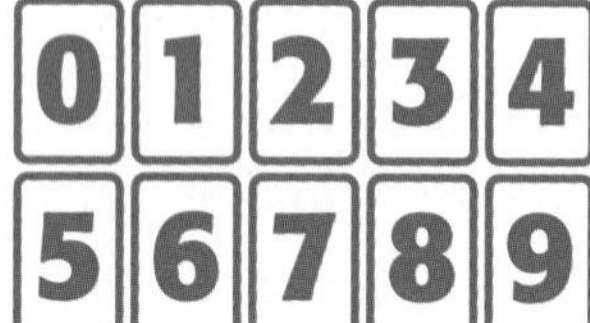

Object
The object of the game is to make a multiplication problem with the greatest product.

How to Play

1. Each player draws a multiplication grid like the one below. Shuffle the cards and lay them face down.

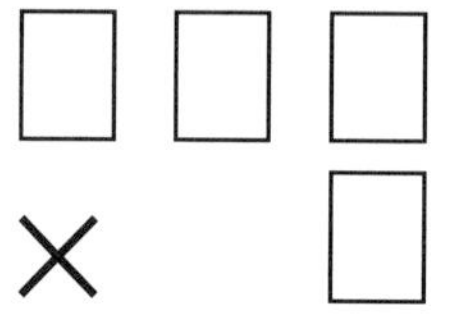

2. One player turns over a card. Each player writes that number in any box on his or her multiplication grid.

Jan's Grid

Jim's Grid

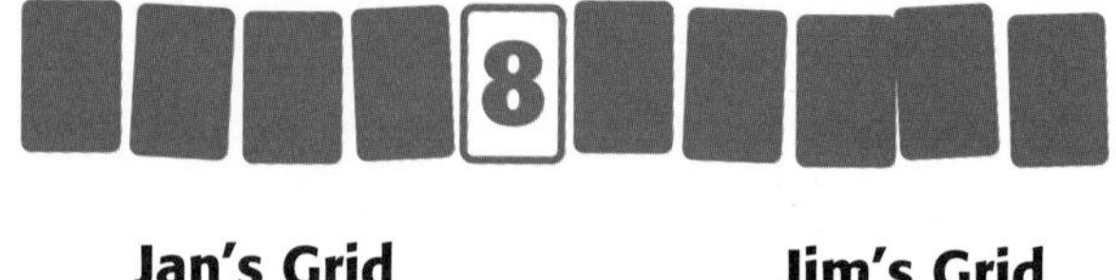

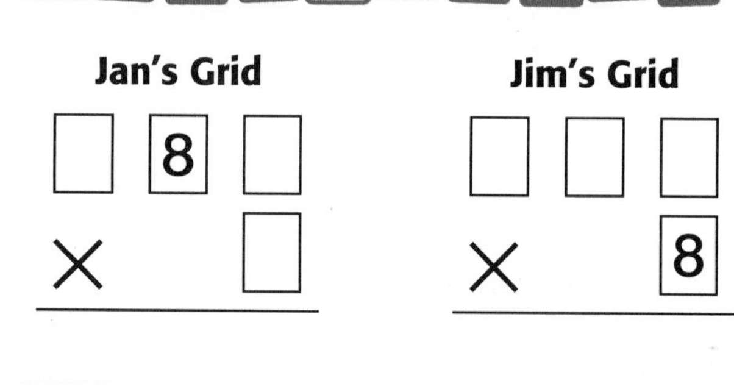

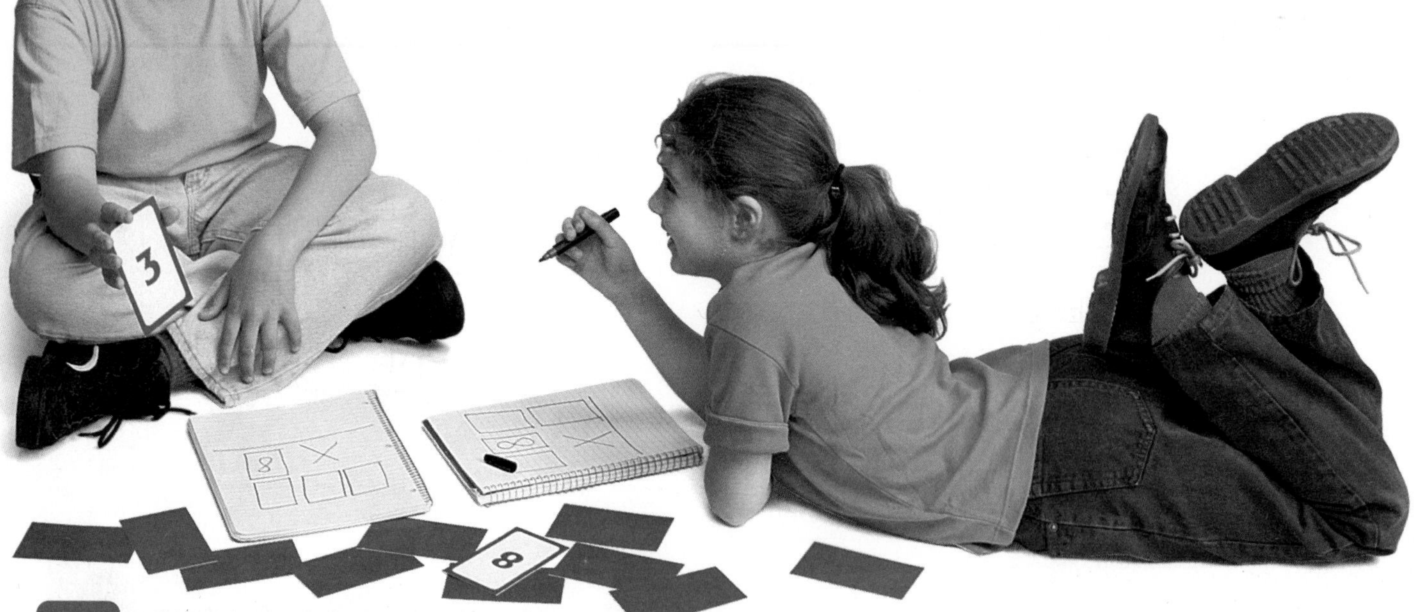

3. A player continues turning over cards until players have placed numbers in all of the boxes on the grid.

4. Multiply. The player with the greatest product wins.

5. Play five or more games. Look for winning strategies.

Talk About It

1. What strategies did you use to get the greatest product?
2. Which card did you least like to turn over? Why?

More Ways to Play

- Play again. Use a grid like this.

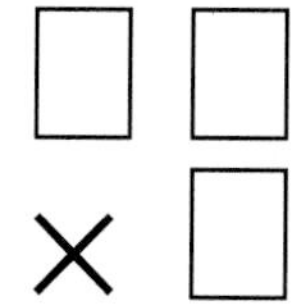

- Play another game. Use either grid. This time the winner is the player with the least product.
- Play the game using this grid.

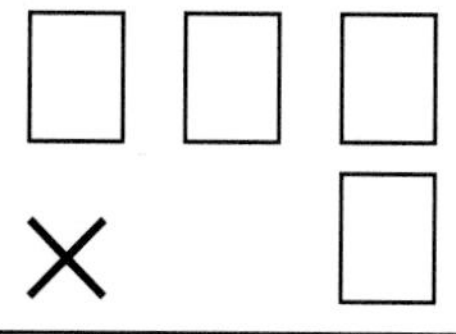

The winner is the player who gets closest to 3,000 or any number players choose.

Reasoning

1. Suppose an 8 were turned over and you could put it in any box on this grid. What strategy would you use if you were playing the Greatest Product Game?

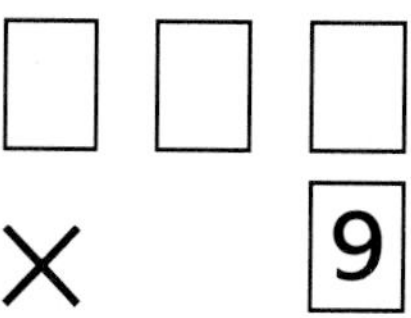

2. Suppose you turned over a 9 to put on this grid. What strategy would you use if you were playing the Greatest Product Game?

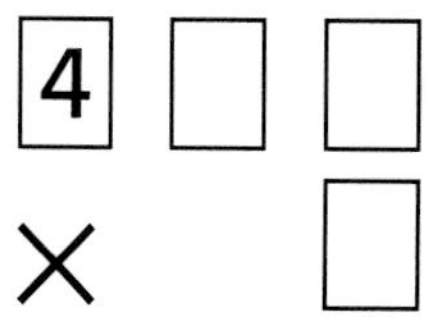

3. Suppose your grid looks like this in the Least Product Game. What number do you hope to pick next so that you get the least product? Explain why it is the best number.

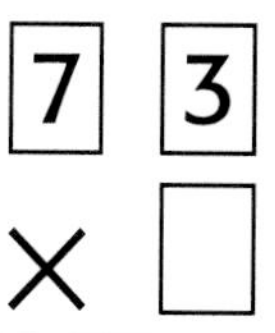

4. **What If** You are playing a game called Closest to 3,000. How can you arrange the digits in this grid to get closest to 3,000?

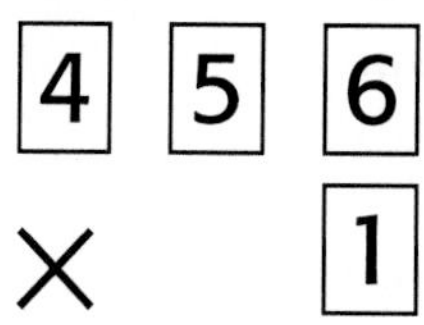

SECTION B

Review and Practice

Vocabulary Choose the word that best completes each sentence.

1. Addition, subtraction, multiplication, and division are ____.

Ⓐ estimates   Ⓑ products   Ⓒ operations   Ⓓ factors

2. You can ____ 32 ones as 3 tens and 2 ones.

Ⓐ multiply   Ⓑ estimate   Ⓒ regroup   Ⓓ add

(Lesson 5) Find each product. Estimate to check.

3. 37×4 **4.** 18×9 **5.** 29×6 **6.** 86×7 **7.** 34×8

8. 2×53 **9.** 64×5 **10.** 76×4 **11.** 3×92 **12.** 6×47

13. Find the product of 58 and 6.   **14.** Find the product of 8 and 46.

(Lesson 6) Multiply.

15. 236×3 **16.** 756×2 **17.** 709×6 **18.** 450×3 **19.** 805×5

20. 347×4 **21.** 406×6 **22.** 812×6 **23.** Find the product of 805 and 5.

(Lesson 7) Solve each problem.

24. Four students baked 16 muffins each. How many muffins did they bake in all?

25. Joel ate 4 carrots and had 16 left. How many carrots did he start with?

(Lesson 8) Multiply.

26. $1{,}347 \times 7$ **27.** $6{,}058 \times 8$ **28.** $5{,}608 \times 4$

29. $5{,}079 \times 8$ **30.** $2{,}489 \times 2$ **31.** $1{,}235 \times 6$

32. **Critical Thinking** Suppose you used a calculator to find $8{,}562 \times 7$ and got 5,992. How could you tell that this is not the right answer?

33. **Journal** Describe each step you would follow to find $4{,}539 \times 6$.

Skills Checklist

In this section, you have:

- ☑ Multiplied 2-Digit Numbers
- ☑ Multiplied 3-Digit Numbers
- ☑ Solved Problems by Making Decisions
- ☑ Learned to Choose a Calculation Method

REVIEW AND PRACTICE

Extending Multiplication

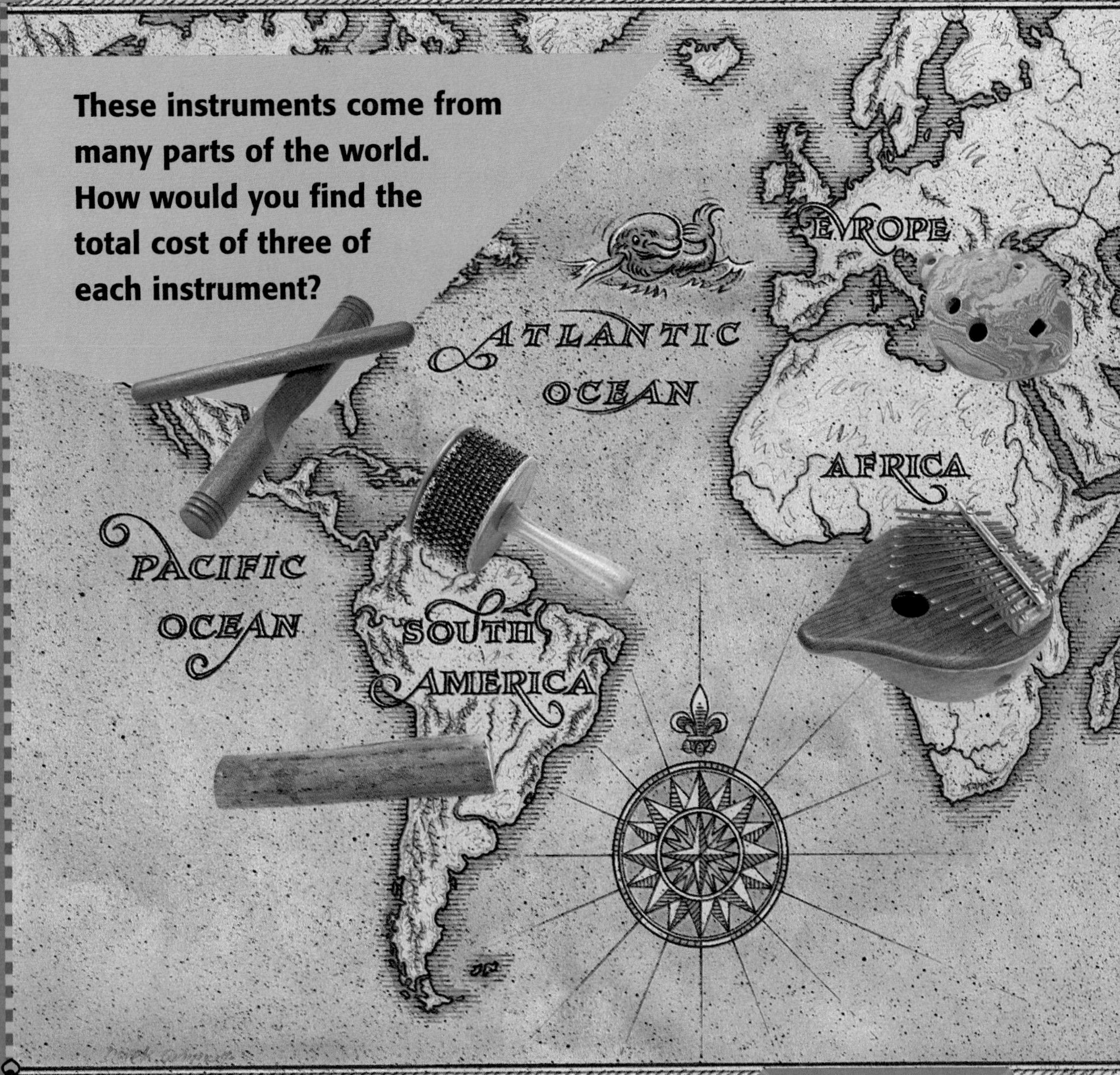

GET READY!

Multiplying Money

Review how to add money. Find each sum.

1. \$3.75 + \$3.75 + \$3.75
2. \$1.50 + \$1.50 + \$1.50 + \$1.50 + \$1.50
3. \$12.25 + \$12.25 + \$12.25 + \$12.25
4. \$15.75 + \$15.75 + \$15.75 + \$15.75

Skills Checklist

In this section, you will:

- ❒ Multiply Money
- ❒ Find Special Products
- ❒ Multiply Three Factors
- ❒ Solve Multiple-Step Problems
- ❒ Solve Problems by Making a Table

Chapter 5
Lesson
9

Multiplying Money

You Will Learn
how to multiply amounts of money

Learn

"Swimmers, take your marks," the starter shouts. BANG! The swimmers spring into action and dive into the pool. The Seahawks Swim Team sells T-shirts and other items to raise money to travel to its swim meets.

Multiplying amounts of money is like multiplying whole numbers.

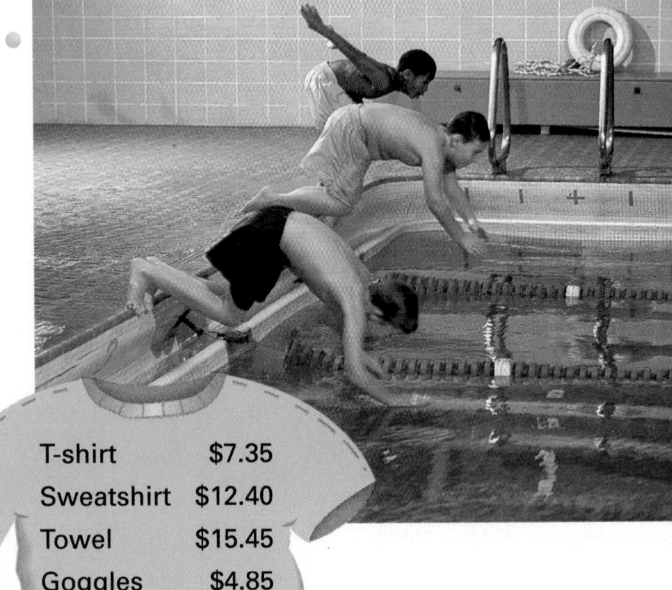

T-shirt	$7.35
Sweatshirt	$12.40
Towel	$15.45
Goggles	$4.85

Example

Rob wants to buy 3 T-shirts. How much money does he need?

To find the cost of 3 T-shirts, multiply $7.35 by 3.

Step 1

```
  1 1
 $7.35
×    3
 2205
```

Multiply the same way as with whole numbers.

Step 2

```
   1 1
 $7.35
×    3
$22.05
```

Write the answer in dollars and cents.

Rob needs $22.05 to buy 3 T-shirts.

Math Tip
2205 is not the same as $22.05.

Talk About It

Suppose you forgot to write the answer in dollars and cents. Would your answer make sense? Explain.

Check

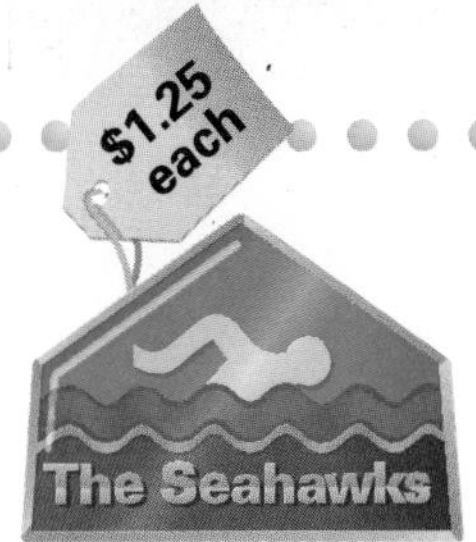

Find each cost.

1. 3 pins **2.** 8 pins **3.** 5 pins **4.** 6 pins

5. Reasoning Is $8.00 enough to buy 7 pins? Explain.

Practice

Skills and Reasoning

Find each product.

6.	**7.**	**8.**	**9.**	**10.**
$1.37 × 7	$2.70 × 4	$34.75 × 5	$20.04 × 6	$14.99 × 8

11. 5 × $32.75 **12.** 9 × $2.21 **13.** 3 × $4.75 **14.** 4 × $51.25

Find each cost.

15. 2 fish magnets **16.** 4 fish magnets

17. 9 bird magnets **18.** 7 bird magnets

19. Is $12.00 enough to buy 5 fish magnets?

Problem Solving and Applications

20. How much would 5 sweatshirts cost? Use the data on page 224.

21. Logic Who was last to swim in the relay race? Raúl swam after Jamal. Toby started the race. Nick was not the fourth swimmer.

Using Data Use the table to answer **22** and **23.**

22. How much more did 6 energy bars cost in 1996 than in 1991?

23. Would $5.00 have bought 4 comic books and a hamburger in 1991? Explain.

	1991 Price	1996 Price
Comic Book	$0.75	$1.45
Hamburger	$1.45	$1.65
Energy Bar	$0.99	$1.69

Mixed Review and Test Prep

STAY SHARP!

Patterns Copy and complete.

24. 12, 36, 108, ■, ■, ■ **25.** 10, 40, 160, ■, ■, ■ **26.** 4, 20, 100, ■, ■, ■

27. Find the number that means 3 thousands, 8 tens, 7 ones.

Ⓐ 18 Ⓑ 315 Ⓒ 387 Ⓓ not here

STOP and Practice

Find each product. Estimate to check.

1. 63 × 4	**2.** 43 × 8	**3.** 98 × 3	**4.** 46 × 5	**5.** 68 × 7
6. 58 × 5	**7.** 93 × 3	**8.** 59 × 7	**9.** 83 × 6	**10.** 39 × 5
11. 712 × 6	**12.** 204 × 8	**13.** 647 × 4	**14.** 408 × 8	**15.** 534 × 9
16. 1,879 × 6	**17.** 2,302 × 7	**18.** 3,604 × 7	**19.** 4,523 × 5	**20.** 7,968 × 6
21. $8.79 × 6	**22.** $2.02 × 7	**23.** $6.04 × 4	**24.** $5.20 × 9	**25.** $7.08 × 8
26. $18.79 × 6	**27.** $24.02 × 7	**28.** $65.04 × 7	**29.** $25.20 × 5	**30.** $70.08 × 8
31. 68 × 4	**32.** 6 × 932	**33.** 893 × 9	**34.** 8 × 592	**35.** 219 × 3
36. 403 × 2	**37.** 806 × 4	**38.** 6 × 2,932	**39.** 8,893 × 9	**40.** 409 × 8
41. 8 × 5,092	**42.** 4,803 × 3	**43.** 8 × $3.92	**44.** $9.03 × 5	**45.** 7 × $21.99
46. 6 × $46.32	**47.** $59.03 × 7	**48.** 2,124 × 3	**49.** 6 × 78	**50.** 8 × 555

Error Search

Find each product that is not correct. Write it correctly and explain the error.

51. 234 × 9 = 1,876	**52.** 1,207 × 6 = 7,242	**53.** $3.96 × 5 = $1,980.00	**54.** $32.90 × 8 = $246.20	**55.** 880 × 3 = 2,640

Something Fishy!

Multiply to solve the riddle. Match each letter to its answer in the blank below. Some letters are not used.

A group of fish is called a school. What is a group of toads called?

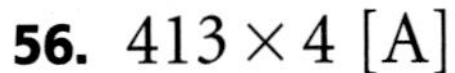

56. 413×4 [A] **57.** 312×8 [M] **58.** 105×4 [H] **59.** 41×9 [T]

60. 453×2 [N] **61.** 270×7 [C] **62.** 512×9 [W] **63.** 214×5 [R]

64. 71×6 [O] **65.** 633×3 [K] **66.** 139×3 [D] **67.** 704×5 [P]

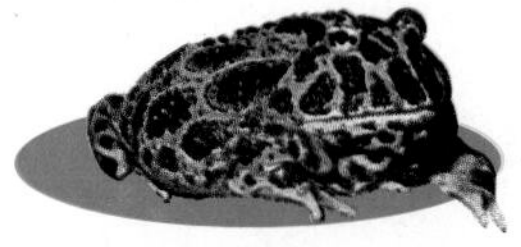

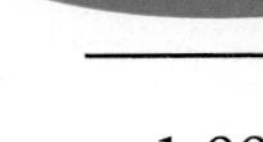

______ ______ ______ ______ ______

1,652 1,899 906 426 369

Number Sense Estimation and Reasoning

Write whether each statement is true or false. Explain your answer.

68. The product of 4 and 22 is greater than 100.

69. The product of 7 and 800 is less than 5,000.

70. The product of 5 and 400 is greater than 1,500.

71. The product of 3 and 52 is 6 more than 150.

72. The product of 6 and 73 is closer to 420 than 430.

73. The product of 8 and 600 is 800 more than 4,800.

74. The product of 2 and 301 is greater than the product of 3 and 201.

Chapter 5 Lesson 10

Mental Math: Special Products

You Will Learn
two different methods of using mental math to multiply

Learn

Adam and Patti play the computer game "Insect Power." Each insect they collect scores 3 points.

Adam collected 32 insects.
To find his score, he multiplies 32 and 3.

I think of 32 as $30 + 2$.
30×3 is 90.
2×3 is 6.
$90 + 6 = 96$. So, $32 \times 3 = 96$.
My score is 96.

Patti collected 49 insects.
To find her score, she multiplies 49 and 3.

I think of 49 as almost 50.
50×3 is 150.
Subtract 1 group of 3.
$150 - 3 = 147$.
So, $49 \times 3 = 147$.
My score is 147.

Did You Know?
One of the first popular video games was Pong, which was developed in the 1970s. A winning score was 21.

Talk About It

How do these methods make it easier to multiply mentally?

Check

Use Adam's method to find each product.

1. 41×6 **2.** 8×52 **3.** 63×2 **4.** 81×4 **5.** 4×92

Use Patti's method to find each product.

6. 3×39 **7.** 28×5 **8.** 4×79 **9.** 58×3 **10.** 8×59

11. Reasoning Which method would you use to find 48×6? Explain.

Practice

Skills and Reasoning

Mental Math Find each product.

12. 32×6	**13.** 7×19	**14.** 8×61	**15.** 59×5	**16.** 9×81
17. 51×6	**18.** 99×8	**19.** 3×72	**20.** 32×5	**21.** 5×29
22. 51×2	**23.** 49×6	**24.** 22×6	**25.** 6×71	**26.** 88×3
27. 7×39	**28.** 59×3	**29.** 38×6	**30.** 2×91	**31.** 9×21

32. Find the product of 42 and 5 mentally.

33. Multiply 6 and 39 mentally.

34. Would you use addition or subtraction to find 26×8 mentally? Explain.

Problem Solving and Applications

35. Money A computer game costs $19. Use mental math to find how much it will cost for 8 computer games.

Dragonfly

36. Technology In 1990, a CD-ROM could transfer data at about 150 kilobytes per second. By 1996, CD-ROMs could transfer data about 8 times as fast. Estimate the speed of a 1996 CD-ROM.

37. Algebra Readiness A CD rack holds 12 CDs. How many racks would you need to hold 84 CDs?

38. Science There are about 6,500 kinds of dragonflies and 2,000 kinds of praying mantis. How many more kinds of dragonflies are there than praying mantis?

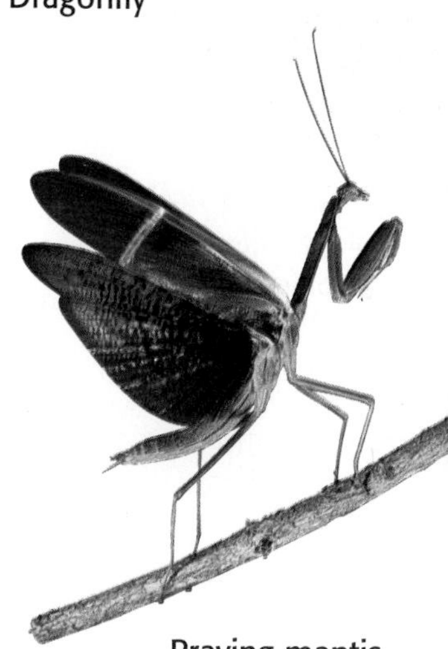

Praying mantis

39. Collecting Data Make a list of 5 video games. Ask your classmates to name their favorites. Then make a bar graph to show the class data.

40. Journal Explain how you would use the mental math strategies in this lesson to find 59×4 and 71×6.

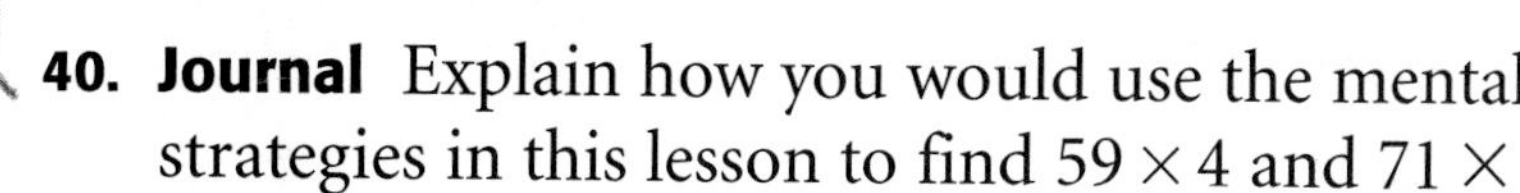

Mixed Review and Test Prep

Find each sum or difference.

41. $2,500 - 375$ **42.** $906 + 48$ **43.** $735 - 217$ **44.** $13,195 + 504$

45. Which has a greater product than 18×7?

Ⓐ 23×4 Ⓑ 16×8 Ⓒ 27×3 Ⓓ 15×8

Chapter 5
Lesson
11

Multiplying 3 Factors

You Will Learn
how to multiply when you have three factors

Vocabulary
grouping property
when the grouping of factors is changed, the product remains the same

Learn

Ashley spends a lot of her free time dancing. She competes in Scottish Highland dance and has won many championships.

The Highland fling can have 6 steps. Each step takes up 8 bars of music. And each bar has 4 counts. How many counts are in the fling?

Ashley lives in Shelby Township, Michigan.

Find $6 \times 8 \times 4$.

Here are some ways you can find the product when there are 3 factors. The parentheses tell which factors to multiply first.

Did You Know?
There are about 3,000 official tartan plaids. A tartan plaid is a kind of woven cloth with different color patterns.

Example 1	**Example 2**	**Example 3**
Multiply these first.	Multiply these first.	Pick any two. Try these.
↓ ↓	↓ ↓	↓ ↓
$(6 \times 8) \times 4$	$6 \times (8 \times 4)$	$6 \times 8 \times 4$
$48 \times 4 = 192$	$6 \times 32 = 192$	$24 \times 8 = 192$

There are 192 counts in this Highland Fling.

The examples show the **grouping property**. Changing the grouping of the factors does not change the product.

In what way are $(3 \times 2) \times 7$ and $3 \times (2 \times 7)$ the same? Different?

Check

Find each product.

1. $4 \times 7 \times 5$ **2.** $3 \times 2 \times 5$ **3.** $4 \times 9 \times 8$ **4.** $6 \times 7 \times 3$

5. Reasoning What is an easy way to multiply $4 \times 8 \times 25$? Explain.

Practice

Skills and Reasoning

Find each product.

6. $(2 \times 14) \times 6$ **7.** $4 \times (9 \times 7)$ **8.** $(11 \times 5) \times 2$ **9.** $8 \times (7 \times 6)$

10. $3 \times (5 \times 4)$ **11.** $(2 \times 5) \times 8$ **12.** $(25 \times 3) \times 3$ **13.** $7 \times (16 \times 5)$

14. $(81 \times 2) \times 4$ **15.** $(3 \times 8) \times 9$ **16.** $(5 \times 6) \times 7$ **17.** $6 \times (2 \times 7)$

Find each product.

18. $12 \times 8 \times 5$ **19.** $6 \times 9 \times 11$ **20.** $4 \times 4 \times 7$ **21.** $5 \times 7 \times 6$

22. Write $5 \times 6 \times 8$ in three different ways.

23. Write $6 \times 9 \times 0$ in three different ways. Then solve.

Problem Solving and Applications

24. Music One version of the Strathspey reel has 2 steps. Each step has 16 bars of music. Each bar has 4 counts. What's the total number of counts?

Use the diagram to answer **25** and **26.**

25. Geometry Readiness Each letter shows a dancer's starting position. Follow the arrows. How many times will dancer A change places to come back to where he or she started?

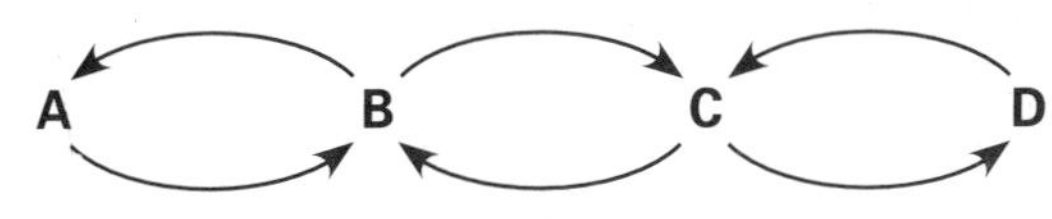

26. Logic When dancers A and B pass each other, which shoulder (right or left) will be nearest the other dancer?

27. Patterns If green is next in this tartan plaid, what color comes after that?

28. Calculator After 23 hours and 44 minutes, Roy Castle stopped tap dancing. How many minutes was that in all?

Mixed Review and Test Prep

Find each answer.

29. $491 + 837$ **30.** $2{,}006 - 1{,}924$ **31.** $1{,}433 + 297$ **32.** $3{,}051 - 2{,}834$

33. Which number sentence is in the same family of facts as $16 - 9 = 7$?

Ⓐ $16 + 7 = 23$ Ⓑ $16 \times 9 = 144$ Ⓒ $9 + 7 = 16$ Ⓓ $16 + 9 = 25$

Skills Practice Bank, page 565, Set 6

Problem Solving

Analyze Word Problems: Multiple-Step Problems

You Will Learn
how to solve problems that have more than one step

Learn

The World Beat band plays instruments from around the world. Joy must order 8 ocarinas, 6 rainsticks, and 2 cabaças (kuh BAS ahs) for the next performance. How much money will she need?

Claves, Haiti $6.90

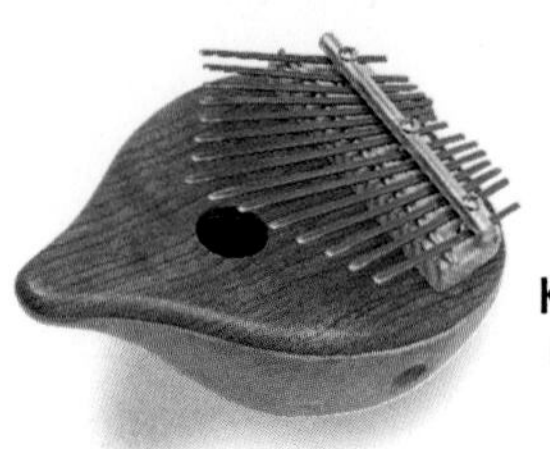
Kalimba, Uganda $18.50

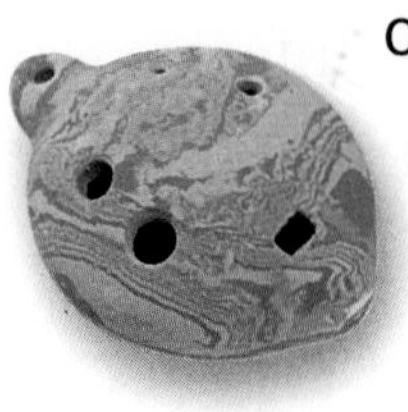
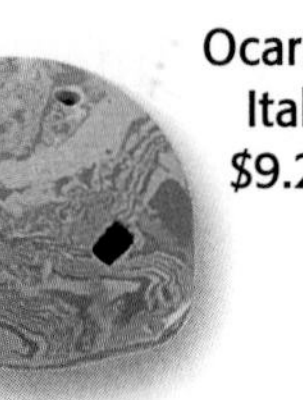
Ocarina, Italy $9.20

Cabaça, South America $9.50

Rainstick, Chile $8.75

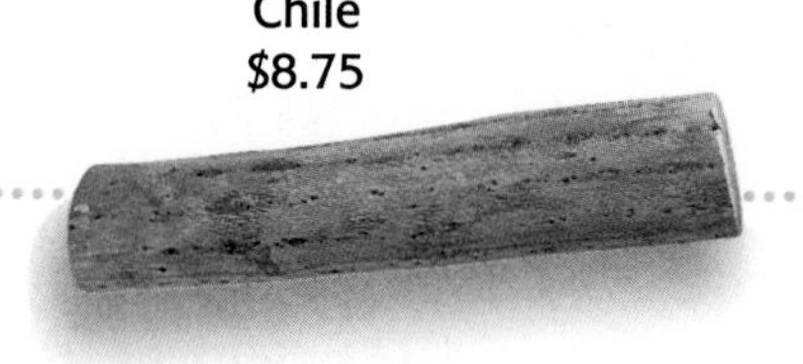

Work Together

▶ Understand

What do you know?

What do you need to find out?

▶ Plan

How can you begin? Multiply to find the cost of each instrument.

What's the next step? Add to find the total cost.

▶ Solve

Step 1: Multiply.

Ocarinas	Rainsticks	Cabaças
$9.20	$8.75	$9.50
× 8	× 6	× 2
$73.60	$52.50	$19.00

Step 2: Add. $73.60 + $52.50 + $19.00 = $145.10

What's the answer? Joy needs $145.10 to buy the instruments.

▶ Look Back

How can you check if your answer makes sense?

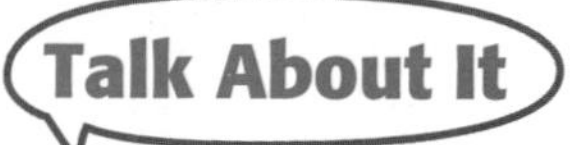

Why does it take two steps to solve this problem?

Check

Use the prices shown on page 232 to solve **1–3**.

1. Suppose Joy wanted 6 ocarinas and 5 cabaças.
   a. How much money would she need for each type of instrument?
   b. How much money would she need in all?
2. How much would it cost to buy 4 ocarinas, 8 kalimbas, and 2 rainsticks?
3. Joy has $100. If she bought 9 sets of claves, how much money would she have left?

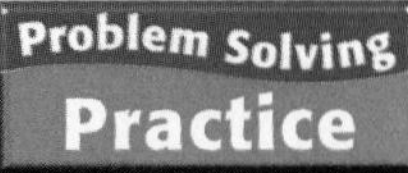

Problem Solving Practice

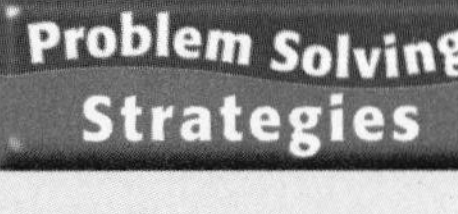

Problem Solving Strategies

- Use Objects/Act It Out
- Draw a Picture
- Look for a Pattern
- Guess and Check
- Use Logical Reasoning
- Make an Organized List
- Make a Table
- Solve a Simpler Problem
- Work Backward

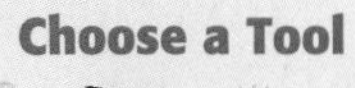

Choose a Tool

Use the prices shown on page 232 to solve **4–7**.

4. How much money do you need for 7 ocarinas, 9 rainsticks, and 1 kalimba?
5. Joy's aunt pays her $1.50 to walk her dog. Could Joy afford a cabaça if she walked the dog 6 times? Explain.
6. Joy has $50. She ordered 5 rainsticks. What is her change?
7. How much more would you pay for 8 cabaças than for 8 rainsticks?
8. **Music** American folk music typically has about 120 beats per minute. Akadinda music played in western Africa can reach about 10 beats *per second.* How many more beats per minute are played in akadinda than in American folk music?
9. In the World Beat band, 3 rows of students wear red T-shirts, 2 rows wear blue T-shirts, and 1 row wears green T-shirts. If there are 12 students in each row, how many students are in the band? What strategy did you use?
10. To raise money for the band, Patti sold 5 boxes of dried fruit. Eddie sold 7 boxes of granola bars. If a box of dried fruit costs $3.20 and a box of granola bars costs $2.75, how much did Patti and Eddie collect?
11. **Time** Craig went to the band practice at 7:30 P.M. Practice had started 45 minutes earlier. What time did the practice start?

Problem Solving

Analyze Strategies: Make a Table

You Will Learn
how to solve problems by making a table

Learn

Put on your creative hat! How many pattern pieces do you need to make a headband with 7 stars? One star has 6 pattern pieces. Two pattern pieces link the stars.

1 star

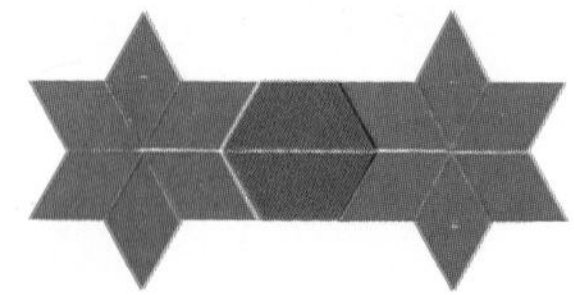
2 stars

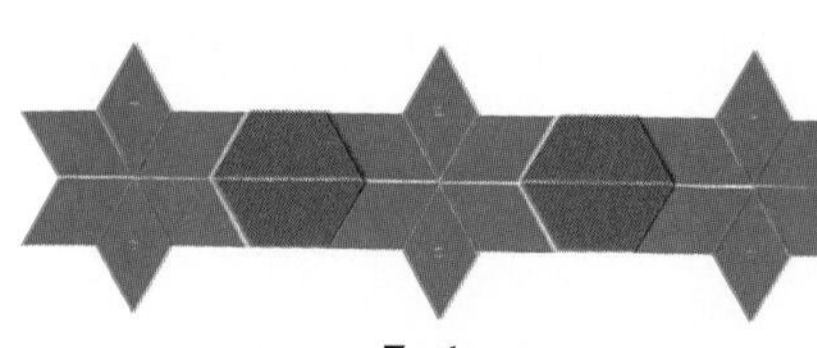
3 stars

Ojibwa (oh JIB wah) headband

Work Together

▶ Understand

What do you know?

What do you need to find out?

▶ Plan

Think how you might organize the data in a table. Decide what it will show.

Label a column *Number of Stars.* Label another column called *Number of Pieces.*

▶ Solve

Make the table. Fill in what you know.

Keep filling in the table.

Use the table to complete the pattern.

Number of Stars	Number of Pieces
1	6
2	14
3	22
4	30
5	38
6	46
7	54

Problem Solving Hint
You can use Power Polygons or draw a picture to help you see a pattern.

What is the answer?

With 7 stars, there are 54 pieces in all.

▶ Look Back

How can you check your answer?

Another Example

If you continue this pattern until there are 5 stars, how many pieces will you need?

Make a table.

What You See

a. A star is made up of 6 pieces.

b. A star is linked to another star by 6 green triangles.

c. Continue the pattern until there are 5 stars.

What You Do

Number of Stars	Number of Pieces
1	6
2	18
3	30
4	42
5	?

When this pattern has 5 stars, there will be 54 pieces in all.

Talk About It

1. How do the tables help you solve the problems?
2. What patterns did you find in the second table?

Check

Copy and complete the table. Use Power Polygons or draw a picture to help you see a pattern.

1. If your pattern has 4 blue rectangles, how many pieces will it have in all?
2. If you use 5 blue rectangles, how many pieces will you have?
3. **Reasoning** How could you make a table that shows how the number of squares changes with the growing pattern?

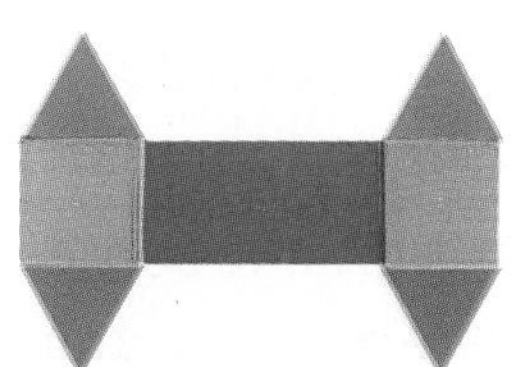

Number of Blue Rectangles	Number of Pieces
1	7
2	11
3	15
4	
5	

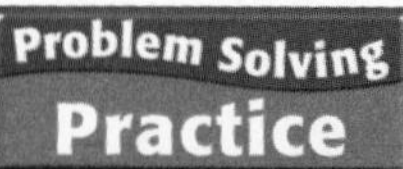

Apply the Strategy

Copy and complete each table to help you solve the problems.

Number of Squares	Number of Pieces
1	4
2	9
3	14
4	

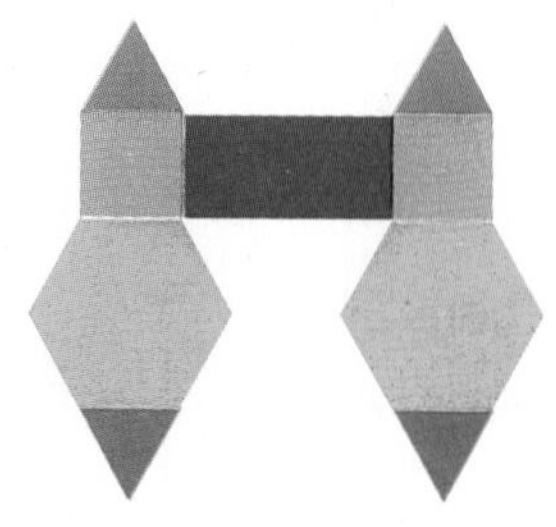

Problem Solving Strategies

- Use Objects/Act It Out
- Draw a Picture
- Look for a Pattern
- Guess and Check
- Use Logical Reasoning
- Make an Organized List
- Make a Table
- Solve a Simpler Problem
- Work Backward

Choose a Tool

4. If your pattern has 4 squares, how many pieces will it have in all?

5. If your pattern has 5 squares, how many pieces will it have in all?

6. If your pattern has 8 blue rectangles, how many squares will it have?

7. A drummer played traditional tribal music at the fair. He gave 6 shows. Each one lasted 15 minutes. By the end of the fourth show, how many minutes had he played?

Performance	Minutes
1	15
2	

Choose a Strategy

Use any strategy to solve each problem.

8. A 9-inch piece of trimming has a pattern of 27 triangles.

   a. Suppose you make some trimming with the same pattern and the same size triangles, but make it 18 inches long. How many triangles will there be?

   b. Suppose you want to make some trimming that is 27 inches long. How many triangles will there be?

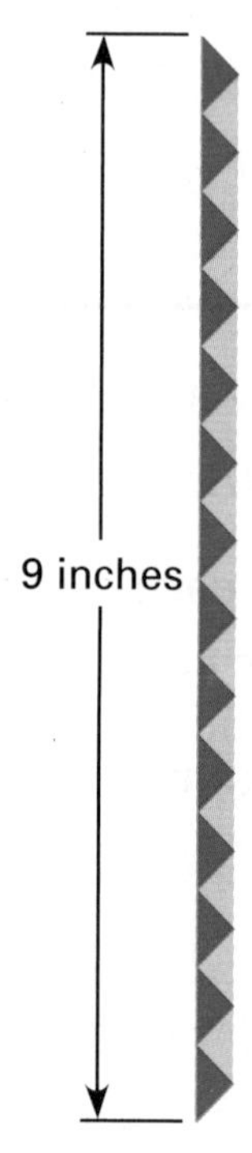

9. **Using Data** Use the Data File on page 197 for the meatless pemmican recipe.

   a. If you want to serve 24 people, how would you increase the amount of each ingredient?

   b. What will change as you increase the recipe, the number of ingredients or the amount of each ingredient?

Problem Solving and FINE ARTS

Navajo create fine handweaving. Many regions have their own designs.

In any Navajo rug, the wool threads are pulled tightly and evenly. Typically, a Wide Ruins rug has about 8 vertical (warp) threads per inch. Typically, there are about 44 horizontal (weft) threads per inch.

Using Data Use the data and pictures for **10** and **11**.

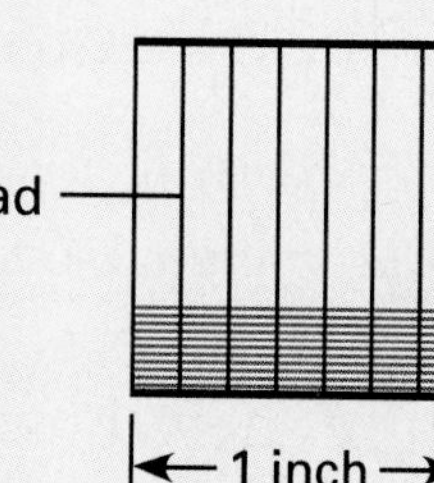

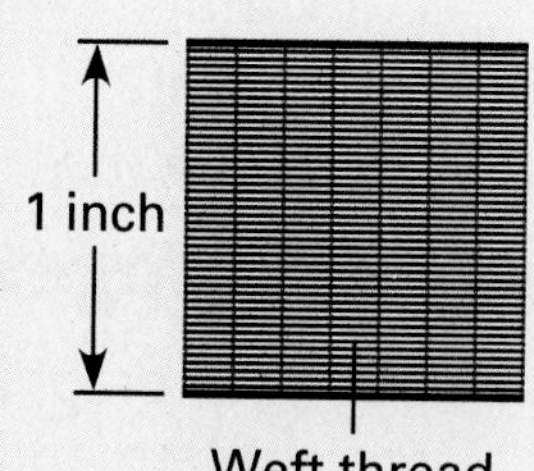

10. If a weaver wants to make a rug that is 23 inches wide, how many warp threads will be needed?

11. Typically, how many weft threads should there be in 5 inches?

12. Write Your Own Problem Draw your own design that has a pattern. Explain it.

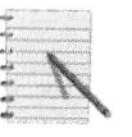

13. Journal Write your favorite recipe. Tell how you would change the recipe to serve the number of students in your class. Explain how making a table could help you change the recipe.

Mixed Review and Test Prep

Find each product.

14. $6 \times 3 \times 4$ **15.** $8 \times 2 \times 7$ **16.** $2 \times 9 \times 4$ **17.** $5 \times 7 \times 4$

Find each quotient.

18. $54 \div 6$ **19.** $49 \div 7$ **20.** $42 \div 6$ **21.** $48 \div 8$ **22.** $36 \div 9$

Patterns Copy and complete each pattern.

23. 7, 14, 21, ■, ■, ■ **24.** 2, 6, 18, ■, ■, ■ **25.** 15, ■, 45, 60, ■, ■

26. Admission to the fair is $3.00 per adult and $1.50 per child. How much would it cost for a family of 3 children and 2 adults?

Ⓐ $10.50 Ⓑ $15.00 Ⓒ $7.50 Ⓓ $12.50

Technology

Comparing Costs

When the curtain lifts, all you'll see are eyes! That's the effect the Drama Club wants for the opening scene of "Eyes on You." The club plans to order plastic eyeballs.

Materials

DataWonder! or other graphing software

The Drama Club needs to order:

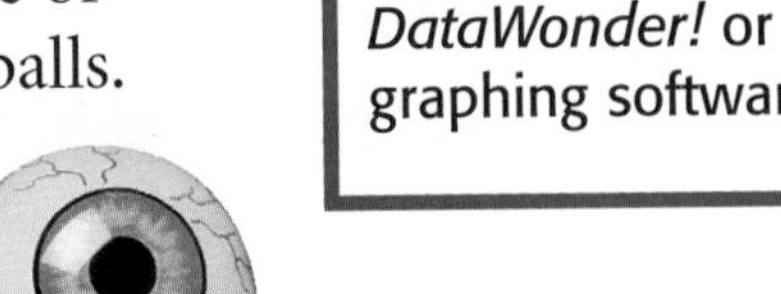

3 Glow-in-the-Dark Eyeballs
9 Eyeballs with Veins
3 Cat's Eyeballs
7 Extra-Large Eyeballs

How much will each order cost?

Work Together

Use your graphing software to calculate and graph data.

1. Open a **Full Data Table.** Copy the data table shown here. Remember, you can change the width of the columns.

2. Find the item totals. For each item:
   - From the **Calculate** menu, choose **Multiply.**
   - Select the cells of the Cost and the Number Ordered, then press Return.
   - Click on the cell in the Total column to enter the product on the form.
   - Find the total cost.

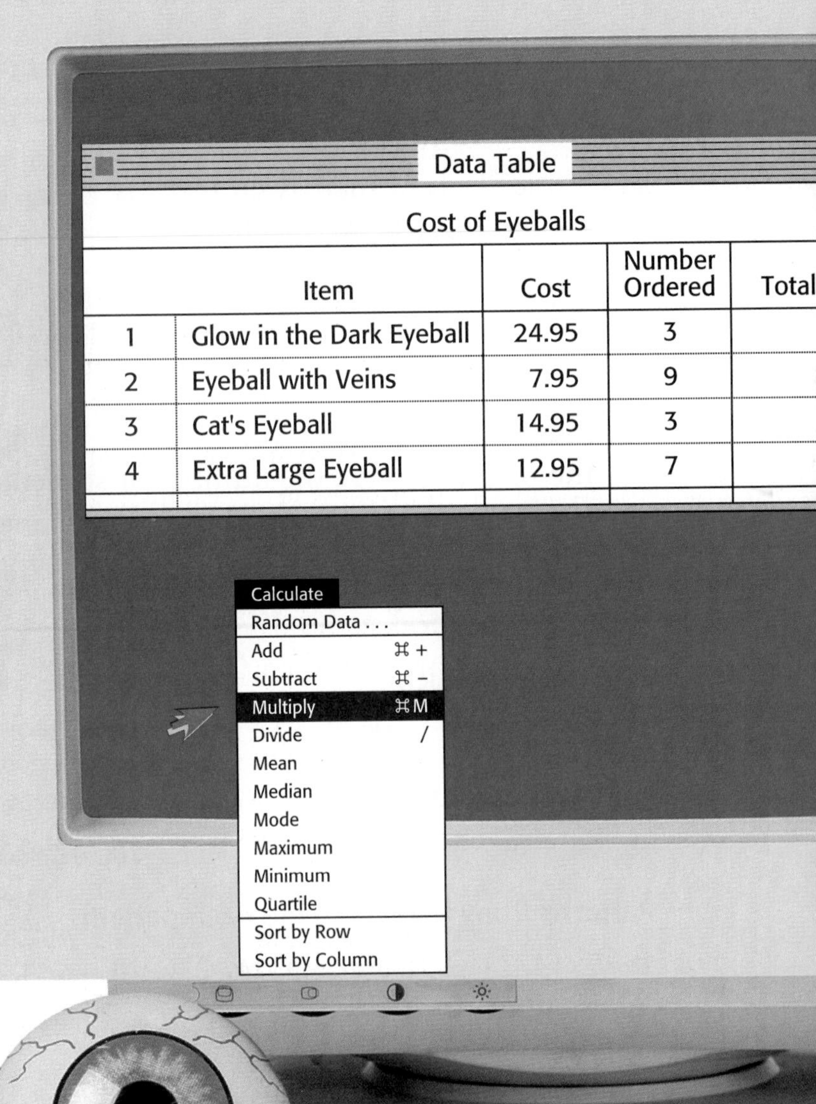

Data Table

Cost of Eyeballs

	Item	Cost	Number Ordered	Total
1	Glow in the Dark Eyeball	24.95	3	
2	Eyeball with Veins	7.95	9	
3	Cat's Eyeball	14.95	3	
4	Extra Large Eyeball	12.95	7	

3 Graph the item totals.

- From the **Graph** menu, choose **Show Graph.**
- Select the four products.
- Drag the selected products onto the Graph window.
- Make a bar graph.

4 Insert the table and graph into the Report window.

Graph
Show Graph ⌘G
Choose Scale ⌘H
Vertical Bar . . .
Line Graph
Pictograph
Histogram
Scattergram
Circle Graph
Horizontal Bar
Stem and Leaf
Box Plot

Exercises

Answer **1–3** in the Report window. **Print Report** when you are finished.

1. What was the total cost for all the orders?

2. Which orders cost about the same amount?

3. The Drama Club has $70 to spend on special props for "Eyes on You." About how many times as much is the cost of the eyeballs?

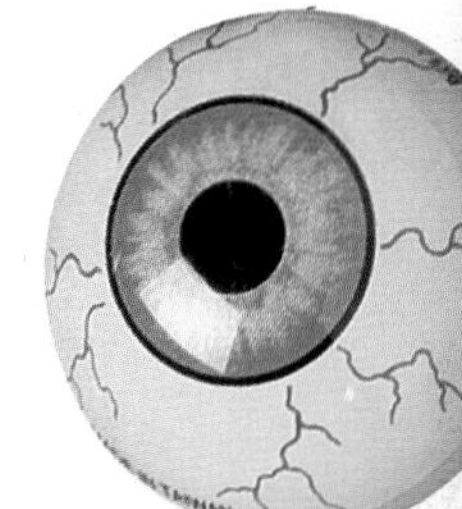

Extensions

Using Data Answer **4** and **5** using the table at the right and the prices in the table on page 238. **Print Report** when you are finished.

Item Ordered	Number
Glow-in-the-Dark Eyeball	4
Eyeball with Vein	8
Cat's Eyeball	2
Extra-Large Eyeball	2

4. If the summer school actors sell 60 tickets at $7 each for their play, will they have enough money to buy the eyeballs and spend $120 on other props and costumes? Explain.

5. Reasoning If you used a calculator, what numbers could you leave off the data tables and still make the same bar graphs?

Copy and complete the table below. How many of each item were sold?

	Item	Cost ($)	Number Sold	Item Total ($)
6.	Fluorescent Green Eyeball	34.95		209.70
7.	Orange Eyeball	18.95		94.75
8.	Silver Eyeball	24.95		199.60
9.	Gold Eyeball	29.95		89.85

SECTION C

Review and Practice

(Lesson 9) Find each product.

1. $\$5.26 \times 8$
2. $\$3.48 \times 5$
3. $\$27.39 \times 4$
4. $\$46.52 \times 7$
5. $\$31.95 \times 3$

6. **Reasoning** Would $35.00 be more than or less than enough to buy 9 books at $4.25 each? Explain.

(Lesson 10) **Mental Math** Find each product.

7. 41×3
8. 6×19
9. 4×71
10. 3×99
11. 7×21

12. Explain how you would find 3×72 mentally.

(Lesson 11) Find each product.

13. $6 \times 6 \times 3$
14. $4 \times 11 \times 3$
15. $5 \times 9 \times 4$
16. $2 \times 5 \times 4$
17. $6 \times 8 \times 5$

18. Write $4 \times 8 \times 6$ three different ways. Solve.
19. Write $3 \times 9 \times 3$ three different ways. Solve.

(Lesson 12) Solve each problem.

20. Monica had $45. She bought 8 harmonicas for $3.50 each. How much money did she have left?

21. At a cook-out, 7 students ate hamburger meals, 8 ate hot dog meals, and 5 ate chicken meals. If each student had 3 cookies with his or her meal, how many cookies were eaten?

(Lesson 13) Make a table or use any strategy to help you solve.

Tosh is making a fruit shake for an after-school party.

22. How many scoops of ice cream does Tosh need if he uses 8 cans of fruit juice?

23. How many cups of water will he need for 8 cans of fruit juice?

24. **Journal** Explain how multiplying money is like multiplying whole numbers. How is it different?

Skills Checklist

In this section, you have:

- Multiplied Money
- Found Special Products
- Multiplied Three Factors
- Solved Multiple-Step Problems
- Solved Problems by Making a Table

REVIEW AND PRACTICE

YOUR CHOICE

Choose at least one. Use what you have learned in the chapter.

1 Clean Up!

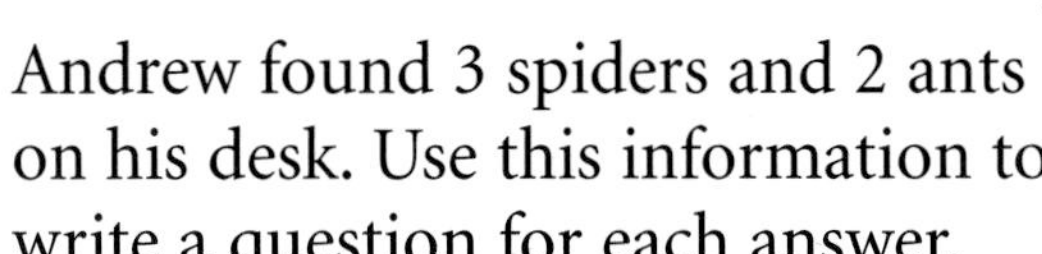

Andrew found 3 spiders and 2 ants on his desk. Use this information to write a question for each answer.

a. 24 b. 12 c. 36 d. 38 e. 6

Go to **www.mathsurf.com/4/ch5** to find information about spiders and ants. Write your own questions and answers.

2 A Trunkful

Mimi has a 28-gallon trunk and Bobo has a 29-gallon trunk. About how many trips will they take to fill a 200-gallon tank? Explain.

3 Multiplication Collage

At Home Use magazines or newspapers to find photos that show multiplication. Cut out the photos and make a collage. Write the multiplication number sentence for each photo. Ask a friend or family member, to see if they can match the multiplication sentence with the photo.

4 Number Detective

Find the rule and write the missing numbers. Then make an In–Out table of your own. Ask a classmate to find the rule.

In	20		70	60	
Out	100	150	350		200

5 Texas Trail

The average pencil can draw a line 35 miles long! Could 7 pencils draw the distance from San Antonio to Dallas? Explain.

REVIEW AND PRACTICE

CHAPTER 5

Review/Test

Vocabulary Match each word with its meaning.

1. array
2. factors
3. multiples
4. product
5. regroup

a. numbers being multiplied
b. the answer in multiplication
c. to name a number in a different way
d. data arranged in rows and columns
e. products of a given number and a whole number

(Lessons 1, 2) **Mental Math** Find each product using mental math.

6. 9×90 7. 4×500 8. 2×80 9. $4 \times 6{,}000$ 10. 8×10

11. 3×300 12. 9×600 13. $7 \times 2{,}000$ 14. 5×900 15. 8×600

(Lesson 3) Estimate each product.

16. 6×81 17. 52×3 18. 6×503 19. 2×402 20. 2×27

(Lessons 4–6, 8, 9) Find each product.

21. 26×8 22. 31×9 23. 605×2 24. $\$7.61 \times 8$ 25. 714×5

26. $3{,}007 \times 6$ 27. $2{,}521 \times 9$ 28. $3{,}506 \times 8$ 29. $\$75.00 \times 3$ 30. $8{,}552 \times 7$

(Lesson 10) **Mental Math** Answer the question.

31. Explain how would you find 4×52 mentally.

(Lesson 11) Answer the question.

32. Write $9 \times 3 \times 4$ in three different ways. Then solve.

(Lessons 12-13) Solve.

33. Six tickets to the play cost $4.50. How much would it cost to buy tickets for a class of 36 students and a class of 30 students?

Number of Tickets	6	12	18
Price	$4.50	$9.00	$13.50

REVIEW/TEST

Performance Assessment

Suppose at the end of the year your art club has $100 to spend on craft supplies. How would you spend the $100?

Craft Supplies

Poster board	$3 per box	Fabric paints	$4 per bottle
Clay	$12 per bag	Paint markers	$2 per marker
Papier mâché	$18 per bottle	Beads	$11 per box
Colored sand	$6 per bag	Colored markers	$5 per box

1. **Decision Making** Decide which items you will buy. Decide how many of each item.

2. **Recording Data** Copy and fill out the table below. Remember that your total can be close to $100, but cannot go over.

Description of Item	How Many	Price of One	Total Price
		Total Price of All Items	

3. **Explain Your Thinking** How did you decide which items to buy? How did you decide how many of each item?

4. **Critical Thinking** Find another combination of items that gives you a total closer to $100.

REVIEW/TEST

Math Magazine

Grid Lock **Unlock the secret to solving tough multiplication problems the way people in ancient India did. The key is using a special grid. Here's how they did it.**

Multiply 647 x 59

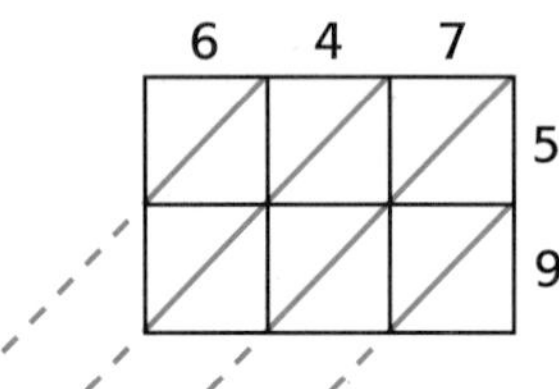

Use a grid like this one to multiply a 3-digit number by a 2-digit number.

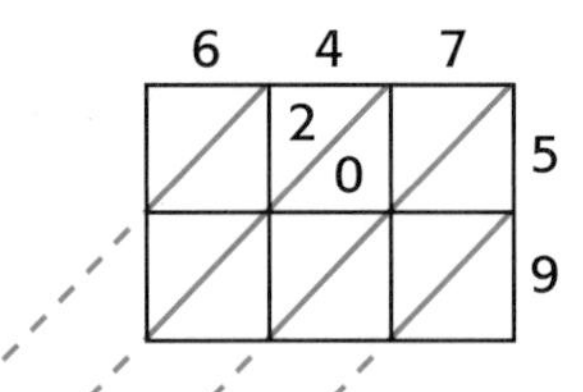

Each square in the grid shows the product of two digits. Record the tens in the top part of the square and the ones in the bottom part.

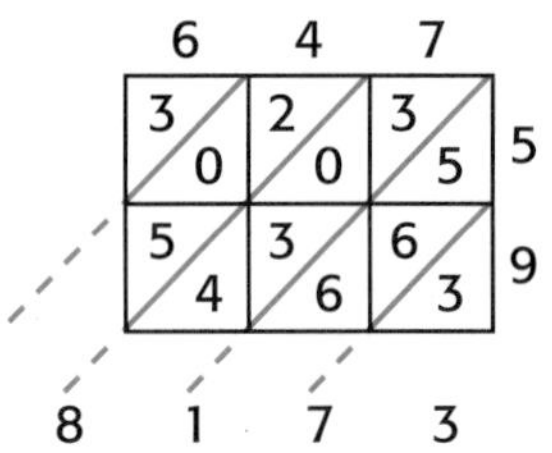

Fill in all products. To find the answer, begin in the bottom right corner and add the diagonals. Regroup as needed.

$647 \times 59 = 38{,}173$

Try These!

1. 35×24

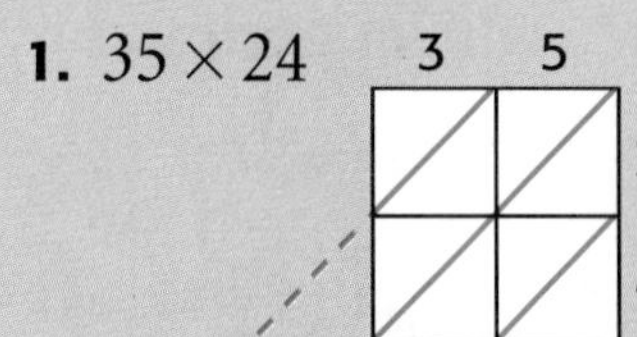

2. 682×25

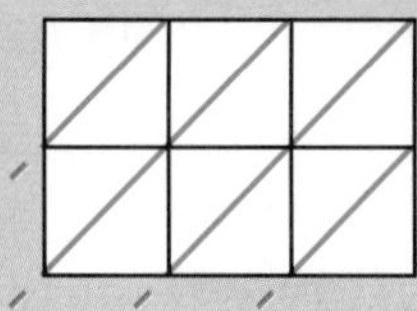

3. 42×56 **4.** 758×93 **5.** 89×67 **6.** 73×94

CHAPTERS 1–5

Cumulative Review

Test Prep Strategy: Eliminate Choices!

Estimate.
What is the product of 7 and 307?

Ⓐ 214 Ⓑ 2,149 Ⓒ 21,490 Ⓓ 314

307 is close to 300.

$7 \times 300 = 2{,}100$.

214 and 314 are too low. 21,490 is too great. The answer is Ⓑ 2,149.

Write the letter of the correct answer. You may estimate or use any strategy to help.

Test Prep Strategies

- Read Carefully
- Follow Directions
- Make Smart Choices
- Eliminate Choices
- Work Backward from an Answer

1. For her club meeting, Teresa bought 6 boxes of cookies. If each box held 19 cookies, how many cookies did she bring?

   Ⓐ 25 Ⓑ 13 Ⓒ 114 Ⓓ 240

2. The gym at Emerson school holds 3,123 people. The gym at King school holds 1,521 people. How many people can both gyms hold?

   Ⓐ 4,644 Ⓑ 1,602 Ⓒ 13,644 Ⓓ 644

3. What is the product of 5 and 689?

   Ⓐ 345 Ⓑ 694 Ⓒ 1,445 Ⓓ 3,445

4. The members of the drama club each paid $7 to go to a play. If there are 49 members, how much money did they spend?

   Ⓐ $56 Ⓑ $713 Ⓒ $343 Ⓓ $127

5. Rodrigo put 9 baseball cards on each page of an album. If there are 29 pages in the album, how many cards does he have?

   Ⓐ 38 Ⓑ 162 Ⓒ 261 Ⓓ 181

6. While playing jump rope, Inez jumped 492 times and Alison jumped 611 times. How many more times did Alison jump than Inez?

   Ⓐ 119 Ⓑ 1,103 Ⓒ 321 Ⓓ 27

7. If a concert starts at 8:00 and it takes 55 minutes to get to the concert hall, what time should you leave?

   Ⓐ 6:00 Ⓑ 7:05 Ⓒ 7:15 Ⓓ 7:25

DATA FILE

Chapter 6
Multiplying by 2-Digit Factors

On the Move!

SECTION

Multiplication Number Sense 249

Buses, trains, subways, and trolleys are different forms of public transportation. In which city do the most people use public transportation?

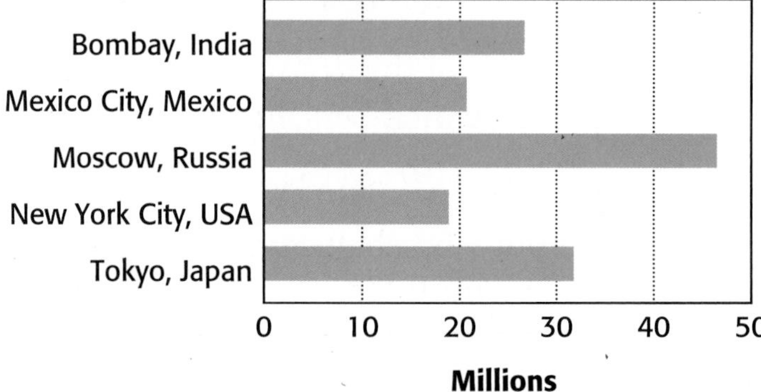

Dragon boat racing
Page 249

Surfing the World Wide Web!

Find some other ways that people stay on the move. Check out **www.mathsurf. com/4/ch6.**

Multiplying

259

Sometimes the form of transportation you use depends on how quickly you want to get where you are going. Which form of transportation is fastest? Which is slowest?

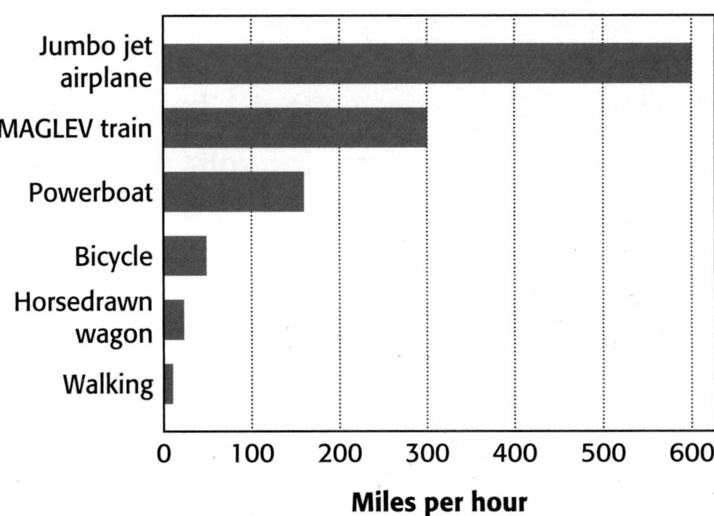

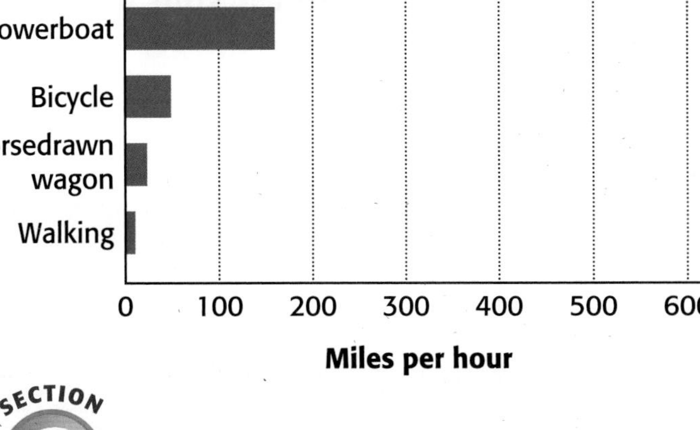

SECTION C

Extending Multiplication

273

The New York subway began operating in the late 1800s. In 1904, it cost just five cents to ride the subway. How have fares changed since then?

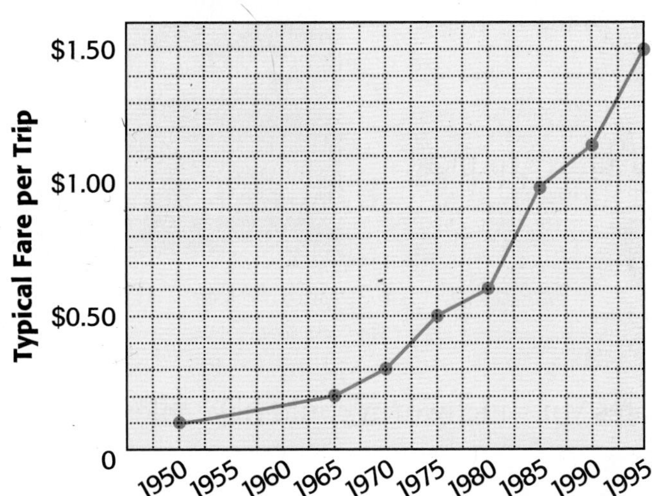

In the air
Page 259

Inline skating
Page 273

Team Project: Inchworm Traveler

Materials
ruler, yardstick

Early explorers drew landmarks such as mountains and lakes on maps. This helped them find their way.

Think of a tiny inchworm traveling across your classroom. To move forward, an inchworm stretches out its body, then scrunches itself end-to-end. With each "step" forward, it moves about 1 inch.

Make a map of your classroom for your inchworm traveler. Show at least three landmarks.

Make a Plan

- Where will the inchworm start and end its trip?
- Choose landmarks your inchworm might see.
- Place the landmarks about where they would be along the inchworm's path.

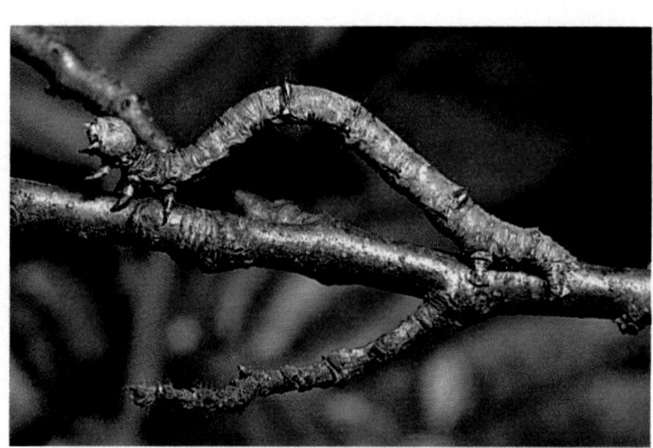

Carry It Out

1. Measure distances between the landmarks in feet or yards, using whole numbers only.
2. Draw the map showing the distances.
3. Find how many inch-long "steps" your inchworm will take from place to place.

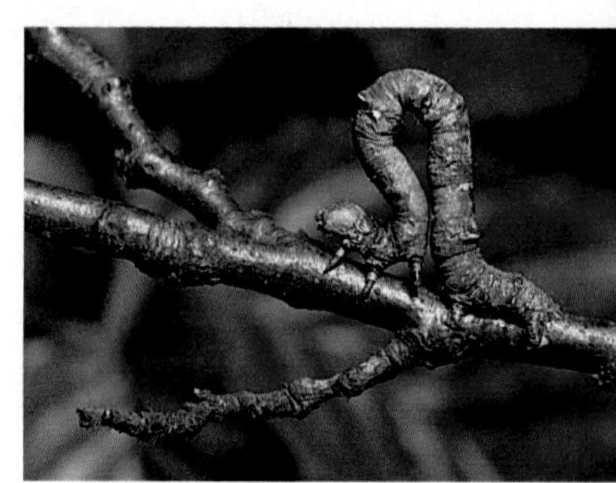

Talk About It

- How did you find the distances in inches?
- How are maps helpful?

Present the Project

- Show your map to the class.
- Talk about different routes your inchworm could have taken.

CHAPTER 6

SECTION A

Multiplication Number Sense

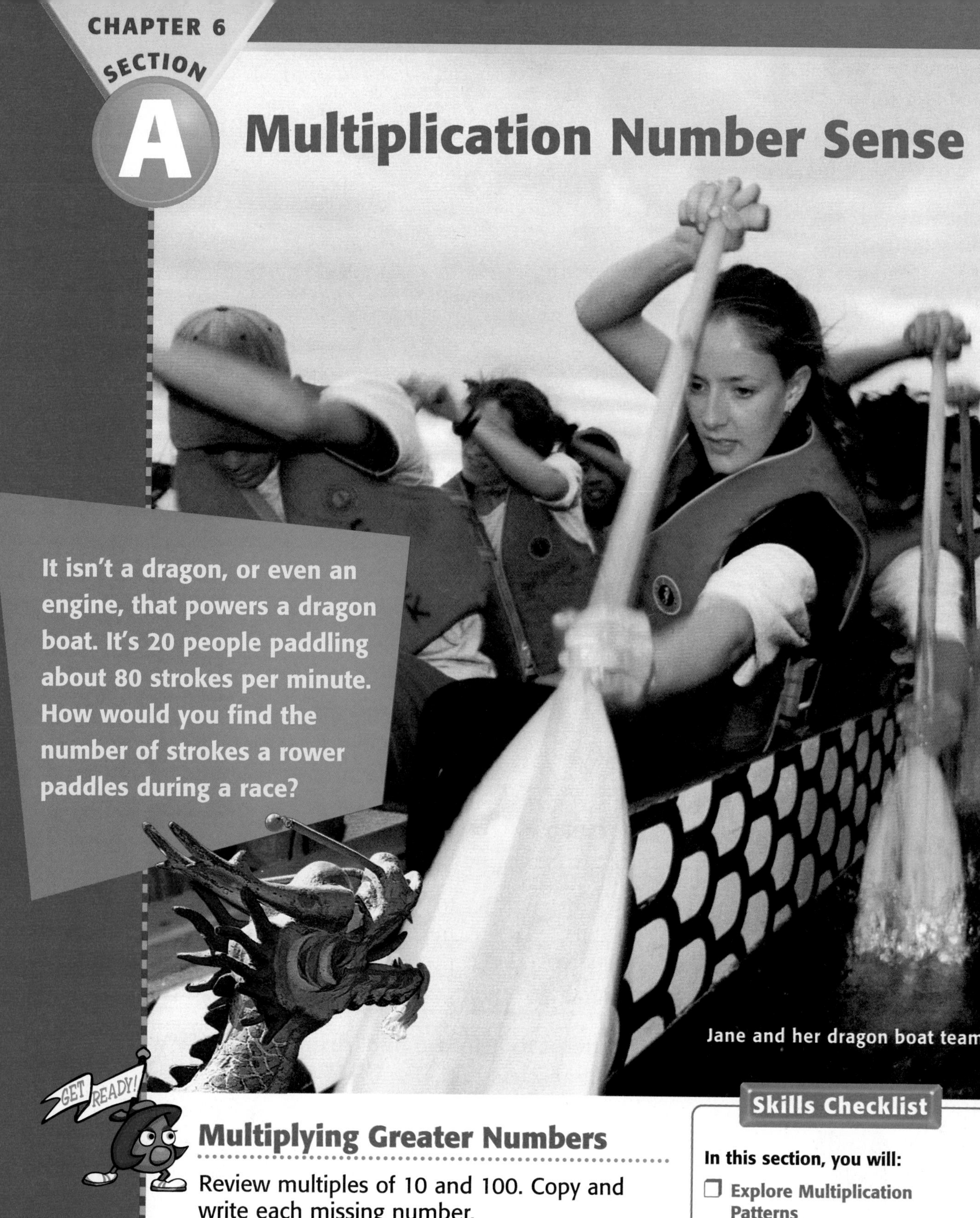

It isn't a dragon, or even an engine, that powers a dragon boat. It's 20 people paddling about 80 strokes per minute. How would you find the number of strokes a rower paddles during a race?

Jane and her dragon boat team

GET READY!

Multiplying Greater Numbers

Review multiples of 10 and 100. Copy and write each missing number.

1. 10, ■, 30, 40, ■, 60, ■

2. 140, 150, ■, 170, ■, 190, ■

3. 100, 200, 300, ■, ■, 600, ■

Skills Checklist

In this section, you will:

- ❒ Explore Multiplication Patterns
- ❒ Estimate Products
- ❒ Multiply by Multiples of 10
- ❒ Explore Multiplying with 2-Digit Factors

Chapter 6
Lesson
1

Exploring Multiplication Patterns

Problem Solving Connection
Look for a Pattern

Materials
calculator

Vocabulary

multiple
the product of a given whole number and any other whole number

product
the number obtained after multiplying

factors
numbers that are multiplied together to obtain a product

Explore

You can use basic facts and multiples of 10 to explore multiplication patterns.

Work Together

1. Use a calculator to find each product. Look for patterns.

a.	b.	c.
$20 \times 3 = n$	$40 \times 5 = n$	$30 \times 1 = n$
$20 \times 30 = n$	$40 \times 50 = n$	$30 \times 10 = n$
$20 \times 300 = n$	$40 \times 500 = n$	$30 \times 100 = n$
$20 \times 3{,}000 = n$	$40 \times 5{,}000 = n$	$30 \times 1{,}000 = n$

Remember
The numbers 10, 20, 30, 40, ... are multiples of 10.

2. Look for patterns to help you find each product. Use a calculator to check your answers.

a.	b.	c.
$40 \times 2 = n$	$30 \times 3 = n$	$50 \times 2 = n$
$40 \times 20 = n$	$30 \times 30 = n$	$50 \times 20 = n$
$40 \times 200 = n$	$30 \times 300 = n$	$50 \times 200 = n$
$40 \times 2{,}000 = n$	$30 \times 3{,}000 = n$	$50 \times 2{,}000 = n$

Talk About It

3. What patterns did you notice?
4. Why does the product of 40×50 have three zeros instead of two?

Connect

You can use basic facts, mental math, and place value to help you multiply by multiples of 10, 100, and 1,000.

	Multiple of 10	Multiple of 100	Multiple of 1,000
Find	60×80	60×800	$60 \times 8{,}000$
Basic fact	Think: $6 \times 8 = 48$	Think: $6 \times 8 = 48$	Think $6 \times 8 = 48$
Zeros in factors	2	3	4
Product	$60 \times \mathbf{80} = 4{,}8\mathbf{00}$	$60 \times \mathbf{800} = 48{,}\mathbf{000}$	$60 \times 8{,}\mathbf{000} = 480{,}\mathbf{000}$

Practice

Look for patterns to help you find each product. Use a calculator to check your answers.

1. $20 \times 2 = n$
   $20 \times 20 = n$
   $20 \times 200 = n$
   $20 \times 2{,}000 = n$
2. $80 \times 4 = n$
   $80 \times 40 = n$
   $80 \times 400 = n$
   $80 \times 4{,}000 = n$
3. $50 \times 6 = n$
   $50 \times 60 = n$
   $50 \times 600 = n$
   $50 \times 6{,}000 = n$

Mental Math Find each product. Use mental math.

4. 30×10
5. 50×20
6. 40×70
7. 100×90
8. 60×30
9. 60×200
10. $30 \times 8{,}000$
11. $500 \times 3{,}000$

12. **Time** Joshua rode a bus 6 times. Each trip took 10 minutes. How long did he spend on the bus?

13. **Careers** Suppose a travel agent earns \$50 for each trip that is planned for a customer. How much would the travel agent earn for 20 trips?

14. **Money** Mark got 8 twenty-dollar bills from the bank machine. Write the total amount of money using a dollar sign.

15. **Geometry Readiness** A square piece of cloth is wide enough and tall enough for the sail on this dhow (DOW), a boat used in Africa and Asia. How many sails could you cut from the cloth?

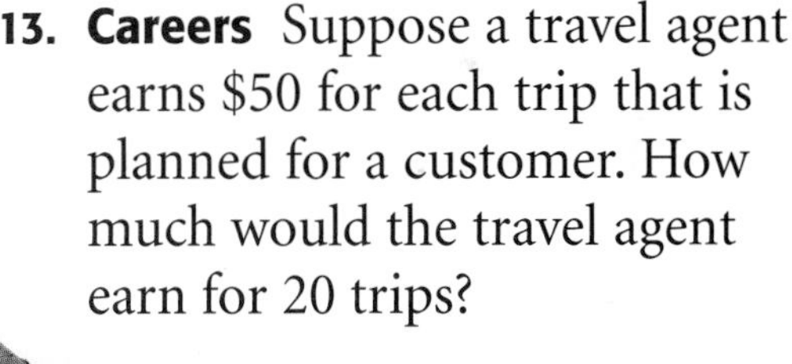

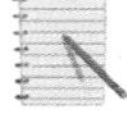

16. **Journal** Describe how you can find the product of 20 and 400 using basic facts and mental math.

Chapter 6
Lesson
2

Estimating Products

You Will Learn
how to estimate products of 2-digit factors

Learn

In Dayton, Ohio, electric trolleys help people on the move. A trolley can carry 64 people at one time. Between 2:30 P.M. and 6:30 P.M., trolleys travel along Salem Avenue 23 times. About how many people can be transported during that time?

Tammy Maxwell drives trolleys in Dayton, Ohio.

Did You Know?
Electric trolleys can be found in only five U.S. cities: Boston, Dayton, Philadelphia, San Francisco, and Seattle.

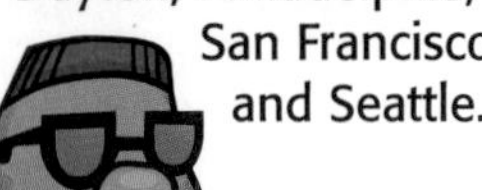

You can estimate the product to find about how many people can be transported.

Example

Estimate 23×64.

Round each factor to the nearest multiple of 10.

Number of people	23	×	64	Number of trips
	↓		↓	
	20	×	60 = 1,200	

About 1,200 people can be transported in 23 trolley trips.

Talk About It

1. Without computing, do you think the exact answer is greater or less than the estimate? How can you decide?
2. What would be your estimate if a trolley carried 65 people? Why?

Check

Estimate each product.

1. 26×31
2. 45×23
3. 87×49
4. 56×53
5. 73×97
6. **Reasoning** How can you estimate to find the number of digits in the product of 53 and 66?

Practice

Skills and Reasoning

Estimate each product.

7. 21×31
8. 48×45
9. 16×11
10. 9×39
11. 75×55
12. 33×35
13. 77×83
14. 44×97
15. 19×29
16. 23×94
17. 74×65
18. 59×26
19. 38×27
20. 85×84
21. 49×62
22. 41×15
23. 67×22
24. 92×47
25. 54×42
26. 81×36
27. Estimate 9×45.
28. Estimate the product of 86 and 34.
29. Would an estimate for the product of 35 and 47 be greater or less than the exact answer? Explain.
30. Would an estimate for 23×41 be greater or less than the exact answer? Explain.

Problem Solving and Applications

31. Although 64 people can fit on each Dayton trolley, only 46 people can be seated at one time. Estimate how many passengers in all of the 23 trolleys would get to sit down.
32. About 4,600 people ride the Route 7 trolley each day in Dayton. About 5,200 people ride the Route 8 trolley. In all, how many people ride these two trolley routes each day?
33. **Time** If it costs Cliff $48 a month to travel on public transportation, about how much will it cost in a year?

Using Data Use the Data File on page 246 for **34** and **35.**

34. Which city has fewer than 20 million people using public transportation each week?
35. About how many more people in Moscow use public transportation than people in Bombay?

The Metro in Moscow, Russia

Mixed Review and Test Prep

STAY SHARP!

Algebra Readiness Find each missing number.

36. $67 - n = 20$
37. $526 + n = 750$
38. $n + 621 = 1{,}000$
39. **Time** Which is the seventh month of the year?

Ⓐ June Ⓑ November Ⓒ August Ⓓ July

Chapter 6
Lesson
3

Multiplying by Multiples of 10

You Will Learn
how to multiply by multiples of 10

Learn

"Faster! Go!" cry the on-lookers. Fierce reptiles glide with the splash of paddles.

Each dragon boat team like Jane's has a crew of 22 people. If 60 teams compete in a race, how many crew members are there in all?

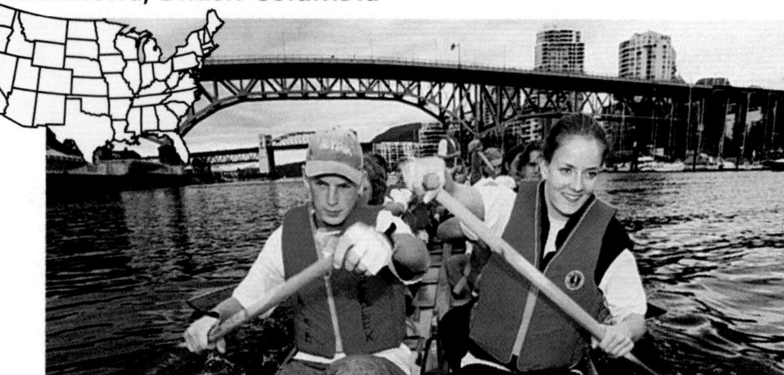

Jane rows for her dragon boat team in Richmond, British Columbia, in Canada.

You can multiply to find the total number of crew members.

Remember
You can use basic facts and patterns to help you multiply by multiples of 10.

Example

Find 60×22.

Step 1

Multiply by the digit in the ones place.

$$\begin{array}{r} 22 \\ \times 60 \\ \hline 0 \end{array}$$

Step 2

Multiply by the digit in the tens place.

$$\begin{array}{r} \scriptstyle 1 \\ 22 \\ \times 60 \\ \hline 1{,}320 \end{array}$$

Estimate to check.

$60 \times 20 = 1{,}200$

Since 1,320 is close to 1,200, the answer is reasonable.

There are 1,320 crew members in the race.

Talk About It

Why do you write 132 next to the 0 in Step 2?

Check

Find each product.

1. 32×10 **2.** 23×20 **3.** 16×10 **4.** 58×40 **5.** 73×80

6. Reasoning How many zeros are in the product of 37 and 20? How can you tell before you multiply?

Practice

Skills and Reasoning

Find each product.

7. 21×30 **8.** 58×20 **9.** 10×49 **10.** 72×90 **11.** 85×40

12. 70×50 **13.** 67×80 **14.** 54×10 **15.** 90×12 **16.** 40×98

17. 60×63 **18.** 89×60 **19.** 30×99 **20.** 10×75 **21.** 46×50

22. Find the product of 20 and 35. **23.** Multiply 66 by 80.

24. Reasoning How many zeros are in the product of 25 and 40? Explain.

Problem Solving and Applications

25. Forty teams competed at the sixth annual Dragon Boat Festival in New York. With 22 crew members on each boat, how many people competed in all?

26. Measurement The course for the Dragon Boat Festival in New York is 640 meters long. If a crew finishes the course, turns around, and paddles back to the starting line, how many meters does it travel?

Dragon boat drum

27. Critical Thinking In a dragon boat team, 20 people row, 1 person beats a drum and yells to the rowers, and 1 person steers. If 60 teams compete in a race, how many crew members are not rowing?

28. Time A rower paddles 80 strokes per minute. Is this faster than 1 stroke per second? Explain.

29. History Dragon boat racing began in China about 24 centuries ago. How many years is that? (Hint: A century is 100 years.)

30. Journal Without finding the exact answer, how do you know the product of 30 and 7,975 will have a zero in the ones place?

Mixed Review and Test Prep

STAY SHARP!

Find each sum or difference.

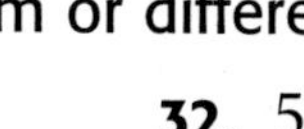

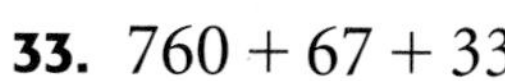

31. $409 + 38$ **32.** $532 - 485$ **33.** $760 + 67 + 33$ **34.** $300 - 145$

35. Mental Math What is the sum of 80 and 8 and 800?

Ⓐ 88 Ⓑ 888 Ⓒ 8,880 Ⓓ not here

Chapter 6
Lesson
4

Exploring Multiplying with 2-Digit Factors

Problem Solving Connection
- Use Objects/ Act It Out
- Draw a Picture

Materials
place-value blocks

Remember
An array is data arranged in rows and columns.

Explore

For 18 months of 1860 and 1861, the Pony Express delivered mail between St. Joseph, Missouri, and Sacramento, California. Suppose a rider traveled 12 hours a day at a speed of 15 mi/hr. How many miles could the rider travel in a day?

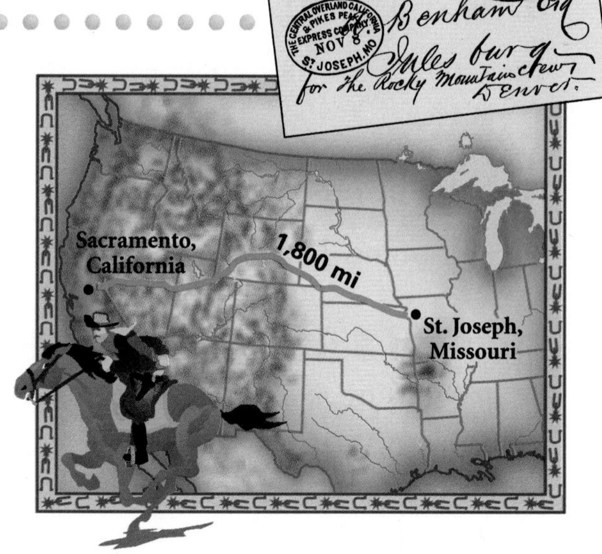

Work Together

1. Use place-value blocks to show 12×15 in an array.
   a. Show 1 ten and 5 ones in a row.
   b. Make 11 more rows of 15. (Hint: You can use a hundred block to show 10 rows of 10.)
   c. How many hundreds are there? How many tens? How many ones?
   d. How many ones are in the whole array?
   e. How many miles could the rider travel in one day?

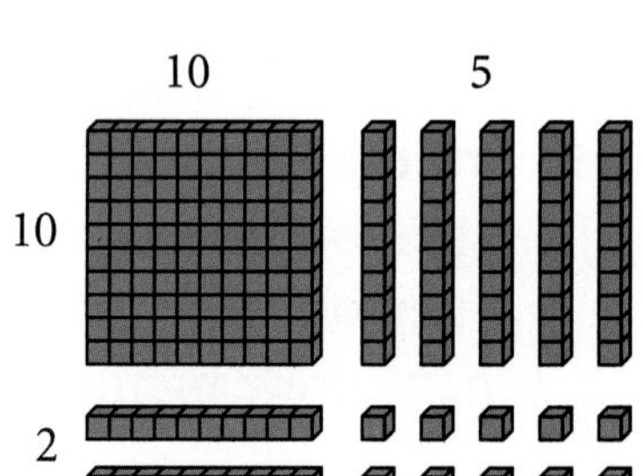

2. Use place-value blocks to show each amount in an array. How many ones are in the whole array?
   a. 13×14 b. 14×21 c. 11×15

Talk About It

3. Can you show 12×15 using 1 hundred block and 8 tens? Explain.
4. Describe how you used place-value blocks to show 13×14.

Connect

You can use place-value blocks to help find a product.

Find 13×23.

What You See

$10 \times 20 = 200$

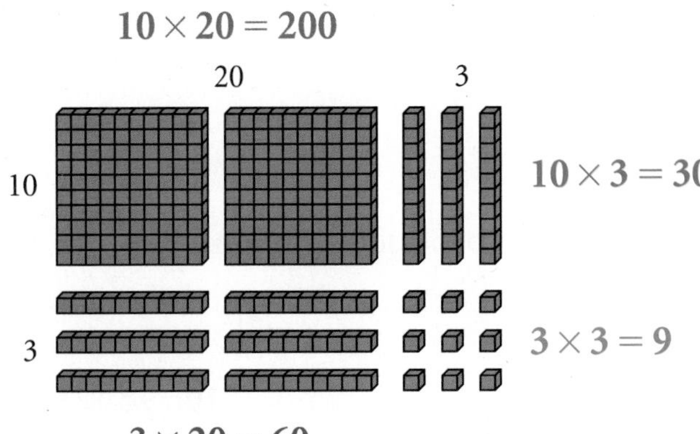

$10 \times 3 = 30$

$3 \times 3 = 9$

$3 \times 20 = 60$

What You Write

$$\begin{array}{rl} 23 & \\ \times 13 & \\ \hline 9 & \leftarrow 3 \times 3 \\ 60 & \leftarrow 3 \times 20 \\ 30 & \leftarrow 10 \times 3 \\ 200 & \leftarrow 10 \times 20 \\ \hline 299 & \leftarrow 9 + 60 + 30 + 200 \end{array}$$

$13 \times 23 = 299$

Practice

Copy and complete. Draw a picture or use place-value blocks to help.

1.
$$\begin{array}{rl} 35 & \\ \times 13 & \\ \hline 15 & \leftarrow 3 \times 5 \\ 90 & \leftarrow 3 \times 30 \\ 50 & \leftarrow 10 \times 5 \\ 300 & \leftarrow 10 \times 30 \\ \hline ■■■ & \end{array}$$

2.
$$\begin{array}{rl} 46 & \\ \times 29 & \\ \hline 54 & \leftarrow 9 \times 6 \\ 360 & \leftarrow 9 \times 40 \\ 120 & \leftarrow 20 \times 6 \\ ■■■ & \leftarrow 20 \times 40 \\ \hline ■,■■■ & \end{array}$$

3.
$$\begin{array}{rl} 28 & \\ \times 37 & \\ \hline 56 & \leftarrow 7 \times 8 \\ 140 & \leftarrow 7 \times 20 \\ ■■■ & \leftarrow 30 \times 8 \\ ■■■ & \leftarrow 30 \times 20 \\ \hline ■,■■■ & \end{array}$$

4.

$$\begin{array}{r} 53 \\ \times 12 \\ \hline ■ \\ ■■■ \\ ■■ \\ ■■■ \\ \hline ■■■ \end{array}$$

5.
$$\begin{array}{r} 64 \\ \times 17 \\ \hline ■■ \\ ■■■ \\ ■■ \\ ■■■ \\ \hline ■,■■■ \end{array}$$

6.
$$\begin{array}{r} 36 \\ \times 52 \\ \hline ■■ \\ ■■ \\ ■■■ \\ ■,■■■ \\ \hline ■,■■■ \end{array}$$

7.
$$\begin{array}{r} 79 \\ \times 25 \\ \hline ■■ \\ ■■■ \\ ■■■ \\ ■,■■■ \\ \hline ■,■■■ \end{array}$$

8.
$$\begin{array}{r} 14 \\ \times 48 \\ \hline ■■ \\ ■■ \\ ■■■ \\ ■■■ \\ \hline ■■■ \end{array}$$

9. $\begin{array}{r} 45 \\ \times 37 \\ \hline \end{array}$ **10.** $\begin{array}{r} 38 \\ \times 19 \\ \hline \end{array}$ **11.** $\begin{array}{r} 42 \\ \times 35 \\ \hline \end{array}$ **12.** $\begin{array}{r} 38 \\ \times 42 \\ \hline \end{array}$ **13.** $\begin{array}{r} 57 \\ \times 16 \\ \hline \end{array}$

14. 62×48 **15.** 19×57 **16.** 32×14 **17.** 26×17 **18.** 67×39

19. History A Pony Express rider typically traveled 75 miles a day. How many miles could a rider travel in a week?

20. Journal Draw a picture to show how to find the product of 14 and 21. Describe each step in multiplying ones and tens.

SECTION A

Review and Practice

(Lesson 1) Patterns Look for patterns to help you find each product.

1. $50 \times 4 = n$
   $50 \times 40 = n$
   $50 \times 400 = n$
   $50 \times 4{,}000 = n$
2. $30 \times 7 = n$
   $30 \times 70 = n$
   $30 \times 700 = n$
   $30 \times 7{,}000 = n$
3. $80 \times 3 = n$
   $80 \times 30 = n$
   $80 \times 300 = n$
   $80 \times 3{,}000 = n$
4. Find the product of 90 and 60.
5. Find the product of 30 and 500.

(Lesson 2) Estimation Estimate each product.

6. 43×27
7. 18×22
8. 51×55
9. 28×73
10. 96×34
11. 25×62
12. 86×33
13. 45×29
14. 94×12
15. 16×38
16. Tina needs 4 pieces of 28-inch wood to make a picture frame. Estimate the total amount of wood she needs.

(Lessons 3 and 4) Find each product.

17. 18×86
18. 37×38
19. 74×15
20. 19×24
21. 62×22
22. 49×10
23. 27×46
24. 32×13
25. 64×12
26. 53×57
27. 57×14
28. 88×25
29. 61×29
30. 72×44
31. 96×39
32. 30×72
33. 84×60
34. 50×56
35. 40×78
36. 90×33
37. **History** The *Apollo 11* spacecraft carried the first humans to walk on the moon. Each Apollo flight held 3 astronauts. There were 13 Apollo space flights. How many astronauts were there on the Apollo flights?
38. **Money** If a sheet of 20¢ stamps has 4 rows with 5 stamps in each row, how much does the sheet cost?
39. **Journal** Estimate the product of 47 and 35. Then find the exact answer. Explain why your estimate is greater or less than the exact answer.

Skills Checklist

In this section, you have:

- ☑ **Explored Multiplication Patterns**
- ☑ **Estimated Products**
- ☑ **Multiplied by Multiples of 10**
- ☑ **Explored Multiplying with 2-Digit Factors**

CHAPTER 6

SECTION

B Multiplying

A ride in the sky can be quiet ... except for the engine roar and the hum of the propeller. How can you use multiplication to find out how far you travel?

Liesl is a member of the International Wheelchair Aviators.

GET READY!

Finding Greater Products

Review multiplication by 1-digit factors. Find each product.

1. 28×9	**2.** 59×8	**3.** 42×5
4. 46×7	**5.** 37×4	**6.** 81×3
7. 16×2	**8.** 32×6	**9.** 77×8

Skills Checklist

In this section, you will:

- ❒ Multiply with 2-Digit Factors
- ❒ Estimate Greater Products
- ❒ Choose a Calculation Method
- ❒ Solve Problems by Making Decisions

Chapter 6
Lesson
5

Multiplying with 2-Digit Factors

You Will Learn
how to multiply with 2-digit factors

Did You Know?
The longest regular airline flight is from New York City to Johannesburg, South Africa. It covers a distance of 7,967 miles.

Learn

Liesl gets off the ground as often as possible. She's a member of the International Wheelchair Aviators, a group of pilots who fly small airplanes.

Liesl flies from the airport at Saginaw, Michigan.

Pilots keep logbooks of how many hours they fly. If Liesl flies 26 hours each month, how many hours will she log in one year?

Bryan and Arianna solved the problem in different ways.

I found 12 × 26 this way. First, I multiplied 6 by 2 and 20 by 2. Next, I multiplied 6 by 10 and 20 by 10. Then I added the products.

I got the same answer, but I did it differently. First, I multiplied by 2 ones. Next, I multiplied by 1 ten. Then I added the products.

Bryan's Way

$$\begin{array}{r} 26 \\ \times 12 \\ \hline 12 \\ 40 \\ 60 \\ 200 \\ \hline 312 \end{array}$$

Arianna's Way

$$\begin{array}{r} \overset{1}{2}6 \\ \times 12 \\ \hline 52 \\ 260 \\ \hline 312 \end{array}$$

Liesl will log 312 miles

How are Arianna and Bryan's ways alike? How are they different?

Another Example

Use Arianna's way to find 36×47.

Step 1	Step 2	Step 3
Multiply by ones.	Multiply by tens.	Add the products.
$\begin{array}{r} {\scriptstyle 4} \\ 47 \\ \times 36 \\ \hline 282 \end{array}$	$\begin{array}{r} {\scriptstyle 2} \\ {\scriptstyle 4} \\ 47 \\ \times 36 \\ \hline 282 \\ 1410 \end{array}$	$\begin{array}{r} {\scriptstyle 2} \\ {\scriptstyle 4} \\ 47 \\ \times 36 \\ \hline 282 \\ 1410 \\ \hline 1{,}692 \end{array}$

$36 \times 47 = 1{,}692$ **Estimate** to check.

36×47 is close to 40×50. $40 \times 50 = 2{,}000$

Since 1,692 is close to 2,000, the answer is reasonable.

Talk About It

1. In the Example above, what do the small numbers in Step 2 stand for?
2. How would you multiply 60 and 15 mentally?

Check

Copy and complete.

1. $\begin{array}{r} 23 \\ \times 12 \\ \hline \square 6 \\ \square\square\square \\ \hline 2\square 6 \end{array}$
2. $\begin{array}{r} 48 \\ \times 21 \\ \hline \square\square \\ \square 6 \square \\ \hline 1{,}\square 08 \end{array}$
3. $\begin{array}{r} 36 \\ \times 17 \\ \hline 25\square \\ 3\square\square \\ \hline 61\square \end{array}$
4. $\begin{array}{r} 52 \\ \times 43 \\ \hline \square 56 \\ 2\,\square\square\square \\ \hline \square{,}236 \end{array}$
5. $\begin{array}{r} 45 \\ \times 34 \\ \hline 1\square 0 \\ \square\,\square\square\square \\ \hline \square{,}\square 30 \end{array}$

Find each product.

6. $\begin{array}{r} 17 \\ \times 14 \\ \hline \end{array}$
7. $\begin{array}{r} 39 \\ \times 22 \\ \hline \end{array}$
8. $\begin{array}{r} 51 \\ \times 35 \\ \hline \end{array}$
9. $\begin{array}{r} 28 \\ \times 16 \\ \hline \end{array}$
10. $\begin{array}{r} 66 \\ \times 47 \\ \hline \end{array}$
11. $\begin{array}{r} 10 \\ \times 72 \\ \hline \end{array}$
12. $\begin{array}{r} 43 \\ \times 56 \\ \hline \end{array}$
13. $\begin{array}{r} 69 \\ \times 40 \\ \hline \end{array}$
14. $\begin{array}{r} 86 \\ \times 19 \\ \hline \end{array}$
15. $\begin{array}{r} 75 \\ \times 70 \\ \hline \end{array}$
16. 44×58
17. 28×43
18. 74×39
19. 36×15
20. 55×97
21. **Reasoning** How can you tell from estimating that the product of 25 and 25 is less than 1,000?
22. **Reasoning** Write a multiplication sentence that has 4,000 as its product.

Practice

Skills and Reasoning

Find each product. Estimate to check.

23. $\begin{array}{r} 44 \\ \times 31 \\ \hline \end{array}$ **24.** $\begin{array}{r} 32 \\ \times 15 \\ \hline \end{array}$ **25.** $\begin{array}{r} 49 \\ \times 39 \\ \hline \end{array}$ **26.** $\begin{array}{r} 26 \\ \times 39 \\ \hline \end{array}$ **27.** $\begin{array}{r} 73 \\ \times 23 \\ \hline \end{array}$

28. $\begin{array}{r} 41 \\ \times 22 \\ \hline \end{array}$ **29.** $\begin{array}{r} 83 \\ \times 13 \\ \hline \end{array}$ **30.** $\begin{array}{r} 34 \\ \times 83 \\ \hline \end{array}$ **31.** $\begin{array}{r} 72 \\ \times 11 \\ \hline \end{array}$ **32.** $\begin{array}{r} 53 \\ \times 91 \\ \hline \end{array}$

33. $\begin{array}{r} 32 \\ \times 51 \\ \hline \end{array}$ **34.** $\begin{array}{r} 61 \\ \times 18 \\ \hline \end{array}$ **35.** $\begin{array}{r} 45 \\ \times 13 \\ \hline \end{array}$ **36.** $\begin{array}{r} 89 \\ \times 12 \\ \hline \end{array}$ **37.** $\begin{array}{r} 15 \\ \times 75 \\ \hline \end{array}$

38. 65×43 **39.** 81×12 **40.** 96×27 **41.** 19×19 **42.** 78×65

43. 38×38 **44.** 21×43 **45.** 78×63 **46.** 81×26 **47.** 16×88

48. Multiply 59 and 29. **49.** Find the product of 18 and 62.

50. How many digits are in the product of 25 and 47?

Problem Solving and Applications

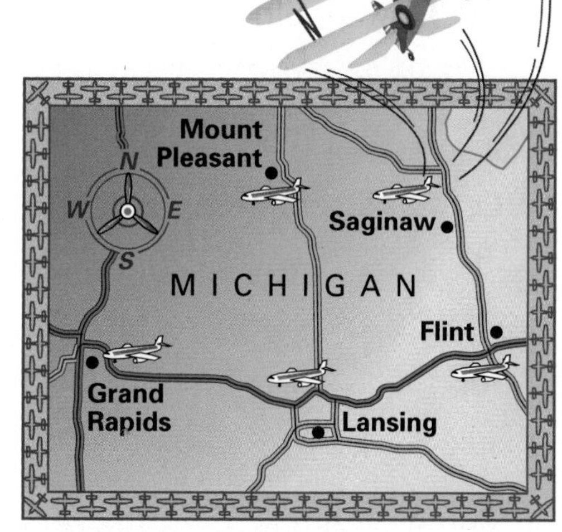

51. Geography Liesl flies from Saginaw, Michigan, to Defiance, Ohio—a distance of 196 miles. She also flies to Sheboygan, Wisconsin—a distance of 155 miles. How much farther is the trip to Defiance?

52. Suppose Liesl flies from Saginaw to Mount Pleasant and back once a week for 15 weeks. The round trip distance is 76 miles. How many miles would she fly in all?

53. Geometry Readiness Use the map. Suppose Liesl flies from Saginaw to Flint, then to Lansing, and then back to Saginaw. What would be the shape of her route?

Using Data Use the Data File on page 247 for **54 and 55.**

54. History The plane that Orville and Wilbur Wright built in 1903 flew at 30 miles per hour. Which form of transportation shown on the bar graph is closest to this speed?

55. The speed of a MAGLEV train is about twice as fast as which form of transportation?

Problem Solving and MATH HISTORY

The ancient Incas of Peru kept records using knots on strings. The strings were called *quipus.* The knots stood for animals, people, and plots of land. Even through the 1800s, herders in Peru used knotted strings to keep track of their animals. Ancient Greeks and Persians used similar systems of knotted strings to count.

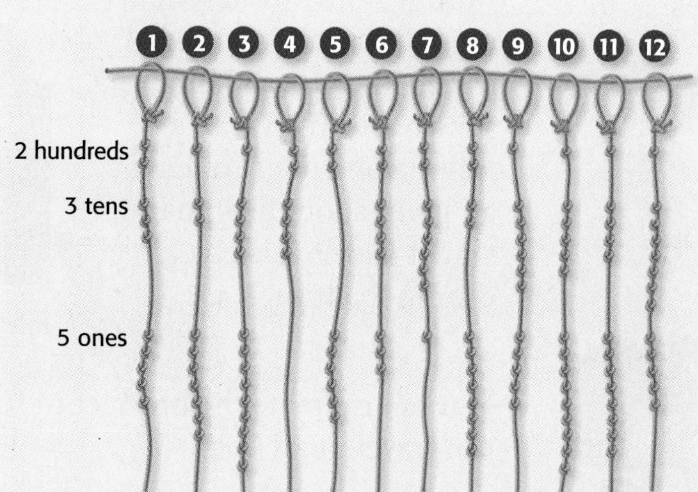

Each string on the *quipu* stands for 1 herd.

56. Each string stands for a different herd of animals. The first string shows 235 animals in one herd. How many animals are in the herd shown by the second string?

57. Which herd has the most animals? How many does it have?

58. How many herds does this *quipu* show?

59. Critical Thinking What is the greatest number of knots that could be shown in the tens group? Explain.

60. If 14 calves are born in each herd, how many knots would have to be added to the *quipu?*

61. Critical Thinking Why do you think farmers and herders used this system of keeping records?

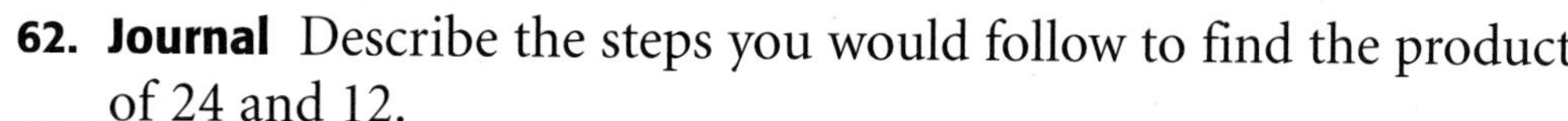

62. Journal Describe the steps you would follow to find the product of 24 and 12.

Mixed Review and Test Prep

Find each quotient.

63. $8 \div 4$ **64.** $12 \div 2$ **65.** $6 \div 3$ **66.** $14 \div 2$ **67.** $9 \div 3$

Find each difference.

68. \$11.01 − \$9.92 **69.** \$43.20 − \$0.75 **70.** \$14.95 − \$1.24 **71.** \$3.87 − \$2.19

72. Which number is a multiple of 9?

Ⓐ 33 Ⓑ 72 Ⓒ 22 Ⓓ 46

Estimating Greater Products

You Will Learn
how to estimate greater products

Learn

Kyle and Julian take the subway home from school every day. The train they travel on can seat 396 passengers. If 18 trains travel along their route in an hour, about how many seated passengers can travel during that time?

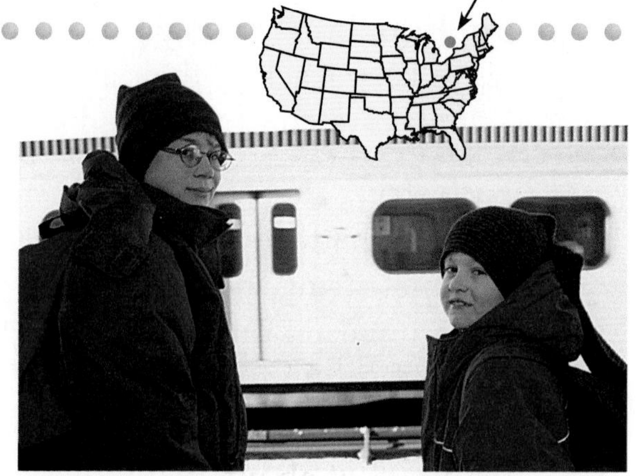

Kyle and Julian live in Toronto, Ontario, in Canada.

You can estimate the product to find about how many passengers can travel in an hour.

Math Tip
Estimate to find if your answer is reasonable.

Example

Estimate 18×396.

Step 1

Round each factor.

18×396

Round to tens ↓ ↓ Round to hundreds

20×400

Step 2

Multiply the rounded factors.

$20 \times 400 = 8{,}000$

About 8,000 seated passengers can travel in an hour.

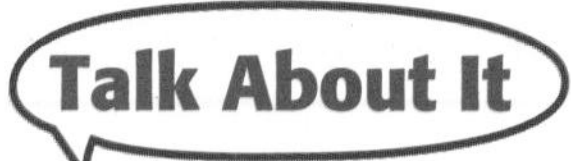

Is the estimate greater or less than the exact answer? Explain.

Check

Estimate each product.

1. 126×32 **2.** 608×43 **3.** 73×564 **4.** 36×390

5. **Reasoning** Name two factors that have an estimated product of 10,000.

Practice

Skills and Reasoning

Estimate each product.

6. 185 × 18 7. 525 × 63 8. 149 × 21 9. 542 × 25

10. 342 × 19 11. 417 × 23 12. 950 × 48 13. 322 × 35 14. 661 × 78

15. 120 × 42 16. 869 × 59 17. 981 × 53 18. 357 × 16 19. 456 × 38

20. Estimate the product of 635 and 68. 21. Estimate 671 by 45.

22. Write two different sets of factors you could estimate to have a product of about 20,000.

Problem Solving and Applications

23. About 180 people in each Toronto subway car can stand. Usually there are 6 cars on a train. Estimate how many riders per train might be standing.

24. **Money** If Kyle and Julian's parents spend $34 per week for their childrens' subway tokens, about how much will they spend in a school year of 33 weeks?

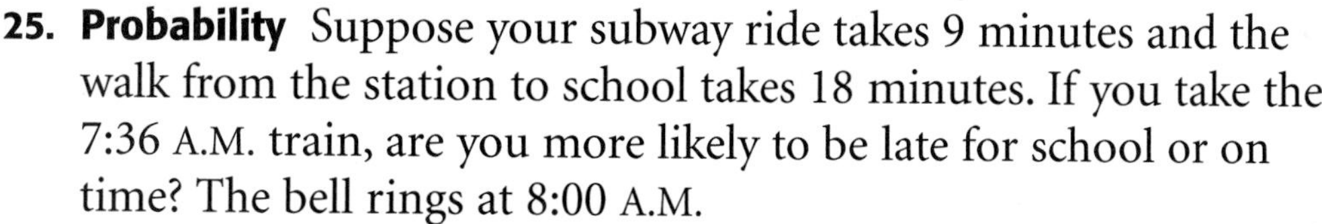

25. **Probability** Suppose your subway ride takes 9 minutes and the walk from the station to school takes 18 minutes. If you take the 7:36 A.M. train, are you more likely to be late for school or on time? The bell rings at 8:00 A.M.

26. **Using Data** Use the Data File on page 247. About how many miles could a bicyclist travel in 6 hours, based on the speed shown?

27. **Critical Thinking** What is the greatest whole number factor that you could multiply by 50 to get a product less than 10,000? Explain how you know.

Mixed Review and Test Prep

Find each quotient.

28. 36 ÷ 6 29. 25 ÷ 5 30. 20 ÷ 2 31. 63 ÷ 9 32. 49 ÷ 7

33. Which number is a factor of 96?

Ⓐ 5 Ⓑ 7 Ⓒ 8 Ⓓ 9

Chapter 6
Lesson
7

Choosing a Calculation Method

You Will Learn
how to multiply numbers in the thousands

Learn

Choi Jong-yul was on the move for seven months. His journey took him 4,500 miles across the Sahara Desert in northern Africa. How would it feel to walk that far?

Choi Jong-yul from South Korea likes adventure in the wilderness.

In one mile, you would walk the length of about 15 football fields. How many football-field lengths did Choi Jong-yul walk?

Math Tip
When you multiply greater numbers, it's good to know more than one way to find the answer.

Tanya and Dave used different methods to find $15 \times 4,500$.

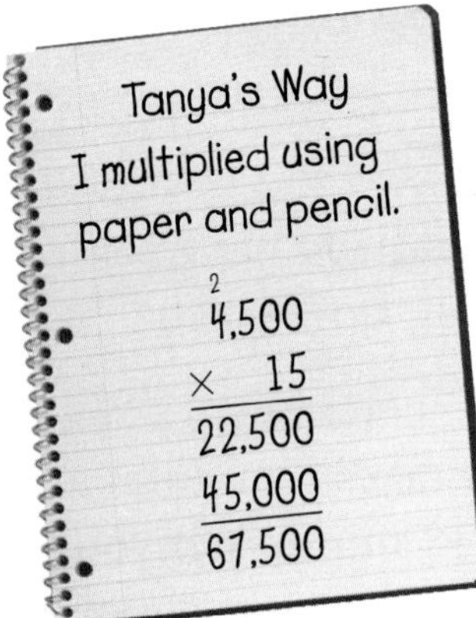

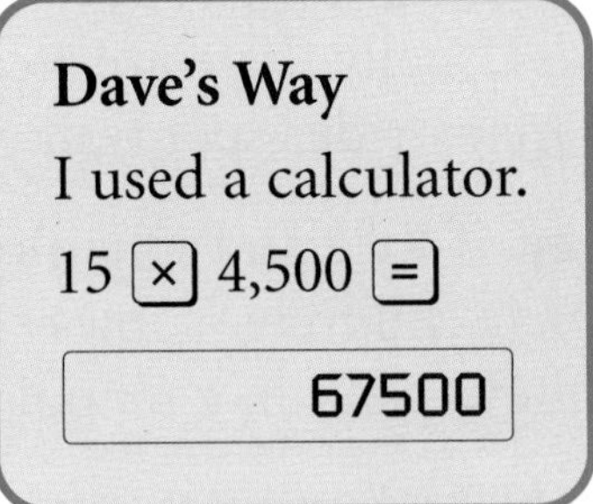

Choi Jong-yul walked about 67,500 football-field lengths.

What does the small 2 mean in the first method?

Check

Find each product.

1. 423×26
2. 309×19
3. $5,000 \times 20$
4. $2,966 \times 33$
5. $1,983 \times 41$
6. $3,002 \times 10$
7. $68 \times 5,172$
8. $19 \times 7,758$
9. $40 \times 1,200$
10. **Reasoning** How many digits are in the product of 2,999 and 12?

Practice

Skills and Reasoning

Choose a tool

Find each product. Estimate to check.

11. 343×59 **12.** 118×13 **13.** $2{,}096 \times 21$ **14.** $6{,}000 \times 90$ **15.** $1{,}789 \times 16$

16. $3{,}739 \times 12$ **17.** $3{,}855 \times 15$ **18.** $2{,}021 \times 54$ **19.** $4{,}223 \times 18$ **20.** $1{,}440 \times 33$

21. $23 \times 3{,}174$ **22.** $14 \times 2{,}000$ **23.** 320×39 **24.** $16 \times 3{,}285$

25. Find the product of 249 and 14. **26.** Find the product of 3,989 and 12.

27. Mental Math How would you use mental math to find the product of 4,000 and 12?

28. How many digits are in the product of 1,111 and 11?

Problem Solving and Applications

29. Social Studies Suppose you walked from Washington, D.C., to San Francisco, California, or about 2,922 miles. About how many football-field lengths would you walk, if there are 15 in a mile?

30. Geography The desert across northern Africa grows by about 6 miles a year. About how many miles farther south will it be after 75 years?

31. Time Choi Jong-yul got to the Red Sea on June 6, 1996, after traveling 7 months. About when did he begin his trip?

32. Measurement The temperature in the Sahara can be as low as 5°F in the high mountains or as high as 136°F elsewhere. What is the range of temperature?

Choi Jong-yul began here.
Sahara Desert
He ended here.
Nouakchott
Suakin
AFRICA
Atlantic Ocean
Indian Ocean

33. Journal Explain which calculation method you would use to find $2{,}000 \times 22$.

Mixed Review and Test Prep

Find each quotient.

34. $48 \div 8$ **35.** $35 \div 7$ **36.** $66 \div 6$ **37.** $64 \div 8$ **38.** $27 \div 3$

39. Money If you give \$10 for a \$7.61 item, how much change will you get?

Ⓐ \$2.39 Ⓑ \$2.84 Ⓒ \$3.39 Ⓓ \$7.61

Skills Practice Bank, page 567, Set 5

and Practice

Find each product.

1. 72 × 15	**2.** 74 × 24	**3.** 42 × 55	**4.** 81 × 14	**5.** 60 × 35
6. 41 × 10	**7.** 65 × 85	**8.** 89 × 27	**9.** 47 × 34	**10.** 56 × 18
11. 419 × 29	**12.** 245 × 26	**13.** 153 × 75	**14.** 463 × 28	**15.** 218 × 90
16. 900 × 73	**17.** 539 × 43	**18.** 67 × 111	**19.** 19 × 663	**20.** 935 × 30
21. 4,571 × 13	**22.** 1,776 × 58	**23.** 6,210 × 61	**24.** 1,122 × 25	**25.** 4,506 × 30
26. 707 × 22	**27.** 86 × 54	**28.** 166 × 12	**29.** 5,284 × 68	**30.** 3,019 × 77
31. 31 × 49	**32.** 460 × 53	**33.** 588 × 59	**34.** 2,963 × 44	**35.** 591 × 98

36. 82 × 753	**37.** 39 × 3,206	**38.** 263 × 87	**39.** 66 × 1,089
40. 2,225 × 71	**41.** 3,220 × 51	**42.** 5,432 × 16	**43.** 5,678 × 36
44. 629 × 33	**45.** 37 × 1,834	**46.** 57 × 88	**47.** 23 × 5,479

Error Search

Find each incorrect product. Write it correctly and explain the error.

48. 5,332 × 50	**49.** 8,005 × 48	**50.** 4,190 × 17	**51.** 1,828 × 32	**52.** 1,034 × 21
266,600	384,000	80,000	57,496	23,714

Find the Ancient Riddler!

Can you name this flying creature from ancient Greek mythology? It has the body of a lion and the head of a person. Sometimes it has wings, but it always speaks in riddles.

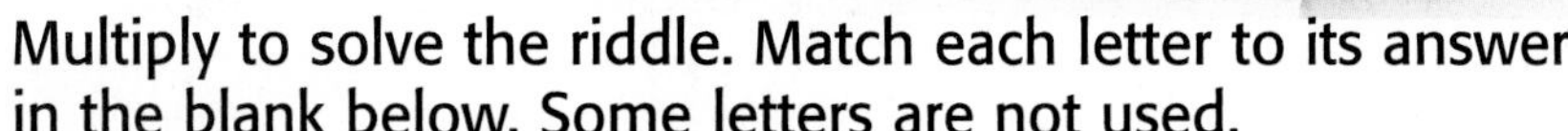

Multiply to solve the riddle. Match each letter to its answer in the blank below. Some letters are not used.

53. 419×24 [H]

54. 324×17 [E]

55. 72×12 [G]

56. 421×90 [I]

57. 587×45 [X]

58. $5{,}317 \times 15$ [O]

59. 628×39 [S]

60. $9{,}170 \times 29$ [B]

61. 691×15 [N]

62. 63×99 [P]

■	■	■	■	■	■
24,492	6,237	10,056	37,890	10,365	26,415

Number Sense Estimation and Reasoning

Copy and complete. Write <, >, or =.

63. 1,200 × 40 ● 4,000 × 30

64. 2,000 × 30 ● 700 × 99

65. 500 × 33 ● 300 × 55

66. 4,000 × 42 ● 997 × 98

67. 205 × 80 ● 90 × 195

68. 808 × 80 ● 880 × 80

69. 5,000 × 20 ● 2,000 × 50

70. 600 × 600 ● 6,000 × 60

Chapter 6
Lesson
8

Problem Solving

Decision Making: Worth the Wait?

You Will Learn
how to analyze data to make a decision

Explore

Cedar Point Park has some of the tallest, fastest, and scariest roller coasters in the world. There are 12 roller coasters to choose from!

Your group decides to ride the same roller coasters. There are lots of people in line, so you may have to wait a long time. Which ones will you choose on this busy summer day?

Wild rides at Cedar Point Park in Sandusky, Ohio

Facts and Data

You don't want to wait more than 25 minutes for a ride. But you may decide to wait longer for a ride that is special.

You want to ride 3 roller coasters.

If you wait more than 25 minutes in line for any 1 ride, you will be able to ride only 2 roller coasters.

Name	People in Line	Ride Capacity (per min)	Speed (mi/hr)	Greatest Height (ft)	Whole Loops
Mantis	910	30 people	60	145	4
Raptor	780	30 people	57	137	6
Mean Streak	635	26 people	65	161	0
Magnum	845	33 people	72	205	0
Gemini	975	55 people	60	125	0
Corkscrew	670	30 people	38–48	85	3

Work Together

Understand

1. What do you know?
2. What do you need to find out?
3. What is the main decision you have to make?

Plan and Solve

4. Find out how many people in line will get on each roller coaster within 25 minutes.
5. Find out which roller coasters you would be able to ride after standing in line for less than 25 minutes.
6. Which roller coaster is fastest? Which coasters have loops?
7. Which roller coasters would you most like to ride?
8. Why might you want to wait in line longer for a certain roller coaster?

Problem Solving Hint
Multiply the number of people per minute by 25 minutes. Compare this with the number of people in line.

Make a Decision

9. Write a list of the roller coasters you would like to ride.
10. What is the total amount of time you would spend waiting to ride all of the roller coasters you choose?

Present Your Decision

11. Tell how you decided which roller coasters to ride.
12. Check out **www.mathsurf.com/4/ch6** for more information on roller coasters. Compare the data.

Skills Practice Bank, page 566, Set 4

SECTION B

Review and Practice

(Lesson 5) Find each product.

1. $\begin{array}{r} 56 \\ \times 15 \\ \hline \end{array}$
2. $\begin{array}{r} 91 \\ \times 23 \\ \hline \end{array}$
3. $\begin{array}{r} 47 \\ \times 11 \\ \hline \end{array}$
4. $\begin{array}{r} 35 \\ \times 32 \\ \hline \end{array}$
5. $\begin{array}{r} 76 \\ \times 18 \\ \hline \end{array}$

6. 65×17
7. 82×14
8. 22×31
9. 75×49

10. **Reasoning** Write a multiplication sentence with 2-digit factors that has 5,600 as its product.

(Lesson 6) Estimation Estimate each product.

11. 456×19
12. 946×53
13. 359×28
14. 521×33

15. **Time** Danielle is training for a bike race. If she rides 38 miles each week, about how many miles will she ride in 1 year?

(Lesson 7) Find each product. Choose a tool 

16. $\begin{array}{r} 476 \\ \times \; 44 \\ \hline \end{array}$
17. $\begin{array}{r} 1{,}007 \\ \times \quad 25 \\ \hline \end{array}$
18. $\begin{array}{r} 4{,}018 \\ \times \quad 16 \\ \hline \end{array}$
19. $\begin{array}{r} 2{,}603 \\ \times \quad 69 \\ \hline \end{array}$
20. $\begin{array}{r} 3{,}284 \\ \times \quad 57 \\ \hline \end{array}$

Using Data Use the table for **21–23.**

Sweetwater City Buses	
Bus Number	**One-Way Trips per Week**
31	281
66	280
15	704
27	477

21. If Bus 31 carries about 55 people each trip, how many passengers will it carry in a week?
22. If Bus 15 carries about 46 people each trip, how many passengers will it carry in a week?
23. **Write Your Own Problem** Use the data to write a multiplication problem using 2-digit factors.
24. **Reasoning** Which set of factors has the greater product: 1,330 and 22, or 1,311 and 24?
25. **Journal** Suppose you need to find the products for $2{,}400 \times 10$ and $2{,}420 \times 18$. If you could use a calculator for only one problem, which would it be? Explain.

Skills Checklist

In this section, you have:

- **Multiplied with 2-Digit Factors**
- **Estimated Greater Products**
- **Chosen a Calculation Method**
- **Solved Problems by Making Decisions**

REVIEW AND PRACTICE

CHAPTER 6

SECTION

C Extending Multiplication

Some inline skaters belong to teams that compete in races. If you know how many skaters are on each team and how many teams are in a race, how could you find the number of skaters in a race?

Inline skater, Allen MacDonald

Multiplying Money

Review writing dollars and cents. Write the amount of money in dollars and cents.

1. 3 quarters
2. 1 dime, 1 nickel, 2 pennies
3. 2 nickels, 3 pennies, 2 quarters

Skills Checklist

In this section, you will:

- ❒ Multiply Money
- ❒ Solve Problems Needing Overestimates or Underestimates
- ❒ Solve Problems by Drawing a Picture

Chapter 6
Lesson
9

Multiplying Money

You Will Learn
how to multiply amounts of money

Learn

Allen MacDonald is one of the fastest seniors around. He competes as an inline skater. He has competed on his own and as part of a 16-member team.

New brakes for a pair of skates cost \$8.99. How much would it cost for Allen's whole team to buy new brakes?

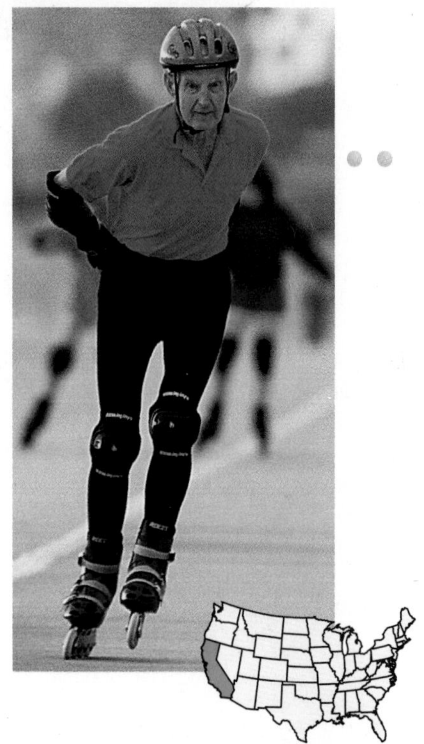

Allen MacDonald lives in Seal Beach, California.

Math Tip
Multiplying with money is like multiplying with whole numbers.

You can multiply to find out.

Example

Find $16 \times \$8.99$.

Step 1

$$\begin{array}{r} \overset{5\ 5}{\$8.99} \\ \times \quad 16 \\ \hline 5394 \\ 8990 \\ \hline 14384 \end{array}$$

Multiply.

Step 2

$$\begin{array}{r} \overset{5\ 5}{\$8.99} \\ \times \quad 16 \\ \hline 5394 \\ 8990 \\ \hline \$143.84 \end{array}$$

Write the answer in dollars and cents.

Estimate to check. $16 \times \$9 = \$144$

Since \$143.84 is close to \$144, it is a reasonable answer.

It would cost \$143.84 to buy new brakes for the team's skates.

Talk About It

What rule can you think of for writing an answer in dollars and cents?

Check

Inline skate wheel

Use the picture to find each cost.

1. 11 wheels
2. 12 wheels
3. 24 wheels
4. 17 wheels
5. **Reasoning** Is \$100 enough to buy 10 skate wheels? Explain.

Practice

Skills and Reasoning

Multiply. Estimate to check.

6. $5.68 × 19	**7.** $2.10 × 24	**8.** $5.68 × 17	**9.** $7.06 × 23	**10.** $24.69 × 11
11. $4.25 × 66	**12.** $12.34 × 21	**13.** $14.08 × 25	**14.** $19.99 × 37	**15.** $16.67 × 51
16. $32.13 × 9	**17.** $17.01 × 12	**18.** $20.99 × 20	**19.** $9.78 × 22	**20.** $17.35 × 42

21. $2.45 × 10 **22.** $1.98 × 14 **23.** 13 × $12.50 **24.** 16 × $20.98

25. Find the product of $13.99 and 26. **26.** Multiply $2.86 by 15.

27. Could you buy 18 wheels, at $9.50 each, with $165.00? Explain.

Problem Solving and Applications

Using Data Use the prices in the picture and data from page 274 for **28–31.**

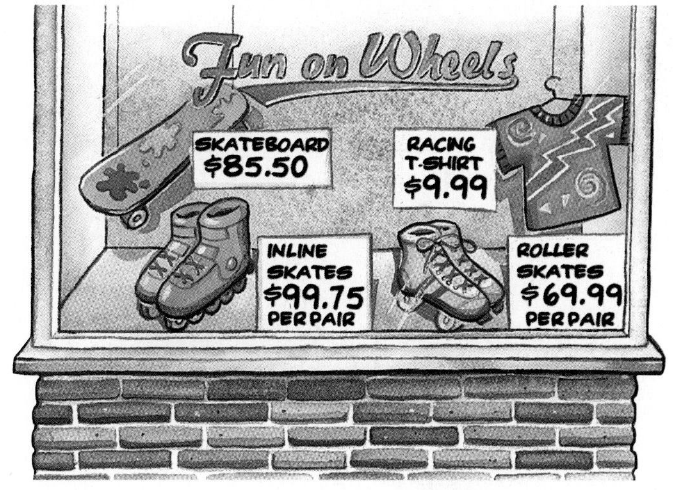

28. How much would it cost Allen MacDonald's team to buy racing T-shirts for all team members?

29. How much more does a pair of inline skates cost than a pair of roller skates?

30. Which costs more, 2 pairs of inline skates or 20 T-shirts?

31. How much would 3 skateboards cost?

32. **Using Data** Use the Data File on page 247. What was the total fare for 5 people in 1980? In 1995?

Mixed Review and Test Prep

STAY SHARP!

Algebra Readiness Find the value of each *n*.

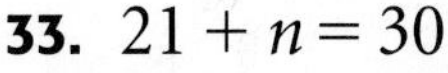

33. $21 + n = 30$ **34.** $14 + n = 19$ **35.** $n + 6 = 18$ **36.** $58 + n = 75$

37. **Time** How many minutes are in 3 hours?

38. **Time** How many days are in 26 weeks?

Ⓐ 168 days Ⓑ 172 days Ⓒ 182 days Ⓓ 260 days

Around the World Multiplication Game

Players

2 or more players

Materials

- 2 number cubes, each labeled 3–8
- world map or globe

Object

The object of the game is to find products which, when added together have a sum that is equal to or greater than 24,902—the distance in miles round Earth at the equator.

How to Play

1. Players take turns rolling the two number cubes to make one 2-digit number. Each player chooses which digit will be ones and which will be tens. Repeat to make another 2-digit number.

2. Each player records the two numbers on paper and then multiplies them. The product stands for the number of miles traveled around the earth.

3. Players continue to roll the number cubes, forming 2-digit numbers and multiplying them.

4. Players total their products, trying to get a sum that is equal to or greater than 24,902—the distance in miles around Earth at the equator.

5. Players count how many times they roll the cubes and multiply.

Talk About It

1. How many rolls did it take you to reach the total of 24,902?

2. Do you think it's possible to reach 24,902 without going beyond? Explain.

3. What strategy could you use to reach the total of 24,902 in the fewest tries?

More Ways to Play

- Play again. This time, subtract your first product from 24,902. Then subtract your next product from the difference. And so on.

- Play another game. For each product, find a place on a map that is about that distance from your home state. Keep track of the places you "visit."

Reasoning

1. Suppose you get 4 and 3 on the first roll and 3 and 5 on the second roll. How would you arrange your digits if you want to reach the total of 24,902 in the fewest tries? What would be the product?

2. What is the greatest product possible with the number cubes? How would you get it?

3. How many rolls of a 5 and 6 will give you a product that is close to the distance around the earth in miles? Explain.

Chapter 6
Lesson
10

Problem Solving

Analyze Word Problems: Overestimating and Underestimating

You Will Learn
how to decide when to overestimate or underestimate

Reading Tip
First read all the information to find the main idea. Then find the facts you need.

Learn

Neighbors want to put a merry-go-round in the park. They buy one that holds 14 children.

The neighbors decide to make a sign that tells how many pounds the merry-go-round can support. The typical weight for a child who rides on merry-go-rounds is 75 pounds. Should the sign overestimate or underestimate the weight allowed?

Work Together

Understand

What do you know?

What do you need to find out?

Plan

Decide if you should overestimate or underestimate.

To make sure the merry-go-round can support the weight of 14 children, you should underestimate the weight allowed.

Solve

To underestimate, round one or both factors down. Then multiply.

Round 14 to 10.
$10 \times 75 = 750$
The sign should list 750 pounds as the maximum weight allowed.

Look Back

How can you check to see if your answer is reasonable?

Why does it make sense to underestimate in this situation?

Check

Decide if you should overestimate or underestimate. Solve.

1. **Money** You need about 28 ft of lumber to build a car body for a soapbox derby. Lumber costs $0.85 a foot at your local lumber yard. To make sure you have enough lumber, about how much should you plan to spend?

2. You set aside 15 hours to read a book for a book report. You can read about 12 pages an hour. To make sure you have enough time to read the whole book, what is the greatest number of pages the book can have?

Problem Solving Practice

Problem Solving Strategies

- Use Objects/Act It Out
- Draw a Picture
- Look for a Pattern
- Guess and Check
- Use Logical Reasoning
- Make an Organized List
- Make a Table
- Solve a Simpler Problem
- Work Backward

Choose a Tool

Solve each problem.

3. You want to find how long it will take to earn enough money to buy a skateboard. You earn $3.50 for mowing a lawn. You can mow 12 lawns a month.
   a. Should you underestimate or overestimate? Why?
   b. Estimate how much you might earn in a month.

4. Most cars need an oil change about every 5,000 miles. Suppose a family drives about 238 miles each week.
   a. Will the car need an oil change after 23 weeks? How do you know?
   b. Why would you overestimate to find out?

5. **Critical Thinking** Elheran can walk 30 yd a minute in snowshoes. He wants to make sure he can get to a friend's house before dark. The sun goes down in 65 minutes. Three friends live nearby. To which friend's house should Elheran go? Explain.

Friend	Distance to House
Sebastian	1,900 yd
Andrew	1,750 yd
Janos	2,050 yd

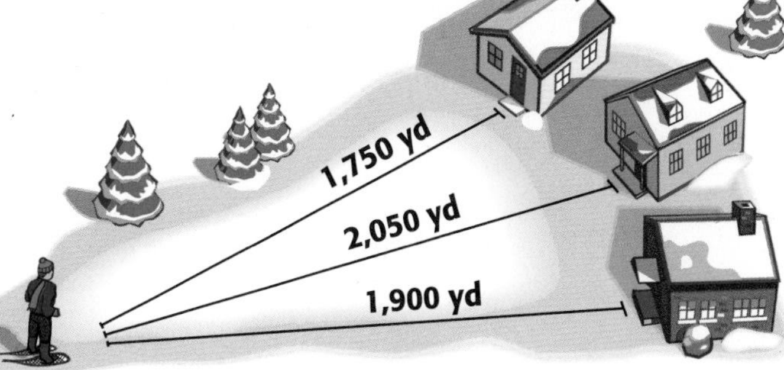

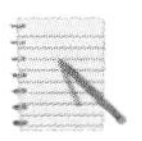

6. **Journal** Write about a situation in which you overestimated an amount. Explain why it made sense to overestimate. Then tell how you solved the problem.

PROBLEM SOLVING PRACTICE

Chapter 6
Lesson
11

Problem Solving

Analyze Strategies: Draw a Picture

You Will Learn
how to solve a problem by drawing a picture

Learn

Suppose you enter a bike race. There are 12 racers in each row. There are 11 rows. You are in the seventh row.

How many racers start ahead of you? How many racers are there in all?

Work Together

▶ Understand

What do you know?

What do you need to find out?

▶ Plan

Think of a picture that will help. Decide what it will show.

Write an A for each racer ahead of you.
Write a B for each racer in your row.
Write a C for each racer behind you.

▶ Solve

Draw the picture.
Use labels as needed.

Use the picture to solve the problem.

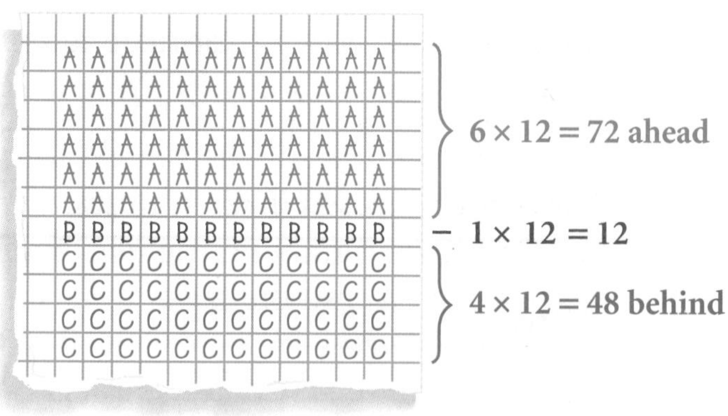

$72 + 12 + 48 = 132$

What are the answers? There are 72 racers ahead and 132 in all.

▶ Look Back

How can you check your answers?

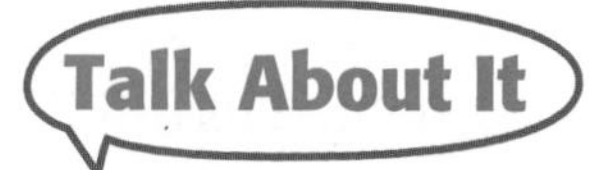

How did the picture help you solve the problem?

Check

Problem Solving
Understand
Plan
Solve
Look Back

Draw a picture to help you solve each problem.

1. Regina enters a bike race that has 7 rows of racers, with 15 racers in each row.
   a. How many racers are in the race?
   b. If Regina starts in the second row, how many racers will start after her?
   c. If Regina starts in the fifth row, how many racers will start ahead of her?
   d. If 3 racers in each row belong to Speedy Bicycle Club, how many of their club members are in the race?

2. Max lines up his baseball cards with the same number of cards in each row. The card in the middle of the array has 8 cards to its left, 8 to its right, 8 above, and 8 below.
   a. How many cards are in each row?
   b. How many are there in all?

Problem Solving Practice

Draw a picture or use any strategy to solve each problem.

3. If 150 racers enter a race, what are two ways they could line up in rows with the same number of riders in each row?

4. Roberto is part of a 14-member racing club. When the club members train, they ride in pairs. If the whole club rides together, how many rows do they form?

5. A group of runners is ready to start a race. All rows have the same number of people. The seventh person from the left is also the seventh person from the right. There are six rows of people ahead of that person and six rows behind. How many racers are there in all?

6. Tori and Kim are training for a bike race. Tori rides 12 miles a day, 5 days a week. Kim rides 9 miles a day, 6 days a week. Who rides more miles each week?

7. Leda finished ahead of Aris in a bicycle race. Sophie finished behind Leda. Aris finished ahead of Sophie. Who finished in second place? What strategy did you use to solve the problem?

Problem Solving Strategies

- Use Objects/Act It Out
- Draw a Picture
- Look for a Pattern
- Guess and Check
- Use Logical Reasoning
- Make an Organized List
- Make a Table
- Solve a Simpler Problem
- Work Backward

Choose a Tool

SECTION C

Review and Practice

(Lesson 9) Multiply.

1. $6.75 × 13	**2.** $1.41 × 41	**3.** $3.01 × 18	**4.** $5.35 × 62	**5.** $2.76 × 44
6. $19.22 × 71	**7.** $30.01 × 12	**8.** $6.83 × 15	**9.** $27.89 × 31	**10.** $36.00 × 29

11. Reasoning Which could you buy with $20: 12 boxes of crayons for $1.85 each, or 15 rubber spiders for $1.25 each?

Using Data Use the Data File on page 247.

12. How much would someone have spent for 16 subway rides in 1995?

13. How much would someone have paid for 16 subway rides in 1950?

(Lesson 10) Decide if you should overestimate or underestimate. Solve.

14. Money You need about 16 yd of cloth for a sail. The cloth costs $5.79 a yard. To make sure you have enough cloth, about how much should you plan to spend?

15. Suppose a car's gas tank holds 12 gallons of gasoline. The car usually travels about 27 miles per gallon. Estimate the greatest number of miles the driver can go before stopping to get gasoline.

(Lesson 11) Draw a picture to help you solve each problem.

16. Jars of strawberry and plum jam are packed in a box, with the same number of jars in each row. The jar in the middle is the only one that has strawberry jam. There are 5 jars to the left, right, above, and below it. How many jars have plum jam?

17. At the start of a race, there are 14 rows of 12 runners. If Ben is in the ninth row, how many runners are ahead of him?

18. Journal If you walked 9 blocks to school every day, each way, how many blocks would you walk in 2 weeks of school days? Explain how you would find the answer.

Skills Checklist

In this section, you have:

- ☑ **Multiplied Money**
- ☑ **Solved Problems Needing Overestimates or Underestimates**
- ☑ **Solved Problems by Drawing a Picture**

REVIEW AND PRACTICE

Choose at least one. Use what you have learned in this chapter.

1 Unlock the Door

To unlock, on which panels should you knock?

a. Knock on 2 panels that have a product of exactly 800.

b. Knock on 2 panels that have a product greater than 700 and less than 800.

c. Knock on 2 panels that have a product that is an even number greater than 1,000.

3 Tour Organizer

You are the class tour organizer! Check out **www.mathsurf.com/4/ch6** to find prices of different kinds of public transportation. How much will it cost for your class to travel from where you live to a nearby city? Which is the least expensive way to travel? The most expensive?

2 Mosaic of Glass

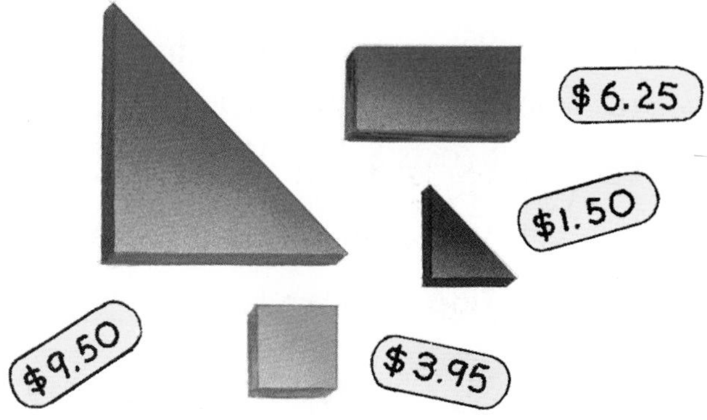

Suppose you buy these figures to make a stained glass window. Use at least 12 figures in your window. Use Power Polygons to make your window, or draw a picture of it. What is the cost of your window?

4 A Case Study

At Home With a family member or friend, find several boxes or cans of food. Make a table. List each item of food, the weight of the item, and the cost of the item. Find out how much a case of 24 of those items would weigh. How much would each case cost?

REVIEW AND PRACTICE

CHAPTER 6

Review/Test

(Lessons 1, 3, 4, and 5) Find each product.

1. 14×23 **2.** 27×40 **3.** 31×34 **4.** 15×75 **5.** 60×20

6. 61×19 **7.** 36×18 **8.** 60×30 **9.** 49×60 **10.** 19×18

(Lessons 2, 6, 10) Estimate each product.

11. 43×95 **12.** 36×78 **13.** 82×74 **14.** 198×61 **15.** 234×55

16. Your class of 28 is going on a field trip to the museum. Each ticket costs $2.75. About how much money does your class need? Would you overestimate or underestimate? Explain.

(Lesson 7) Find each product.

17. $1{,}438 \times 12$ **18.** 100×21 **19.** $5{,}422 \times 42$ **20.** $3{,}683 \times 14$ **21.** 200×26

22. 291×14 **23.** 841×27 **24.** $1{,}100 \times 80$ **25.** $2{,}000 \times 41$

26. History In 1903, a typical car traveled at 12 miles per hour. Now, the speed limit on many highways is 65 miles per hour.

a. How far would you travel in 12 hours at 12 miles per hour?

b. How far would you travel in 12 hours at 65 miles per hour?

(Lesson 9) Find each product.

27. $\$1.78 \times 32$ **28.** $\$3.21 \times 72$ **29.** $\$2.01 \times 37$ **30.** $\$1.50 \times 29$

31. Money In 1889, a meal in a train car cost $0.75. If 23 customers went to dinner one night, how much would they pay all together?

32. Reasoning Which costs more, 2 tickets at $3.50 or 3 tickets at $2.50?

(Lesson 11) Solve.

33. A marching band has 15 rows of 12 members. If you are in the tenth row from the front, how many band members march before you?

Performance Assessment

Angel's Flight, a funicular (fyoo nik yoo lar), is a cable railway that climbs up steep hills. It runs between Hill Street and a plaza in downtown Los Angeles, 298 feet high.

Angel's Flight Tickets	
1 ticket	\$0.25
Book of 10 tickets	\$1.00
Book of 40 tickets	\$7.50

Angel's Flight is the shortest railway in the world.

If you built a funicular to climb a hill, how much would you charge?

1. **Decision Making** Decide what you would call your funicular railway. Then decide on a cost for a single ride and for books of tickets.

2. **Recording Data** Copy and complete the table to show how much you would charge for a single ride, a round-trip ticket, and booklets of 15, 25, and 45 tickets.

Funicular Railway	Ticket Cost
One-way ticket	
Round-trip ticket	
Book of 15 tickets	
Book of 25 tickets	
Book of 45 tickets	

3. **Explain Your Thinking** How did you use multiplication to decide on ticket costs? In what ways could you use estimation to help you?

4. **Critical Thinking** How much does a single ride on Angel's Flight cost if you buy a book of 10 tickets? How can you find out? Why do you think it costs less per ticket if you buy 10 tickets?

Math Magazine

A market in Nigeria, western Africa

Cowrie Shells What if the only money we had was pennies? If something cost $15.00, you would have to count and carry a lot of pennies to the store!

One of the earliest and most widely used kinds of money was the cowrie shell. It was used in many parts of Africa and Asia.

Here are some cowrie shell amounts in the language of the Yoruba, which is spoken in western Africa.

ogoji = 1 string = 40 cowrie shells
ogwao = bunch of 5 strings = 200 cowrie shells
egwegwa = group of 10 bunches = 2,000 cowrie shells
oke = bag of 10 groups = 20,000 cowrie shells

Try These!

1. How are cowrie shells like pennies?
2. Which Yoruba word could mean 2 dollars?
3. Why do you think in big markets people were hired just to count cowries?
4. If something cost about 30 *ogwao,* about how many cowrie shells would it cost?

CHAPTERS 1–6

Cumulative Review

Test Prep Strategy: Eliminate Choices

Estimate.

What is the product of 57 and 34?

Ⓐ 3,208 Ⓑ 1,938 Ⓒ 18,698 Ⓓ 871

STAY SHARP!

Use your estimate to eliminate unreasonable choices. Estimate 57×34. $60 \times 30 = 1,800$. Ⓐ, Ⓒ, and Ⓓ are not close to 1,800. The answer is Ⓑ.

Write the letter of the correct answer. Eliminate choices or use any other strategy to help.

Using Data Use the graph for **1** and **2**.

1. What is the total number of miles Jennifer trained each week?

Ⓐ 4 mi Ⓑ 10 mi

Ⓒ 70 mi Ⓓ 160 mi

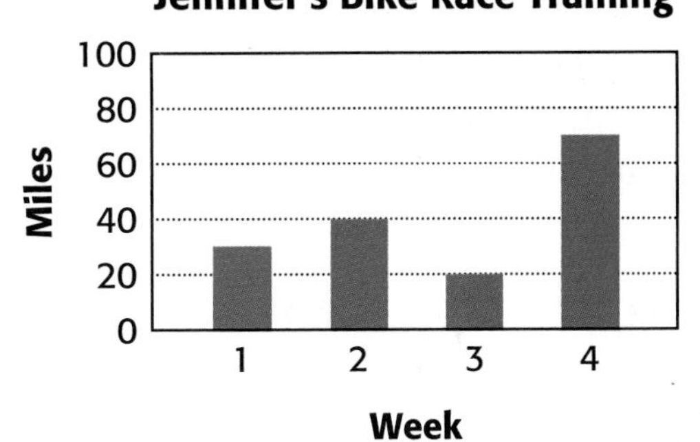

2. Suppose Jennifer trained the same number of miles each week as she trained in week 2. If she did this for a year, how many miles would she train?

Ⓐ 160 mi Ⓑ 1,040 mi Ⓒ 2,080 mi Ⓓ 2,342 mi

3. Which number is between 2,351,298 and 2,361,928?

Ⓐ 2,362,928 Ⓑ 2,361,982 Ⓒ 2,351,289 Ⓓ 2,359,892

4. Subtract 2,789 from 5,121.

Ⓐ 1,668 Ⓑ 2,332 Ⓒ 3,668 Ⓓ not here

5. Find the product of $4 \times 8 \times 5$.

Ⓐ 17 Ⓑ 28 Ⓒ 37 Ⓓ 160

6. Which numbers complete this pattern? 30, 45, 60, ■, ■

Ⓐ 70, 80 Ⓑ 85, 100 Ⓒ 75, 90 Ⓓ 65, 70

7. Which product is the least?

Ⓐ 55×41 Ⓑ 18×27 Ⓒ 54×23 Ⓓ 87×2

8. Which product is greater than $100.00?

Ⓐ 5.50×13 Ⓑ $\$40.98 \times 2$ Ⓒ $3 \times \$34.21$ Ⓓ $12 \times \$7.87$

Test Prep Strategies

- Read Carefully
- Follow Directions
- Make Smart Choices
- Eliminate Choices
- Work Backward from an Answer

REVIEW AND PRACTICE

DATA FILE

Chapter 7

Dividing by 1-Digit Divisors

Soup to Nuts

SECTION A

Developing Division Number Sense

291

How many people might share the lasagna?

Record Weights of Food

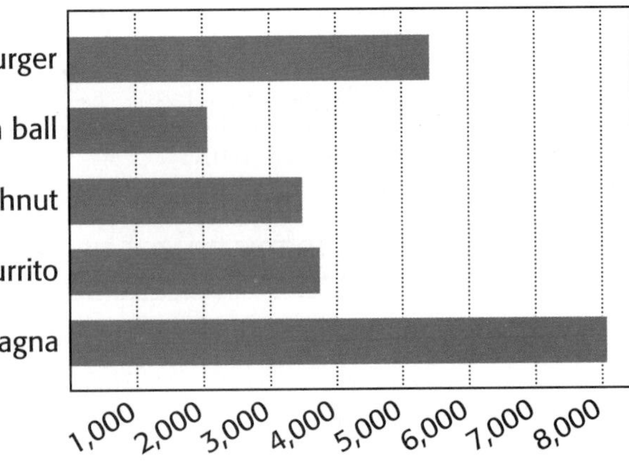

Cranberries from Maine
Page 291

Surfing the World Wide Web!

Choose a favorite food. Check out **www.mathsurf.com/4/ch7** to find out an amazing fact about it. Share the fact with other students in your class.

SECTION **B**

Dividing

299

Which food do you think is more popular—apples or oranges?

What the Average American Eats In a Year	
Watermelon	○○○○○○○○
Lettuce	○○○○○○○○○○○○○○○
Oranges	○○○○○○◖
Chocolate	○○○○○○○○○◖
Celery	○○○○
Peanut butter	○◖
Ground beef	○○○○○○○○○○○○○○○
Apples	○○○○○○○○○○

○ = 2 pounds

Delicious rice cakes
Page 299

SECTION **C**

Extending Division

319

What other costs do we pay for our food, in addition to the farmers' cost?

What the Farmer Earns		
Foods	**You Pay**	**The Farmer Earns**
1 pound of lemons	$1.23	$0.38
1 pound of green beans	$1.02	$0.11
1 pound of sugar	$0.40	$0.15
1 pound of potato chips	$1.96	$0.31
1 pound of oatmeal	$3.31	$0.19

Chili cook-off
Page 319

Team Project: Label a Salsa Jar

Materials
crayons, markers

Colorful food labels can grab your attention in the supermarket. They also list important food facts.

Help the Chili Company design a label for its new salsa. Include the food facts per serving.

Make a Plan

- Each jar of Hot Chili Salsa is 16 ounces. Each serving is 2 ounces. How will you use this data on your label?
- Salsa is made from tomatoes, chili peppers, and other ingredients. What pictures might you want to include on your label?

Carry It Out

1. Find the number of servings per jar.
2. Here are some food facts for a jar of salsa. Use division to find the food facts per serving.

Food Facts for 1 Jar of Hot Chili Salsa					
Calories	**Fat**	**Salt**	**Protein**	**Carbohydrates**	**Sugar**
120	0 grams	600 milligrams	8 grams	16 grams	16 grams

3. Draw your label. Include the food facts per serving.

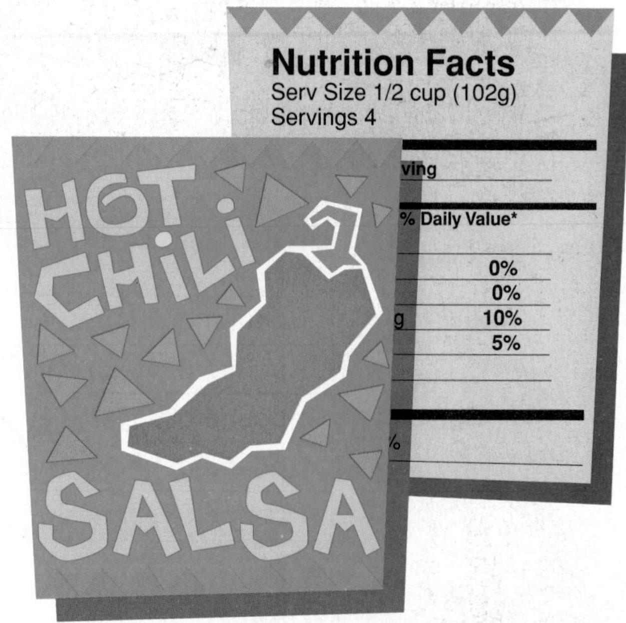

Talk About It

- How did you decide what to put on your label?

Present the Project

- Display the salsa labels. Which salsa might you reach for on a supermarket shelf? Explain.

CHAPTER 7

SECTION

A Developing Division Number Sense

Cranberries grow in bogs. What are some ways to estimate how many cranberries you will get per acre from a cranberry bog?

Christine DiRienzo
Plymouth,
Massachusetts

Division Patterns

Review multiplying by 10.

1. 6×10
2. 8×10
3. 7×10
4. 90×10
5. 50×10
6. 10×10
7. 200×10
8. 300×10
9. 400×10
10. $7{,}000 \times 10$
11. $9{,}000 \times 10$

Skills Checklist

In this section, you will:

- ❐ Explore Division Patterns
- ❐ Estimate Quotients
- ❐ Explore Division with Remainders

Chapter 7
Lesson
1

Exploring Division Patterns

Problem Solving Connection
Look for a Pattern

Materials
calculator

Explore

Place-value patterns can help you divide greater numbers.

$$8 \div 4 = 2$$
$$80 \div 4 = 20$$

Math Tip
Think of basic division facts to help.

Work Together

1. Use a calculator to find each quotient. Look for patterns.

a. $8 \div 4 = n$
$80 \div 4 = n$
$800 \div 4 = n$

b. $9 \div 3 = n$
$90 \div 3 = n$
$900 \div 3 = n$

c. $8 \div 2 = n$
$80 \div 2 = n$
$800 \div 2 = n$

2. Use patterns to find each quotient. Check with a calculator.

a. $7 \div 7 = n$
$70 \div 7 = n$
$700 \div 7 = n$

b. $10 \div 2 = n$
$100 \div 2 = n$
$1{,}000 \div 2 = n$

c. $18 \div 2 = n$
$180 \div 2 = n$
$1{,}800 \div 2 = n$

d. $48 \div 6 = n$
$480 \div 6 = n$
$4{,}800 \div 6 = n$

e. $24 \div 4 = n$
$240 \div 4 = n$
$2{,}400 \div 4 = n$

f. $35 \div 5 = n$
$350 \div 5 = n$
$3{,}500 \div 5 = n$

Talk About It

3. Describe the patterns you found.

4. Explain how you can divide 540 by 6 mentally.

Connect

You can use basic facts and place-value patterns to help you divide mentally.

Find 280 ÷ 4.

Think: $28 \div 4 = 7$

28 tens ÷ 4 = 7 tens
$280 \div 4 = 70$

Find 2,800 ÷ 4.

Think: $28 \div 4 = 7$

28 hundreds ÷ 4 = 7 hundreds
$2{,}800 \div 4 = 700$

Practice

Copy and complete.

1. $12 \div 3 = n$
   $120 \div 3 = n$
   $1{,}200 \div 3 = n$
2. $16 \div 8 = n$
   $160 \div 8 = n$
   $1{,}600 \div 8 = n$
3. $32 \div 4 = n$
   $320 \div 4 = n$
   $3{,}200 \div 4 = n$
4. $21 \div 7 = n$
   $210 \div 7 = n$
   $2{,}100 \div 7 = n$
5. $36 \div 6 = n$
   $360 \div 6 = n$
   $3{,}600 \div 6 = n$
6. $63 \div 9 = n$
   $630 \div 9 = n$
   $6{,}300 \div 9 = n$

Mental Math Find each quotient.

7. $140 \div 7$
8. $300 \div 5$
9. $1{,}800 \div 3$
10. $810 \div 9$
11. $7{,}200 \div 8$
12. $560 \div 7$
13. $4{,}200 \div 6$
14. $120 \div 6$
15. $1{,}600 \div 2$
16. $5{,}400 \div 6$
17. $490 \div 7$
18. $2{,}500 \div 5$

Algebra Readiness Copy and complete.

19. $40 \div 8 = n$
    $400 \div n = 50$
    $n \div 8 = 500$
20. $20 \div 5 = n$
    $n \div 5 = 40$
    $2{,}000 \div n = 400$
21. $15 \div 3 = n$
    $n \div 3 = 50$
    $1{,}500 \div n = 500$

22. **Geometry Readiness** Copy and complete the pattern.

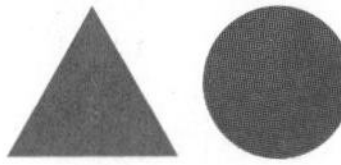      ___ ___ ___

23. **Critical Thinking** What do you notice about quotients for pairs like $420 \div 6$ and $420 \div 7$?

24. **Health** Infants need 2,800 milligrams of calcium a week. How much is that a day?

25. **Journal** Explain how basic facts and place value help you find $2{,}400 \div 4$.

Chapter 7 Lesson 2

Estimating Quotients

You Will Learn
how to use basic facts to estimate quotients

Learn

Have you ever been part of a piece of art?

This Native American portrait was created by mowing a farmer's field in Kansas. The "beads" on the 300-foot long headband were really 450 schoolchildren.

If the children stood in 8 equal groups on the band, about how many were in each group?

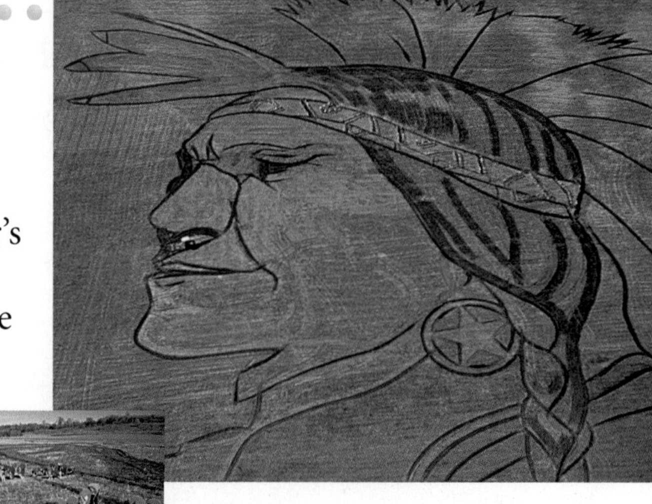

Field in Kansas with crop art of Saginaw Grant by Stan Herd

Here are two ways to estimate $450 \div 8$.

Remember
Think of basic division facts, such as $48 \div 8 = 6$ and $40 \div 8 = 5$.

Bonita's Way

450 is close to 480.

I know that $48 \div 8 = 6$.

So, $480 \div 8$ is 60.

There were about 60 children in each group.

Pedro's Way

I'll use $400 \div 8$.

I know that $40 \div 8 = 5$.

So, $400 \div 8$ is 50.

There were about 50 children in each group.

Talk About It

Could there have been more than 60 children in each group? Fewer than 50? Explain.

Check

Estimate each quotient.

1. $47 \div 3$ **2.** $96 \div 4$ **3.** $222 \div 5$ **4.** $299 \div 4$ **5.** $332 \div 6$

6. **Reasoning** Cal's estimate of $383 \div 5$ was 80. Marsha's estimate was 70. Are both estimates reasonable? Explain.

Practice

Skills and Reasoning

Estimate each quotient.

7. $115 \div 2$ **8.** $131 \div 5$ **9.** $136 \div 3$ **10.** $151 \div 6$

11. $263 \div 4$ **12.** $529 \div 7$ **13.** $365 \div 8$ **14.** $192 \div 3$

15. $388 \div 6$ **16.** $600 \div 8$ **17.** $512 \div 6$ **18.** $680 \div 8$

19. $315 \div 9$ **20.** $533 \div 7$ **21.** $767 \div 9$ **22.** $305 \div 4$

23. $599 \div 2$ **24.** $408 \div 5$ **25.** $350 \div 4$ **26.** $493 \div 7$

27. If you give an estimate of 50 for $272 \div 5$, is your estimate greater than or less than the exact answer? Explain.

Problem Solving and Applications

28. Rob has 124 cans of sweet corn to stack on the shelf. If he puts 6 cans in each row, about how many rows will he make?

29. Science The typical ear of corn has 800 kernels, arranged in 16 rows. About how many kernels would there be on 20 ears of corn?

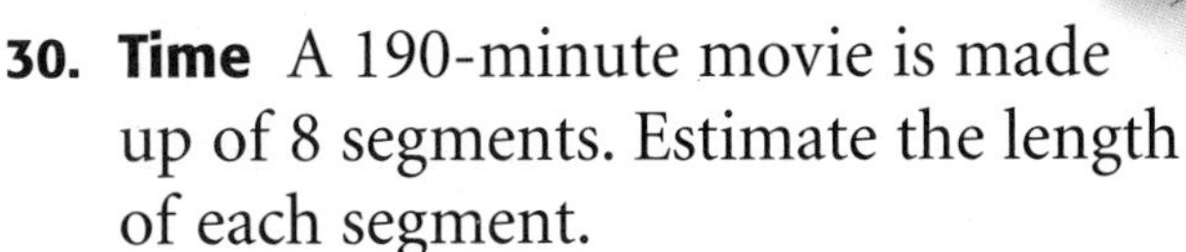

30. Time A 190-minute movie is made up of 8 segments. Estimate the length of each segment.

31. Literature L. Frank Baum wrote *The Wizard of Oz* and 13 other books about the Land of Oz. Ruth P. Thompson wrote 19 Oz books. Other authors wrote 7 more books about Oz. How many Oz books were written?

Mixed Review and Test Prep

STAY SHARP!

Find each product.

32. 70×2 **33.** 500×5 **34.** 80×6 **35.** 800×4

36. 60×7 **37.** 300×8 **38.** 20×9 **39.** 400×6

40. Find the sum of 199 and 203.

Ⓐ 403 Ⓑ 303 Ⓒ 402 Ⓓ not here

Exploring Division with Remainders

Problem Solving Connection
Guess and Check

Materials
counters

Vocabulary
remainder
the number less than the divisor that remains after the division is complete

Explore

It's a chilly autumn day. There is a warm smell of bread baking in the oven.

Suppose you make cranberry bread. A recipe calls for 5 ounces of cranberries per loaf. You have 24 ounces. How many loaves of bread can you make?

Christine DiRienzo harvests cranberries on the family bog in Plymouth, Massachusetts.

Did You Know?
Small family farms in Massachusetts produce about half of the world's cranberries.

Work Together

1. Use 1 counter for each ounce of cranberries in a loaf of bread.
   a. How many 5-ounce groups of cranberries are there?

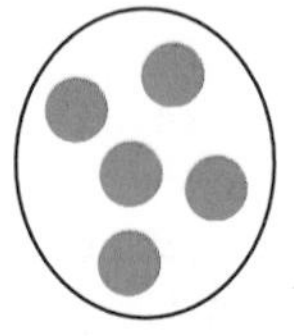 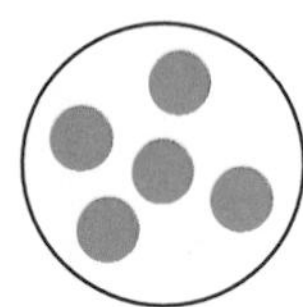 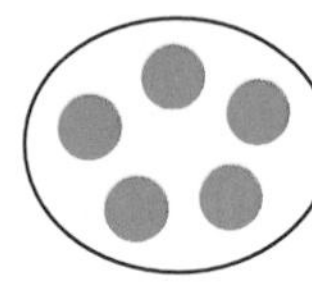 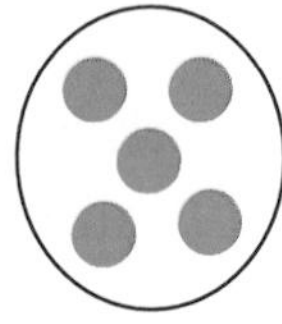 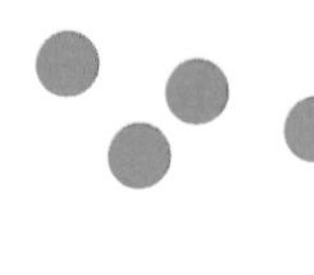

   b. How many loaves of bread can you make with 24 ounces of cranberries?
   c. How many ounces are left over?
2. Suppose you want to decorate some mashed sweet potatoes with cranberries. You have 33 cranberries.
   a. How many rows of 6 cranberries can you put on top of the mashed sweet potatoes?
   b. How many cranberries are left over?

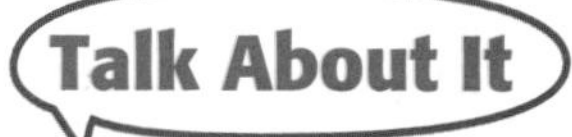

Tell how you found the number of rows of cranberries.

Connect

Sometimes when you divide, there are leftovers.
Leftovers are called **remainders**.

Find 23 ÷ 3.

What You See

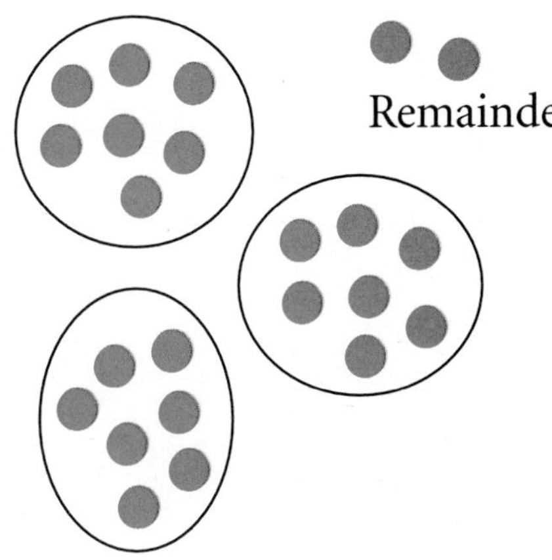

What You Write

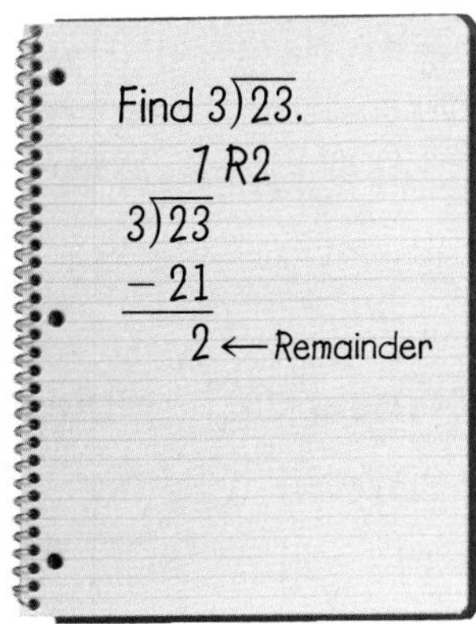

So, 23 ÷ 3 = 7 with 2 left over, or 7 R2.

Practice

Divide. You may use counters to help you.

■ R ■	■ R ■	■ R ■	■ R ■	■ R ■
1. 3)28	**2.** 4)18	**3.** 5)24	**4.** 6)30	**5.** 7)32
6. 7)13	**7.** 8)44	**8.** 7)50	**9.** 8)35	**10.** 8)64
11. 3)29	**12.** 5)48	**13.** 9)81	**14.** 8)70	**15.** 9)51
16. 7)66	**17.** 4)25	**18.** 7)18	**19.** 6)58	**20.** 9)83

21. Social Studies Wetlands help support sandy cranberry bogs. Massachusetts has about 36,300 acres of wetlands and 13,200 acres of cranberry bogs. How much land is this in all?

22. Using Data Use the Data File on page 288. In 1990, some Canadians baked a 37,740-pound cherry pie. About how many times as heavy is the cherry pie than the doughnut?

23. A Plymouth cranberry pie that serves 8 is made with 16 ounces of cranberries. How many ounces of cranberries will each person eat?

24. Christine's family bog covers about 6 acres. If the family harvests 150 barrels of cranberries per acre, how many barrels will they get in all?

25. Journal Explain how you would divide 50 cranberries equally among 8 muffins.

SECTION A

Review and Practice

(Lesson 1) Mental Math Find each quotient.

1. 200 ÷ 4 **2.** 180 ÷ 6 **3.** 270 ÷ 3 **4.** 420 ÷ 7

5. 3,600 ÷ 9 **6.** 2,100 ÷ 3 **7.** 6,400 ÷ 8 **8.** 3,200 ÷ 4

9. 240 ÷ 6 **10.** 4,000 ÷ 5 **11.** 810 ÷ 9 **12.** 1,200 ÷ 3

13. 4,200 ÷ 6 **14.** 210 ÷ 7 **15.** 300 ÷ 5 **16.** 6,000 ÷ 2

(Lesson 2) Estimation Estimate each quotient.

17. 142 ÷ 4 **18.** 227 ÷ 5 **19.** 323 ÷ 9 **20.** 597 ÷ 8

21. 162 ÷ 3 **22.** 333 ÷ 4 **23.** 491 ÷ 8 **24.** 510 ÷ 7

25. 502 ÷ 6 **26.** 553 ÷ 9 **27.** 377 ÷ 5 **28.** 335 ÷ 4

29. Reasoning Suppose you have 136 bagels. You want to put 6 bagels in each bag. Will you have more or less than 20 bags with exactly 6 bagels ? Explain.

(Lesson 3) Divide.

30. 14 ÷ 6 **31.** 27 ÷ 5 **32.** 44 ÷ 8 **33.** 52 ÷ 7 **34.** 42 ÷ 6

35. 37 ÷ 5 **36.** 35 ÷ 6 **37.** 75 ÷ 8 **38.** 43 ÷ 7 **39.** 29 ÷ 4

40. 57 ÷ 8 **41.** 65 ÷ 9 **42.** 50 ÷ 7 **43.** 27 ÷ 9 **44.** 22 ÷ 3

45. $2\overline{)17}$ **46.** $9\overline{)76}$ **47.** $3\overline{)14}$ **48.** $9\overline{)64}$ **49.** $4\overline{)38}$

50. $4\overline{)32}$ **51.** $5\overline{)29}$ **52.** $3\overline{)20}$ **53.** $9\overline{)76}$ **54.** $6\overline{)55}$

55. Critical Thinking "I need 3 cups of milk for each pudding. I have 14 cups of milk, so I can make 5 puddings," says Shira. Is she correct? Explain.

56. Reasoning 982 ÷ 5 = 196 R2. How can this help you find what number divided by 5 is 196? Explain.

57. Journal Suppose you have 40 apples. You put 6 in a bag. How many bags can you fill? Explain why the answer is not 5 R10.

Skills Checklist

In this section, you have:

- ☑ **Explored Division Patterns**
- ☑ **Estimated Quotients**
- ☑ **Explored Division with Remainders**

REVIEW AND PRACTICE

CHAPTER 7

SECTION

B Dividing

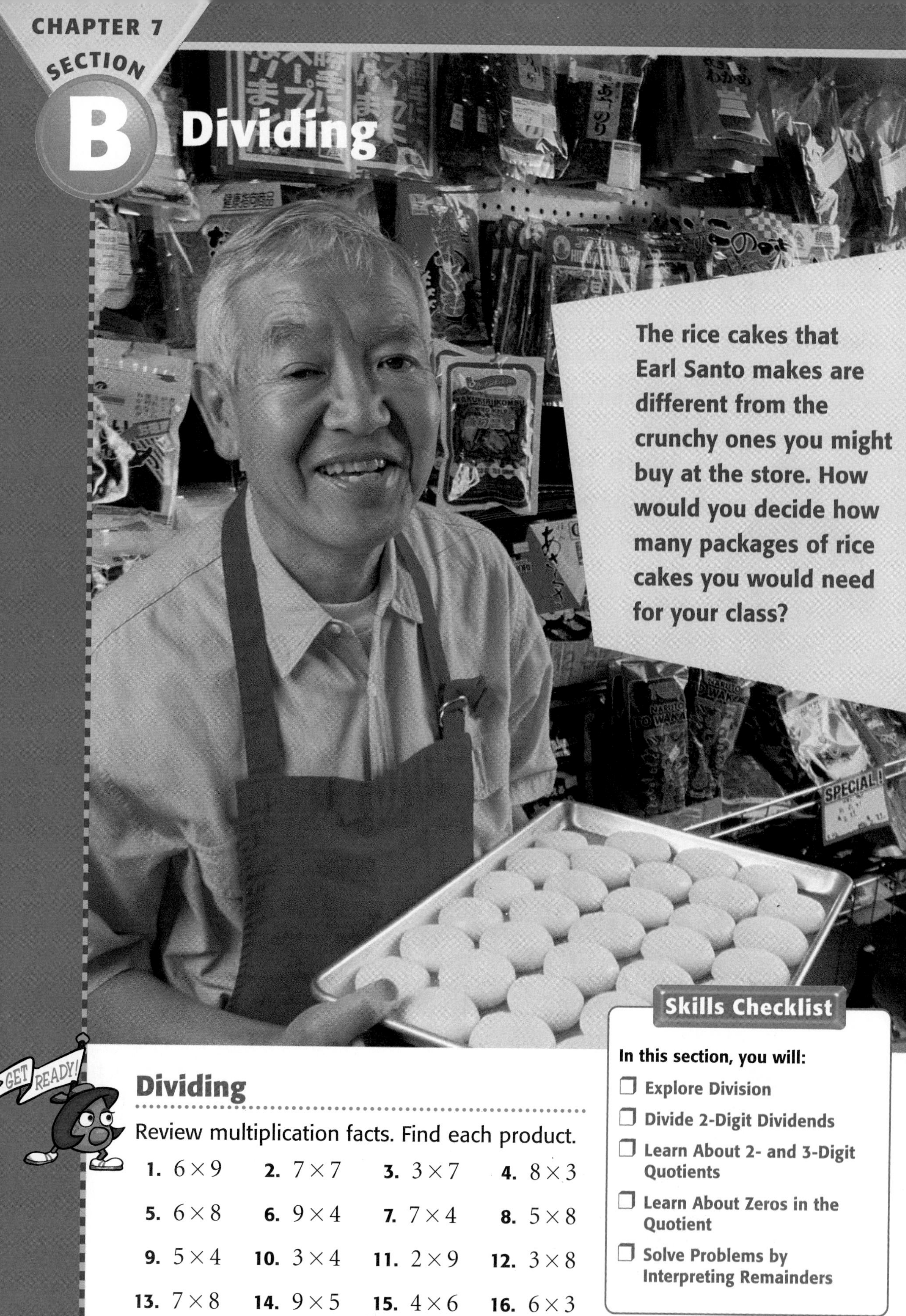

The rice cakes that Earl Santo makes are different from the crunchy ones you might buy at the store. How would you decide how many packages of rice cakes you would need for your class?

Dividing

Review multiplication facts. Find each product.

1. 6 × 9	**2.** 7 × 7	**3.** 3 × 7	**4.** 8 × 3
5. 6 × 8	**6.** 9 × 4	**7.** 7 × 4	**8.** 5 × 8
9. 5 × 4	**10.** 3 × 4	**11.** 2 × 9	**12.** 3 × 8
13. 7 × 8	**14.** 9 × 5	**15.** 4 × 6	**16.** 6 × 3

Skills Checklist

In this section, you will:

- ❒ Explore Division
- ❒ Divide 2-Digit Dividends
- ❒ Learn About 2- and 3-Digit Quotients
- ❒ Learn About Zeros in the Quotient
- ❒ Solve Problems by Interpreting Remainders

Chapter 7
Lesson
4

Exploring Division

Problem Solving Connection
Use Objects/
Act It Out

Materials
place-value blocks

Explore

Wisconsin produces more than a million tons of cheese a year. That's almost a third of all cheese that Americans eat.

If you have 46 Wisconsin cheese logs to pack in 3 boxes, how many should you pack in each box?

You can use place-value blocks to show division.

Work Together

1. Use place-value blocks to find $46 \div 3$.
   a. Show 46 as 4 tens and 6 ones.
   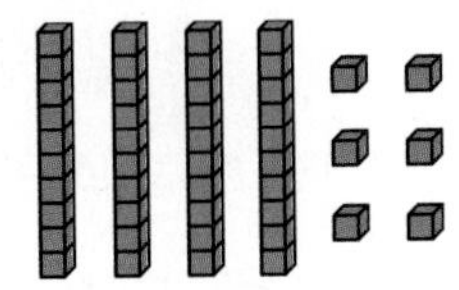
   b. Divide the tens into three groups. Put an equal number in each group. How many are in each group? How many extra tens do you have?
   c. Regroup the extra ten. How many ones do you now have?
   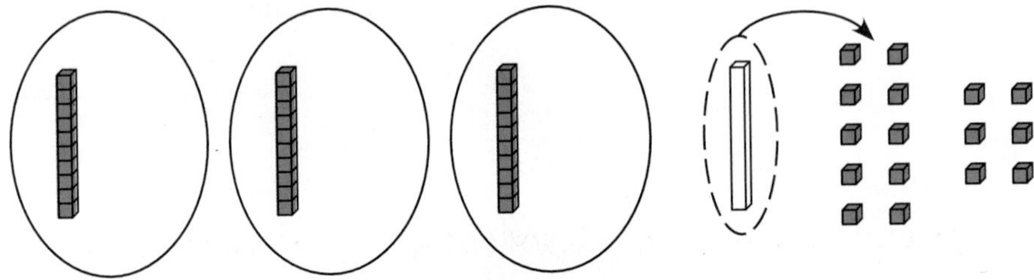
   d. Divide the ones into three groups. Put an equal number of ones in each group. How many ones are in each group? How many extra ones do you have?
   e. If you wanted to pack 46 cheese logs into 3 boxes, how many would you pack in each box? How many would be left over?

Remember
The remainder must be less than the divisor.

2. Use place-value blocks to divide.
   a. $19 \div 3$ b. $51 \div 4$ c. $29 \div 6$ d. $36 \div 9$

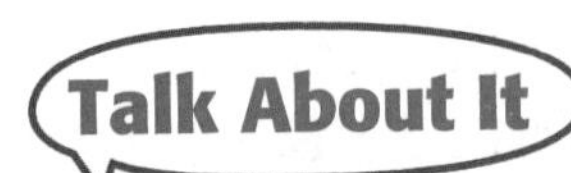

Why did you have to regroup to find $46 \div 3$?

Connect

Here is a way to record division shown with place-value blocks.

What You See

What You Write

Find 31 ÷ 2

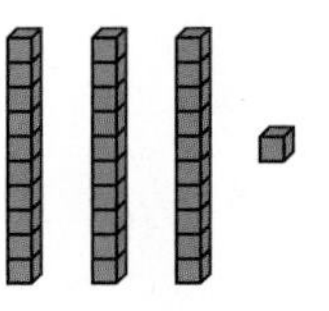

$2\overline{)31}$

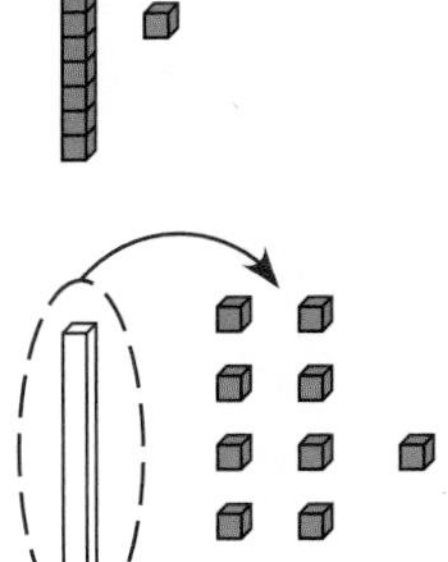

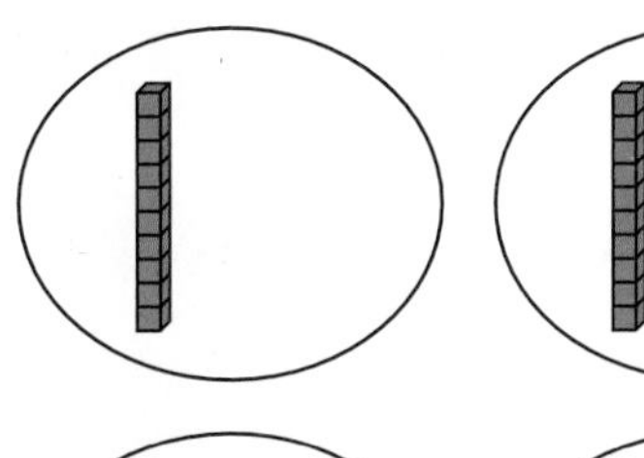

```
   1      1 ten in each group
2)31
 - 2      2 tens used
   1      1 ten left over
```

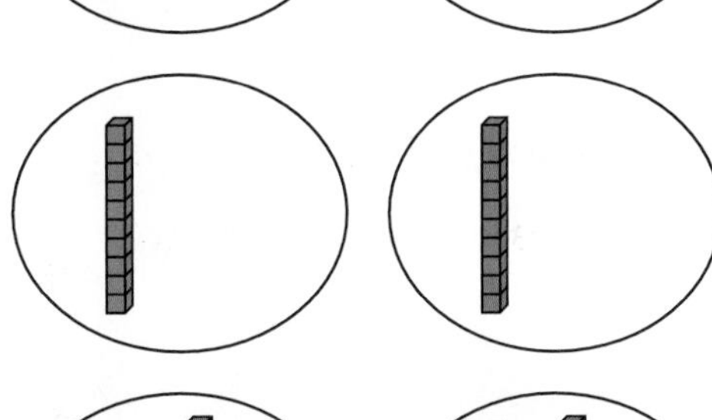

```
   1
2)31
 - 2↓     Bring down 1 one.
   11     11 ones in all
```

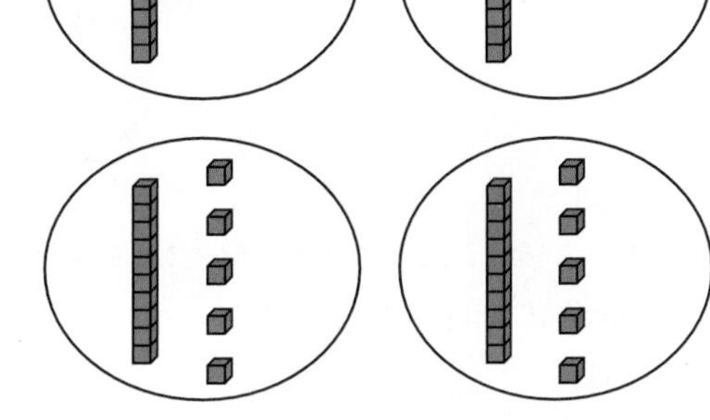

```
   15     5 ones in each group
2)31
 - 2
   11
 - 10     10 ones used
    1     1 one left over
```

So, 31 ÷ 2 = 15 R1.

Practice

Copy and complete. You may use place-value blocks to help.

```
1.   1■          2.  ■4 R■         3.  ■■ R1         4.  ■■ R■
   5)8 0           4)5 8             3)7 9             6)8 1
   - 5↓            - 4↓              - ■↓              - ■↓
     ■■              ■■                ■■                ■■
   - ■■            - ■■              - ■■              - ■■
      ■               ■                 ■                 ■
```

Divide. You may use place-value blocks to help.

5. $3\overline{)36}$ **6.** $5\overline{)71}$ **7.** $4\overline{)49}$ **8.** $2\overline{)33}$ **9.** $5\overline{)64}$

10. Suppose you have 48 cheese logs. How many can you put in 5 boxes, if you put an equal number of logs in each box?

11. Journal Explain how to divide 68 by 3 with place-value blocks.

Chapter 7
Lesson
5

Dividing 2-Digit Dividends

You Will Learn
how to divide 2-digit dividends

Learn

Boiled peanuts are a tasty Southern treat. They're crunchy and juicy at the same time. Peanuts are an important crop in Alabama and Georgia. Farmers plant them in rows.

If Scott plants 4 rows of peanuts and has a total of 76 plants, how many plants are in each row?

You can divide to find out how many plants are in each row.

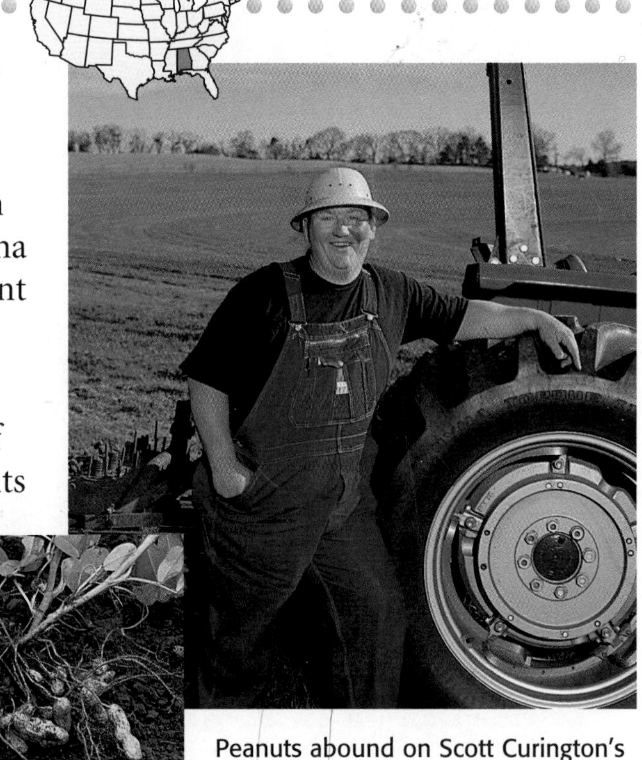

Peanuts abound on Scott Curington's farm in Enterprise, Alabama.

Did You Know?
About 540 peanuts go into making a medium-size jar of peanut butter.

Example 1

Find 76 ÷ 4.

Step 1

Estimate. It will help you decide where to start dividing.

Think: $4\overline{)80}$ = 20

You need an answer in the tens.

Start by dividing tens.

Step 2

Divide the tens.

$$\begin{array}{r} 1 \\ 4\overline{)76} \\ -4 \\ \hline 3 \end{array}$$

Multiply. $1 \times 4 = 4$
Subtract. $7 - 4 = 3$
Compare the remainder with the divisor. $3 < 4$

Step 3

Bring down the ones and divide.

$$\begin{array}{r} 19 \\ 4\overline{)76} \\ -4\downarrow \\ \hline 36 \\ -36 \\ \hline 0 \end{array}$$

Multiply. $9 \times 4 = 36$
Subtract. $36 - 36 = 0$
Compare. $0 < 4$

You can use multiplication to check your answer.

$$\begin{array}{r} 19 \\ \times\ 4 \\ \hline 76 \end{array}$$ 19 ← Quotient, 4 ← Divisor

$$\begin{array}{r} 76 \\ +\ 0 \\ \hline 76 \end{array}$$ 0 ← Remainder, 76 ← Dividend

Scott has 19 peanut plants in each row.

Example 2

Suppose you have 65 boiled peanuts and want to divide them among 3 friends. How many peanuts will each person get?

Find 65 ÷ 3.

Step 1

Estimate so you can decide where to start dividing.

Think: $3\overline{)60}$ = 20

Step 2

Start by dividing tens.

$$\begin{array}{r} 2 \\ 3\overline{)65} \\ -6 \\ \hline 0 \end{array}$$

Multiply. $2 \times 3 = 6$
Subtract. $6 - 6 = 0$
Compare. $0 < 3$

Step 3

Bring down the ones and divide.

$$\begin{array}{r} 21 \text{ R2} \\ 3\overline{)65}\phantom{\text{ R2}} \\ -6\downarrow\phantom{\text{ R2}} \\ \hline 05\phantom{\text{ R2}} \\ -\ 3\phantom{\text{ R2}} \\ \hline 2\phantom{\text{ R2}} \end{array}$$

Multiply. $1 \times 3 = 3$
Subtract. $5 - 3 = 2$
Compare. $2 < 3$

You can use multiplication to check your answer.

$$\begin{array}{r} 21 \\ \times\ 3 \\ \hline 63 \end{array} \begin{array}{l} \leftarrow \text{Quotient} \\ \leftarrow \text{Divisor} \\ \end{array} \qquad \begin{array}{r} 63 \\ +\ 2 \\ \hline 65 \end{array} \begin{array}{l} \\ \leftarrow \text{Remainder} \\ \leftarrow \text{Dividend} \end{array}$$

You could give each person 21 boiled peanuts and have 2 left over.

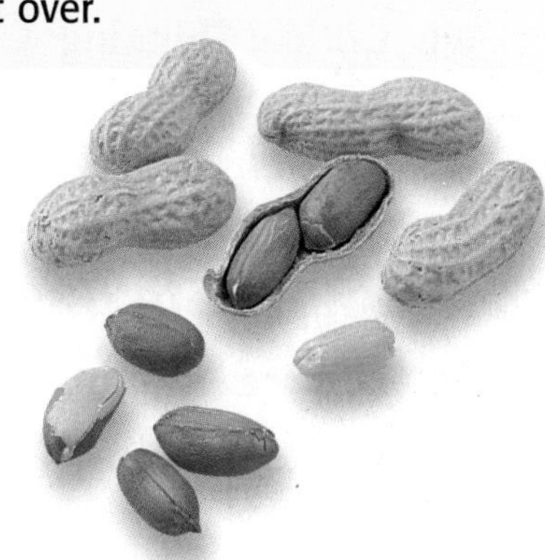

Talk About It

1. How did you decide where to start dividing?
2. In steps 2 and 3, why do you need to compare the remainder to the divisor?

Check

Copy and complete.

1. $\begin{array}{r} \blacksquare 8 \\ 3\overline{)54} \\ -3 \\ \hline 2\blacksquare \\ -24 \\ \hline 0 \end{array}$

2. $\begin{array}{r} 2\blacksquare \text{ R1} \\ 4\overline{)85}\phantom{\text{ R1}} \\ -\blacksquare\phantom{\text{ R1}} \\ \hline 0\blacksquare\phantom{\text{ R1}} \\ -\ 4\phantom{\text{ R1}} \\ \hline \blacksquare\phantom{\text{ R1}} \end{array}$

3. $\begin{array}{r} \blacksquare 1 \text{ R3} \\ 5\overline{)58}\phantom{\text{ R3}} \\ -\blacksquare\phantom{\text{ R3}} \\ \hline \blacksquare 8\phantom{\text{ R3}} \\ -\ 5\phantom{\text{ R3}} \\ \hline \blacksquare\phantom{\text{ R3}} \end{array}$

4. $\begin{array}{r} \blacksquare\blacksquare \text{ R}\blacksquare \\ 3\overline{)41}\phantom{\text{ R}\blacksquare} \\ -3\phantom{\text{ R}\blacksquare} \\ \hline \blacksquare\blacksquare\phantom{\text{ R}\blacksquare} \\ -\ \blacksquare\phantom{\text{ R}\blacksquare} \\ \hline 2\phantom{\text{ R}\blacksquare} \end{array}$

Divide. Check your answer.

5. $3\overline{)46}$
6. $4\overline{)56}$
7. $4\overline{)75}$
8. $5\overline{)62}$
9. $6\overline{)87}$
10. $6\overline{)74}$
11. $8\overline{)97}$
12. $2\overline{)58}$
13. $7\overline{)83}$
14. $6\overline{)81}$
15. **Reasoning** What is the greatest remainder you can have if the divisor is 4?

Practice

Skills and Reasoning

Divide. Check your answer.

16. $2\overline{)42}$	**17.** $3\overline{)45}$	**18.** $4\overline{)60}$	**19.** $2\overline{)70}$	**20.** $4\overline{)88}$
21. $4\overline{)53}$	**22.** $6\overline{)68}$	**23.** $4\overline{)89}$	**24.** $3\overline{)72}$	**25.** $7\overline{)85}$
26. $8\overline{)98}$	**27.** $3\overline{)81}$	**28.** $4\overline{)67}$	**29.** $9\overline{)99}$	**30.** $4\overline{)65}$
31. $2\overline{)79}$	**32.** $6\overline{)84}$	**33.** $7\overline{)96}$	**34.** $5\overline{)69}$	**35.** $3\overline{)88}$
36. $5\overline{)93}$	**37.** $6\overline{)74}$	**38.** $3\overline{)71}$	**39.** $8\overline{)88}$	**40.** $9\overline{)92}$

41. Find 76 divided by 6.

42. Divide 50 by 4.

43. Suppose you divided 76 by 3 and got 24 R4. How would you check your answer? What clue would tell you the answer was wrong?

44. **Critical Thinking** Corwin divided a number between 55 and 60 by 5. The remainder was 4. What number did Corwin divide?

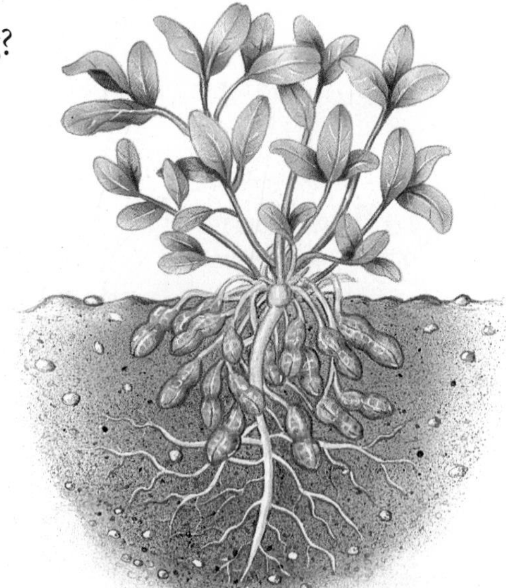

Problem Solving and Applications

45. **Science** Peanuts grow underground in pods. Each pod is attached to the stem. Suppose you dug up 3 peanut plants and gathered 88 pods. How many pods might have been attached to each plant?

46. **Time** Scott Curington grows Southern Runners, a special variety of peanuts. He plants seeds the third week of April and harvests about 154 days later. In which month will he harvest?

47. **Health** One tablespoon of peanut butter has 5 grams of protein. How many tablespoons of peanut butter would you need to eat to get the daily protein requirement of 45 grams?

48. In 1996, Scott planted 72 acres of peanuts. If he used 95 pounds of seed for each acre, how much seed did he use in all?

49. Suppose you make 4 dozen peanut butter cookies for a party. You invite 9 people. How many cookies have you allowed per person? How many are left over?

50. **Using Data** Use the Data File on page 289. About how much peanut butter does a person eat in a year?

Problem Solving and SOCIAL STUDIES

In 1919, the town of Enterprise, Alabama, built an unusual statue. It's a monument to the boll weevil, an insect that destroyed cotton crops. Before 1915, farmers grew about 35,000 bales of cotton a year. In 1916, they grew only about 21,000 bales! Farmers turned to growing peanuts. The statue is a symbol that good times can spring from bad luck.

Using Data Use the data in the paragraph and picture for **51–53.**

51. The monument is 108 inches from the street to the feet of the statue. How high is the monument from the street to the top of the boll weevil?

52. About how much less, in bales, was the cotton harvest of 1916 than the harvest before 1915?

53. In what year did the town of Enterprise celebrate the 75th birthday of the boll weevil statue?

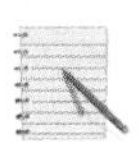

54. Journal Explain how to find the quotient and remainder of a problem like 74 ÷ 8.

Mixed Review and Test Prep

Find each sum or difference.

55. $\begin{array}{r} 339 \\ -\ 287 \\ \hline \end{array}$ **56.** $\begin{array}{r} 487 \\ 1{,}908 \\ +\ 3{,}227 \\ \hline \end{array}$ **57.** $\begin{array}{r} 1{,}077 \\ -\ 399 \\ \hline \end{array}$ **58.** $\begin{array}{r} 489 \\ 487 \\ +\ 486 \\ \hline \end{array}$ **59.** $\begin{array}{r} 1{,}300 \\ -\ 987 \\ \hline \end{array}$

60. 4,700 − 3,947 **61.** 137 + 4,187 + 23 **62.** 1,402 − 84

Find each product.

63. $\begin{array}{r} 47 \\ \times\ 9 \\ \hline \end{array}$ **64.** $\begin{array}{r} 83 \\ \times\ 18 \\ \hline \end{array}$ **65.** $\begin{array}{r} 26 \\ \times\ 19 \\ \hline \end{array}$ **66.** $\begin{array}{r} 45 \\ \times\ 23 \\ \hline \end{array}$ **67.** $\begin{array}{r} 317 \\ \times\ 8 \\ \hline \end{array}$

68. 84 × 3 **69.** 109 × 8 **70.** 34 × 35 **71.** 23 × 18

72. Which of the following is the product of 377 × 99?

Ⓐ 37,700 Ⓑ 37,699 Ⓒ 30,723 Ⓓ 37,323

Finding 3-Digit Quotients

You Will Learn
how to find 3-digit quotients

Learn

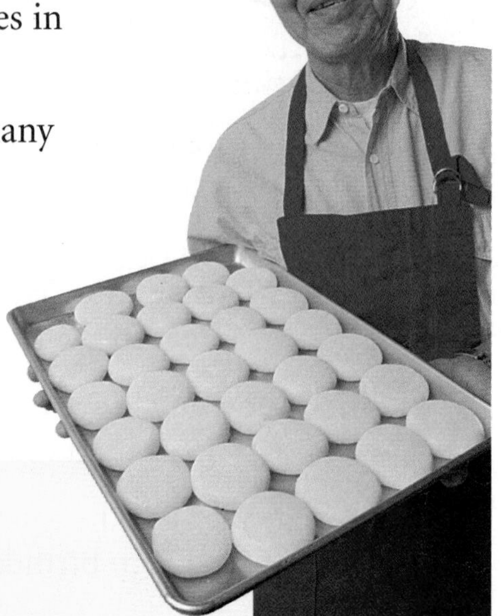

Earl Santo shapes the sweet rice dough into small, soft mounds. He packs the cakes in groups of 8 to sell in his market.

If an order calls for 896 cakes, how many packages will Earl need?

Earl Santo's food market in San Jose, California, has been serving the neighborhood for more than 50 years.

Example

Divide 896 by 8.

Step 1

Estimate to decide where to start dividing.

Think:

```
   100
8)800
```

Start by dividing hundreds.

Step 2

Divide the hundreds.

```
   1
8)896
 -8        Multiply. 1 × 8 = 8
  0        Subtract. 8 − 8 = 0
           Compare. 0 < 8
```

Step 3

Bring down the tens and divide.

```
   11
8)896
 -8        Multiply. 1 × 8 = 8
  09       Subtract. 9 − 8 = 1
 - 8       Compare. 1 < 8
   1
```

Step 4

Bring down the ones and divide.

```
   112
8)896
 -8
  09
 - 8
   16      Multiply. 2 × 8 = 16
  -16      Subtract. 16 − 16 = 0
    0      Compare. 0 < 8
```

Check. $112 \times 8 = 896$

Earl will need 112 packages.

How did you decide where to start dividing?

Check

Divide. Check your answer.

1. $2\overline{)312}$
2. $4\overline{)528}$
3. $3\overline{)458}$
4. $5\overline{)677}$
5. $7\overline{)808}$
6. **Reasoning** Without finding an exact answer, how can you tell $786 \div 6$ will have a 3-digit quotient? Explain.

Practice

Skills and Reasoning

Divide. Check your answer.

7. $2\overline{)628}$
8. $4\overline{)792}$
9. $3\overline{)954}$
10. $4\overline{)869}$
11. $5\overline{)614}$
12. $6\overline{)726}$
13. $5\overline{)712}$
14. $7\overline{)849}$
15. $3\overline{)594}$
16. $4\overline{)685}$
17. $871 \div 7$
18. $728 \div 4$
19. $999 \div 9$
20. $865 \div 4$
21. $789 \div 6$
22. $564 \div 4$
23. $398 \div 3$
24. $832 \div 6$
25. Find 647 divided by 4.
26. Divide 934 by 8.
27. How can you tell how many digits the quotient of $645 \div 3$ will have?

Problem Solving and Applications

28. Suppose Earl packed rice cakes in groups of 6. How many packages would he need to fill an order for 738 cakes?
29. **Measurement** A cup of uncooked brown rice makes 4 cups of cooked rice. If you want to serve 12 people, and each person eats 1 cup of rice, how many cups of uncooked rice will you need?
30. **Time** Brown rice takes about 45 minutes to cook. If you start cooking at 6:30 P.M., what time will the rice be done?
31. **Literature** The recipe for Rajit's biryani in *Everybody Cooks Rice* by Norah Dooley calls for 3 cups of rice. How much rice is needed to double the recipe?

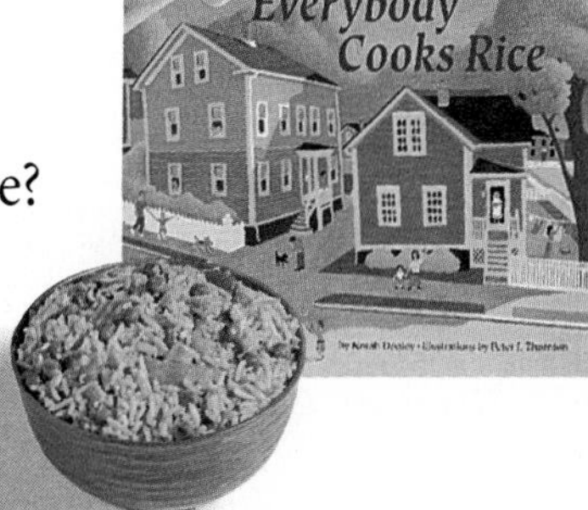

Mixed Review and Test Prep

Find each product.

32. 327×4
33. 598×7
34. 42×35
35. 145×22
36. 39×99

37. **Algebra Readiness** Find the missing number. $517 \times n = 0$

Ⓐ 51 Ⓑ 0 Ⓒ 1 Ⓓ 517

and Practice

Find each quotient. Check your answer.

1. $2\overline{)34}$	**2.** $3\overline{)57}$	**3.** $6\overline{)96}$	**4.** $4\overline{)76}$
5. $5\overline{)65}$	**6.** $4\overline{)91}$	**7.** $7\overline{)89}$	**8.** $2\overline{)49}$
9. $6\overline{)89}$	**10.** $4\overline{)97}$	**11.** $4\overline{)78}$	**12.** $3\overline{)59}$
13. $4\overline{)93}$	**14.** $7\overline{)87}$	**15.** $8\overline{)91}$	**16.** $2\overline{)246}$
17. $8\overline{)896}$	**18.** $6\overline{)888}$	**19.** $3\overline{)417}$	**20.** $9\overline{)999}$
21. $2\overline{)783}$	**22.** $5\overline{)926}$	**23.** $5\overline{)999}$	**24.** $6\overline{)927}$
25. $7\overline{)846}$	**26.** $4\overline{)712}$	**27.** $5\overline{)645}$	**28.** $4\overline{)566}$
29. $5\overline{)719}$	**30.** $3\overline{)547}$	**31.** $773 \div 4$	**32.** $527 \div 4$
33. $964 \div 7$	**34.** $758 \div 6$	**35.** $916 \div 5$	**36.** $93 \div 4$
37. $283 \div 2$	**38.** $745 \div 4$	**39.** $944 \div 7$	**40.** $958 \div 3$
41. $593 \div 4$	**42.** $761 \div 6$	**43.** $825 \div 7$	**44.** $988 \div 8$
45. $694 \div 3$	**46.** $37 \div 4$	**47.** $627 \div 6$	**48.** $972 \div 4$
49. $540 \div 3$	**50.** $688 \div 7$	**51.** $29 \div 7$	**52.** $84 \div 9$

Error Search

Find each answer that is not correct. Write it correctly and explain the error.

53. $\overset{14 \text{ R1}}{6\overline{)83}}$	**54.** $\overset{100 \text{ R56}}{7\overline{)756}}$	**55.** $\overset{24 \text{ R1}}{3\overline{)73}}$	**56.** $\overset{157 \text{ R11}}{6\overline{)953}}$
57. $\overset{79}{5\overline{)395}}$	**58.** $\overset{150 \text{ R2}}{2\overline{)301}}$	**59.** $\overset{3113}{2\overline{)826}}$	**60.** $\overset{69 \text{ R2}}{4\overline{)278}}$

Happy 100!

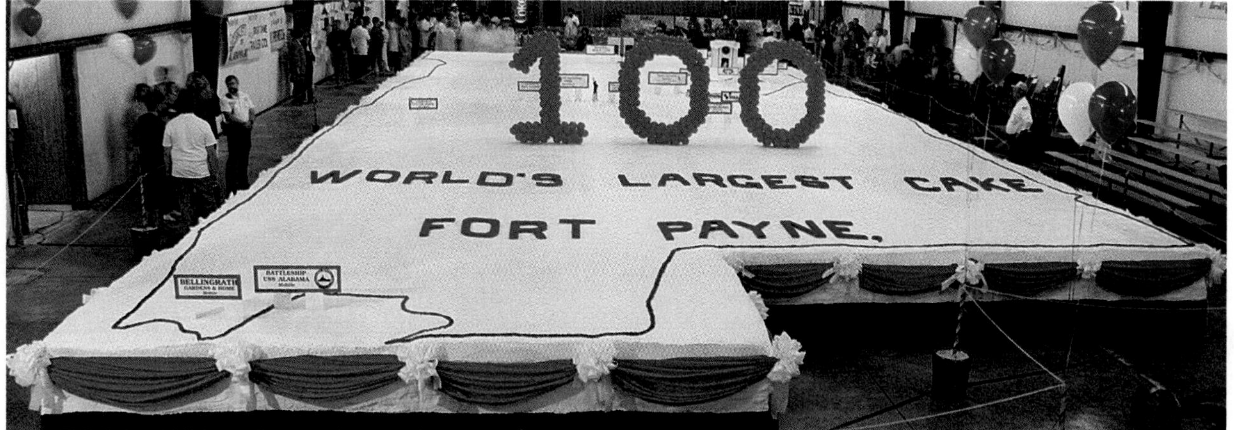

The world's largest cake was baked to celebrate a town's 100th birthday.
The cake weighed 128,238 lb 8 oz.

In what shape is this tasty "state"ment? Divide to solve the riddle. Match each letter to its answer in the blanks below. Some letters are not used.

61. $4\overline{)65}$ [A] **62.** $5\overline{)695}$ [H] **63.** $2\overline{)98}$ [B] **64.** $6\overline{)790}$ [L]

65. $6\overline{)802}$ [A] **66.** $4\overline{)81}$ [A] **67.** $7\overline{)918}$ [Q] **68.** $3\overline{)555}$ [E]

69. $8\overline{)893}$ [U] **70.** $5\overline{)67}$ [D] **71.** $3\overline{)82}$ [A] **72.** $6\overline{)775}$ [M]

___	___	___	___	___	___	___
133 R4	131 R4	27 R1	49	20 R1	129 R1	16 R1

Number Sense Mental Math and Reasoning

Write whether each statement is true or false. Explain your answer.

73. The quotient of 400 divided by 4 is greater than 250 divided by 5.

74. The quotient of 360 divided by 4 is greater than 720 divided by 9.

75. The quotient of 300 divided by 6 is less than 200 divided by 4.

76. The quotient of 540 divided by 9 is less than 350 divided by 7.

77. The quotient of 810 divided by 9 is equal to 270 divided by 3.

Chapter 7
Lesson
7

2- or 3-Digit Quotients

You Will Learn
how to find 2- or 3-digit quotients

Learn

What does a lime fruit drink have in common with a coral reef in Florida? How about a mango drink and a rain forest? Lots of cents!

The fruit drink company that Catherine Page works for gives part of its profits to environmental groups. The money will help save endangered sites.

Catherine Page works for a natural fruit drink company in Charlotte, North Carolina.

Math Tip
Always estimate the quotient to see if you can start dividing a 3-digit dividend in the hundreds place.

Example

Catherine's company stacks 114 cases onto pallets. Cases are stacked 6 layers high. How many cases are in each layer?

Find 114 ÷ 6.

Step 1	Step 2	Step 3
Estimate to decide where to start dividing. **Think:** 114 is close to 120. $6\overline{)120}$ = 20 Start by dividing tens. Your quotient will have 2 digits.	Divide the tens. $6\overline{)114}$, quotient 1 -6 5 Multiply. $1 \times 6 = 6$ Subtract. $11 - 6 = 5$ Compare. $5 < 6$	Bring down the ones and divide. $6\overline{)114}$, quotient 19 -6 54 -54 0 Multiply. $9 \times 6 = 54$ Subtract. $54 - 54 = 0$ Compare. $0 < 6$

There are 19 cases in each layer on the pallet.

Talk About It

1. How did estimating help you make sure you divided in the right place?
2. How can you tell that 375 ÷ 7 will have a 2-digit quotient?

Check

Divide. Check your answer.

1. $5\overline{)115}$ 2. $3\overline{)556}$ 3. $4\overline{)328}$ 4. $5\overline{)177}$ 5. $7\overline{)838}$

6. **Reasoning** Explain why estimating 495 ÷ 5 might give a 3-digit quotient but the exact answer gives a 2-digit quotient.

Practice

Skills and Reasoning

Divide. Check your answer.

7. $2\overline{)128}$ 8. $4\overline{)192}$ 9. $3\overline{)834}$ 10. $7\overline{)689}$ 11. $4\overline{)169}$

12. $8\overline{)223}$ 13. $9\overline{)153}$ 14. $5\overline{)625}$ 15. $6\overline{)336}$ 16. $6\overline{)825}$

17. 659 ÷ 8 18. 511 ÷ 4 19. 999 ÷ 9 20. 265 ÷ 3 21. 491 ÷ 5

22. 585 ÷ 5 23. 294 ÷ 6 24. 401 ÷ 2 25. 198 ÷ 7 26. 642 ÷ 4

27. Find 569 divided by 8.

28. Explain how you know where to start dividing to find 372 divided by 5.

Problem Solving and Applications

29. Eight pallets of cases are loaded onto a truck. In all, there are 816 cases of fruit drink bottles. How many cases are on each pallet, if each pallet holds an equal amount?

30. Suppose the cases were stacked 5 layers high, for a total of 115 cases. How many cases would be in each layer?

31. **Social Studies** Part of the profits from fruit drink sales help Cape Hatteras Lighthouse in North Carolina. At 190 feet, it may be the world's tallest brick lighthouse. Built in 1870, it is 30 feet taller than the first lighthouse built on that site in 1803. How tall was the 1803 lighthouse?

Look at the label on the bottle on page 310. Can you see the lighthouse?

Mixed Review and Test Prep

STAY SHARP!

Money Write the change from a $10 bill.

32. $5.25 33. $8.90 34. $2.56 35. $0.31 36. $1.99

37. What is the product of 3 and $2.75?

Ⓐ $7.25 Ⓑ $8.75 Ⓒ $7.55 Ⓓ $8.25

Chapter 7
Lesson
8

Zeros in the Quotient

You Will Learn
how to divide when there are zeros in the quotient

Did You Know?
A medium-size strawberry has about 200 seeds.

Learn

"May is our busiest time," Patrick explains. "The plants grow all year round, but the biggest crop of berries come in late spring."

One strawberry patch at Patrick's family farm has 824 plants, arranged in 8 rows. How many strawberry plants are in each row?

You can divide to find out how many strawberry plants are in each row.

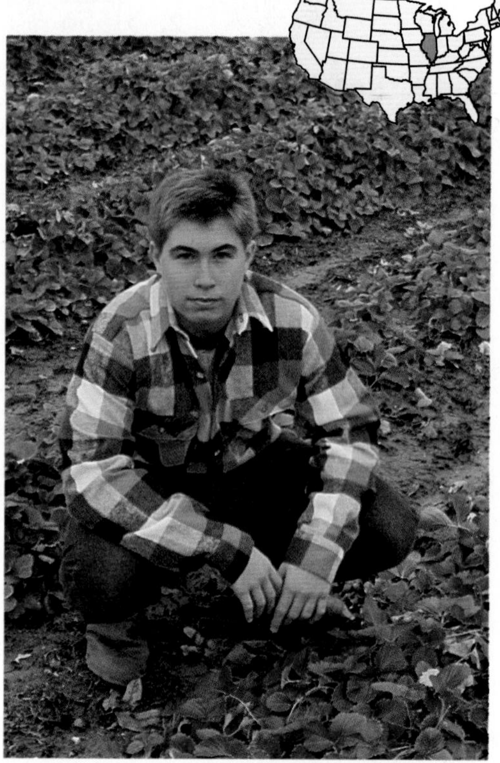

Patrick and his family grow strawberries in Mulkeytown, Illinois.

Example 1

Divide 824 by 8.

Step 1

Estimate to decide where to start dividing.

824 is close to 800.

Think: $8\overline{)800}$ = 100

Start by dividing hundreds.

Step 2

Divide the hundreds.

```
    1
 8)824   Multiply.
  -8     Subtract.
   0     Compare. 0 < 8
```

Step 3

Bring down the tens and divide.

```
   10    Write a zero.
 8)824
  -8
   02    Multiply.
  - 0    Subtract.
    2    Compare. 2 < 8
```

Step 4

Bring down the ones and divide.

```
   103
 8)824
  -8
   02
  - 0
    24   Multiply.
   -24   Subtract.
     0   Compare. 0 < 8
```

Compare your quotient with your estimate.

Each row has 103 strawberry plants.

Other Examples

You can also have zeros in quotients when there are remainders.

A.
80 R5
7)565
−56
05
− 0
5

B.
40 R2
4)162
−16
02
− 0
2

C.
107 R3
6)645
−6
04
− 0
45
−42
3

Talk About It

1. What does the zero in the quotient of Example 1 show?
2. What would happen with your quotient if you didn't write the zero for Example 1?
3. Examples A, B, and C also have zeros in the quotient. In what way are these zeros alike or different from the zero in Example 1?

Check

Copy and complete.

1.
■0 1
4)8 0 4
− 8
0■
− 0
0 4
− 4
0

2.
2 0■
3)6 1 5
− 6
■1
− 0
1■
− 1 5
0

3.
3■ R2
3)9 2
− ■
0 2
− ■
2

4.
1■8 R■
3)3 2 5
− ■
■2
− ■
2 5
− 2 4
■

5.
■■ R■
6)1 2 1
− 1 2
■1
− 0
1

Divide. Check your answer.

6. 4)80
7. 4)414
8. 7)210
9. 5)253
10. 3)926
11. 2)219
12. 3)392
13. 9)453
14. 8)848
15. 6)902
16. Find the quotient of 945 divided by 9.
17. Divide 272 by 3.
18. **Reasoning** Without finding the exact answer, how can you tell that you will get a 0 in the quotient for 423 ÷ 4?
19. **Reasoning** Explain how the quotients of 840 ÷ 7 and 84 ÷ 7 are alike and different.
20. **Social Studies** An acre of farmland can produce about 21 tons of strawberries. How many strawberries can a 15 acre farm produce?

Practice

Skills and Reasoning

Divide. Check your answer.

21. $6\overline{)607}$	**22.** $4\overline{)163}$	**23.** $3\overline{)182}$	**24.** $7\overline{)725}$	**25.** $5\overline{)301}$
26. $6\overline{)363}$	**27.** $4\overline{)826}$	**28.** $5\overline{)454}$	**29.** $5\overline{)533}$	**30.** $4\overline{)523}$
31. $7\overline{)215}$	**32.** $8\overline{)857}$	**33.** $9\overline{)547}$	**34.** $4\overline{)818}$	**35.** $7\overline{)706}$
36. $2\overline{)216}$	**37.** $7\overline{)423}$	**38.** $5\overline{)254}$	**39.** $3\overline{)612}$	**40.** $9\overline{)945}$

41. $726 \div 8$	**42.** $923 \div 3$	**43.** $407 \div 8$	**44.** $614 \div 6$
45. $645 \div 8$	**46.** $324 \div 8$	**47.** $841 \div 7$	**48.** $253 \div 5$
49. $220 \div 4$	**50.** $819 \div 2$	**51.** $305 \div 6$	**52.** $547 \div 9$

53. Find the quotient and the remainder of 607 divided by 3.

54. Find the quotient and the remainder of 415 divided by 4.

55. Mental Math Find $401 \div 2$, $602 \div 3$, and $803 \div 4$.

Problem Solving and Applications

56. Time Strawberries must be refrigerated within 30 minutes of being picked. Suppose it takes 4 hours to pick one strawberry patch. How many trips to the refrigerator will be necessary?

57. Using Data About how many seeds would you swallow if you ate 7 strawberries? Use the data from *Did You Know?* on page 312.

58. Write Your Own Problem Write a division problem about serving strawberry shortcake. Think about how many strawberries you might include for each person.

59. Science Look closely at a strawberry plant, and you'll see 4 stages of growth: white flowers, buds, green berries, and ripe berries. That's why plants are picked twice a week. How many times will a plant be picked in 112 days?

60. Social Studies Illinois and Indiana are known for growing soybeans. In 1994, Illinois farmers harvested 9,530,000 acres of soybeans. That same year, Indiana harvested 8,770,000 acres of soybeans. How many acres of soybeans did these two states harvest?

Problem Solving and HEALTH

Everyone needs vitamin C for healthy bones, blood vessels, and body cells. Children need 50 to 60 milligrams of vitamin C each day.

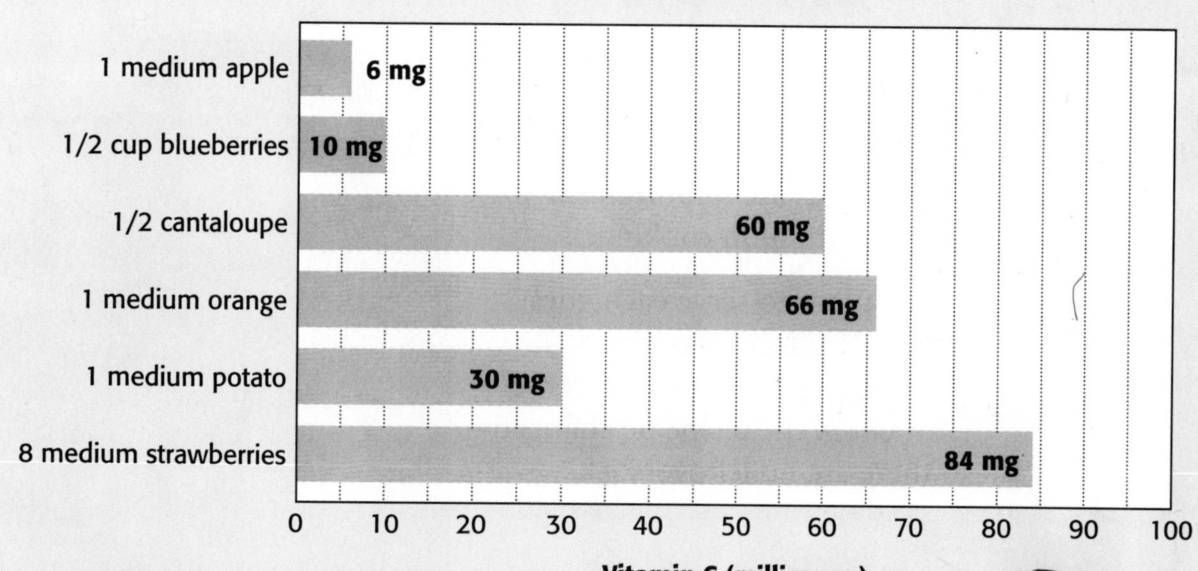

Using Data Use the bar graph for **61–63.**

61. Which foods would you eat to get enough vitamin C for the day?

62. How many apples would you have to eat to get 60 milligrams of vitamin C?

63. About how many milligrams of vitamin C are in 1 medium strawberry?

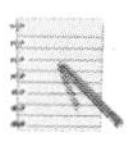

64. Journal Explain how estimating helps you decide if there is a zero in the quotient.

Mixed Review and Test Prep

Find each product.

65. 348×6 **66.** 403×8 **67.** 694×8 **68.** 287×9

Find each sum or difference.

69. $2,396 + 584$ **70.** $903 - 87$ **71.** $5,004 - 2,318$ **72.** $\$2.55 + \$3.45$

73. Patterns What are the next three numbers in this pattern? 3, 4, 6, 9, 13, ■, ■, ■

Ⓐ 14, 16, 18 Ⓑ 17, 22, 28 Ⓒ 17, 21, 25 Ⓓ 18, 24, 31

Chapter 7
Lesson
9

Problem Solving

Analyze Word Problems: Interpreting Remainders

You Will Learn
how to interpret remainders to solve problems

Learn

Kombo! Gombo! Gumbo!

These words are important to Creole and Cajun cooking.

A chef plans to serve each guest 2 cups of gumbo. How many guests will a 45-cup recipe serve? How could the recipe be changed so there are no leftovers?

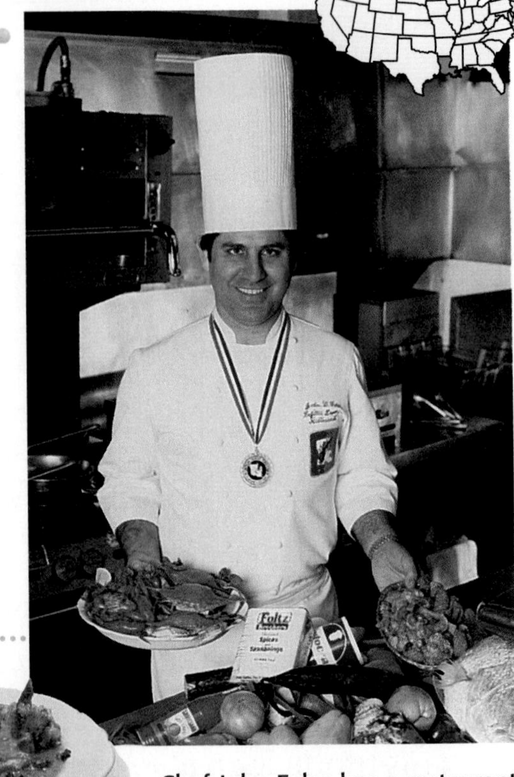

Chef John Folse has a restaurant in Donaldsonville, Louisiana.

Work Together

Understand What do you know about the recipe?
What do you need to find?

Plan How will you find out? Choose an operation that fits the situation.
Divide the pot of gumbo into equal servings of 2 cups. Find the number of leftover cups.

Solve Divide 45 by 2.
$45 \div 2 = 22$ servings with a remainder of 1 cup. If the recipe made 1 more cup, it would serve 23 guests with no leftovers.

Look Back How did you check your answer?

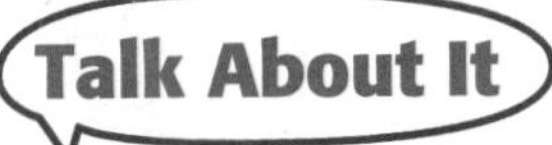

Explain why the chef would have to make 8 pecan pies to serve the 45 guests, if each pie serves 6.

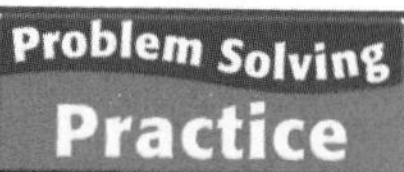

Check

Solve each problem.

1. Find the number of baskets a waiter needs for 18 rolls, if each basket holds 4 rolls.
   a. Write the division sentence for this problem.
   b. Explain what the remainder represents.
2. If a 17-inch-long loaf of bread is cut into 3-inch pieces, how much of the end of the loaf can the chef use for bread crumbs?

Problem Solving Practice

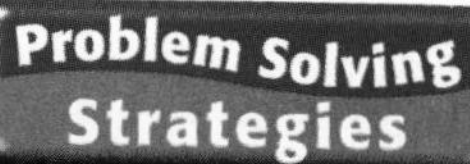

Problem Solving Strategies

- Use Objects/Act It Out
- Draw a Picture
- Look for a Pattern
- Guess and Check
- Use Logical Reasoning
- Make an Organized List
- Make a Table
- Solve a Simpler Problem
- Work Backward

Choose a Tool

Solve each problem.

3. A party of 45 people celebrates at a restaurant. Each table in the dining room seats 8 people.
   a. How many tables will the party take up?
   b. In counting the tables, did you include the remainder? Explain.
   c. How many full groups of 8 will be seated?
   d. In counting the full groups, did you include the remainder? Explain.
4. A tray holds 6 plates at one time. The waiters need to carry 68 plates of food into the dining room.
   a. How many trays will the waiters carry?
   b. Does your answer include a remainder? Explain.
5. When serving gumbo, the chef always puts 4 large shrimp in each bowl. Suppose the restaurant kitchen has 130 large shrimp.
   a. How many bowls of gumbo could be served?
   b. If the restaurant serves that many, how many extra shrimp will there be?
6. A gumbo recipe that serves 30 people calls for 45 ounces of canned tomatoes, 12 celery stalks, 3 green peppers, and 6 cups of okra, among other ingredients. Suppose you want to make enough for only 10 people.
   a. How much of each ingredient will you need?
   b. What strategy did you use to solve the problem?

PROBLEM SOLVING PRACTICE

SECTION B

Review and Practice

(Lessons 4 and 5) Divide. Check your answer.

1. $3\overline{)54}$ **2.** $5\overline{)78}$ **3.** $4\overline{)89}$ **4.** $6\overline{)67}$ **5.** $7\overline{)82}$

6. $2\overline{)48}$ **7.** $3\overline{)76}$ **8.** $4\overline{)59}$ **9.** $6\overline{)86}$ **10.** $5\overline{)85}$

11. If you have 37 cookies to share equally among 7 people, how many does each person get?

(Lessons 6, 7, and 8) Divide. Check your answer.

12. $2\overline{)364}$ **13.** $5\overline{)585}$ **14.** $4\overline{)336}$ **15.** $3\overline{)169}$ **16.** $4\overline{)225}$

17. $903 \div 5$ **18.** $476 \div 7$ **19.** $817 \div 9$ **20.** $984 \div 3$ **21.** $566 \div 4$

22. $194 \div 7$ **23.** $435 \div 5$ **24.** $501 \div 5$ **25.** $327 \div 8$ **26.** $259 \div 6$

27. $7\overline{)495}$ **28.** $6\overline{)624}$ **29.** $8\overline{)943}$ **30.** $2\overline{)839}$ **31.** $3\overline{)387}$

Using Data Use the table for **32–34.**

Food	Servings	Calories from Fat
Tortilla chips	4	244
Popcorn	3	198
Toaster tart	8	310
Potato chips	9	545

32. How many calories from fat does one serving of tortilla chips have?

33. Which snack food has the fewest calories from fat per serving?

34. **Critical Thinking** How many calories from fat would 8 servings of popcorn have?

(Lesson 9) Use any strategy to solve.

35. How many dining tables are needed for 59 people, if 4 people can sit at each table?

36. Marc is decorating sweatshirts. He has 40 beads. If he puts 7 beads on each sweatshirt, how many sweatshirts can he decorate? How many more beads does he need if he wants to decorate another sweatshirt?

37. **Journal** How would you share 127 pumpkin seeds equally among 9 people? How many would each person get?

Skills Checklist

In this section, you have:

- ☑ **Explored Division**
- ☑ **Divided 2-Digit Dividends**
- ☑ **Learned About 2- and 3-Digit Quotients**
- ☑ **Learned About Zeros in the Quotient**
- ☑ **Solved Problems by Interpreting Remainder**

CHAPTER 7

SECTION

C Extending Division

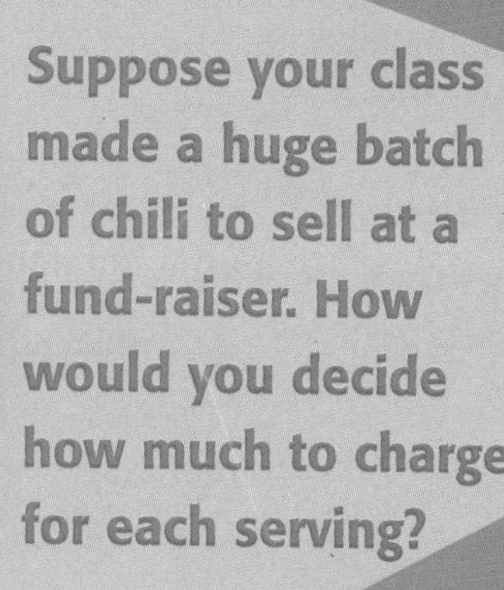

Elizabeth
Fort Worth, Texas

Dividing Money

Review regrouping money.
How many pennies?

1. 6 dimes, 5 nickels, 3 pennies
2. 8 dimes, 3 nickels, 7 pennies
3. 2 dollars, 3 dimes, 6 nickels, 4 pennies

Skills Checklist

In this section, you will:

- ❐ Explore Division with Money
- ❐ Divide Money Amounts
- ❐ Explore Finding the Mean
- ❐ Explore Divisibility
- ❐ Solve Problems by Working Backward

Chapter 7
Lesson
10

Exploring Division with Money

Problem Solving Connection
Use Objects/
Act It Out

Materials
play money: dollars, dimes, pennies

Explore

Suppose you buy a bag of popcorn that costs $1.32 with tax. You decide to share it with three friends who want to help pay. To share the cost equally, how much should each person pay?

Work Together

1. Divide $1.32 by 4.
   a. Show $1.32.

   b. Regroup $1 as dimes. How many dimes are there?
   c. Put the dimes in 4 equal groups. How many dimes are in each group? How many dimes are left over?

   d. Regroup any leftover dimes as pennies. How many pennies are there?
   e. Put the pennies in 4 equal groups. How much money is in each group?
   f. How much should each person pay?
2. Find each quotient. Use play money to help.
   a. $1.62 ÷ 3   b. $2.34 ÷ 2   c. $1.25 ÷ 5

Did You Know?
Paper money was first used in China more than 4,000 years ago.

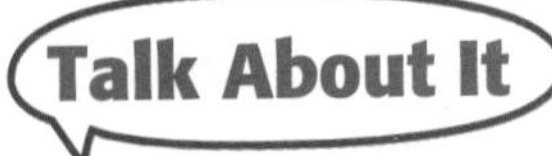

How is dividing money like dividing with place-value blocks?

Connect

Here is a way to record dividing with money.

What You See | **What You Write**

```
2)$1.14
```

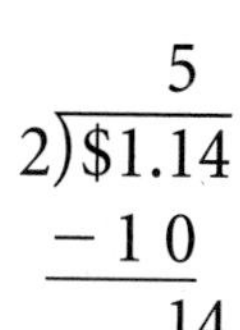

Regroup the dollar as dimes.
Divide the dimes.

```
     5
2)$1.14
  -1 0
    14
```

Regroup the dime as pennies.
Divide the pennies.

```
  $0.57
2)$1.14
  -1 0
    14
   -14
     0
```

Practice

Copy and complete. Find each quotient. Use play money to help.

```
1.   $0.■5        2.   $■.6■        3.   $■.■■        4.   $■.■4        5.   $1.2■
   3)$1.65          2)$3.26          4)$4.48          3)$2.22          5)$6.25
    -15              -2               -4               -21              -■
      ■5              ■■               ■4               ■2               ■2
     -15             -12              -■               -■■              -10
       ■               06               ■8                0                2■
                      - 6              -■                                -25
                        ■                0                                 ■
```

6. **Reasoning** Is it cheaper to share the $1.32 bag of popcorn with 2 or 3 friends? Explain.

7. **Journal** Explain how you would divide $4.62 equally among three people.

PRACTICE AND APPLY

Chapter 7
Lesson
11

Dividing Money Amounts

You Will Learn
how to divide money amounts

Learn

"I enjoy helping my mom cook," says Elizabeth. "Sometimes I make chili for my family."

Math Tip
$4.25 is the same as 425 cents.

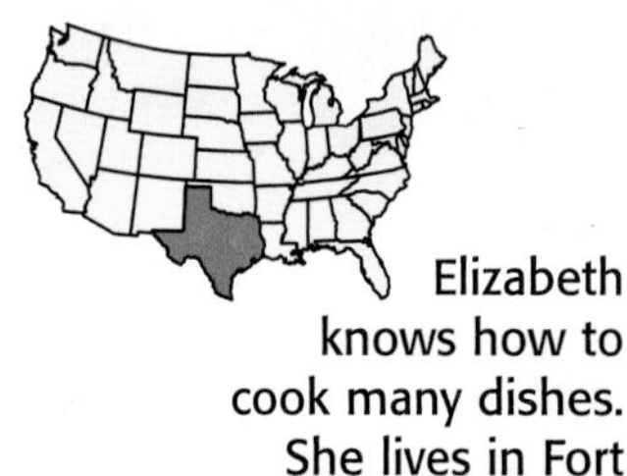

Elizabeth knows how to cook many dishes. She lives in Fort Worth, Texas.

Example 1

Suppose Elizabeth helped at a chili cook-off fund-raiser. She sold 5 small bowls of chili and collected \$4.25. How much did each small bowl cost?

Find \$4.25 ÷ 5.

Step 1

Divide the way you would with whole numbers.

```
     85
 5)$4.25
  -4 0
     25
    -25
      0
```

Step 2

Show dollars and cents in the quotient.

```
  $0.85
 5)$4.25
  -4 0
     25
    -25
      0
```

Each small bowl of chili cost \$0.85.

Example 2

Suppose Elizabeth sold 2 large bowls of chili for \$3.28. How much did each large bowl cost?

Find \$3.28 ÷ 2.

```
  $1.64
 2)$3.28
  -2
   1 2
  -1 2
     08
    -08
      0
```

Check by multiplying.

```
   1
 $1.64
 ×   2
 $3.28
```

Each large bowl of chili cost \$1.64.

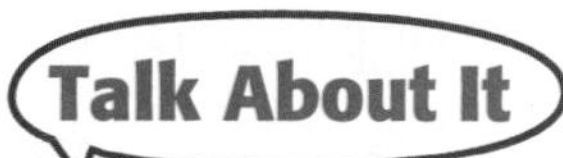

Talk About It

How would you write a quotient of 5 cents in dollars and cents?

Check

Divide and check.

1. $4\overline{)\$2.56}$ **2.** $3\overline{)\$5.22}$ **3.** $2\overline{)\$9.48}$ **4.** $6\overline{)\$1.92}$ **5.** $8\overline{)\$3.76}$

6. Reasoning Suppose 3 bowls of chili cost \$3.45. Is the cost of each bowl more or less than \$1.00? Explain.

Practice

Skills and Reasoning

Divide and check.

7. $2\overline{)\$6.90}$ **8.** $5\overline{)\$4.55}$ **9.** $4\overline{)\$9.44}$ **10.** $5\overline{)\$1.05}$ **11.** $9\overline{)\$0.99}$

12. $7\overline{)\$3.43}$ **13.** $4\overline{)\$2.60}$ **14.** $8\overline{)\$0.64}$ **15.** $2\overline{)\$9.82}$ **16.** $7\overline{)\$4.90}$

17. $3\overline{)\$6.21}$ **18.** $7\overline{)\$3.92}$ **19.** $2\overline{)\$8.82}$ **20.** $5\overline{)\$3.60}$ **21.** $6\overline{)\$9.00}$

22. $6\overline{)\$6.12}$ **23.** $9\overline{)\$5.67}$ **24.** $4\overline{)\$7.28}$ **25.** $9\overline{)\$5.31}$ **26.** $3\overline{)\$2.97}$

27. Find the quotient of \$5.45 divided by 5.

28. How is $\$7.25 \div 5$ like $725 \div 5$? How is it different?

Problem Solving and Applications

29. Del Rio's chili cook-off collected \$918 from ticket sales. If tickets cost \$9 each, how many tickets were sold?

30. Jani bought 6 jalapeño pepper plants for \$7.50. How much did one plant cost?

Using Data Use the table to answer **31** and **32**.

Pepper Jelly	Price
2-pack	\$1.58
4-pack	\$2.76
8-pack	\$5.28

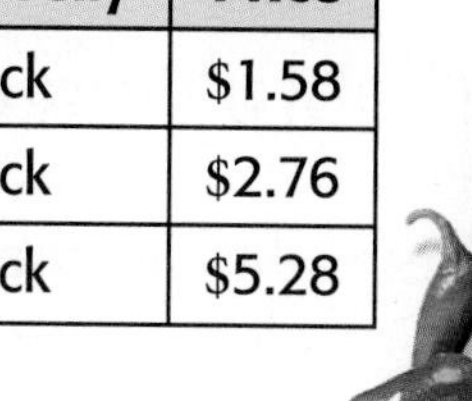

31. Which pack has the lowest price per bottle?

32. Critical Thinking How much would you save by buying one 8-pack of jelly rather than four 2-packs?

Mixed Review and Test Prep

STAY SHARP!

Find each sum or difference.

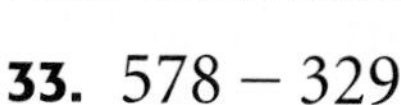

33. $578 - 329$ **34.** $388 + 914$ **35.** $1{,}205 - 563$ **36.** $4{,}403 + 387$

37. There are 38 students in the art club. Each student pays \$6 for supplies. How much is collected from all the students?

Ⓐ \$2,808 Ⓑ \$498 Ⓒ \$228 Ⓓ not here

Skills Practice Bank, page 569, Set 5

The Greatest Quotient Game

Players
2 or more

Materials
set of digit cards

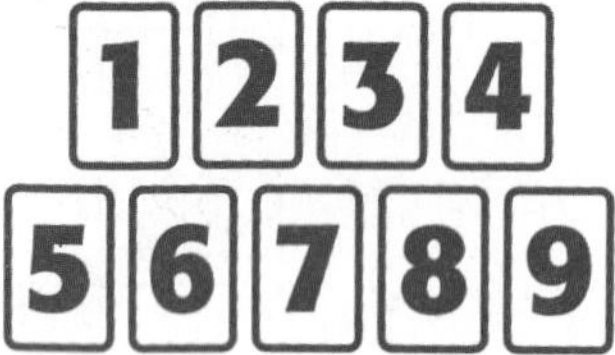

Object
The object of the game is to make a division problem with the greatest quotient.

How to Play

1. Each player draws a division grid like the one below. Shuffle the cards and place them face down.

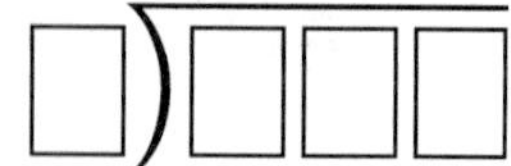

2. One player turns over a card. Each player writes the number in any box on his or her division grid.

Nina's Grid

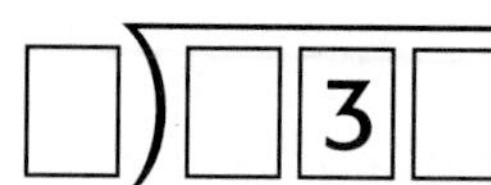

Zach's Grid

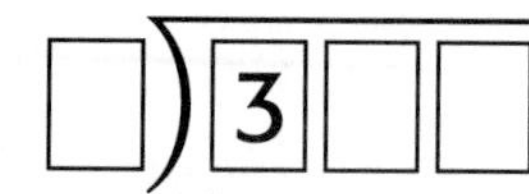

3. Continue turning over the cards until there are numbers in all of the boxes on the grids.
4. Divide. The player with the greatest quotient wins.
5. Play 5 or more games.

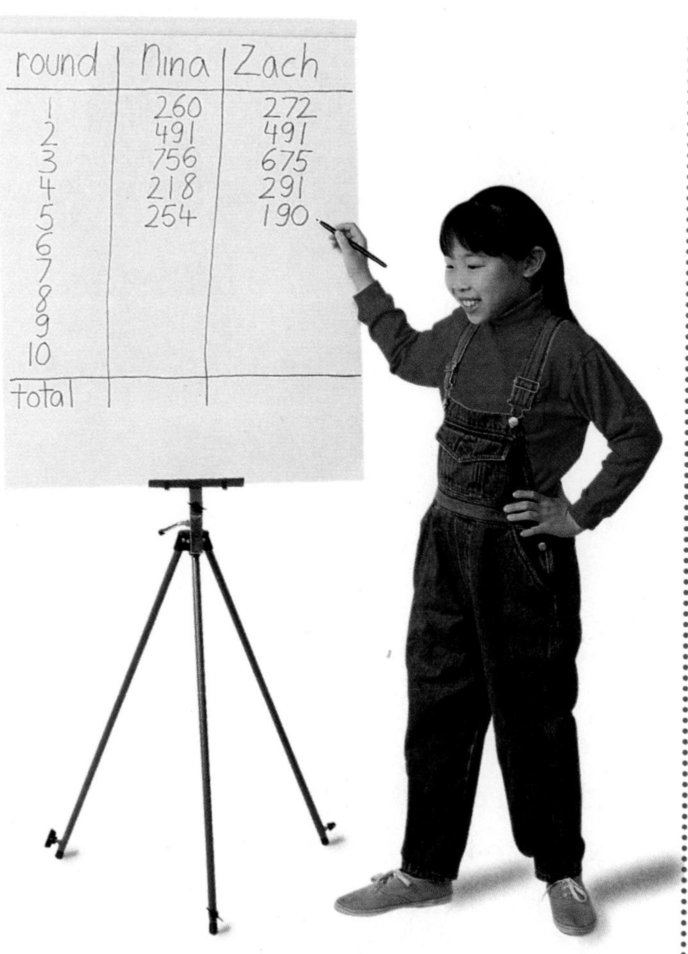

More Ways to Play

- Play again, using a grid like this.

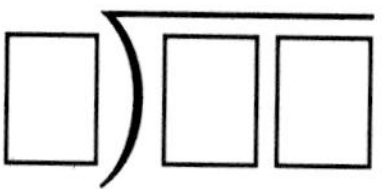

- Play the Least Quotient Game using either grid. In this game, the player with the least quotient wins.
- Hold a Greatest Quotient Game championship. Play 10 or more rounds. Ignore the remainders and total the quotients for all rounds. The player with the greatest total wins the championship.

Reasoning

1. In the Greatest Quotient Game, where on this grid would you place a 2? Explain your strategy.

2. Suppose your grid looks like this. What number do you hope to turn over next so that you get the least quotient?

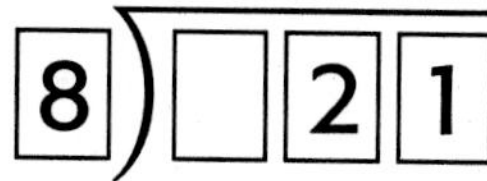

Talk About It

1. What strategy worked best for getting the greatest quotient?
2. Suppose you got a 9. Where on the grid would you place it to get the greatest quotient?

Chapter 7
Lesson
12

Exploring Mean

Problem Solving Connection
Use Objects/
Act It Out

Materials
- potatoes
- paper strips
- scissors
- tape
- ruler

Vocabulary
mean
quotient when the sum of two or more numbers is divided by the number of addends

average
another word for *mean*

Explore

Idaho produces almost one-third of all potatoes grown in the United States. How big is a typical potato? You can get a good idea by measuring several.

Work Together

1. Find the typical length of four potatoes.
   a. Cut a strip of paper the length of each potato.
   b. Tape the four strips together to form one long strip.
   c. Now, fold the long strip in half twice. Open it and cut along the folds to get four equal lengths.
   d. Use a ruler to measure the length of your strips.
   e. How long is one typical length of your group's potatoes? Record this length.
2. Find the typical length of the potatoes measured by the different groups in your class.
   a. Collect one typical length strip from each of 3 other groups. Tape the strips together.
   b. Fold this long strip in half twice, open it, and cut along the folds.
   c. Record the typical length of the potatoes measured by four groups.

Talk About It

3. What was the typical length for your group? For the four groups?
4. Using strips of paper, how could you find the typical length of 32 potatoes?

Connect

The typical number in a set of data is called the **mean**, or **average**.

To find the mean, or average, of a set of numbers, add the numbers and divide by the number of addends.

Find the mean of 18, 21, 25, and 20.

Add:

$$\begin{array}{r} 18 \\ 21 \\ 25 \\ +\,20 \\ \hline 84 \end{array}$$

Divide:

$$\begin{array}{r} 21 \\ 4\overline{)84} \\ -\,8 \\ \hline 04 \\ -\,4 \\ \hline 0 \end{array}$$

The mean for this set of numbers is 21.

Practice

Find the mean, or average, for each set of data for 1–3.

1. **Language Arts** The letters in some of the longest words in the Oxford English Dictionary:

Pneumonoultramicroscopicsilicovolcanoconiosis	45 letters
Supercalifragilisticexpialidocious	34 letters
Pseudopseudohypoparathyroidism	30 letters
antidisestablishmentarianism	28 letters
octamethylcyclotetrasiloxane	28 letters

2. **Time** 55 min, 43 min, 1 hr 7 min

3. **Money** \$1.30, \$0.65, \$1.15, \$1.10

4. **Using Data** Use the Data File on page 289. What is the difference between what you pay for potato chips and what the farmer earns?

5. **Reasoning** The mean of this set of numbers: 8, 3, 4, 7, 2, 6 is 5. What two numbers can you add to the set of numbers so the mean will still be 5?

6. Find the mean price received by farmers in 1995.

Price Received by Farmers for 1995 Fall Potato Crop					
State	California	Idaho	Indiana	New York	Ohio
Price (per 100 lb)	\$9.65	\$6.20	\$6.10	\$7.45	\$6.90

7. **Logic** The mean of five numbers is 60. Four of the numbers are 50, 60, 40, and 80. Find the fifth number.

8. **Journal** Explain how to find the mean hat size of four students.

Technology

Finding the Mean

PAPAS FRITAS Fritten French fries Chips Kentang goreng

Materials

DataWonder! or other graphing software

They are eaten almost everywhere.

Use your computer to find the mean number of french fries in a bag. Which restaurant gives you the most fries for your money?

Work Together

Use your graphing software to calculate the mean and to graph data.

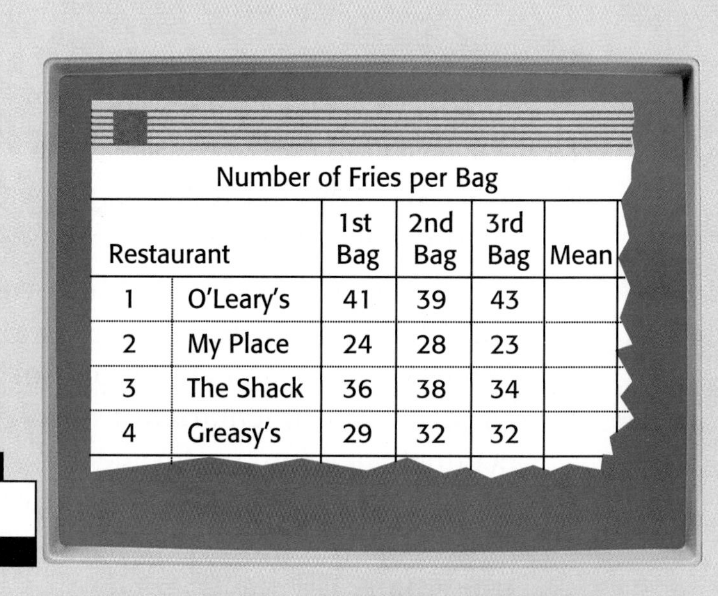

Number of Fries per Bag

Restaurant		1st Bag	2nd Bag	3rd Bag	Mean
1	O'Leary's	41	39	43	
2	My Place	24	28	23	
3	The Shack	36	38	34	
4	Greasy's	29	32	32	

1. Open a **Full Data Table.** Copy the table of the number of fries per bag.
2. From the **Graphs** menu, select **Show Graph** to graph the data.
3. Find the mean number of fries per bag for each restaurant.

Calculate
Multiply
Divide
Mean

   - Type *Mean* in the column to the right of *3rd Bag.*
   - Pull down the **Calculate** menu. Select Mean.
   - Click and drag to select the number-of-fries cells for O'Leary's. Press Return.
   - Click on Insert Result.
   - Click on the *Mean* cell for O'Leary's restaurant.
   - Notice the new *Mean* bar in the graph.
4. Find the mean numbers of fries for the other restaurants.
5. Pull down the **Report** menu and select Show Report. Insert the table and graph in your Report. Don't forget to give your report a title.

Exercises

Answer **1–3** in the Report window. **Print Report** when you are finished.

1. Which restaurant serves, on average, the most fries per bag? The least?
2. How many fries were in the three bags from My Place?
3. **Reasoning** Suppose you recount the first bag from The Shack and find it has 6 more fries. How will the mean number of fries change?

Extensions

Use your graphing software. Copy the table of lengths of french fries. Then answer **4** and **5** in the Report Window. **Print Report** when you are finished.

Lengths of French Fries (cm)					
	1st Fry	**2nd Fry**	**3rd Fry**	**4th Fry**	**5th Fry**
O'Leary's	4	4	5	4	3
My Place	10	7	11	8	9
The Shack	6	8	6	8	7
Greasy's	9	7	10	8	6

4. Which restaurant serves, on average, the longest french fry? The shortest?
5. Explain how you can find the mean length of the fries from Greasy's using *add* in the Calculate menu, and mental math.

Chapter 7
Lesson
13

Exploring Divisibility

Problem Solving Connection
Use Logical Reasoning

Materials
calculator

Vocabulary

even number
whole number divisible by 2

odd number
whole number not divisible by 2

divisible
a number is divisible by another number, if there is no remainder

Explore

Even numbers end with the digits 0, 2, 4, 6, or 8.

Odd numbers end with the digits 1, 3, 5, 7, or 9.

A number is **divisible** by another number if there is no remainder.

Work Together

1. Copy and complete the table. You may use your calculator.
   a. Write *Y* (yes) when a number is divisible by a factor.
   b. Write *N* (no) when a number is not divisible by a factor.

Factor	2	10	12	15	16	25	30	64	75	100
2	Y									
5										
10										

2. Look for patterns in your data. Write a rule for deciding whether a number is divisible:
   a. by 2 b. by 5 c. by 10

How do divisibility rules help you decide if a number is divisible by another number?

Remember
A factor is a number that divides into another number without a remainder.

Connect

You can use these rules to test if 108 is divisible by 3, 6, or 9.

A whole number is divisible by ...	Example
3 if the sum of the digits is divisible by 3.	$1 + 0 + 8 = 9$ and $9 \div 3 = 3$. There is no remainder. So, 108 is divisible by 3.
6 if the number is divisible by both 2 and 3.	You know 108 is divisible by 3. It is also divisible by 2 because it is an even number. So, 108 is divisible by 6.
9 if the sum of the digits is divisible by 9.	$1 + 0 + 8 = 9$ and $9 \div 9 = 1$. There is no remainder. So, 108 is divisible by 9.

Practice

Copy and complete. Test each number to see if it is divisible by 2, 3, 5, 6, 9, or 10. If it is, write the quotient.

		48	60	200	153	123	58	93	540	225	134	29
1.	By 2?	24										
2.	By 3?	16										
3.	By 5?											
4.	By 6?											
5.	By 9?											
6.	By 10?											

7. Without dividing, can you tell if you can share $4.29 equally among 3 friends? Explain.

8. Without dividing, do you know if you can cut a 144 in. ribbon into 9 equal pieces? Explain.

9. **Reasoning** Write an even number that is divisible by 3.

10. **Reasoning** Write an odd number that is divisible by 9.

11. **Journal** Explain how you decide whether a number is divisible by 2, 3, 5, 6, 9, or 10.

Chapter 7
Lesson
14

Problem Solving

Analyze Strategies: Work Backward

You Will Learn
how working backward can help you solve problems

Did You Know?
Bananas, apples, grapes, and oranges, in that order, are the most favorite fruit in the United States.

Learn

Florida mangoes were donated for a Teacher Appreciation lunch. Two mangoes were too ripe to use. Three groups of four students cut up the remaining fruit. Each student cut up five mangoes. How many mangoes were donated?

Work Together

▶ Understand

What do you know?

What do you need to find?

▶ Plan

Try working backward. Find how many mangoes were cut up. Add the number of mangoes that were not used.

▶ Solve

How many mangoes were cut up? students × mangoes × groups:
$4 \times 5 \times 3 = 60$

How many mangoes were donated? cut-up + 2 unused:
$60 + 2 = 62$ 62 mangoes were donated.

▶ Look Back

How can you check your answer?

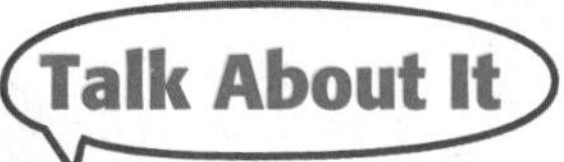

How did working backward help you solve the problem?

Check

Problem Solving
Understand
Plan
Solve
Look Back

Work backward to solve.

1. Inez made a sandwich with two 1-oz slices of bread, 3 oz of cheese, and an unmeasured amount of meat. She weighed the sandwich and found it weighed 8 ounces. How much meat did she use?

2. Jack made fruit punch with 15 ounces of orange juice and an unknown amount of Florida grapefruit juice. He divided the mixture into four 6-ounce glasses with 1 ounce left over. How much grapefruit juice did he use?

Problem Solving Practice

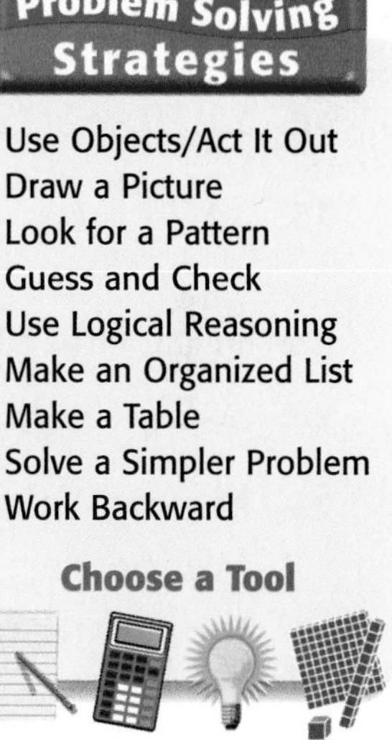

Work backward or use any strategy to help solve.

3. Wayne spread lemon frosting on 2 cakes. He put 3 times as much frosting on the second cake as the first. He put 15 ounces of frosting on the second cake. How much frosting did Wayne use in all?

4. Wendy mixed 24 ounces of tomato sauce with some olive oil. She spread 3 ounces of the mixture on each of 6 pizzas. How much of the mixture did she have left over?

5. **Social Studies** When Minnesota became a state, there were eight times as many states as there were when Georgia became a state. Oregon, the 33rd state, was the next state after Minnesota to become a state. How many states were there when Georgia became a state?

6. **Money** Glen spent $12. Then he had 3 ten-dollar bills and 2 one-dollar bills left. How much money did he start with?

7. **Geography** Key lime pie is named after small yellow limes that grow in the Florida Keys. The juice is sold in 12-ounce bottles. It takes 4 ounces to make a pie. How many bottles does it take to make 76 pies?

Atlantic Ocean
FLORIDA
Gulf of Mexico
Florida Keys

SECTION C

Review and Practice

Vocabulary Complete each sentence with one of the words listed.

Word List
even
odd
divisible
mean

1. The numbers 5, 17, and 43 are ____.
2. Another word for *average* is ____.
3. The number 20 is ____ by 4 and 5, but not by 3.
4. The numbers 4, 26, and 88 are ____.

(Lessons 10 and 11) Divide and check.

5. $3\overline{)\$1.35}$
6. $5\overline{)\$2.65}$
7. $4\overline{)\$6.48}$
8. $6\overline{)\$7.26}$
9. $2\overline{)\$1.26}$
10. $1.70 ÷ 2
11. $5.91 ÷ 3
12. $4.68 ÷ 4
13. $8.35 ÷ 5
14. $9.81 ÷ 9
15. $3.24 ÷ 6
16. $5.88 ÷ 7
17. $4.86 ÷ 9
18. $9.84 ÷ 8
19. $3.25 ÷ 5

(Lesson 12) Find the mean, or average, of each set of numbers.

20. 8, 12, 15, 9, 10, 6
21. 58, 70, 91, 66, 57, 53, 60
22. 279, 189, 243, 305

23. **Money** Yolanda spent $2.12 for lunch on Tuesday, $2.48 on Wednesday, $3.45 on Thursday, and $1.91 on Friday. What was the mean amount she spent on lunch?

(Lesson 13) Copy and complete. Test each number to see if it is divisible by 2, 3, or 9. If it is, write the quotient.

		45	144	90	360	357	32	180	81	138	545	261
24.	By 2?											
25.	By 3?											
26.	By 9?											

(Lesson 14) Solve. Use any strategy.

27. Sean handed out 18 award ribbons at the Junior Olympics. There were 3 awards for each event and 3 awards for the overall high scores. How many events were there?

28. **Journal** The cost of oranges per pound were $0.45, $0.55, $0.35, $0.65, and $0.35. How would you find the mean, or average, cost per pound of the oranges?

Skills Checklist

In this section, you have:

- ☑ Explored Division with Money
- ☑ Divided Money Amounts
- ☑ Explored Finding the Mean
- ☑ Explored Divisibility
- ☑ Solved Problems by Working Backward

REVIEW AND PRACTICE

Choose at least one. Use what you have learned in this chapter.

1 Photo Time

It is class photo day. The photographer has asked you to arrange your class in groups of 2, 3, 5, 6, 9, and 10. Write on index cards the names of the students in your class. Use the cards to show how you can arrange the class into different sized groups. Explain which arrangement you think works the best.

2 Sing-a-long

Choose a favorite song. Time how many seconds it takes you to sing it three different times. Then calculate the mean amount of time it took you to sing the song once.

3 Robo-Teach

At Home Write directions for programming a robot to find $426 \div 8$. Check your directions by asking friends or family members to use them to find the answer.

4 Homework Machine

Keep a log for a week and find the mean amount of time you spend doing homework. Compare your results with those of other students at **www.mathsurf.com/4/ch7.**

5 Mapmaker

Your teacher needs help rearranging your classroom desks. Draw maps to show how you would arrange the desks and divide the class into teams.

CHAPTER 7

Review/Test

Vocabulary Match each word with its meaning.

1. remainder	**a.** a typical number in a set of data
2. divisible	**b.** result when one number is divided by another
3. mean	**c.** number leftover after division
4. dividend	**d.** number that is being divided
5. quotient	**e.** when a number divides into another number with no remainder

(Lesson 2) Estimation Estimate each quotient.

6. $256 \div 4$ **7.** $224 \div 5$ **8.** $524 \div 7$ **9.** $444 \div 6$ **10.** $395 \div 4$

(Lessons 3, 5–8, 10, and 11) Divide.

11. $4\overline{)63}$ **12.** $2\overline{)75}$ **13.** $5\overline{)85}$ **14.** $6\overline{)94}$

15. $3\overline{)46}$ **16.** $3\overline{)561}$ **17.** $6\overline{)684}$ **18.** $8\overline{)937}$

19. $7\overline{)878}$ **20.** $5\overline{)679}$ **21.** $5\overline{)352}$ **22.** $5\overline{)724}$

23. $638 \div 9$ **24.** $453 \div 7$ **25.** $745 \div 7$ **26.** $\$8.25 \div 3$

27. $\$4.76 \div 7$ **28.** $\$7.56 \div 6$ **29.** $\$9.65 \div 5$ **30.** $\$48.60 \div 6$

(Lessons 9 and 14) Solve. Use any strategy.

31. Six eggs fit in a mini-carton. How many mini-cartons can be filled with 110 eggs?

32. If you multiply the number of ounces a potato weighs by 9, and then divide the product by 3, you get 39. How many ounces does the potato weigh?

33. Reasoning Without finding an exact answer, how can you tell how many digits are in the quotient and what the greatest possible remainder could be for $7\overline{)654}$?

REVIEW/TEST

CHAPTER 7

Performance Assessment

Sneak a peek inside the food basket. Plan a picnic lunch for 8 people.

1. **Decision Making** Decide on a picnic lunch for each person. The meals can be different, but make sure each person has 3 different kinds of food. Find out how much food is left over, if any.

2. **Recording Data** Copy and fill out the table below to keep track of the food amounts. Use only the food that is in the basket.

	Lunch
Person 1	
Person 2	
Person 3	
Person 4	
Person 5	
Person 6	
Person 7	
Person 8	

3. **Explain Your Thinking** How did you use division to plan the meals? What other math operations did you use?

4. **Critical Thinking** How could you adjust the lunches so there are no leftovers?

REVIEW/TEST

Math Magazine

Sweet Tooth **The first sugar to satisfy a sweet tooth was probably honey. For thousands of years, people have known how to "borrow" the sweet liquid from the busy honey bees.**

People are willing to go to great lengths to find wild honey. In Nepal, this hunter climbs a 400-foot cliff to get honey from the nests of the largest honey bees in the world.

A worker bee collects nectar from flowers to make honey. One worker bee makes about a $\frac{1}{2}$ teaspoon of honey in its lifetime.

Try These!

1. If it takes 144 worker bees to fill a 6-ounce jar of honey, how many bees would it take to make only 1 ounce of honey?
2. A honey hunter can collect 2,800 ounces of honey in one trip.
   a. How many 4-ounce jars can he fill with the honey?
   b. How many bees would it take to make that many jars of honey?

3. Check out **www.mathsurf.com/4/ch7** for more data on honey and bees.

CHAPTERS 1–7

Cumulative Review

STAY SHARP!

The sum of two numbers is \$6.00. \$6.00 − \$2.56 = \$3.44. The answer is Ⓑ.

Test Prep Strategy: Work Backward from an Answer

Replace the missing number with each choice.

\$6.00 is the sum of \$2.56 and ______?

Ⓐ \$6.44 Ⓑ \$3.44 Ⓒ \$3.56 Ⓓ \$2.44

Test Prep Strategies

- Read Carefully
- Follow Directions
- Make Smart Choices
- Eliminate Choices
- Work Backward from an Answer

Write the letter of the correct answer. You may work backward from an answer or use any other strategy to solve the problem.

1. The number 62 is equal to:
   Ⓐ 60 tens, 2 ones Ⓑ 62 tens
   Ⓒ 6 tens Ⓓ 6 tens, 2 ones
2. What is the rule for this set of numbers? 4, 7, 10, 13, 16
   Ⓐ multiply by 3 Ⓑ add 3
   Ⓒ subtract 3 Ⓓ add 10
3. For the number sentence, $n + 27 = 35$, what is the value of n?
   Ⓐ 15 Ⓑ 8 Ⓒ 7 Ⓓ $n + 7$
4. Bo gave the clerk a dollar bill for a \$0.45 bagel and received \$0.35 change. In what way was Bo's change incorrect?
   Ⓐ \$0.20 too much Ⓑ \$0.30 too little
   Ⓒ \$0.20 too little Ⓓ \$0.30 too much
5. Which of the following does not equal the product of 48 and 9?
   Ⓐ 54×8 Ⓑ 72×6 Ⓒ 132×3 Ⓓ 108×4
6. The quotient is 52 and the remainder is 1. The divisor is 4. What is the dividend?
   Ⓐ 210 Ⓑ 209 Ⓒ 208 Ⓓ 13
7. Which one of these has a remainder of 4?
   Ⓐ $236 \div 3$ Ⓑ $102 \div 7$ Ⓒ $135 \div 4$ Ⓓ $198 \div 6$
8. Juan cut a 200-cm wire into 6-cm pieces. How many 6-cm pieces did he get?
   Ⓐ 33 Ⓑ 60 Ⓒ 34 Ⓓ 100

Chapter 8
Using Geometry

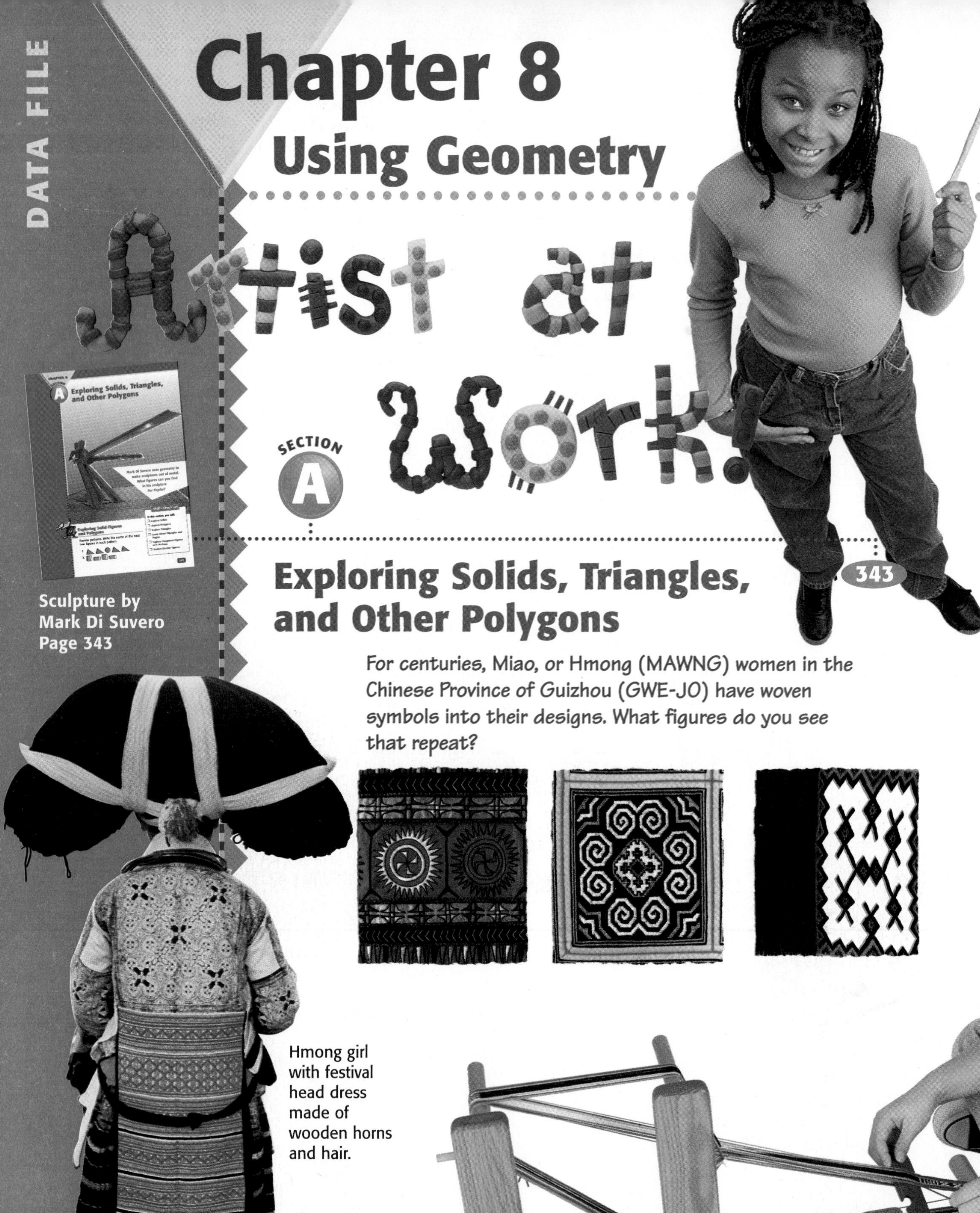

Exploring Solids, Triangles, and Other Polygons

Sculpture by Mark Di Suvero Page 343

For centuries, Miao, or Hmong (MAWNG) women in the Chinese Province of Guizhou (GWE-JO) have woven symbols into their designs. What figures do you see that repeat?

Hmong girl with festival head dress made of wooden horns and hair.

SECTION

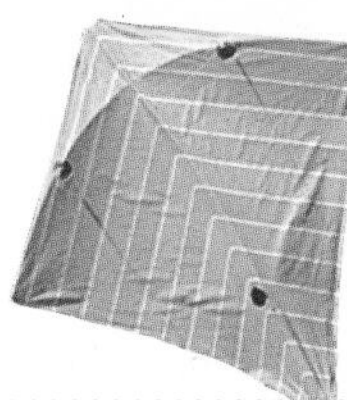

Diamond Kite flies well in 6–15 mph winds.

Exploring Quadrilaterals

357

If the wind is blowing at 20 mph, which kite would you choose to fly? Why?

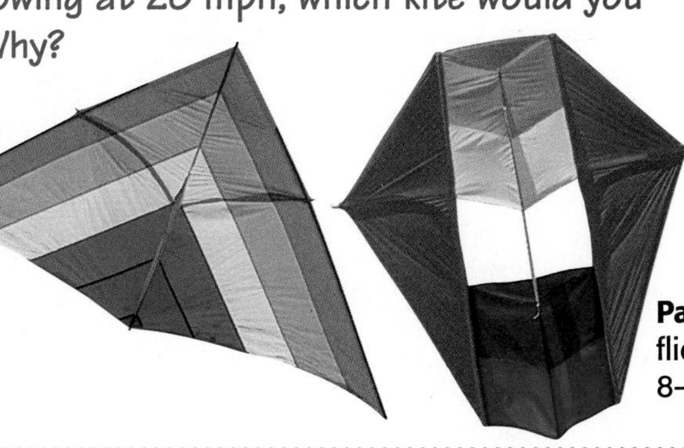

Delta Kite flies well in 6–15 mph winds.

Parafoil Kite flies well in 8–25 mph winds.

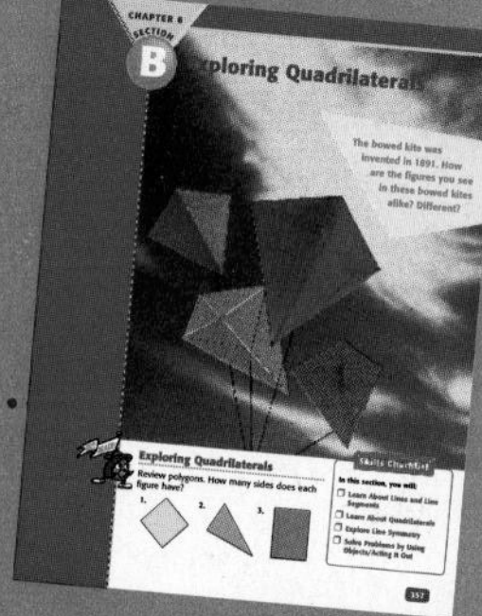

Bowed kites
Page 357

SECTION C

Exploring Perimeter, Area, and Volume

367

Some places are important for their culture or history. The United Nations listed 469 natural sites and places built by humans that need protection. When were natural sites in the U.S. listed?

World Heritage Sites in the U.S.	Year Listed
Everglades, Florida	1979
Taos Pueblo, New Mexico	1992
Great Smoky Mountains, North Carolina	1983
Monticello, Virginia	1987
Statue of Liberty, New York	1984

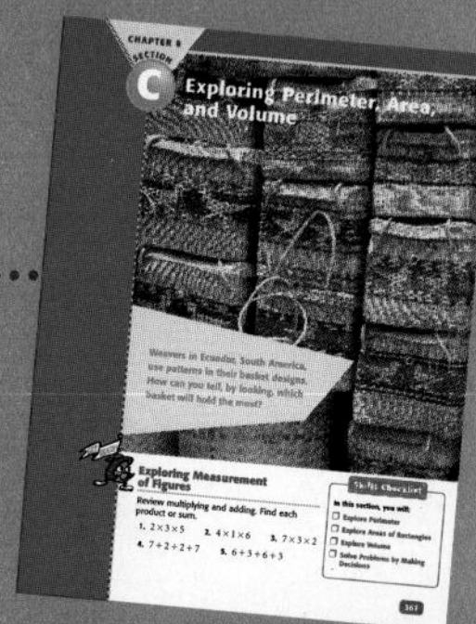

Baskets from Ecuador
Page 367

The conical tower of the Great Zimbabwe ruins was built about 700 years ago. The ruins are protected as a World Heritage site.

Surfing the World Wide Web!

Find out about World Heritage sites at **www.mathsurf.com/4/ch8.** Share with your classmates a site you would like to visit.

Materials
grid paper, ruler, scissors

Use what you have learned about solids. Make a pattern that you can fold into a box.

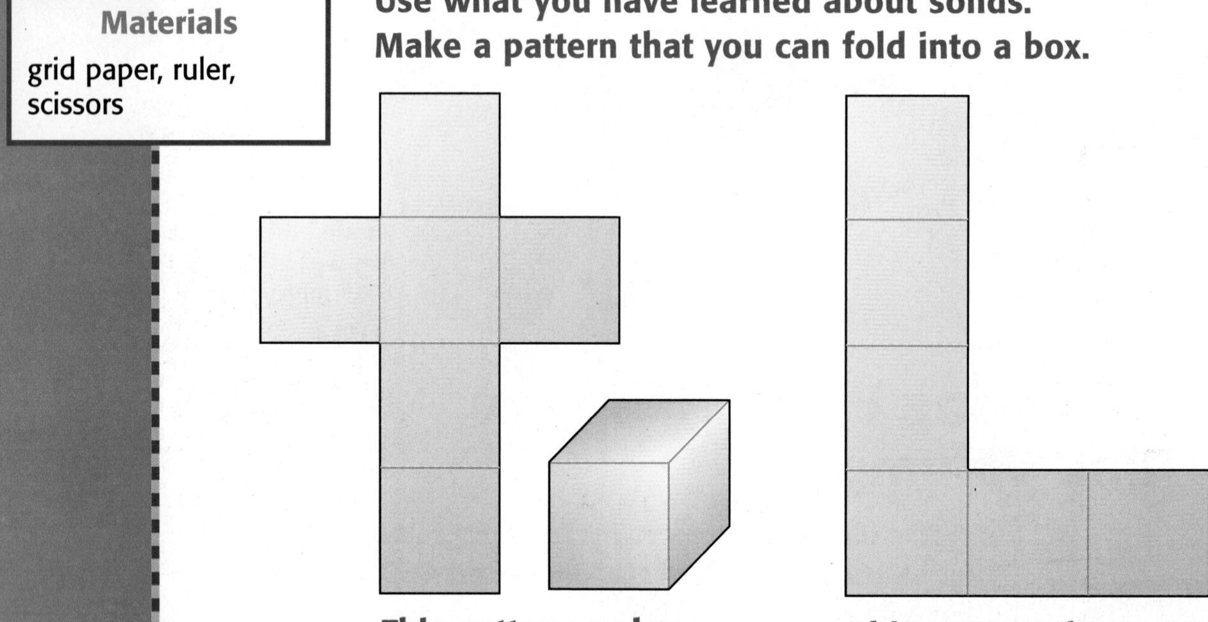

This pattern makes this box.

This pattern does not fold into a box.

Make a Plan

- What will your box look like?
- How many faces will you need to show on your pattern?

Carry It Out

1. Use grid paper to draw your pattern.
2. Cut out and fold your pattern. See if it folds into a box.

Talk About It

- Look at the patterns made by your classmates. How are they alike? How are they different?
- Is there only one possible pattern for the same box? Explain.

Present the Project

- Share your pattern. Show how you can fold it.

CHAPTER 8

SECTION

A Exploring Solids, Triangles, and Other Polygons

Mark Di Suvero uses geometry to make sculptures out of metal. What figures can you find in his sculpture *For Kepler?*

Exploring Solid Figures and Polygons

Review patterns. Write the name of the next two figures in each pattern.

1. ▲ ▲ ● ▲ ▲
2. ■ ▬ ■ ▬

Skills Checklist

In this section, you will:

- ❒ Explore Solids
- ❒ Explore Polygons
- ❒ Explore Triangles
- ❒ Learn About Triangles and Angles
- ❒ Explore Congruent Figures and Motions
- ❒ Explore Similar Figures

Chapter 8
Lesson
1

Exploring Solids

Problem Solving Connection
Use Objects/
Act It Out

Vocabulary
Solid Figures
cube
rectangular prism
pyramid
cone
sphere
cylinder

face
If a solid figure has only flat surfaces, then we call each surface a face.

edge
a line segment where two faces of a solid meet

vertex
a point where two or more edges meet

Explore

More than 4,000 years ago, sculptors carved huge blocks of stone at Stonehenge in England. Some blocks weigh about 50 tons. Each stone block is a **solid figure**. Many solids have only flat surfaces. They are made up of **faces**, **edges**, and **vertices**.

Work Together

1. Find four solids that have only flat surfaces in your classroom. Trace and label each face on paper.

2. Copy and complete the table using your four solids.

Solid	Number of Faces	Number of Edges	Number of Vertices
Book	6	12	

Talk About It

3. Which of your solids has the most edges? Which has the most vertices?

4. Are any of the faces that you traced alike?

Connect

You can describe solids in different ways. These solids have only flat surfaces.

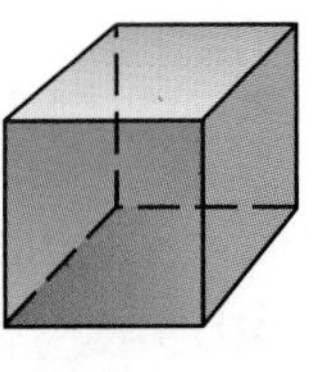
Cube

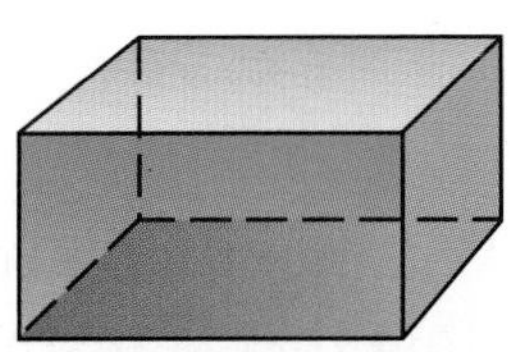
Rectangular prism

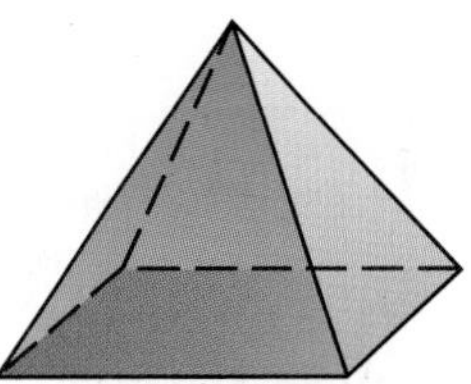
Pyramid

Some solids have a curved surface. Some have both curved and flat surfaces.

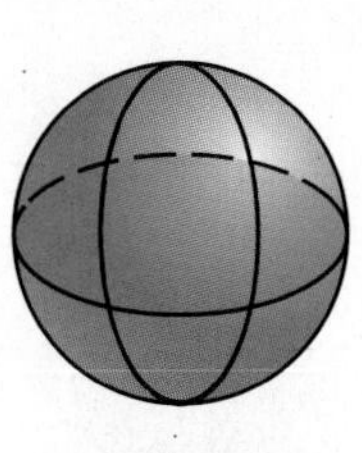
Sphere

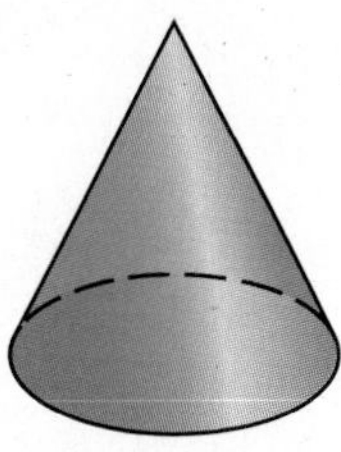
Cone

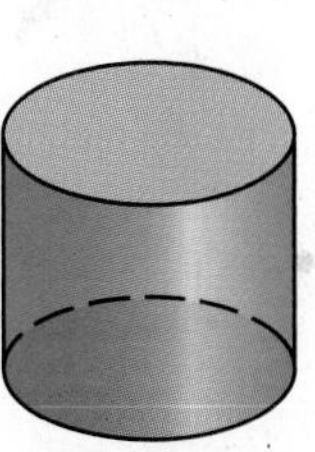
Cylinder

Practice

Name the solid that each object looks like.

1. 

2. 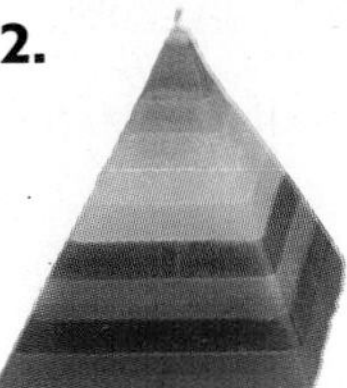

3. 

4. 

5. Which could be a flat surface of a cone? Of a cylinder? Of a cube?

a. 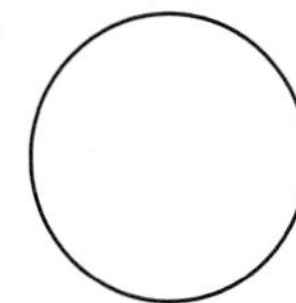

b. 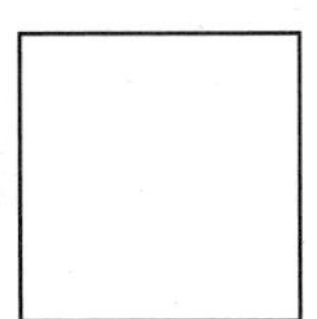

c. 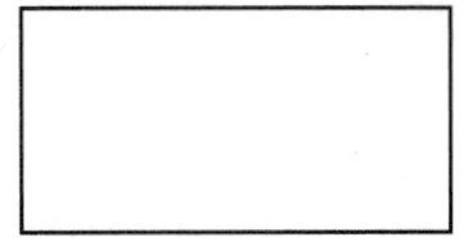

Reasoning Solve each riddle. Name the solid.

6. I have no vertices or flat surfaces. What am I?

7. I have six faces that are all the same size. What am I?

8. My faces are four triangles and one rectangle. What am I?

9. I have two flat surfaces shaped like circles. What am I?

10. **Journal** Which of the solids are easiest to stack? Explain.

Chapter 8
Lesson
2

Exploring Polygons

Problem Solving Connection
Make a Table

Materials
ruler

Vocabulary

plane figure
a figure that lies on a flat surface

polygon
a closed plane figure made of line segments

Polygons
triangle
quadrilateral
pentagon
hexagon
octagon

Explore

Inca sculptors in Peru built walls out of huge rocks. They carved the rocks so perfectly that they fit together with no space between them.

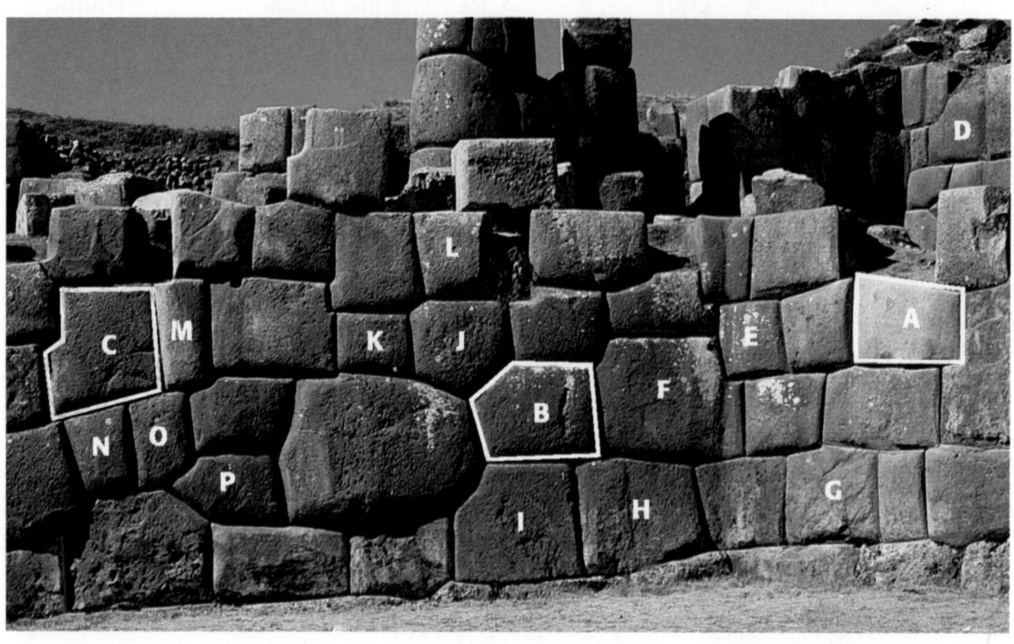

Stones used in the terraces of the Inca fort of Sacsahuaman are almost polygon-shaped.

Work Together

1. Study the 3 figures outlined in the photo. Record each figure's letter and the number of sides it has.

Outlined Figures	Number of Sides	Other Figures
A	4	*K*
B		
C		

2. For each outlined figure, find other figures in the photo with the same number of sides. Record their letters.

3. Use a ruler to draw a wall with five blocks. Draw blocks with 3 sides, 4 sides, 5 sides, 6 sides, and 8 sides.

Did You Know?
Each of the four triangular faces of the Great Pyramid at Giza, Egypt, were once 481 feet high, about as high as a 40-story building.

Talk About It

Look at some figures in the photo with the same number of sides. How are the figures different?

Connect

The face of a solid is a **plane figure**. A **polygon** is a closed plane figure formed by line segments. Here are some polygons.

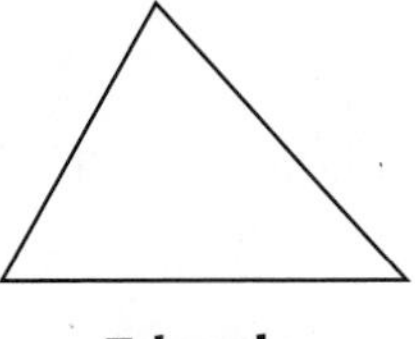

Triangle
3 sides

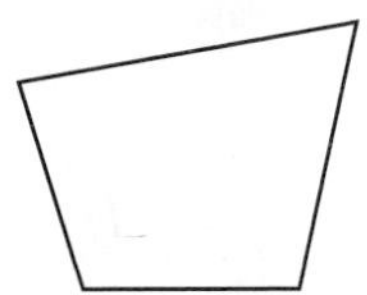

Quadrilateral
4 sides

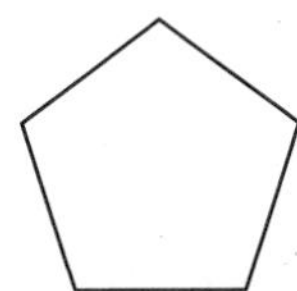

Pentagon
5 sides

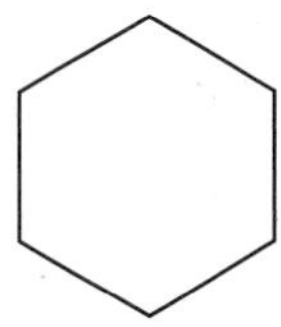

Hexagon
6 sides

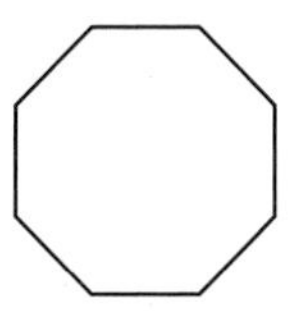

Octagon
8 sides

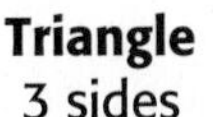

Here are some plane figures that are *not* polygons.

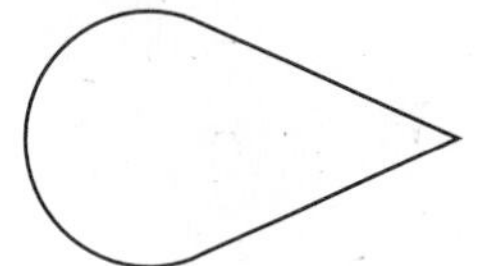

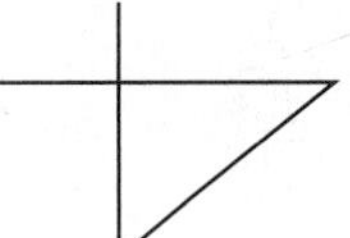

Practice

Write the name of each polygon.

1. 

2. 

3 

4. 

5. **Measurement** A 1,350-yard-long path runs around a pentagon-shaped park. All the sides of the park except one measure 200 yards. How long is the unequal side?

6. **Using Data** Use the data from the *Did You Know?* on page 346. Was the base of the Great Pyramid a quadrilateral? Explain.

7. Jacob and Kelly make a park plan. Jacob draws a circular path around a lake. Kelly draws a three-sided figure from the pond to the swings, to the gardens, and back to the pond. Which path is a polygon? Explain.

8. **Reasoning** What is the name of a figure that is 48 inches around and that has equal sides, each 6 inches long?

9. **Critical Thinking** If you cut a square in half with a straight line, what different figures could you make?

10. **Journal** Draw and label a square and a cube. Explain the difference between the two figures.

PRACTICE AND APPLY

Chapter 8
Lesson
3

Exploring Triangles

Problem Solving Connection
Use Objects/
Act It Out

Materials
Power Polygons

Vocabulary
Triangles
equilateral
isosceles
scalene

Explore

Piet Mondrian used polygons in many of his paintings. In this painting he used only quadrilaterals.

Use Power Polygons to "paint" your own designs.

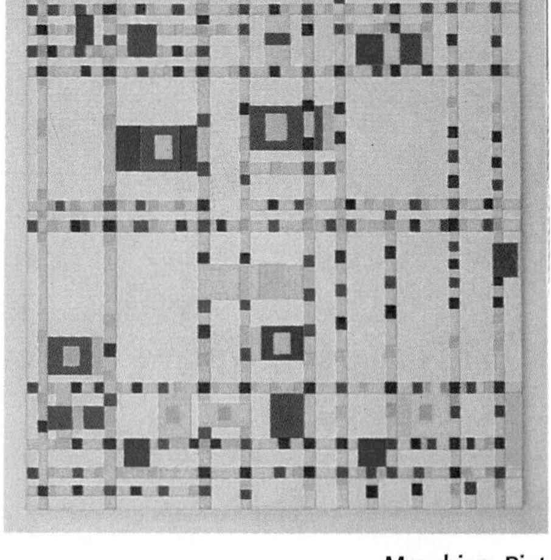

Mondrian, Piet
Broadway Boogie Woogie.
1942–1943

Work Together

Remember
Triangles, quadrilaterals, pentagons, hexagons, and octagons are polygons.

1. a. Choose six triangles the same size. All three sides of each triangle should be the same length.
   b. Make a polygon using your six triangles. Trace the triangles to record your design. What polygon did you make?
2. a. Choose six triangles the same size. Only two sides of each triangle should be the same length. The third side should be a different length.
   b. Make a polygon using your six triangles. Trace the triangles to record your design. What polygon did you make?

Talk About It

3. You used triangles that had three equal sides. You also used triangles that had two equal sides. Are there any other kinds of triangles? If so, describe them.
4. How many triangles with two equal sides would you need to make a hexagon?

Connect

You can name triangles by the lengths of their sides.

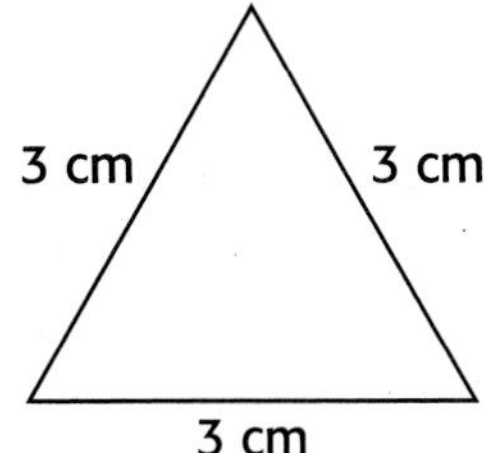

Equilateral triangle
All sides are the same length.

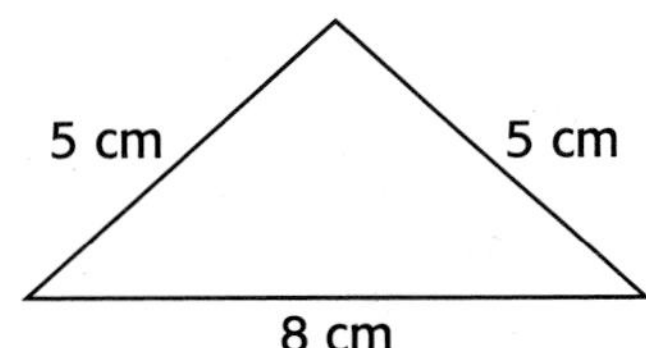

Isosceles triangle
At least two sides are the same length.

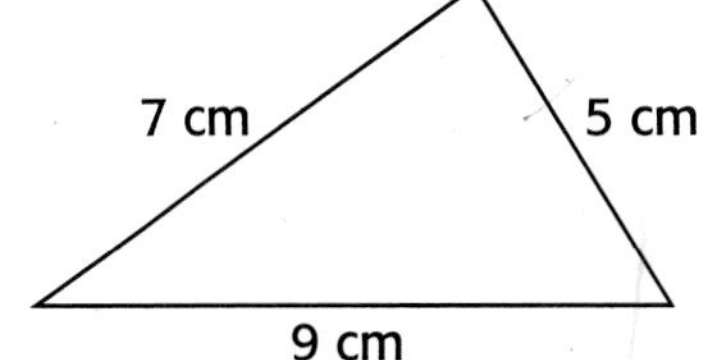

Scalene triangle
No sides are the same length.

PRACTICE AND APPLY

Practice

The lengths of the sides of a triangle are given. Name each triangle.

1. 5 in., 6 in., 5 in. **2.** 8 cm, 10 cm, 7 cm **3.** 4 ft, 4 ft, 4 ft

4. 20 mi, 20 mi, 2 mi **5.** 6 cm, 5 cm, 5 cm **6.** 2 ft, 3 ft, 4 ft

7. 6 in., 6 in., 6 in. **8.** 12 in., 12 in., 12 in. **9.** 10 cm, 14 cm, 11 cm

10. Draw a design using the three types of triangles you learned about. Name each triangle you use.

11. Two sides of an isosceles triangle measure 2 in. and 3 in. How long is the third side? Give all possible answers.

12. Tri-City Auto Supply uses an equilateral triangle as its symbol. One side of a Tri-City symbol measures 14 in. How long are the other two sides?

Geography Name each lettered triangle by the lengths of its sides.

13.

Papua New Guinea

14.

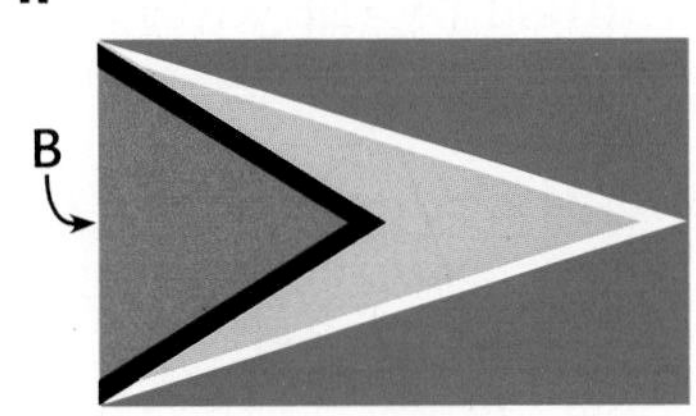

Guyana

15.

São Tomé and Príncipe

16. Critical Thinking Marcus drew a line connecting two opposite vertices of a square. What kind of triangles did he make?

17. Journal Sketch and name triangles with no sides the same length, at least two sides the same length, and all sides the same length.

Chapter 8
Lesson
4

Triangles and Angles

You Will Learn
how to classify angles and triangles

Vocabulary

ray
part of a line having only one endpoint

angle
two rays with a common endpoint

vertex
the common endpoint of two rays forming an angle

Angles
right
acute
obtuse
straight

Triangles
right
acute
obtuse

Learn

Mark Di Suvero makes huge sculptures out of metal. In this sculpture, intersecting steel beams form **angles**.

Mark Di Suvero *For Kepler*. 1995. Courtesy of the Artist and Gagosian Gallery, New York

You can name an angle by the size of its opening.

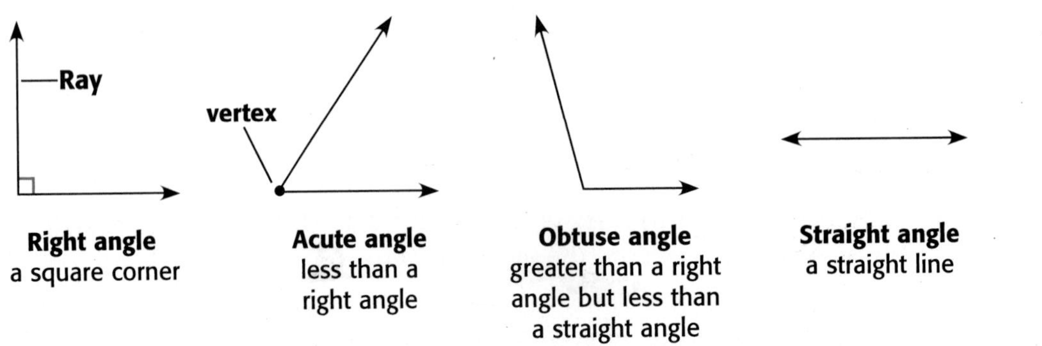

Right angle
a square corner

Acute angle
less than a right angle

Obtuse angle
greater than a right angle but less than a straight angle

Straight angle
a straight line

You know how to name a triangle by the length of its sides. You can also name a triangle by the kinds of angles it has.

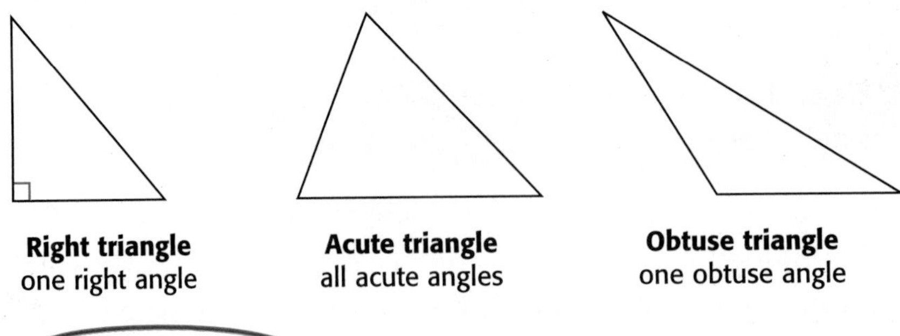

Right triangle
one right angle

Acute triangle
all acute angles

Obtuse triangle
one obtuse angle

Talk About It

How can you use the corner of an index card to decide if an angle is right, acute, or obtuse?

Check

Name each triangle as right, acute, or obtuse.

1. 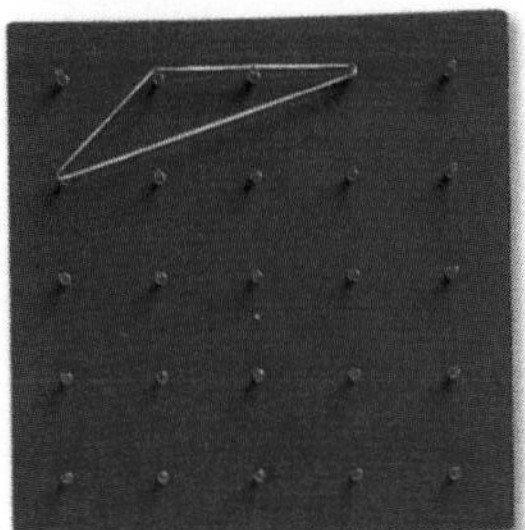

2. 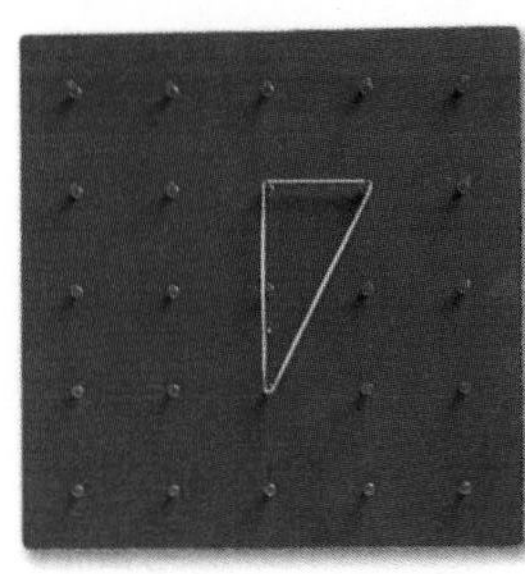

3. 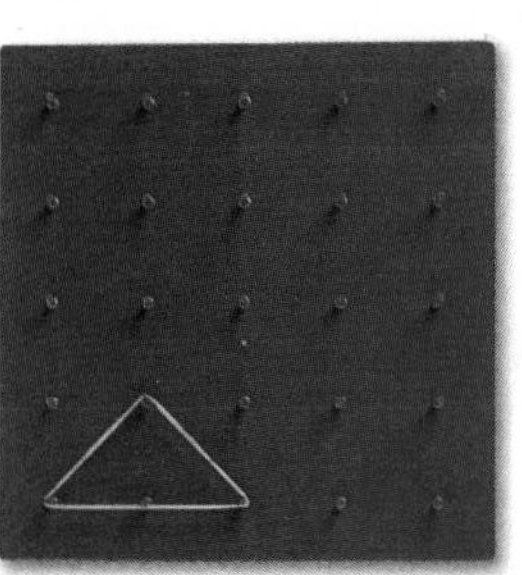

4. **Reasoning** Can a triangle have two right angles? Explain.

Practice

Skills and Reasoning

Name each triangle as right, acute, or obtuse.

5. 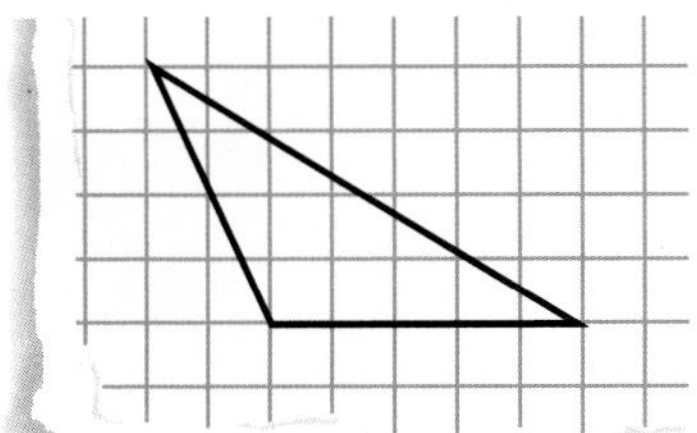

6. 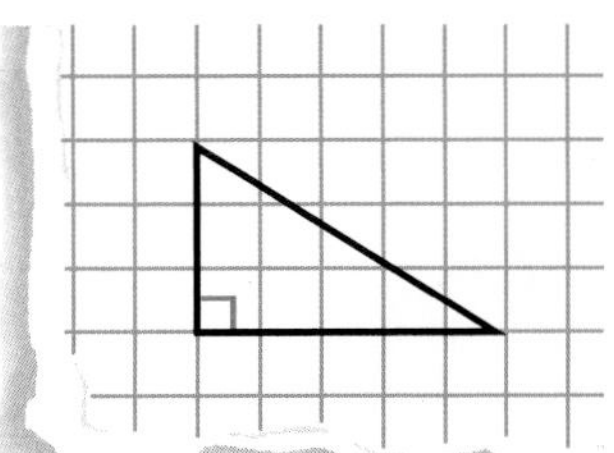

7. 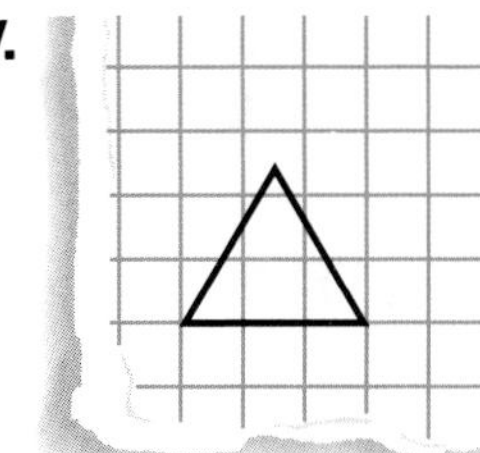

Problem Solving and Applications

Time Name the shaded angle between each clock's hands as right, acute, or obtuse.

8. 

9. 

10. 

11. **Using Data** Use the Data File on page 340. What angles can you see in the third design?

Mixed Review and Test Prep

STAY SHARP!

 **Algebra Readiness** Find the missing number.

12. $90 + n = 180$
13. $30 + n = 180$
14. $60 + n = 180$

15. Find the quotient of 291 divided by 3.

Ⓐ 90 Ⓑ 96 R3 Ⓒ 97 Ⓓ 103

Chapter 8
Lesson
5

Exploring Congruent Figures and Motions

Problem Solving Connection
- Use Objects/ Act It Out
- Draw a Picture

Materials
Power Polygons

Vocabulary
congruent having the same size and shape
flip to turn a figure over
turn to rotate a figure
slide to move a figure in one direction

Math Tip
An acrobat *flips*.
A skater *slides*.
A wheel *turns*.

Explore

Can you make designs that look alike but are in different positions?

Work Together

Use Power Polygons.

1. Sit across from another student. One student makes and traces a design at one end of a sheet of paper. The second student copies the design on the other end.

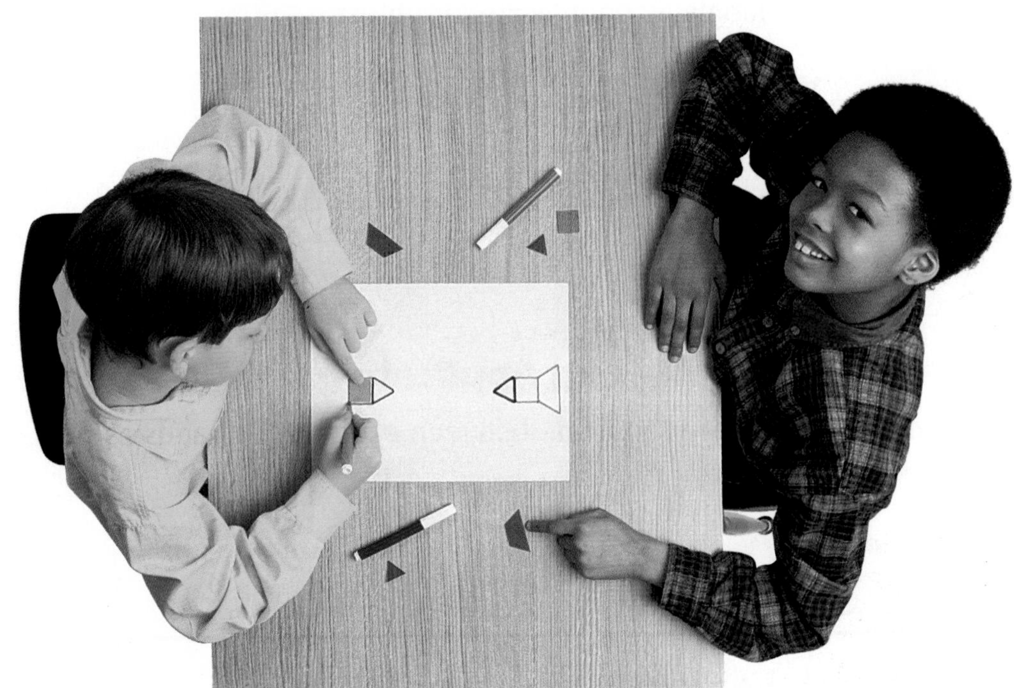

2. Sit side-by-side. Draw the designs beside each other.
3. Sit side-by-side. One student makes and traces a design along the width of a sheet of paper. The second student copies the design along the length of the same sheet of paper.

How are your designs alike?
How are they different?

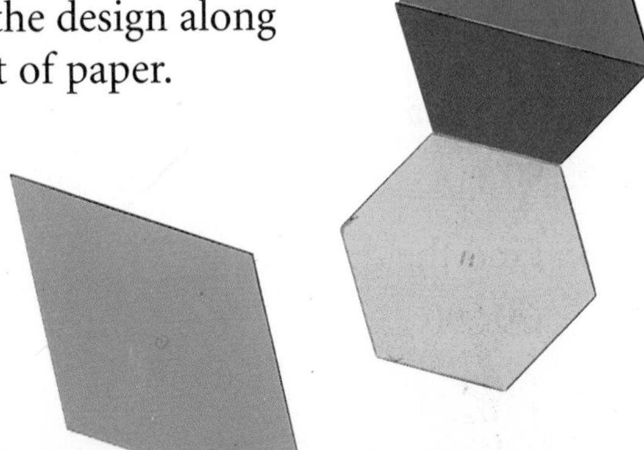

Connect

Two figures that have the same size and shape are **congruent**.

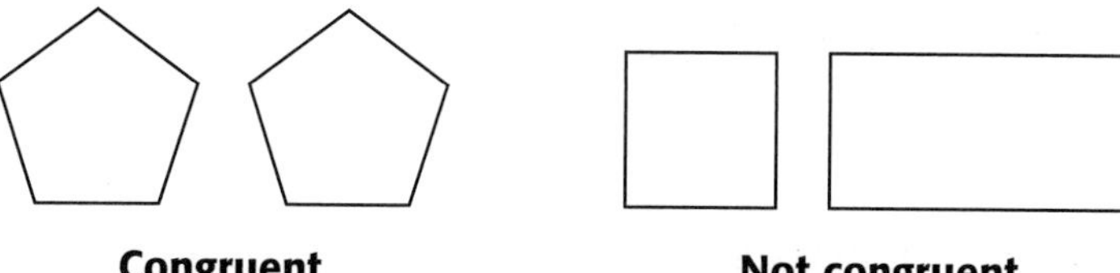

Congruent **Not congruent**

You can **flip** (or reflect), **turn** (or rotate), and **slide** (or translate) a figure to test if two figures are congruent.

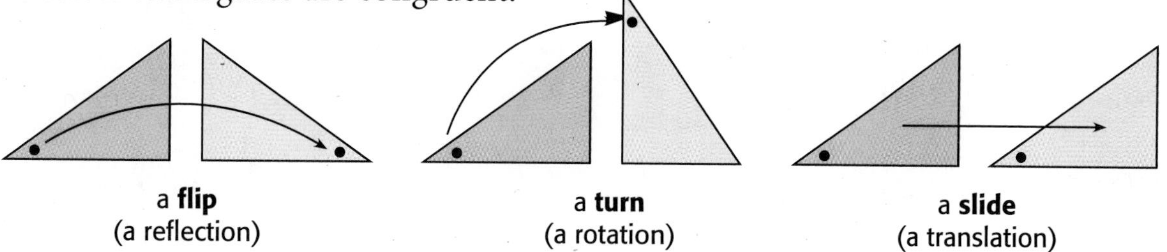

a **flip** (a reflection) a **turn** (a rotation) a **slide** (a translation)

Each pair of triangles fit on top of each other exactly.

Practice

Write whether each picture shows a translation, reflection, or rotation.

1. 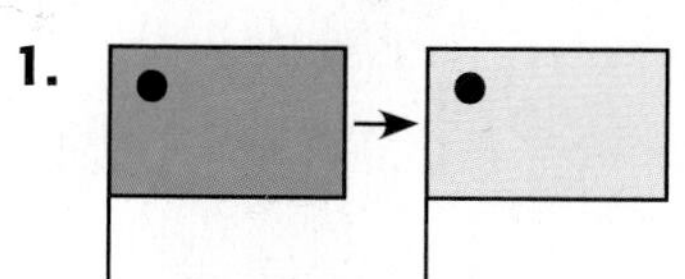

2. 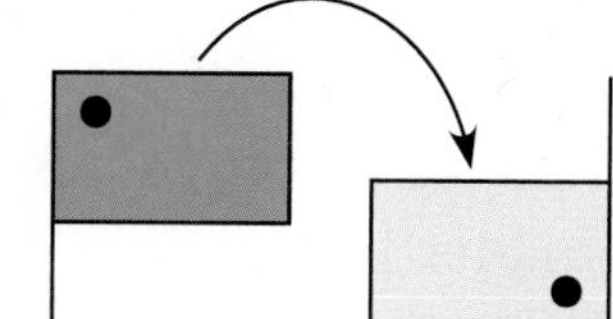

3. 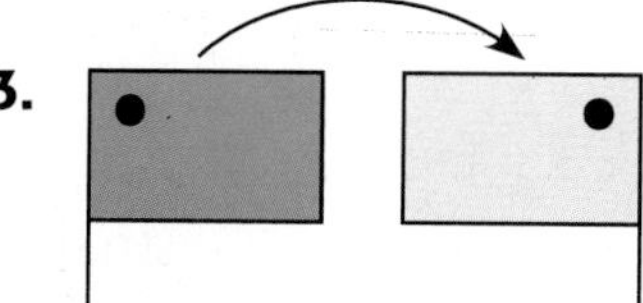

4. Reasoning Brian says that a square looks the same whether he translates it, reflects it, or rotates it 90°. Is he right? Explain.

5. Fine Arts Draw a part of the design in the tile that shows:

a. a translation.

b. a reflection.

c. a rotation.

Mexican tile makers are known for the beauty of their designs.

6. Do two triangles drawn side by side always show a slide? Explain.

7. Language Arts If you turn a lower-case b, you get a q. Find letters that look like other letters after they are flipped or turned. (Don't forget capital letters.)

8. Journal How can you use slides, flips, and turns to decide whether two figures are congruent?

Chapter 8
Lesson
6

Exploring Similar Figures

Problem Solving Connection
Use Objects/
Act It Out

Materials
- geoboard
- dot paper

Vocabulary
similar
having the same shape

Explore

Russian folk artists make hollow dolls that nest inside each other. The different-sized dolls must be the same shape so that they fit inside one another.

Work Together

Use a geoboard to solve each riddle. Then record your answer on dot paper.

1. It is a polygon with four right angles. It has four equal sides, each four units long. Inside is another polygon. It has four equal sides, each two units long. Inside the smaller polygon is one peg. What polygons did you make?

2. It is a 5-sided polygon with a peg inside. Outside is another 5-sided polygon. Each side is twice as long as the same side of the inside polygon. What polygons did you make?

3. Make up your own riddle with two polygons that are the same shape. Ask a classmate to solve it.

Remember
Congruent figures have the same size and shape.

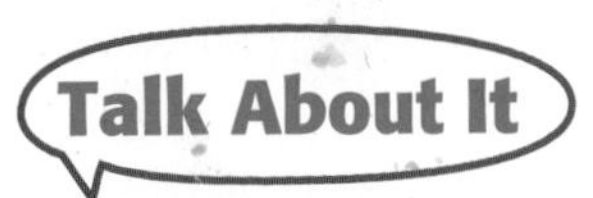

What did you notice about the shape and size of the polygons in riddles 1 and 2?

Connect

Similar figures have the same shape, but not necessarily the same size.

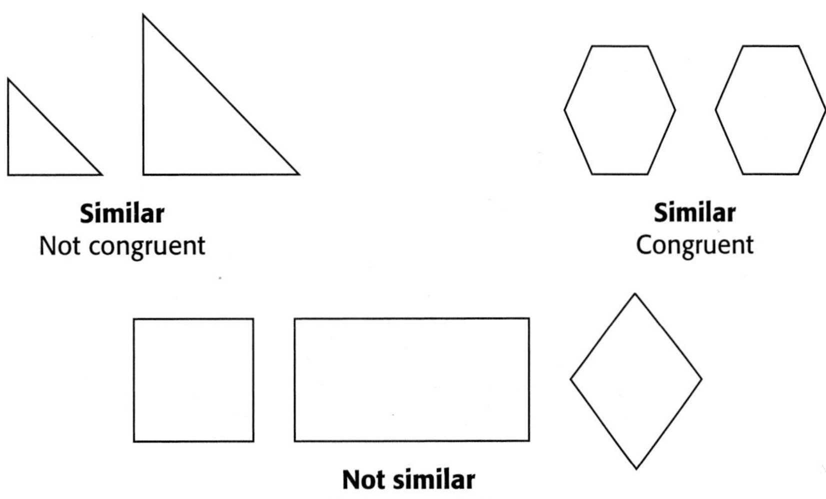

Practice

Write whether each set of figures is congruent, similar, or neither.

1. 

2. 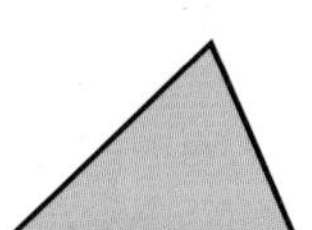 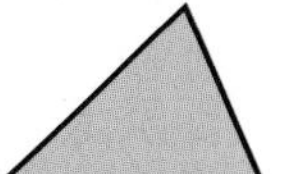

3. 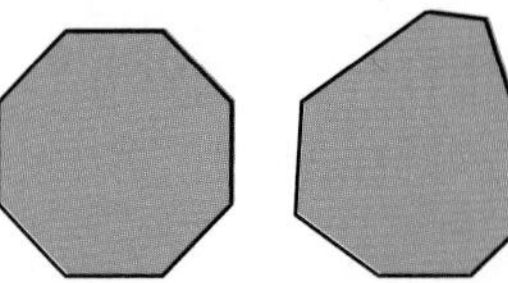

4. 

5. 

6. 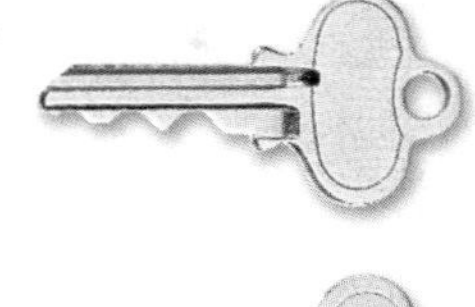

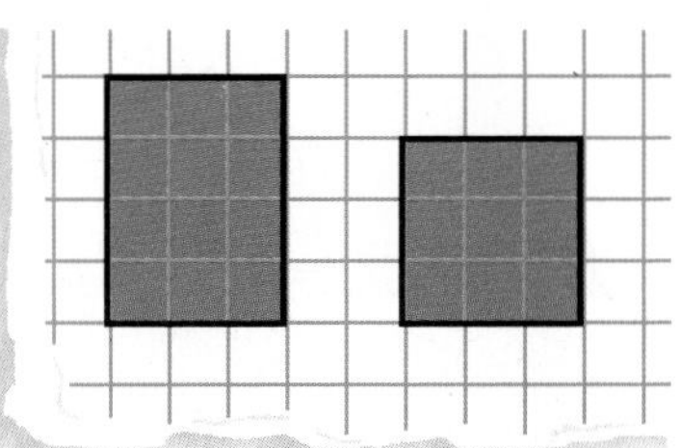

7. **Reasoning** Victoria says that these two figures are similar because all of the angles are right angles. Is she right? Explain.

8. **Collecting Data** Find plane figures in your classroom that are congruent, similar, or neither. Explain your choices.

9. **Journal** In your own words, explain the difference between congruent and similar figures.

SECTION A

Review and Practice

(Lesson 1) Name the solid that each object looks like.

1. 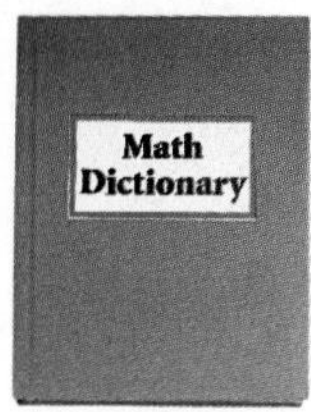

2. 

3. 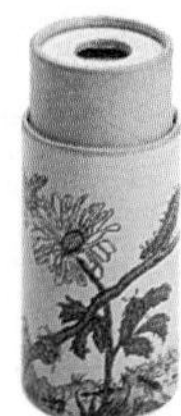

(Lesson 2) Write the name of each polygon.

4. 

5. 

6. 

(Lesson 3) The lengths of the sides of a triangle are given. Name each triangle.

7. 8 in., 6 in., 8 in. **8.** 5 ft, 5 ft, 5 ft **9.** 3 yd, 4 yd, 2 yd

(Lesson 4) Name each triangle as right, acute, or obtuse.

10. 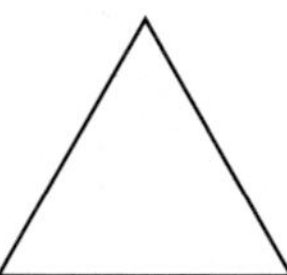

11. 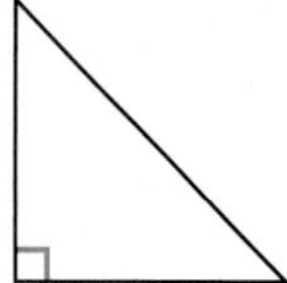

12. 

(Lesson 5) Write whether each picture shows a slide, flip, or turn.

13. 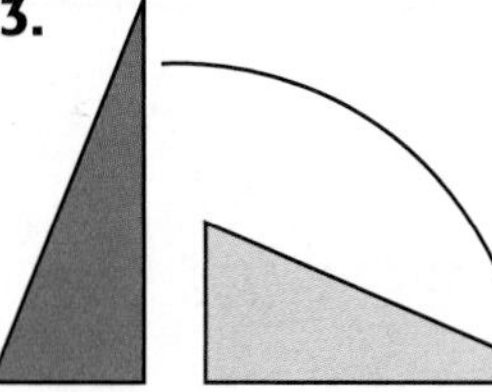

14. 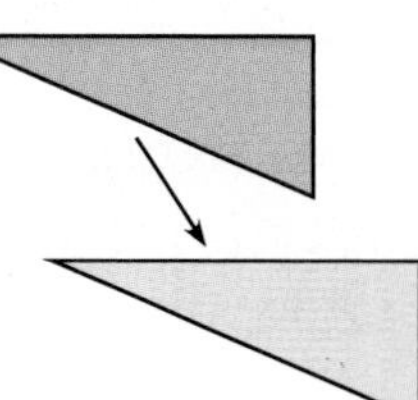

(Lessons 5 and 6) Write whether each set of figures appears to be congruent, similar, or neither.

15. 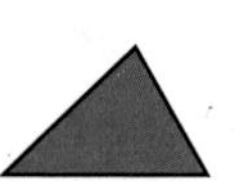

16. 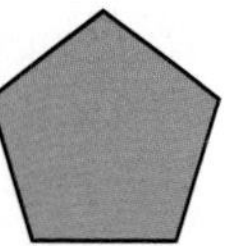 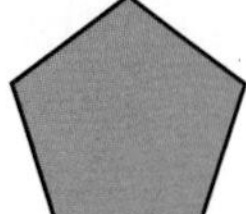

17. Journal Are all triangles similar figures? Explain.

Skills Checklist

In this section, you have:

- ☑ **Explored Solids**
- ☑ **Explored Polygons**
- ☑ **Explored Triangles**
- ☑ **Learned About Triangles and Angles**
- ☑ **Explored Congruent Figures and Motions**
- ☑ **Explored Similar Figures**

CHAPTER 8

SECTION

B Exploring Quadrilaterals

The bowed kite was invented in 1891. How are the figures you see in these bowed kites alike? Different?

Exploring Quadrilaterals

Review polygons. How many sides does each figure have?

1. 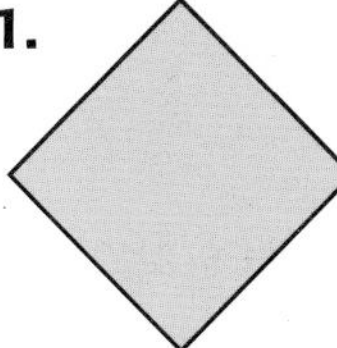

2. 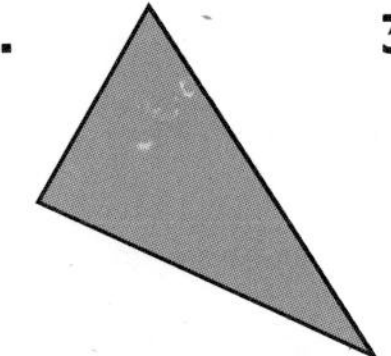

3. 

Skills Checklist

In this section, you will:

- ❑ Learn About Lines and Line Segments
- ❑ Learn About Quadrilaterals
- ❑ Explore Line Symmetry
- ❑ Solve Problems by Using Objects/Acting It Out

Chapter 8
Lesson
7

Lines and Line Segments

You Will Learn
how to identify intersecting, parallel, and perpendicular lines

Vocabulary

line
a straight path that goes on forever in both directions

line segment
part of a line with two endpoints

point
a location in space

Lines or Line Segments
intersecting
parallel
perpendicular

Learn

Artists use grids. The intersecting lines or line segments help them to enlarge or shrink drawings.

Line

Endpoints

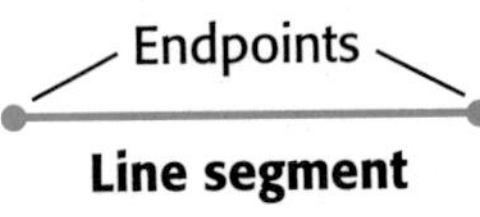

Line segment

Endpoint

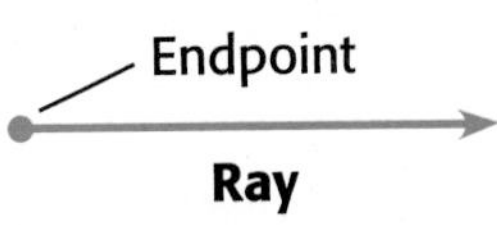

Ray

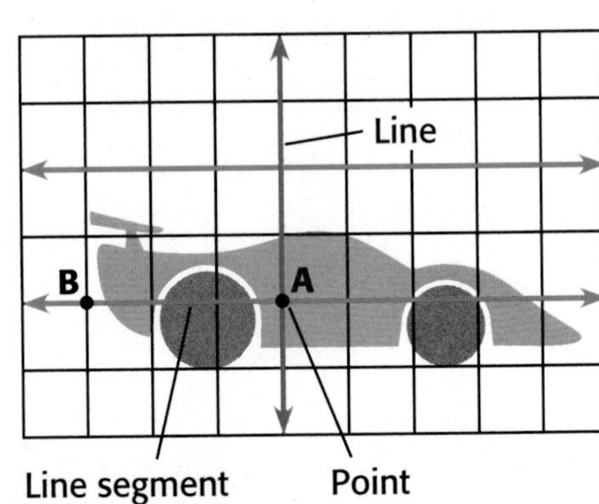

In the grid two **intersecting** lines cross at **point** *A*.

Parallel lines never intersect. The red grid lines are parallel.

Perpendicular lines intersect at right angles. The blue grid line is perpendicular to each red line.

Remember
A ray is part of a line with only one end point.

Talk About It

Name pairs of intersecting, perpendicular, and parallel lines or line segments in your classroom.

Check

Write intersecting, parallel, or perpendicular for each.

1. 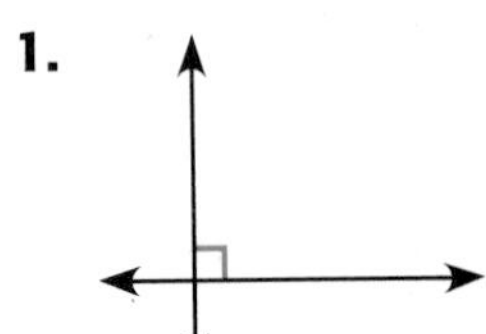

2. 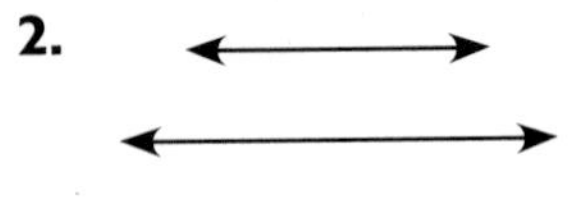

3. 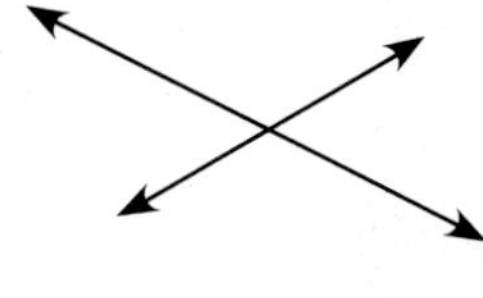

4. Reasoning Raoul says perpendicular lines are always intersecting lines. Is he right? Explain.

Practice

Skills and Reasoning

Write intersecting, parallel, or perpendicular for each.

5.

6.

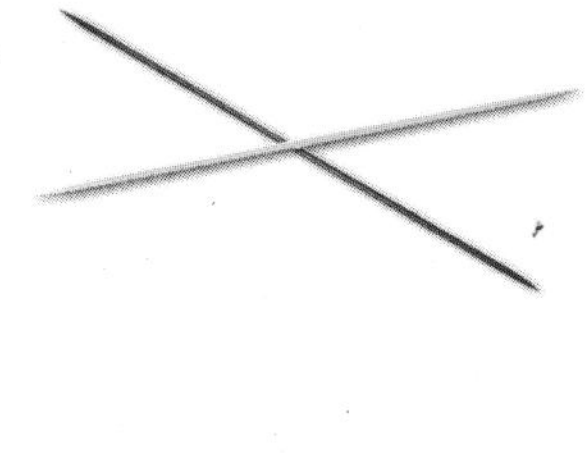

7.

8. Write a capital letter of the alphabet that has:
   a. intersecting lines. b. perpendicular lines. c. parallel lines.

Problem Solving and Applications

9. Corey is 1 mile from Stoney Creek. He wants to get to the creek as quickly as possible. Should he walk on a line that is parallel to the creek, perpendicular to the creek, or neither? Explain.

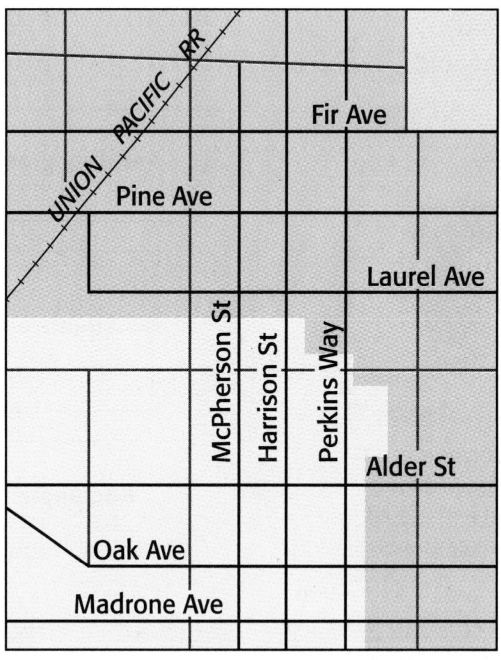

Fort Bragg, California

Using Data Use the map of Fort Bragg to answer **10** and **11.**

10. **Geography** Write if each pair of streets appears to be parallel or perpendicular.
    a. Pine Ave. and Perkins Way
    b. Alder St. and Madrone Ave.
11. **Critical Thinking** Could you get from the corner of McPherson and Laurel to the corner of Fir and Perkins Way without crossing Harrison? Explain.

Mixed Review and Test Prep

STAY SHARP!

Multiply or divide.

12. 467×5 13. $871 \div 7$ 14. 392×36 15. $543 \div 8$

16. There are 25 students in a class. Each student has 5 books. Which number sentence shows how many books there are in all?
    Ⓐ $25 + 5 = 30$ Ⓑ $25 - 5 = 20$ Ⓒ $25 \times 5 = 125$ Ⓓ $25 \div 5 = 5$

Chapter 8
Lesson
8

Quadrilaterals

You Will Learn
how to name quadrilaterals by their side lengths and angle sizes

Vocabulary
quadrilateral
a polygon with 4 sides

Quadrilaterals
parallelogram
square
rectangle
rhombus
trapezoid

Learn

Kite makers often use four-sided polygons in their designs. This kite was made in Japan. It is handpainted on rice paper and bamboo.

Edo, or Warrior Face kite.

You can name **quadrilaterals** by the lengths of their sides and the sizes of their angles.

Parallelogram — There are two pairs of opposite parallel sides.

Square — All sides are the same length. There are four right angles.

Rectangle — Opposite sides are parallel and the same length. There are four right angles.

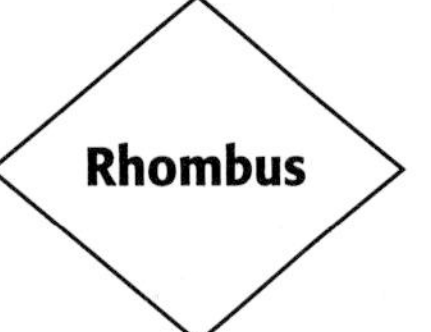

There are two pairs of parallel sides. All sides are the same length.

There is only one pair of parallel sides.

Remember
A polygon is a closed plane figure made of line segments.

Talk About It

How can you tell a trapezoid from a parallelogram? A rhombus from a rectangle?

Check

Write the name of each quadrilateral.

1. 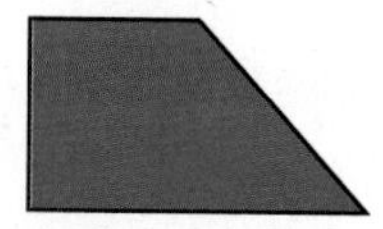
2. 
3. 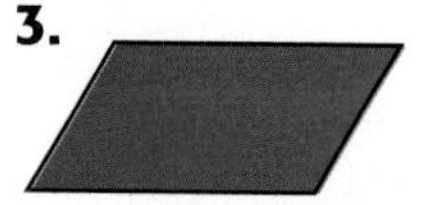
4. 

5. **Reasoning** Can a quadrilateral be both a square and a rectangle? Can it be both a parallelogram and a rhombus? Explain.

Practice

Skills and Reasoning

Write the name of each quadrilateral.

6. 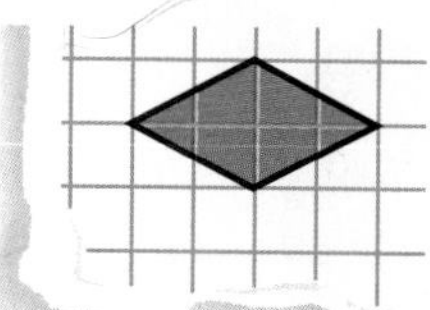
7. 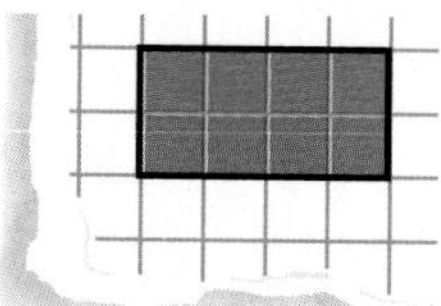
8. 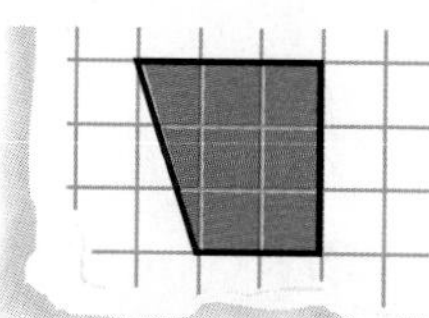
9. 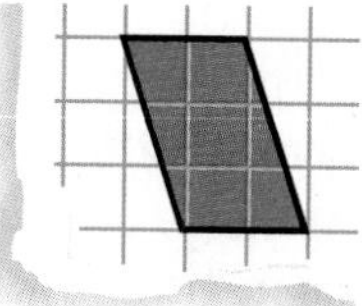

10. Draw a quadrilateral that is not a square, a rectangle, a parallelogram, a rhombus, or a trapezoid.

Problem Solving and Applications

11. **Sports** A baseball "diamond" is actually a square. It is 90 ft from first base to second base. How far is it from second base to third base?

12. **Using Data** Use the Data File on page 341. What figures do you see in the kites?

13. **Critical Thinking** Look at the kite from Japan on page 360. Decide which figure, or figures, it is. Explain.

    a. Square b. Rhombus c. Rectangle d. Parallelogram

Mixed Review and Test Prep

STAY SHARP!

Find each answer.

14. 255×43

15. $912 \div 7$

16. 614×29

17. $438 \div 6$

18. If 8 people share 16 ounces of frozen yogurt equally, how many ounces will each person get?

    Ⓐ 6 ounces Ⓑ 4 ounces Ⓒ 2 ounces Ⓓ not here

Chapter 8
Lesson
9

Exploring Line Symmetry

Problem Solving Connection
- Use Objects/ Act It Out
- Guess and Check

Materials
square and rectangular pieces of paper

Vocabulary
line of symmetry line on which a figure can be folded so that both halves are congruent
diagonal line segment, other than a side, connecting two vertices of a polygon

Explore

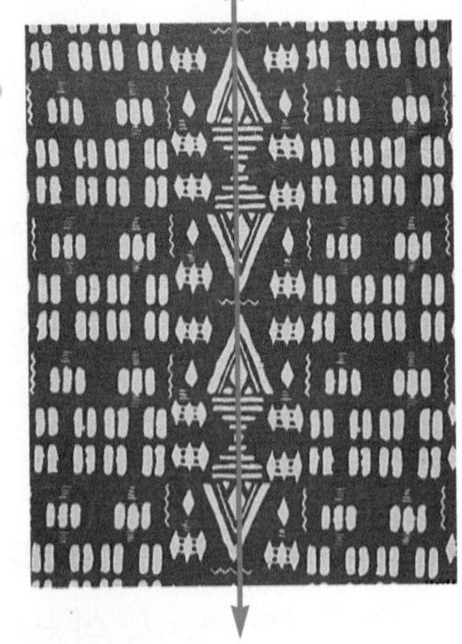

This batik from West Africa can be folded into two congruent halves.

You can use folded sheets of paper to make your own congruent figures.

Work Together

1. Fold a piece of square paper in half.

   a. Do the two halves match? Draw a line along the fold.
   b. Try to find other lines that divide the square in half. Fold to see if you are right. Draw along the fold lines.

Remember
Congruent figures have the same shape and size.

2. Fold a piece of rectangular paper in half.
   a. Do the two halves match? Draw along the fold line.
   b. Try to find other lines that divide the rectangle in half. Fold to see if you are right. Draw along the fold lines.

3. Draw a figure other than a square or rectangle that can be folded into two halves that match exactly. Then draw one that can't.

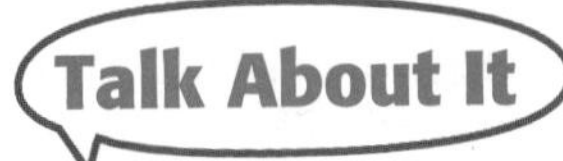

Do the lines on your square divide the square into congruent halves? Explain.

Connect

This mask has one **line of symmetry**.

You can see that half of the mask has been flipped to create the other half.

Some figures have more than one line of symmetry.

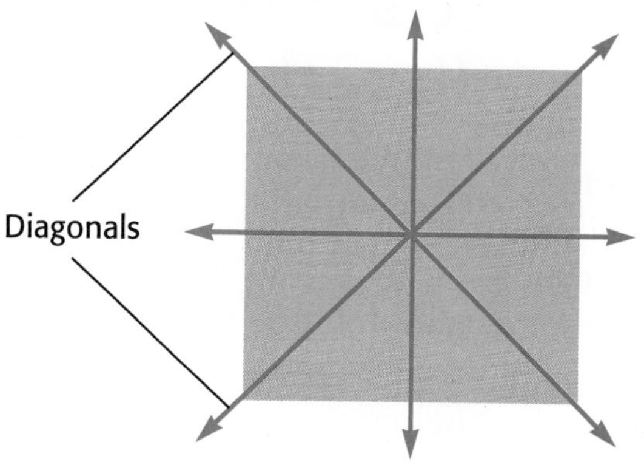

Some **diagonals** are lines of symmetry.

Practice

How many lines of symmetry for each? You may trace each figure.

1. 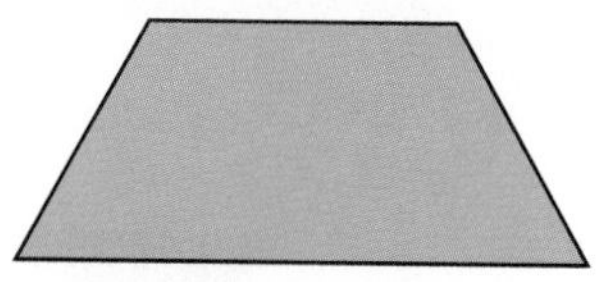

2. 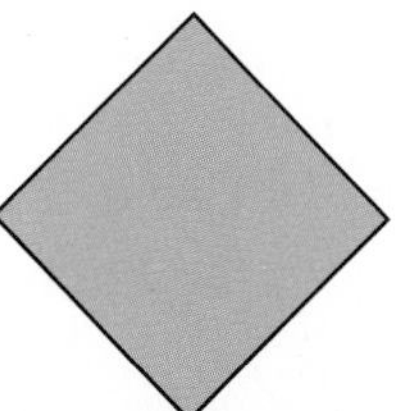

3. 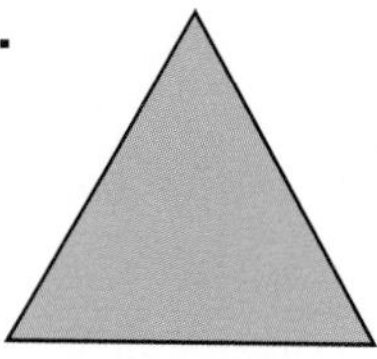

4. 

5. 

6. 

7. Half of a figure and its line of symmetry are shown.

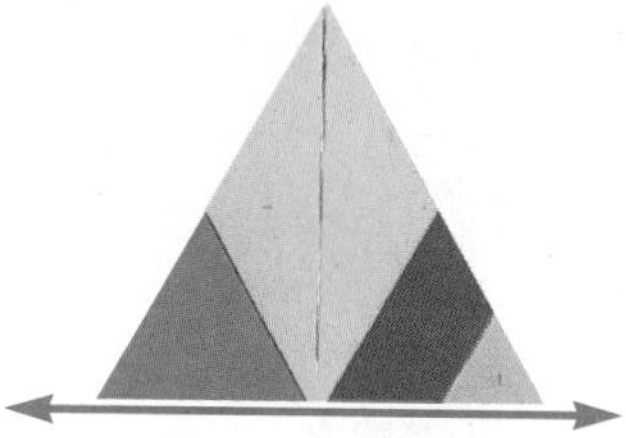

a. Sketch the whole figure.

b. Did you slide, flip, or turn the half figure to make the whole? Explain.

8. Write Your Own Problem Draw half of a figure and a line of symmetry. Challenge a friend to draw the whole figure.

9. Journal Make drawings of items that have one line of symmetry, two lines of symmetry, and more than two lines of symmetry.

Skills Practice Bank, page 570, Set 3

Chapter 8
Lesson
10

Problem Solving

Analyze Strategies: Use Objects/Act It Out

You Will Learn
how to use objects to solve problems

Materials
Power Polygons

Learn

Suppose a totem pole has a raven, a dog, a bear, and a walrus. The walrus is above the raven but below the bear. The dog is below the walrus but above the raven. In what order are the animals?

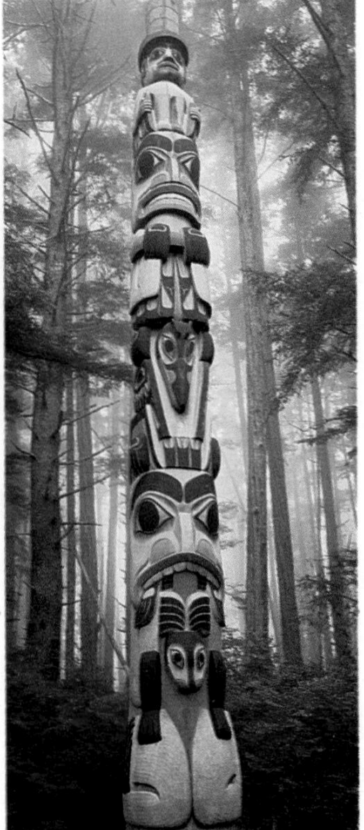

Yaadaas Crest Corner Pole made by the Haida Clan in Prince of Wales Island, Alaska.

Work Together

Understand

What do you know?

What do you need to find out?

Plan

How will you find out? Use a different Power Polygon piece to stand for each animal.

Solve

Move the pieces until you have the right order.

The walrus is above the raven but below the bear.

The dog is below the walrus but above the raven.

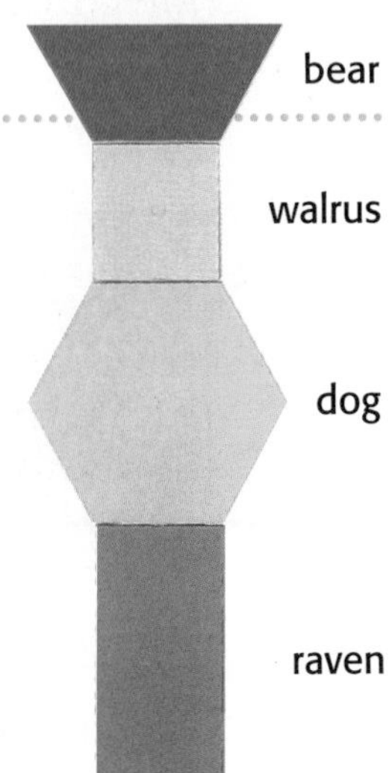

What is the answer? The order of the animals is bear, walrus, dog, and raven.

Look Back

How can you check your answer?

1. How did the Power Polygons help you solve the problem?
2. How did you know the dog is below the bear?

Check

Use objects to help solve the problem.

1. An Arctic animal mural has a polar bear, a walrus, a blue fox, and an Arctic hare. The polar bear is in front of the walrus but behind the blue fox. The Arctic hare is behind the blue fox but in front of the polar bear.
   a. What objects will you choose to stand for each animal?
   b. Use the first clue. What is the order of the three animals?
   c. Use the second clue. Where should you put the Arctic hare?
   d. What is the order of the animals in the mural?

Arctic hares are found in Alaska and Canada. They have thick fur on the soles of their feet.

2. Four polygons are lined up. The quadrilateral is next to the triangle and pentagon. The hexagon has only one polygon next to it. The triangle is not first or fourth. In what order are the polygons?

Problem Solving Practice

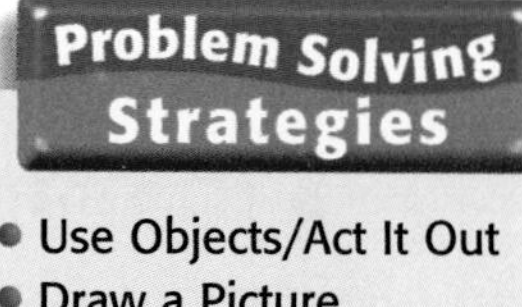

- Use Objects/Act It Out
- Draw a Picture
- Look for a Pattern
- Guess and Check
- Use Logical Reasoning
- Make an Organized List
- Make a Table
- Solve a Simpler Problem
- Work Backward

Choose a Tool

Use objects or any strategy to help you solve each problem.

3. Mark's birthday is before Alex's but after Beth's. Ellen's birthday is before Beth's but after Orlando's. Whose birthday is first?
4. Zac has to choose an outfit. He has 1 yellow shirt, 1 blue shirt, 1 pair of blue jeans, and 1 pair of black pants. How many different outfits can he wear?
5. Zelda bought some fabric for $32.00. Then she bought lunch for $7.50. She has 50 cents left. How much money did she start with?
6. **Money** Mike has the same number of nickels and quarters. He has $1.50. How many nickels and quarters does he have?
7. Remove 4 toothpicks so that exactly 1 square remains.

SECTION B

Review and Practice

Vocabulary Choose the word that best completes each sentence.

Word List
perpendicular
quadrilateral
parallel

1. _____ lines never intersect.
2. _____ lines intersect at right angles.
3. A _____ is a 4-sided polygon.

(Lesson 7) Write intersecting, parallel, or perpendicular.

4. 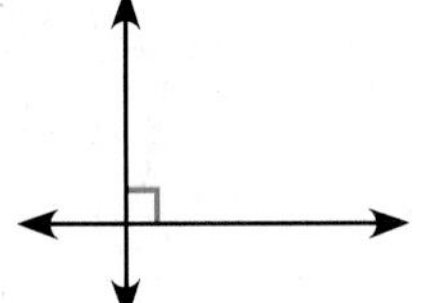

5. 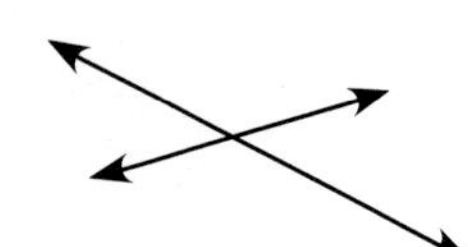

6. 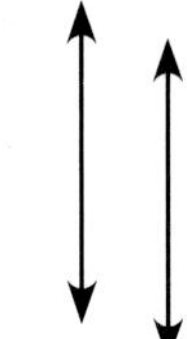

(Lesson 8) Write the name of each quadrilateral.

7. 

8. 

9. 

(Lesson 9) How many lines of symmetry does each figure have?

10. Rectangle

11. Square

12. Isosceles triangle

13. 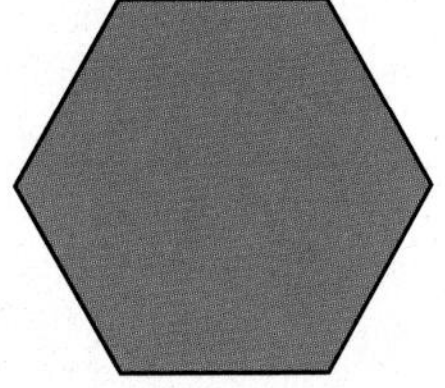

14. 

15. 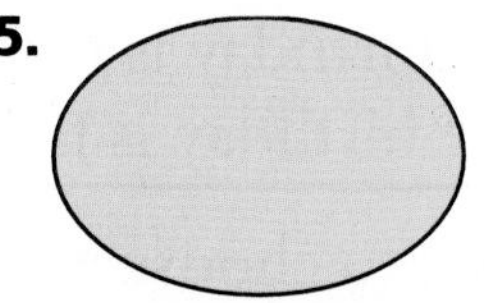

(Lesson 10) Use objects or any other strategy to solve.

16. In the family photo, Mr. Simms stood to the left of his son Tom and to the right of Mrs. Simms. Daughter Julie stood to the left of her father and to the right of her mother. In what order were the four family members standing?

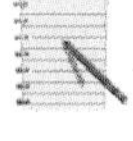

17. Journal Do all quadrilaterals have a line of symmetry? Explain.

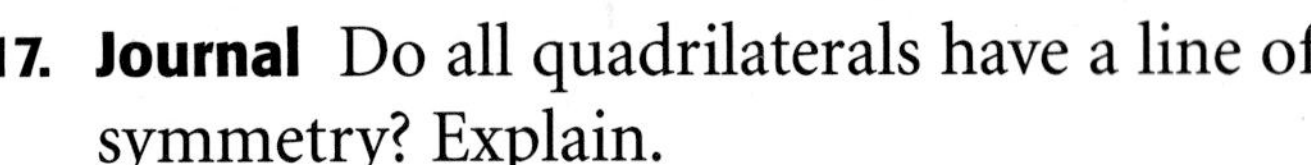

Skills Checklist

In this section, you have:

- ☑ Learned About Lines and Line Segments
- ☑ Learned About Quadrilaterals
- ☑ Explored Line Symmetry
- ☑ Solved Problems by Using Objects/Acting It Out

CHAPTER 8

SECTION

C Exploring Perimeter, Area, and Volume

Weavers in Ecuador, South America, use patterns in their basket designs. How can you tell, by looking, which basket will hold the most?

Exploring Measurement of Figures

Review multiplying and adding. Find each product or sum.

1. $2 \times 3 \times 5$ **2.** $4 \times 1 \times 6$ **3.** $7 \times 3 \times 2$

4. $7 + 2 + 2 + 7$ **5.** $6 + 3 + 6 + 3$

Skills Checklist

In this section, you will:

- ❐ Explore Perimeter
- ❐ Explore Areas of Rectangles
- ❐ Explore Volume
- ❐ Solve Problems by Making Decisions

Chapter 8 Lesson 11

Exploring Perimeter

Problem Solving Connection

- Use Objects/ Act It Out
- Draw a Picture

Materials

- geoboard
- rubberbands
- dot paper

Vocabulary

perimeter the distance around a figure

Explore

Kirsten designs travel posters. To buy materials to frame a poster, she first finds the **perimeter** of, or distance around, the poster.

The perimeter of this poster is 22 in. + 34 in. + 22 in. + 34 in., or 112 in.

22 in.

34 in.

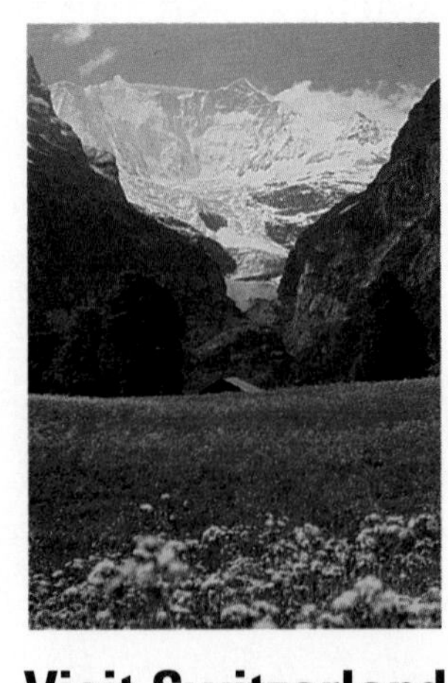

Visit Switzerland

34 in.

22 in.

Work Together

Find the perimeter.

1. Use a geoboard and rubberbands.
   a. Make this figure.
   b. Count the units along the outside of the figure.
   c. What is its perimeter?

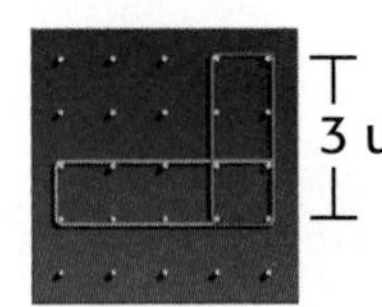
3 units

2. Make a rectangle with the same perimeter as the figure above.
3. Make a rectangle with a perimeter of 12 units.

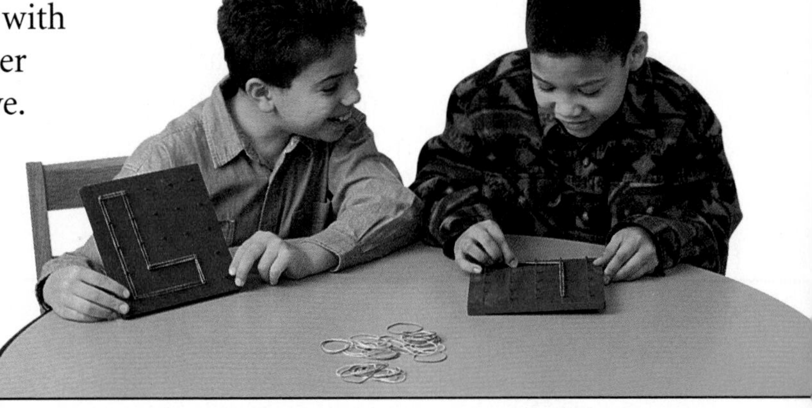

Math Tip

When finding perimeter, mark your starting point. Count each unit once.

4. How many different figures can you find with a perimeter of 12? Draw each figure on dot paper.

Talk About It

5. How did you find the perimeter of your figures?
6. Can two different figures have the same perimeter? Explain.

Connect

You can find the perimeter of a polygon by adding the lengths of its sides.

Perimeter = 5 in. + 5 in. + 3 in. + 3 in. + 5 in.

Perimeter = 21 inches

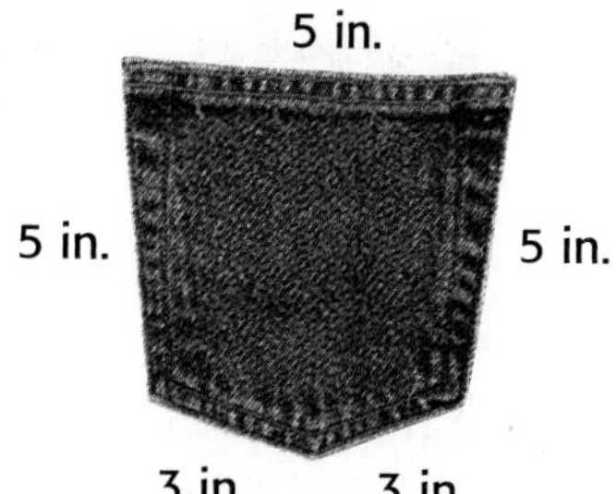

Practice

Find the perimeter of each polygon.

1.

2.

3.

4. 

5. 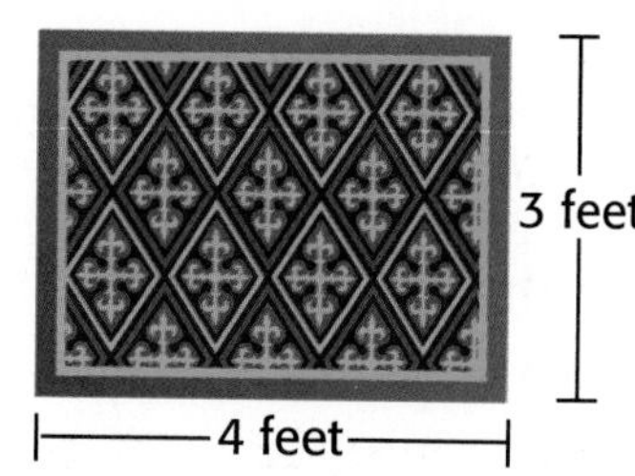

6. 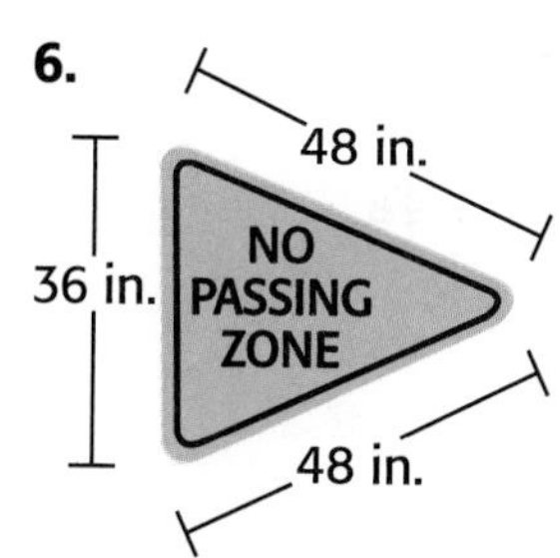

7. **Reasoning** How are the polygons in **1–3** the same? How are they different?

8. **Fine Arts** One of the world's largest quilts was made by 7,000 people in North Dakota. The quilt was a rectangle measuring 85 ft by 134 ft. What was the perimeter of the quilt?

9. **Critical Thinking** Using units from 1–9, how many rectangles with a perimeter of 20 units can you find? Give the measurements of each.

10. This rectangle has the measurements shown.
    a. What is the length of the missing side?
    b. What is the rectangle's perimeter?

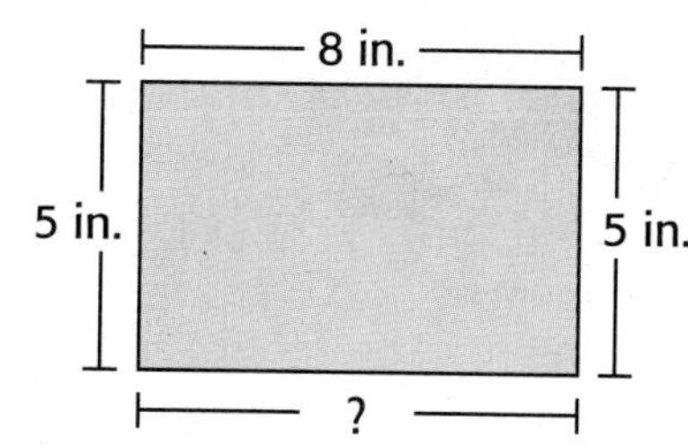

11. **Algebra Readiness** The perimeter of a square measures 36 inches. How long is each side?

12. **Journal** Use the Data File on page 341. Explain how you would find the perimeter of one of the stone blocks in the Great Zimbabwe tower.

PRACTICE AND APPLY

Chapter 8
Lesson
12

Exploring Areas of Rectangles

Problem Solving Connection
Use Objects/
Act It Out

Materials
grid paper

Vocabulary

area
number of square units needed to cover a figure

Some Units for Measuring Area
square unit
square inch
square centimeter

Explore

The **area** of a figure is the number of **square units** needed to cover it.

This is a square unit. This is about half of a square unit.

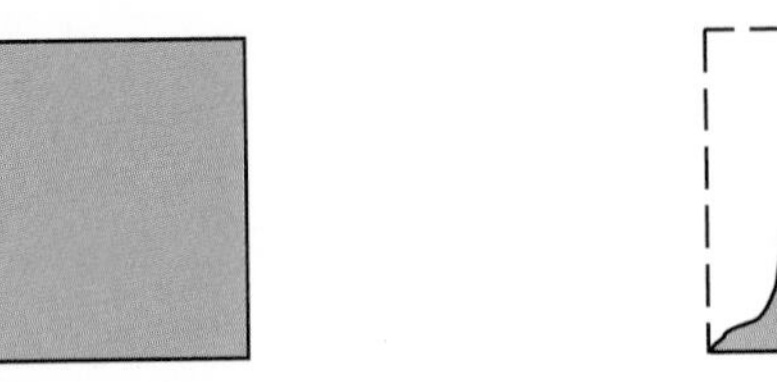

Work Together

Estimate the area of the bottom of your shoe. Use grid paper.

1. a. Trace the outline of your shoe on grid paper.
   b. Count the whole squares and almost-whole squares.
   c. Count the half squares and almost-half squares.
   d. Estimate the total area.

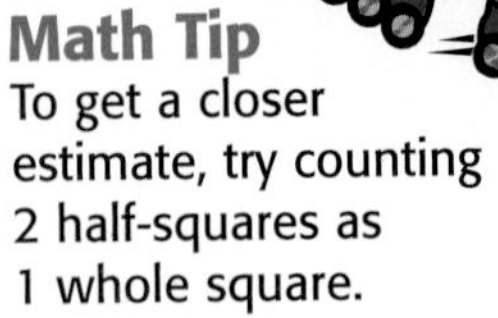

Math Tip
To get a closer estimate, try counting 2 half-squares as 1 whole square.

2. How did you estimate the total area of your shoe?
3. If someone else estimated the area of your shoe, would they get the same answer? Explain.

Connect

You use square units to measure area. You can count the number of **square centimeters** or **square inches** to find the area.

The area is 5 square centimeters.

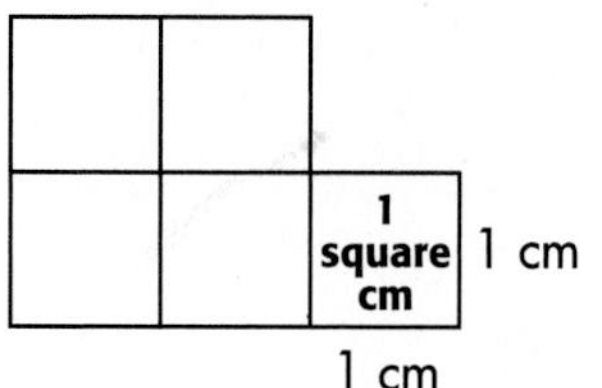

The area is 2 square inches.

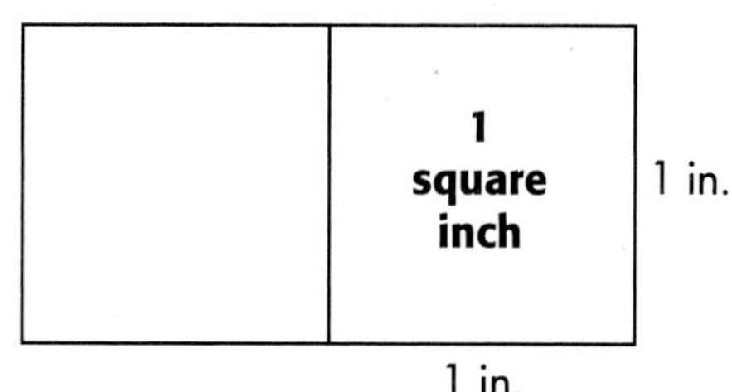

You can also find the area of a rectangle by using a formula.

Area = length × width

Area = 3 units × 2 units

Area = 6 square units

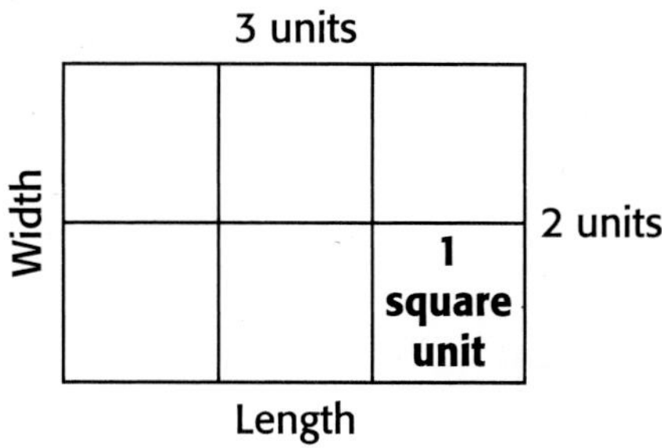

Practice

Find the area of each rectangle.

1. 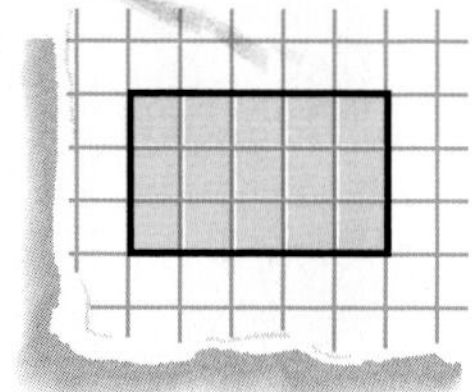

2. 

3. 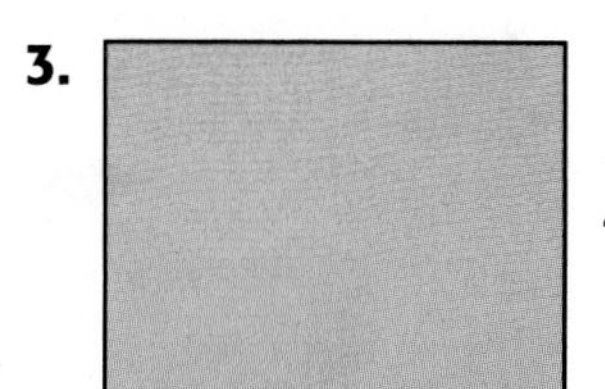

4. **Sports** Badminton is played on a rectangular court measuring 44 ft by 20 ft. What is the area of a badminton court?

5. Keith Witt is the world's fastest window cleaner! In 10 seconds, he cleaned 3 rectangular windows each measuring about 47 in. by 42 in. Estimate the total area he washed.

6. **Mental Math** The area of a rectangle is 24 square inches. Its length is 8 inches. What is its width?

7. **What If** The sides of a 5 in.-by-11 in. rectangle are doubled. Is the area of the new figure twice as large? Explain.

8. **Journal** Explain how to find the area of this page.

Skills Practice Bank, page 570, Set 4

Exploring Volume

Problem Solving Connection
Use Objects/
Act It Out

Materials
- color cubes
- calculator

Vocabulary
volume
number of cubic units needed to fill a solid

Units for Measuring Volume
cubic unit
cubic centimeter
cubic inch

Remember
A rectangular prism is a solid with a right angle at each vertex.

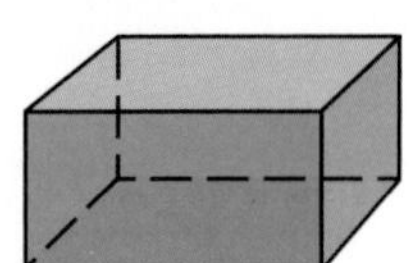

Explore

The **volume** of a solid is the number of **cubic units** it contains. This is one cubic unit.

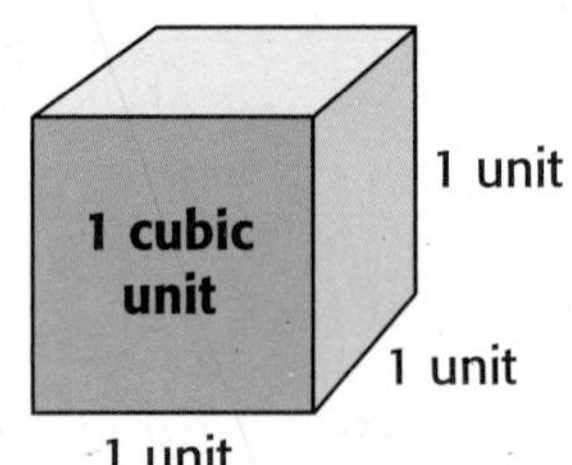

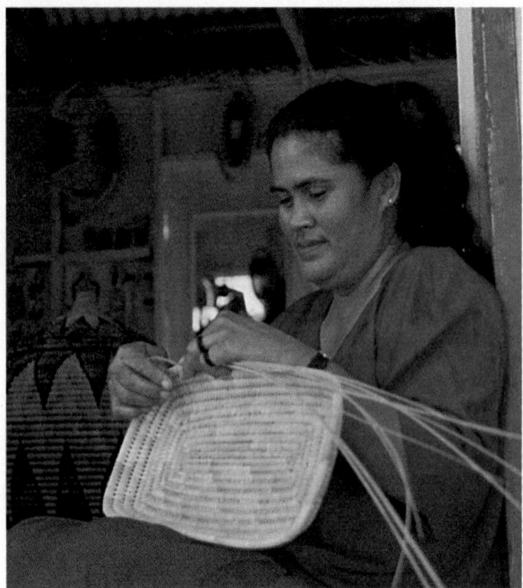

People of many cultures handweave patterned baskets.

Work Together

Each of your cubes stands for a basket.

1. How many baskets are in each rectangular prism?

a.

b.

c.
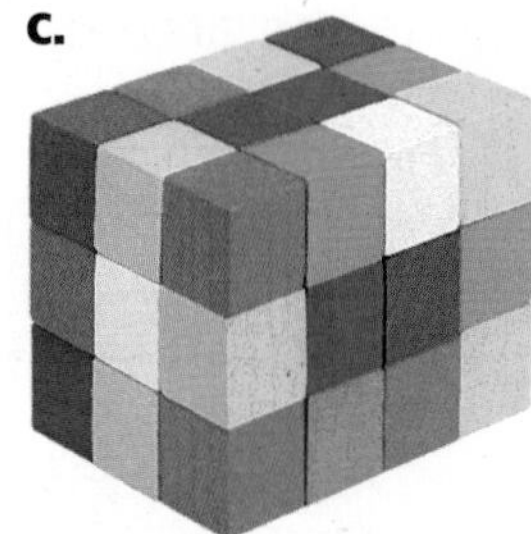

2. Suppose each basket is 1 cubic unit. What is the length, width, and height of each rectangular prism above?
3. How many different rectangular prisms can you make with:
   a. 6 baskets **b.** 15 baskets **c.** 16 baskets **d.** 24 baskets

Talk About It

4. How did you find the number of cube-shaped baskets in each rectangular prism?
5. Can you think of another way to find the number of baskets in each rectangular prism?

Connect

You use cubic units to measure the volume of a solid. You can count the number of **cubic centimeters** or **cubic inches** to find the volume.

The volume is 5 cubic centimeters.

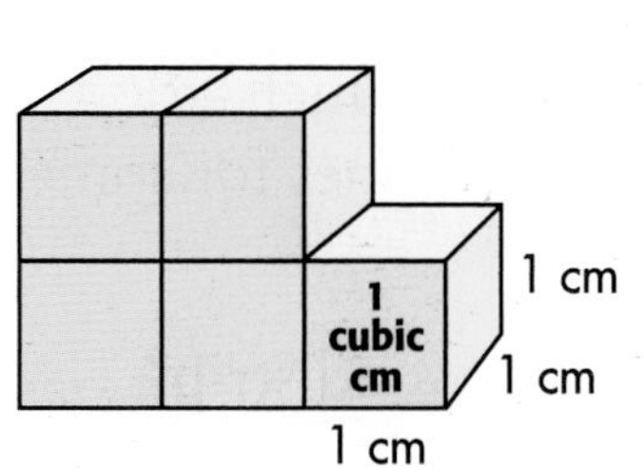

The volume is 2 cubic inches.

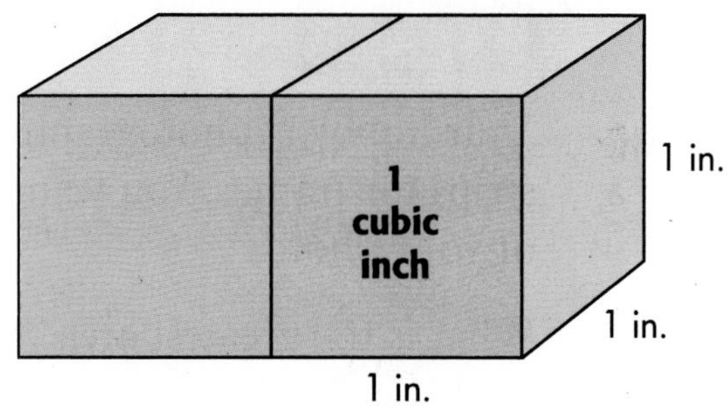

You can also find the volume of a rectangular prism by using a formula.

Volume = length × width × height

Volume = 3 units × 2 units × 2 units

Volume = 12 cubic units

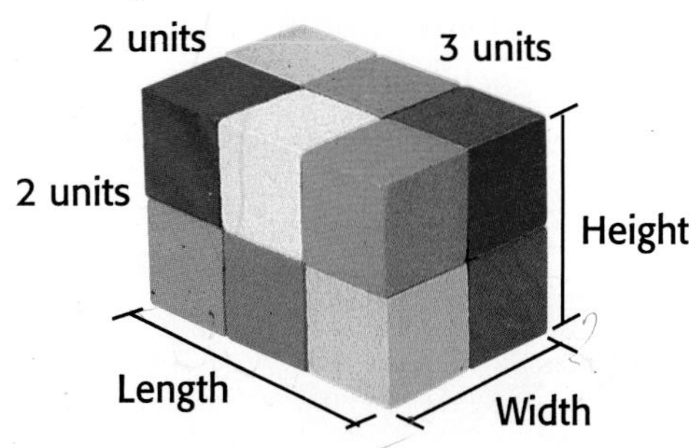

Practice

Find the volume of each rectangular prism.

1. 

2. 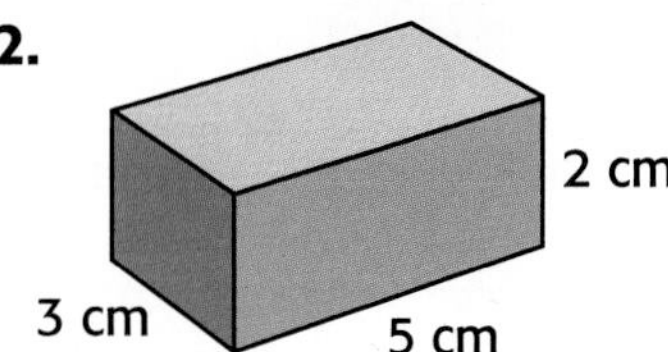

3. 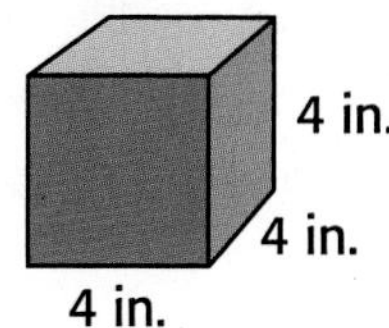

4. Find the volume of a rectangular prism that has a length of 8 ft, a width of 5 ft, and a height of 2 ft.
5. **Critical Thinking** A swimming pool is shaped like a rectangular prism, 30 ft by 20 ft by 10 ft.
   a. How deep is the pool?
   b. What is the area of the pool cover?
   c. How much dirt was removed from the hole to make the pool?

6. **Journal** Explain how to find the volume of a box that is 3 in. by 2 in. by 4 in.

Skills Practice Bank, page 570, Set 5

Chapter 8
Lesson
14

Problem Solving

Decision Making: The Greatest Area

You Will Learn
how to make decisions about the perimeter and area of a rectangle.

Explore

Your hobby is photography. The Photo Shop sells 48-inch wood strips for frames. You want to buy strips to make frames for some of your photos.

What is the greatest area you can frame with one wood strip?

Some Facts and Data
Each frame must be made from one 48-inch strip of wood. Use all 48 inches in each frame. All your frames should be rectangles. Each width and length must be a whole number.

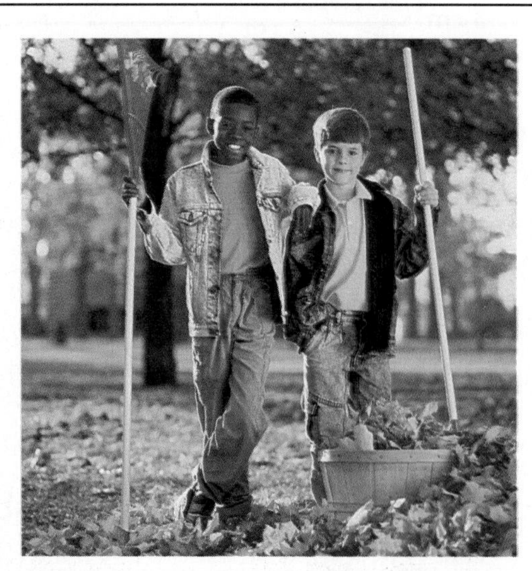

Work Together

▶ Understand

1. What do you know?
2. What are you asked to do?

▶ Plan and Solve

3. How can you find the length and width of a rectangle with a perimeter of 48 inches?
4. Find different rectangles that have perimeters of 48 inches. Then record data about the rectangles in a table. Your table should show the length, width, and area of each rectangle.

▶ Make a Decision

5. Do all of the rectangles have the same perimeter? Do they have the same area?
6. Which rectangle has the greatest area?
7. Do you think there is another rectangle with an even greater area than the one you found?

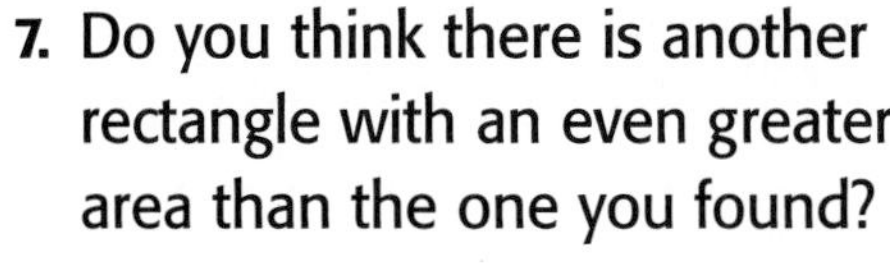

Perimeter = 48inches		
Length	Width	Area

▶ Present Your Decision

8. How did you decide which rectangle has the greatest area?
9. What patterns do you see in your table?

Skills Practice Bank, page 570, Set 6

SECTION C

Review and Practice

Vocabulary Write true or false.

1. Perimeter is the distance around a figure.
2. Volume is the number of square units needed to cover a region.
3. Area is the number of cubic units in a solid figure.

(Lesson 11) Find the perimeter of each polygon.

4.

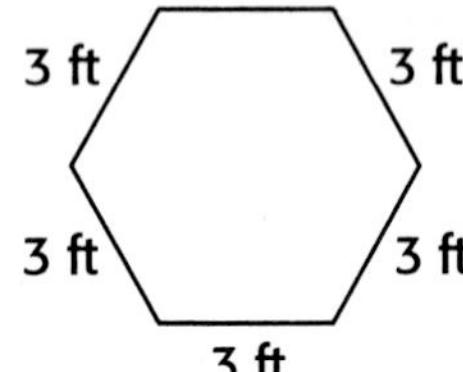

5.

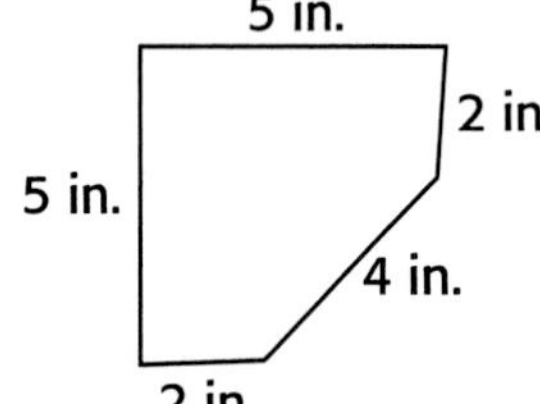

6.

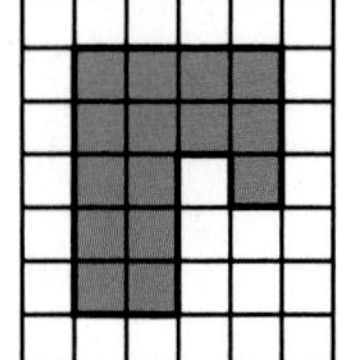

(Lesson 12) Find the area of each rectangle.

7.

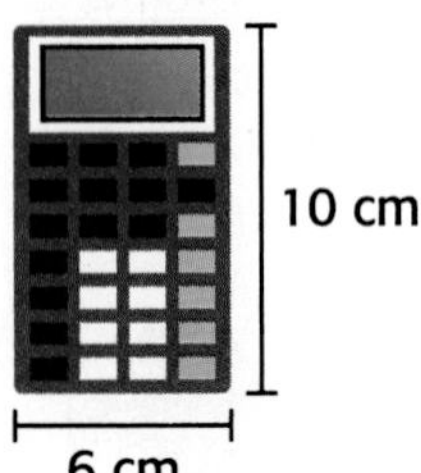

8.

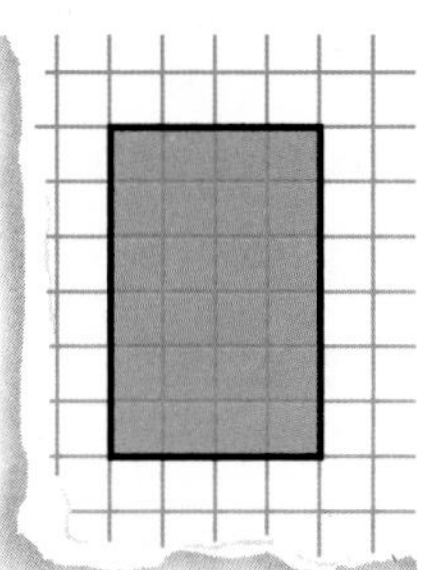

9.

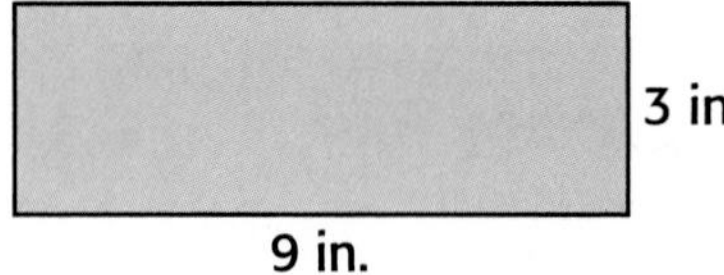

(Lesson 13) Find the volume of each rectangular prism.

10.

11.

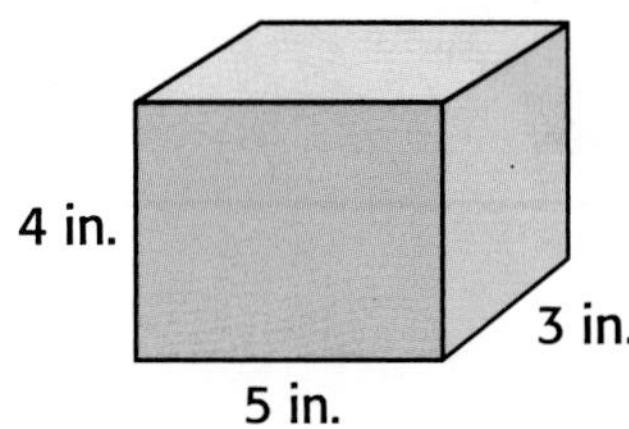

12. A rectangular prism is 5 inches long, 3 inches wide, and 2 inches high. Find its volume.
13. **Reasoning** Juanita framed a square painting with a perimeter of 64 in. What was the area of the painting?
14. **Journal** Two rectangles have the same perimeter. Do they have the same area? Explain.

Skills Checklist

In this section, you have:

- Explored Perimeter
- Explored Areas of Rectangles
- Explored Volume
- Solved Problems by Making Decisions

Choose at least one. Use what you have learned in this chapter.

1 Ship Shape

The sailboat is made from a right triangle, a line segment, and a trapezoid. Can you make a drawing containing at least five of the figures you have learned about in this chapter?

How do artists use geometric figures in their art? To find out more about geometric figures in art, check out **www.mathsurf.com/4/ch8.**

2 What's Your Angle?

This student is acting out the word *angle.* Take turns with other students acting out geometry words. Give yourself 1 point for guessing a word correctly. Give yourself 2 points if another student guesses your word.

3 The L-Shaped Room

What is the perimeter of the room?
What is the area?
(Hint: Draw the room on grid paper.)

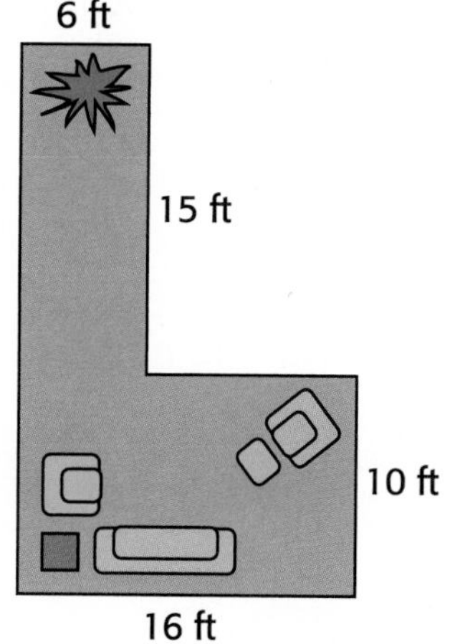

4 Half and Half

At Home Work with a family member or friend. Find magazine photos with lines of symmetry. Cut each photo along the line of symmetry. Paste half the photo on a piece of paper. Draw in the missing half of the photo. Or, paste the whole photo and draw the lines of symmetry on it.

CHAPTER 8

Review/Test

Vocabulary Match each with its meaning.

1. congruent	**a.** two lines that never intersect
2. angle	**b.** figures with the same size and shape
3. polygon	**c.** closed plane figure made of line segments
4. parallel	**d.** two rays with a common end point

(Lesson 2) Write the name of each polygon.

5. 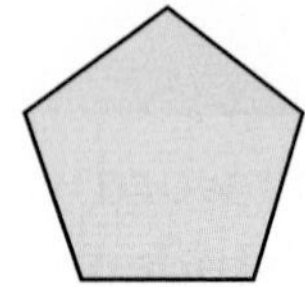

6. 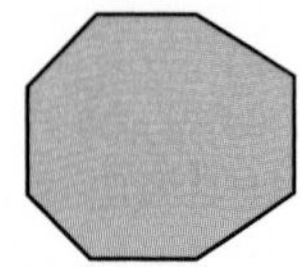

7. 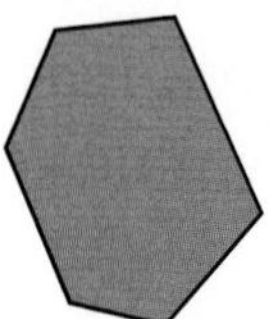

(Lesson 3) The lengths of the sides of triangles are given. Name each triangle.

8. 9 cm, 11 cm, 8 cm **9.** 5 ft, 5 ft, 5 ft **10.** 6 in., 14 in., 14 in.

(Lesson 7) Write intersecting, parallel, or perpendicular for each.

11. 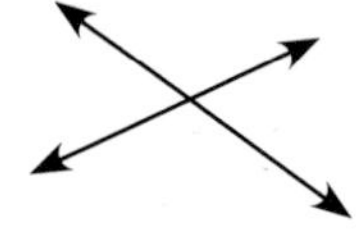

12. 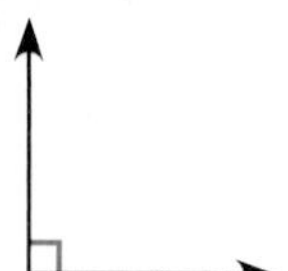

13. 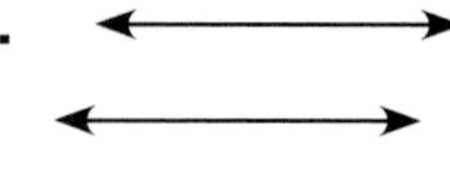

(Lesson 8) Write the name of each quadrilateral.

14. 

15. 

16. 

(Lesson 9) Solve.

17. How many lines of symmetry does an equilateral triangle have?

(Lesson 10) Solve. Use any strategy.

18. Mark was in front of Shilo but behind Nika. Dana was in front of Vi but behind Shilo. Find the order of the students.

(Lessons 11–12) A rectangle has length 8 cm and width 6 cm.

19. Find its perimeter. **20.** Find its area.

REVIEW/TEST

CHAPTER 8

Performance Assessment

A. Geometry

This painting by the Cuban painter Carmen Herrera uses geometric figures. It does not use a flip or turn, but it does use a slide. It does not have a line of symmetry.

Use two or more geometric shapes to make your own design. It should show a flip, slide, or turn. It should have one or more lines of symmetry.

1. **Decision Making** Decide which figures you will use.
2. **Critical Thinking** Where can you place the figures in your design? They must show a flip, slide, or turn and a line of symmetry.
3. Make your design.
4. **Explain Your Thinking** Why did you choose the figures you used? How did you decide where to place them?

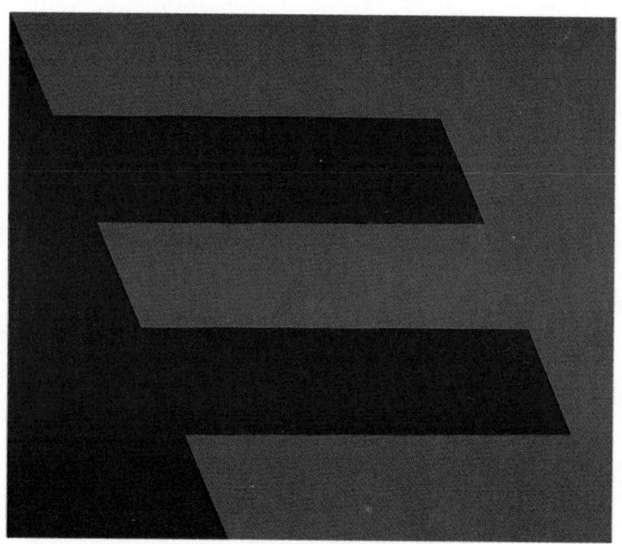

Carmen Herrera *Green and Orange*.
Photo by Tony Velez.

B. Perimeter, Area, and Volume

Trish's new computer was packed in this carton.

5. **Recording Data** Record the length, width, and height of the carton.
6. **Decision Making** Decide what each face looks like. Make a sketch of each face showing its dimensions.
7. **Using Data**
   a. Find the perimeter of each face.
   b. Find the area of each face.
   c. Find the volume of the carton.

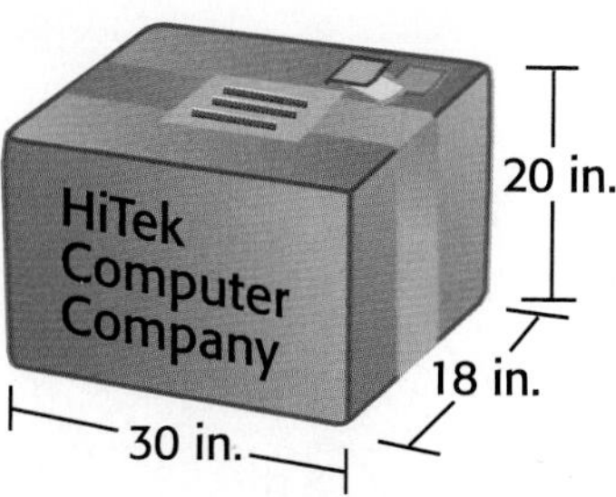

REVIEW/TEST

Math Magazine

Take a Walk Around the Pool **A rectangular swimming pool measures 90 ft by 50 ft. A sidewalk around the outside "frames" the pool. The sidewalk makes a rectangle measuring 100 ft by 60 ft.**

You can find the area of the sidewalk.

1. Area of large rectangle $= 100 \times 60$
   $= 6{,}000$ sq ft
2. Area of small rectangle $= 90 \times 50$
   $= 4{,}500$ sq ft
3. Area of sidewalk = Area of large rectangle − Area of small rectangle

$$\begin{array}{r} 6{,}000 \\ -\ 4{,}500 \\ \hline 1{,}500 \end{array}$$

The area of the sidewalk is 1,500 sq ft.

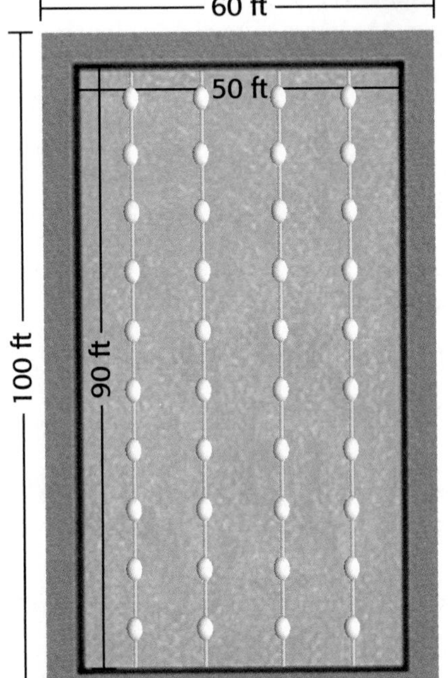

Try These!

Find each shaded area.

1. 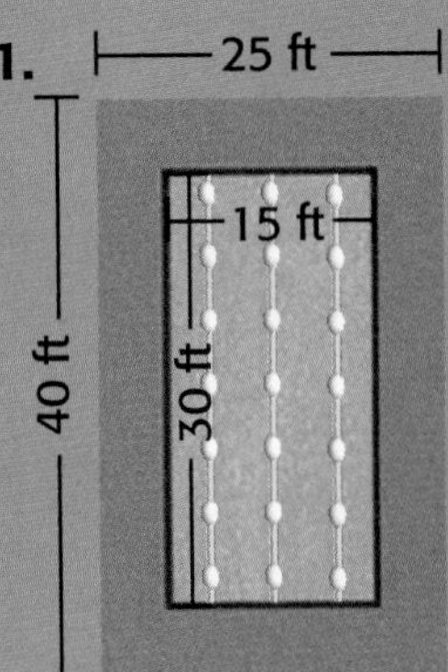

2. 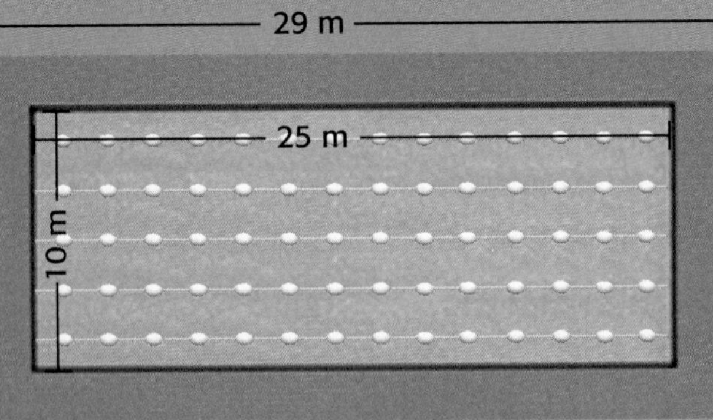

3. What other way could you find the area of the sidewalk around the pool?

Cumulative Review

Test Prep Strategy: Eliminate Choices!

Check the ones digit first.

What is $41.12 + $99.19?

Ⓐ $140.32 Ⓑ $140.24 Ⓒ $140.31 Ⓓ $140.29

STAY SHARP! Add the ones digit first. 9 + 2 = 11. The ones digit is 1. Eliminate Ⓐ $140.32, Ⓑ $140.24, and Ⓓ $140.29. The answer is Ⓒ!

Test Prep Strategies

- Read Carefully
- Follow Directions
- Make Smart Choices
- Eliminate Choices
- Work Backward from an Answer

Write the letter of the correct answer. You may eliminate choices or use any strategy to help.

1. On Saturday 531 people visited a museum and on Sunday 439 visited it. About how many people visited in all?

   Ⓐ 900 Ⓑ 800 Ⓒ 1,100 Ⓓ 1,200

2. You can find the point (2, 4) by starting at 0, then moving:

   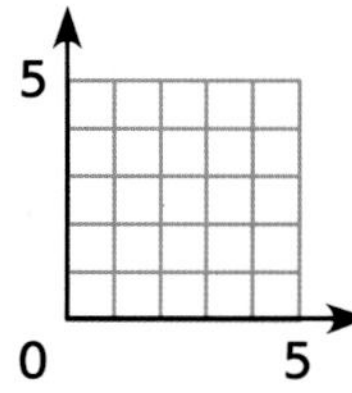

   Ⓐ right 4, up 2 Ⓑ right 2, up 4
   Ⓒ left 2, up 4 Ⓓ right 2, down 4

3. What is 412 – 368?

   Ⓐ 38 Ⓑ 40 Ⓒ 52 Ⓓ not here

4. In what place is the digit 3 in this number? 531,482

   Ⓐ tens Ⓑ hundreds
   Ⓒ thousands Ⓓ ten-thousands

5. A pack of batteries costs $4.29. How much would 3 packs cost?

   Ⓐ $12.88 Ⓑ $12.78 Ⓒ $12.67 Ⓓ $12.87

6. What is the area of the rectangle?

   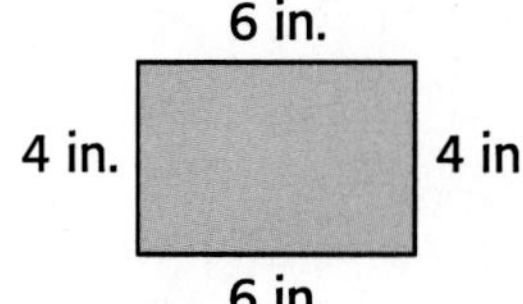

   Ⓐ 10 square in. Ⓑ 12 square in.
   Ⓒ 20 square in. Ⓓ 24 square in.

7. Name the triangle.

   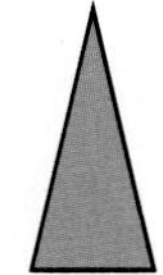

   Ⓐ isosceles Ⓑ equilateral
   Ⓒ right Ⓓ scalene

8. What is the quotient of 312 ÷ 4?

   Ⓐ 72 Ⓑ 78 Ⓒ 83 Ⓓ 88

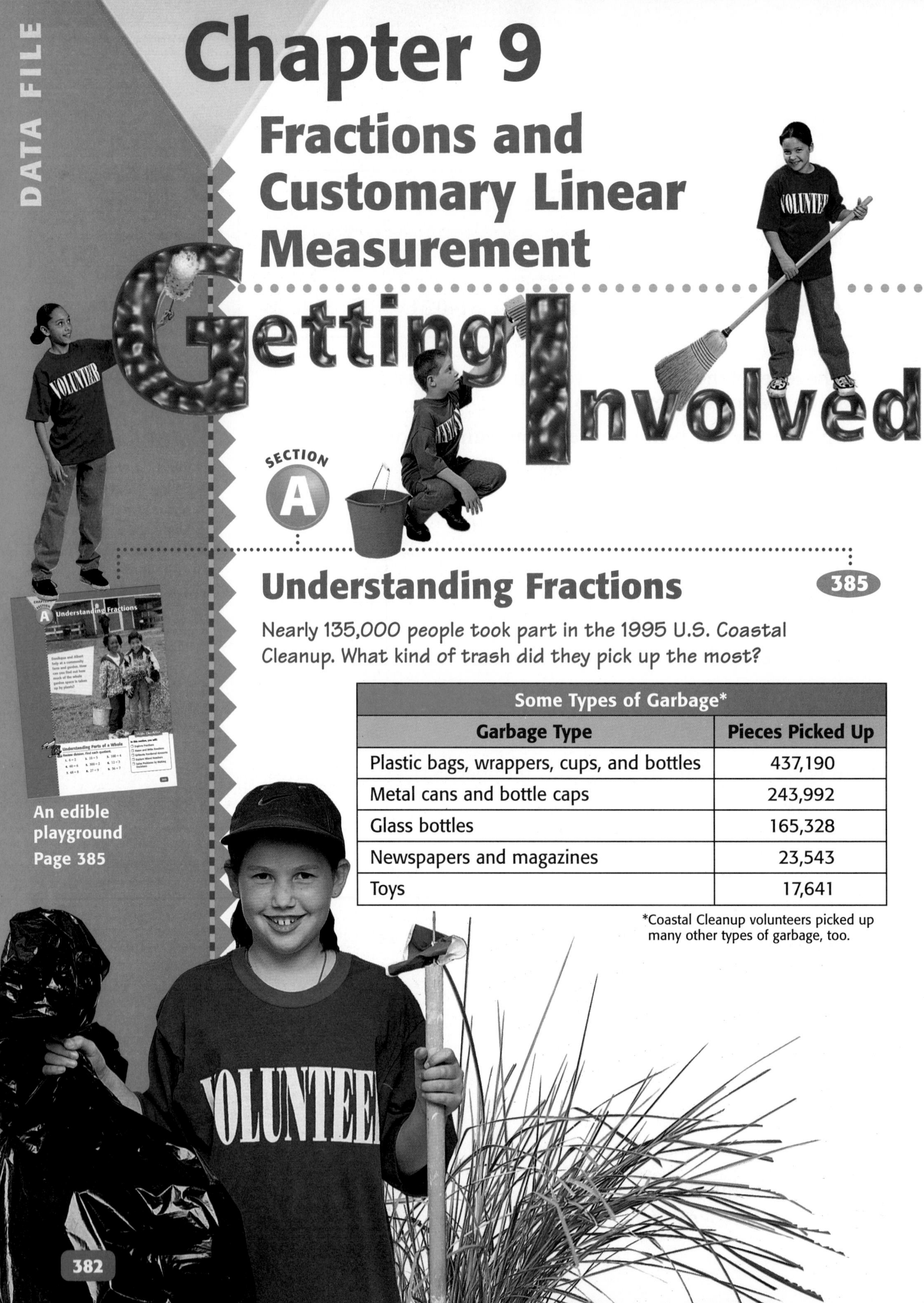

Chapter 9

Fractions and Customary Linear Measurement

SECTION A

Understanding Fractions

385

Nearly 135,000 people took part in the 1995 U.S. Coastal Cleanup. What kind of trash did they pick up the most?

Some Types of Garbage*	
Garbage Type	**Pieces Picked Up**
Plastic bags, wrappers, cups, and bottles	437,190
Metal cans and bottle caps	243,992
Glass bottles	165,328
Newspapers and magazines	23,543
Toys	17,641

*Coastal Cleanup volunteers picked up many other types of garbage, too.

An edible playground
Page 385

Extending Fraction Concepts

397

Animal lovers can get involved by helping care for animals that need homes. About how many pets get adopted each week in the United States?

Daily Statistics for U.S. Pets	
Dogs and cats born	132,000
Pets taken to animal shelters	41,000
Pets adopted	10,000

Pet care
Page 397

Using Customary Linear Measurement

413

Based on this survey, are people more likely to get involved if they are asked or not asked? How can you tell?

What It Takes to Get People Involved

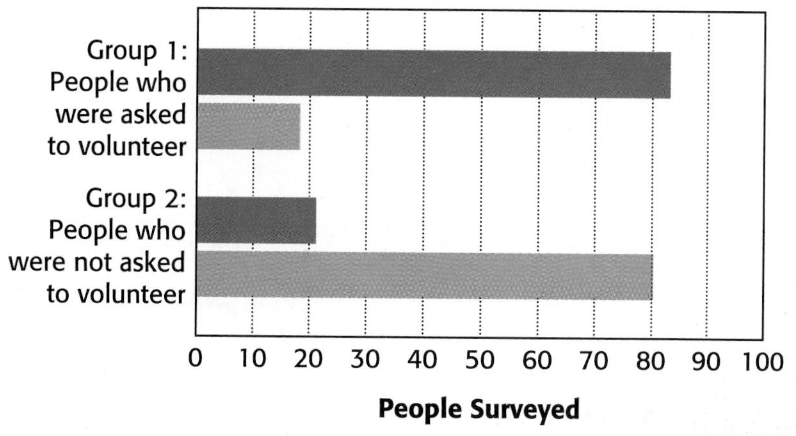

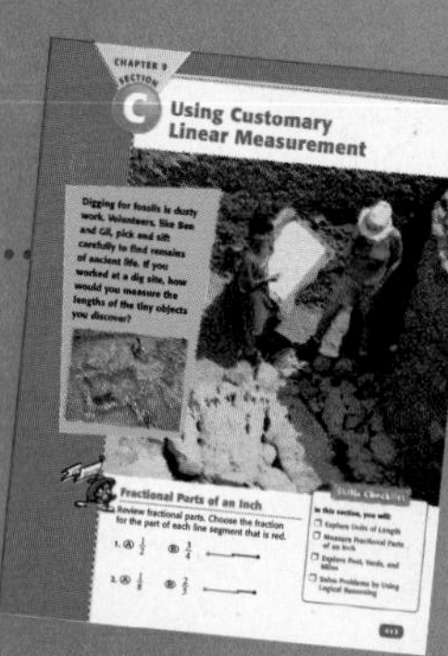

Can you dig it?
Page 413

Surfing the World Wide Web!

How involved are you in your community? What are other students around the country doing to get involved? Head over to **www.mathsurf.com/4/ch9** to find out.

Materials
paper or posterboard, markers or crayons

If you want people to volunteer, let them know how much you need their help.Your team has been asked to advertise a volunteer activity. How will you do it?

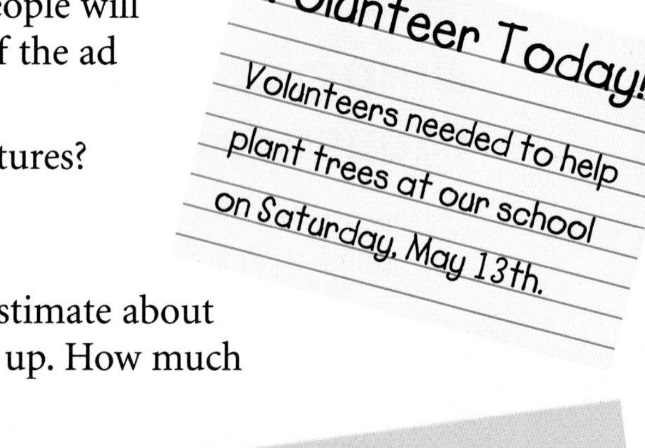

Make a Plan

- Design an ad that asks for volunteers. It can be a poster, flyer, newspaper page, or button.
- How can you attract people's attention? If your ad has too many words, people will not read it. About what fraction of the ad will you use for words?
- What fraction will you use for pictures?

Carry It Out

Design your ad. Use fractions to estimate about how much space the pictures take up. How much do the words take up?

Talk About It

- Do you think your ad will attract attention? Explain.
- If you change the amount of space taken up by pictures or words, will the ad attract more attention? Explain.

Present the Project

- Post your ad in your classroom or your community. Compare your design with those made by other teams.

CHAPTER 9

SECTION A

Understanding Fractions

Danikqua and Albert help at a community farm and garden. How can you find out how much of the whole garden space is taken up by plants?

GET READY!

Understanding Parts of a Whole

Review division. Find each quotient.

1. $6 \div 2$ **2.** $10 \div 5$ **3.** $100 \div 4$

4. $60 \div 6$ **5.** $300 \div 2$ **6.** $12 \div 3$

7. $48 \div 8$ **8.** $27 \div 9$ **9.** $56 \div 7$

Skills Checklist

In this section, you will:

- ❐ Explore Fractions
- ❐ Name and Write Fractions
- ❐ Estimate Fractional Amounts
- ❐ Explore Mixed Numbers
- ❐ Solve Problems by Making Decisions

Chapter 9
Lesson
1

Exploring Fractions

Problem Solving Connection
- Use Objects/ Act It Out
- Draw a Picture

Materials
- geoboard
- rubber bands
- dot paper

Vocabulary
fraction
a comparison of parts to a whole or to a set

Explore

You can divide a geoboard into equal parts in many different ways.

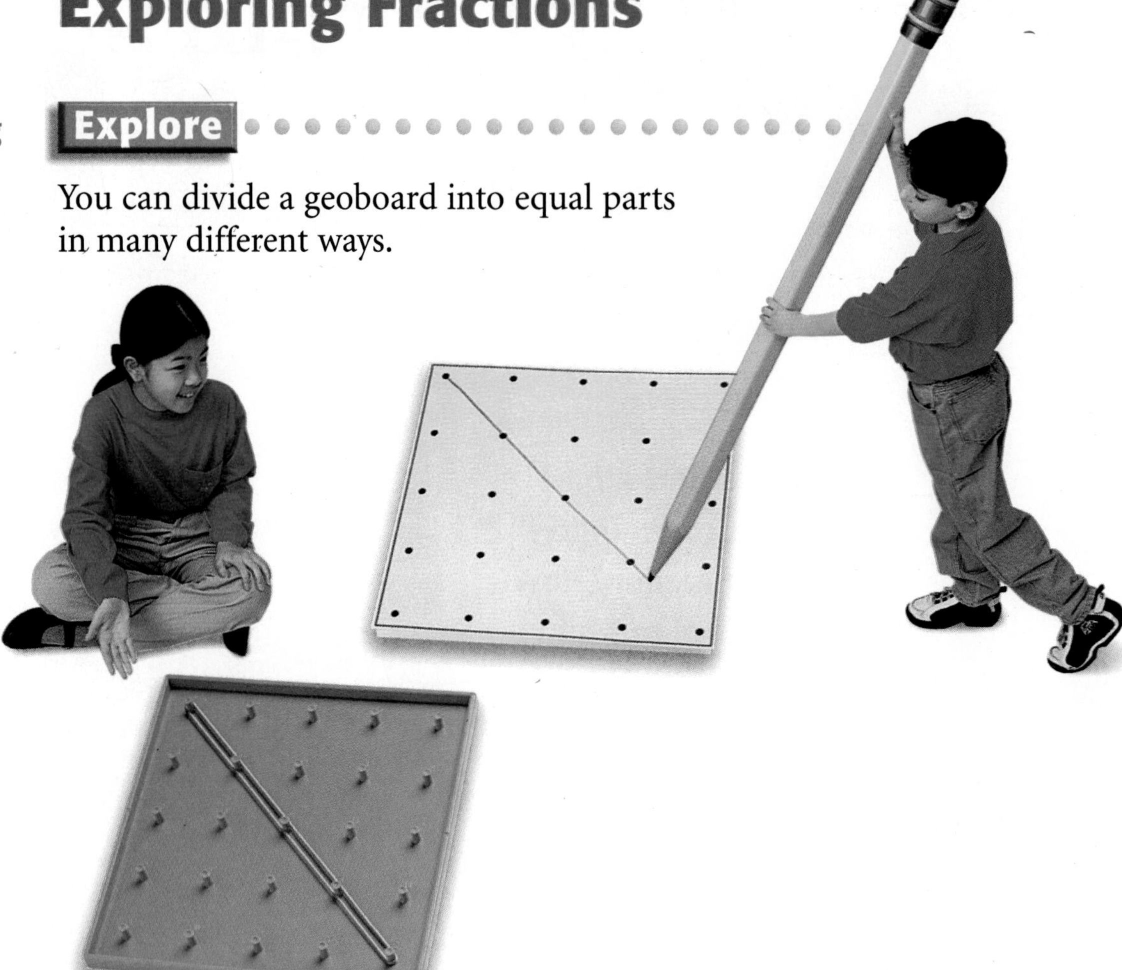

Math Tip
Try dividing the square by making triangles.

Work Together

Use a geoboard and rubber bands.

1. Find 2 ways to divide a geoboard into 2 equal parts.
2. Find some more ways to show 2 equal parts of a square. Record the different ways on dot paper.
3. Find 2 ways to divide a geoboard into 4 equal parts.
4. Find some more ways to show 4 equal parts of a square. Record the different ways on dot paper.
5. Find at least 2 ways to show 8 equal parts of a square. Record the different ways on dot paper.

Talk About It

6. How can you tell if the parts are the same size?
7. Can equal parts be the same size but not the same shape?

Connect

A **fraction** is a way to name equal parts of a whole.

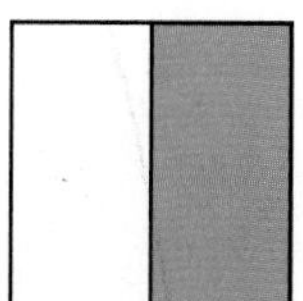

1 of **2** equal parts

$\frac{1}{2}$ or one-half

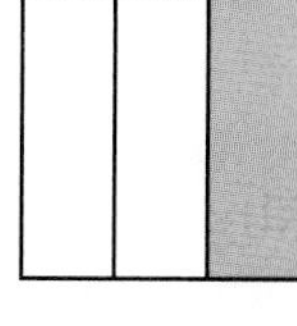

1 of **3** equal parts

$\frac{1}{3}$ or one-third

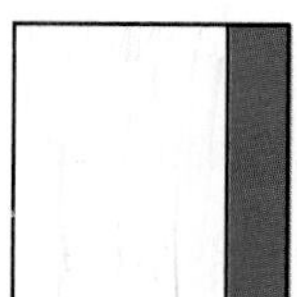

This does not show $\frac{1}{2}$.

The parts are not equal.

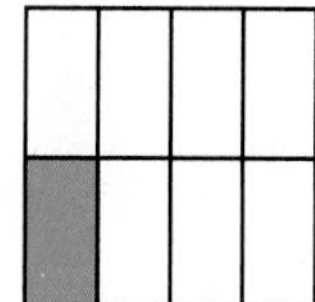

1 of **8** equal parts

$\frac{1}{8}$ or one-eighth

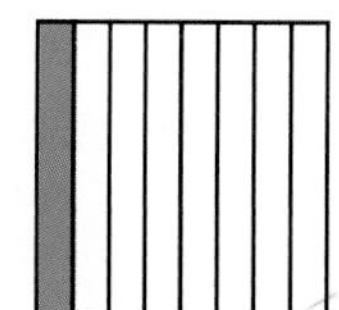

1 of **8** equal parts

$\frac{1}{8}$ or one-eighth

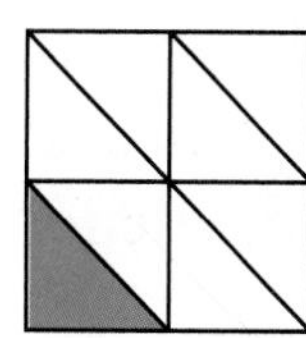

1 of **8** equal parts

$\frac{1}{8}$ or one-eighth

Math Tip
Equal parts can have different shapes.

Practice

Write a fraction for each shaded part.

1. 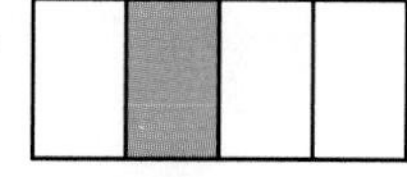

2. 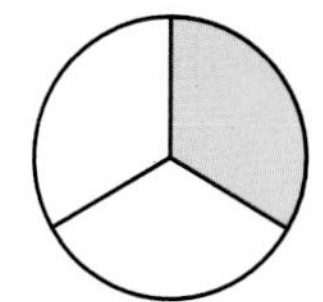

3. 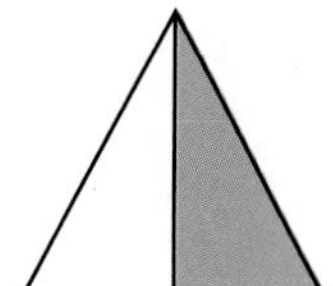

4. 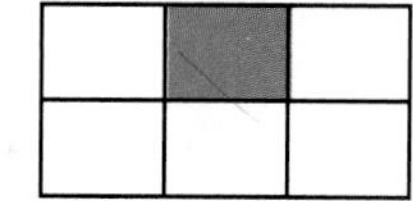

5. Critical Thinking These two dot paper squares are the same size. Is part *A* of the first square the same size as part *B* of the second square? Explain.

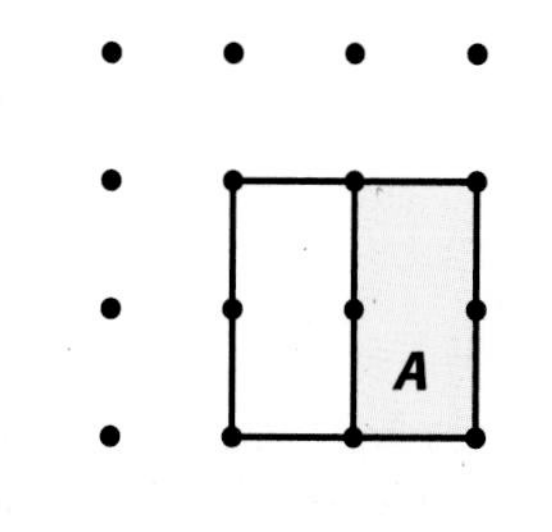

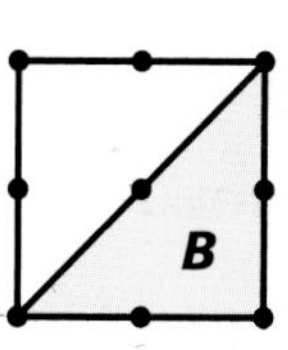

6. Geometry Readiness How many different ways can you divide a parallelogram into equal halves? Draw pictures and use shading to show the different ways.

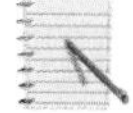

7. Journal Describe how you would divide a square into sixths. Use grid paper or dot paper and shading to help.

Chapter 9
Lesson
2

Naming and Writing Fractions

You Will Learn
how to name and write fractions of a set or region

Vocabulary

numerator
the number above the line in a fraction; the number of equal parts in a fractional amount

denominator
the number below the line in a fraction; the number of equal parts in the whole

Learn

Crisgeromie and Danikqua dig in to plant a community garden. Their hard work pays off in fresh vegetables for the school.

They use fractions to show how much of the garden to use for different kinds of plants. A fraction has a **numerator** and a **denominator**.

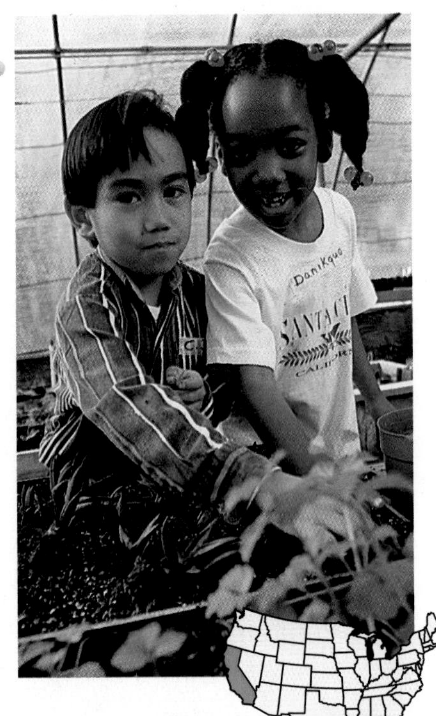

Crisgeromie and Danikqua help out at the Loma Vista Farm and Garden in Vallejo, California.

You can use fractions to name equal parts of a region.

Example 1

Students planted carrots in part of the garden plot. What fraction shows this part?

Numerator → 1 ← Part planted with carrots
Denominator → 3 ← Equal parts in all

$$\frac{1}{3}$$

They planted $\frac{1}{3}$, or one-third, of the plot with carrots.

You can use fractions to name part of a set or group.

Did You Know?
Since the 1500s, three-fourths of the food plant varieties in North and South America are now extinct because farmers do not grow them.

Example 2

What fraction of the onions are purple?

Numerator → 5 ← Purple onions
Denominator → 7 ← Onions in all

$$\frac{5}{7}$$

Five-sevenths, or $\frac{5}{7}$, of the onions are purple.

Talk About It

1. In Example 1, how many thirds make up the whole garden?
2. What fraction of the garden does not have carrots?

Check

Write a fraction for each.

1. What fraction is planted with corn?
2. What fraction of the peppers are green?

3. **Reasoning** How many sixths make up the whole set of peppers in the picture above?

Practice

Skills and Reasoning

Write a fraction that shows what part of each field is planted.

4. 
5. 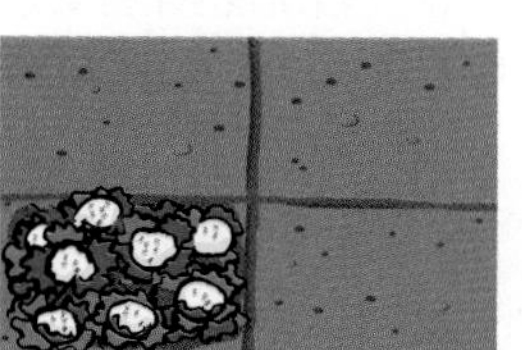
6. 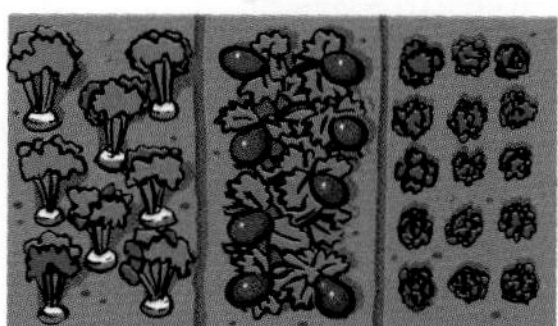

Write a fraction that compares the different tools to the whole set.

7. Rake
8. Shovels
9. Tools with one handle
10. What number shows how many tools are in the whole set? In **7–9**, did you use this number as a numerator or a denominator?

Problem Solving and Applications

11. **Time** Together, Saturday and Sunday form what fraction of the days in a week?
12. Suppose you plant 12 bean seeds and 5 do not grow into seedlings. What fraction of the bean seeds grow?

Mixed Review and Test Prep

Find each product.

13. 14×24
14. 31×47
15. 526×3
16. 229×8
17. 194×4

18. **Money** Which group of coins is the most money?

Ⓐ 3 quarters Ⓑ 6 dimes Ⓒ 8 nickels Ⓓ 7 dimes

Skills Practice Bank, page 571, Set 1

Estimating Fractional Amounts

You Will Learn
to estimate fractional amounts

Vocabulary
benchmark
a known measurement used to estimate other measurements

Learn

Grab your hat and sneakers. It's time for the annual Coastal Cleanup.

Coastal Cleanup volunteers pick up garbage on beaches all over the world.

Students pick up trash along the Gulf Coast of Texas.

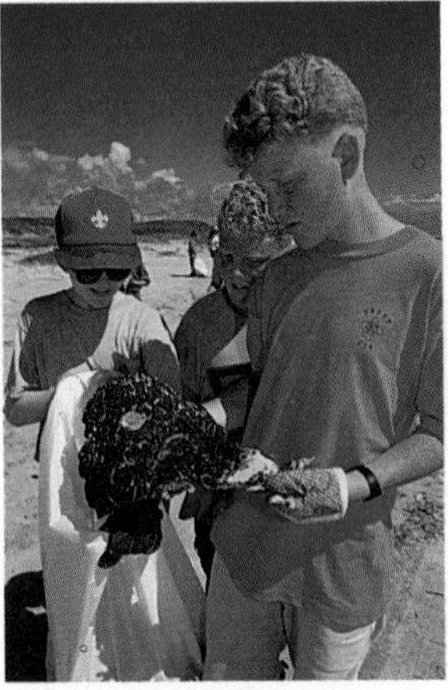

Adopt-a-Beach program, Corpus Christi, Texas

Use **benchmarks** like $\frac{1}{4}$, $\frac{1}{3}$, $\frac{1}{2}$, $\frac{2}{3}$, and $\frac{3}{4}$ to estimate fractional amounts.

About how full is each trash can?

About $\frac{1}{2}$ full

About $\frac{1}{4}$ full

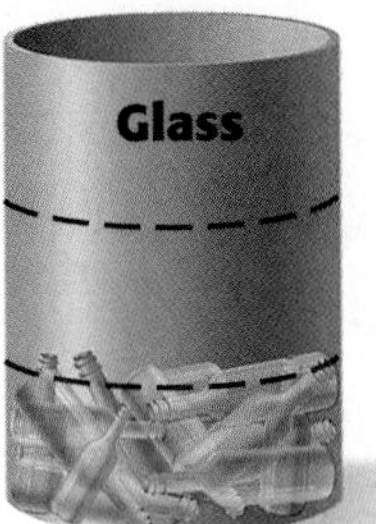

About $\frac{1}{3}$ full

Talk About It

How did you use benchmarks to estimate the fractional amounts?

Math Tip
Estimating $\frac{1}{2}$ of something can help you estimate other fractional amounts.

Check

Write a fraction that shows about how full each container is.

1.

Ⓐ $\frac{1}{2}$

Ⓑ $\frac{2}{3}$

2.

Ⓐ $\frac{1}{2}$

Ⓑ $\frac{1}{4}$

3. Reasoning A carton is $\frac{3}{4}$ full. Is it closer to being empty or full? Explain.

Practice

Skills and Reasoning

Choose a fraction that shows about how full each container is.

4. 

Ⓐ $\frac{1}{2}$

Ⓑ $\frac{1}{3}$

5. 

Ⓐ $\frac{3}{4}$

Ⓑ $\frac{1}{3}$

Draw a picture for each fractional amount.

6. $\frac{3}{4}$ of a pie **7.** A glass $\frac{1}{4}$ full **8.** $\frac{1}{3}$ of a pizza **9.** A milk carton $\frac{2}{3}$ full

10. A glass is almost completely full. Which benchmark fraction. $\frac{3}{4}$ or $\frac{1}{4}$, better describes how full the glass is? Why?

Problem Solving and Applications

11. Using Data Use the Data File on page 382. How many more metal cans and bottle caps than glass bottles did Coastal Cleanup volunteers pick up?

Science Use the Lifetime of Litter sign for **12–14.**

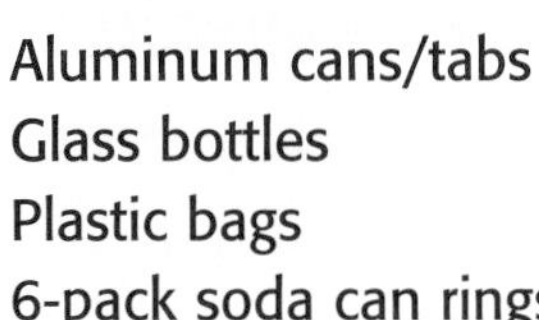

Lifetime of Litter

Aluminum cans/tabs	500 yr
Glass bottles	1,000 yr
Plastic bags	Up to 20 yr
6-pack soda can rings	100 yr

12. A sign at Enchanted Rock Natural Area near Fredericksburg, TX warns visitors how long litter lasts. How many times as long do glass bottles last than plastic 6-pack rings?

13. What fraction of time do aluminum cans last compared to glass bottles?

14. Wool socks take as long as 5 years to decay. What litter takes about 4 times as long?

Mixed Review and Test Prep

Divide.

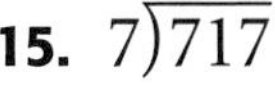

15. 7)717	**16.** 5)989	**17.** 3)340	**18.** 2)610
19. 4)412	**20.** 2)225	**21.** 3)697	**22.** 2)506

23. Time How does a digital clock show the same time that is on this clock?

Ⓐ 6:48 Ⓑ 6:09 Ⓒ 9:63 Ⓓ 9:33

Chapter 9
Lesson
4

Exploring Mixed Numbers

Problem Solving Connection
- Use Objects/ Act It Out
- Draw a Picture

Materials
fraction strips

Vocabulary
mixed number
a number that has a whole number and a fractional part

improper fraction
a fraction in which the numerator is greater than or equal to the denominator

Math Tip
If two sets of fraction strips are the same length, they show the same amount.

Explore

A bowl of Brand D cereal has $2\frac{1}{2}$ teaspoons of sugar. The number $2\frac{1}{2}$ is a **mixed number**. If you use a $\frac{1}{2}$ teaspoon to show this amount of sugar, you will fill the spoon five times.

The **improper fraction** $\frac{5}{2}$ also shows this amount.

You can use fraction strips and number lines to explore mixed numbers and improper fractions.

Work Together

1. Use fraction strips to show $1\frac{3}{4}$.
   a. How many $\frac{1}{4}$ strips are in 1?
   b. How many $\frac{1}{4}$ strips are in $\frac{3}{4}$?
   c. How many $\frac{1}{4}$ strips are in $1\frac{3}{4}$?
   d. What improper fraction shows how many $\frac{1}{4}$ strips are in $1\frac{3}{4}$?
2. Use fraction strips to show $1\frac{1}{8}$ on a number line.
   a. How many $\frac{1}{8}$ strips are in $1\frac{1}{8}$?
   b. Draw a number line below the fraction strips. Label the number line.

Talk About It

1. How many $\frac{1}{8}$ fraction strips are in $2\frac{1}{8}$.
2. On a number line does $\frac{8}{3}$ come before $2\frac{1}{3}$? Explain.

Connect

To write a mixed number as an improper fraction, break the whole number into fractional parts and add the parts.

For $1\frac{2}{3}$:

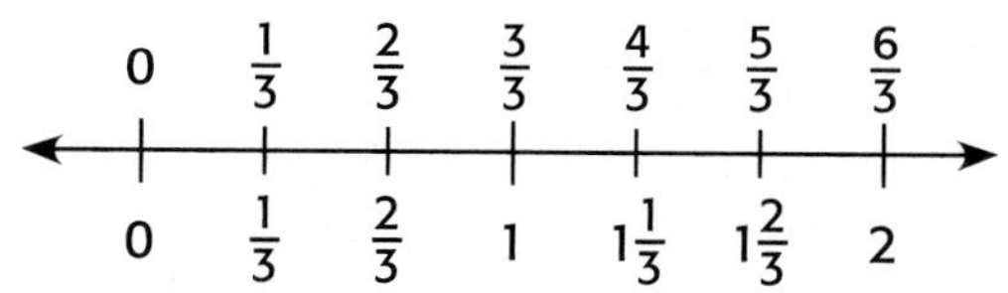

You can show mixed numbers or improper fractions on a number line.

0 $\frac{1}{3}$ $\frac{2}{3}$ $\frac{3}{3}$ $\frac{4}{3}$ $\frac{5}{3}$ $\frac{6}{3}$

0 $\frac{1}{3}$ $\frac{2}{3}$ 1 $1\frac{1}{3}$ $1\frac{2}{3}$ 2

Practice

Write each improper fraction as a whole or mixed number. Use fraction strips or a number line to help.

1. $\frac{3}{2}$ **2.** $\frac{7}{4}$ **3.** $\frac{9}{8}$ **4.** $\frac{6}{3}$ **5.** $\frac{10}{7}$ **6.** $\frac{11}{5}$

Write each mixed number as an improper fraction.

7. $2\frac{1}{4}$ **8.** $1\frac{1}{3}$ **9.** $3\frac{2}{5}$ **10.** $1\frac{1}{2}$ **11.** $2\frac{5}{6}$ **12.** $4\frac{2}{7}$

13. Patterns Copy and complete the pattern. Use the number line to help.

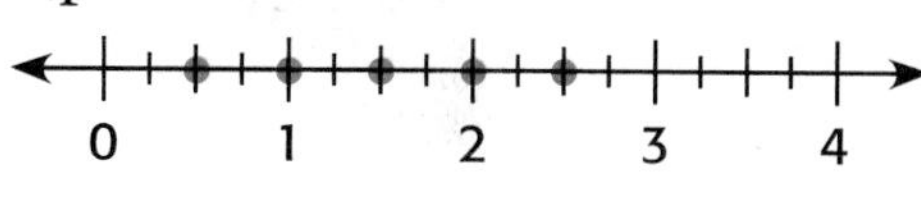

$\frac{1}{2}$, 1, $\frac{3}{2}$, 2, $\frac{5}{2}$, ■, ■, ■

14. Science The Center for Science in the Public Interest tested cereal. Brand X had $\frac{13}{4}$ tsp of sugar. Brand Z had 3 tsp of sugar. Which cereal had more sugar per serving?

15. What If You have only a $\frac{1}{4}$-cup measuring cup. How many times do you have to fill it to measure $5\frac{1}{4}$ cups of flour?

16. Critical Thinking Write the number 5 as an improper fraction with a denominator of 2.

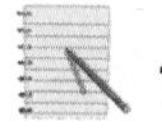

17. Journal Describe how you would change $\frac{18}{5}$ to a mixed number. Explain which number is easier to picture in your mind.

Skills Practice Bank, page 571, Set 2

Chapter 9 Lesson 5

Problem Solving

Decision Making: Can You Volunteer Some Time?

You Will Learn
how to answer a question by using facts

Explore

More than 25 million people in the United States volunteer 5 or more hours a week. Do you think students your age could give up that much of their free time?

Work together to plan a week's schedule of your activities. Use it to keep track of how much free time you have and what you choose to do with your time. Decide how you could fit volunteer activities into your weekly schedule.

Teens paint houses in San Antonio, Texas.

Volunteers serve Thanksgiving dinner in San Antonio, Texas.

Youth volunteer with the Special Friends Program reads with a friend.

Facts and Data

There are 168 hours in a week.

You spend about 114 hours sleeping, eating, and going to school.

You can count the remaining 54 hours per week as free time. Keep in mind activities such as chores and homework when planning your schedule.

Youths clean a petroglyph in Coconino National Forest, Arizona.

Work Together

▶ Understand

1. What do you know?
2. What do you need to find out?
3. What is the main decision you have to make?

▶ Plan and Solve

4. Make a schedule like the one below. End your schedule at 9:00 P.M.
5. List the activities you do each week. Be sure to count time you already spend doing volunteer work!
6. Write the activities in the schedule. Color the blocks, using a different color for each activity.
7. Find the fractional part of your free time each week that you spend doing each activity. For example, if you spend 1 hour every day reading, that would be $\frac{7}{54}$ of your free time.

▶ Make a Decision

8. What fractional part of your free time each week would be 5 hours? Could you spend that much time volunteering? Explain.
9. Which activities could you cut back on if you wanted to make time for volunteer work?

▶ Present Your Decision

10. Compare your schedule with those of other class members. Do most students have 5 free hours to volunteer each week? Explain.

My Activities

Time	Mon.	Tues.	Wed.	Thurs.	Fri.	Sat.	Sun.
9:00–10:00 A.M.							
10:00–11:00 A.M.						read to sister	
11:00–12:00 P.M.							
12:00–1:00 P.M.			Time at School				
1:00–2:00 P.M.							
2:00–3:00 P.M.							
3:00–4:00 P.M.							
4:00–5:00 P.M.		walk dog					
5:00–6:00 P.M.							
6:00–7:00 P.M.							
7:00–8:00 P.M.							
8:00–9:00 P.M.							

Skills Practice Bank, page 571, Set 6

SECTION A

Review and Practice

Vocabulary Match each word with its meaning.

1. fraction
2. mixed number
3. improper fraction
4. numerator
5. denominator

a. a whole number and a fractional part
b. a comparison of parts to a whole
c. the number above the line in a fraction
d. the number below the line in a fraction
e. a fraction in which the numerator is greater than or equal to the denominator

(Lesson 1) Write a fraction for each shaded part.

6. 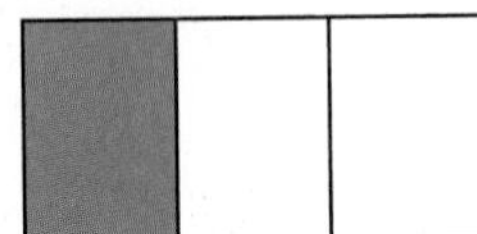

7. 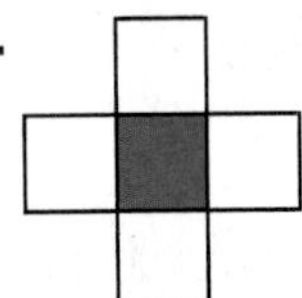

8. 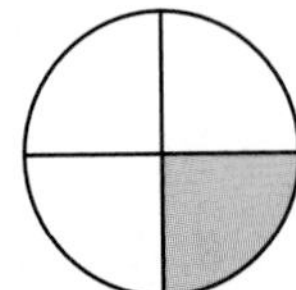

(Lesson 2) Write a fraction for each.

9. What fraction of the pots contain flowers?

10. What fraction of the umbrella is striped?

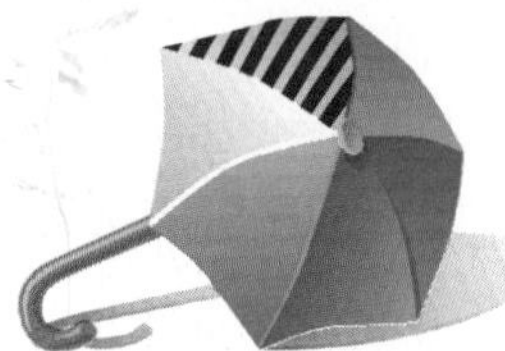

11. What fraction of the books are red?

(Lesson 3) Choose the fraction that shows about how full each container is.

12. 

Ⓐ $\frac{1}{4}$

Ⓑ $\frac{2}{3}$

13. 

Ⓐ $\frac{1}{2}$

Ⓑ $\frac{3}{4}$

(Lesson 4) Write each improper fraction as a whole or mixed number.

14. $\frac{7}{5}$ **15.** $\frac{8}{3}$ **16.** $\frac{5}{2}$ **17.** $\frac{12}{4}$

Write each mixed number as an improper fraction.

18. $3\frac{3}{4}$ **19.** $1\frac{1}{6}$ **20.** $2\frac{5}{8}$ **21.** $1\frac{7}{8}$

22. Journal Describe how to write a mixed number as an improper fraction.

Skills Checklist

In this section, you have:

- ☑ Explored Fractions
- ☑ Named and Written Fractions
- ☑ Estimated Fractional Amounts
- ☑ Explored Mixed Numbers
- ☑ Solved Problems by Making Decisions

CHAPTER 9

SECTION

B Extending Fraction Concepts

Kendall volunteers 8 hours a week, including 6 hours at an animal shelter and 2 hours for a radio talk show. What fractions tell how many of her volunteer hours go to each activity?

Equivalent Fractions

Review factors. Write all factors of each.

1. 12 **2.** 9 **3.** 16 **4.** 18 **5.** 24

Copy and complete each pattern.

6. 2, 4, 6, 8, ■, ■

7. 3, 6, 9, ■, ■

8. 5, 10, ■, 20, ■, 30

9. ■, 4, ■, 16, 32

Skills Checklist

In this section, you will:

- ❒ Explore Equivalent Fractions
- ❒ Name and Write Equivalent Fractions
- ❒ Learn About Simplest Form Fractions
- ❒ Compare and Order Fractions
- ❒ Explore a Fraction of a Set

Chapter 9
Lesson
6

Exploring Equivalent Fractions

Problem Solving Connection

- Use Objects/ Act It Out
- Look for a Pattern

Materials

fraction strips

Vocabulary

equivalent fractions
fractions that name the same region, part of a set, or part of a segment

Explore

Can two fractions name the same amount? Use fraction strips to find out.

Work Together

1. Find different ways to show the fraction $\frac{1}{2}$. Start with a $\frac{1}{2}$ strip.
   a. Line up $\frac{1}{4}$ strips beneath the $\frac{1}{2}$ strip.
   How many $\frac{1}{4}$ strips put together match the $\frac{1}{2}$ strip?
   Write the fraction that names the same amount as $\frac{1}{2}$.
   b. Line up $\frac{1}{8}$ strips beneath the $\frac{1}{2}$ strip.
   How many $\frac{1}{8}$ strips match the $\frac{1}{2}$ strip?
   Write the fraction that names the same amount as $\frac{1}{2}$.
   c. Line up $\frac{1}{12}$ strips beneath the $\frac{1}{2}$ strip.
   How many $\frac{1}{12}$ strips match the $\frac{1}{2}$ strip?
   Write the fraction that names the same amount as $\frac{1}{2}$.
2. Find different ways to show the fraction $\frac{2}{3}$.
   Start with two $\frac{1}{3}$ strips, placed end to end.
   Line up other fraction strips beneath the $\frac{2}{3}$ strip.
   a. What strips can you use to match the $\frac{2}{3}$ strip?
   b. What fractions name the same amount as $\frac{2}{3}$?

Math Tip

Drawing pictures for two fractions can help you see if they are equivalent.

Talk About It

3. Look at the fractions that name the same amount as $\frac{1}{2}$. What patterns do you see with the denominators and numerators?
4. What strips will have the same length as $\frac{1}{3}$?

Connect

Fractions that name the same amount are called **equivalent fractions**.

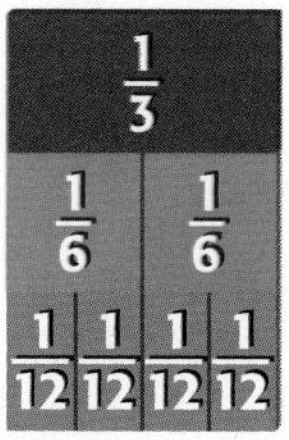

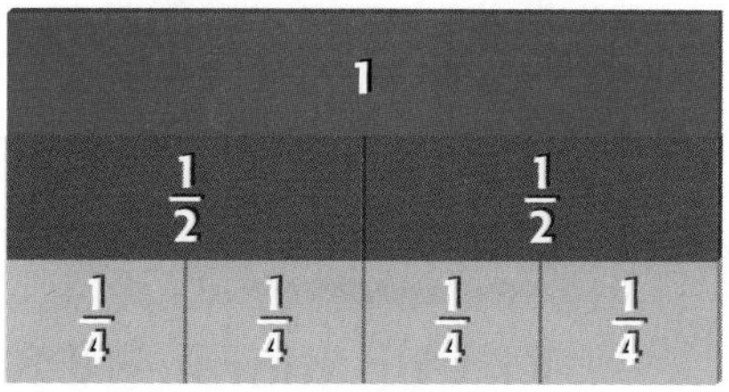

$\frac{2}{6}$ and $\frac{4}{12}$ are equivalent fractions.
They are also equivalent to $\frac{1}{3}$.

$\frac{2}{2}$ and $\frac{4}{4}$ are equivalent fractions.
They are also equivalent to 1.

Practice

Write if each pair of fractions is equivalent or not. Use fraction strips to help.

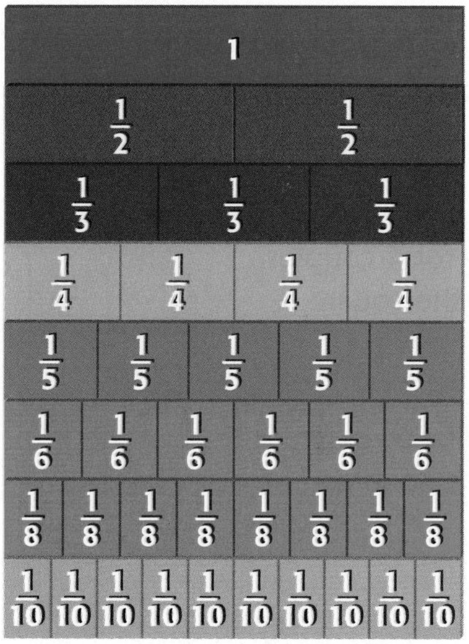

1. $\frac{2}{5}$ and $\frac{4}{10}$

2. $\frac{5}{8}$ and $\frac{2}{3}$

3. $\frac{4}{8}$ and $\frac{3}{6}$

4. $\frac{5}{6}$ and $\frac{7}{8}$

5. $\frac{1}{2}$ and $\frac{5}{10}$

6. $\frac{2}{3}$ and $\frac{5}{6}$

Find an equivalent fraction for each. You may use fraction strips to help.

7. $\frac{3}{4}$ **8.** $\frac{3}{5}$ **9.** $\frac{1}{6}$ **10.** $\frac{2}{3}$ **11.** $\frac{6}{8}$ **12.** $\frac{1}{2}$

13. Logic Emmett cut a pan of baked brownies into 12 equal pieces. How many pieces were in one-third of the pan?

14. Copy and complete the number line. Write two equivalent fractions for each missing point.

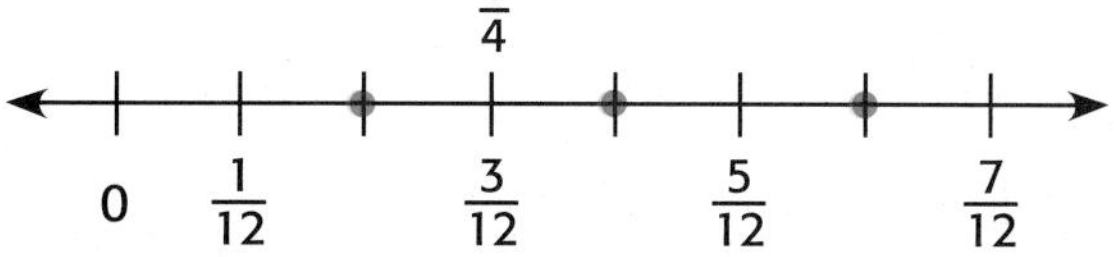

15. Journal Draw a picture to show two equivalent fractions for $\frac{1}{5}$. Describe how the numerators and denominators are related.

Chapter 9
Lesson
7

Naming and Writing Equivalent Fractions

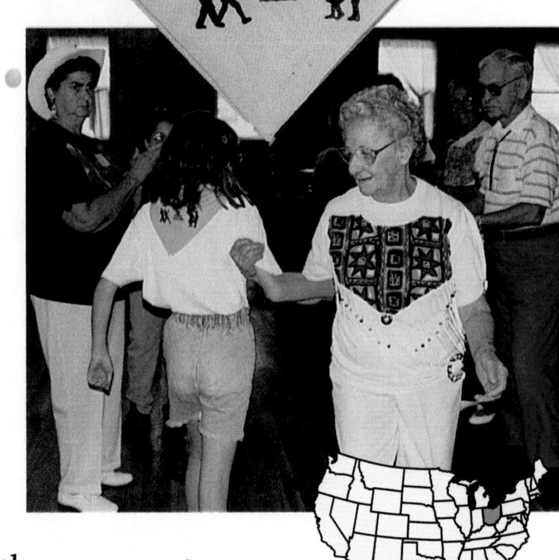

You Will Learn
how to name and write equivalent fractions

Remember
Equivalent fractions name the same amount of a set or region.

Learn

Kick up your heels! Barn dances are popular events for Sidekicks, a program that brings young people and seniors together. The dancers can be represented by fractions.

Sidekicks is a volunteer program that began in Batavia, Ohio.

To find equivalent fractions, multiply the numerator and denominator by the same number.

Example 1

Many square dances are for 4 couples. A couple makes up $\frac{1}{4}$ of the square. What fraction of the square do 2 dancers form?

There are 8 dancers in all. So, 2 dancers make up $\frac{2}{8}$ of the square.

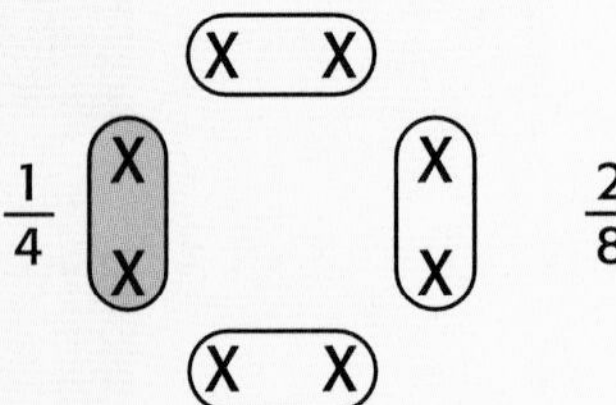

$$\frac{1}{4} \xrightarrow{\times 2} = \frac{2}{8}$$

$\frac{1}{4}$ and $\frac{2}{8}$ are equivalent fractions.

You can also find equivalent fractions by dividing the numerator and denominator by the same number.

Example 2

If 6 dancers make up $\frac{6}{8}$ of the square, how many couples is that? What fraction of the square is that?

So, 3 couples make up $\frac{3}{4}$ of the square.

$$\frac{6}{8} \xrightarrow{\div 2} = \frac{3}{4}$$

$\frac{6}{8}$ and $\frac{3}{4}$ are equivalent fractions.

Talk About It

1. Four dancers represent what fraction of the square?
2. Two couples represent what fraction of the square?

Check

Multiply or divide to find equivalent fractions.

1. $\frac{2}{3} = \frac{■}{■}$ (×3 numerator and denominator)
2. $\frac{12}{15} = \frac{■}{■}$ (÷3 numerator and denominator)
3. $\frac{3}{5} = \frac{■}{■}$ (×4 numerator and denominator)
4. $\frac{4}{12} = \frac{■}{■}$ (÷2 numerator and denominator)
5. $\frac{1}{7} = \frac{■}{■}$ (×8 numerator and denominator)

6. **Reasoning** Can you multiply the numerator and denominator of a fraction by zero to find an equivalent fraction? Why or why not?

PRACTICE AND APPLY

Practice

Skills and Reasoning

Multiply or divide to find equivalent fractions.

7. $\frac{3}{8} = \frac{■}{■}$ (×2 numerator and denominator)
8. $\frac{25}{30} = \frac{■}{■}$ (÷5 numerator and denominator)
9. $\frac{4}{12} = \frac{■}{■}$ (÷4 numerator and denominator)
10. $\frac{4}{9} = \frac{■}{■}$ (×5 numerator and denominator)
11. $\frac{12}{18} = \frac{■}{■}$ (÷6 numerator and denominator)

12. $\frac{5}{7}$ 13. $\frac{8}{12}$ 14. $\frac{3}{10}$ 15. $\frac{4}{6}$ 16. $\frac{6}{9}$

17. Give three fractions equivalent to two-eighths.

18. If a fraction is equivalent to $\frac{1}{2}$, is its denominator always an even number? Explain.

Problem Solving and Applications

19. One square dance is for 8 couples. There are 16 dancers in all. Three of the couples represent what fraction of the whole square?

Dancing at a Sidekicks event

20. **Science** Of the nine planets in the solar system, Mercury and Venus are the only planets that do not have moons. Write a fraction that names the fraction of planets that have moons.

Mixed Review and Test Prep

STAY SHARP!

Find each product.

21. 12×8 22. 10×9 23. 12×12 24. 11×9 25. 10×8

26. Which of the following is **not** divisible by 4?

Ⓐ 16 Ⓑ 24 Ⓒ 30 Ⓓ 100

Simplest Form Fractions

You Will Learn
how to write fractions in simplest form

Vocabulary
simplest form
when the numerator and denominator of a fraction have no common factors other than 1

Learn

Kendall gives advice to pet owners during a weekly radio talk show. She also works at an animal shelter.

One week the shelter had 18 puppies. Six got adopted. So, $\frac{6}{18}$ of the puppies found homes. How can you write the fraction $\frac{6}{18}$ in **simplest form**?

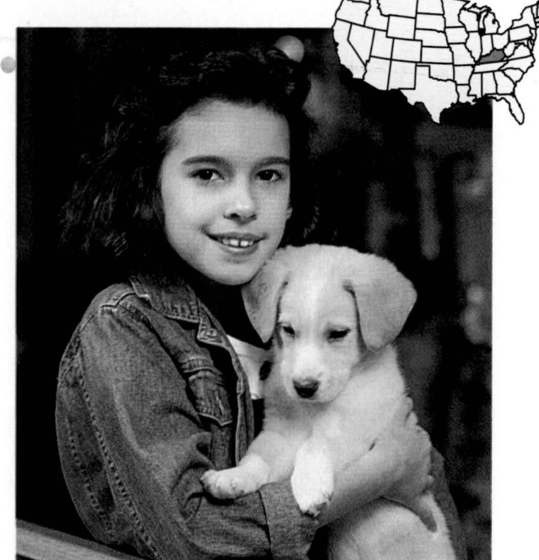

Kendall lives in Louisville, Kentucky.

Remember
A common factor divides two or more numbers with no remainder.

Derek's Way
First I divided by 2.

$$\frac{6}{18} = \frac{3}{9} \quad (\div 2)$$ Not simplest form

Then I divided by 3.

$$\frac{3}{9} = \frac{1}{3} \quad (\div 3)$$ Simplest form

Kendall's Way
I divided the numerator and denominator by 6.

$$\frac{6}{18} = \frac{1}{3} \quad (\div 6)$$

$\frac{1}{3}$ is in simplest form.

Talk About It

How are Derek and Kendall's ways alike? How are they different?

Check

Is each fraction in simplest form? If not, write it in simplest form.

1. $\frac{2}{8}$ **2.** $\frac{8}{10}$ **3.** $\frac{4}{7}$ **4.** $\frac{12}{15}$ **5.** $\frac{1}{7}$ **6.** $\frac{5}{6}$

7. Reasoning Which is in simplest form: $\frac{2}{3}$, $\frac{4}{6}$, $\frac{6}{9}$, or $\frac{8}{12}$? Explain.

Practice

Skills and Reasoning

Is each fraction in simplest form? If not, write it in simplest form.

8. $\frac{5}{10}$ **9.** $\frac{5}{9}$ **10.** $\frac{6}{8}$ **11.** $\frac{9}{21}$ **12.** $\frac{4}{5}$ **13.** $\frac{9}{12}$

14. $\frac{3}{17}$ **15.** $\frac{9}{10}$ **16.** $\frac{5}{50}$ **17.** $\frac{11}{22}$ **18.** $\frac{14}{20}$ **19.** $\frac{5}{9}$

20. $\frac{7}{14}$ **21.** $\frac{8}{10}$ **22.** $\frac{10}{15}$ **23.** $\frac{12}{16}$ **24.** $\frac{8}{15}$ **25.** $\frac{16}{21}$

26. How can you find the simplest form for the fraction $\frac{21}{35}$?

Problem Solving and Applications

27. A pet shelter can find homes for only about 9 out of every 30 pets they get. Write the simplest form fraction for this data.

28. Science Animals inherit hair and eye color from their parents. In a litter of 8 kittens, 2 have orange fur like their father's. The others have fur like their mother's. What fraction of the kittens has fur like their mother's? Write the fraction in simplest form.

Algebra Readiness Copy and complete. Write each rule.

29.

In	$\frac{1}{2}$	1	$1\frac{1}{2}$	2	$2\frac{1}{2}$
Out	$2\frac{1}{2}$	3	$3\frac{1}{2}$		

30.

In	$8\frac{1}{4}$	$7\frac{3}{4}$	$7\frac{1}{4}$	$6\frac{3}{4}$	$6\frac{1}{4}$
Out	$5\frac{1}{4}$	$4\frac{3}{4}$	$4\frac{1}{4}$		

Using Data Use the Data File on page 383 for **31** and **32.**

31. About how many dogs and cats are born each week?

32. Mental Math About how many pets are adopted each year?

Mixed Review and Test Prep

Money Order each set of dollar amounts from greatest to least.

33. \$2.25, \$1.95, \$2.75, \$2.55 **34.** \$8.75, \$10.00, \$7.95, \$8.95

35. Find 721 divided by 4.

Ⓐ 18 R1 Ⓑ 180 R1 Ⓒ 2,884 Ⓓ not here

Technology

Finding Simplest Form Fractions

Materials

calculator

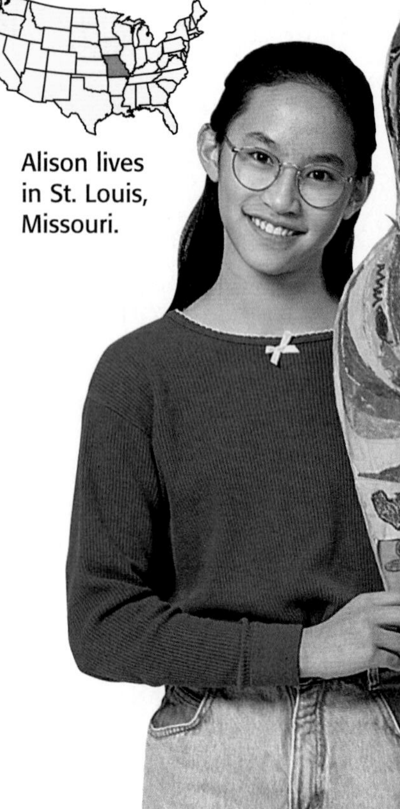

Alison lives in St. Louis, Missouri.

Alison volunteers one hour each week as an art assistant. The circle graph shows how she spent her time helping out one week. Find the simplest form of the fraction of time she spent cutting mats.

One Hour a Week as an Art Assistant

Cutting Art Mats $\frac{24}{60}$

Sharpening Pencils $\frac{15}{60}$

Gathering Art Materials $\frac{21}{60}$

Some calculators can find the simplest form of a fraction.

Work Together

Use a calculator to write fractions in simplest form.

1. Turn on the calculator. Enter the fraction $\frac{24}{60}$ by entering 24 [/] 60.
2. Next, press the [Simp] key followed by [=].
3. The calculator will display [N/D → n/d]. This means that the fraction is still not in its simplest form. To keep simplifying, keep pressing [Simp] and [=].
4. What is the simplest form of the fraction $\frac{24}{60}$?

Exercises

Answer **1–4** using a calculator.

1. Find the simplest form fraction for the part of the hour Alison spent sharpening pencils.

2. Find the simplest form fraction for the part of the hour Alison spent gathering art materials.

3. What does pressing [Simp] [=] do?

4. Why would you want to find the simplest form of a fraction instead of using the fraction as it is?

Extensions

5. This time, enter 24 [/] 60 [Simp] 4 [=]. What does the calculator do?

6. How many times must you press [Simp] [=] to find the simplest form fraction for $\frac{30}{60}$? What is it?

7. Suppose you wanted to find the simplest form fraction for $\frac{30}{60}$ in one step. What divisor would you use? Why?

8. What divisor would you use to simplify each of the following fractions in one step?

a. $\frac{20}{25}$ **b.** $\frac{16}{24}$ **c.** $\frac{9}{15}$ **d.** $\frac{18}{27}$

9. Raul spent an hour helping clean up the parks in his neighborhood.

a. How many minutes did he spend at each park?

b. What fraction of an hour, in simplest form, did he spend at each park?

Raul's Park Cleanup Time	
59th St. Park	$\frac{30}{60}$ hr
Columbus Park	$\frac{15}{60}$ hr
Martin Luther King, Jr., Park	$\frac{15}{60}$ hr

Chapter 9
Lesson
9

Comparing and Ordering Fractions

Greenland Pines students in Jacksonville, Florida.

You Will Learn
how to compare and order fractions

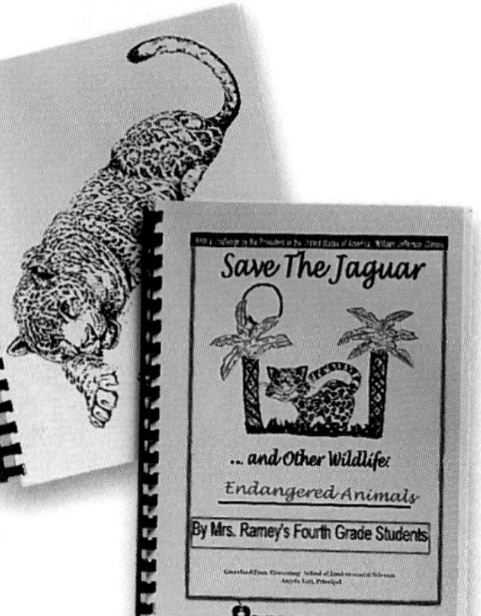

Learn

These students wrote and sold a book about endangered wildlife. They used the money for environmental projects.

You can use fraction strips to compare fractions.

Example 1

Mrs. Ramey's class sold $\frac{3}{4}$ of their books. Mrs. Smith's sold $\frac{5}{8}$ of theirs. If they had the same number of books, which sold more?

$\frac{1}{4}$	$\frac{1}{4}$	$\frac{1}{4}$

$\frac{1}{8}$	$\frac{1}{8}$	$\frac{1}{8}$	$\frac{1}{8}$	$\frac{1}{8}$

Compare $\frac{3}{4}$ and $\frac{5}{8}$.

$\frac{3}{4} > \frac{5}{8}$

Mrs. Ramey's class sold more books.

Did You Know?
Greenland Pines students are members of Kids for a Clean Environment. This group helps young people save the earth's resources.

You can use fraction strips or a number line to order fractions.

Example 2

Order the fractions $\frac{3}{4}$, $\frac{3}{8}$, and $\frac{5}{8}$ from greatest to least.

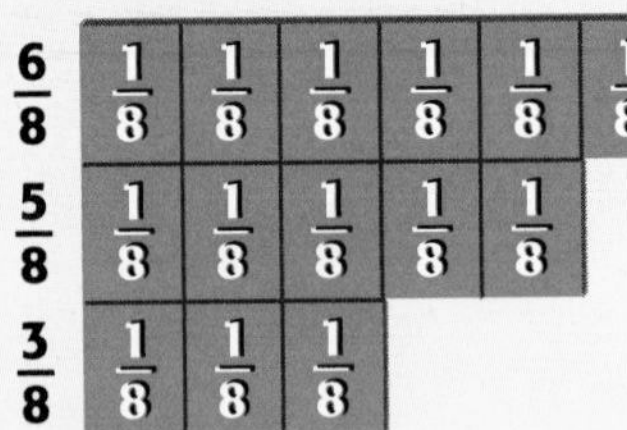

Think: $\frac{3}{4}$ is equivalent to $\frac{6}{8}$.

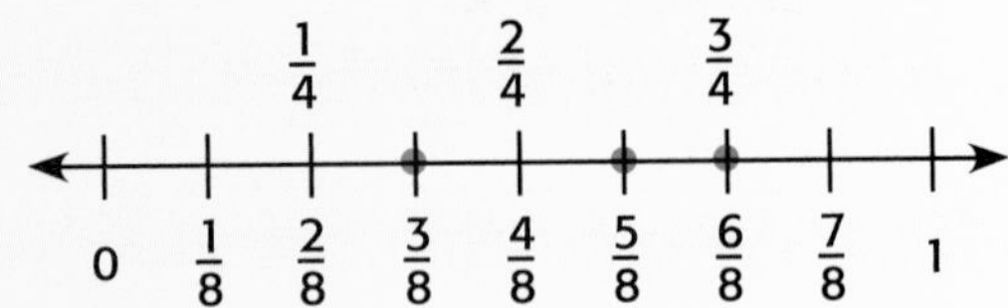

So, the order from greatest to least is $\frac{3}{4}$, $\frac{5}{8}$, $\frac{3}{8}$.

Talk About It

How can you use equivalent fractions to order $\frac{2}{3}$, $\frac{1}{6}$, and $\frac{1}{3}$ from greatest to least?

Check

Copy and complete. Write >, <, or =.

1. $\frac{1}{2}$ ● $\frac{1}{4}$ **2.** $\frac{2}{3}$ ● $\frac{2}{6}$ **3.** $\frac{4}{4}$ ● $\frac{8}{8}$ **4.** $\frac{1}{3}$ ● $\frac{5}{8}$ **5.** $\frac{1}{3}$ ● $\frac{5}{12}$

Order each group of fractions from least to greatest.

6. $\frac{1}{4}, \frac{1}{8}, \frac{3}{8}$ **7.** $\frac{2}{10}, \frac{4}{10}, \frac{1}{2}$ **8.** $\frac{2}{9}, \frac{8}{9}, \frac{2}{3}$ **9.** $\frac{6}{10}, \frac{4}{5}, \frac{5}{5}$

10. Reasoning How could you compare $\frac{5}{8}$ and $\frac{1}{2}$ by finding just one equivalent fraction?

Practice

Skills and Reasoning

Copy and complete. Write >, <, or =.

11. $\frac{1}{2}$ ● $\frac{2}{3}$ **12.** $\frac{5}{6}$ ● $\frac{5}{8}$ **13.** $\frac{4}{7}$ ● $\frac{1}{7}$ **14.** $\frac{12}{16}$ ● $\frac{3}{4}$ **15.** $\frac{1}{3}$ ● $\frac{4}{5}$

16. $\frac{3}{5}$ ● $\frac{6}{6}$ **17.** $\frac{3}{10}$ ● $\frac{2}{5}$ **18.** $\frac{7}{10}$ ● $\frac{1}{2}$ **19.** $\frac{3}{4}$ ● $\frac{3}{16}$ **20.** $\frac{6}{9}$ ● $\frac{2}{3}$

Order each group of fractions from greatest to least.

21. $\frac{3}{4}, \frac{7}{8}, \frac{5}{8}$ **22.** $\frac{5}{10}, \frac{3}{10}, \frac{3}{5}$ **23.** $\frac{3}{15}, \frac{2}{5}, \frac{4}{5}$ **24.** $\frac{7}{12}, \frac{11}{12}, \frac{3}{6}$

25. Which is greater, four-fifths or three-fourths?

26. To compare $\frac{4}{5}$ and $\frac{5}{7}$, what equivalent fractions can you use?

Problem Solving and Applications

Using Data Use the graph for **27** and **28**.

27. Which event got the most money?

28. Which two events got the same amount of money?

Environmental Club Budget

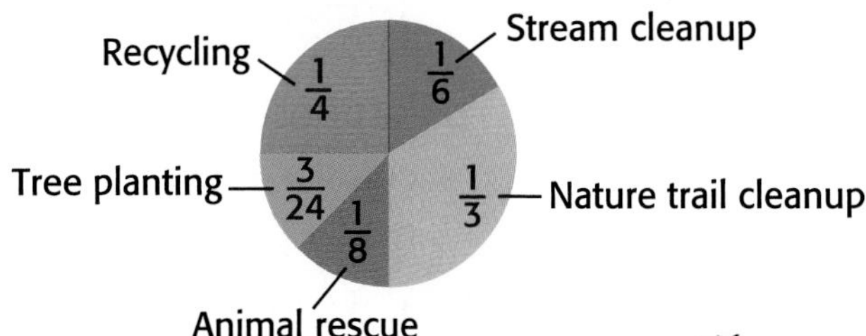

Mixed Review and Test Prep

STAY SHARP!

Mental Math Find each product.

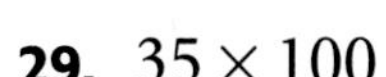

29. 35×100 **30.** 10×40 **31.** 10×400 **32.** 35×200

33. Which of the following is the sum of 87 and 341?

Ⓐ 254 Ⓑ 328 Ⓒ 400 Ⓓ 428

Chapter 9
Lesson
10

Exploring a Fraction of a Set

Problem Solving Connection
- Use Objects/ Act It Out
- Look for a Pattern

Materials
counters

Explore

Volunteers help the staff at museums in many ways.

The Wheelright Museum of The American Indian is preparing a 12-piece art exhibit. If three people help, each person will set up $\frac{1}{3}$ of the art. How many pieces will each person set up?

Laverne Pinnecoose works at the Wheelright Museum of The American Indian in Santa Fe, New Mexico.

You can use counters to help find a fractional part of a set.

Remember
$\frac{4}{12} = \frac{1}{3}$

Work Together

1. Use counters to find $\frac{1}{3}$ of 12.
   a. Put 12 counters in 3 equal groups. How many counters are in each group?
   b. How many counters are in $\frac{1}{3}$ of 12?
   c. How many of the 12 pieces of art does each person set up?
   d. Find $\frac{2}{3}$ of 12.
2. Suppose 3 people share the work equally to set up 9 pieces of art. How many pieces does 1 person set up? 2 people?
   a. Find $\frac{1}{3}$ of 9. b. Find $\frac{2}{3}$ of 9.
3. Suppose 4 people share the work equally to set up 8 pieces of art. How many pieces does 1 person set up? 3 people?
   a. Find $\frac{1}{4}$ of 8. b. Find $\frac{3}{4}$ of 8.

How many equal groups of counters show $\frac{1}{4}$ of 8?

Connect

You can use division and multiplication to find a fraction of a set.

Find $\frac{2}{3}$ of 15.

Example

Step 1

First find $\frac{1}{3}$ of 15. Divide the total by the denominator. So, divide 15 by 3.

15	÷	3	=	5
Total in the set		Number of groups		Number in each group

$\frac{1}{3}$ of 15 = 5

Step 2

Multiply the numerator by the number in each group. So, multiply 5 by 2.

2	×	5	=	10
Number of groups		Number in each group		Total in part of the set

$\frac{2}{3}$ of 15 = 10

Counters can help you show fractions of a set.

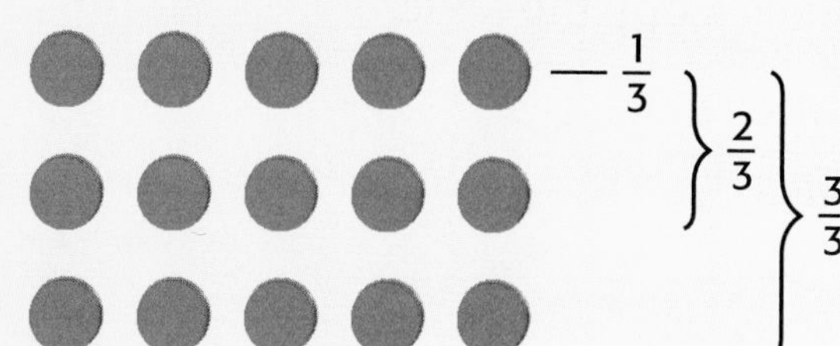

Practice

Find the number for each fraction of a set. You may use counters to help.

1. $\frac{1}{5}$ of 10 **2.** $\frac{5}{6}$ of 12 **3.** $\frac{3}{4}$ of 20 **4.** $\frac{3}{8}$ of 16 **5.** $\frac{1}{2}$ of 18

6. $\frac{2}{3}$ of 30 **7.** $\frac{1}{4}$ of 24 **8.** $\frac{1}{10}$ of 10 **9.** $\frac{3}{7}$ of 21 **10.** $\frac{2}{9}$ of 27

11. Critical Thinking Sandi set up 8 pieces of art. At the museum, 5 co-workers shared equally the work of setting up 35 pieces of art. Sandi said she set up more pieces than any of her co-workers. Is she right? Explain.

Language Arts Choose letters from the box. Use each letter only one time in a word.

A	U	L	O	B
N	K	T	M	I

12. Write a word that uses $\frac{3}{10}$ of the letters.

13. Write a word that uses $\frac{1}{2}$ of the letters.

14. Write a word that uses $\frac{2}{5}$ of the letters.

15. Journal Explain how you would find $\frac{2}{5}$ of 10.

"Untitled," 1997, acrylic on wood by Gregory Lomayesva. Wheelright Museum of The American Indian.

Technology

Finding a Fraction of a Set

Materials
DataWonder! or other graphing software

At one school, some students volunteer at a day-care center. Some help at an animal shelter. Others pack groceries at the community food bank. You can use fractions to compare what Ms. Kane's class and Mr. Clay's class are doing.

Work Together

Use your graphing software to graph and compare this data.

1. Open a **Full Data Table.** Copy the table.
2. Display a graph of your data.
   - Set to **Long Menus.**
   - Pull down the **Graphs** menu and select **Circle Graph.**

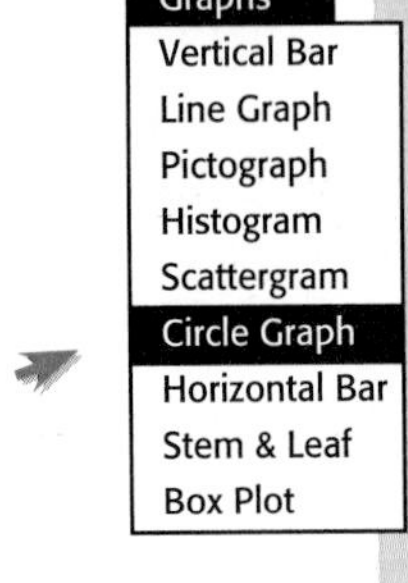

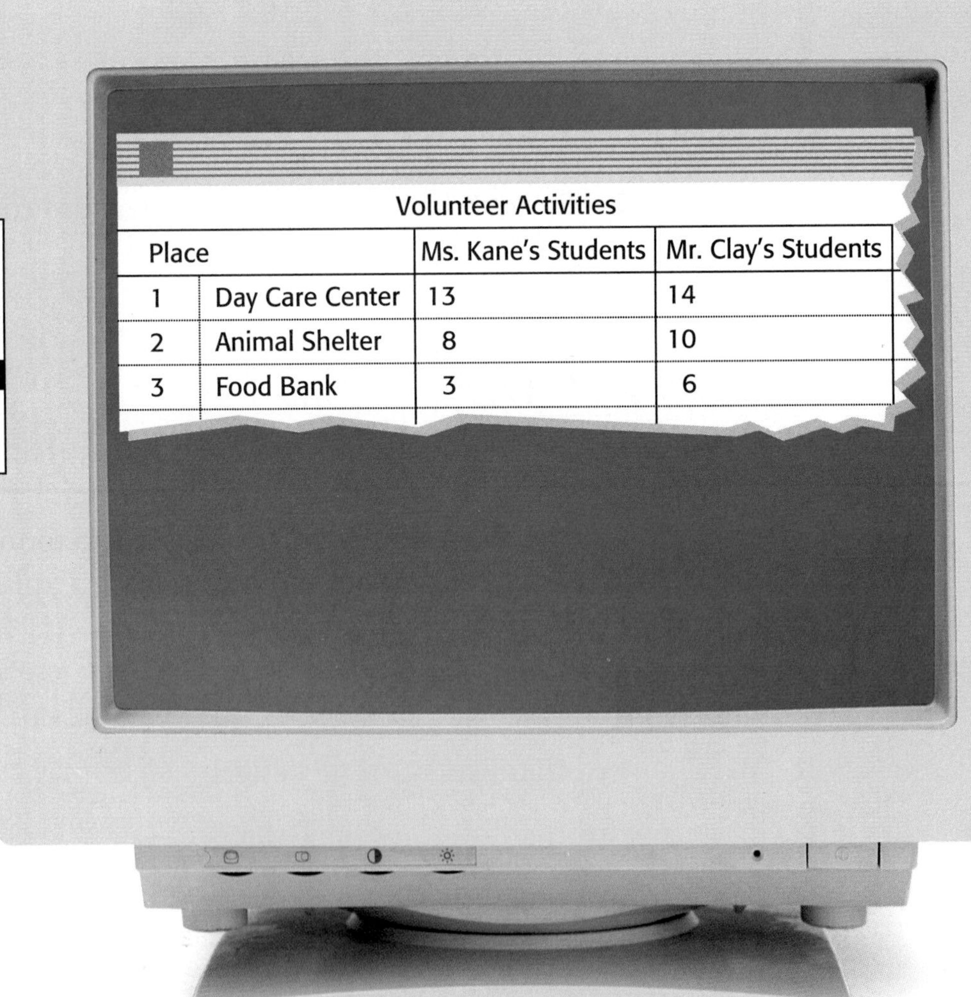

Volunteer Activities

Place		Ms. Kane's Students	Mr. Clay's Students
1	Day Care Center	13	14
2	Animal Shelter	8	10
3	Food Bank	3	6

3. Pull down the **Report** menu and select **Show Report.** Insert the graph and the table. Give your report a title.

Exercises

Answer **1–4** in the Report window. When you are finished, choose **Print Report** from the File menu.

1. What is the total number of students in each class? (Hint: Use the **Calculate** menu to Add, but do not insert the result in the data table.)
2. What fraction of Ms. Kane's class volunteers at each of the three different places?
3. What fraction of Mr. Clay's class volunteers at each of the three different places?
4. Look at the data table and the fractions. Do more than half of the students in either class volunteer at the same place? Explain.

Extensions

Use the circle graphs for **5–7.** Write your answers in the Report window. Print your report when you are finished.

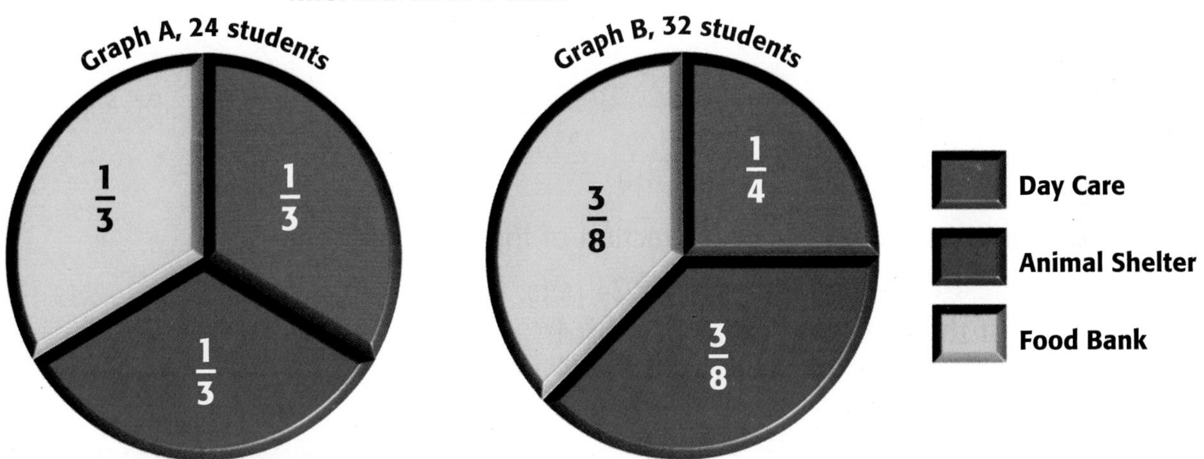

5. Graph A shows the fraction of Mrs. Martinez's class that volunteers at the day-care center, the animal shelter, and the food bank. If Mrs. Martinez has 24 students in all, how many volunteer at the day-care center?
6. Suppose 8 more students join Mrs. Martinez's class. Graph B shows what fraction of the class now works at each place. How many of the new students decided to work at the day-care center?
7. Use the graphing software to create a data table to go with Graph B. Remember, Mrs. Martinez's class now has 32 students. (Hint: Make your own circle graph to check your answer.)

SECTION B

Review and Practice

Vocabulary Copy and complete.

Word List
equivalent fractions
simplest form

1. Fractions that name the same amount are ____.
2. A fraction is in ____ when the numerator and denominator have no common factor greater than 1.

(Lesson 6) Write two equivalent fractions for each.

3. $\frac{6}{8}$ **4.** $\frac{3}{6}$ **5.** $\frac{4}{10}$ **6.** $\frac{1}{3}$ **7.** $\frac{5}{7}$

(Lesson 7) Multiply or divide to find equivalent fractions.

8. $\frac{5}{6}$ **9.** $\frac{4}{16}$ **10.** $\frac{2}{5}$ **11.** $\frac{6}{10}$ **12.** $\frac{7}{8}$

(Lesson 8) Is each fraction in simplest form? If not, write it in simplest form.

13. $\frac{7}{10}$ **14.** $\frac{4}{12}$ **15.** $\frac{2}{13}$ **16.** $\frac{6}{15}$ **17.** $\frac{2}{6}$

(Lesson 9) Copy and complete. Write $>$, $<$, or $=$.

18. $\frac{2}{9}$ ● $\frac{3}{4}$ **19.** $\frac{2}{3}$ ● $\frac{5}{6}$ **20.** $\frac{3}{5}$ ● $\frac{6}{10}$ **21.** $\frac{3}{8}$ ● $\frac{1}{4}$ **22.** $\frac{2}{3}$ ● $\frac{4}{6}$

23. Order from least to greatest. $\frac{3}{10}, \frac{9}{10}, \frac{2}{5}$

(Lesson 10) Find the number for each fraction of the set.

On Friday, the animal hospital treated 24 pets. One-fourth of the pets were cats. One-third of the pets were dogs.

24. How many cats were there?

25. How many dogs were there?

26. How many animals were neither cats or dogs?

27. Journal Suppose you took a survey to find out which of your classmates have different types of pets. Explain how you would write each number as a fraction.

Skills Checklist

In this section, you have:

- **Explored Equivalent Fractions**
- **Named and Written Equivalent Fractions**
- **Learned About Simplest Form Fractions**
- **Compared and Ordered Fractions**
- **Explored a Fraction of a Set**

CHAPTER 9

SECTION C

Using Customary Linear Measurement

Digging for fossils is dusty work. Volunteers, like Ben and Gil, pick and sift carefully to find remains of ancient life. If you worked at a dig site, how would you measure the lengths of the tiny objects you discover?

Fractional Parts of an Inch

Review fractional parts. Choose the fraction for the part of each line segment that is red.

1. Ⓐ $\frac{1}{2}$ Ⓑ $\frac{3}{4}$

2. Ⓐ $\frac{1}{8}$ Ⓑ $\frac{2}{3}$

Skills Checklist

In this section, you will:

- ❒ Explore Units of Length
- ❒ Measure Fractional Parts of an Inch
- ❒ Explore Feet, Yards, and Miles
- ❒ Solve Problems by Using Logical Reasoning

Chapter 9
Lesson
11

Exploring Units of Length

Problem Solving Connection
Use Objects/
Act It Out

Materials
- ruler
- yardstick

Vocabulary
Customary Units of Length
inch
foot
yard

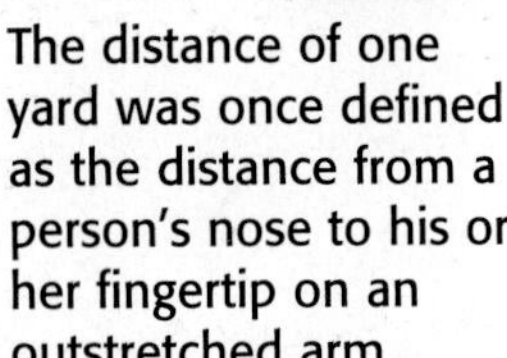

Did You Know?
The distance of one yard was once defined as the distance from a person's nose to his or her fingertip on an outstretched arm.

Explore

Susan measures the leaf at between 3 and 4 inches. It is closer to 4 inches. So it is about 4 inches long.

You can use a ruler to measure the lengths of small objects. You can use a yardstick to measure greater lengths.

Work Together

1. Use rulers or yardsticks to measure classroom objects.
   a. Estimate the length of a pencil in inches. Then measure it to the nearest inch. About how long is the pencil? How does your measurement compare with your estimate?
   b. Estimate the length of one side of your desk. Then measure it to the nearest inch. About how long is it? Check your estimate.
2. Find other classroom objects. Estimate their lengths. Then measure each one to the nearest inch.

Talk About It

3. About how far is it from the boy's chin to the end of his outstretched finger?
4. About what fraction of a yard is this?

Connect

Inch, **foot**, and **yard** are customary units of length.

12 inches (in.) = 1 foot (ft)

3 feet (ft) = 1 yard (yd)

1 yd = 36 in.

Here are some ways to think about inches, feet, and yards.

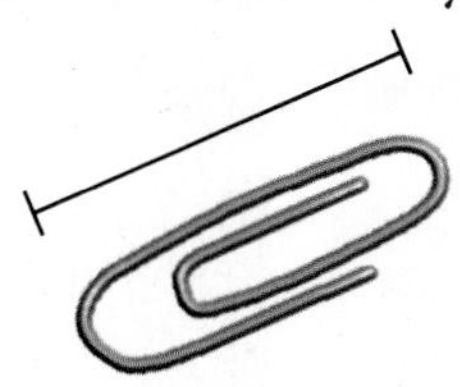

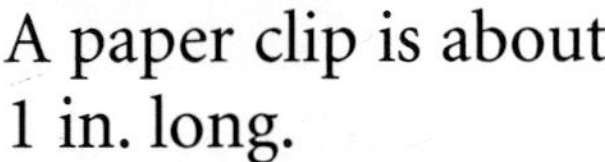

A paper clip is about 1 in. long.

A man's shoe is about 1 ft long.

A door is about 1 yd wide.

Practice

Find each measurement to the nearest inch.

1. Width of your math book
2. Height of your math book

Choose the better measure for each object.

3. 

   Ⓐ 2 yd
   Ⓑ 2 in.

4. 

   Ⓐ 3 ft
   Ⓑ 3 in.

5. 

   Ⓐ 45 ft
   Ⓑ 45 in.

6. Which is longer: 9 in. or $\frac{1}{2}$ ft? Explain.
7. Which is longer: 1 foot or $\frac{1}{2}$ yd? Explain.
8. **Science** The General Sherman Tree is a 272-ft tall giant sequoia in California's Sequoia National Park. Is this more or less than 100 yd? How much more or less?

9. **Journal** List two items from your home that you think could best be measured in inches. Then list two items that could best be measured in feet, and two that could best be measured in yards. Explain your choices.

Chapter 9
Lesson
12

Measuring Fractional Parts of an Inch

You Will Learn
how to measure fractional parts of an inch

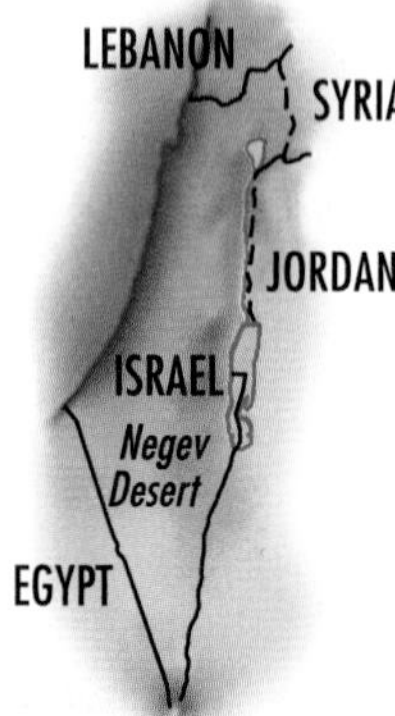

Learn

Each summer, Gil and Ben help their dad look for coins, bones, and pottery of earlier civilizations. Their dad is an archaeologist, a scientist who studies ancient remains.

Measure these pottery fragments to the nearest $\frac{1}{2}$ in., $\frac{1}{4}$ in., and $\frac{1}{8}$ in.

Gil and Ben live in San Diego, California, but get involved by helping dig for fossils in the Negev Desert in Israel.

Math Tip
On a ruler, you can count $\frac{1}{8}$, $\frac{2}{8}$ or $\frac{1}{4}$, $\frac{3}{8}$, $\frac{4}{8}$ or $\frac{1}{2}$, $\frac{5}{8}$, and so on.

Example 1

Measure to the nearest $\frac{1}{2}$ in.
The fragment is about 2 in.

Example 2

Measure to the nearest $\frac{1}{4}$ in.
The fragment is about $1\frac{1}{4}$ in.

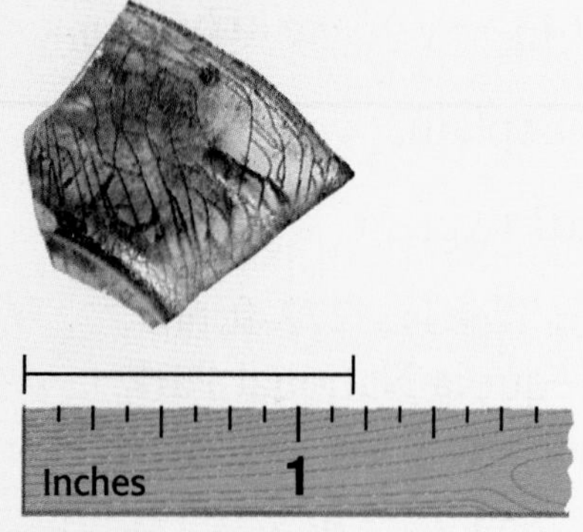

Example 3

Measure to the nearest $\frac{1}{8}$ in.
The fragment is about $1\frac{1}{8}$ in.

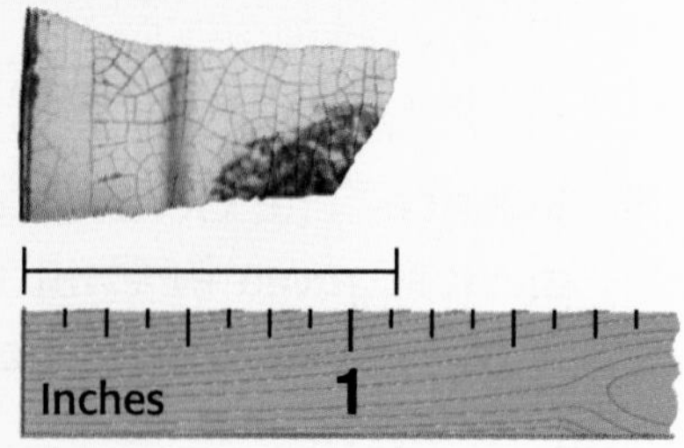

Which fractional part of an inch would you use for the closest measurement: $\frac{1}{2}$, $\frac{1}{4}$, or $\frac{1}{8}$?

Check

Measure each item to the nearest:

1. $\frac{1}{2}$ in.

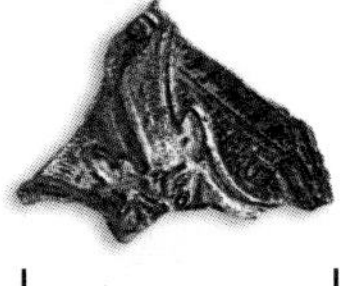

2. $\frac{1}{4}$ in.

3. $\frac{1}{8}$ in.

4. **Reasoning** Gil and Ben both measure the same object to the nearest $\frac{1}{2}$ inch. Gil says it is 1 in. Ben says it is $1\frac{1}{2}$ in. Can Gil and Ben both be right? Explain.

Practice

Skills and Reasoning

Measure the bracelet and one coin to the nearest:

5. $\frac{1}{2}$ in.

6. $\frac{1}{8}$ in.

7. **Patterns** You have measured in fractions of an inch: $\frac{1}{2}, \frac{1}{4}, \frac{1}{8}$. What fractional part of an inch is measured by the marks between the $\frac{1}{8}$ marks?

Problem Solving and Applications

8. Suppose you find a piece of pottery that is $2\frac{5}{8}$ in. long. Is its length closer to 2 in. or 3 in.?

9. **Math History** The 1 foot measure was once determined by the length of the measurer's foot.
   a. Measure your foot to the nearest $\frac{1}{4}$ inch, and to the nearest inch.
   b. What fraction of 1 foot is the length of your foot?

Mixed Review and Test Prep

Find each quotient.

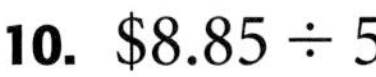

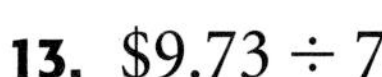

10. \$8.85 ÷ 5 11. \$2.52 ÷ 3 12. \$2.76 ÷ 6 13. \$9.73 ÷ 7

14. **Geometry** Which of the following is a parallelogram?

 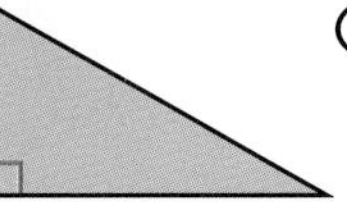  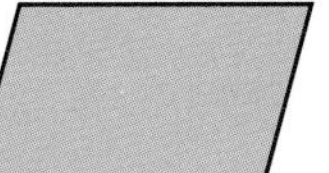 Ⓒ   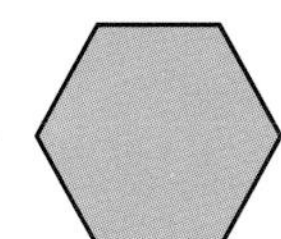

Chapter 9
Lesson
13

Exploring Feet, Yards, and Miles

Problem Solving Connection
- Guess and Check
- Use Objects/ Act It Out

Materials
- yardstick
- calculator

Vocabulary
mile
a distance equal to 5,280 ft or 1,760 yd

Explore

Students at North Ridge Primary School helped raise money just by taking a walk. They took part in the Kids for Kids Walk-a-Thon. Their goal was to walk twice around a one-mile course in Sunken Meadows State Park.

How long is a mile?

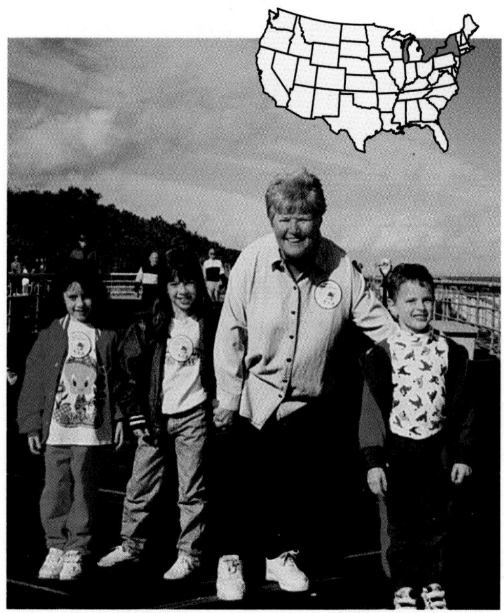

Students at North Ridge Primary School in Commack, New York, raised $1,000 for the Ronald McDonald House during the Walk-a-Thon.

Did You Know?
There are about 20 city blocks in a mile.

Work Together

Use a calculator and measurements to figure out how long a mile is.

1. How many steps do you think it would take to walk a mile?
   a. Measure the distance you walk in one step to the nearest foot.
   b. Divide 5,280 (the number of feet in a mile) by the distance you walk in one step. About how many steps would you take if you walked a mile?
2. How many times do you think you would have to walk back and forth across the classroom to walk a mile?
   a. Measure the width of your classroom to the nearest yard.
   b. Divide 1,760 (the number of yards in a mile) by the width of the classroom. How many times would you have to walk across the room to walk a mile?

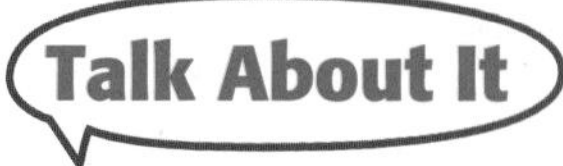

Talk About It

3. How could you estimate how long it would take to walk a mile?
4. Give an example of a distance from your school to somewhere that you think is about a mile.

Connect

A **mile** is a customary unit of length used to measure long distances.

1 mile = 5,280 feet
1 mile = 1,760 yards

Here are some ways to think about a mile.

132 buses lined up end to end is about 1 mile.

15 football fields placed end to end is about 1 mile.

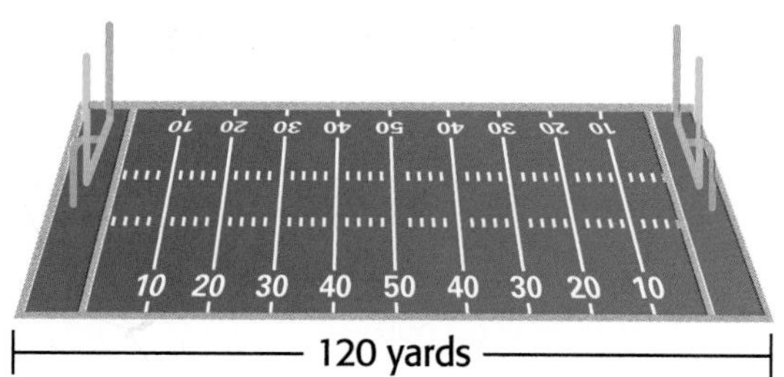

Practice

1. **Estimation** A jet airplane is flying at 30,000 feet. About how many miles high is it?
2. A bicycle travels about 7 feet with each turn of its wheels. About how many times would a bicycle wheel turn if you rode for 1 mile?
3. **Time** If it takes a bicyclist 10 minutes to travel a mile, how many miles would she travel in an hour and a half?
4. **Math History** Around 1600, the length of a mile was made law by England's Queen Elizabeth I. A mile was defined as 8 furlongs, or 5,280 feet. How many feet are in 1 furlong?

Using Data Use the Walk-a-Thon map for **5–7.**

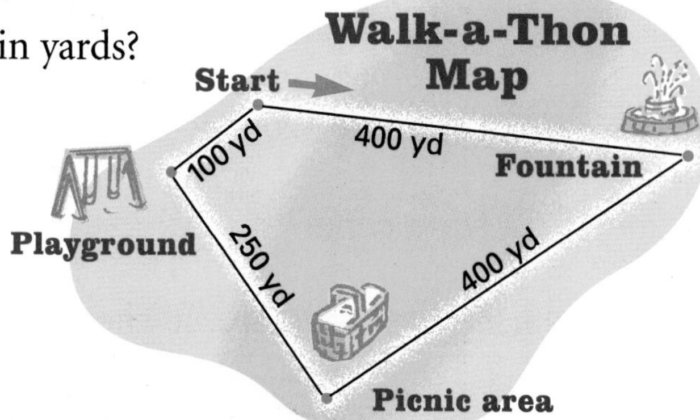

5. What is the total distance of the course in yards?
6. George walked around the course one time but then stopped when he reached the fountain the second time. Did he walk more than a mile? Explain.
7. How many times would you have to complete the course to walk 3 miles?

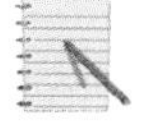

8. **Journal** How would you describe how long a mile is without using numbers?

Skills Practice Bank, page 571, Set 5

Chapter 9
Lesson
14

Problem Solving

Analyze Strategies: Use Logical Reasoning

You Will Learn
how to use logical reasoning to help solve problems

Reading Tip
Find clues that help you narrow your choices.

Learn

The mountains pictured are Kilimanjaro, Elbrus, Mount Everest, Aconcagua, and Mount McKinley. They are not in order. Read the clues. Then use them to identify each mountain by its height.

29,028 ft | 22,834 ft | 20,320 ft | 19,340 ft | 18,510 ft

a. Mount Everest is the world's tallest mountain.
b. Aconcagua is only 2,514 ft taller than Mount McKinley.
c. Kilimanjaro is about 1,000 ft shorter than Mount McKinley.

Work Together

▶ Understand

What do you know?

What do you need to find out?

▶ Plan

How will you find out? Use the clues to identify the mountains.

▶ Solve

Find the greatest height. Mount Everest is 29,028 ft.

Find two numbers that have a difference of 2,514 ft.
$22{,}834 - 20{,}320 = 2{,}514$
So, Aconcagua is 22,834 ft and Mount McKinley is 20,320 ft.

Find a height that is about 1,000 less than 20,320.
$20{,}320 - 1{,}000 = 19{,}320$
19,340 ft is close to 19,320 ft.
So, Kilimanjaro is 19,340 ft.

Elbrus must be 18,510 ft tall.

▶ Look Back

How can you check your answer?

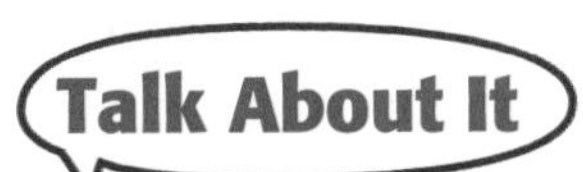

How could you change the clues to include Elbrus?

Check

Problem Solving: Understand, Plan, Solve, Look Back

Copy and complete the table. Use logical reasoning to solve the problem.

1. Four student volunteers cleaned up the trash on four nature trails. Who cleaned each trail?
   - Mauricio cleaned one more mile of trail than James.
   - Herman has never been on either of the lake trails.
   - Suzanne cleaned the most miles of trail.

Volunteer	Trail Name	Miles Cleaned
	Riverhead	6
	Gray Mountain	5
	Lake Tyrell	2
	Lake Green	3

Problem Solving Practice

Problem Solving Strategies

- Use Objects/Act It Out
- Draw a Picture
- Look for a Pattern
- Guess and Check
- Use Logical Reasoning
- Make an Organized List
- Make a Table
- Solve a Simpler Problem
- Work Backward

Choose a Tool

Use any strategy to solve each problem.

2. A crew of 28 volunteers plant trees to protect a hillside. 16 volunteers plant pine trees. 22 plant oak trees. How many people plant both kinds of trees?
3. **Using Data** Use the Data File on page 383.
   a. About what fraction of those in Group 1 volunteered?
   b. About what fraction of those in Group 2 volunteered?
4. A group of 50 climbers took part in this year's mountain cleanup. For 29 climbers this was their second year helping. 10 had never helped before. How many of the 50 climbers had helped before last year?
5. Fifty climbers were carried to the base of the mountain by three vehicles—a bus, a van, and a car. Use these clues to find out how many climbers were in each vehicle.
   - The bus carried three times as many climbers as the van.
   - The van carried five more climbers than the car.

Climbers repair trails in California.

6. Every year, climbers set a goal to collect twice as much trash as the year before. This year's goal is 1,200 pounds of trash.
   a. What was their goal two years ago? Three years ago?
   b. What strategy did you use? Explain.

PROBLEM SOLVING PRACTICE

SECTION C

Review and Practice

(Lesson 11) Choose the better measure for each object.

1. 

Ⓐ 14 in.
Ⓑ 14 ft

2. 

Ⓐ 4 in.
Ⓑ 4 yd.

3. 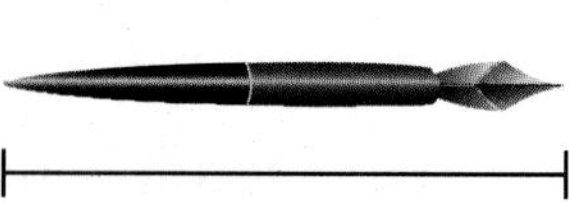

Ⓐ 7 ft
Ⓑ 7 in.

4. Which is longer: 5 in. or $\frac{1}{2}$ ft? Explain.
5. Which is longer: 2 ft or $\frac{1}{2}$ yd? Explain.
6. **Reasoning** To measure the width of a doorway, you place the end of a yardstick at one edge. The other edge is at $35\frac{1}{4}$ inches. What is the width of the doorway to the nearest inch? Explain.

(Lesson 12) Measure the pencil to the nearest:

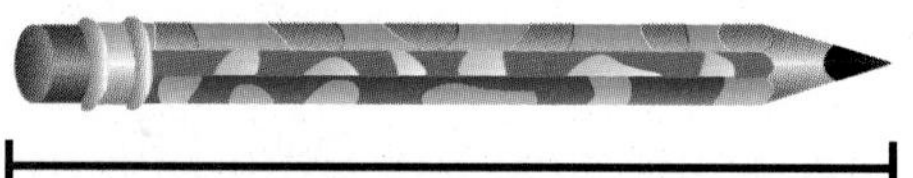

7. $\frac{1}{2}$ in.
8. $\frac{1}{4}$ in.

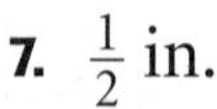

(Lesson 13) Solve.

9. **Literature** In William Brooke's story *The Working of John Henry,* John Henry races against a steam hammer to tunnel through a mountain. By Saturday night, John Henry has tunneled 90 feet. The steam hammer has tunneled 48 yards. Which tunneled farther, man or machine? Explain.
10. **Estimation** One runner ran a 1,500-yd race, a 5,000-yd race, and a 10,000-yd race. About how many miles did she run in all?

(Lesson 14) Use any strategy to solve the problem.

11. Four students picked up cans. Al picked up neither the most nor the least. Beth picked up more than Al but fewer than Carl. Di picked up the least. Put the students in order from least to most cans picked up.

12. **Journal** Why do we measure the distance a car goes in miles rather than in yards or feet?

Skills Checklist

In this section, you have:

- ☑ **Explored Units of Length**
- ☑ **Measured Fractional Parts of an Inch**
- ☑ **Explored Feet, Yards, and Miles**
- ☑ **Solved Problems by Using Logical Reasoning**

REVIEW AND PRACTICE

Choose at least one. Use what you have learned in this chapter.

1 Sock Survey

Take a survey of the sock colors in your class. Find what fraction of the class is wearing socks. Of the sock-wearers, find the fraction that shows how many people wear each color. What does the denominator in each fraction stand for? What does each numerator stand for?

3 Going Places

At Home Think about the places you go in a typical day. When do you travel miles? When do you travel yards? Ask a family member to help you estimate the distances you travel in a day. Write a short journal entry using different measurement words.

2 Word Play

How long was a Roman mile? The English word *mile* comes from *milia passum,* a Latin term that means "1,000 paces." A Roman pace was 2 steps. Measure a pace and guess the length of a Roman mile. How much longer or shorter is it than a mile? Use a dictionary to find other words that come from *mil.* List the words and their meanings. Tell how they relate to 1,000.

4 Fraction Notes

Music relies on the use of fractions to show the amount of time to hold a note. Do you read music? If so, show an equivalent fraction for each of the following amounts, using whole notes, half notes, quarter notes, or eighth notes.

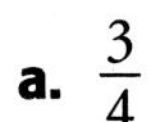

a. $\frac{3}{4}$ **b.** $\frac{6}{3}$ **c.** $\frac{5}{2}$ **d.** $\frac{10}{16}$

Go to **www.mathsurf.com/4/ch9** for more about music.

CHAPTER 9

Review/Test

(Lessons 1–3) Write a fraction for each shaded part.

1. 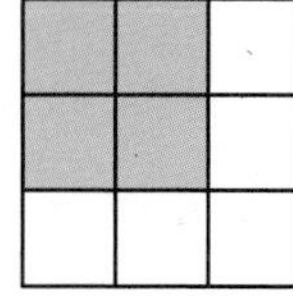

2. 

3. 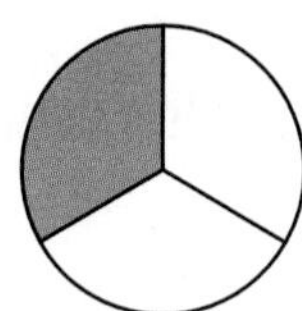

(Lesson 4) Write each improper fraction as a mixed number. Write each mixed number as an improper fraction.

4. $\frac{7}{2}$ **5.** $\frac{5}{3}$ **6.** $1\frac{3}{4}$ **7.** $2\frac{1}{8}$ **8.** $\frac{11}{10}$

(Lessons 6 and 7) Write an equivalent fraction for each.

9. $\frac{3}{4}$ **10.** $\frac{2}{16}$ **11.** $\frac{1}{3}$ **12.** $\frac{3}{10}$ **13.** $\frac{1}{6}$

14. Logic $\frac{4}{5} = \frac{▲}{■}$. If ▲ is 20, what is ■? **15.** Find n if $\frac{3}{8} = \frac{n}{32}$.

(Lesson 8) Is each fraction in simplest form? If not, write it in simplest form.

16. $\frac{2}{10}$ **17.** $\frac{7}{10}$ **18.** $\frac{2}{8}$ **19.** $\frac{9}{15}$ **20.** $\frac{3}{9}$

(Lesson 9) Copy and complete. Write <, >, or =.

21. $\frac{1}{2}$ ● $\frac{3}{5}$ **22.** $\frac{2}{3}$ ● $\frac{3}{4}$ **23.** $\frac{4}{6}$ ● $\frac{2}{3}$ **24.** $\frac{3}{8}$ ● $\frac{1}{4}$

(Lesson 10) Find the number for each fraction of a set.

25. $\frac{1}{5}$ of 15 **26.** $\frac{2}{6}$ of 12 **27.** $\frac{3}{4}$ of 8 **28.** $\frac{5}{8}$ of 24

(Lesson 11) Measurement Copy and complete.

29. 12 in. = ■ ft **30.** 1 yd = ■ in. **31.** 1 yd = ■ ft

(Lessons 12–14) Solve.

32. Terrell jumped $50\frac{1}{2}$ in. in a long-jumping contest. His brother jumped $50\frac{5}{8}$ in. Who jumped farther?

33. Geography Potosí, Bolivia, has an elevation of just more than 13,000 feet. About how many miles high is Potosí?

REVIEW/TEST

CHAPTER 9

Performance Assessment

A. Fractions

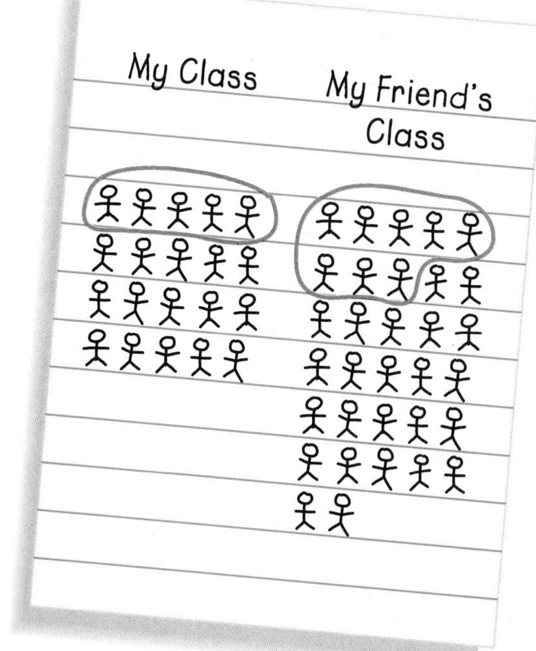

You sign up 5 students in your class of 20 as volunteers for the cleanup club. A friend in a different class signs up 8 students from his class of 32. Which of you does a better job of signing up volunteers? Use equivalent fractions to find out.

1. **Decision Making** Decide how to rename each fraction.

2. **Explain Your Thinking** Which method did you choose? Explain your thinking.

3. **Recording Data** Write or draw each step of your solution to show all of your work. Are the two fractions equivalent? Explain.

B. Customary Linear Measurement

Draw a map for a walking tour of the area near your home or school. The total distance of the tour should be about a mile, in your estimation. Mark the beginning and the end of the tour. Mark and label two places along the way. Label the distances in yards between each point you label.

1. **Decision Making** Decide where your tour will begin and end and where your stops will be along the way.

2. **Estimation** Estimate the distance of each segment of the tour in yards.

3. **Recording Data** Mark and label two places. Label the length of each segment of the tour in yards. Make sure they total about a mile.

Math Magazine

Mostly Mosaic **Making a mosaic is like creating a puzzle. Mosaics may be made of pebbles, shells, jewels, or wood. Some have geometric pieces of stone, glass, or tile.**

Small polygons can be fractions of larger polygons. In this mosaic there are small triangles in the hexagons.

Try These!

Use Power Polygons to explore making different mosaic patterns.

1. What shapes fit together well?
2. How many green triangle pieces fit on a hexagon? What fraction of the hexagon is covered by 1 triangle?
3. If you used only triangles in a mosaic, how many more pieces would you need than if you used only hexagons?
4. Create different mosaic designs using hexagons and triangles.

CHAPTERS 1–9

Cumulative Review

Test Prep Strategy: Work Backward from an Answer

Replace the missing number with each choice.

Sheila and Paul each bought notebooks. The total cost of their notebooks was \$4.50. Sheila's cost twice as much as Paul's. How much did her notebook cost?

Ⓐ \$2.00   Ⓑ \$3.00   Ⓒ \$4.00   Ⓓ \$5.00

STAY SHARP!

You can work backward from the total of \$4.50 to find how much Sheila's notebook cost. If Sheila paid \$3.00, Paul paid \$1.50. The total would be \$4.50, so the answer is Ⓑ.

Write the letter of each correct answer. You may work backward from an answer or use any strategy to help.

Test Prep Strategies

- Read Carefully
- Follow Directions
- Make Smart Choices
- Eliminate Choices
- Work Backward from an Answer

1. Roberto had \$3.50 after his brother gave him \$1.25. How much money did he have before his brother gave him the money?

   Ⓐ \$5.00   Ⓑ \$4.75   Ⓒ \$2.25   Ⓓ \$2.00

2. 850 people went to 3 shows in all. 300 people went to each of the last 2 shows. How many people went to the first show?

   Ⓐ 150   Ⓑ 250   Ⓒ 550   Ⓓ 1,150

3. Kathy picked a square plot of land for a garden. She put a stake at each corner and used a 32-ft length of string to go around the plot. How long is each side of the square?

   Ⓐ 128 ft   Ⓑ 64 ft   Ⓒ 4 ft   Ⓓ not here

4. Shawn, Rebecca, and Carlos shared a submarine sandwich. Shawn ate $\frac{1}{3}$. Rebecca ate $\frac{1}{2}$. Carlos ate $\frac{2}{12}$. Who ate the most?

   Ⓐ Carlos   Ⓑ Rebecca
   Ⓒ Shawn   Ⓓ Rebecca and Carlos

5. Which of the following is equal to 1,200?

   Ⓐ 3×4 Ⓑ 6×20 Ⓒ 30×40 Ⓓ 600×200

6. Brenda and four friends paid \$140 for five bus tickets. How much was each ticket?

   Ⓐ \$28   Ⓑ \$35   Ⓒ \$560   Ⓓ not here

7. How many 3-ft pieces of rope placed end to end would be as long as one 10-yd piece of rope?

   Ⓐ 4   Ⓑ 5   Ⓒ 10   Ⓓ 30

DATA FILE

Chapter 10

Fraction Operations and Customary Measurement

SECTION A

Adding Fractions

Suppose you ride the New York City subway from Union Square station to Times Square station. About what fraction of the distance will you have gone when you pass the Empire State building?

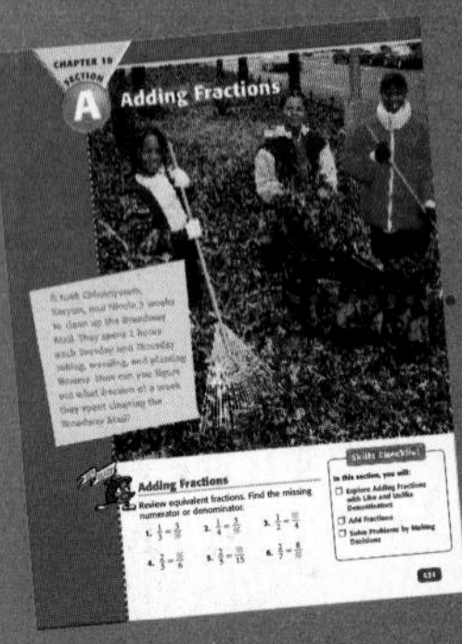

Clean up at the Broadway Mall!
Page 431

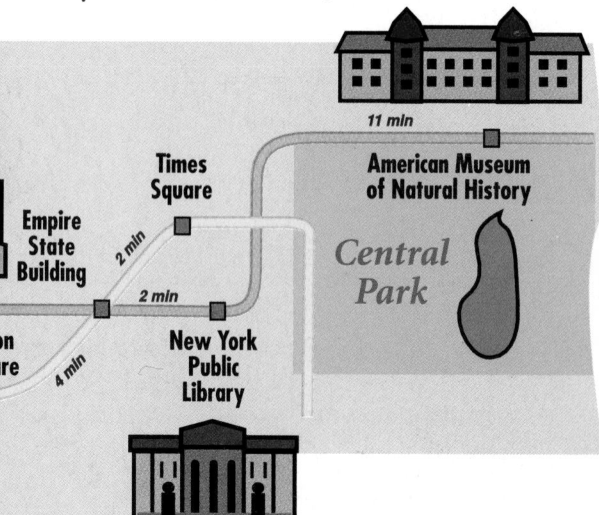

431

Subtracting Fractions

443

The total population of the top 8 U.S. cities in 1990 was about 20 million people. About what fraction of the total population lived in Chicago?

Population of U.S. Cities (1990)	
New York, NY	7,322,564
Los Angeles, CA	3,485,398
Chicago, IL	2,783,726
Houston, TX	1,630,553
Philadelphia, PA	1,585,577
San Diego, CA	1,110,549
Detroit, MI	1,027,974
Dallas, TX	1,007,618

Surfing the World Wide Web!

Check out **www.mathsurf.com/4/ch10** to find data about cities you would like to visit.

Farming in Chicago Page 443

Aquarium life Page 455

Using Customary Measurement

455

Many cities have a special site that symbolizes the city. Which monument is about the height of the St. Louis Arch?

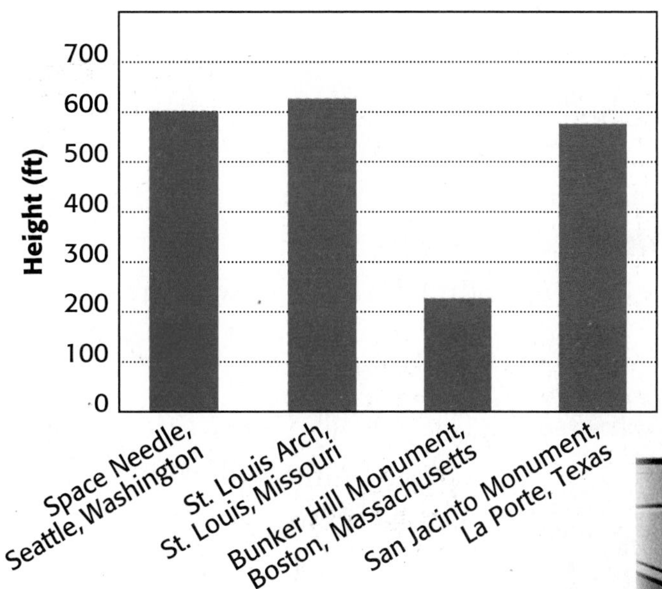

Benjamin Banneker (1731–1806) was an important part of the surveying project of Washington, D.C. He helped design the layout of the city.

Materials

large piece of paper, markers, scissors, grid paper, glue stick

Washington, D.C., was a planned city laid out on a grid. Other cities, such as Los Angeles, California, grew without a plan as people slowly moved in.

Help design a city of the future: $\frac{1}{2}$ of the city should be homes, $\frac{1}{4}$ should be parks, $\frac{1}{8}$ should be industry, and $\frac{1}{8}$ should be stores.

Make a Plan

- Talk with your team about how cities are laid out.
- Will you plan a downtown or will stores be next to homes?
- Will you design one large park or several small ones?

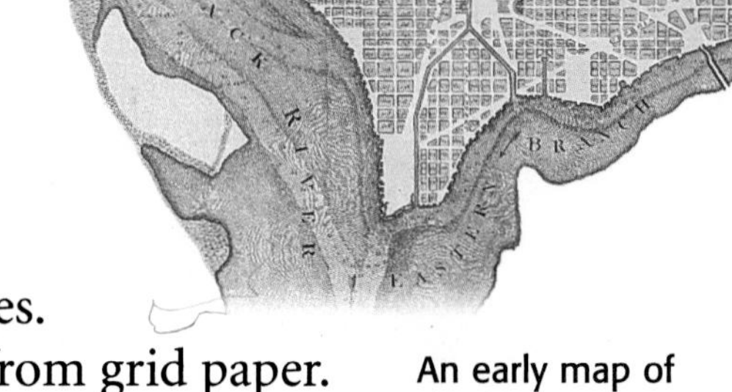

An early map of Washington, D.C., about 1791

Carry It Out

1. Make your city a total of 24 squares. Cut out 24 squares the same size from grid paper.
2. If $\frac{1}{2}$ of the city is to be homes, how many squares will be homes? Figure out how many squares can be used for parks, stores, and industry.
3. Color in or draw on the squares to show what they are.
4. To make your city plan, glue the squares onto a large piece of paper.

Talk About It

- How did you figure out how many squares would be used for each part of the city?

Present the Project

- Display the plans on the wall. How are the cities different? Which city would you like to live in?

CHAPTER 10

SECTION

A Adding Fractions

It took Chinonyerem, Karyms, and Nicole 2 weeks to clean up the Broadway Mall. They spent 2 hours each Tuesday and Thursday raking, weeding, and planting flowers. How can you figure out what fraction of a week they spent cleaning the Broadway Mall?

GET READY!

Adding Fractions

Review equivalent fractions. Find the missing numerator or denominator.

1. $\frac{1}{3} = \frac{3}{\square}$ **2.** $\frac{1}{4} = \frac{3}{\square}$ **3.** $\frac{1}{2} = \frac{\square}{4}$

4. $\frac{2}{3} = \frac{\square}{6}$ **5.** $\frac{2}{5} = \frac{\square}{15}$ **6.** $\frac{2}{7} = \frac{8}{\square}$

Skills Checklist

In this section, you will:

- ❒ Explore Adding Fractions with Like and Unlike Denominators
- ❒ Add Fractions
- ❒ Solve Problems by Making Decisions

Chapter 10
Lesson
1

Exploring Adding Fractions with Like Denominators

Problem Solving Connection
Use Objects/
Act It Out

Materials
fraction strips

Remember
$\frac{3}{4} \begin{array}{l}\rightarrow \text{numerator} \\ \rightarrow \text{denominator}\end{array}$

Explore

You can use fraction strips to add fractions when they have like denominators.

Work Together

1. Use $\frac{1}{6}$ fraction strips to find $\frac{3}{6} + \frac{2}{6}$.
   a. How many $\frac{1}{6}$ strips do you need to show $\frac{3}{6}$? To show $\frac{2}{6}$?
   b. How many $\frac{1}{6}$ strips do you need to show the sum of $\frac{3}{6}$ and $\frac{2}{6}$?
   c. Write the sum as a fraction. Use the number of $\frac{1}{6}$ strips as the numerator. Since each strip is a sixth, what number would you use as the denominator?
2. Use $\frac{1}{8}$ fraction strips to find $\frac{1}{8} + \frac{5}{8}$. How many $\frac{1}{8}$ strips do you need to show $\frac{5}{8}$? To show $\frac{1}{8} + \frac{5}{8}$? Write the sum as a fraction.
3. Find $\frac{5}{12} + \frac{7}{12}$. Use fraction strips to check.

Talk About It

4. If two fractions each have 4 as a denominator, how would you find their sum?
5. What fraction strips would you use to find $\frac{3}{10} + \frac{7}{10}$? Explain.

Connect

To add fractions with like denominators, first add the numerators. Use the same denominator. Simplify if possible.

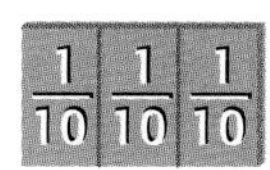

$$\frac{5}{10} + \frac{3}{10} = \frac{8}{10} \text{ or } \frac{4}{5}$$

Math Tip
To simplify means to write a fraction in simplest form.

Practice

Copy and complete.

1. $\frac{1}{3} + \frac{1}{■} = \frac{■}{3}$

2. $\frac{2}{■} + \frac{■}{■} = \frac{■}{■}$

Find each sum. Simplify. Use fraction strips or draw pictures to help.

3. $\frac{2}{4} + \frac{1}{4}$
4. $\frac{2}{6} + \frac{1}{6}$
5. $\frac{3}{8} + \frac{1}{8}$
6. $\frac{1}{12} + \frac{7}{12}$
7. $\frac{5}{8} + \frac{1}{8}$
8. $\frac{7}{10} + \frac{1}{10}$
9. $\frac{1}{6} + \frac{5}{6}$
10. $\frac{1}{5} + \frac{1}{5}$
11. $\frac{1}{3} + \frac{2}{3}$
12. $\frac{1}{8} + \frac{1}{8}$
13. $\frac{1}{4} + \frac{1}{4}$
14. $\frac{1}{6} + \frac{1}{6}$
15. $\frac{1}{12} + \frac{5}{12}$

Algebra Readiness Copy and complete.

16. $\frac{1}{5} + n = \frac{4}{5}$
17. $n + \frac{3}{12} = \frac{10}{12}$
18. $n + \frac{3}{10} = \frac{5}{10}$
19. $\frac{1}{8} + n = \frac{5}{8}$
20. How many addition problems can you write that use two fractions and have a sum of $\frac{7}{7}$? Explain.

Using Data Use the Data File on page 428.

21. What fraction of an hour does it take to ride the subway from the Washington Square Park to the Empire State Building?

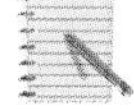

22. **Journal** Describe the steps you use when you add fractions that have like denominators.

Exploring Adding Fractions with Unlike Denominators

Problem Solving Connection
Use Objects/
Act It Out

Materials
fraction strips

Remember
You can match fraction strips to show equivalent fractions.

Explore

You can use fraction strips to add fractions when they have unlike denominators.

Work Together

1. Use fraction strips to find $\frac{1}{8} + \frac{1}{4}$.
   - a. You need like denominators to add. Rename $\frac{1}{4}$ as an equivalent fraction $\frac{2}{8}$.
   - b. Find the sum of $\frac{1}{8} + \frac{2}{8}$.
2. Use fraction strips to find $\frac{3}{10} + \frac{2}{5}$.
   - a. Decide which fraction, $\frac{3}{10}$ or $\frac{2}{5}$, to rename as an equivalent fraction.
   - b. Find an equivalent fraction.
   - c. Write the sum of $\frac{3}{10} + \frac{2}{5}$.

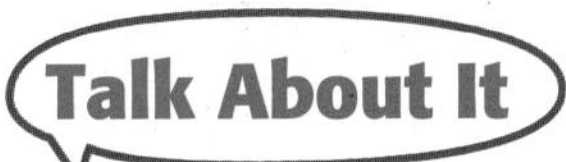

Which fraction would you rename to add $\frac{1}{2}$ and $\frac{3}{8}$? Explain.

Connect

To add fractions with unlike denominators, first find equivalent fractions that have like denominators.

$\frac{1}{3}$	$\frac{1}{6}$	$\frac{1}{6}$	$\frac{1}{6}$

$\frac{1}{3} + \frac{3}{6} = \blacksquare$

↓

$\frac{1}{6}$	$\frac{1}{6}$	$\frac{1}{6}$	$\frac{1}{6}$	$\frac{1}{6}$

$\frac{2}{6} + \frac{3}{6} = \frac{5}{6}$

Here are some fraction strips you can use to rename fractions as equivalent fractions.

1							
$\frac{1}{2}$				$\frac{1}{2}$			
$\frac{1}{4}$		$\frac{1}{4}$		$\frac{1}{4}$		$\frac{1}{4}$	
$\frac{1}{8}$	$\frac{1}{8}$	$\frac{1}{8}$	$\frac{1}{8}$	$\frac{1}{8}$	$\frac{1}{8}$	$\frac{1}{8}$	$\frac{1}{8}$

1											
$\frac{1}{3}$				$\frac{1}{3}$				$\frac{1}{3}$			
$\frac{1}{6}$		$\frac{1}{6}$		$\frac{1}{6}$		$\frac{1}{6}$		$\frac{1}{6}$		$\frac{1}{6}$	
$\frac{1}{12}$	$\frac{1}{12}$	$\frac{1}{12}$	$\frac{1}{12}$	$\frac{1}{12}$	$\frac{1}{12}$	$\frac{1}{12}$	$\frac{1}{12}$	$\frac{1}{12}$	$\frac{1}{12}$	$\frac{1}{12}$	$\frac{1}{12}$

Practice

Use fraction strips or draw pictures to help find each sum. Simplify.

$\frac{1}{2}$			$\frac{1}{6}$
$\frac{1}{6}$	$\frac{1}{6}$	$\frac{1}{6}$	$\frac{1}{6}$

$\frac{1}{4}$		$\frac{1}{8}$
$\frac{1}{8}$	$\frac{1}{8}$	$\frac{1}{8}$

1. $\frac{1}{2} + \frac{1}{6}$ or $\frac{\blacksquare}{6} + \frac{1}{6} = \frac{\blacksquare}{\blacksquare} = \frac{\blacksquare}{\blacksquare}$

2. $\frac{1}{4} + \frac{1}{8}$ or $\frac{\blacksquare}{8} + \frac{1}{8} = \frac{\blacksquare}{\blacksquare}$

3. $\frac{1}{2} + \frac{2}{6}$

4. $\frac{1}{3} + \frac{1}{6}$

5. $\frac{1}{4} + \frac{3}{8}$

6. $\frac{5}{12} + \frac{1}{3}$

7. Social Studies Of Los Angeles' 3,500,000 people, $\frac{4}{10}$ are of Hispanic origin and $\frac{1}{10}$ are of Asian origin. These two groups combined make up what fraction of Los Angeles' population?

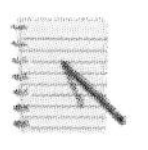

8. Journal How is adding fractions with unlike denominators different from adding with like denominators?

Chapter 10 Lesson 3

Adding Fractions

You Will Learn
how to add fractions with like and unlike denominators

Remember
You can rename a fraction by multiplying.

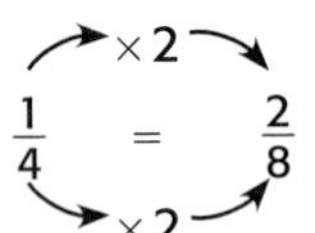

Learn

"You can do it. You can make it look better. Don't give up," says Nicole. Her special interest is to make her community look better.

Nicole lives in New York City. When she was in fourth grade, her class at Ralph Bunche School helped clean up the Broadway Mall.

Example 1

Nicole's class used rakes, big shovels, and small shovels to pick up leaves. If $\frac{1}{5}$ of the tools were big shovels and $\frac{3}{5}$ were small shovels, what fraction of the tools were shovels?

Find $\frac{1}{5} + \frac{3}{5}$.

$$\frac{1}{5} + \frac{3}{5} = \frac{4}{5}$$

$\frac{4}{5}$ of the tools were shovels.

Example 2

Some students found little creatures at the Broadway Mall. Suppose $\frac{1}{4}$ were worms and $\frac{5}{8}$ were beetles. What fraction of the creatures were worms or beetles?

Find $\frac{1}{4} + \frac{5}{8}$.

Rename $\frac{1}{4}$ as $\frac{2}{8}$.

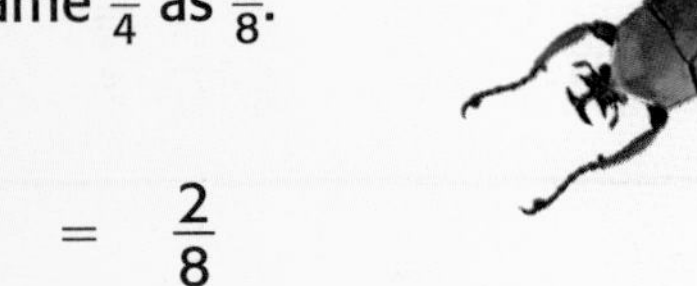

$$\begin{array}{rcr} \frac{1}{4} & = & \frac{2}{8} \\ +\frac{5}{8} & = & +\frac{5}{8} \\ \hline & & \frac{7}{8} \end{array}$$

$\frac{7}{8}$ of the creatures were worms or beetles.

Talk About It

Why did you need to rename $\frac{1}{4}$ as $\frac{2}{8}$?

Check

Copy and complete.

1. $\frac{1}{2} + \frac{1}{4} = \frac{\square}{4}$ **2.** $\frac{1}{4} + \frac{3}{8} = \frac{\square}{8}$ **3.** $\frac{5}{12} + \frac{1}{4} = \frac{\square}{12} = \frac{\square}{3}$

4. Reasoning To add $\frac{2}{3} + \frac{1}{9}$, would you rename $\frac{2}{3}$ or $\frac{1}{9}$? Explain.

Practice

Skills and Reasoning

Find each sum. Simplify.

5. $\frac{1}{2} + \frac{1}{8}$ **6.** $\frac{1}{3} + \frac{1}{6}$ **7.** $\frac{1}{10} + \frac{1}{5}$ **8.** $\frac{2}{3} + \frac{1}{9}$ **9.** $\frac{3}{5} + \frac{1}{5}$

10. $\frac{2}{5} + \frac{5}{10}$ **11.** $\frac{5}{8} + \frac{1}{4}$ **12.** $\frac{3}{10} + \frac{3}{5}$ **13.** $\frac{3}{4} + \frac{1}{4}$ **14.** $\frac{1}{7} + \frac{3}{14}$

15. How much is five-twelfths plus one-half?

Mental Math What would you add to each to get a sum of 1?

16. $\frac{1}{4} + \frac{\square}{\square}$ **17.** $\frac{2}{5} + \frac{\square}{\square}$ **18.** $\frac{7}{9} + \frac{\square}{\square}$ **19.** $\frac{3}{10} + \frac{\square}{\square}$

Problem Solving and Applications

20. What If Nicole spent $\frac{1}{2}$ of an hour raking leaves and $\frac{1}{4}$ of an hour weeding. What fraction of an hour did she spend raking and weeding?

Using Data Use the table to answer **21–23.**

21. How many horses are listed in the table?

22. What fraction of all the horses are Arabians? Palominos?

23. What fraction of all the horses are Arabians or Palominos?

Sunnyside Stables

Breed of Horses	Number
Arabian	18
Saddlebred	8
Palomino	6
Thoroughbred	4

Mixed Review and Test Prep

Copy and complete.

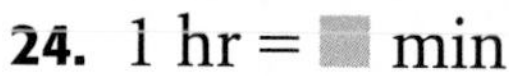

24. 1 hr = $\square$ min **25.** 2 wk = $\square$ days **26.** 60 sec = $\square$ min **27.** 1 yr = $\square$ days

28. Measurement The lengths of the sides of a triangle are given in centimeters. Which triangle has the greatest perimeter?

Ⓐ 3, 4, 5 Ⓑ 3, 3, 4 Ⓒ 3, 5, 7 Ⓓ 2, 5, 6

Cube-er-ators GAME

Players

2 or more

Materials

2 number cubes, each labeled 1–6

Object

The object of the game is to use two fractions and find the greatest sum less than or equal to 1.

Remember

$\frac{5}{2} = 2\frac{1}{2}$

How to Play

1. Choose one player to roll the number cubes.
2. Each player writes two fractions.
   - Use the numbers on the cubes for the two numerators.
   - Choose two *different* numbers from this list to use as denominators: 2, 4, 8, 16.
3. The players add their fractions.

Sample Game

Beth		**Tony**
$\frac{2}{4}, \frac{5}{16}$	←cubes→	$\frac{5}{8}, \frac{2}{16}$
$\frac{2}{4}$	←list→	$\frac{5}{8}$
↓		↓
$\frac{8}{16} + \frac{5}{16} = \frac{13}{16}$		$\frac{10}{16} + \frac{2}{16} = \frac{12}{16}$

Beth's fraction $\frac{13}{16}$ is closest to 1. She scores 1 point.

4 The player with the sum closest to 1, *but not greater than 1,* scores 1 point.

5 A game consists of several rounds. Players take turns rolling the cubes.

Talk About It

1. Why are fractions with denominators of 2, 4, 8, and 16 easy to add?
2. What strategies can you use to find a sum closest to 1?

More Ways to Play

- Play again. Use one of these groups of denominators.

  3, 6, 12, 24
  5, 10, 20, 40
  6, 12, 24, 48

- Use three number cubes. Each player writes and adds three fractions. Use 2, 4, 8, and 16 as denominators.

Reasoning

1. Who scores a point? Why?

Ted	**Etta**
$\frac{2}{4} + \frac{3}{8}$	$\frac{2}{8} + \frac{3}{4}$

2. What fractions would you make with these rolls to get a sum of exactly 1? Use 2, 4, 8, and 16 as denominators.

   a.  

   b.  

Chapter 10
Lesson
4

Problem Solving

Decision Making: Which City Mural to Paint?

You Will Learn
how to use data to make a decision

Explore

Some cities collect unused cans of paint. They give the paint to groups that are doing community projects, such as painting murals. Decide which site you want to paint. Help plan a mural using donated paint.

Paint Collected
Yellow–$\frac{1}{12}$ container
Red–$\frac{1}{6}$ container
Light blue–$\frac{1}{3}$ container
Dark blue–$\frac{1}{4}$ container
Green–$\frac{1}{12}$ container
Purple–$\frac{1}{12}$ container

Paint Coverage
2 containers–720 square feet
$1\frac{1}{2}$ containers–540 square feet
1 container–360 square feet
$\frac{1}{2}$ container–180 square feet
$\frac{1}{4}$ container–90 square feet

Possible Mural Site
School entrance 240 square feet
Bank construction site 420 square feet
Library patio 300 square feet

Murals can add color and beauty to a city. This mural is in San Francisco, California, and was painted by Junipero Serra students.

Work Together

Understand

1. What do you know?
2. What do you need to decide?
3. What information will you need to help you make a decision?

Plan and Solve

4. How many square feet will the paint cover?
5. What color do you have the most of? How much of it do you have?

Make a Decision

6. Decide which mural site to paint.
7. Decide what kind of mural to make. For example, do you have enough green paint to make a mural of a forest?

Present Your Decision

8. Share your decision and sketch a plan for your mural. Explain how the paint available helped you decide which site to paint and what design to use.

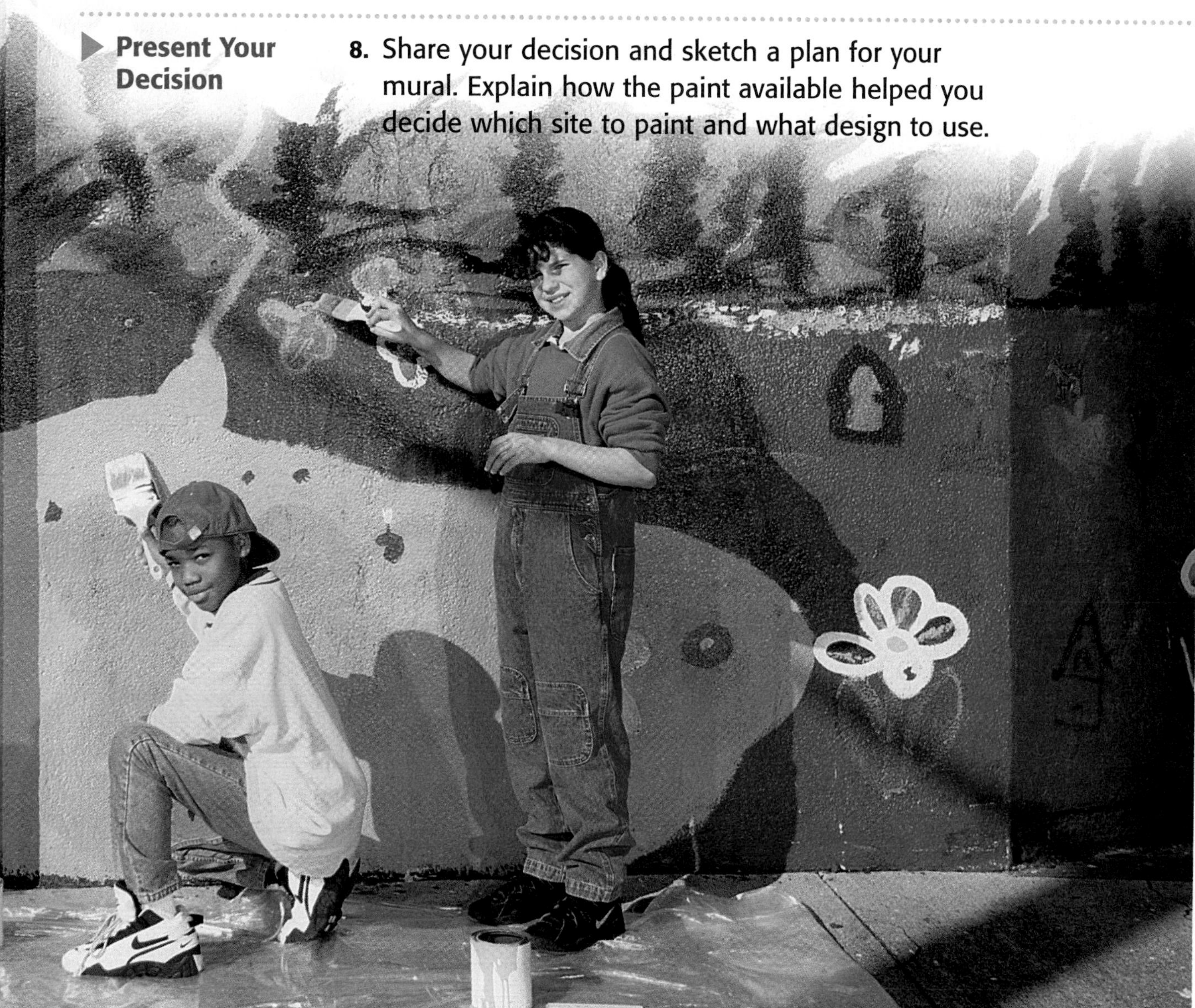

SECTION A

Review and Practice

(Lesson 1) Find each sum. Simplify.

1. $\frac{1}{3} + \frac{2}{3}$ **2.** $\frac{3}{5} + \frac{1}{5}$ **3.** $\frac{1}{8} + \frac{5}{8}$ **4.** $\frac{5}{6} + \frac{1}{6}$

5. $\frac{3}{7} + \frac{2}{7}$ **6.** $\frac{2}{9} + \frac{4}{9}$ **7.** $\frac{3}{10} + \frac{6}{10}$ **8.** $\frac{1}{4} + \frac{2}{4}$

Algebra Readiness Copy and complete.

9. $\frac{4}{9} + n = \frac{7}{9}$ **10.** $\frac{3}{7} + n = 1$ **11.** $n + \frac{2}{6} = \frac{5}{6}$ **12.** $n + \frac{1}{5} = \frac{4}{5}$

(Lessons 2 and 3) Find each sum. Simplify.

13. $\frac{2}{3} + \frac{1}{6}$ **14.** $\frac{3}{8} + \frac{2}{4}$ **15.** $\frac{2}{8} + \frac{1}{4}$ **16.** $\frac{1}{10} + \frac{1}{5}$

17. $\frac{1}{8} + \frac{3}{4}$ **18.** $\frac{3}{8} + \frac{7}{16}$ **19.** $\frac{1}{4} + \frac{5}{12}$ **20.** $\frac{1}{9} + \frac{2}{3}$

21. $\frac{4}{9} + \frac{1}{3}$ **22.** $\frac{1}{3} + \frac{5}{12}$ **23.** $\frac{3}{16} + \frac{3}{8}$ **24.** $\frac{1}{10} + \frac{4}{5}$

25. $\frac{2}{3} + \frac{1}{12}$ **26.** $\frac{1}{6} + \frac{5}{12}$ **27.** $\frac{3}{5} + \frac{1}{10}$ **28.** $\frac{7}{12} + \frac{1}{4}$

Mental Math What would you add to each to get a sum of 1?

29. $\frac{1}{5} + \frac{■}{■}$ **30.** $\frac{5}{6} + \frac{■}{■}$ **31.** $\frac{3}{8} + \frac{■}{■}$ **32.** $\frac{4}{7} + \frac{■}{■}$

33. Social Studies Of New York City's 7,300,000 people, $\frac{24}{100}$ are of Hispanic origin and $\frac{7}{100}$ are of Asian origin. These two groups combined make up what fraction of New York City's population?

34. Journal Charles has 3 one-gallon containers, each $\frac{2}{5}$ filled with juice. He wants to pour them all into 1 one-gallon container. Explain whether or not this can be done.

Skills Checklist

In this section, you have:

- ☑ **Explored Adding Fractions with Like and Unlike Denominators**
- ☑ **Added Fractions**
- ☑ **Solved Problems by Making Decisions**

CHAPTER 10

SECTION

B Subtracting Fractions

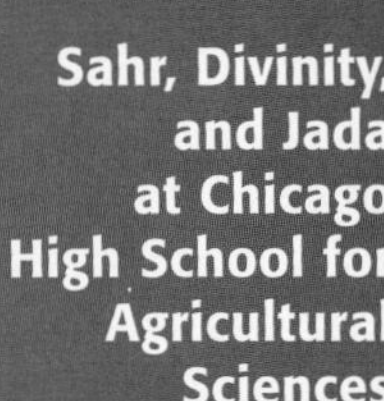

Sahr, Divinity, and Jada at Chicago High School for Agricultural Sciences

In this Chicago classroom there are flowers, lawn mowers, several farm animals, and bags of dirt. In what careers do you think the students are interested?

GET READY!

Subtracting Fractions

Review fractions. Simplify each.

1. $\frac{3}{6}$ **2.** $\frac{6}{12}$ **3.** $\frac{2}{8}$ **4.** $\frac{10}{12}$

5. $\frac{16}{24}$ **6.** $\frac{6}{9}$ **7.** $\frac{3}{15}$ **8.** $\frac{8}{32}$

Skills Checklist

In this section, you will:

- ❒ Explore Subtracting Fractions
- ❒ Subtract Fractions
- ❒ Solve Problems by Choosing an Operation

Exploring Subtracting Fractions

Problem Solving Connection
Use Objects/
Act It Out

Materials
fraction strips

Explore

You can use fraction strips to subtract fractions.

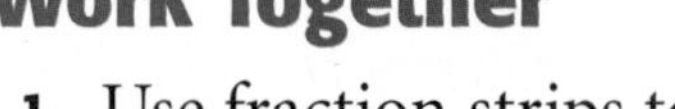

Work Together

1. Use fraction strips to find $\frac{4}{5} - \frac{2}{5}$.
   a. Are the denominators in the fractions alike? Explain.
   b. Compare the number of strips for $\frac{4}{5}$ and $\frac{2}{5}$. What is the difference in the number of strips?
   c. Write the difference of $\frac{4}{5} - \frac{2}{5}$ as a fraction.
2. Use fraction strips to find $\frac{2}{3} - \frac{1}{6}$.
   a. Are the denominators in the fractions alike? Explain.
   b. How can you rewrite one fraction so the fractions have like denominators?
   c. Write the difference of $\frac{2}{3} - \frac{1}{6}$.

Remember
$\frac{4}{5}$ 4 → four parts; 5 → each part is a fifth

Talk About It

3. How would you use fraction strips to find $\frac{1}{2} - \frac{1}{4}$?
4. To subtract $\frac{3}{8}$ from 1, describe which fraction strips you would use for 1.
5. How is subtracting fractions with unlike denominators different from subtracting fractions with like denominators?

Connect

To find the difference of $\frac{3}{4} - \frac{1}{4}$, you can use fraction strips.

$$\frac{3}{4} - \frac{1}{4} = \frac{2}{4} = \frac{1}{2}$$

You can also use fraction strips when you subtract fractions with unlike denominators.

Find $\frac{7}{8} - \frac{1}{2}$.

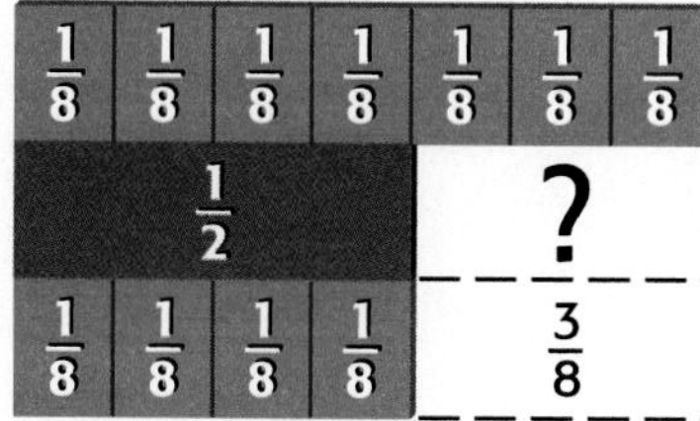

$$\frac{7}{8} - \frac{1}{2} = \blacksquare$$

$$\downarrow$$

$$\frac{7}{8} - \frac{4}{8} = \frac{3}{8}$$

Practice

Write a subtraction problem for each. Find each difference.

1.

2.

3. 

Find each difference. Simplify. Use fraction strips or pictures to help.

4. $\frac{5}{8} - \frac{1}{8}$ **5.** $\frac{9}{10} - \frac{2}{5}$ **6.** $\frac{2}{3} - \frac{1}{3}$ **7.** $\frac{4}{5} - \frac{1}{5}$ **8.** $\frac{7}{8} - \frac{1}{2}$

9. $\frac{7}{12} - \frac{1}{6}$ **10.** $\frac{11}{12} - \frac{3}{4}$ **11.** $\frac{7}{8} - \frac{3}{4}$ **12.** $\frac{5}{6} - \frac{1}{2}$ **13.** $\frac{3}{4} - \frac{1}{2}$

14. Patterns Find each difference.

a. $1 - \frac{1}{4}$ **b.** $1 - \frac{1}{6}$ **c.** $1 - \frac{1}{8}$ **d.** $1 - \frac{1}{12}$ **e.** $1 - \frac{1}{5}$

f. What patterns do you see?

15. Journal Explain how you can use fraction strips to subtract $\frac{1}{6}$ from $\frac{2}{3}$.

Chapter 10
Lesson
6

Subtracting Fractions

You Will Learn
how to subtract fractions

Did You Know?
One-fifth of all jobs in the United States are related to agriculture.

Some Agriculture Jobs:
Farmer
Market researcher
Veterinarian
Florist
Chemist
Environmental scientist
Dietitian
Food scientist

Learn

Chicago's "Farmer High School" is one of two city schools in the United States that focuses on skills needed for careers in agriculture. Students grow gardens, tend animals, and work on lab experiments.

Corn takes up $\frac{3}{8}$ of a school garden. Tomatoes take up $\frac{1}{8}$ of a garden. How much more of the garden is taken up by corn than by tomatoes?

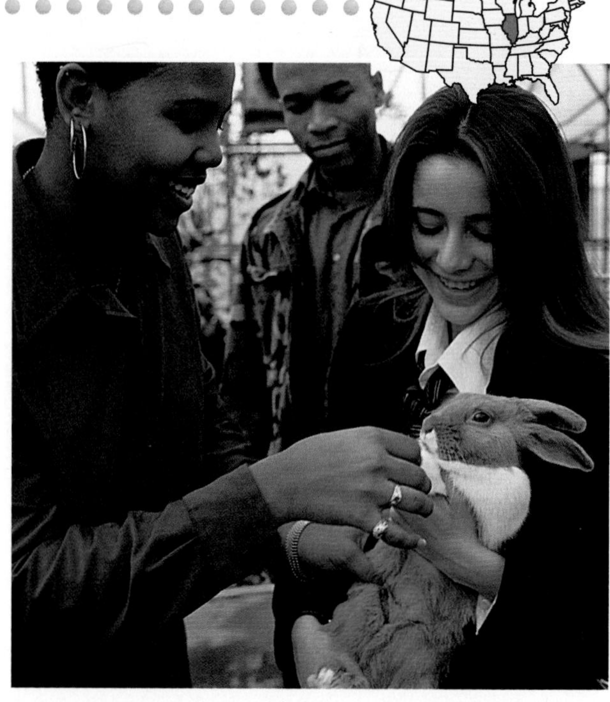

Although Sahr, Divinity, and Jada live in Chicago, Illinois, they share some of the same experiences of students in small towns.

You can use what you know about adding fractions to subtract fractions with like denominators.

Example 1

Find $\frac{3}{8} - \frac{1}{8}$.

$\frac{1}{8}$	$\frac{1}{8}$	$\frac{1}{8}$
$\frac{1}{8}$	?	

$$\frac{3}{8} - \frac{1}{8} = \frac{2}{8}$$

Simplify the answer.

$$\frac{2}{8} = \frac{1}{4} \quad (\div 2)$$

The garden has $\frac{1}{4}$ more corn than tomatoes.

Sometimes, you need to rename a fraction before you can subtract.

Example 2

Jada spends $\frac{1}{12}$ of each day working in the school garden. She spends $\frac{1}{6}$ of each day in class. How much more time does she spend in class than she spends in the garden?

Subtract $\frac{1}{12}$ from $\frac{1}{6}$.

Rename $\frac{1}{6}$ as $\frac{2}{12}$.

$$\begin{array}{rcr} \frac{1}{6} & = & \frac{2}{12} \\ -\frac{1}{12} & = & -\frac{1}{12} \\ \hline & & \frac{1}{12} \end{array}$$

Jada spends $\frac{1}{12}$ more time in class.

Talk About It

1. How would you rename $\frac{3}{5}$ to find $\frac{3}{5} - \frac{3}{10}$?
2. How can you decide whether you need to rename before subtracting?

Check

Copy and complete.

1. $\begin{array}{r} \frac{3}{5} \\ -\frac{2}{5} \\ \hline \frac{\blacksquare}{5} \end{array}$

2. $\begin{array}{r} \frac{5}{8} \\ -\frac{3}{8} \\ \hline \frac{2}{\blacksquare} = \frac{\blacksquare}{4} \end{array}$

3. $\begin{array}{rcr} \frac{3}{4} & = & \frac{3}{4} \\ -\frac{1}{2} & = & -\frac{2}{\blacksquare} \\ \hline & & \frac{\blacksquare}{4} \end{array}$

4. $\begin{array}{rcr} \frac{2}{3} & = & \frac{4}{\blacksquare} \\ -\frac{1}{6} & = & -\frac{1}{6} \\ \hline & & \frac{\blacksquare}{6} = \frac{\blacksquare}{2} \end{array}$

Find each difference. Simplify.

5. $\begin{array}{r} \frac{5}{12} \\ -\frac{1}{12} \\ \hline \end{array}$

6. $\begin{array}{r} \frac{1}{2} \\ -\frac{1}{6} \\ \hline \end{array}$

7. $\begin{array}{r} \frac{5}{6} \\ -\frac{1}{3} \\ \hline \end{array}$

8. $\begin{array}{r} \frac{5}{8} \\ -\frac{1}{4} \\ \hline \end{array}$

9. $\begin{array}{r} \frac{8}{9} \\ -\frac{1}{3} \\ \hline \end{array}$

10. $\frac{3}{4} - \frac{1}{4}$

11. $\frac{5}{7} - \frac{3}{7}$

12. $\frac{2}{3} - \frac{1}{3}$

13. $\frac{4}{5} - \frac{1}{10}$

14. $\frac{1}{2} - \frac{1}{4}$

15. **Reasoning** Jody wants to subtract $\frac{3}{5}$ from 1. How should she rename 1?

Practice

Skills and Reasoning

Find each difference. Simplify.

16. $\begin{array}{r} \frac{2}{3} \\ -\frac{1}{3} \\ \hline \frac{\square}{3} \end{array}$

17. $\begin{array}{r} \frac{5}{8} \\ -\frac{1}{8} \\ \hline \frac{\square}{8} = \frac{\square}{2} \end{array}$

18. $\begin{array}{rcr} \frac{5}{6} & = & \frac{5}{6} \\ -\frac{2}{3} & = & -\frac{\square}{6} \\ \hline & & \frac{\square}{6} \end{array}$

19. $\begin{array}{rcr} \frac{7}{12} & = & \frac{7}{12} \\ -\frac{1}{4} & = & -\frac{3}{\square} \\ \hline & & \frac{\square}{12} = \frac{\square}{3} \end{array}$

20. $\frac{6}{10} - \frac{1}{2}$ **21.** $\frac{7}{10} - \frac{1}{5}$ **22.** $\frac{2}{3} - \frac{1}{6}$ **23.** $\frac{5}{9} - \frac{2}{9}$ **24.** $\frac{7}{10} - \frac{2}{5}$

25. $\frac{3}{4} - \frac{5}{8}$ **26.** $\frac{5}{6} - \frac{2}{3}$ **27.** $\frac{5}{8} - \frac{1}{4}$ **28.** $\frac{11}{12} - \frac{1}{6}$ **29.** $\frac{6}{7} - \frac{2}{7}$

30. $\frac{7}{12} - \frac{1}{6}$ **31.** $\frac{11}{12} - \frac{3}{4}$ **32.** $\frac{7}{8} - \frac{3}{4}$ **33.** $\frac{5}{6} - \frac{1}{2}$ **34.** $\frac{8}{9} - \frac{2}{3}$

35. Without subtracting, explain which is greater, $\frac{7}{8} - \frac{1}{2}$ or $\frac{5}{8} - \frac{1}{2}$.

Problem Solving and Applications

Use the garden plan for **36–39.**

36. What fraction of the plot is tomatoes and zucchini?

37. How much more of the plot is taken up by corn than by peppers?

38. What fraction of the plot is pumpkins?

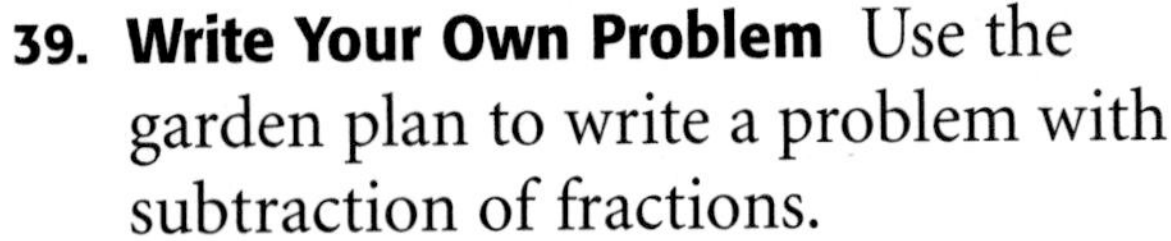

39. Write Your Own Problem Use the garden plan to write a problem with subtraction of fractions.

40. Geography New York City is made up of five boroughs. Two boroughs are on Long Island, one is on Manhattan Island, and one is on Staten Island. What fraction of the boroughs is not on an island?

Problem Solving and HISTORY

Rosa Parks won a Peace Prize for her role in the civil rights movement.

1913	1945	1955	1955
Born August 4, in Tuskegee, Alabama	Allowed to vote, after being denied twice	Arrested for not giving up her seat on a Montgomery city bus	Bus boycott began and lasted 381 days
1956	**1987**	**1991**	**1994**
Supreme Court declared bus segregation unconstitutional	Co-founded the Institute for Self-Development	Statue of Parks is placed in the Smithsonian Museum	Received the Peace Prize in Stockholm, Sweden

41. a. About how many weeks did the bus boycott last?

b. Is that closer to $\frac{1}{2}$ year, 1 year, or $1\frac{1}{2}$ years?

42. Make a time line for the events shown in Parks' life.

a. If each inch stands for 10 years, about how long would your time line be?

b. Would 5 years be shown as $\frac{1}{2}$ in., 1 in., or $1\frac{1}{2}$ in.?

43. How many years after the boycott ended did Rosa Parks receive the Peace Prize?

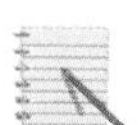

44. Journal How is subtracting fractions with unlike denominators the same as subtracting fractions with like denominators?

Mixed Review and Test Prep

Find each product.

45. 16×5 **46.** 24×8 **47.** 12×12 **48.** 25×20 **49.** 16×33

Find each quotient.

50. $\$8.40 \div 4$ **51.** $\$15 \div 3$ **52.** $\$3.50 \div 5$ **53.** $\$5.40 \div 6$

54. Time Anjali rode the subway for 40 minutes. She got off at 6:14 P.M. What time did she begin her trip?

Ⓐ 4:34 P.M. Ⓑ 5:34 P.M. Ⓒ 6:54 P.M. Ⓓ 5:36 P.M.

Skills Practice Bank, page 572, Set 3

and Practice

Find each sum or difference. Simplify.

1. $\frac{3}{8} + \frac{1}{2}$
2. $\frac{4}{7} - \frac{2}{7}$
3. $\frac{1}{2} + \frac{1}{2}$
4. $\frac{5}{6} + \frac{1}{6}$
5. $\frac{1}{6} + \frac{1}{3}$
6. $\frac{9}{16} - \frac{3}{16}$
7. $\frac{1}{4} + \frac{1}{2}$
8. $\frac{1}{4} + \frac{5}{12}$
9. $\frac{7}{12} - \frac{3}{6}$
10. $\frac{3}{5} + \frac{2}{10}$
11. $\frac{1}{9} + \frac{2}{3}$
12. $\frac{5}{6} - \frac{1}{3}$
13. $\frac{9}{10} - \frac{4}{5}$
14. $\frac{3}{8} + \frac{1}{4}$
15. $\frac{6}{7} - \frac{3}{7}$
16. $\frac{8}{9} - \frac{1}{3}$
17. $\frac{2}{3} + \frac{1}{6}$
18. $\frac{10}{12} - \frac{3}{4}$
19. $\frac{1}{5} + \frac{4}{10}$
20. $\frac{7}{10} - \frac{1}{2}$
21. $\frac{1}{6} + \frac{2}{3}$
22. $\frac{1}{7} + \frac{5}{7}$
23. $\frac{11}{16} - \frac{1}{4}$
24. $\frac{5}{8} - \frac{1}{4}$
25. $\frac{8}{9} - \frac{2}{3}$
26. $\frac{7}{16} - \frac{3}{8}$
27. $\frac{3}{7} + \frac{3}{7}$
28. $\frac{3}{5} + \frac{3}{10}$
29. $\frac{1}{2} + \frac{3}{10}$
30. $\frac{3}{7} + \frac{2}{7}$
31. $\frac{11}{12} - \frac{5}{6}$
32. $\frac{3}{4} - \frac{5}{12}$

Error Search

Find each sum or difference that is not correct. Write it correctly and explain the error.

33. $\frac{1}{6} + \frac{2}{3} = \frac{5}{6}$
34. $\frac{1}{5} + \frac{2}{5} = \frac{3}{10}$
35. $\frac{8}{16} - \frac{2}{8} = \frac{1}{12}$
36. $\frac{5}{8} - \frac{1}{2} = \frac{4}{6}$
37. $\frac{7}{9} - \frac{1}{3} = \frac{9}{4}$

Dusty Riddle!

Add or subtract to solve the riddle. Which ancient city was completely buried by volcanic lava? Match each letter to its answer in the blank below. Some letters are not used.

38. $\frac{3}{5} + \frac{1}{5}$ [B] **39.** $\frac{6}{9} - \frac{1}{3}$ [I]

40. $\frac{5}{16} + \frac{1}{16}$ [S] **41.** $\frac{1}{3} + \frac{3}{12}$ [M]

42. $\frac{8}{9} - \frac{2}{3}$ [R] **43.** $\frac{8}{12} - \frac{2}{4}$ [A]

44. $\frac{2}{7} + \frac{3}{7}$ [V] **45.** $\frac{1}{3} + \frac{1}{6}$ [I]

46. $\frac{10}{12} - \frac{1}{12}$ [O] **47.** $\frac{1}{3} + \frac{1}{15}$ [P]

48. $\frac{5}{9} - \frac{1}{3}$ [F] **49.** $\frac{3}{4} - \frac{1}{2}$ [E]

50. $\frac{8}{12} - \frac{2}{3}$ [L] **51.** $\frac{4}{6} - \frac{1}{2}$ [W]

52. $\frac{6}{16} + \frac{1}{4}$ [P] **53.** $\frac{6}{7} - \frac{1}{7}$ [J]

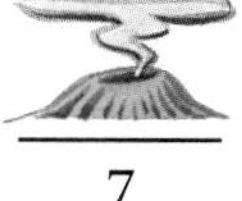

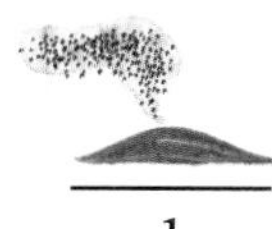

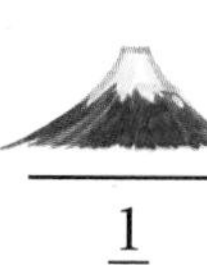

$\frac{2}{5}$	$\frac{3}{4}$	$\frac{7}{12}$	$\frac{5}{8}$	$\frac{1}{4}$	$\frac{1}{2}$	$\frac{1}{3}$

Number Sense Estimation and Reasoning

Replace each fraction with 0, $\frac{1}{2}$, or 1 to estimate the sum or difference.

54. $\frac{11}{12} + \frac{1}{9}$ **55.** $\frac{4}{9} - \frac{5}{12}$ **56.** $\frac{8}{9} + \frac{1}{12}$ **57.** $\frac{12}{12} - \frac{4}{9}$

58. $\frac{12}{12} - \frac{8}{9}$ **59.** $\frac{9}{9} - \frac{7}{12}$ **60.** $\frac{3}{8} + \frac{2}{9}$ **61.** $\frac{5}{6} - \frac{1}{5}$

62. Which is greater in volume, one-half of a pear or one-half of a watermelon?

Analyze Word Problems: Choose an Operation

You Will Learn
how to choose an operation to solve problems

Reading Tip
The action in the problem is to put together the groups of hummingbirds.

Learn

You can visit the hummingbird aviary at the Arizona-Sonora Desert Museum near Tucson.

Suppose $\frac{3}{8}$ of the hummingbirds are violet-crowns, and $\frac{7}{16}$ are blue-throats. What fractional part of the hummingbirds in the aviary are violet-crowns or blue-throats?

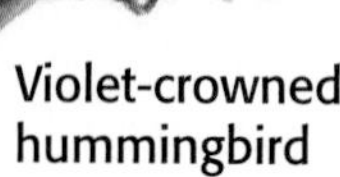

Violet-crowned hummingbird

Work Together

▶ Understand

What do you know?

What do you need to find out?

▶ Plan

Which operation should you use? Since you are finding the total number, you add.

▶ Solve

Find the sum.

$$\frac{7}{16} + \frac{3}{8} = n$$

The denominators are unlike, so rename $\frac{3}{8}$.

$$\downarrow$$

$$\frac{7}{16} + \frac{6}{16} = \frac{13}{16}$$

$\frac{13}{16}$ of all the hummingbirds in the aviary are violet-crowns or blue-throats.

▶ Look Back

How can you check your answer?

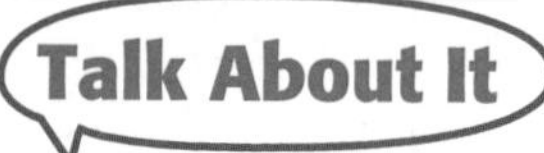

What are some words that tell you to add? To subtract?

Check

Write the operation you would use. Then solve each problem.

1. Michelle practiced the piano for $\frac{1}{2}$ of an hour. Seth practiced for $\frac{1}{4}$ of an hour.
   a. How much total time did they spend practicing?
   b. How much longer did Michelle practice than Seth?

2. Kindra spent $\frac{1}{12}$ of Saturday baby-sitting. Then she spent $\frac{1}{6}$ of the day at the Desert Museum.
   a. Find the difference between the part of the day she visited the museum and the part of the day she baby-sat.
   b. Find the sum of the two parts of the day.
   c. What fraction of Saturday was Kindra not baby-sitting or visiting the museum?

Problem Solving
Understand
Plan
Solve
Look Back

Problem Solving Practice

Use any strategy to solve each problem.

3. David read $\frac{2}{3}$ of a book. He plans to finish the book later. What fraction of the book does he still have to read?

4. **Time** Sarah has lunch at 12:10 P.M. She leaves to go to the park 25 minutes later. She gets there after a 10-minute walk. What time does she arrive at the park?

5. Wilbur buys a bag of popcorn just before boarding the train. By the time he gets to his stop, the bag is about $\frac{1}{4}$ full. What part of the popcorn has he eaten on the train?

6. **Using Data** Use the Data File on page 429. In 1960, New York City's population was 7,781,984.
   a. Find the decrease in New York City's population between 1960 and 1990.
   b. About what fractional part of a million was this decrease?

7. **Science** How much longer is the wingspan of a Western pipistrelle bat than the wingspan of a hog-nosed bat?

Problem Solving Strategies

- Use Objects/Act It Out
- Draw a Picture
- Look for a Pattern
- Guess and Check
- Use Logical Reasoning
- Make an Organized List
- Make a Table
- Solve a Simpler Problem
- Work Backward

Choose a Tool

Western pipistrelle bat

Smallest Bats
World record: Hog-nosed bat Location: Thailand Wingspan: $\frac{13}{24}$ ft
U.S. record: Western pipistrelle Wingspan: $\frac{2}{3}$ ft

Skills Practice Bank, page 572, Set 6

SECTION B

Review and Practice

(Lessons 5 and 6) Find each difference. Simplify.

1. $\frac{6}{7} - \frac{2}{7}$
2. $\frac{11}{12} - \frac{5}{12}$
3. $\frac{4}{5} - \frac{2}{5}$
4. $\frac{3}{4} - \frac{1}{2}$
5. $\frac{5}{7} - \frac{1}{7}$
6. $\frac{7}{9} - \frac{2}{3}$
7. $\frac{7}{12} - \frac{1}{4}$
8. $\frac{2}{3} - \frac{1}{6}$
9. $\frac{4}{8} - \frac{1}{2}$
10. $\frac{3}{5} - \frac{1}{10}$
11. $\frac{3}{4} - \frac{1}{4}$
12. $\frac{5}{8} - \frac{1}{4}$
13. $\frac{2}{7} - \frac{3}{14}$
14. $\frac{5}{6} - \frac{2}{3}$
15. $\frac{1}{4} - \frac{1}{8}$
16. $\frac{9}{16} - \frac{5}{16}$
17. $\frac{3}{4} - \frac{1}{8}$
18. $\frac{1}{2} - \frac{1}{4}$
19. $\frac{5}{7} - \frac{2}{7}$
20. $\frac{7}{15} - \frac{1}{3}$
21. $\frac{7}{10} - \frac{2}{5}$
22. $\frac{3}{4} - \frac{9}{16}$
23. $\frac{7}{8} - \frac{3}{4}$
24. $\frac{11}{12} - \frac{5}{6}$
25. $\frac{7}{9} - \frac{1}{3}$
26. $\frac{5}{12} - \frac{1}{4}$
27. $\frac{7}{12} - \frac{2}{4}$
28. $\frac{5}{10} - \frac{1}{5}$
29. $\frac{7}{8} - \frac{1}{8}$
30. $\frac{9}{10} - \frac{1}{2}$
31. **Reasoning** What fraction must be subtracted from $\frac{11}{12}$ to equal $\frac{3}{4}$?

(Lesson 7) Write the operation you would use. Then solve each problem.

32. Jeremy ran $\frac{2}{5}$ of a mile on Monday. He ran $\frac{4}{5}$ of a mile on Tuesday. How much farther did he run on Tuesday?
33. Alicia walked her dog $\frac{1}{4}$ of a mile on Wednesday and $\frac{3}{8}$ of a mile on Friday. How far is that all together?
34. Troy ate $\frac{1}{4}$ of an apple pie. Later, he ate another $\frac{1}{8}$ of the pie. How much of the pie was left?
35. Ashley needs $\frac{7}{8}$ of a yard of fabric. She buys 2 pieces of fabric measuring $\frac{3}{8}$ and $\frac{1}{4}$ of a yard. Did she buy enough? Explain.
36. **Journal** Explain how subtracting fractions with unlike denominators is the same as adding fractions with unlike denominators.

Skills Checklist

In this section, you have:

- ☑ Explored Subtracting Fractions
- ☑ Subtracted Fractions
- ☑ Solved Problems by Choosing an Operation

REVIEW AND PRACTICE

CHAPTER 10

SECTION

C Using Customary Measurement

Jason Crighton works with these fish in Baltimore's National Aquarium. What units could you use to measure the size of a fish? What units could you use to measure the size of a tank at the aquarium?

GET READY!

Using Customary Measurement

Review comparing fractions. Copy and complete. Write >, <, or =.

1. $\frac{1}{2}$ ● $\frac{3}{4}$
2. $\frac{2}{3}$ ● $\frac{4}{5}$
3. $\frac{2}{5}$ ● $\frac{1}{4}$
4. $\frac{3}{5}$ ● $\frac{5}{6}$
5. $\frac{2}{3}$ ● $\frac{6}{9}$
6. $\frac{3}{8}$ ● $\frac{3}{4}$

Skills Checklist

In this section, you will:

- ❒ Explore Weight and Capacity
- ❒ Change Units of Length, Weight, and Capacity
- ❒ Solve Problems by Drawing a Picture and Making a Table
- ❒ Explore Algebra Using a Balance Scale Model

Chapter 10
Lesson
8

Exploring Weight

Problem Solving Connection
- Use Objects/ Act It Out
- Guess and Check

Materials
- balance scale
- classroom objects

Vocabulary

Customary Units of Weight
ounce (oz)
pound (lb)
ton (T)

scale
instrument used to measure an object's weight

Did You Know?
Our customary units of measure were brought to this country from England more than 300 years ago.

Explore

How can you find out whether one object is heavier than another?

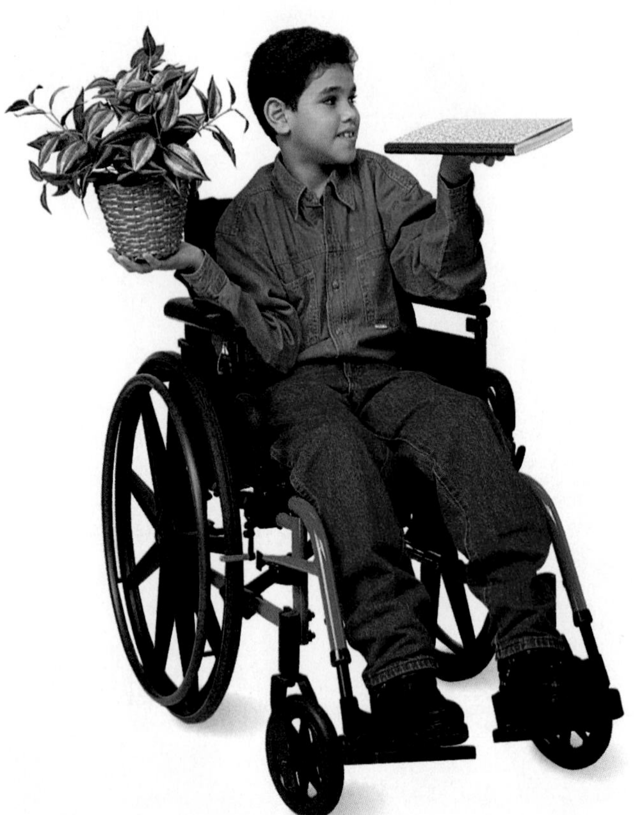

Work Together

Use 5 objects in your classroom and compare their weights.

1. Pick up the objects and decide which is the heaviest, which is the next heaviest, and so on.
2. Arrange the objects in order from heaviest to lightest.
3. Now use a balance **scale**. Compare the weights of the objects you chose. Did you arrange the objects in the correct order?

Talk About It

4. Which weighs more, a dollar bill or a quarter? Does the larger object always weigh more? Explain.
5. Did any of your objects weigh the same? How could you tell?

Connect

Customary units for measuring **weight** are **ounce (oz)**, **pound (lb)** and **ton (T)**. You can use the weights of these common objects to estimate the weights of other objects.

16 oz = 1 lb
2,000 lb = 1 T

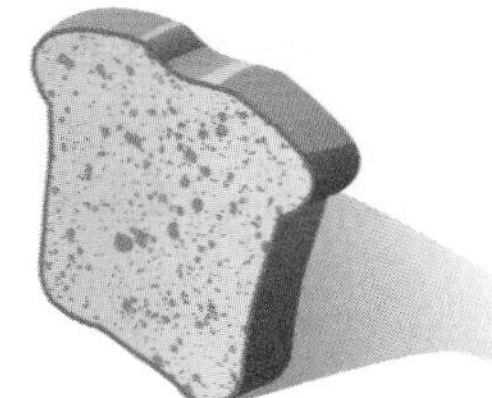

Slice of bread, about 1 oz

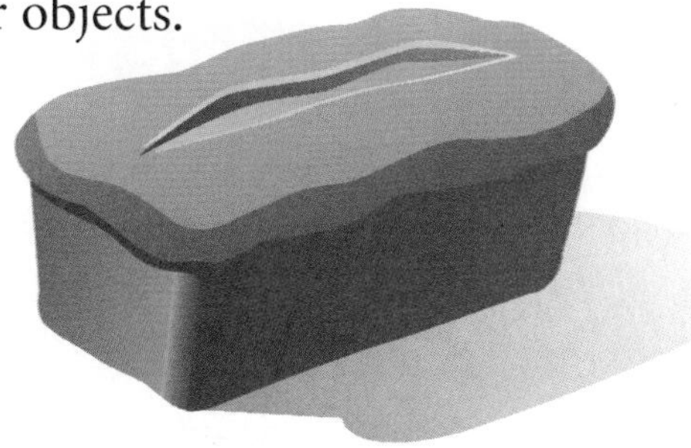

Loaf of bread, about 1 lb

Small bread truck, about 1 T

Practice

Choose a reasonable unit of weight for each. Write oz, lb, or T.

1. 

2. 

3. 

Choose the better estimate for each weight.

4. Cat
7 oz or 7 lb

5. Rat
15 oz or 15 lb

6. Whale
2 T or 2 lb

7. Which weighs more: 10 oz or $\frac{1}{2}$ lb? Explain.

8. Which weighs less: 900 lb or $\frac{1}{2}$ T? Explain.

9. "This box of books weighs a ton!" said Erica's father. What do you think he meant? What do you think a box of 24 math books might weigh?

10. Journal Make a list or draw pictures of grocery items. Explain which unit of measure you would use to weigh each item.

Chapter 10
Lesson
9

Exploring Capacity

Problem Solving Connection

- Use Objects/ Act It Out
- Guess and Check

Materials

- standard containers (c, pt, qt, gal)
- sand

Vocabulary

capacity
the amount a container can hold

Customary Units of Capacity
cup (c)
pint (pt)
quart (qt)
gallon (gal)
fluid ounce (fl oz)
teaspoon (tsp)
tablespoon (tbsp)

Did You Know?

The unit of capacity in the oil industry is the barrel.

1 barrel = 42 gal of oil

Explore

Capacity is the amount a container can hold.
Customary units for measuring capacity are **cup (c)**, **pint (pt)**, **quart (qt)**, and **gallon (gal)**.

1 cup

1 pint

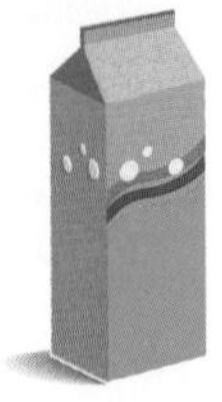
1 quart

1 gallon

Work Together

Find out how much a container can hold.

1. Fill a measuring cup with sand and pour it into a pint container. Can you pour a second cup of sand into the pint container? How many cups does a pint hold?
2. Fill a pint container with sand and pour it into a quart container. How many pints does a quart hold?
3. Fill a quart container with sand and pour it into a gallon container. How many quarts does a gallon hold?

Talk About It

4. How can you tell how many cups there are in 1 quart?
5. How can you tell how many pints there are in 1 gallon?

Connect

A **fluid ounce (fl oz)**, a **teaspoon (tsp)**, and a **tablespoon (tbsp)** are also customary units of capacity. They are often used in cooking.

You can use a table of measures to help you find equivalent units of capacity.

3 teaspoons = 1 tablespoon
2 tablespoons = 1 fluid ounce
8 fluid ounces = 1 cup

2 cups = 1 pint
2 pints = 1 quart
4 quarts = 1 gallon

Practice

Choose a reasonable unit of capacity for each. Write cup, pint, quart, or gallon.

1. 

2. 

3. 

Choose the better estimate for each capacity.

4. Bowl of soup
2 c or 2 gal

5. Can of soda
12 fl oz or 12 c

6. Full bathtub
56 gal or 56 pt

7. Which holds less juice: a gallon container or a 2 quart container?

8. Critical Thinking You can save about 5 gallons of water every day, just by turning off the water while you brush your teeth. Suppose you save 5 gallons of water a day. About how many years will it take you to save enough water to fill a swimming pool that holds 7,000 gallons of water?

9. Journal If you were cooking or shopping for groceries, what cup, pint, quart, and gallon containers might you use or buy?

Skills Practice Bank, page 572, Set 4

Chapter 10 Lesson 10

Changing Units: Length, Weight, and Capacity

You Will Learn
how to change from one unit of length, weight, or capacity to another unit of length, weight, or capacity

Learn

Explore a frosty Icelandic coast, a misty rain forest, or a coral reef in the National Aquarium in Baltimore, Maryland. It has more than 5,000 creatures living in about 2 million gallons of water.

Yellowtail Blue Damsel Fish

When you change smaller units to larger units, you divide.

When you change larger units to smaller units, you multiply.

Example 1

A fish tank in the aquarium is 27 feet long. What is its length in yards?

27 ft = ■ yd

3 feet = 1 yard

$27 \div 3 = 9$

The fish tank is 9 yards long.

Example 2

A fish bowl weighs 2 pounds. Find its weight in ounces.

2 lb = ■ oz

1 pound = 16 ounces

$2 \times 16 = 32$

The fish bowl weighs 32 ounces.

Did You Know?
You need about 5 gallons of water for every 1 inch of fish in a home saltwater aquarium.

Talk About It

Would you multiply or divide to change cups to quarts? Why?

Check

Copy and complete.

1. 4 qt = ■ pt **2.** 3 lb = ■ oz **3.** 15 ft = ■ yd

4. Reasoning Is a quart of fish food greater or less than 6 cups? Explain.

Practice

Skills and Reasoning

Copy and complete. Use the table of measures on page 575.

5. 6 c = ▪ pt **6.** 6,000 lb = ▪ T **7.** 8 ft = ▪ in.

8. 4 tbsp = ▪ tsp **9.** 2 yd = ▪ in. **10.** 8 qt = ▪ gal

11. 3 gal = ▪ qt **12.** 12 tbsp = ▪ fl oz **13.** 12 ft = ▪ yd

14. Would you multiply or divide to change ounces to pounds? Gallons to quarts?

Problem Solving and Applications

An Otter's Meal
10 oz of rock cod
5 oz of shrimp
10 oz of surf clam
4 oz of squid
2 oz of white smelt

Estimation Use the data in the table to answer **15** and **16.**

15. About how many pounds of food does 1 otter eat at each feeding?

16. The otters at the Monterey Aquarium in California eat 4 times per day. About how many pounds of food does 1 otter eat each day?

17. Robbie used 100 quarts of water to fill his fish tank. How many gallons did he use?

18. **Using Data** Use the Data File on page 429. Estimate the height in yards of the San Jacinto Monument in Texas.

19. The table lists the weights of 3 butterfly fish.

a. Write each weight as a fraction of a pound.

b. What fractional part of a pound is the total weight of the three fish?

Fish	Weight
Long-nosed	4 oz
Copperband	6 oz
Raccoon	5 oz

Mixed Review and Test Prep

Copy and complete. Write <, >, or =.

20. $\frac{5}{7}$ ● $\frac{1}{2}$ **21.** $\frac{3}{8}$ ● $\frac{5}{16}$ **22.** $\frac{1}{3}$ ● $\frac{5}{6}$ **23.** $\frac{3}{4}$ ● $\frac{5}{12}$

24. Find the quotient and remainder for 537 ÷ 8.

Ⓐ 4,296 Ⓑ 76 Ⓒ 66 R9 Ⓓ 67 R1

Problem Solving

Compare Strategies: Draw a Picture/ Make a Table

You Will Learn
how to compare strategies

Learn

Out of every six students who visit a museum, two admissions are free. How many tickets are free if 22 students go on a field trip to the museum?

Kelsey and Tanner solved this problem in different ways.

Kelsey's Way

I'll draw 3 rows of 6 students each and have 4 students left over. I'll circle 2 students in each row of 6.

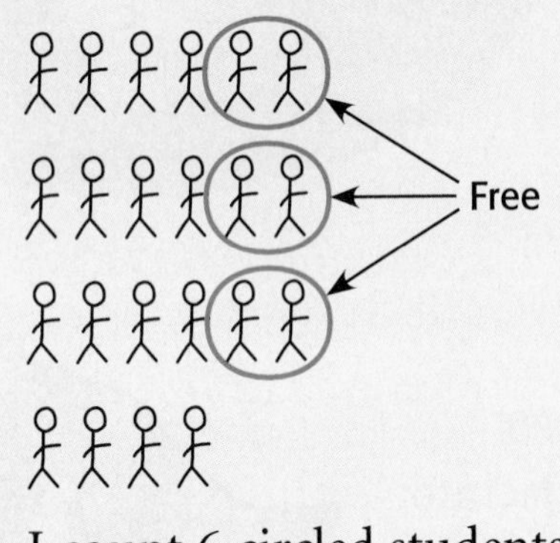

I count 6 circled students. Six students get in free.

Tanner's Way

I can make a table of multiples of 6 students and multiples of 2 free tickets.

Students	6	12	18	24
Free Tickets	2	4	6	8

A group of 22 students is not enough for 8 free tickets.

That's 6 free tickets.

Talk About It

1. Which strategy would be the most helpful to you in solving the problem? Explain.
2. If you were taking 76 students to the museum, which strategy would be most helpful to use? Explain.

Check

Copy and complete the table to help solve the problem.

1. A school required three adult leaders for every 24 students. If 168 students signed up for a field trip to the Alamo, how many adults were needed?

Students	24	48	72	96		144	168	192
Adult leaders	3			12	15			

Problem Solving Practice

Problem Solving Strategies

- Use Objects/Act It Out
- Draw a Picture
- Look for a Pattern
- Guess and Check
- Use Logical Reasoning
- Make an Organized List
- Make a Table
- Solve a Simpler Problem
- Work Backward

Choose a Tool

Use any strategy to solve each problem.

2. For every $75 worth of food receipts, a grocery store gives a school library two new books.
   a. After a class collected $335 worth of receipts, how many new books would they receive?
   b. If the library receives 20 books, how many dollars worth of food receipts were collected?
3. The visitor's center in San Antonio, Texas gives tourists coupons. A trolley tour usually costs $4.50 per child and $8.95 per adult. A family of 2 adults and 3 children plans to use the trolley tour coupon. How much will the tour cost? Use the trolley coupon to solve.

4. In Austin, Texas, Lavaca Street is 4 blocks away from San Jacinto. Congress is between Los Brazos and Colorado. Los Brazos is 1 block from San Jacinto and 2 blocks from Colorado. Write the names of the streets in order.
5. To solve use the coupon from the Witte Museum of Natural Science and History in San Antonio. Which family group would save more: A family with 1 adult and 3 children, or a family with 3 adults and 1 child? Explain.

PROBLEM SOLVING PRACTICE

Chapter 10 Lesson 12

Exploring Algebra: Using a Balance Scale Model

Problem Solving Connection

Use Logical Reasoning

Remember

A number sentence balances when the value of the left side equals the value of the right side.

Explore

A scale is balanced when each side has the same value or weight. You can use this idea and number sense to help you find an unknown value.

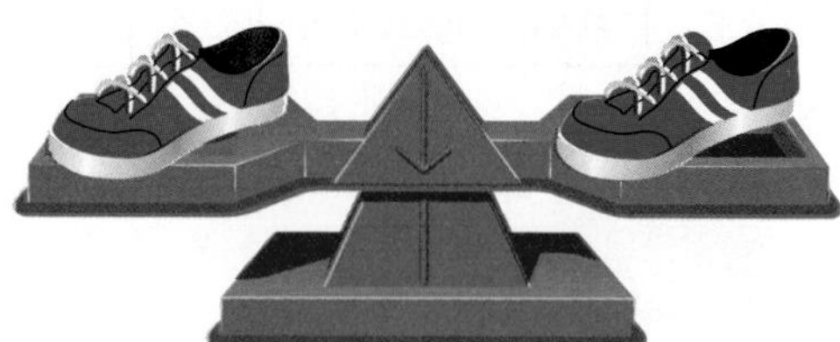

Work Together

1. Look at the scale in the drawing. Is it balanced? Explain.
2. The calculator weighs n ounces. Find the value of n.
3. What would happen to the scale if another calculator with the same weight of n was added to the same side of the scale?
4. Draw a picture to show what happens to the scale if the stapler is taken off the left side of the scale.
5. Draw a scale that is balanced. Show 3 objects on one side and 2 objects on the other side. Label the weights of the objects.

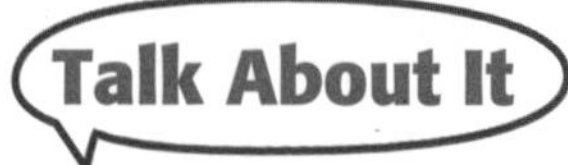

In Step 2, how did you find the weight of the calculator?

Connect

When a scale is balanced, the weight of one side of the scale is equal to the weight of the other side. A scale can be used as a model for a number sentence.

You can write a number sentence for a scale model. Then you can use number sense to find the value of *n*.

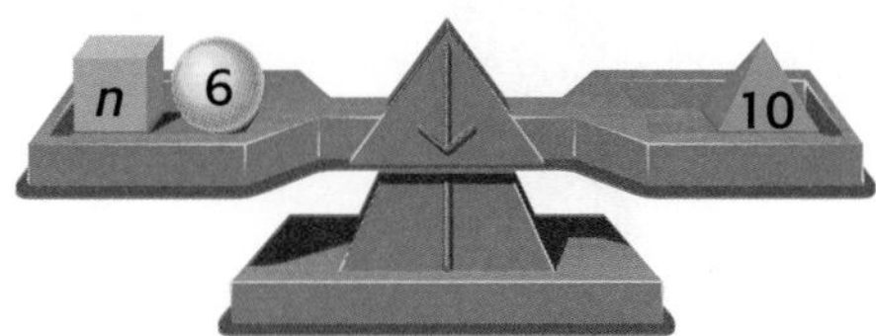

$n + 6 = 10$
So, $n = 4$

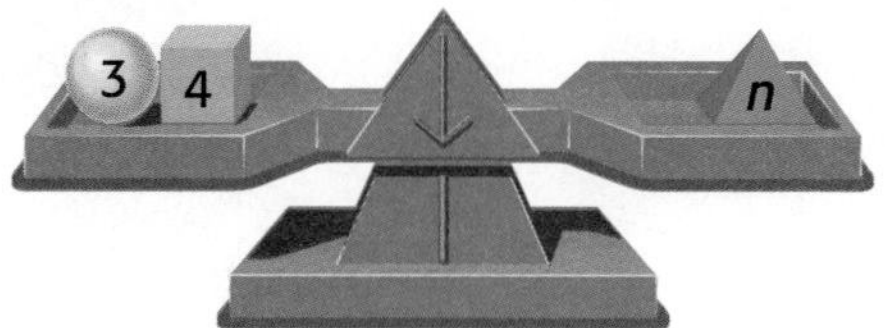

$3 + 4 = n$
So, $n = 7$

Practice

Write a number sentence for each scale model. Then find the value of each *n*.

1.

2.

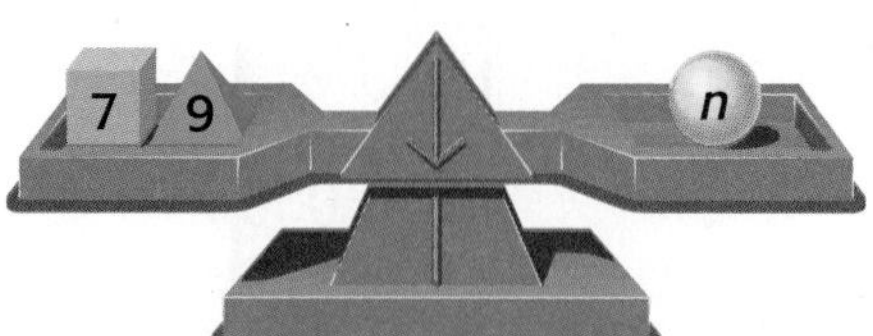

3.

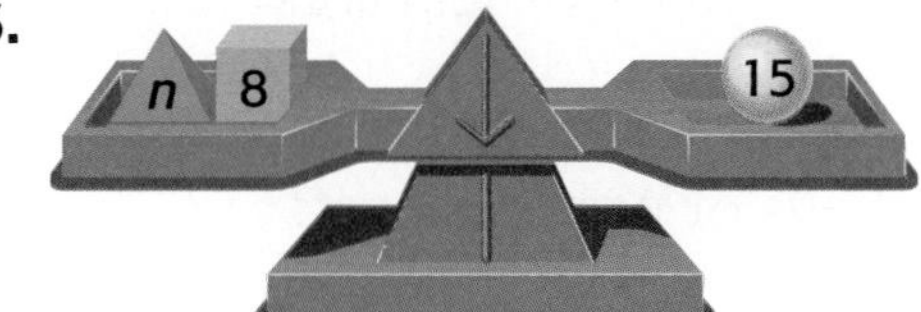

4.

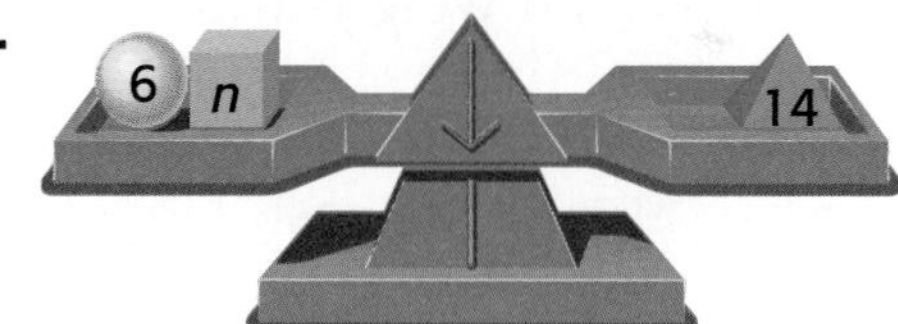

Draw a scale model for each number sentence. Label the weight or value of each object on your scale. Find the value for *n*.

5. $n + 5 = 7$ **6.** $10 + n = 13$ **7.** $7 + 6 = n$ **8.** $3 + n = 11$

9. Critical Thinking Draw a scale model for the number sentence: $n + n = 12$. What is the value for *n*?

Calculator Find the value for *n* in each.

10. $n + 336 = 1{,}048$ **11.** $139 + n = 642$ **12.** $785 + 615 = n$ **13.** $3{,}008 + n = 5{,}374$

14. If you start with a balanced scale and add the same amount of weight to each side, what happens to the scale?

15. Journal Write three different addition number sentences with *n*, 9, and 5. Explain how they are alike and different.

SECTION C

Review and Practice

(Lesson 8) Choose a reasonable unit of weight for each. Write oz, lb, or T.

1. 

2. 

3. 

Choose the better estimate for each weight.

4. Fire helmet
5 T or 5 lb

5. Taxi
1,900 lb or 1,900 oz

6. Brick
4 lb or 4 oz

(Lessons 9 and 10) Copy and complete.

7. 8 pt = ▇ qt

8. 3 gal = ▇ qt

9. 3 yd = ▇ ft

10. 5 ft = ▇ in.

11. 5 yd = ▇ in.

12. 10 lb = ▇ oz

13. 16 c = ▇ gal

14. 6,000 lb = ▇ T

15. 2 qt = ▇ c

16. Would you multiply or divide to change from pounds to ounces?

17. **Reasoning** Which weighs more: 3 lb of apples or 50 oz of feathers?

18. A 10-lb bag of oranges costs $3.50. If you buy 3 bags, you can buy another bag at half the cost. How much do 4 bags of oranges cost?

(Lesson 11) **Patterns** Copy and complete the table. Look for patterns.

19. How many tokens could you get for $10?

Tokens	2	4	6	8		
Cost	$1	$2	$3	$4	$5	$6

(Lesson 12) Draw a scale model for each number sentence. Label the weight or value of each object on your scale. Find the value of *n*.

20. $n + 2 = 8$

21. $4 + n = 7$

22. **Journal** When you weigh an object, explain how you decide whether to use pounds or ounces.

Skills Checklist

In this section, you have:

- ☑ Explored Weight and Capacity
- ☑ Changed Units of Length, Weight, and Capacity
- ☑ Solved Problems by Drawing a Picture and Making a Table
- ☑ Explored Algebra Using a Balance Scale Model

REVIEW AND PRACTICE

Choose at least one. Use what you have learned in this chapter.

1 What's It Worth?

If the green triangle is worth $\frac{1}{2}$¢, what is the value of the fish?

If the yellow hexagon is worth $3.00, what is the value of the green triangle? The red trapezoid?

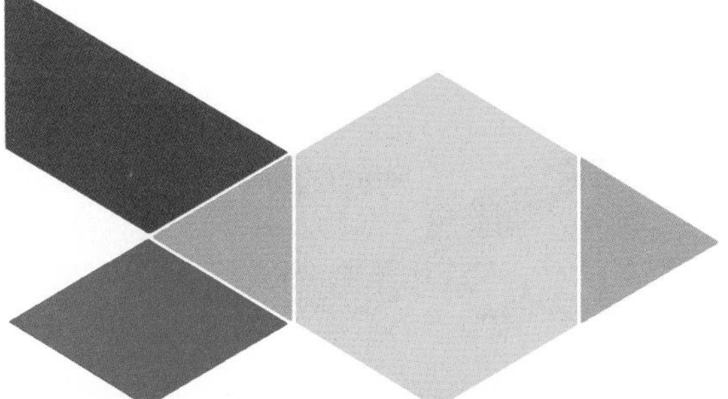

Make your own design with Power Polygons. Give one shape a value. Find the total value of your design.

2 Tile Maker

Design your own square tile on grid paper. Use a variety of figures in the tile. Half of your design should be colored green.

3 Have It Your Way

Choose two objects, such as paper clips, coins, or number cubes to create your own system of weight measurement. Estimate how many of one object it takes to equal the weight of another. Then write three problems asking for one unit to be changed to the other.

1 ruler = 3 crayons

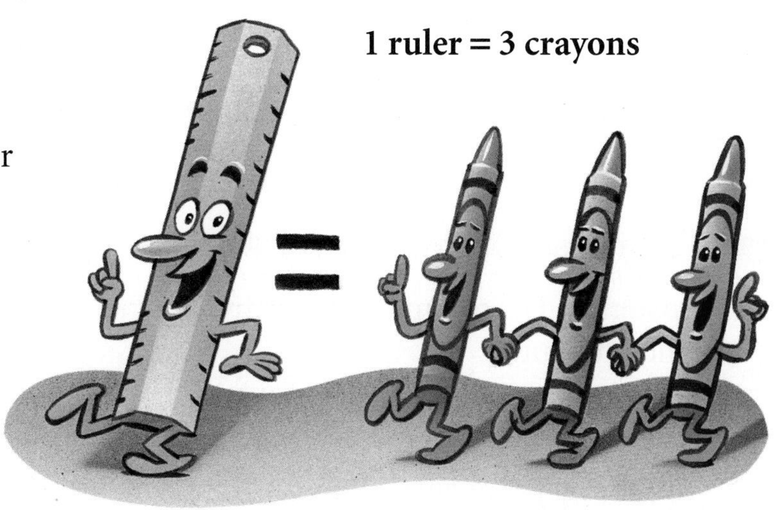

Check out **www.mathsurf.com/4/ch10** to discover some different ways people have measured objects in the past.

4 Grocery List

At Home Work with a friend or family member. Find grocery items with labels of either capacity or weight. Make a list of the measurements. What unit or capacity appears most often in your list? Did you find fractions, decimals, or whole numbers?

CHAPTER 10

Review/Test

(Lessons 1–7) Find each sum or difference. Simplify.

1. $\frac{1}{6} + \frac{4}{6}$ **2.** $\frac{3}{8} + \frac{5}{8}$ **3.** $\frac{1}{10} + \frac{5}{10}$ **4.** $\frac{8}{9} - \frac{2}{9}$ **5.** $\frac{4}{5} - \frac{2}{5}$

6. $\frac{1}{2} - \frac{3}{8}$ **7.** $\frac{2}{3} - \frac{1}{6}$ **8.** $\frac{5}{6} - \frac{1}{12}$ **9.** $\frac{1}{12} + \frac{5}{12}$ **10.** $\frac{1}{3} + \frac{4}{6}$

11. $\frac{4}{5} + \frac{2}{10}$ **12.** $\frac{3}{16} + \frac{3}{4}$ **13.** $\frac{9}{12} - \frac{1}{3}$ **14.** $\frac{3}{5} - \frac{3}{10}$ **15.** $\frac{5}{9} + \frac{1}{3}$

16. James has to walk $\frac{7}{9}$ of a mile to school. If he has walked $\frac{2}{3}$ of a mile, how much farther does he have to walk?

(Lesson 8) Choose the better estimate for each weight.

17.

Ⓐ About 6 lb
Ⓑ About 6 T

18.

Ⓐ About 7 lb
Ⓑ About 7 oz

19.

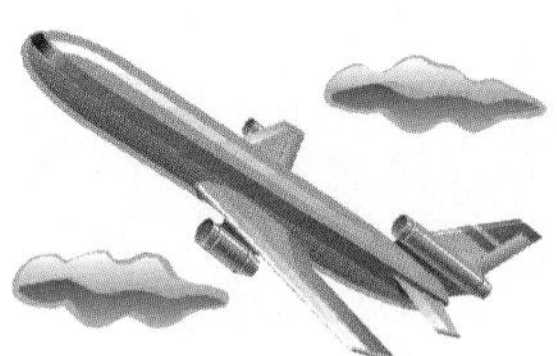

Ⓐ About 200 lb
Ⓑ About 200 T

(Lessons 9–10) Copy and complete.

20. 4,000 lb = ■ T **21.** 7 lb = ■ oz **22.** 16 oz = ■ lb

23. 6 ft = ■ in. **24.** 8 tbsp = ■ fl oz **25.** 18 ft = ■ yd

26. 2 qt = ■ c **27.** 9 yd = ■ in. **28.** 5 gal = ■ qt

29. Which weighs more: 5 T or 1,500 lb? **30.** Which holds less: 5 tsp or 2 tbsp?

31. **Reasoning** Do you multiply or divide when you change fluid ounces to cups?

(Lesson 11) Use any strategy to solve the problem.

32. Out of every 5 people who visit the town fair, 2 admissions are free. How many tickets are free if 16 classmates go together to the fair?

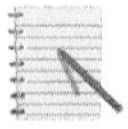

33. **Journal** Explain how you would change 5 pounds to ounces, and how you would change 6 feet to yards.

REVIEW/TEST

CHAPTER 10

Performance Assessment

An old song starts, "Lucky, lucky, lucky me." Two of the lines in the song are:

> "I work 8 hours, I sleep 8 hours,
> I leave 8 hours for fun."

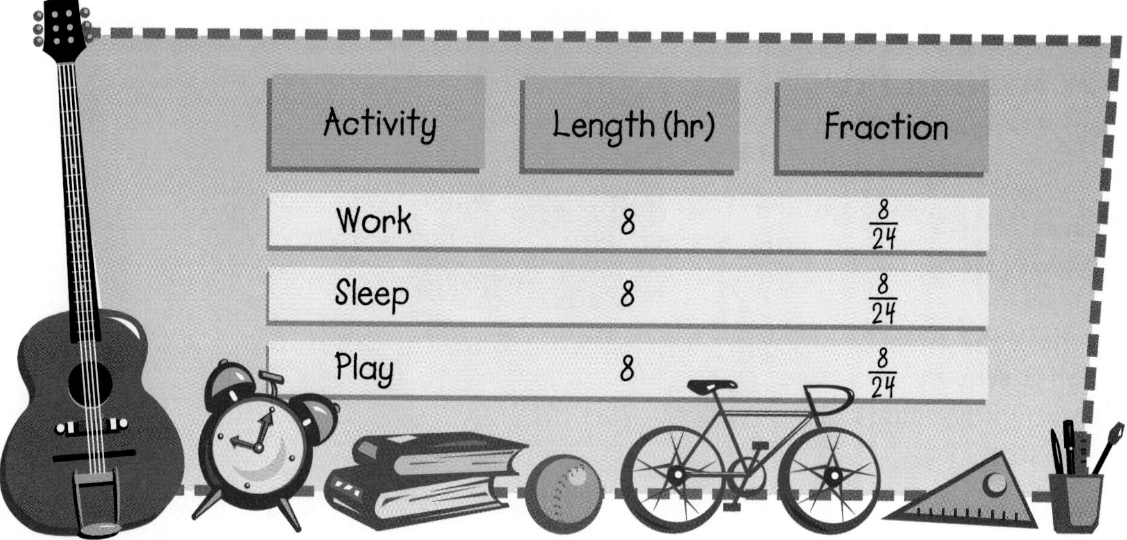

Activity	Length (hr)	Fraction
Work	8	$\frac{8}{24}$
Sleep	8	$\frac{8}{24}$
Play	8	$\frac{8}{24}$

Most people don't have days that divide up quite so neatly. How is a typical day for you divided?

1. **Decision Making** Decide on at least five activities, such as eating and sleeping, into which a typical day for you is divided.

2. **Recording Data** Estimate the length of time (in whole hours) you spend on each activity. The total should equal 24 hours. Then write the fraction of a day you spend on each activity. Use 24 as the denominator.

3. **Using Data**
   - **a.** Choose two activities. Show how to add their fractions to find the fraction of a day you spend on those activities combined.
   - **b.** Choose two other activities. Show how to subtract their fractions to find how much more time is spent on one activity than the other.

4. **Critical Thinking** What is the sum of the fractions for all your activities? Why does that make sense?

Math Magazine

Anasazi Apartments

The idea of building homes on top of one another is an old one. The Anasazi (ah-nuh-SAH-zee), Native Americans lived in the southwest United States 800 years ago. They built their homes under steep cliffs.

Why do you think the Anasazi chose to build on cliffs? Why do you think they chose to build dwellings with more than one story?

Try These!

How do the tallest Anasazi buildings compare with other tall buildings?

Anasazi Dwellings
50 feet tall

Great Pyramid of Cheops
500 feet tall

Sears Tower
1,454 feet tall

1. The Anasazi apartment is $\frac{1}{10}$ the height of the Great Pyramid of Cheops. How many Anasazi apartments would you have to add together to equal the height of the Great Pyramid?

2. The Anasazi apartment is $\frac{1}{30}$ the height of the Sears Tower. How many Anasazi apartments would you have to add together to equal the height of the Sears Tower?

Cumulative Review

The question asks for the difference, so find $\frac{4}{5} - \frac{1}{5}$. The answer is Ⓑ.

Test Prep Strategy: Follow Directions

Answer the question asked.

What is the difference between $\frac{4}{5}$ and $\frac{1}{5}$?

Ⓐ $\frac{5}{5}$ Ⓑ $\frac{3}{5}$ Ⓒ $\frac{5}{10}$ Ⓓ 3

Write the letter of the correct answer. Choose any strategy.

1. What is the median of: 24, 22, 23, 22, 34?
   Ⓐ 23 Ⓑ 22 Ⓒ 12 Ⓓ 25
2. What digit is in the hundreds place in the sum of 1,236 and 9,999?
   Ⓐ 1 Ⓑ 2 Ⓒ 3 Ⓓ 5
3. Which number is divisible by 9?
   Ⓐ 82 Ⓑ 37 Ⓒ 111 Ⓓ 333
4. The tennis coach gave each of her 12 students 6 tennis balls. How many tennis balls is that all together?
   Ⓐ 72 Ⓑ 2 Ⓒ 18 Ⓓ 108
5. Find the product of $3 \times 2 \times 5$.
   Ⓐ 6 Ⓑ 10 Ⓒ 60 Ⓓ 30
6. Peter receives $5.50 for each driveway he shovels. Last week he shoveled 9 driveways. How much money did he earn?
   Ⓐ $55.00 Ⓑ $49.50 Ⓒ $550 Ⓓ $4,950
7. What is the answer when 235 is divided by 8?
   Ⓐ 29 R3 Ⓑ 23 R1 Ⓒ 29 R19 Ⓓ 12 R19
8. Which fraction is not equivalent to $\frac{12}{36}$?
   Ⓐ $\frac{1}{6}$ Ⓑ $\frac{4}{12}$ Ⓒ $\frac{6}{18}$ Ⓓ not here
9. How many pennies would you have if you took $\frac{2}{3}$ of these?
   Ⓐ 3 Ⓑ 9 Ⓒ 6 Ⓓ 4

Test Prep Strategies

- Read Carefully
- Follow Directions
- Make Smart Choices
- Eliminate Choices
- Work Backward from an Answer

REVIEW AND PRACTICE

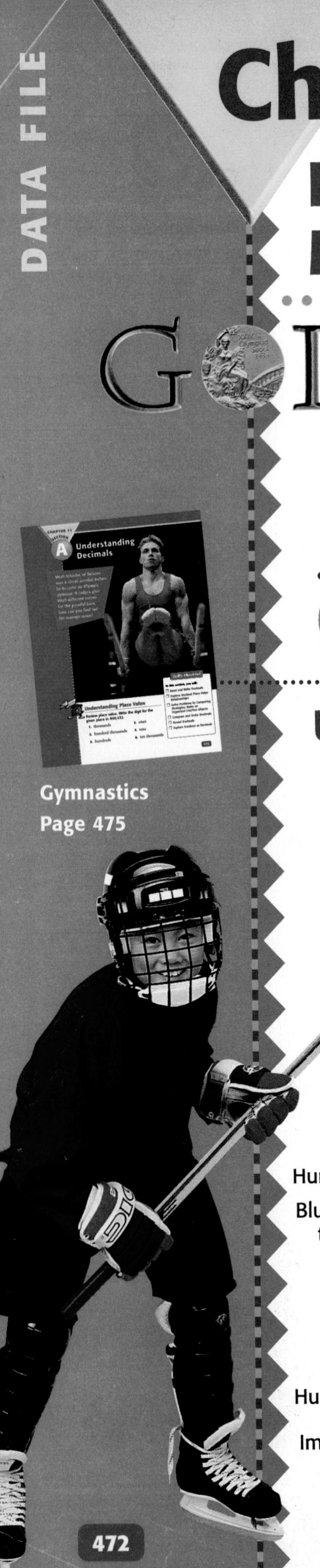

Gymnastics
Page 475

Chapter 11
Decimals and Metric Measurement

SECTION A

Understanding Decimals

475

Olympic athletes strive to be the best. How would they compare, though, if they competed against animals? The bar graphs show records for humans and animals. Who would win each event?

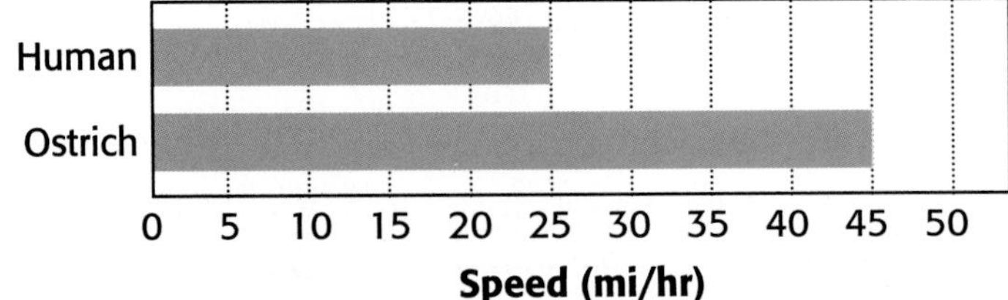

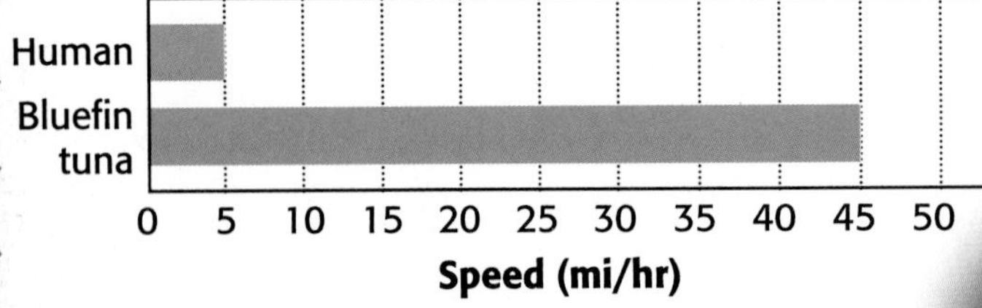

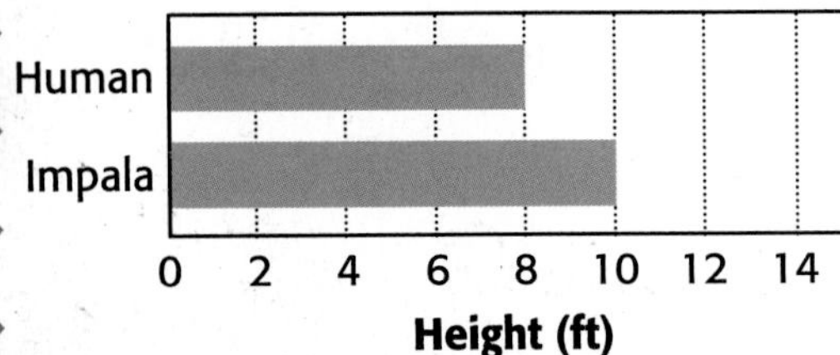

Adding and Subtracting Decimals 491

In the Olympics, first-place winners get gold medals. Second-place winners get silver medals. Third-place winners get bronze medals. In which year did U.S. athletes bring home more silver medals than gold?

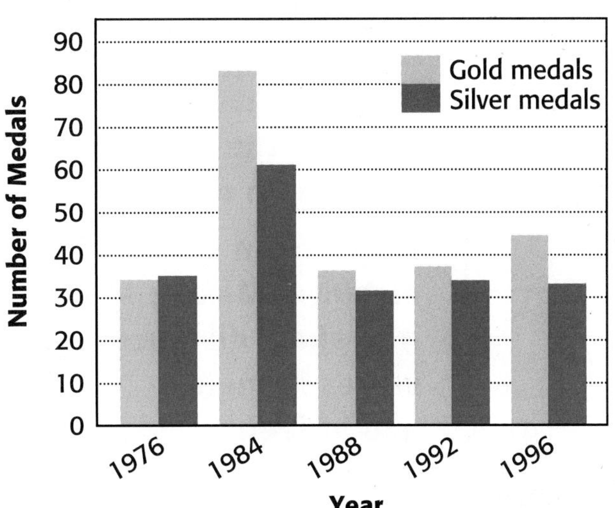

Speed skating
Page 491

Cycling
Page 503

Surfing the World Wide Web!

Which sports would you like to see in the next Olympics? Check out **www.mathsurf.com/4/ch11** to compare your choices with other students' choices.

Using Metric Measurement 503

During the Paralympic Games, physically challenged athletes from all over the world compete in 17 different sports. Which year shows the greatest increase in the number of nations represented?

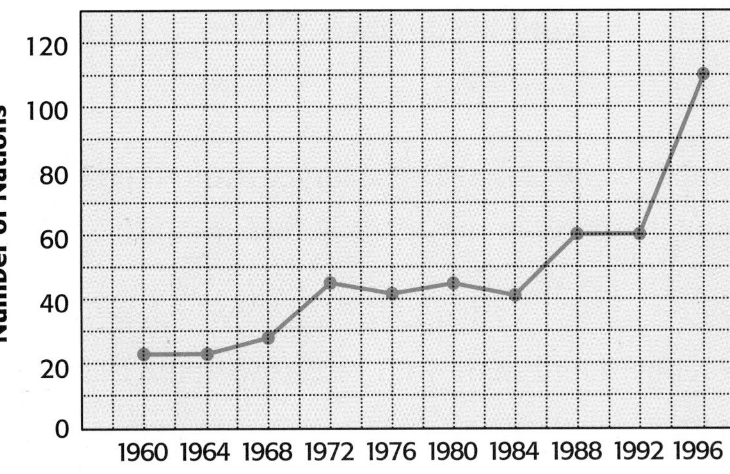

TEAM PROJECT

Olympic Scoreboard

Materials
2-meter sheet of butcher paper, tape, crayon or felt-tip marker, plastic fork, counter, yardstick, meter stick

Robert Beamon set a world record long jump in 1968. Many Americans didn't realize how far he had jumped, because the scoreboard showed the distance in meters.

Play a team game where you measure distance. Make a scoreboard and use it to show distance scores in meters and in feet.

Make a Plan

- Find a good location for your game paper. Tape it to the floor.
- Where will you mark the start line and target point?

Carry It Out

1. Take turns playing this game. Put a counter at the start line. Use a fork to push the counter once toward the target. See how close you can get to the target without passing it.
2. Measure each distance to the nearest hundredth of a meter.
3. Measure again in feet and inches to the nearest $\frac{1}{4}$ inch.
4. Make a scoreboard and record the distances.

Talk About It

- Which team member came closest to the target without passing it?
- Is it easier to compare scores in meters or in feet and inches? Why?

Present the Project

- Display your scoreboard and share your results with the class.
- Discuss why Olympic events are scored the way they are.

CHAPTER 11

SECTION

A Understanding Decimals

Vitali Scherbo of Belarus was a circus acrobat before he became an Olympic gymnast. If judges give Vitali different scores for the parallel bars, how can you find out his average score?

Skills Checklist

In this section, you will:

- ❒ Read and Write Decimals
- ❒ Explore Decimal Place-Value Relationships
- ❒ Solve Problems by Comparing Strategies: Make an Organized List/Use Objects
- ❒ Compare and Order Decimals
- ❒ Round Decimals
- ❒ Explore Fractions as Decimals

GET READY!

Understanding Place Value

Review place value. Write the digit for the given place in 890,432.

1. thousands
2. ones
3. hundred thousands
4. tens
5. hundreds
6. ten thousands

Chapter 11
Lesson
1

Reading and Writing Decimals

You Will Learn
how to read and write decimals using tenths and hundredths

Vocabulary
decimal
a number that uses a decimal point to separate the ones place from the tenths place

Learn

Table tennis is one of the world's most popular games. It became an Olympic sport in 1988. A table tennis ball weighs between 2.4 grams and 2.53 grams. These weights are **decimals**.

You can use a place-value chart to show decimals.

Ones		Tenths	Hundredths
2	.	4	
2	.	5	3

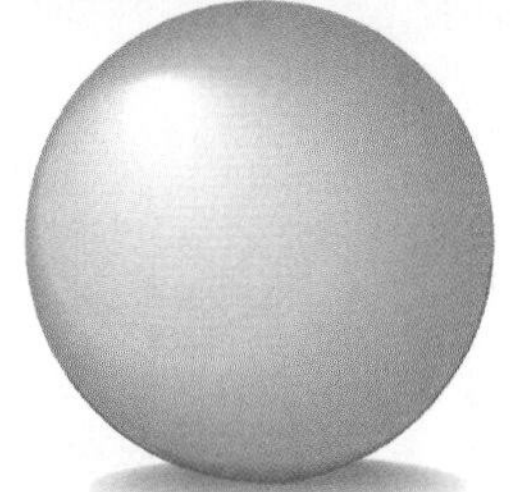

You can write decimals in tenths.

Example 1

In 2.4, the place to the right of the decimal point shows how many tenths.

Read 2.4 as two and four tenths.

You can write the mixed number $2\frac{4}{10}$ as the decimal 2.4.

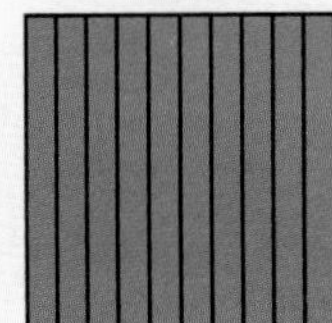 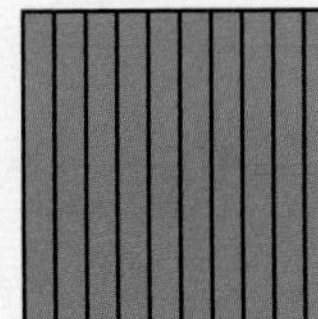 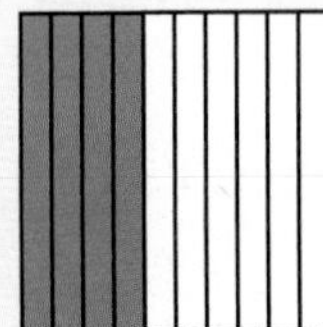

You can also write decimals in hundredths.

Example 2

In 2.53, the places to the right of the decimal point show how many hundredths.

Read 2.53 as two and fifty-three hundredths.

You can write the mixed number $2\frac{53}{100}$ as the decimal 2.53.

  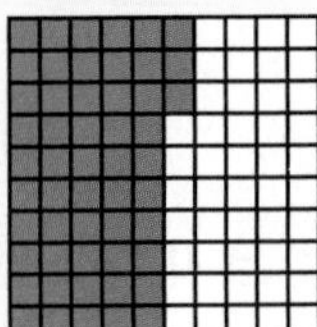

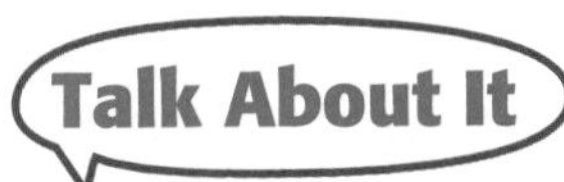

What is the value of each 5 in 2.55?

Check

Write the word name, fraction, and decimal for each shaded part.

1. 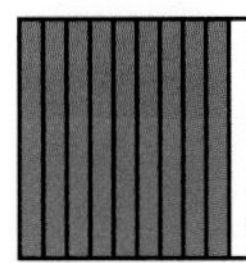

2. 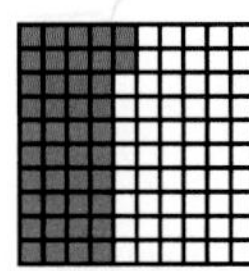

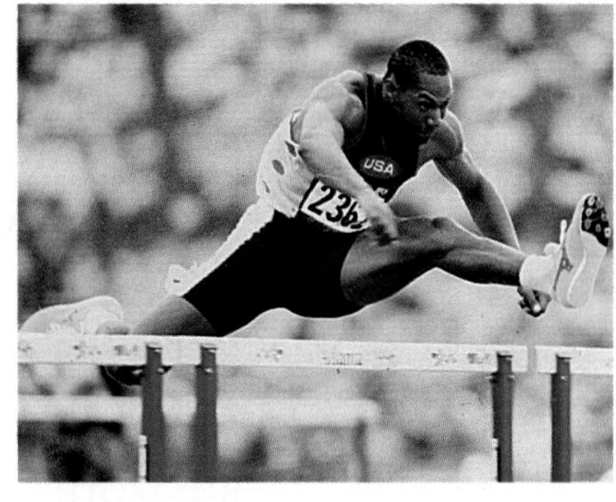

Chris Huffins

3. **Reasoning** The 110-meter hurdles is an Olympic track and field event. Which scores of these top hurdlers have a 5 in the hundredths place?

13.72	13.56	13.45	13.48
13.55	13.95	13.62	

Practice

Skills and Reasoning

Write the word name, fraction, and decimal for each shaded part.

4. 

5. 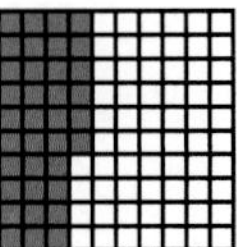

6. 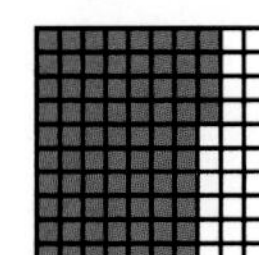

Write the decimal for each.

7. $\frac{58}{100}$ 8. $2\frac{7}{10}$ 9. three and five tenths 10. eighty hundredths

Problem Solving and Applications

Write the decimal for each.

11. yellow tennis balls, compared with the total
12. white tennis balls, compared with the total
13. Copy the number line. Write the missing decimals.

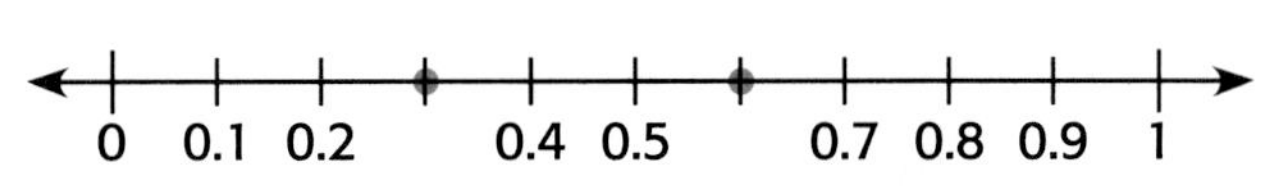

Mixed Review and Test Prep

Algebra Readiness Copy and complete each equivalent fraction.

14. $\frac{1}{2} = \frac{n}{10}$ 15. $\frac{3}{7} = \frac{n}{14}$ 16. $\frac{4}{4} = \frac{n}{8}$ 17. $\frac{3}{4} = \frac{n}{100}$

18. **Geometry** Which polygon has five sides?

Ⓐ pentagon Ⓑ trapezoid Ⓒ rectangle Ⓓ hexagon

Exploring Decimal Place-Value Relationships

Problem Solving Connection
Draw a Picture

Materials
- tenths grid
- hundredths grid

Did You Know?
The *heptathlon* is a 7-event competition for women. The *decathlon* is a 10-event competition for men.

Explore

In 1988, Jackie Joyner-Kersee ran a 200-meter race in 22.3 seconds.

Running times usually are written in hundredths. The decimal 0.3 means three tenths. How can you rewrite 0.3 in hundredths?

In 1988, Jackie Joyner-Kersee won gold medals in the heptathlon and long jump.

Work Together

Use grids to explore tenths and hundredths.

1. Show 0.3 and 0.30.
   - **a.** Shade 3 columns of a tenths grid. How many tenths are shaded?
   - **b.** Shade 3 columns of a hundredths grid. How many hundredths are shaded?
   - **c.** Rewrite 0.3 in hundredths.

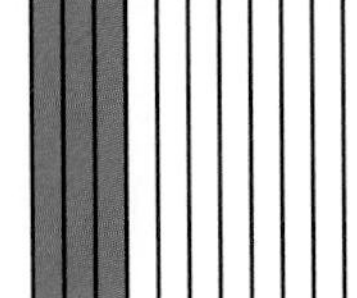

2. Shade 20 squares of a hundredths grid.
   - **a.** How many *tenths* is that?
   - **b.** How can you rewrite 7.20 in tenths?
3. Shade six tenths of a hundredths grid.
   - **a.** How many *hundredths* is that?
   - **b.** Shade more squares until 67 hundredths are shaded. How many more hundredths did you have to shade?

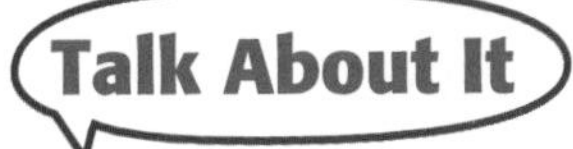

Explain why 3 tenths is the same as 30 hundredths.

Connect

Tenths can be written as hundredths.

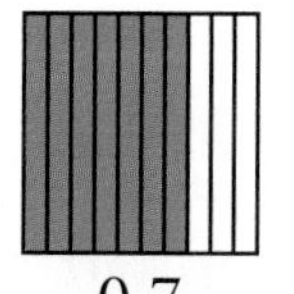

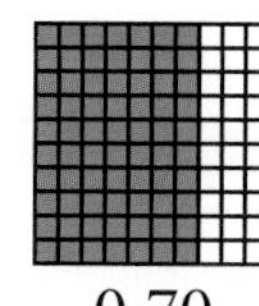

0.7 = 0.70

Money amounts can also be written as hundredths.

$1.00 $0.10 $0.01

Practice

Write two decimals for each.

1. 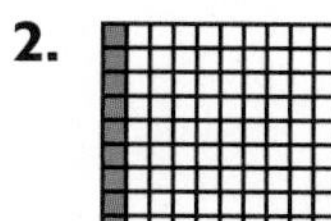

2. 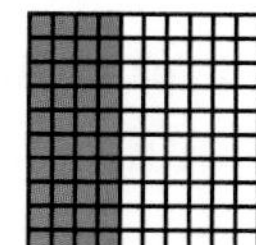

3.

Rewrite each in hundredths.

4. 0.5
5. 4.9
6. 2.6
7. 1.7
8. 13.2
9. 8.3
10. four tenths, one hundredth
11. 8 dimes, 3 pennies

Rewrite each in tenths.

12. 0.20
13. 3.60
14. 5.30
15. 2.40
16. 14.10
17. six and ninety hundredths
18. three dollars and one dime
19. Write $\frac{9}{10}$ in two ways, once with one decimal place, the other with two decimal places.
20. **Using Data** Jackie Joyner-Kersee's best time for the 100-meter race is 12.61 seconds.
    a. Write her time in words.
    b. Did she run the 100-meter race in more or less than 12.5 seconds? Explain.
21. **Math History** The word *decimal* comes from the Latin word *decimus,* meaning "ten." Find two words with the prefix *dec*-. Explain their relationship to ten.

22. **Journal** Greg said that 5.20 is greater than 5.2, because 20 is greater than 2. Was he right? Explain.

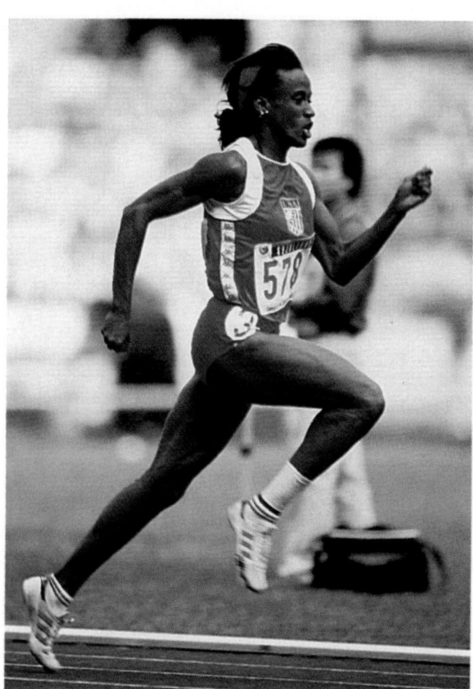

Problem Solving

Compare Strategies: Make an Organized List/Use Objects

You Will Learn
how to compare problem solving strategies

Learn

Many visitors at the 1996 Atlanta Olympics rode buses. A bus ticket cost $1.50. What combinations of some quarters and some dimes could a visitor use to buy a ticket?

Opening ceremonies in 1996 Olympics

Amina and Rebecca solved the problem in different ways.

Amina's Way

I made a list. For each number of quarters, I figured out how much more money was needed. Then I could see which combinations worked.

Quarters	Value	Need	Dimes
1	$0.25	$1.25	Not possible
2	$0.50	$1.00	10
3	$0.75	$0.75	Not possible
4	$1.00	$0.50	5
5	$1.25	$0.25	Not possible

Two combinations:
2 quarters and 10 dimes
4 quarters and 5 dimes

Rebecca's Way

I used objects to find different combinations. I started with 1 quarter and counted up with dimes. I got $1.45 and $1.55 but not $1.50.

Then I started with 2 quarters and counted up with dimes.

"That's $0.50." "$0.60, $0.70, $0.80, ..., $1.50."

Then I tried counting up with dimes from 3, 4, and 5 quarters.

I found two combinations:
2 quarters and 10 dimes
4 quarters and 5 dimes

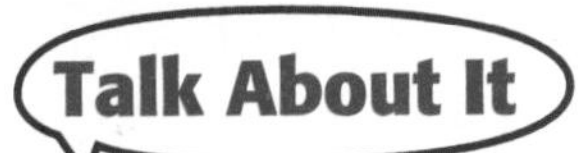

What combinations of some quarters and some dimes total $1.55?

Check

Solve using an organized list or objects.

1. Suppose you have $1.08 in dimes and pennies. What is the fewest coins you could have? What are they?
2. Suppose you have 16 dimes and pennies that total $0.52. How many of each coin do you have?

- Use Objects/Act It Out
- Draw a Picture
- Look for a Pattern
- Guess and Check
- Use Logical Reasoning
- Make an Organized List
- Make a Table
- Solve a Simpler Problem
- Work Backward

Choose a Tool

Use any strategy to solve.

3. Suppose you have the same number of pennies and dimes. The coins total $1.21. How many of each coin do you have?
4. Robert has 1 dollar, 5 quarters, and 3 dimes. Can he buy a sandwich that costs $2.65? Explain.
5. **Logic** To get from the airport to the stadium, the bus driver headed west for 2 miles. He turned right and headed north for 1 mile. Then he turned left and drove 3 miles west until he got to the stadium. How many miles west of the airport is the stadium?

Using Data Use the data from the picture for **6** and **7.**

6. A group of five tourists spent $21.00 to get to the airport. How many children and adults were there?
7. A tour guide paid for 6 adult round trips on the airport stadium bus. He started with $100. How much money did he have left?
8. **Measurement** A girl jogged from her house to the park, a distance of 800 ft. Then she jogged around the 550-ft path in the park twice and jogged home. How many yards did she jog?
9. **Journal** When is making an organized list a good strategy to use?

PROBLEM SOLVING PRACTICE

Comparing and Ordering Decimals

You Will Learn
how to compare and order decimals

Remember
The decimal 0.3 is the same as 0.30.

Learn

Safety comes first, then comfort. All these helmets provide the same protection.

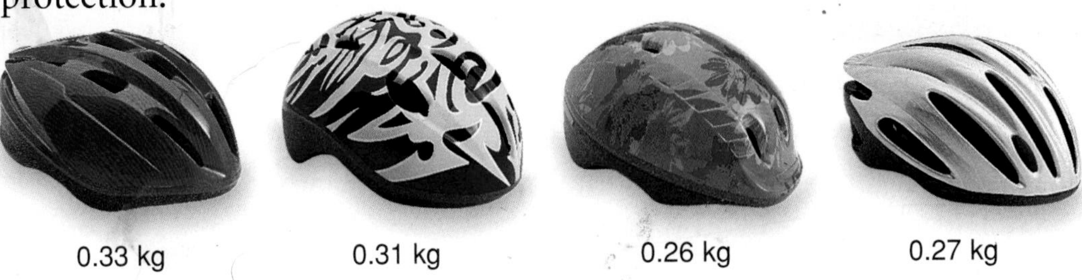

Which is lighter, the 0.33 kg bike helmet or the 0.31 kg skating helmet?

You can use a hundredths grid to compare and order decimals.

Example 1

Compare 0.33 and 0.31.

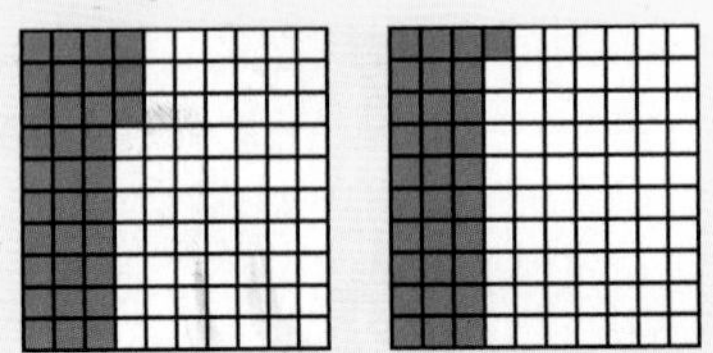

31 hundredths $<$ 33 hundredths
0.31 is less than 0.33.

The skating helmet is lighter.

You can use a number line to compare and order decimals.

Example 2

Order the weights of the four helmets on a number line.

The weights from lightest to heaviest are 0.26 kg, 0.27 kg, 0.31 kg, and 0.33 kg.

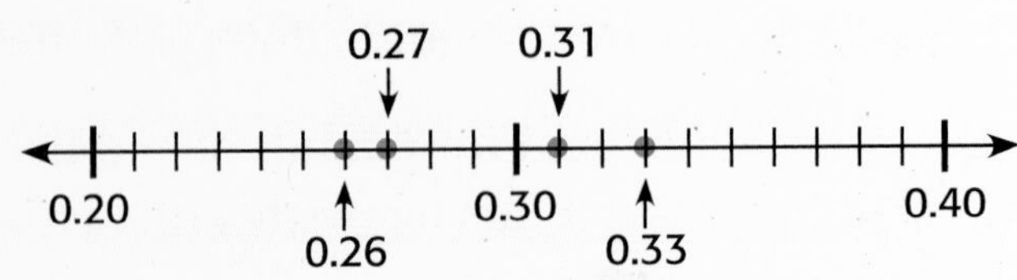

Talk About It

Since $6 > 5$, is $0.26 > 0.35$? Explain.

Check

Copy and complete. Write >, <, or =.

1. 1.26 ● 1.29 **2.** 6.2 ● 6.35 **3.** 0.4 ● 0.40 **4.** 1.3 ● 0.15

5. **Reasoning** Latasha says that since 50 > 5, 0.50 > 0.5. Do you agree? Explain.

Practice

Skills and Reasoning

Copy and complete. Write >, <, or =.

6. 0.60 ● 0.6 **7.** 4.14 ● 3.99 **8.** 2.07 ● 2.12

9. 1.84 ● 1.48 **10.** 3.08 ● 3.80 **11.** 6.41 ● 6.8

Order the decimals from least to greatest. Draw a number line to help.

12. 1.48, 1.82, 1.09, 1.01, 1.98 **13.** 0.84, 0.73, 1.15, 1.51, 0.8

14. Can a number with a 3 in the hundredths place be greater than a number with a 9 in the hundredths place? If so, give an example.

Problem Solving and Applications

Using Data Use the data in the table for **15–17.**

Women's All-Around Gymnastics 1976 Olympics	
Gymnast	**Score**
Olga Korbut	78.03
Lyudmila Tourischeva	78.63
Nelli Kim	78.68
Nadia Comăneci	79.28
Teodora Ungureanu	78.38

15. Copy the number line. Write the name of the gymnast who got each score.

16. Which gymnast got the greatest score?

17. Whose score was greater than Ungureanu's, but less than Kim's?

Mixed Review and Test Prep

STAY SHARP!

Mental Math Find each sum or difference.

18. 187 + 100 **19.** 475 − 325 **20.** 532 + 70 **21.** 200 − 74

22. Find the sum of $\frac{1}{4}$ and $\frac{1}{8}$.

Ⓐ $\frac{3}{8}$ Ⓑ $\frac{2}{32}$ Ⓒ $\frac{3}{12}$ Ⓓ not here

Skills Practice Bank, page 573, Set 1

Chapter 11
Lesson
5

Rounding Decimals

You Will Learn
how to round decimals to a whole number

Remember
If less than 5, round down. If 5 or greater, round up.

Learn

Mary T. Meagher won a gold medal in the 100-meter butterfly with a time of 59.26 seconds. Her best time, however, was 57.93 seconds.

How can you round these times to the nearest whole number?

Mary T. Meagher won three gold medals at the 1984 Olympics.

Example 1

Round 57.93 seconds to the nearest whole number.

57.93

Look at the tenths place.

9 > 5, so round to the next greatest whole number.

57.93 rounds to 58.

To the nearest whole number, her best time was 58 seconds.

Example 2

You can use a number line to round decimals. Round 59.26 seconds to the nearest whole number.
59.26 is between 59 and 60. It is closer to 59.

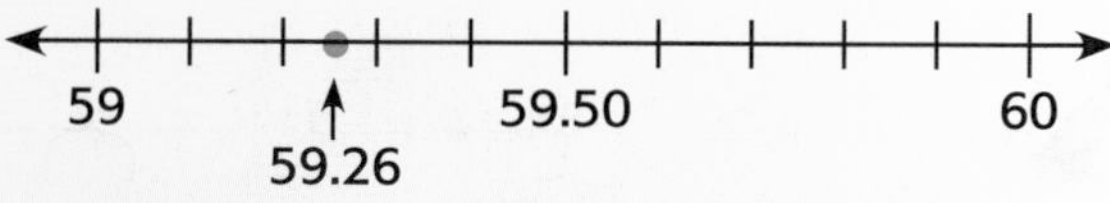

59.26 seconds round to 59 seconds.

If you round 59.99, would you get 59 or 60? Explain.

Check

Round to the nearest whole number. Use a number line to help.

1. 4.7 **2.** 8.2 **3.** 2.93 **4.** 75.28 **5.** 0.81

6. Reasoning Think of decimals that you can round to 15. Write one that is less than 15. Write one that is greater than 15. Both decimals should be in the hundredths.

Practice

Skills and Reasoning

Round to the nearest whole number. Use a number line to help.

7. 5.77	**8.** 4.01	**9.** 0.50	**10.** 109.4	**11.** 4.49
12. 13.13	**13.** 1.25	**14.** 14.51	**15.** 9.99	**16.** 999.89
17. 2.70	**18.** 49.45	**19.** 50.5	**20.** 3.3	**21.** 400.1

22. two and thirty-five hundredths **23.** seven and six hundredths

24. A swimmer's time in the 100-meter backstroke is 58 seconds when rounded to the nearest whole number. Name the fastest and slowest times possible, in decimals to the hundredths place.

Problem Solving and Applications

Choose the two decimals in each set that round to the same whole number. Write the whole number.

25. 3.49, 3.54, 3.44 **26.** 0.53, 1.51, 1.48

Using Data Use the table for **27–29**.

Top Medal Winners, 1992 Olympics			
Team	**Gold**	**Silver**	**Bronze**
Unified Team	45	38	29
United States	37	34	37
Germany	33	21	28
China	16	22	16

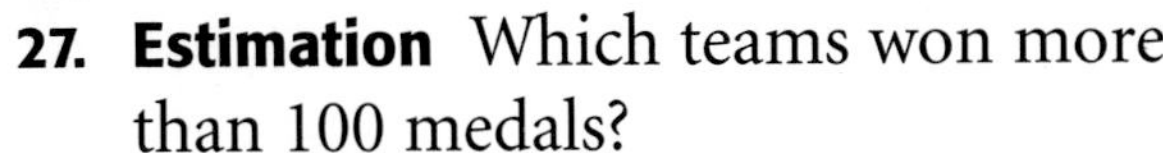

27. Estimation Which teams won more than 100 medals?

28. Which teams won the same number of bronze medals as gold medals?

29. How many total medals did each team get?

30. Mental Math An Olympic swimming pool must be 50 meters long. How many times would an athlete swim the length of the pool during a 1,500 meter race?

Mixed Review and Test Prep

Find each sum.

31. $\frac{3}{10} + \frac{6}{10}$ **32.** $\frac{5}{10} + \frac{5}{10}$ **33.** $\frac{5}{8} + \frac{2}{8}$ **34.** $\frac{5}{12} + \frac{2}{6}$

35. Measurement Two gallons is equal to:

Ⓐ 2 pints Ⓑ 8 pints Ⓒ 2 quarts Ⓓ not here

Exploring Fractions as Decimals

Problem Solving Connection
Draw a Picture

Materials
- hundredths grid
- colored pencils or crayons

Remember
Use multiplication or division to find equivalent fractions.

Explore

You can use grid paper to show fractions as decimals.

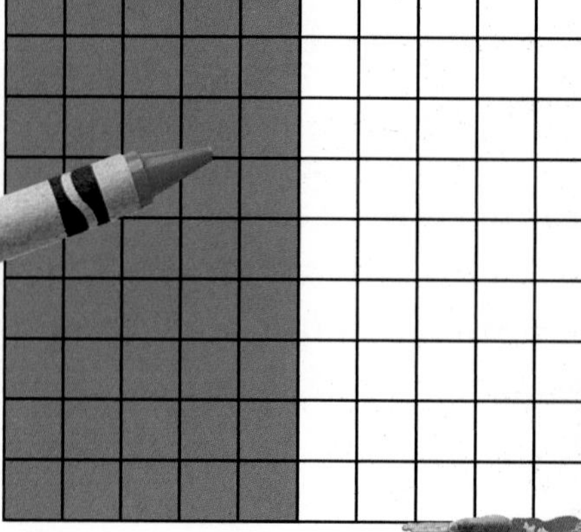

Work Together

1. Find a decimal for $\frac{1}{2}$.
   a. Divide the hundredths grid into two equal parts. Shade one part. What fraction of the grid is shaded?
   b. How many hundredths are shaded?
   c. Write the number of shaded hundredths as a fraction and as a decimal.
2. Find a decimal for $\frac{1}{4}$.
   a. Divide the hundredths grid into four equal parts. Shade one part. What fraction of the grid is shaded?
   b. How many hundredths are shaded?
   c. Write the number of shaded hundredths as a fraction and as a decimal.
   d. What fraction of the grid is not shaded?
   e. How many hundredths are not shaded?
   f. Write the number of unshaded hundredths as a fraction and as a decimal.

Talk About It

3. What decimal amount does each small grid square show?
4. How are fractions and decimals related?

Connect

You can use equivalent fractions to help you write fractions as decimals.

Write $\frac{3}{4}$ as a decimal.

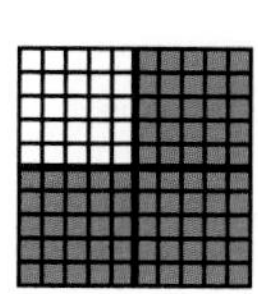

$$\frac{3}{4} \xrightarrow{\times 25} = \frac{75}{100}$$

$\frac{3}{4} = \frac{75}{100}$, or 0.75

Write $\frac{3}{5}$ as a decimal.

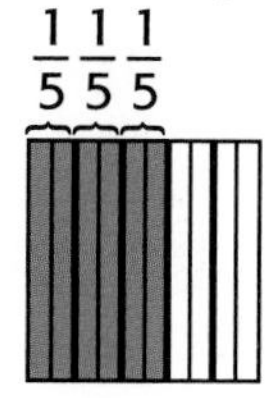

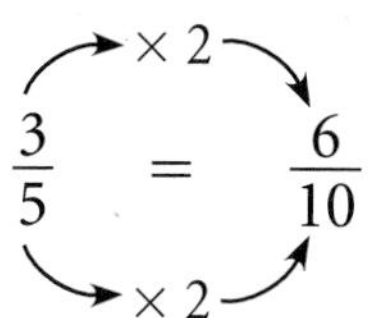

$$\frac{3}{5} \xrightarrow{\times 2} = \frac{6}{10}$$

$\frac{3}{5} = \frac{6}{10}$, or 0.6

Practice

Write the decimal for each fraction. Use the grid to help.

1. $\frac{90}{100}$ 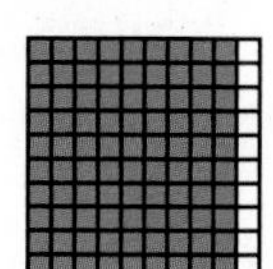

2. $\frac{7}{10}$ 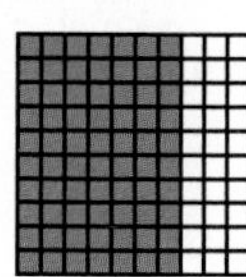

3. $\frac{4}{100}$ 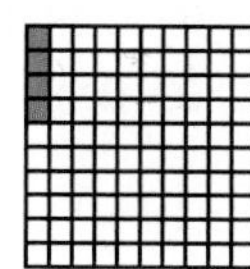

Write the decimal for each fraction. Find an equivalent fraction in tenths or hundredths or draw a grid to help.

4. $\frac{3}{20}$ **5.** $\frac{7}{25}$ **6.** $\frac{4}{5}$ **7.** $\frac{7}{20}$ **8.** $\frac{2}{5}$

9. $\frac{8}{10}$ **10.** $\frac{3}{12}$ **11.** $\frac{9}{25}$ **12.** $\frac{3}{10}$ **13.** $\frac{2}{4}$

14. Which is greater, $\frac{5}{25}$ or 0.24? Explain.

15. Money What fraction of a dollar is 20 pennies? How would you write the fraction? How would you write the amount using a decimal point?

Using Data Use the Data File on page 472 for **16** and **17.**

16. Time A springbok runs at 50 mi/hr. Which animal could run 5 miles in the least amount of time, a springbok or an ostrich?

17. Suppose a bluefin tuna and a human swim for 1 hour. How much farther would the tuna travel than the human?

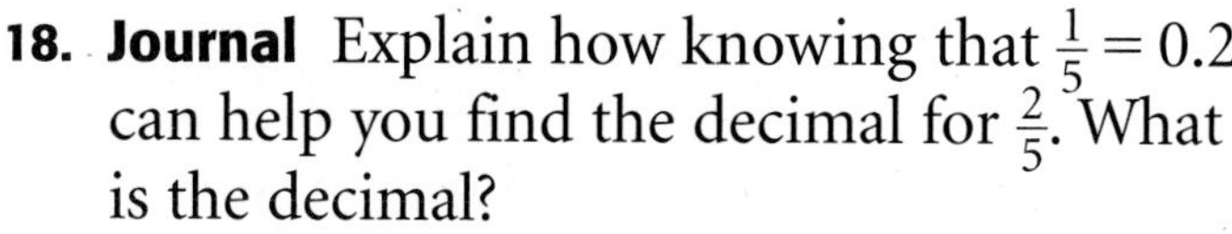

18. Journal Explain how knowing that $\frac{1}{5} = 0.2$ can help you find the decimal for $\frac{2}{5}$. What is the decimal?

Technology

Finding Decimal Patterns on a Calculator

Emilio was reading some old pole vault and high jump Olympic records. They were written as fractions. Modern records are written as decimals.

Materials
calculator

To compare the records more easily, Emilio changed the fractions to decimals. That's when he noticed interesting patterns with the decimals. You can explore these patterns using a calculator.

Work Together

Use a calculator to change fractions to decimals and to explore patterns.

1. Use the F⊃D key to find the decimal equivalent for $\frac{1}{20}$.
   a. Turn on the calculator. Enter the fraction $\frac{1}{20}$ by pressing 1 [/] 20.
   1/20
   b. Press F⊃D.
   0.05

2. You can also use division to find the decimal equivalent for a fraction.
   a. Divide the numerator by the denominator.
   b. Press 1 [÷] 20 [=].
   0.05

3. Each of these fractions has a denominator of 20: $\frac{2}{20}$, $\frac{3}{20}$, $\frac{4}{20}$, $\frac{5}{20}$
   a. Find the decimal equivalent for each fraction.
   b. What pattern do you notice?

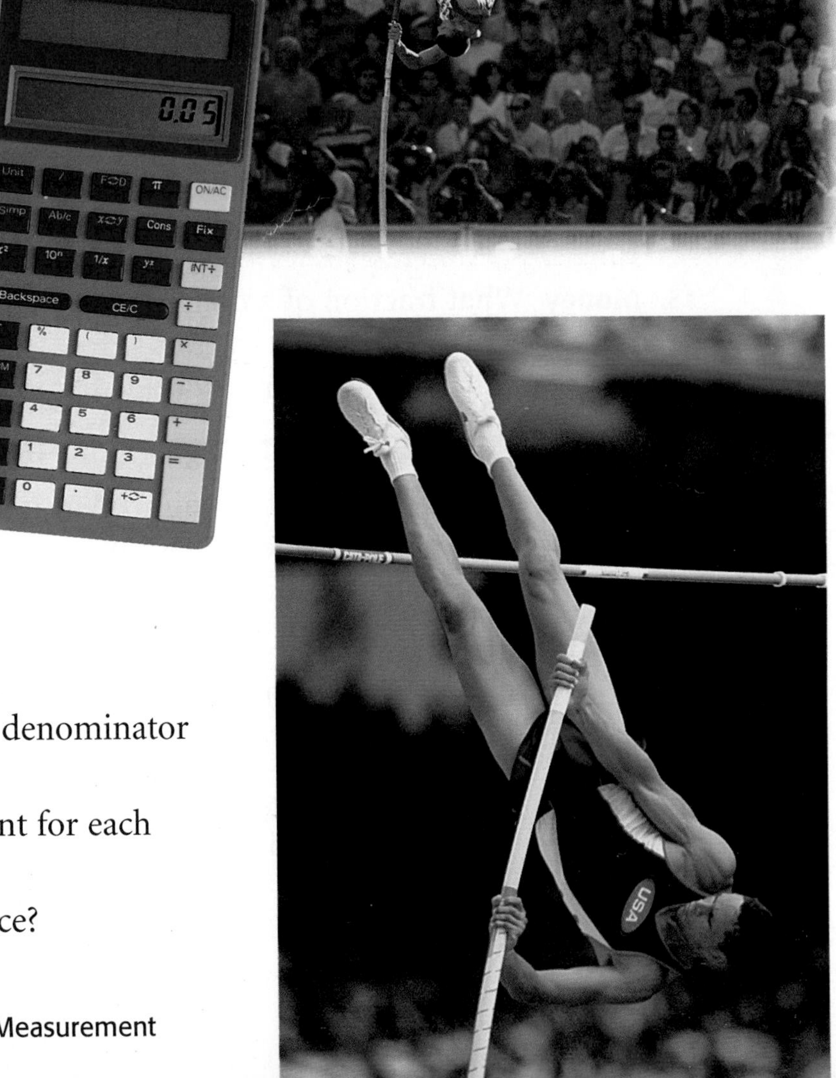

Exercises

Use either method on your calculator for **1** and **2.**

1. Each of these fractions has a denominator of 5: $\frac{4}{5}, \frac{5}{5}, \frac{6}{5}, \frac{7}{5}, \frac{8}{5}, \frac{9}{5}, \frac{10}{5}, \frac{11}{5}$

a. Find the decimal equivalent for each fraction. Look for a pattern.

b. Describe the decimal pattern.

2. Each of these fractions has a denominator of 9: $\frac{1}{9}, \frac{2}{9}, \frac{3}{9}, \frac{4}{9}$

a. Find the decimal equivalent for each fraction. Look for a pattern.

b. Describe the pattern.

c. Try $\frac{5}{9}, \frac{6}{9}, \frac{7}{9}$, and $\frac{8}{9}$. How would you describe the pattern these decimals create?

Extensions

Use your calculator for **3** and **4.**

3. The numbers below show the Fibonacci sequence, a series of numbers that form a special pattern. Each number is the sum of the two numbers before it.

1, 1, 2, 3, 5, 8, 13, 21, 34, 55, 89

a. These fractions use numbers from the Fibonacci sequence. Find the decimal equivalent for each fraction.

$\frac{13}{8}, \frac{21}{13}, \frac{34}{21}, \frac{55}{34}, \frac{89}{55}$

You can see the Fibonacci sequence in many patterns in nature. The shapes on some shells spiral out from the center in a Fibonacci sequence.

b. What pattern do you see?

4. Reasoning Emilio says, "If the denominator of a fraction is a factor of 100, the decimal will not have more than two places." Do you agree? Test his statement using fractions that have 1 as the numerator. Then explain.

SECTION A

Review and Practice

(Lessons 1 and 2) Write the word name, fraction, and decimal for each shaded part.

1. 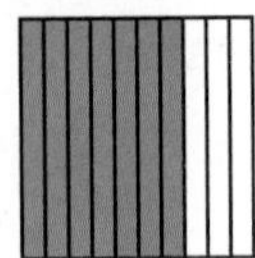

2. 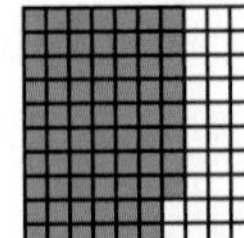

3. 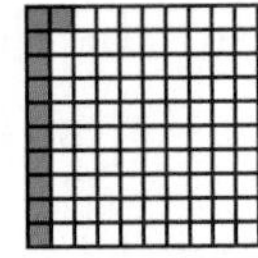

4. **Patterns** Give the next three decimals. 0.01, 0.03, 0.05, ■, ■, ■

5. **Logic** What decimal am I? My digit in the tenths place is twice my digit in the hundredths place. My digit in the hundredths place is odd, but not 1.

Write the decimal for each.

6. $4\frac{2}{10}$ 7. four and thirty-six hundredths   8. $\frac{81}{100}$

(Lesson 3) Use any strategy to solve.

9. Suppose you have $1.76 in dimes and pennies. You have the same number of dimes as pennies. How many of each do you have?

(Lesson 4) Copy and complete. Write $>$, $<$, or $=$.

10. 0.35 ● 0.3   11. 8.01 ● 7.99   12. 0.07 ● 1.2   13. 6.60 ● 6.6

Order the decimals from greatest to least.

14. 0.5, 0.93, 0.15, 1.04, 0.9   15. 8.3, 7.09, 8.19, 7.9, 7.91

(Lesson 5) Round each decimal to the nearest whole number.

16. 10.49   17. 0.52   18. 3.66   19. 98.9

(Lesson 6) Write the decimal for each fraction.

20. $\frac{5}{20}$ 21. $\frac{9}{25}$ 22. $\frac{3}{5}$ 23. $\frac{11}{20}$

24. **Measurement** A discus is a round object that is thrown in an Olympic track and field event. Write the weight of each discus as a decimal.

Men's discus $4\frac{1}{2}$ lb

Women's discus $2\frac{1}{4}$ lb

25. **Journal** Explain how to change $\frac{1}{2}$ to a decimal.

Skills Checklist

In this section, you have:

- ☑ Read and Written Decimals
- ☑ Explored Decimal Place-Value Relationships
- ☑ Solved Problems by Comparing Strategies: Make an Organized List/Use Objects
- ☑ Compared and Ordered Decimals
- ☑ Rounded Decimals
- ☑ Explored Fractions as Decimals

REVIEW AND PRACTICE

CHAPTER 11

SECTION

B Adding and Subtracting Decimals

First Olympic U.S. speed skating team, 1924

Bonnie Blair races against the clock in the 1992 Winter Olympics speed skating competition. What does a time of 6.65 seconds mean?

GET READY!

Adding and Subtracting Decimals

Review adding fractions. Find the sums.

1. $\frac{3}{4} + \frac{1}{8}$
2. $\frac{3}{10} + \frac{7}{10}$
3. $\frac{2}{3} + \frac{1}{6}$
4. $\frac{1}{10} + \frac{3}{5}$
5. $\frac{2}{5} + \frac{3}{5}$
6. $\frac{1}{9} + \frac{2}{3}$

Skills Checklist

In this section, you will:

- ❒ Estimate Sums and Differences
- ❒ Explore Adding and Subtracting Decimals
- ❒ Add and Subtract Decimals

Chapter 11
Lesson
7

Estimating Sums and Differences

You Will Learn
to estimate decimal sums and differences

Remember
When rounding to the nearest whole number, round down if the decimal is less than 0.50. Round up if it is 0.50 or greater.

Learn

Bonnie Blair is fast on ice. In the 1994 Olympics, she skated the 500-meter race in 39.25 seconds. That was 6.65 seconds faster than the gold medalist in the 1960 Olympics, the first year for this event. The winner that year was Helga Haase.

About how long did it take Helga Haase to skate 500 meters?

Bonnie Blair won five Olympic gold medals in speed skating.

Example 1

Estimate the sum of 39.25 and 6.65.

Round each decimal to the nearest whole number.

$$39.25 + 6.65$$

Round down to the nearest whole number. ↓ 39 ↓ 7 Round up to the nearest whole number.

Add. $39 + 7 = 46$

It took Helga Haase about 46 seconds to skate 500 m.

Example 2

In 1994, Bonnie Blair skated the 1,000-m race in 78.74 seconds. About how much longer was that time compared with her 500-m time?

Estimate the difference of 78.74 and 39.25.

$$78.74 - 39.25$$

Round up. ↓ ↓ Round down.

Subtract. $79 - 39 = 40$

It took Bonnie Blair about 40 seconds longer to skate 1,000 m.

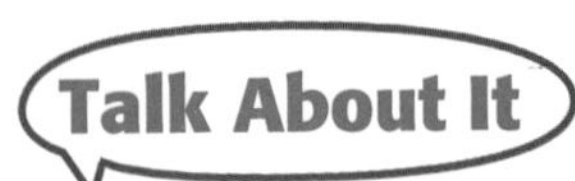

Do you think the exact answer for Example 2 is greater or less than 40 seconds? Explain.

Check

Estimate each sum or difference. Round to the nearest whole number.

1. 3.2 + 5.4 **2.** 10.64 + 1.45 **3.** 9.9 + 10.9 **4.** 40.03 + 51.86

5. 6.20 − 3.9 **6.** 14.04 − 1.40 **7.** 23.6 − 12.5 **8.** 49.99 − 15.09

9. **Reasoning** How could you use fractions to help you estimate the sum of 0.49 and 0.46?

Practice

Skills and Reasoning

Estimate each sum or difference. Round to the nearest whole number.

10. 0.64 + 8.66 **11.** 20.3 + 34.9 **12.** 2.03 + 11.02 **13.** 7.4 + 6.30

14. 4.2 − 1.95 **15.** 12.34 − 8.01 **16.** 50.02 − 40.97 **17.** 4.7 − 3.8

18. How could you use fractions to help you estimate the difference between 0.78 and 0.24?

Problem Solving and Applications

19. **Using Data** In 1984, Bonnie Blair took eighth place in the 500-m race. Her time was 42.53 seconds. About how much faster did she skate in 1994? Use the data on page 492.

20. **Science** A flea can hop about 10 in. off the ground. That hop is equal to 130 times a flea's own length. If 6-ft humans could leap 130 times their height, how high could they jump?

Using Data Use the Data File on page 473 for **21** and **22.**

21. About how many gold and silver medals did U.S. athletes win in 1996?

22. About how many more gold medals did U.S. athletes win in 1984 than in 1976?

Mixed Review and Test Prep

Measurement Copy and complete. Write >, <, or =.

23. 2 yd ● 70 in. **24.** 10 yd ● 20 ft **25.** 28 in. ● 2 ft

26. Which number is the quotient of 5,400 divided by 9?

Ⓐ 6 Ⓑ 60 Ⓒ 600 Ⓓ 6,000

Chapter 11
Lesson
8

Exploring Adding and Subtracting Decimals

Problem Solving Connection
Draw a Picture

Materials
- hundredths grid
- 2 colors of crayons or colored pencils

Remember
The decimal 0.2 means 2 tenths, or 20 hundredths.

The decimal 0.02 means 2 hundredths.

Explore

You can use grids to show how to add or subtract decimals.

Work Together

1. Use a hundredths grid to show how to add 0.5 and 0.37.
   a. Shade 5 columns of 10 squares each to show 0.5.
   b. Use a different color. Shade 37 more squares to show 0.37.
   c. Count the shaded squares. How many whole columns are shaded in all? How many extra squares are shaded?
   d. How many hundredths are shaded in all?
   e. Write the decimal for the total squares shaded.
2. Show how to subtract 0.20 from 0.68.
   a. Shade 6 columns and 8 extra squares to show 0.68.
   b. Cross out 2 columns of shaded squares to show 0.20.
   c. Count the squares that are shaded but not crossed out. How many whole columns? How many extra squares?
   d. Write the decimal for total squares shaded but not crossed out.

Talk About It

3. What decimal shows the number of squares in a column of the grid?
4. Explain how you can count the grid squares without having to count each one individually.

Connect

You can use what you know about place value to add or subtract decimals.

Math Tip
Line up the decimal points to add or subtract.

What You See

Find 0.38 + 0.18.

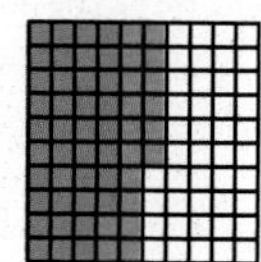

What You Write

Add as you would with whole numbers. Regroup as needed.

$$\begin{array}{r} \overset{1}{} \\ 0.38 \\ +\ 0.18 \\ \hline 0.56 \end{array}$$

Find 0.7 − 0.09.

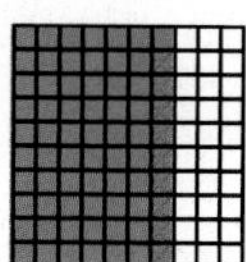

Subtract as you would with whole numbers. Regroup as needed.

$$\begin{array}{r} 0.7 \\ -\ 0.09 \\ \hline \end{array} \qquad \begin{array}{r} 0.\overset{6}{\not 7}\overset{10}{\not 0} \\ -\ 0.09 \\ \hline 0.61 \end{array}$$

← Write zero in the hundredths place.

Practice

Find a sum or difference for each grid.

1. $\begin{array}{r} 0.15 \\ +\ 0.26 \\ \hline \end{array}$

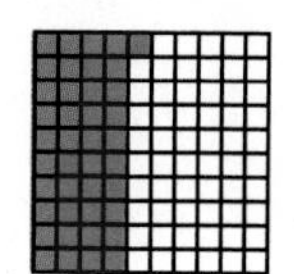

2. $\begin{array}{r} 0.9 \\ -\ 0.28 \\ \hline \end{array}$

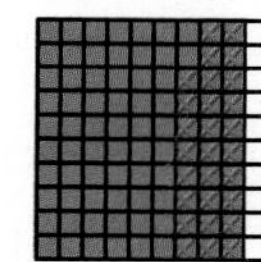

Write an addition or subtraction sentence for each grid.

3. 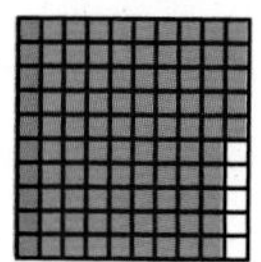

4. 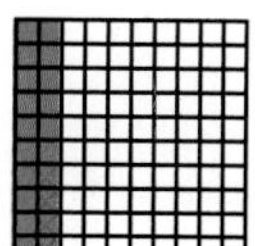

5. 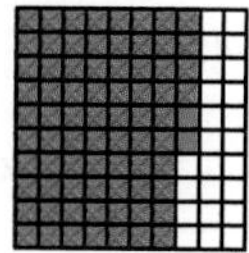

Find each sum or difference. You can use hundredths grids to help.

6. 0.1 + 0.74 **7.** 0.03 + 0.5 **8.** 0.64 + 0.3 **9.** 0.8 + 0.20

10. 0.92 − 0.08 **11.** 0.5 − 0.14 **12.** 0.5 − 0.08 **13.** 0.54 − 0.35

14. 0.2 + 0.47 **15.** 0.7 − 0.21 **16.** 0.63 + 0.09 **17.** 0.61 − 0.29

18. Critical Thinking Sabrina added 0.4 and 0.05 and got the incorrect sum of 0.9. What mistake did she make, and what is the correct answer?

19. Journal Explain how you can add 0.3 and 0.4 on a hundredths grid.

Chapter 11
Lesson
9

Adding and Subtracting Decimals

You Will Learn
how to add and subtract decimals

Learn

The 4×100 meter relay race is a track and field event for teams. Four runners each run 100 meters. The team's score is the sum of all four runners' times.

Did You Know?
The French team had won the bronze medal for the event in the 1988 Olympics.

In 1990, the French team set a world record for the 4×100 meter relay. What was their total time?

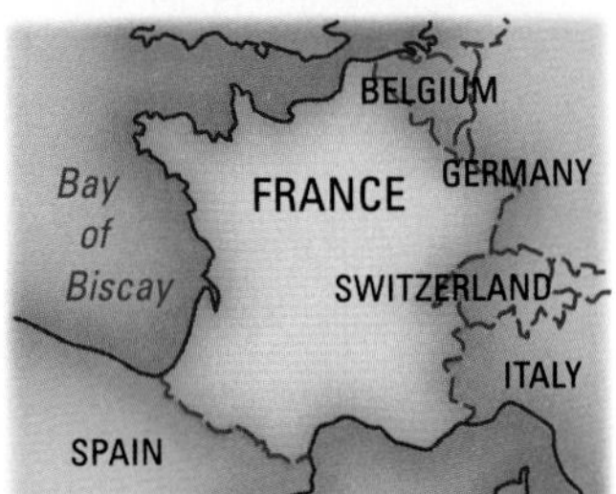

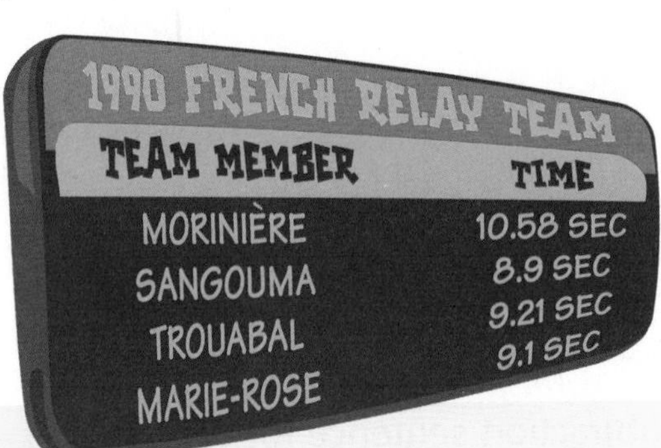

1990 FRENCH RELAY TEAM

TEAM MEMBER	TIME
MORINIÈRE	10.58 SEC
SANGOUMA	8.9 SEC
TROUABAL	9.21 SEC
MARIE-ROSE	9.1 SEC

Example 1

Find the sum of the runners' times.

Step 1

Line up the decimal points.
Write zeros as needed.

$$\begin{array}{r} 10.58 \\ 8.9\mathbf{0} \\ 9.21 \\ +\ 9.1\mathbf{0} \\ \hline \end{array}$$

Step 2

Add as you would with whole numbers.
Regroup as needed.

$$\begin{array}{r} {}^{2\,1} \\ 10.58 \\ 8.90 \\ 9.21 \\ +\ 9.10 \\ \hline 37.79 \end{array}$$

Write the decimal point in the correct place.

Estimate to check. Round each decimal to the nearest whole number.

$11 + 9 + 9 + 9 = 38$

Since 37.79 is close to 38, the answer is reasonable.

The sum of the runners' times is 37.79 seconds.

Example 2

During the 1988 Olympics, the French team ran the 4×100 relay in 38.4 seconds. How much faster did the team run in 1990?

Subtract to find the difference between 38.4 and 37.79.

Step 1

Line up the decimal points.
Write zeros as needed.

$$\begin{array}{r} 38.4\mathbf{0} \\ -\,37.79 \\ \hline \end{array}$$

Step 2

Subtract as you would with whole numbers. Regroup as needed.
Start with hundredths.

$$\begin{array}{r} 13 \\ 7\ \ \cancel{3}\ 10 \\ 3\,\cancel{8}\,.\,\cancel{4}\,\cancel{0} \\ -\,3\,7\,.\,7\,9 \\ \hline 0\,.\,6\,1 \end{array}$$

Estimate to check. Round each decimal to the nearest whole number.

$38 - 38 = 0$

Since 0.61 is close to 0, the answer is reasonable.

The French team ran the relay 0.61 seconds faster in 1990 than in 1988.

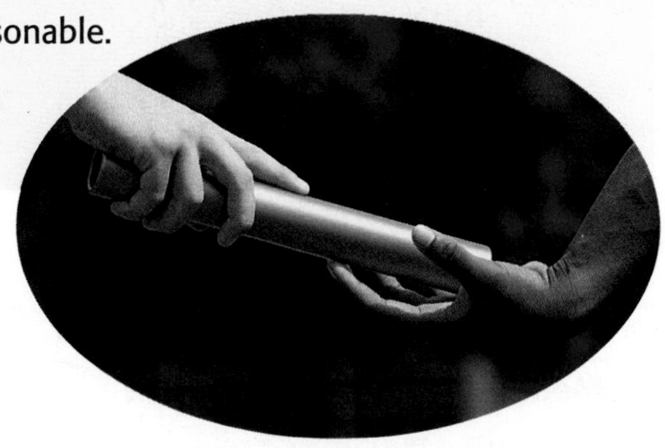

In a relay, each teammate passes the baton to the next runner.

Talk About It

1. In Example 2, why do you need to write 38.4 as 38.40?
2. How do you decide where to put the decimal point in your answer?
3. What is another way that you could check your answer in Example 2?
4. How would you write the number 40 if you subtract 37.79 from it? How would you write it if you subtract 37.7 from it?

Check

Find each sum. Estimate to check your answer.

1. $2.36 + 3.20$ **2.** $4 + 6.5$ **3.** $7.80 + 6.24$ **4.** $0.44 + 1.16$

Find each difference. Estimate to check your answer.

5. $9.55 - 2.33$ **6.** $10 - 0.09$ **7.** $42.58 - 30.8$ **8.** $6.89 - 1.75$

9. **Reasoning** Jeff subtracted 10 from 58.9 and got 57.9 as an answer. What mistake did he make?

Practice

Skills and Reasoning

Find each sum. Estimate to check your answer.

10. 11.91 + 2.16   **11.** \$44.05 + 33.20   **12.** 2.76 + 0.82   **13.** \$30.55 + 19.50   **14.** \$99.92 + 0.83

15. 4 + 96.17 + 0.95   **16.** 0.93 + 0.08 + 0.44   **17.** \$17.75 + 10 + 55.35   **18.** 3.95 + 7.01 + 4.80   **19.** \$24.74 + 6.06 + 52.10

20. 71.57 + 28.43   **21.** 16.6 + 0.93   **22.** 3.04 + 5.2   **23.** 9 + 21.89

Find each difference. Estimate to check your answer.

24. 14.60 − 6.95   **25.** 80.07 − 7.5   **26.** 0.65 − 0.49   **27.** 5.19 − 3.64   **28.** 88 − 67.56

29. 65.11 − 41   **30.** 92.47 − 14.85   **31.** 18.03 − 2.49   **32.** \$76.10 − 74.95   **33.** 26.27 − 4.4

34. 84.1 − 56.03   **35.** 11 − 6.54   **36.** 28.5 − 0.88   **37.** \$16.77 − \$13.84

38. Subtract 35.98 from 94.5.   **39.** Add 4.6, 51.54, and 17.

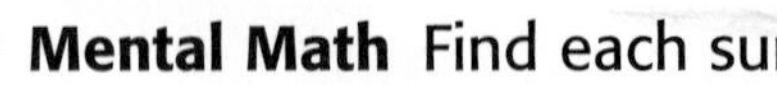

Mental Math Find each sum.

40. 6.07 + 7.07   **41.** 12.2 + 12.2 + 10

42. 3.5 + 4.5

43. Explain how you would estimate the sum of 5.56 + 8.09 + 7.4 + 12.

Problem Solving and Applications

Using Data Use the data in the table for **44** and **45**.

44. What was the difference between the U.S. team's time and the Cuban team's time?

45. How much faster was the Nigerian relay team than the Cuban team?

46. Collecting Data Gather data on at least three teams' times for a relay race. Make a table to compare the decimals.

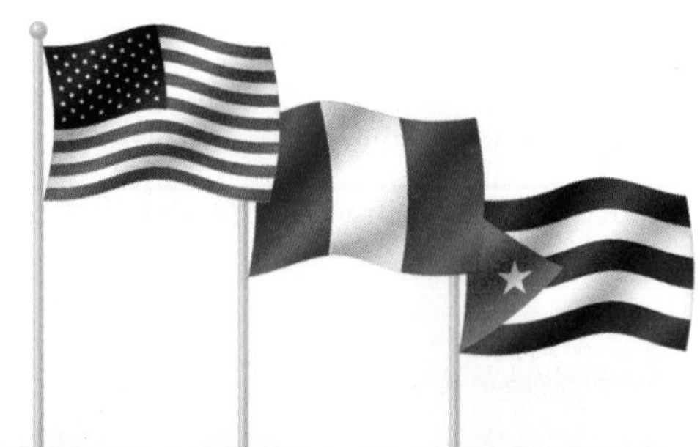

1992 Olympics 4 × 100 Meter Relay

Team	Medal	Time
U.S.A.	Gold	37.40 seconds
Nigeria	Silver	37.98 seconds
Cuba	Bronze	38.00 seconds

Problem Solving and SPORTS

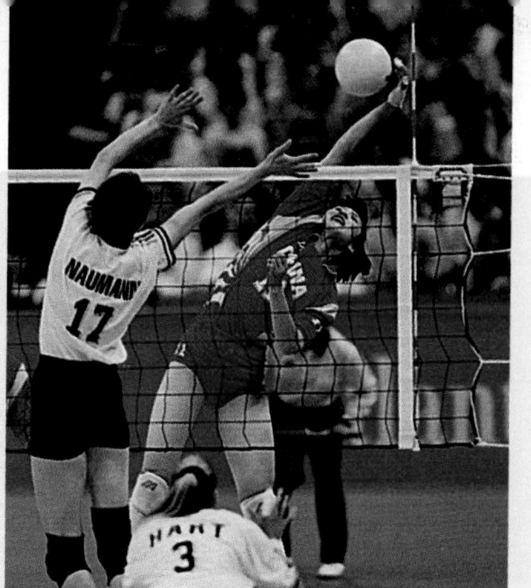

Volleyball was invented in 1895, but it didn't become an Olympic sport until 1964. Olympic volleyball is played on a rectangular court that is 9 meters wide and 18 meters long. For women's volleyball, the top edge of the net is 2.24 meters off the ground.

47. What is the perimeter of a volleyball court?

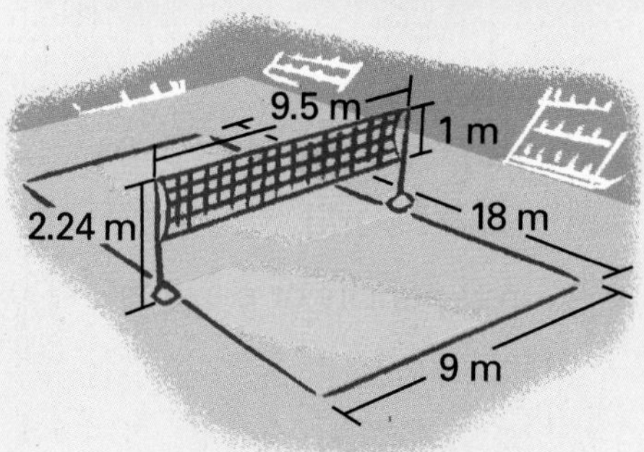

Women's volleyball court

48. In men's volleyball, the top edge of the net is 2.43 m off the ground. How much higher off the ground is the net for the men's game than for the women's game?

49. What is the perimeter of a volleyball net?

50. How many years after volleyball was invented did it become an Olympic sport?

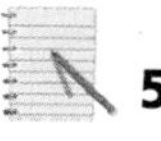

51. Journal Describe how you can estimate to check your answer to a decimal addition or subtraction problem.

Mixed Review and Test Prep

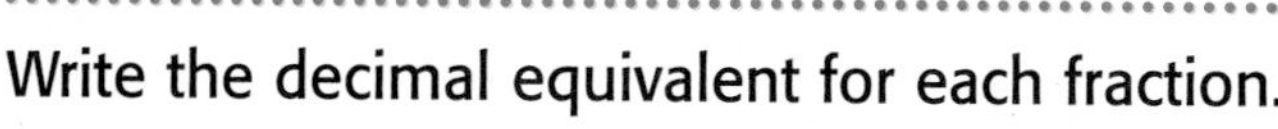

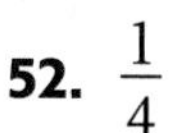

Write the decimal equivalent for each fraction.

52. $\frac{1}{4}$ **53.** $\frac{3}{10}$ **54.** $\frac{2}{5}$ **55.** $\frac{1}{20}$ **56.** $\frac{3}{5}$

Copy and complete.

57. 24 fl oz = ■ c **58.** 1 qt = ■ pt **59.** $1\frac{1}{2}$ gallon = ■ qt

Choose the better unit of measure for each.

60.

Ⓐ 16 oz
Ⓑ 16 lb

61.

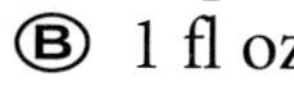

Ⓐ 1 qt
Ⓑ 1 fl oz

62.

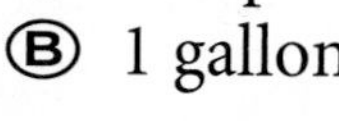

Ⓐ 1 cup
Ⓑ 1 gallon

63. Estimation Lee's friends finished half of a 60-oz bag of cashews. About how much do the remaining cashews weigh?

Ⓐ 2 lb Ⓑ 3 lb Ⓒ 4 lb Ⓓ 40 lb

PRACTICE AND APPLY

Skills Practice Bank, page 573, Set 3

Spinning for Decimals GAME

Players
2 or more

Materials
- spinner with numbers 0–9
- hundredths grid
- colored pencils or crayons

Object
The object of the game is to find a total close to 1 without going over 1.

Math Tip

How to Play

1. Players take turns spinning. When a player spins a number, he or she shades that number on a hundredths grid. For example, if a player spins 3, he or she may shade 3 hundredths or 3 tenths. (You must shade only one kind on each turn.)

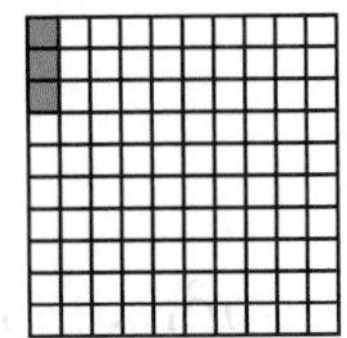

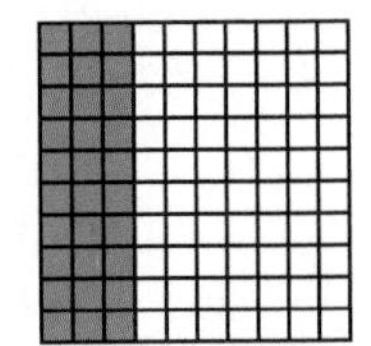

2. If a player spins a zero, no squares are shaded.

3. Each player has three spins and uses one grid to shade in the squares.

4 Each player finds the total of his or her shaded squares.

5 Players compare totals to decide which player is closest to 1 without going over 1. If both players are over 1, the player with the lower score wins.

6 If both players have the same total, each spins again and the player spinning the lower number wins.

7 Play the game several times.

Talk About It

1. If your first spin is a 7, 8, or 9, is it better to shade hundredths or tenths? Explain.

2. Suppose you have shaded 95 hundredths after the second spin. Which numbers on the next spin would give you a total greater than 1?

More Ways to Play

- Play again with 4 spins instead of 3.

- Play to see who can get the lowest score. There is one additional rule: A player cannot shade hundredths squares on every turn.

Reasoning

1. Suppose you spin twice and shade 7 tenths and 3 hundredths. What number would you hope to spin next?

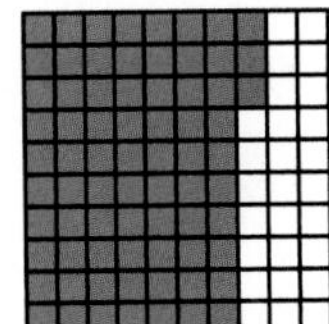

2. Suppose you spin twice and shade 4 tenths and 8 hundredths. What number would you hope to spin next?

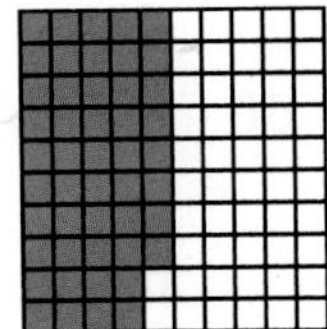

3. Suppose you shade 9 tenths. What two numbers on the spinner could give you a total of 1?

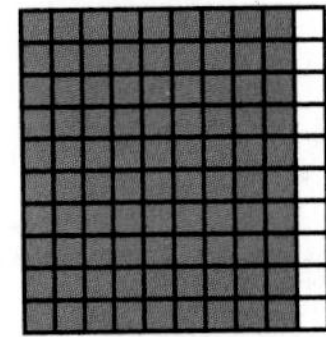

SECTION B

Review and Practice

(Lesson 7) Estimate each sum or difference. Round to the nearest whole number.

1. 14.2 + 15.75 **2.** 7.33 + 11.06 **3.** 10.29 + 4.3 **4.** 2.03 + 5.99

5. 14.7 − 2.98 **6.** 44.63 − 0.85 **7.** 32.6 − 27 **8.** 33.59 − 6.8

(Lesson 8) Write an addition or subtraction sentence for each grid.

9. 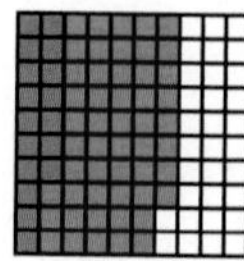

10. 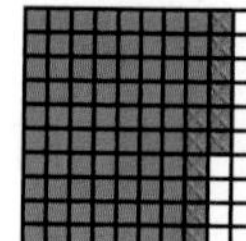

11. 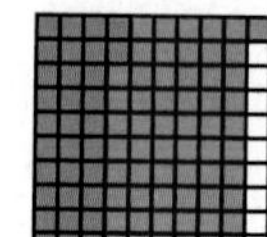

Find each sum or difference.

12. 0.23 + 0.2 **13.** 0.88 − 0.3 **14.** 0.9 − 0.46 **15.** 0.31 + 0.09

16. 0.91 − 0.46 **17.** 0.38 + 0.7 **18.** 0.32 − 0.05 **19.** 0.44 + 0.7

(Lesson 9) Find each sum or difference. Estimate to check your answer.

20. 6.70 + 13.12 **21.** 4.25 + 0.75 **22.** 72.97 + 34.90 **23.** \$10.50 + 20.99 **24.** \$8.15 + 0.68

25. 11.74 − 4.50 **26.** 34.04 − 29.08 **27.** 8.20 − 5.64 **28.** \$76.00 − 35.61 **29.** 51.20 − 0.78

30. 2.5 + 18.77 **31.** 12.21 − 5.40

32. Measurement The bobsled track at the 1994 Winter Olympics was 1.06 miles long. The races were timed over a 0.85-mile long portion of the track. How much of the track was not part of the timed event?

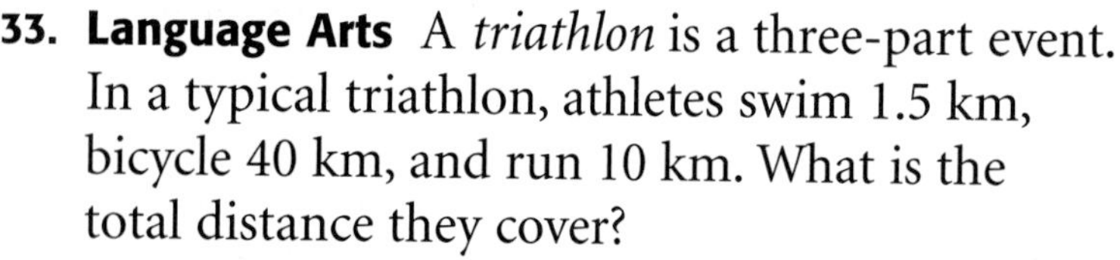

33. Language Arts A *triathlon* is a three-part event. In a typical triathlon, athletes swim 1.5 km, bicycle 40 km, and run 10 km. What is the total distance they cover?

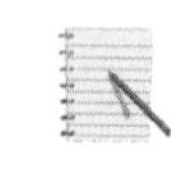

34. Journal Explain how to find sums and differences of decimals. How is it like finding sums and differences of whole numbers?

Skills Checklist

In this section, you have:

- ☑ Estimated Sums and Differences
- ☑ Explored Adding and Subtracting Decimals
- ☑ Added and Subtracted Decimals

CHAPTER 11

SECTION

C

Using Metric Measurement

Cycling is a Special Olympic sport. Twins Rebecca and Laura enter 5 km, 10 km, and 15 km cycling races. Which race do you think takes the most time? Explain.

GET READY!

Understanding Metric Measurement

Review customary units. Copy and complete.

1. 2 gal = ▢ qt
2. 3 c = ▢ fl oz
3. 2 gal = ▢ pt
4. 4 pt = ▢ qt
5. 16 c = ▢ pt
6. 12 c = ▢ qt

Skills Checklist

In this section, you will:

- ❑ Explore Centimeters, Decimeters, and Meters
- ❑ Learn About Meters and Kilometers
- ❑ Explore Length and Decimals
- ❑ Explore Mass and Capacity
- ❑ Learn About Temperature
- ❑ Solve Problems by Making Decisions

Chapter 11
Lesson
10

Exploring Centimeters, Decimeters, and Meters

Problem Solving Connection
- Use Objects/ Act It Out
- Guess and Check

Materials
- string
- felt-tip marker
- meter stick
- baseball, tennis ball, and other sports equipment

Vocabulary
Metric Units of Length
centimeter
decimeter
meter

Math Tip
The prefix *deci-* (as in *decimal*) means 10.
The prefix *cent-* (as in *century*) means 100.

Explore

Handball is a modern sport with ancient roots. A form of handball may have been played in ancient Greece as early as 600 B.C. It became an Olympic sport for the first time in 1936.

Work Together

The distance around a handball is 56 centimeters. You can use this measurement to help you estimate other short distances.

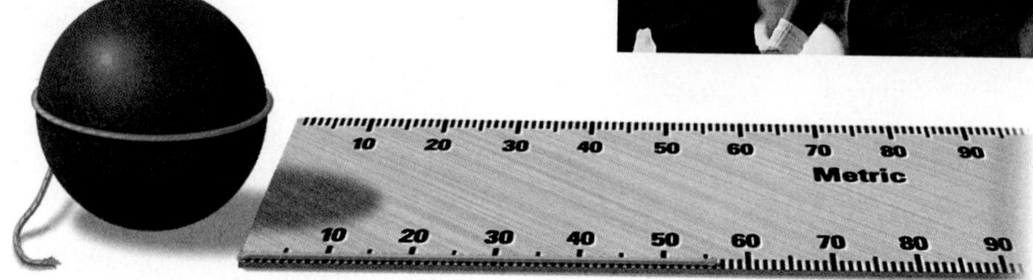

1. Estimate the distance around a baseball. Do you think it is more or less than the distance around a handball?
   a. Wrap string around a baseball and cut it so the ends meet.
   b. Place the string on a meter stick. Measure the length of the string. Record your measurement.
2. Find other sports balls, such as a softball, a tennis ball, a football, and a basketball. Estimate and measure. Record their measurements.

Talk About It

3. Which sports balls have a greater distance around than a handball?
4. How can you tell where 56 cm is on the meter stick above?

Connect

Centimeter (cm), **decimeter** (dm), and **meter** (m) are metric units of length.

10 cm = 1 dm
10 dm = 1 m
100 cm = 1 m

Here are some ways to think about centimeters, decimeters, and meters.

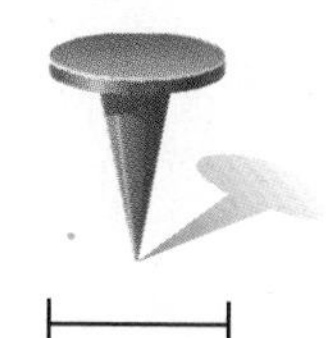

A thumbtack is about 1 cm wide.

A cassette tape is about 1 dm wide.

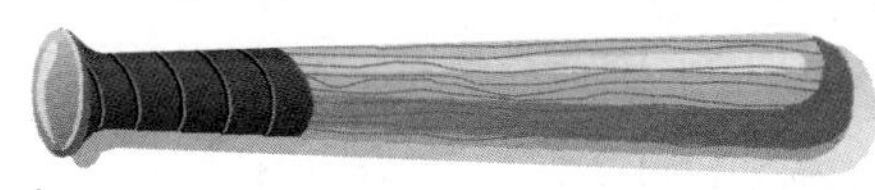

A baseball bat is about 1 m long.

Practice

Choose the better unit of measure for each object.

1. 

decimeters or meters

2. 

centimeters or meters

3. 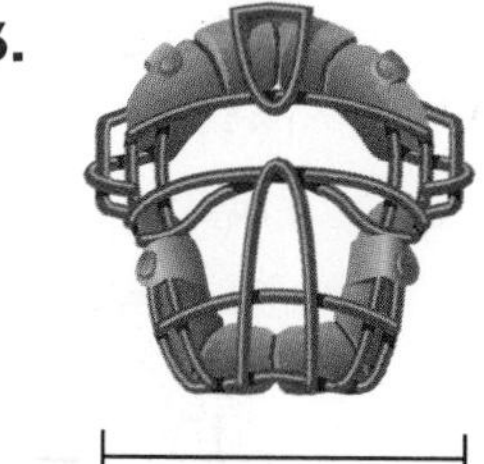

decimeters or meters

Copy and complete. Write >, <, or =.

4. 12 cm ● 12 dm **5.** 4 m ● 4 cm **6.** 50 dm ● 50 m **7.** 2 m ● 2 dm

Geometry Readiness Use a metric ruler to draw each shape.

8. A rectangle 1 dm long and 6 cm wide

9. A parallelogram with two 3-cm sides and two 5-cm sides

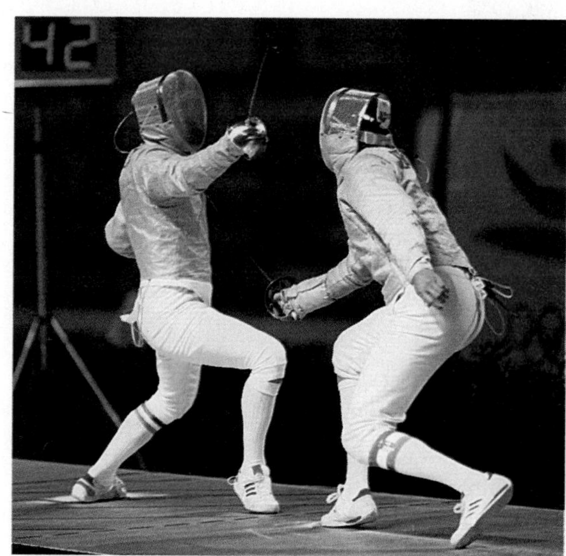

10. History Fencing competitions were held in Egypt and Japan as long as 5,000 years ago. Today, Olympic fencers compete in a rectangular area that is 14 m long and 2 m wide. What is the perimeter of the rectangle?

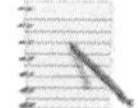

11. Journal Give examples of when you would measure in meters, decimeters, and centimeters.

Chapter 11
Lesson
11

Meters and Kilometers

You Will Learn

how to use and relate meters and kilometers

Vocabulary

kilometer
a distance of 1,000 m

Math Tip

A meter is a little more than a yard. A kilometer is a little more than half a mile.

Learn

Massachusetts

The Olympic sport of cycling is measured in kilometers. Athletes in the Special Olympics can enter road races for 5, 10, and 15 kilometers.

A **kilometer** (km) is a metric unit of length used to measure long distances.

1 km = 1,000 m

Rebecca and Laura, from Stoughton, Massachusetts, won gold medals in cycling at the Special Olympics.

Here are some ways to think about meters and kilometers.

About 1 m

The handlebars of a racing bike are about 1 m off the ground.

547 bicycles placed end-to-end are about 1 km long.

You can change from kilometers to meters by multiplying.

You can change from meters to kilometers by dividing.

Example 1

How many meters are in 5 km?
To find out, multiply.

Think: 1,000 m = 1 km

5 × 1,000 = 5,000

There are 5,000 m in 5 km.

Example 2

How many kilometers are equal to 2,000 m? To find out, divide.

Think: 1,000 m = 1 km

2,000 [÷] 1,000 [=] [2]

2 km are equal to 2,000 m.

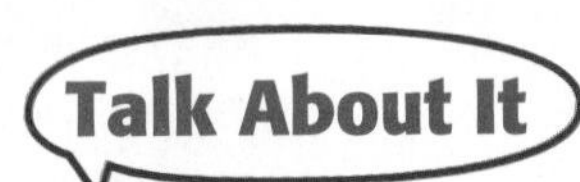

What objects or distances are about a meter or about a kilometer long?

Check

Choose the better measure for each object.

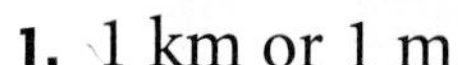

1. 1 km or 1 m
2. 30 m or 10 km
3. 3 m or 3 km

Copy and complete. Write >, <, or =.

4. 200 m ● 2 km
5. 4 m ● 4,000 km
6. 3,000 m ● 3 km
7. **Reasoning** The map shows the distance for each segment of a cross-country race. Is the total length of the course over 4 km?

Practice

Skills and Reasoning

Copy and complete. Write >, <, or =.

8. 40 m ● 4 km
9. 40 km ● 4,000 m
10. 8,000 m ● 8 km
11. 600 m ● 6 km
12. 5,000 m ● 5 km
13. 7,000 km ● 7 m
14. 12 km is how many meters?
15. 15,000 m is how many kilometers?
16. Which event would take longer: A 50-km race or a 4,000-m race?

Problem Solving and Applications

17. **Mental Math** The cycling track for the 1996 Olympics in Atlanta was 250 m long. How many times would a cyclist ride around the track in a 4,000-m race?
18. **History** The cycling road race of the 1896 Olympics was 87 km long. In 1912, it was 320 km long. How much greater was the distance in 1912?

Mixed Review and Test Prep

19. Subtract 70.33 from 90.2
20. Add 29.4, 0.87, and 7.61
21. Find the sum of $\frac{1}{4}$, $\frac{1}{4}$, and $\frac{1}{2}$.

Ⓐ $\frac{3}{4}$ Ⓑ $\frac{3}{6}$ Ⓒ 1 Ⓓ not here

Chapter 11
Lesson
12

Exploring Length and Decimals

Problem Solving Connection
- Use Objects/ Act It Out
- Look for a Pattern

Materials
- string
- scissors
- meter stick

Explore

A ray is a kind of fish that swims along the ocean floor. Its body is flat and almost square-shaped. A giraffe is taller than it is wide. Its shape is more like a rectangle. Are you a square or a rectangle?

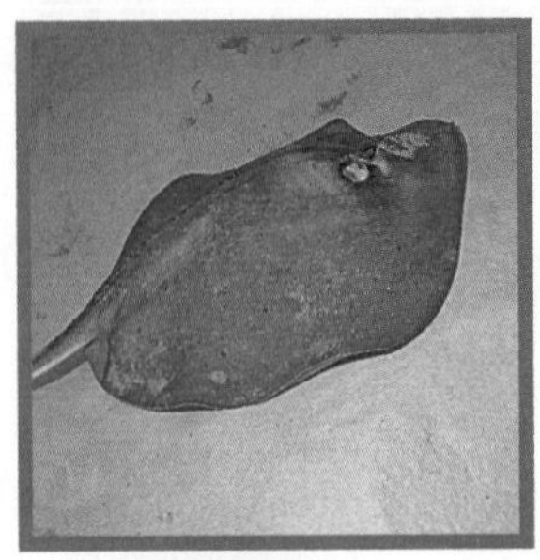

Work Together

Work with a partner.

Remember

$\frac{1}{100} = 0.01$

1. Hold your arms out. Your partner will use string and a meter stick to measure your arm span. Record the measurement.
   a. What is your arm span to the nearest centimeter?
   b. How can you write this length in meters?
2. Stand against a wall. Your partner will measure your height.
   a. What is your height to the nearest centimeter?
   b. What is your height in meters?
3. Compare your height and your arm span. Are you more like a square or a rectangle? Explain.

What patterns do you see in lengths that are measured in both meters and centimeters?

Connect

Here is one way to change centimeters to meters.

35 cm = ▇ m

$1 \text{ cm} = \frac{1}{100} \text{ m}$

So, $35 \text{ cm} = \frac{35}{100}$ of a meter, or 0.35 m

Here is one way to change meters to centimeters.

1.25 m = ▇ cm

1 m = 100 cm

1.25 [×] 100 [=] [125]

So, 1.25 m = 125 cm

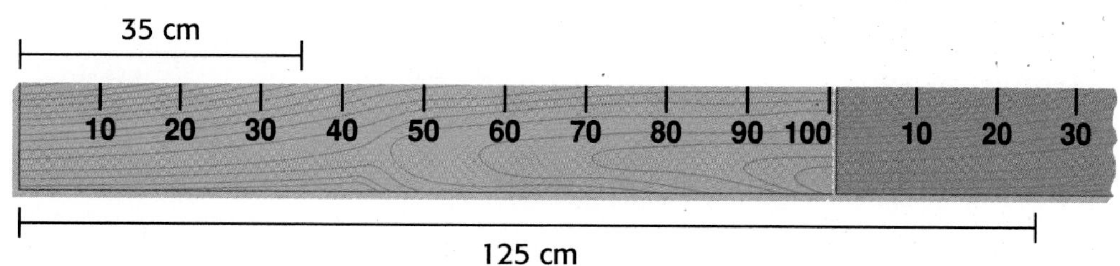

Practice

Choose a tool 

Copy and complete.

1. 27 cm = ▇ m
2. 1.2 m = ▇ cm
3. 84 cm = ▇ m
4. 4 m = ▇ cm
5. 9 cm = ▇ m
6. 0.97 m = ▇ cm
7. 0.6 m = ▇ cm
8. 36 cm = ▇ m
9. 1.55 m = ▇ cm

Write the letter of the measurement that matches.

10. 30 cm
11. 500 cm
12. 8 m
13. 1.17 m
14. 4.6 m
15. 50 cm

a. 5 m	**b.** 800 cm
c. 0.50 m	**d.** 0.30 m
e. 117 cm	**f.** 460 cm

16. At 2.13 m, Daniel Santiago of the Puerto Rican men's basketball team was one of the tallest athletes at the 1996 Summer Olympics. How tall was he in centimeters?

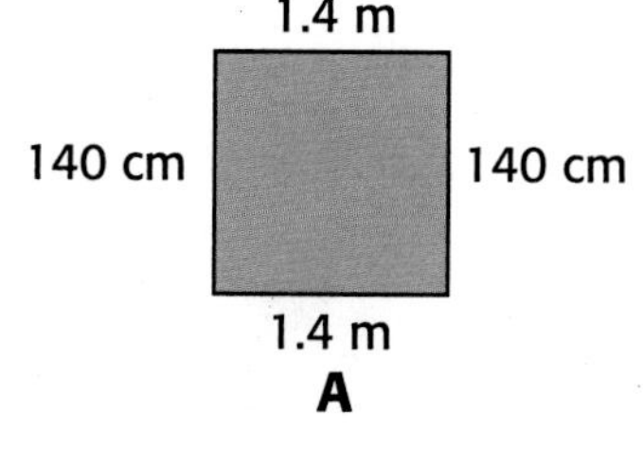

17. **Geometry Readiness** Which of the two rectangles is a square? Explain.

18. **Science** The tallest known giraffe was about 6.1 m tall. The tallest human was about 272 cm tall. Which was taller? How much taller? Give your answer in centimeters and in meters.

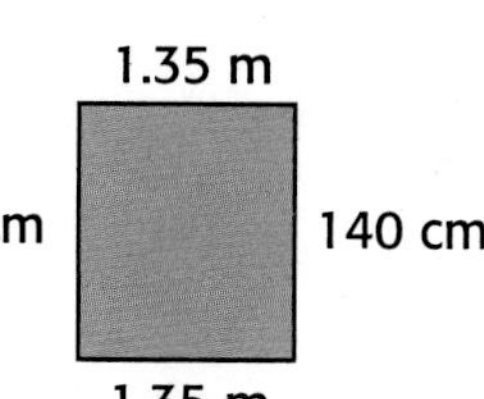

19. **Journal** Explain how 1.2 m, 1.20 m, and 120 cm all name the same length.

Chapter 11
Lesson
13

Exploring Mass

Problem Solving Connection

- Use Objects/Act it Out
- Look for a Pattern

Materials
balance

Vocabulary
Metric Units of Mass
gram (g)
kilogram (kg)

Explore

Kim Brownfield's wheelchair doesn't keep him from setting world records. His record lift of 237 kilograms earned him a gold medal at the Paralympic Games in 1996.

Kim Brownfield lifting weights.

Work Together

Use a balance, gram and kilogram masses, and classroom objects to explore mass.

1. Choose a small object, such as a piece of chalk. Hold it in one hand. Hold a nickel in the other hand. A nickel has a mass of about 5 grams. Do you think the object is greater or less than 5 grams? Use the balance to check.
2. Is a penny greater or less than 5 grams? How can you find out?
3. Choose 5 small objects. Estimate which are less and which are greater than 5 grams. Use a nickel and the balance to check.
4. This book has a mass of about 1 kilogram. Find 3 objects that you think are also about 1 kilogram. Use the balance to check.

Did You Know?
An object weighs $\frac{1}{6}$ as much on the moon as on Earth, but its mass stays the same.

Talk About It

5. Which is greater, a gram or a kilogram?
6. A cotton ball and a marble are about the same size. The cotton ball is less than 1 g, but the marble is about 10 g. How can you explain their difference in mass?

Connect

Grams (g) and **kilograms (kg)** are metric units of mass.

1,000 g = 1 kg

Here are some ways to think about grams and kilograms.

A small grape has a mass of about 1 gram.

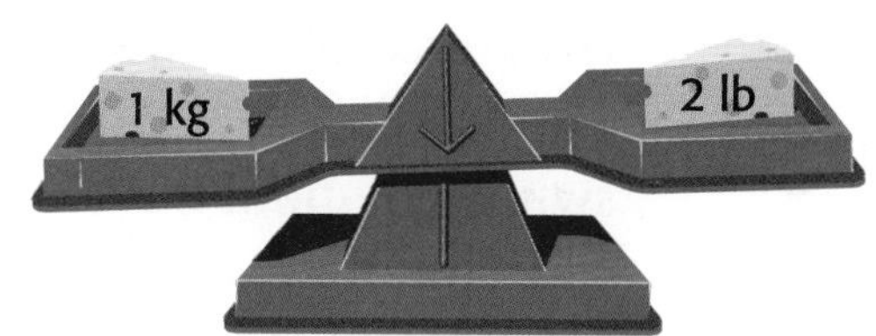

A kilogram is a little more than 2 pounds.

You can change from kilograms to grams by multiplying.

4 kg = ■ g
$4 \times 1{,}000 = 4{,}000$
4 kg = 4,000 g

You can change from grams to kilograms by dividing.

6,000 g = ■ kg
6,000 [÷] 1,000 [=] [6]
6,000 g = 6 kg

Practice

Choose a reasonable unit of mass. Write g or kg.

1. 
2. 
3. 
4. 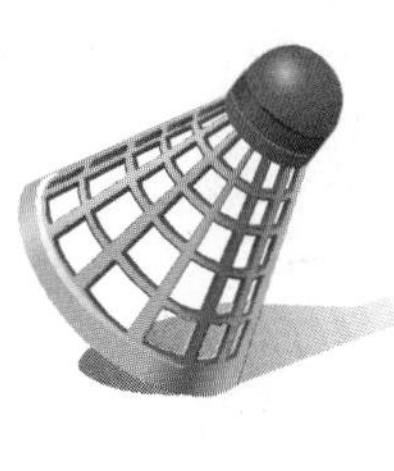

Copy and complete.

5. 3 kg = ■ g
6. 12,000 g = ■ kg
7. 45 kg = ■ g

Choose the better estimate of mass for each object.

8. A carton of milk
   1 g or 1 kg
9. A calculator
   100 g or 10 kg
10. A banana
   400 kg or 40 g
11. **Using Data** Use the Data File on page 473. About how many more nations were represented at the Paralympics in 1996 than in 1960?
12. **Critical Thinking** A cookie recipe calls for 0.5 kg chocolate chips. Will two 340-g bags be enough? Explain.

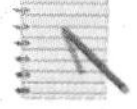

13. **Journal** Describe how you can change kilograms to grams.

Exploring Capacity

Problem Solving Connection
- Use Objects/ Act It Out
- Guess and Check

Materials
- dropper marked in mL
- metric measuring cup
- small spoon
- mug
- 1-liter container
- water

Vocabulary
capacity
the amount a container can hold

Metric Units of Capacity
liter
milliliter

Did You Know?
Athletes and officials at the 1996 Summer Olympics drank about 270,000 liters of milk.

Explore

Liters (L) and **milliliters** (mL) are metric units of **capacity**. An Olympic-size swimming pool has a capacity of about 500,000 liters of water.

Work Together

Use estimation and measurement to explore metric capacity.

1. Find the capacity of the spoon.
   a. Fill the dropper with water. Check the level.
   b. Estimate how many milliliters of water will fit in the spoon.
   c. Use the dropper to fill the spoon with water. What is the spoon's capacity?
2. Find the capacity of a mug.
   a. Fill a measuring cup to 100 mL.
   b. Estimate how many milliliters will fit in the mug. Check.
3. Find how many milliliters are in a liter.
   a. Fill a measuring cup to 250 mL.
   b. Empty the water into a liter container. Estimate how many times it will take to fill 1 liter. Check.
   c. Multiply 250 mL by the number of times you poured. How many milliliters are in a liter?

Talk About It

How did you find how many milliliters are in a liter?

Connect

1 L = 1,000 mL

Here are some ways to think about liters and milliliters.

A liter is a little more than a quart.

You can change from liters to milliliters by multiplying.

7 L = ■ mL
$7 \times 1{,}000 = 7{,}000$
7 L = 7,000 mL

A milliliter is about 4 drops of water.

You can change milliliters to liters by dividing.

3,500 mL = ■ L
3,500 [÷] 1,000 [=] 3.5
3,500 mL = 3.5 L

Practice

Choose a tool

Choose a reasonable unit of capacity for each. Write L or mL.

1. 

2. 

3. 

Copy and complete.

4. 30 mL = ■ L **5.** 4,000 mL = ■ L **6.** 7.5 L = ■ mL

7. 40 L = ■ mL **8.** 610 mL = ■ L **9.** 8.2 L = ■ mL

Choose the better estimate of capacity.

10. A jug of apple juice
4 mL or 4,000 mL

11. A paper cup
2 L or 200 mL

12. A bucket
10 L or 1,000 L

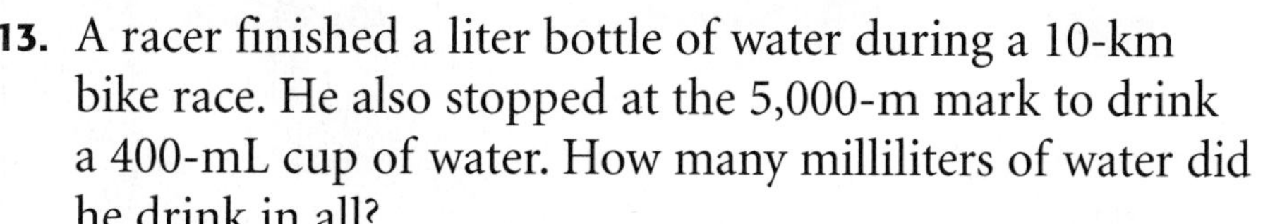

13. A racer finished a liter bottle of water during a 10-km bike race. He also stopped at the 5,000-m mark to drink a 400-mL cup of water. How many milliliters of water did he drink in all?

14. Journal Explain how changing liters to milliliters is like changing kilograms to grams. Give an example.

Chapter 11
Lesson
15

Temperature

You Will Learn

how to read Celsius and Fahrenheit thermometers

Vocabulary

degrees Celsius
metric units of temperature

degrees Fahrenheit
customary units of temperature

Learn

During the opening ceremonies at the 1994 Olympics, the thermometer read 14° Fahrenheit, or −10° Celsius. It was the coldest Winter Olympics ever!

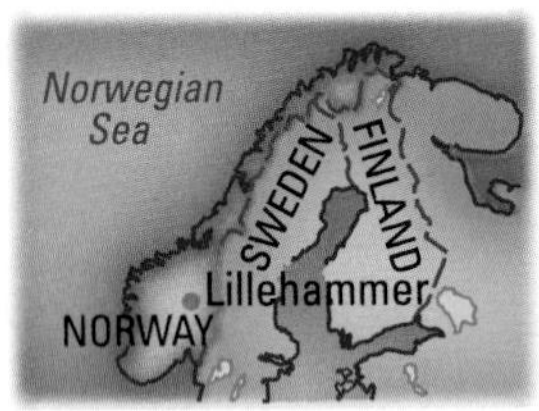

The 1994 Winter Olympics were held in Lillehammer, Norway.

Degrees Celsius are metric units of temperature and are written °C.

Degrees Fahrenheit are customary units of temperature and are written °F.

The thermometer's scale is 2°.

Freezing point is 0°C, or 32°F. We read temperatures that go below 0° as minus. This thermometer shows minus 10° C, the temperature at Lillehammer.

Did You Know?
Normal human body temperature is 98.6°F, or 37°C.

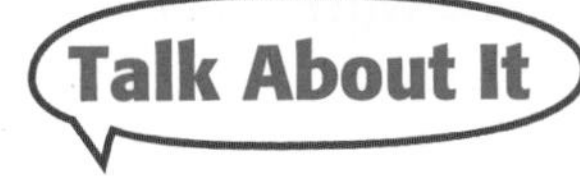

What Celsius temperature is equal to 50°F? How would you describe this temperature?

Check

Read each thermometer. Write the temperature in °C or °F.

1. 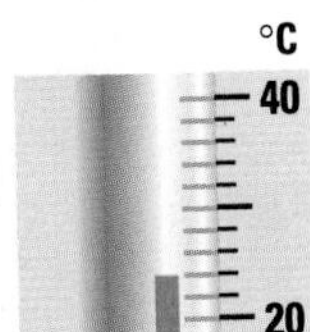

2. 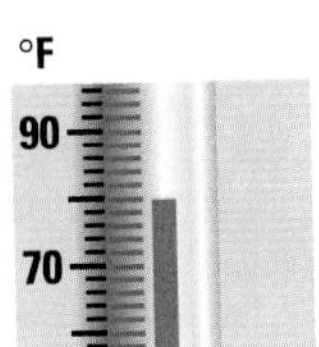

3. 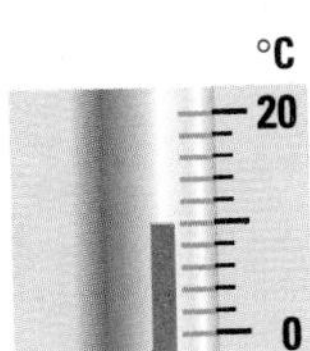

4. 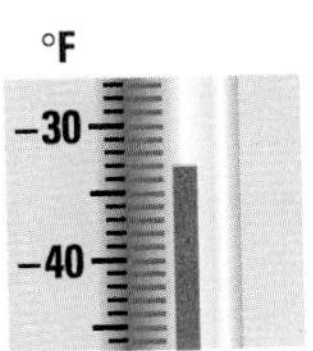

5. **Reasoning** Lee says 30°C is warmer than 30°F, is he correct? Explain.

Practice

Skills and Reasoning

Read each thermometer. Write the temperature in °C or °F.

6. 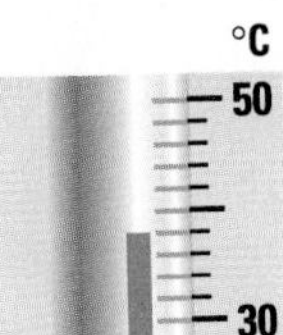

7. 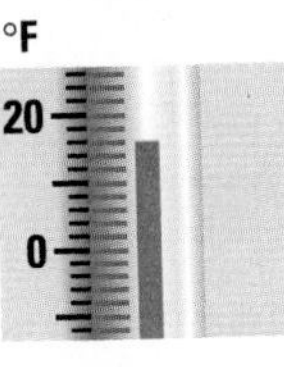

8. 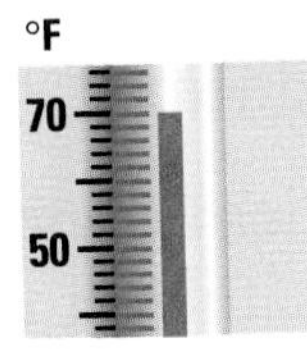

9. 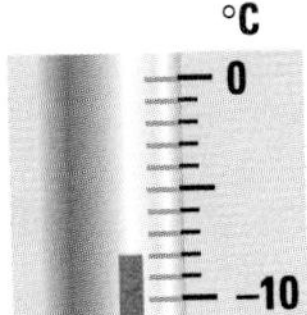

Choose the better estimate for each.

10. Glass of lemonade
 −20°F or 40°F

11. Popsicle
 45°C or −5°C

12. Bowl of hot soup
 60°F or 110°F

13. Which temperature is warmer, −10°C or −5°C?

Problem Solving and Applications

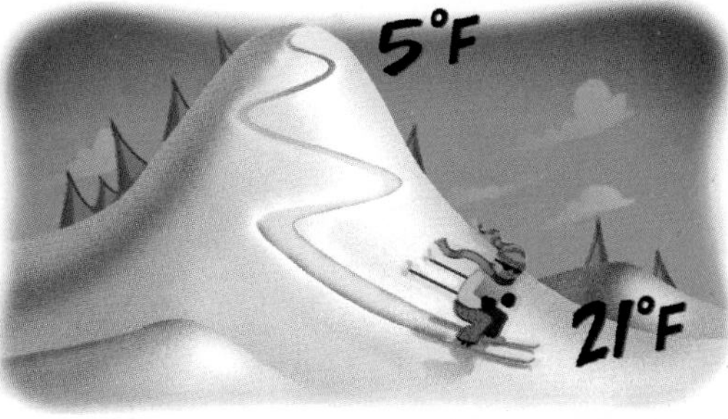

Using Data Use the picture for **14** and **15.**

14. What is the difference in temperature between the top and bottom of the ski slope?

15. Is the temperature above freezing at either location?

16. **Health** Use the *Did You Know?* on page 514. After a race, a marathon runner may have a body temperature of 106°F. How many degrees higher is this than the normal body temperature?

Mixed Review and Test Prep

STAY SHARP!

Find each sum or difference. Write in simplest form.

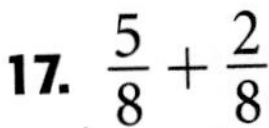

17. $\frac{5}{8} + \frac{2}{8}$ 18. $\frac{3}{4} - \frac{1}{4}$ 19. $\frac{6}{7} - \frac{3}{7}$ 20. $\frac{2}{10} + \frac{6}{10}$

21. **Money** Find the change from $10 if an item costs $8.49.

Ⓐ $2.61 Ⓑ $1.51 Ⓒ $2.51 Ⓓ $1.61

Problem Solving

Decision Making: Plan a New Olympic Track Event

You Will Learn
how to solve problems by making decisions

Materials
- string
- meter stick
- scissors
- large sheet of paper

Explore

The first Olympics in 776 B.C. had only one event, the 200-yard sprint. Later, chariot racing, wrestling, the javelin throw, and other events were added.

Since the modern games began in 1896, there are many more events.

Suppose you bring a new track event to the Olympics, such as human wheelbarrow races or crabwalk races.

Olympia was the home of the Olympic Games in ancient Greece from 776 B.C. to A.D. 393.

Choose a new event. Plan a track for it. Decide the distance the race will cover. How many athletes can race at one time? How can each runner travel the same distance around the track?

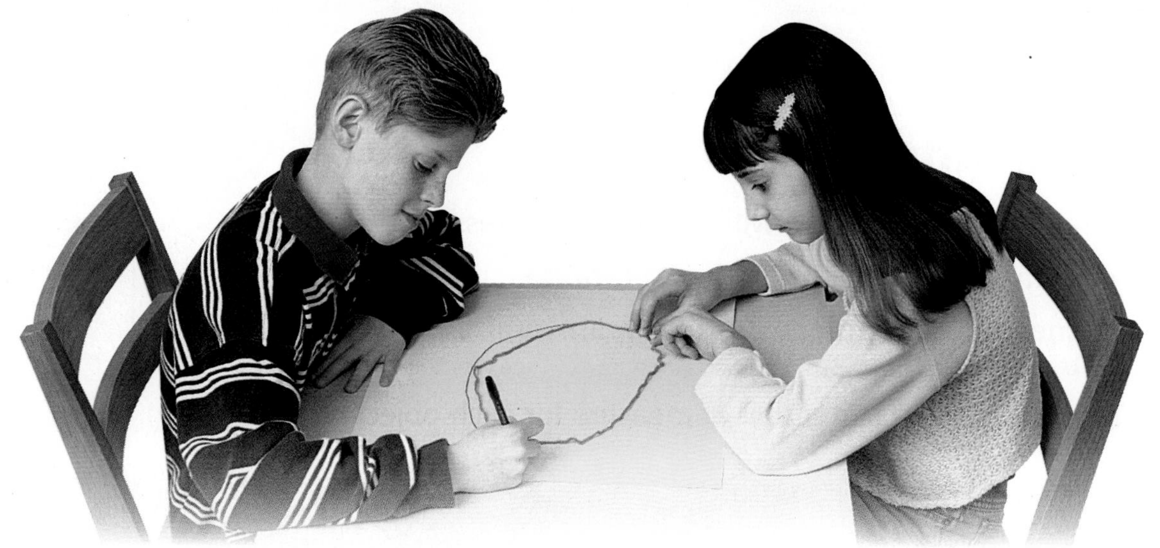

Work Together

Understand

1. Talk about different track events. What do you know about the different lanes of a track?
2. What are the main decisions you need to make?

Plan and Solve

3. Make a model of your track.
   a. Cut a piece of string no longer than 1 meter.
   b. Place it on a large sheet of paper to form the outside lane of the track. Trace around it.
4. Discuss how many lanes your track will need. Each racer will stay in his or her lane throughout the race.
5. Plan where to place a finish line that goes straight across all lanes of the track. Plan where to mark each starting place so that all racers go the same distance. Use the string to help you.

Problem Solving Hint
Running a 1-km race would be like running $\frac{1}{2}$ mile.

Make a Decision

6. Label your track. Show the finish line, the starting places, and the lane numbers. What is the total distance of the race, if racers go just once around the track?
7. Make a list of the race rules.

Present Your Decision

8. Tell the class about your new event. Explain how you decided where to place each start line.
9. What new sports and events are being considered for the Olympics? To find out, take a look at **www.mathsurf.com/4/ch11.**

PROBLEM SOLVING PRACTICE

SECTION C

Review and Practice

Word List
mass
length
capacity

Vocabulary Match each word with what it measures.

1. kilogram **2.** meter **3.** centimeter **4.** liter

5. decimeter **6.** milliliter **7.** gram **8.** kilometer

(Lesson 10) Choose the better unit of measure for each object.

9.

centimeters or meters

10.

centimeters or meters

11.

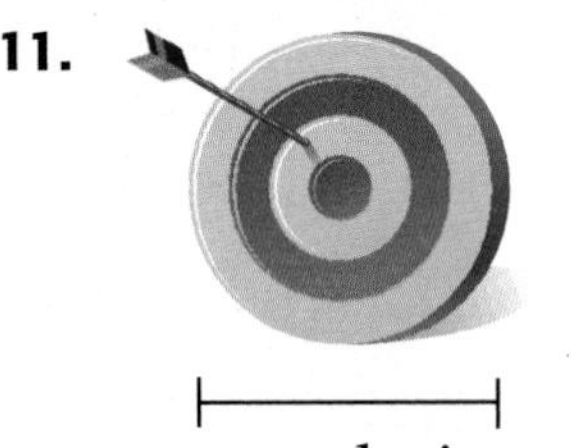

meters or decimeters

(Lesson 11) Copy and complete. Write >, <, or =.

12. 50 m ● 500 cm **13.** 7 km ● 7,000 m **14.** 1,100 m ● 11 km

15. The length of the longest Olympic walking event was 50 kilometers. How many meters was this?

(Lessons 12 and 13) Copy and complete.

16. 2.5 m = ■ cm **17.** 27 cm = ■ m **18.** 15 m = ■ cm

19. 45 kg = ■ g **20.** 5,900 g = ■ kg **21.** 7.6 kg = ■ g

22. Language Arts Olympic rowers use oars, which are 3.82 meters long, or *sculls*, which are 2.98 meters long. What is the difference, in centimeters, between the length of an oar and that of a scull?

(Lesson 14) Choose the better estimate of capacity.

23. Soup bowl
5 mL or 500 mL

24. Garbage can
2.5 L or 250 L

(Lesson 15) Solve.

25. Critical Thinking Mountain temperatures drop 6°C for every 1,000 m you climb. If the temperature is 12°C at the base of a 4,000-m-high mountain, what is it at the peak?

26. Journal Is 14°C above freezing? Is 28°F above freezing? Explain.

Skills Checklist

In this section, you have:

- ☑ **Explored Centimeters, Decimeters, and Meters**
- ☑ **Learned About Meters and Kilometers**
- ☑ **Explored Length and Decimals**
- ☑ **Explored Mass and Capacity**
- ☑ **Learned About Temperature**
- ☑ **Solved Problems by Making Decisions**

Choose at least one. Use what you have learned in this chapter.

1 Olympic Scrapbook

What is your favorite Olympic event? Who is your favorite Olympic athlete? Use magazines, newspapers, an encyclopedia, or other materials to find Olympic data. Make a scrapbook using the data you collect. Write word problems using some of the data. Challenge friends to solve the problems.

110m hurdles
12.91

2 The Pantry

At Home Work with a family member. Read the labels on grocery items in your house or the supermarket. Make a list of the different metric units on the labels. Which information on the labels is only in metric units? Which information on the labels is in metric and customary units?

3 World Wide Weather

The average July temperature is 79°F, or 26°C in Atlanta, Georgia, site of the Summer Olympics in 1996. Check out **www.mathsurf.com/4/ch11** and compare average July temperatures in other U.S. cities. Which city is the hottest?

4 Relay Race

Plan your own relay race. What kind of race will it be? Where will you race? What will the distance be? Use a stopwatch to time each racer. Find the total of each team's time. Make a table of the total times for all of the teams racing.

REVIEW AND PRACTICE

CHAPTER 11

Review/Test

(Lessons 1, 2, and 6) Write the decimal for each.

1. $5\frac{9}{10}$ 2. two and eight hundredths 3. $\frac{91}{100}$ 4. $\frac{4}{20}$

(Lesson 3) Solve.

5. Write 4 ways you can make $1.25 with quarters, dimes, and nickels.

(Lesson 4) Copy and complete. Write >, <, or =.

6. 0.47 ● 0.5 7. 2.11 ● 2.09 8. 5.03 ● 3.05 9. 17.4 ● 17.40

(Lesson 5) Round each decimal to the nearest whole number.

10. 7.39 11. 1.51 12. 14.09 13. 102.7 14. 0.75

(Lesson 7) Estimate each sum or difference.

15. 1.3 + 10.11 16. 40.2 − 20.20 17. 2.58 + 6.17 18. 18 − 0.09

(Lessons 8 and 9) Find each sum or difference.

19. 87.1 − 7.5 20. 36.01 + 11.22 21. 90.07 − 9.50 22. 0.84 + 3.17

(Lessons 10–12) Copy and complete. Write >, <, or =.

23. 8 km ● 800 m 24. 800 cm ● 8 m 25. 2.2 km ● 2,300 m

26. **History** The distance of a marathon race was 42 km until the 1908 Olympics, when England's royal family added about 22 meters to the race. How many meters are now in a marathon?

(Lesson 13) Choose a reasonable unit of mass.

27. Crayon
gram or kilogram

28. Computer monitor
gram or kilogram

29. Eraser
gram or kilogram

(Lesson 14) **Mental Math** Copy and complete.

30. 1,000 mL = ■ L 31. 5 L = ■ mL 32. 68 L = ■ mL

(Lesson 15) Solve.

33. Siobhan had a temperature of 101.4°F. Later, her temperature was 98.6°F. How many degrees did her temperature drop?

CHAPTER 11

Performance Assessment

A. Decimals

Suppose you are a judge at the Snowy Mountain Ski Race. Each skier must ski the course twice. The winner is the skier with the least total time for the two trials.

Race Results		
	Tony	N
Trial 1	40.50	38.8
Trial 2	37.54	38.98

1. **Decision Making** Decide who came in 1st, 2nd, 3rd, and 4th.

2. **Explain Your Thinking** Explain how you reached your decision.

3. **Critical Thinking** Suppose two of these skiers broke the course record. Write a decimal for a possible course record. By how much did the two skiers break the record?

B. Metric Measurement

Kelly is training for a cross-country ski race. She wants to ski the longest possible distance to the ice cave. She wants to carry the heaviest ski pack and the heaviest training weights.

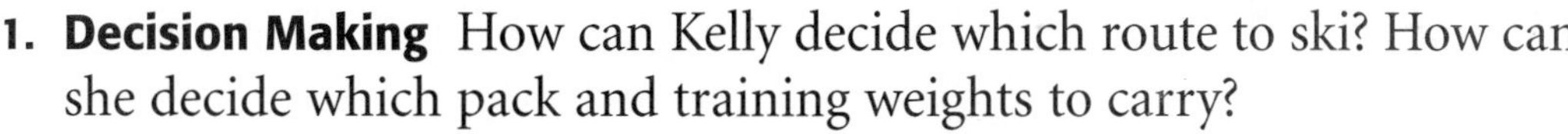

1. **Decision Making** How can Kelly decide which route to ski? How can she decide which pack and training weights to carry?

2. **Recording Data** Make a table to show the distances Kelly can ski.

3. **Explain Your Thinking** Which route has the longest distance? Which ski pack and weights should she carry? What is the total mass of the ski pack and weights?

ath Magazine

Olympic Stories Wilma Rudolph was born into a large family in Tennessee. As a young child, she suffered many illnesses that weakened her legs. As she got older, though, she grew strong and tall and became a fast runner. She qualified for the Olympic track and field team when she was 16.

In the 1960 Olympics, Wilma won a gold medal for her 100-m race. Although her time of 11.0 seconds was fast, it wasn't counted as a world record. That's because her score was "wind-aided." If the wind pushes runners from behind, it helps them go faster.

- A wind speed of 2.00 meters per second or less is allowed.
- On the day of Wilma Rudolph's race, the wind was recorded at 2.75 meters per second.
- How much faster was the wind speed than was allowed?

Wilma Rudolph won three gold medals in the 1960 Olympics.

Try These!

By how many seconds did Wilma beat each of these 100-m scores?

1. 1928 Olympic gold medal score: 12.2 seconds
2. 1948 Olympic gold medal score: 11.9 seconds
3. 1956 Olympic gold medal score: 11.5 seconds
4. **Critical Thinking** What would happen to race results if you couldn't measure races to the nearest tenth of a second?

CHAPTERS 1–11
Cumulative Review

Test Prep Strategy: Read Carefully

Watch for extra information.
Serena scored 8.61 in the floor exercise. The floor exercise was held on a square mat. The length of the mat was 12 m. What was the perimeter of the mat?

Ⓐ 60 m Ⓑ 48 m Ⓒ 36 m Ⓓ 24 m

You do not need to know Serena's score. The mat is square, so the perimeter is 12 + 12 + 12 + 12. The answer is Ⓑ.

Write the letter of the correct answer. Read carefully or use any strategy.

1. In three events at the gymnastics meet, Shaun scored 7.71, 9.35, and 8.02. What is the total of his scores?

   Ⓐ 25.26 Ⓑ 25.10 Ⓒ 25.08 Ⓓ 24.97

2. There were 2 cafeterias. The 43 gymnasts ate in one of them. The cost of lunch for each was $3.00. How much did they spend in all?

   Ⓐ $129 Ⓑ $120 Ⓒ $109 Ⓓ $109.90

3. Six teams took part in a gymnastics meet. There were 48 gymnasts in all. Each team had the same number of gymnasts. How many gymnasts were on each team?

   Ⓐ 42 Ⓑ 54 Ⓒ 6 Ⓓ 8

4. Shaun brought a bag of tangerines. He ate 1, gave away 4, and had 5 left. How many tangerines were in the bag to begin with?

   Ⓐ 20 Ⓑ 12 Ⓒ 10 Ⓓ 5

5. Each team had a school banner hanging on the gymnasium wall. All of the banners except one had 4 sides. This banner could have been shaped like a:

   Ⓐ square Ⓑ triangle Ⓒ rectangle Ⓓ not here

6. The meet ended at 4:30. Shaun and 3 other team members left 35 minutes later. What time did they leave?

   Ⓐ 4:65 Ⓑ 5:10 Ⓒ 5:05 Ⓓ 5:00

7. A gymnastics competition will begin at 9:15 A.M. and is scheduled to last 6 hours. What time will it end?

   Ⓐ 3:15 A.M. Ⓑ 3: 15 P.M. Ⓒ 6:00 P.M. Ⓓ 6:15 P.M.

Test Prep Strategies

- Read Carefully
- Follow Directions
- Make Smart Choices
- Eliminate Choices
- Work Backward from an Answer

DATA FILE

Chapter 12

Dividing by 2-Digit Divisors and Probability

THAT'S ENTERTAINMENT

Rehearsing musicians
Page 527

SECTION A

Dividing by 2-Digit Divisors

527

Which forms of entertainment were available when your grandparents were your age?

Probability

539

The table shows the 10 U.S. parks that attracted the most people in 1995. Suppose you wrote the name of each park on a piece of paper, put all the names in a bag, and then picked one name from the bag. In which state would the park most likely be located?

Park	Location	Attendance (1995)
Disneyland	Anaheim, CA	14,100,000
Magic Kingdom	Lake Buena Vista, FL	12,900,000
EPCOT	Lake Buena Vista, FL	10,700,000
Disney–MGM Studios	Lake Buena Vista, FL	9,500,000
Universal Studios Florida	Orlando, FL	8,000,000
Sea World of Florida	Orlando, FL	4,950,000
Universal Studios Hollywood	Universal City, CA	4,700,000
Six Flags/Great Adventure	Jackson, NJ	4,000,000
Busch Gardens Tampa	Tampa, FL	3,800,000
Sea World of California	San Diego, CA	3,750,000

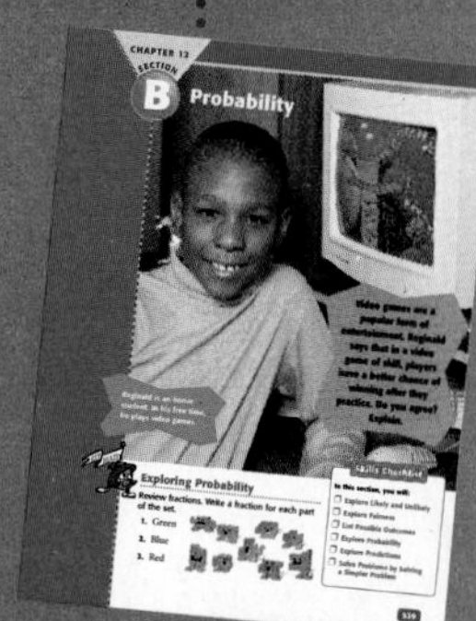

Video fun
Page 539

Surfing the World Wide Web!

Find out more about these theme parks. Check out **www.mathsurf.com/4/ch12**. Use the data you find to plan a trip.

TEAM PROJECT

Activity Survey

A survey of a small group can help you make predictions about a larger group.

Your team will take a sample survey and recommend an end-of-school-year activity: a sports day, an international picnic, or a game day.

Make a Plan

- Will you survey students in your class? In your school? Will you survey teachers and parents?
- What will you ask? How many people will each team member survey?
- How many choices will you record? How will you tally them?

Carry It Out

1. List your questions.
2. Survey the people and tally their choices.
3. Total all the teams' choices.

Talk About It

- How did you decide who to include in your sample survey?
- How can you use the results to decide on an activity?
- If two activities tie for first choice, which will you recommend?

Present the Project

- Tell how you recorded and tallied the data.
- Show your data in a graph.
- Tell which activity you would recommend and why.

CHAPTER 12

SECTION

A Dividing by 2-Digit Divisors

Daniel's school orchestra practices twice a week for an hour before school. About how many hours is that in a school year?

Rebekah received an Outstanding Educational Improvement award from President Clinton.

GET READY!

Dividing with 2-Digit Divisors

Review dividing mentally.

1. $60 \div 2 = n$
2. $80 \div 4 = n$
3. $360 \div 9 = n$
4. $420 \div 7 = n$
5. $630 \div 9 = n$
6. $720 \div 8 = n$
7. $180 \div 3 = n$
8. $200 \div 5 = n$

Skills Checklist

In this section, you will:

- ❒ Explore Division Patterns
- ❒ Estimate Quotients with 2-Digit Divisors
- ❒ Divide by Tens
- ❒ Divide with 2-Digit Divisors
- ❒ Solve Problems by Making Decisions

Chapter 12
Lesson
1

Exploring Division Patterns

Problem Solving Connection
Look for Patterns

Materials
calculator

Explore

Place-value patterns can help you divide greater numbers.

80 ÷ 40 = 2
800 ÷ 40 = 20
8000 ÷ 40 =

Math Tip
Think of basic division facts to help.

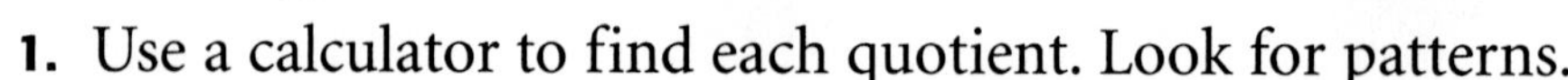

Work Together

1. Use a calculator to find each quotient. Look for patterns.

a. $80 \div 40 = n$
$800 \div 40 = n$
$8{,}000 \div 40 = n$

b. $90 \div 30 = n$
$900 \div 30 = n$
$9{,}000 \div 30 = n$

c. $60 \div 20 = n$
$600 \div 20 = n$
$6{,}000 \div 20 = n$

2. Use patterns to find each quotient. Check with a calculator.

a. $150 \div 50 = n$
$1{,}500 \div 50 = n$
$15{,}000 \div 50 = n$

b. $120 \div 60 = n$
$1{,}200 \div 60 = n$
$12{,}000 \div 60 = n$

c. $210 \div 70 = n$
$2{,}100 \div 70 = n$
$21{,}000 \div 70 = n$

d. $540 \div 90 = n$
$5{,}400 \div 90 = n$
$54{,}000 \div 90 = n$

e. $200 \div 40 = n$
$2{,}000 \div 40 = n$
$20{,}000 \div 40 = n$

f. $320 \div 80 = n$
$3{,}200 \div 80 = n$
$32{,}000 \div 80 = n$

Talk About It

3. Describe the patterns you found.

4. Explain how you can find $640 \div 80$ mentally.

Connect

You can use basic facts and place-value patterns to help you divide greater numbers.

Find $240 \div 30$.
Think: $24 \div 3 = 8$
24 tens ÷ 3 tens = 8
$240 \div 30 = 8$

Find $2{,}400 \div 30$.
Think: $24 \div 3 = 8$
24 hundreds ÷ 3 tens = 80
$2{,}400 \div 30 = 80$

Find $24{,}000 \div 30$.
Think: $24 \div 3 = 8$
24 thousands ÷ 3 tens = 800
$24{,}000 \div 30 = 800$

Practice

Copy and complete.

1. $250 \div 50 = n$
$2{,}500 \div 50 = n$
$25{,}000 \div 50 = n$

2. $280 \div 70 = n$
$2{,}800 \div 70 = n$
$28{,}000 \div 70 = n$

3. $400 \div 50 = n$
$4{,}000 \div 50 = n$
$40{,}000 \div 50 = n$

4. $360 \div 90 = n$
$3{,}600 \div 90 = n$
$36{,}000 \div 90 = n$

5. $420 \div 60 = n$
$4{,}200 \div 60 = n$
$42{,}000 \div 60 = n$

6. $240 \div 40 = n$
$2{,}400 \div 40 = n$
$24{,}000 \div 40 = n$

Mental Math Find each quotient.

7. $40 \div 20$ **8.** $80 \div 20$ **9.** $180 \div 60$ **10.** $810 \div 90$

11. $240 \div 80$ **12.** $270 \div 90$ **13.** $490 \div 70$ **14.** $630 \div 70$

15. $60 \div 30$ **16.** $300 \div 60$ **17.** $180 \div 90$ **18.** $160 \div 20$

Algebra Readiness Copy and complete.

19. $450 \div 90 = n$
$4{,}500 \div n = 50$
$n \div 90 = 500$

20. $210 \div 30 = n$
$n \div 30 = 70$
$21{,}000 \div n = 700$

21. $320 \div 80 = n$
$n \div 80 = 40$
$32{,}000 \div n = 400$

22. Geometry Readiness Copy and complete the pattern.

 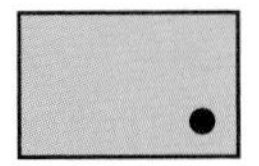 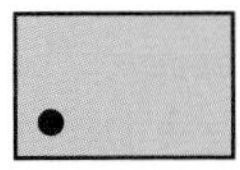 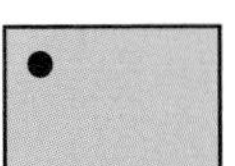 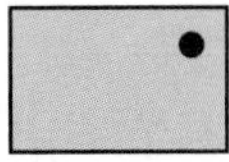 _____ _____ _____

23. Critical Thinking What do you notice about the quotients for pairs like $540 \div 60$ and $540 \div 90$?

24. Money A pair of headsets cost \$40. How many pairs of headsets could you buy with \$160?

25. Journal Explain how basic facts and place-value patterns can help you find $720 \div 80$.

Chapter 12
Lesson
2

Estimating Quotients with 2-Digit Divisors

You Will Learn
how to estimate quotients when dividing by 2-digit numbers

Learn

174 tickets are sold for a school concert that will feature Rebekah and Daniel playing a duet. If there are 21 folding chairs in each row, about how many rows must be set up in the auditorium?

Sister and brother Rebekah and Daniel live in Bay Shore, New York.

Here are two different ways to find $174 \div 21$.

Remember
$160 \div 20 = 8$
$1{,}600 \div 20 = 80$
$16{,}000 \div 20 = 800$

One Way

Think of a basic fact.
You know that $16 \div 2$ is 8.
174 is close to 160.
21 is close to 20.

$160 \div 20 = 8$

So, about 8 rows of chairs are needed.

Another Way

Think of a basic fact.
You know that $18 \div 2$ is 9.
174 is close to 180.
21 is close to 20.

$180 \div 20 = 9$

So, about 9 rows of chairs are needed.

Talk About It

Which estimate would you use if 174 people came to the concert?

Check

Estimate each quotient.

1. $83 \div 38$
2. $152 \div 33$
3. $244 \div 77$
4. $94 \div 31$
5. $271 \div 91$
6. $417 \div 73$
7. $647 \div 76$
8. $198 \div 52$
9. **Reasoning** For $83 \div 38$, do you think the exact answer is greater or less than 2? Explain.

Practice

Skills and Reasoning

Estimate each quotient.

10. $61 \div 22$ **11.** $88 \div 31$ **12.** $124 \div 58$ **13.** $181 \div 91$

14. $242 \div 59$ **15.** $360 \div 95$ **16.** $163 \div 78$ **17.** $272 \div 31$

18. $627 \div 90$ **19.** $237 \div 42$ **20.** $242 \div 29$ **21.** $179 \div 31$

22. $282 \div 41$ **23.** $179 \div 62$ **24.** $476 \div 83$ **25.** $354 \div 49$

Mental Math Copy and complete. Write >, <, or =.

26. $721 \div 80$ ● $722 \div 80$ **27.** $822 \div 90$ ● $811 \div 90$

28. $360 \div 6$ ● $3{,}600 \div 60$ **29.** $560 \div 7$ ● $5{,}600 \div 80$

Problem Solving and Applications

30. For a fund-raiser, the school band must sell at least 220 tickets. If there are 28 students in the band, about how many tickets should each student sell?

31. History The tuba was invented in Germany in 1835. How many years has the tuba been played?

32. Fine Arts An orchestra is divided into 4 groups: string, woodwind, brass, and percussion. If an orchestra has 100 musicians, at least 60 play string instruments. At least what fraction of the orchestra plays strings?

Mixed Review and Test Prep

STAY SHARP!

Find each product.

33. 282×31 **34.** 487×35 **35.** 566×528 **36.** 274×529

Find each sum. Simplify.

37. $\frac{1}{10} + \frac{2}{5}$ **38.** $\frac{2}{3} + \frac{1}{6}$ **39.** $\frac{1}{4} + \frac{3}{8}$ **40.** $\frac{3}{5} + \frac{1}{10}$ **41.** $\frac{1}{4} + \frac{5}{12}$

42. Which product is greater than 20,000?

Ⓐ $2 \times 9{,}123$ Ⓑ $3 \times 5{,}424$ Ⓒ $5 \times 4{,}291$ Ⓓ $9 \times 1{,}988$

Chapter 12
Lesson
3

Dividing by Tens

You Will Learn
how to divide by multiples of ten

Learn

Desiree and 39 other students are producing a school play, *What Fools Mortals Be.* If the auditorium has 335 seats, how many friends and family members can each student invite to the play's opening night?

Desiree from Detroit, Michigan, acts in her school's plays.

You can divide to find the number of people each student can invite.

Example

Find 335 ÷ 40.

Step 1	**Step 2**
Decide where to start dividing. Estimate. **Think:** $40\overline{)320}$ = 8 Start by dividing ones.	Divide the ones. $40\overline{)335}$ = 8 R15 -320 15 Multiply. $8 \times 40 = 320$ Subtract. $335 - 320 = 15$ Compare. $15 < 40$

You can use multiplication to check your answer.

$$\begin{array}{r} 40 \\ \times\ 8 \\ \hline 320 \end{array} \quad \begin{array}{l} \leftarrow \text{Divisor} \\ \leftarrow \text{Quotient} \\ \\ \end{array} \qquad \begin{array}{r} 320 \\ +\ 15 \\ \hline 335 \end{array} \quad \begin{array}{l} \\ \leftarrow \text{Remainder} \\ \leftarrow \text{Dividend} \end{array}$$

Each person can invite 8 friends or family members.

Remember
The remainder must be less than the divisor.

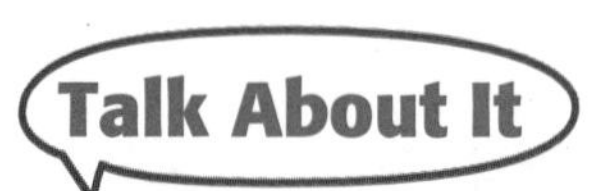

Why would you estimate 320 ÷ 40 rather than 360 ÷ 40?

Check

Divide and check.

1. $326 \div 80$
2. $182 \div 20$
3. $219 \div 70$
4. $271 \div 90$
5. $257 \div 50$
6. $70\overline{)498}$
7. $80\overline{)652}$
8. $30\overline{)194}$
9. $60\overline{)485}$
10. $60\overline{)431}$
11. **Reasoning** Without finding the exact answer, how can you tell that $573 \div 80$ will have a 1-digit quotient?

Practice

Skills and Reasoning

Divide and check.

12. $67 \div 20$
13. $92 \div 30$
14. $124 \div 30$
15. $181 \div 90$
16. $247 \div 60$
17. $375 \div 90$
18. $163 \div 80$
19. $276 \div 30$
20. $378 \div 60$
21. $247 \div 40$
22. $30\overline{)252}$
23. $30\overline{)199}$
24. $80\overline{)724}$
25. $70\overline{)638}$
26. $90\overline{)657}$
27. $60\overline{)149}$
28. $10\overline{)78}$
29. $50\overline{)419}$
30. $40\overline{)339}$
31. $20\overline{)182}$
32. Divide 362 by 70.
33. Divide 448 by 60.
34. Divide 830 by 90.
35. Find 4 numbers that do not have a remainder when divided by 40.

Problem Solving and Applications

36. **Time** Desiree and the other players rehearsed for 9 hours each week, for $2\frac{1}{2}$ months. About how many hours did they rehearse?
37. **Time** Desiree practiced for 35 min on Mon., 25 min on Wed., and 50 min on Sat. About how many hours did she practice?

Using Data Use the Data File on page 524 to answer **38** and **39.**

38. How many years after color TV was introduced were video games available?
39. Technicolor for movies was invented in 1920. Where on the number line would you put *Technicolor Movies?*

Mixed Review and Test Prep

Find each product.

40. 345×25
41. 98×124
42. 40×711
43. 23×742
44. 83×421
45. Choose the number with the same value as $2\frac{1}{2}$.

Ⓐ 22 Ⓑ 2.2 Ⓒ 25 Ⓓ 2.5

Chapter 12
Lesson
4

Dividing with 2-Digit Divisors

You Will Learn
how to divide by 2-digit divisors

Learn

Did You Know?
The *saltwater crocodile* is the longest crocodile. It can grow to about 20 feet.

Jessica's girl scout troop visited a natural history museum. They saw a model of a crocodile. "How many of you would it take, standing hand-to-hand, to equal the length of this 197-inch crocodile?" asked the troop leader.

You can divide to find the number of scouts standing hand-to-hand.

Example

Find 197 ÷ 48.

Step 1

Decide where to start dividing.

Estimate.

Think: $50\overline{)200}$ = 4

Start by dividing ones.

Step 2

Divide the ones.

$$\begin{array}{r} 4\text{ R5} \\ 48\overline{)197} \\ -\,192 \\ \hline 5 \end{array}$$

Multiply. 4 × 48 = 192
Subtract. 197 − 192 = 5
Compare. 5 < 48

You can use multiplication to check your answer.

$$\begin{array}{rl} 48 & \leftarrow \text{Divisor} \\ \times\ 4 & \leftarrow \text{Quotient} \\ \hline 192 & \end{array} \qquad \begin{array}{rl} 192 & \\ +\ \ 5 & \leftarrow \text{Remainder} \\ \hline 197 & \leftarrow \text{Dividend} \end{array}$$

About 4 scouts standing hand-to-hand would equal the length of the crocodile.

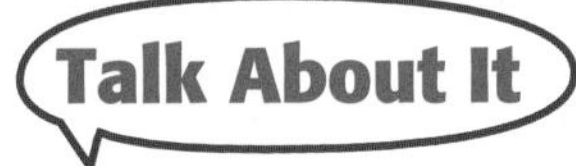

How did you decide where to start dividing?

Check

Divide and check.

1. 325 ÷ 39 **2.** 128 ÷ 21 **3.** 210 ÷ 69 **4.** 271 ÷ 88 **5.** 407 ÷ 49

6. 512 ÷ 73 **7.** 652 ÷ 81 **8.** $32\overline{)198}$ **9.** $41\overline{)373}$ **10.** $22\overline{)159}$

11. Reasoning Suppose you divided 128 by 22 and got 5 R28. How can you tell the answer is incorrect?

Practice

Skills and Reasoning

Divide and check.

12. 67 ÷ 28 **13.** 92 ÷ 64 **14.** 134 ÷ 31 **15.** 184 ÷ 92 **16.** 228 ÷ 38

17. 375 ÷ 93 **18.** 163 ÷ 79 **19.** 276 ÷ 88 **20.** 397 ÷ 66 **21.** 257 ÷ 63

22. $32\overline{)272}$ **23.** $82\overline{)199}$ **24.** $87\overline{)702}$ **25.** $74\overline{)666}$ **26.** $72\overline{)657}$

27. $39\overline{)168}$ **28.** $91\overline{)550}$ **29.** $49\overline{)245}$ **30.** $29\overline{)157}$ **31.** $68\overline{)218}$

32. Without finding the exact answer, how do you know that 450 ÷ 62 will be greater than 7?

Problem Solving and Applications

33. Science A blue whale is 120 feet long. This is about the same length as 18 scuba divers swimming in a line. About how tall is each scuba diver?

34. Money You have $2.27 in bills and pennies that you want to exchange for quarters. How many quarters will you get?

35. Using Data A full-grown Nile crocodile is about 16 feet long. How much longer is a full-grown saltwater crocodile? Use the *Did You Know?* on page 534.

Nile crocodiles are found in Africa and Madagascar.

Mixed Review and Test Prep

STAY SHARP!

Find each sum.

36. 6.7 + 3.9 **37.** 8.9 + 0.5 **38.** 23.4 + 89.6 **39.** 7.6 + 4.8

40. Find the difference between 9,001 and 8,811.

Ⓐ 17,812 Ⓑ 1,810 Ⓒ 190 Ⓓ 188

Chapter 12 Lesson 5

Problem Solving

Decision Making: Videotaping a Fair

You Will Learn how to analyze data to make a decision

Explore

The phone rings. It's the city's fair planners. They want to hire Farukh's team to videotape a community fair at the park.

The fair is outdoors, so Farukh's team will use batteries in the cameras. He has 3 cameras and 9 batteries. Each battery lasts 40 minutes. His team cannot videotape all of every event. The team will film highlights of each event.

How would you plan the job?

Remember There are 60 minutes in an hour.

Farukh Basrai is a video producer in Mountain View, California.

Facts and Data for the Fair Events
• Rock concert: $2\frac{1}{2}$ hours
• Rubber duck race: $\frac{1}{2}$ hour
• Fair food contest: 3 hours
• Antique car rally: $1\frac{3}{4}$ hours
• Pet parade: $1\frac{1}{2}$ hours

Work Together

Understand

1. What do you know?
2. What is the main decision you need to make?

Plan and Solve

3. Which events do you think would be best to videotape? Which ones, if any, would you want to videotape for the entire time?
4. What is the total time, in minutes, that all 9 batteries could supply power?
5. How many minutes does each event last? What is the total?
6. If 3 people divided the videotaping equally, how much time could each person tape?

Make a Decision

7. Decide if the team should use all three cameras and how many batteries each camera person should use.
8. Make a list that shows:
   a. which events each camera person should videotape.
   b. how many minutes each camera person should spend videotaping each event.

Present Your Decision

9. Display your list and explain the decisions you made.
10. Explain how you used division to plan the job. Tell what other operations you used.

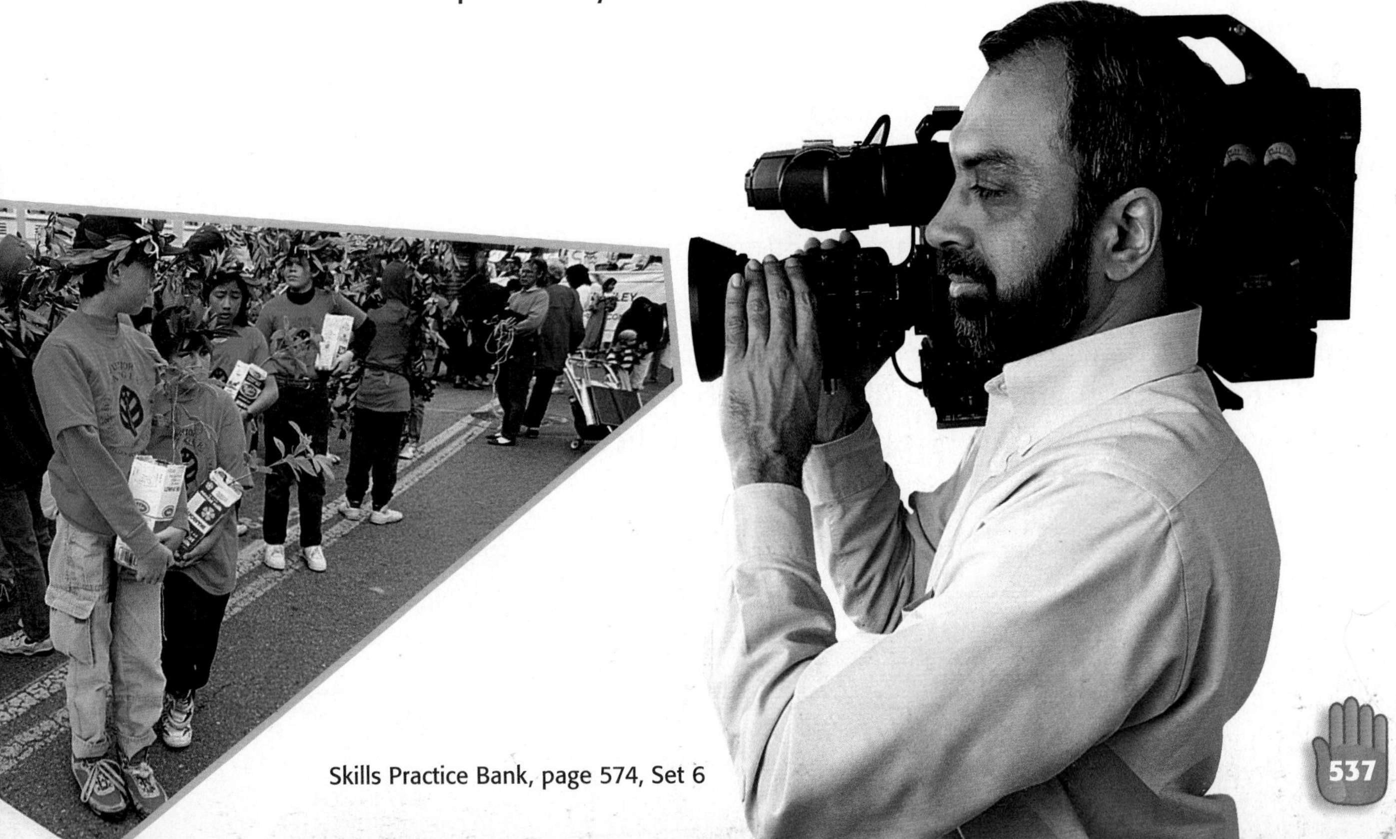

Skills Practice Bank, page 574, Set 6

SECTION A

Review and Practice

(Lesson 1) Mental Math Find each quotient.

1. 60 ÷ 20 **2.** 90 ÷ 30 **3.** 180 ÷ 20 **4.** 210 ÷ 70 **5.** 300 ÷ 50

6. 360 ÷ 60 **7.** 480 ÷ 80 **8.** 160 ÷ 40 **9.** 720 ÷ 80 **10.** 400 ÷ 80

(Lesson 2) Estimate each quotient.

11. 61 ÷ 29 **12.** 217 ÷ 31 **13.** 364 ÷ 39 **14.** 248 ÷ 51 **15.** 273 ÷ 89

16. 257 ÷ 63 **17.** 576 ÷ 72 **18.** 189 ÷ 61 **19.** 122 ÷ 42 **20.** 478 ÷ 81

Mental Math Copy and complete. Write >, <, or =.

21. 258 ÷ 50 ● 259 ÷ 50 **22.** 654 ÷ 80 ● 644 ÷ 80 **23.** 815 ÷ 90 ● 825 ÷ 90

24. 140 ÷ 7 ● 1,400 ÷ 70 **25.** 100 ÷ 5 ● 1,000 ÷ 50 **26.** 540 ÷ 6 ● 5,400 ÷ 90

27. Money You have $4.62 in bills and pennies that you want to exchange at the bank for half-dollar coins. How many half-dollar coins will you get?

28. Time A book has 263 pages. If you read 25 pages each day, could you finish reading the book in a week? Explain.

(Lessons 3 and 4) Divide and check.

29. 183 ÷ 30 **30.** 488 ÷ 60 **31.** 169 ÷ 80 **32.** 251 ÷ 40 **33.** 725 ÷ 80

34. $90\overline{)638}$ **35.** $29\overline{)216}$ **36.** $91\overline{)819}$ **37.** $73\overline{)513}$ **38.** 498 ÷ 69

39. 330 ÷ 82 **40.** 629 ÷ 78 **41.** 129 ÷ 42 **42.** 193 ÷ 33 **43.** 501 ÷ 69

44. Time Alexis watched two movies one after the other. The first one was 132 minutes and the other was 115 minutes long. About how many hours did Alexis watch movies?

45. Measurement The largest tuba is 8 feet high. If its tube was unwound and stretched out it would be about 45 feet long. How many inches long is the tube?

46. Journal How would you find how many boxes you would need to pack 175 toy crocodiles, if each box holds 48 toys?

Skills Checklist

In this section, you have:

- ☑ Explored Division Patterns
- ☑ Estimated Quotients with 2-Digit Divisors
- ☑ Divided by Tens
- ☑ Divided with 2-Digit Divisors
- ☑ Solved Problems by Making Decisions

CHAPTER 12

SECTION

B Probability

Reginald is an honor student. In his free time, he plays video games.

Video games are a popular form of entertainment. Reginald says that in a video game of skill, players have a better chance of winning after they practice. Do you agree? Explain.

GET READY!

Exploring Probability

Review fractions. Write a fraction for each part of the set.

1. Green
2. Blue
3. Red

Skills Checklist

In this section, you will:

- ❒ Explore Likely and Unlikely
- ❒ Explore Fairness
- ❒ List Possible Outcomes
- ❒ Explore Probability
- ❒ Explore Predictions
- ❒ Solve Problems by Solving a Simpler Problem

Chapter 12
Lesson
6

Exploring Likely and Unlikely

Problem Solving Connection
- Draw a Picture
- Use Logical Reasoning

Materials
ruler

Vocabulary
likely
probably will happen
unlikely
probably will not happen
impossible
definitely will not happen
certain
definitely will happen

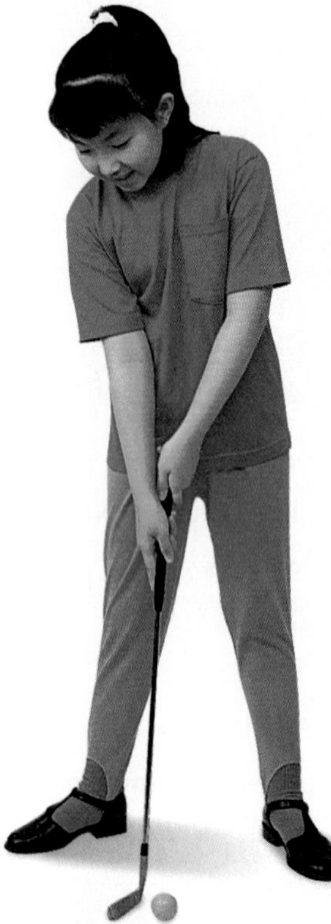

Explore

Kerplunk. It's a hole-in-one! In miniature golf, a player hits a golf ball from the tee into the hole using the fewest tries. The ball must stay inside the boundaries. One try is a hole-in-one. At Max's Golf Town, anyone who gets a hole-in-one on hole A, B, or C wins a free game.

Work Together

1. On each drawing, line up a ruler edge from the golf tee to the hole.
   a. At which hole—A, B, or C—are you most likely to win a free game? Explain.
   b. At which hole are you least likely to win a free game? Explain.
2. Draw a miniature golf course on which a hole-in-one is likely. Draw one on which a hole-in-one is unlikely.
3. Minnie said that it is impossible to get a hole-in-one on hole D. She said that a hole-in-one is certain on hole E. Do you agree?

Talk About It

If it usually snows in the winter where you live, would you say it is *likely* or *certain* to snow this winter? Why?

Connect

Knowing how **likely** or **unlikely** an event is helps you predict whether it will happen. An event that is **impossible** is one that cannot happen. An event that is **certain** is one that must happen. Most events are between *impossible* and *certain.*

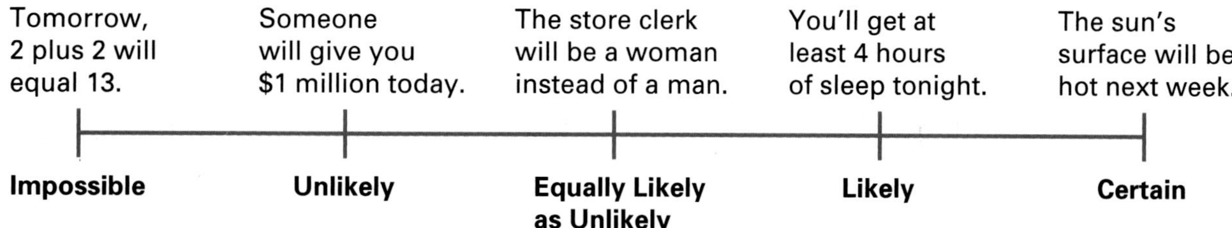

Practice

Read each statement. Write whether the event is impossible, unlikely, equally likely as unlikely, likely, or certain.

1. The day after Thursday will be Friday.
2. A real frog will speak English.
3. It will snow in Florida this year.
4. A new breakfast cereal will be available next year.
5. You will choose a red crayon, if you choose between a blue crayon and a red crayon without looking.
6. You will talk to someone in the next 24 hours.
7. **Geography** Use this map of nine states. If a friend chooses one state, write whether the event below is impossible, unlikely, equally likely as unlikely, likely, or certain. Explain.

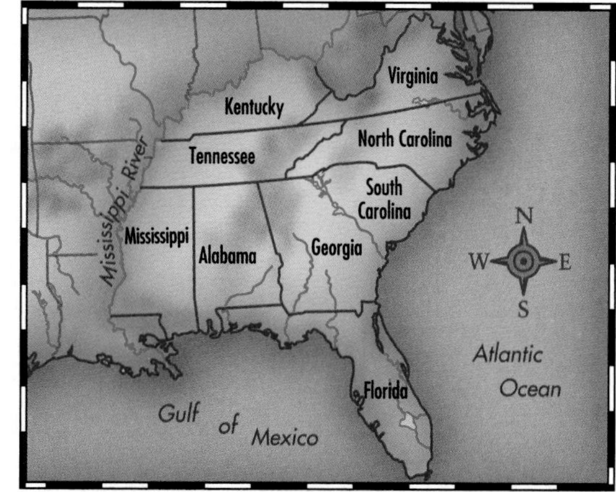

   a. The state will have more than four letters in its full name.
   b. The name of the state will have two words.
   c. The state will be on the coast.
   d. The state will be west of the Mississippi River.

8. **Journal** Think of events in an ordinary school day. Describe one of each kind of event, from impossible to certain.

Exploring Fairness

Problem Solving Connection
- Use Objects/ Act It Out
- Use Logical Reasoning

Materials
number cubes, labeled 1–6

Vocabulary

outcome
the result of an action or event

fair
a game is fair if each player has an equal chance of winning

equally likely
just as likely to happen as not

Explore

"What do I like to do for entertainment? Play video games!" answers Reginald. Sometimes Reginald plays video games with a friend.

In a fair game, players start out with the same chance of winning.

Reginald lives in Little Rock, Arkansas.

Work Together

1. Play a game of Match Me! with a partner. One person tosses a number cube. The partner then tosses another number cube, trying to match the number from the first toss. Repeat 10 times. Tally your scores. Change roles and play again.

Scoring
The first person gets 1 point when the cubes do not match. The partner gets 1 point when the cubes do match.

2. Play a game of Odds and Evens with a partner. Decide who will be "odds" and who will be "evens." Take turns tossing a number cube 10 times. Record each toss.

Scoring
"Odds" gets 1 point for each outcome of 1, 3, or 5. "Evens" gets 1 point for each outcome of 2, 4, or 6.

3. Which of these two games is fair to both partners? Which game is not fair? Explain your answer.

Talk About It

4. What is a "fair" game? Try to use the words *likely* or *unlikely* in your answer.
5. How could you make the unfair game more fair?

Connect

Two people play a game with a spinner. Player A earns 1 point for spinning red. Player B earns 1 point for spinning green. Green and red are each **outcomes** of spinning.

The game is **fair** if the players use this spinner. Both outcomes are **equally likely.**

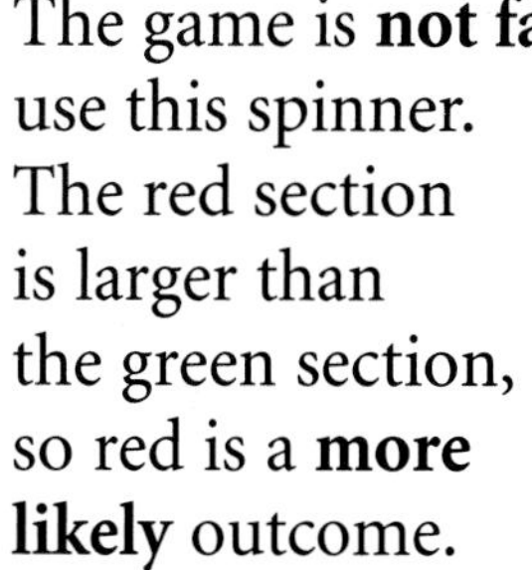

The game is **not fair** if the players use this spinner. The red section is larger than the green section, so red is a **more likely** outcome.

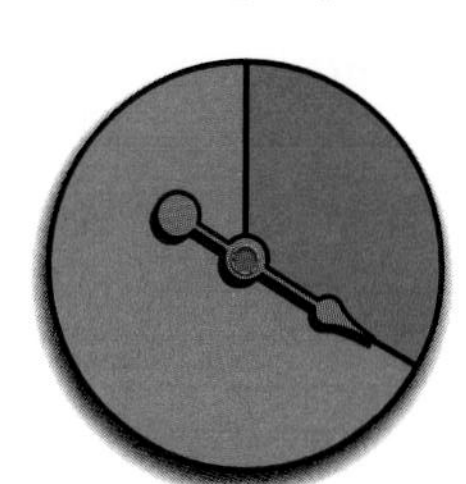

Practice

Write whether each game is fair or unfair. If it is unfair, explain why.

1. Jamal and Cindy toss a penny 20 times. Jamal gets 1 point for each head. Cindy gets 1 point for each tail.

2. **Reasoning** Suppose you play a sock-color game. The winner is the player who has the most socks of one color. You reach into this pile of socks without looking and pull out a sock.

3. **Language Arts** Gwen and Casey play a guessing game with letters. Gwen closes her eyes and picks a word in a book. She wins if the word has a vowel. Casey wins if it doesn't have a vowel.

4. A box contains 12 marbles: 6 are green and 6 are orange. Tran chooses a marble without looking. He wins if the marble is green. Eve wins if it is orange.

5. **Math History** Ancient Babylonians played a game in which a player tossed 3 pyramid pieces. Each pyramid had 2 white tips and 2 red tips. If 3 red tips landed up, the player scored 5 points. If 3 white tips landed up, the player scored 4 points. Players took turns tossing the pyramids.

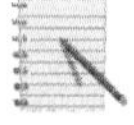

6. **Journal** Draw a spinner with at least two parts. Explain if it is fair or unfair.

Listing Possible Outcomes

You Will Learn
how to list possible outcomes of an event

Vocabulary
tree diagram
a diagram of all possible outcomes of an event (A tree diagram looks like branches of a tree.)

Learn

20
50

Play a bean bag toss game with two targets.

How many possible outcomes are there after two tosses?

To show possible outcomes, you can draw a **tree diagram**.

Bean Bag Toss Rules

Target 1:
50 or 20 points
Target 2:
100, 30, or 10 points

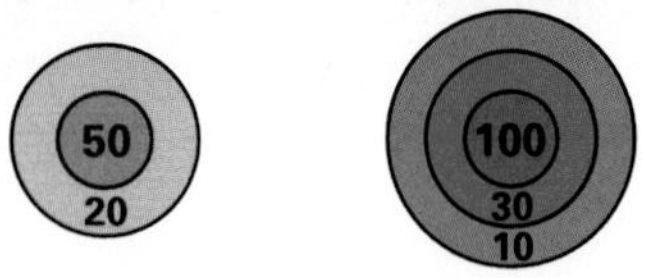
50
20
100
30
10

Each thrower gets two tosses, one to each target. Tosses that do not land on the target are not counted as tosses.

Remember
An outcome is a result of an action or event.

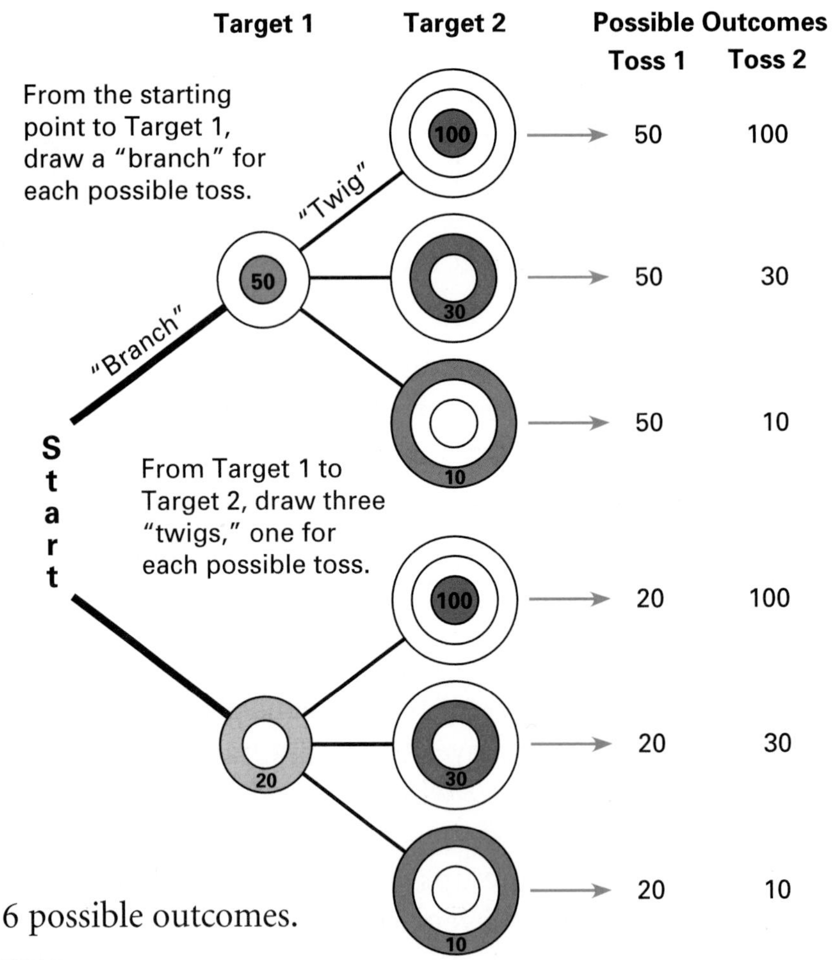
Target 1
Target 2
Possible Outcomes
Toss 1
Toss 2
From the starting point to Target 1, draw a "branch" for each possible toss.
"Twig"
"Branch"
Start
From Target 1 to Target 2, draw three "twigs," one for each possible toss.
50
20
100
30
10
100
30
10
50 100
50 30
50 10
20 100
20 30
20 10

There are 6 possible outcomes.

Talk About It

How many outcomes are possible on the first toss?

Check

Copy and complete the tree diagram. Show all possible outcomes.

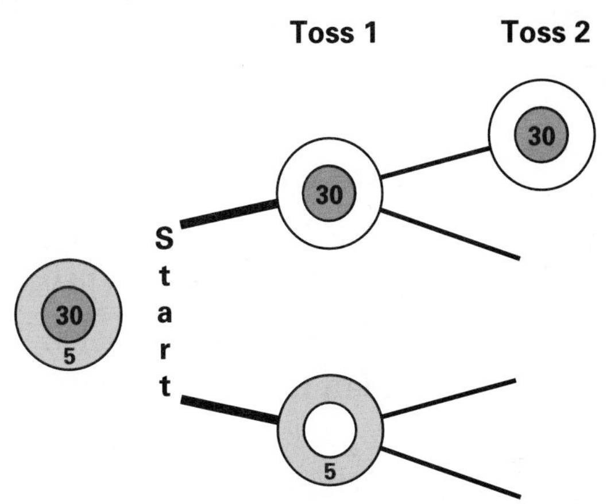
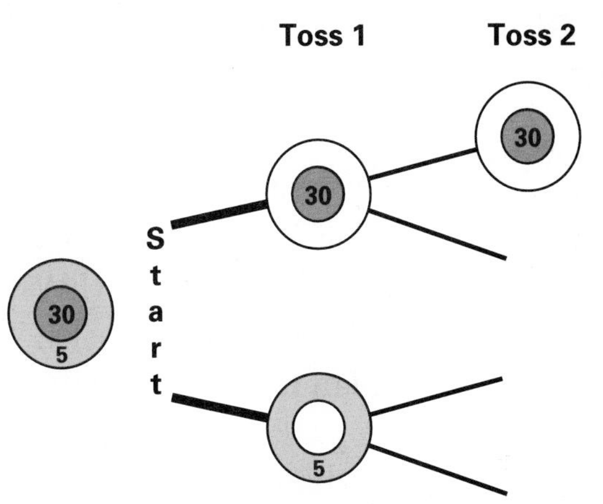

1. Using the target shown, what are the possible outcomes for Toss 1?
2. What are the possible outcomes for Toss 2?
3. **Reasoning** Suppose a player tosses a third time. How many possible outcomes are there for the third toss?

PRACTICE AND APPLY

Practice

Skills and Reasoning

4. What are the possible outcomes for spinning the first spinner?
5. What are the possible outcomes for spinning the second spinner?
6. What are the possible outcomes for spinning both spinners together?
7. Are all possible outcomes for spinning the second spinner equally likely? Explain.

Spinner 1

Spinner 2

Problem Solving and Applications

8. A costume store rents wigs. They come in four colors: purple, yellow, green, or red. Each color comes in short or long hair.
   a. Draw a tree diagram to show all the possible wig choices.
   b. How many possible wig choices are there?
9. **Critical Thinking** Jessie rolled two number cubes each labeled 1–6, and added the numbers. How many ways could she score a sum of 7? A sum of 3? Which outcome is more likely?

Mixed Review and Test Prep

Mental Math Find each quotient.

10. $20\overline{)80}$ 11. $40\overline{)320}$ 12. $30\overline{)210}$ 13. $80\overline{)640}$

14. What is the product of 6 and 6,122?

Ⓐ 360,732 Ⓑ 36,732 Ⓒ 42, 732 Ⓓ 35,732

Chapter 12
Lesson
9

Exploring Probability

Problem Solving Connection
- Use Objects
- Make a List

Materials
- number cube, labeled 1–6
- coin

Vocabulary
probability
the chance that an event will happen

Hikers in south central Alaska

Explore

The Curtis family is visiting the Chugach (CHEW-gatch) Mountains in Alaska. Today, they plan to hike in the Portage Valley. A park ranger says that there are 5 chances in 6 it will rain. Should the family take rain gear?

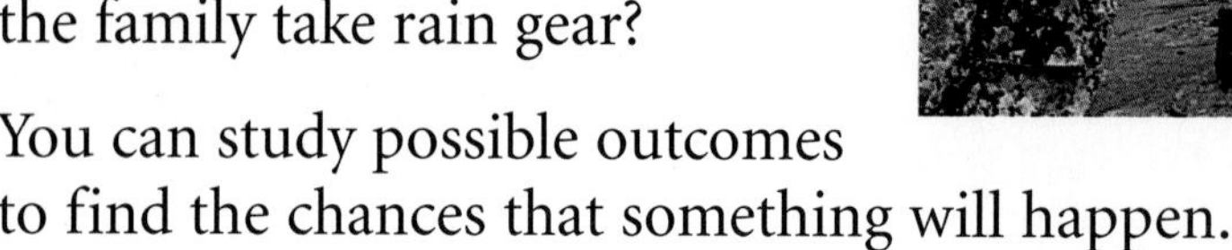

You can study possible outcomes to find the chances that something will happen.

Work Together

Work with a partner. Use a number cube to explore probability.

1. List all of the possible outcomes from rolling the number cube once.
2. Roll the cube 30 times. Use tally marks to record the outcomes.
3. Based on your results, how many chances in 30 are there that someone will roll a 1? Will not roll a 1?
4. Suppose that numbers 1 through 5 stand for rain and 6 stands for clear skies. What does your experiment tell you about whether the Curtis family should expect rain?

Talk About It

5. Is it certain that rain will fall while the Curtis family is hiking? Explain.
6. Is it possible to roll a number cube 10 times and get the same number each time? Is it likely? Explain.

Connect

You can use fractions to describe the **probability** of an event.

What is the probability of rolling a 1 using a number cube labeled 1–6?

Possible outcomes: 1, 2, 3, 4, 5, 6
Probability of rolling a 1:

$\frac{1}{6}$ ← number of ways to roll a 1 / ← total number of outcomes

The probability of rolling a 1 is $\frac{1}{6}$.

What is the probability of *not* rolling a 1 using a number cube labeled 1–6?

Possible outcomes: 1, 2, 3, 4, 5, 6
Probability of not rolling a 1:

$\frac{5}{6}$ ← number of ways *not* to roll a 1 / ← total number of outcomes

The probability of not rolling a 1 is $\frac{5}{6}$.

Practice

Use the spinner for **1–4.** Write the probability of each event.

1. spinning a 5
2. spinning an odd number
3. spinning an even number
4. spinning a number less than 5

Suppose you write each number 1 to 20 on slips of paper and put all of the numbers in a box. Then you close your eyes and draw a number from the box.

5. List all of the possible outcomes.
6. What is the probability of:
   a. drawing a 7?
   b. drawing an even number?
   c. drawing a number less than 10?
   d. drawing either a 2 or a 4?
   e. drawing a number greater than 20?

7. **Journal** Draw a spinner that shows the probability of spinning a 3 is $\frac{1}{4}$. Explain how you know the probability is $\frac{1}{4}$.

Exploring Predictions

Problem Solving Connection
- Use Objects/ Act It Out
- Use Logical Reasoning

Materials
- 10 paper clips of one color
- 10 paper clips of a second color
- envelope

Vocabulary
prediction
a guess about what will happen

Explore

Movie critics predict *The Mighty Probadactyl* will be a box-office hit this summer.

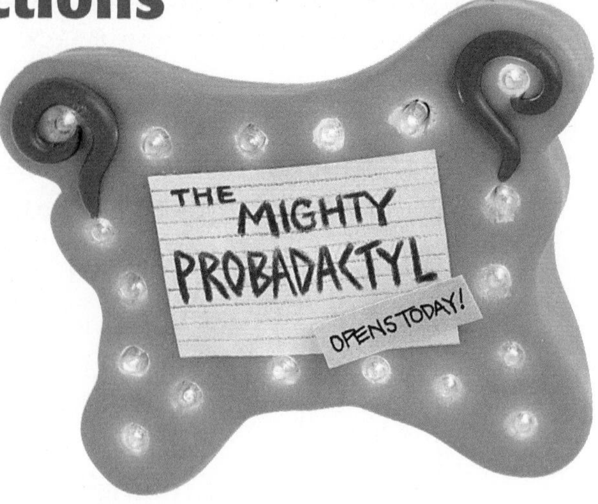

People make predictions based on past events. You can use probability to make **predictions**.

Work Together

Work with a partner to play a game in which you make predictions.

1. One person closes his or her eyes while the partner puts at least 10 paper clips in the envelope, choosing from the two colors.
2. Without looking, the first person takes 1 paper clip from the envelope, records the color, and puts the paper clip back. Repeat 20 times.
3. That person then predicts, based on the results of the experiment, how many paper clips of each color are in the envelope.

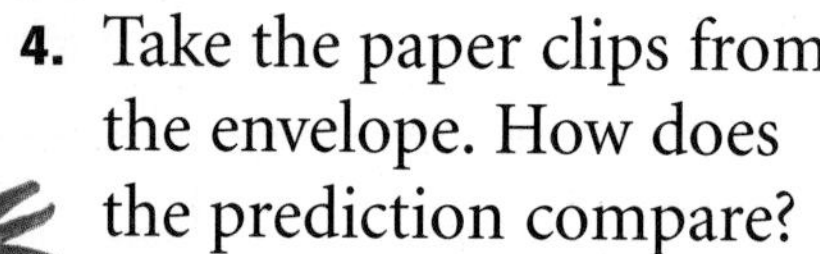

4. Take the paper clips from the envelope. How does the prediction compare?
5. Change roles and repeat the game.

Talk About It

6. How reasonable was your prediction after 20 tries?
7. Would your prediction have been the same after only 5 tries? Explain.

Connect

If you know the probability of an event, you can use this information to make predictions about future events.

In a survey, 50 students were asked which candidate they planned to vote for.

Candidates	Likely Votes
Jessica	4 votes
Bonnie	25 votes
Seth	6 votes
Tom	15 votes

The probability that someone will choose Bonnie as Student of the Year:

$\frac{25}{50} = \frac{1}{2}$

How many students out of 600 would you expect to choose Bonnie?

$\frac{1}{2}$ of $600 = 300$

You could expect that in a survey of 600 students, 300 would choose Bonnie.

Practice

1. Find the probability of spinning A.

2. Suppose you spin 60 times. Predict how many A's you could expect to spin.

3. The table gives the results of a poll of 20 students.

a. Based on these results, what is the probability that a student sleeps fewer than 7 hours?

b. Predict how many students out of 500 would be expected to say they got fewer than 7 hours of sleep in a night.

Hours of Sleep in One Night	
Fewer than 7 hours:	4 students
7 to 9 hours:	13 students
More than 9 hours:	3 students

4. Miko plans to toss a cube numbered 1–6, 60 times. Make a prediction for each outcome.

a. Getting a 2 **b.** Getting a 7 **c.** Getting 1, 2, 3, 4, 5, or 6

5. A reporter questioned 45 people. 15 planned to vote for candidate A. Based on these results, predict how many of River City's 3,000 voters plan to vote for candidate A.

6. **Using Data** Use the Data File on page 525. About how many people would you predict will visit Disneyland next year?

7. **Journal** Describe how to use multiplication to make a prediction for future events.

Skills Practice Bank, page 574, Set 5

Problem Solving

Analyze Strategies: Solve a Simpler Problem

You Will Learn
how to solve problems by solving a simpler problem

Learn

Suppose Nesha displays her favorite dolls from Thailand, Mexico, Germany, and China. How many ways can she arrange 4 dolls on a shelf?

Nesha collects dolls. She lives in Charleston, West Virginia.

Work Together

▶ Understand

What do you know?

What do you need to find out?

▶ Plan

Solve a simpler problem. Arrange the Thai and Mexican dolls.

TM **MT**

There are 2 dolls and 1 way each can be first.

$2 \times 1 = 2$

There are 2 ways to arrange 2 dolls.

Use the pattern to arrange 3 dolls.

TGM **MGT** **GMT**
TMG **MTG** **GTM**

There are 3 dolls and 2 ways each can be first.

$3 \times 2 = 6$

There are 6 ways to arrange 3 dolls.

▶ Solve

Follow the pattern to solve the more difficult problem. Arrange all the dolls.

TCGM **TCMG**
TGCM **TGMC**
TMCG **TMGC**

There are 4 dolls and 6 ways each can be first.

$4 \times 6 = 24$

There are 24 ways to arrange 4 dolls.

▶ Look Back

How can you check your answer?

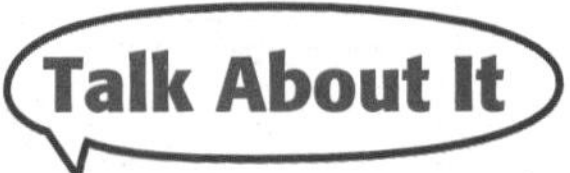

How can solving a simpler problem help solve a more difficult one?

Check

Use a simpler problem to solve.

1. Liza makes a sandwich with a piece of lettuce, a slice of tomato, and a pickle. How many ways could she arrange the contents of her sandwich?
2. Sam, Jo, Kelly, and Brent are deciding in what order to line up for a relay race. In how many ways can they line up?

Problem Solving Practice

Problem Solving Strategies

- Use Objects/Act It Out
- Draw a Picture
- Look for a Pattern
- Guess and Check
- Use Logical Reasoning
- Make an Organized List
- Make a Table
- Solve a Simpler Problem
- Work Backward

Choose a Tool

Use a simpler problem to solve or any other strategy for each.

3. A 2-letter group has A, B, C, or D as its first letter, and E or F as its second letter.
   a. Write all possible 2-letter groups.
   b. How many possibilities are there?
4. Aurora has a box of 3 apples, 6 peaches, and 9 tangerines. She closes her eyes and takes one piece of fruit. What is the probability that it is an apple? A peach? A tangerine?
5. **Science** It takes a beam of light about 500 seconds to travel from the sun to the earth. The sun is 93,000,000 miles from earth. How far does light travel in 1 second?
6. Ellen and Simon played 23 games of checkers. Ellen won 5 more games than she lost. How many games did each player win?
7. **Geometry Readiness** You win tic-tac-toe when you put an X or an O in 3 squares in a row. How many different outcomes are there for winning with Xs?
8. The table lists pitchers and catchers on a baseball team.
   a. How many possible pitcher-catcher pairs are there?
   b. What is the probability that a pitcher-catcher pair will have a player with a 3-letter name?
   c. What is the probability that a pitcher-catcher pair will include Presser?

Pitchers	Catchers
Rabin	Kim
Romero	Monroe
Harvey	Tenney
Presser	Zenas
Flood	

PROBLEM SOLVING PRACTICE

SECTION B

Review and Practice

Vocabulary Write the meaning of each word.

1. outcome **2.** probability

(Lesson 6) Read each statement. Write whether the event is impossible, unlikely, likely, or certain.

3. The Empire State Building will fall over tomorrow morning.

4. Someone will discover a triangle with 4 sides.

(Lesson 7) Write whether each game is fair or unfair. If it is unfair, explain why.

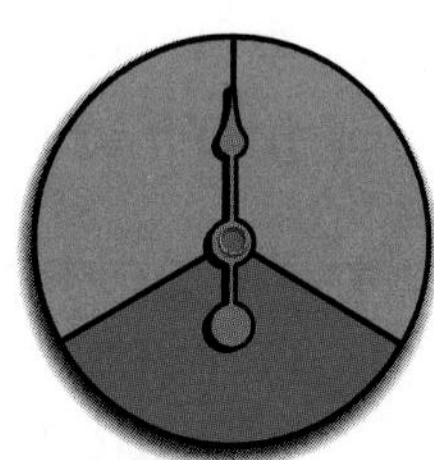

5. Marcus gets 1 point if his spin lands on red. Val gets 1 point if her spin lands on red. A spin landing on blue gives no score.

6. Marcus scores 1 point for any spin that lands on red. Val scores 1 point for any spin landing on blue.

(Lesson 8) List all possible outcomes.

7. A counter has a 2 on one side and a 3 on the other. A second counter has a 5 on one side and a 6 on the other. Find all possible outcomes of flipping both counters.

(Lessons 9 and 10) Write the probability of each outcome.

8. Spinning a 2 **9.** Spinning a 9

10. In a survey of 30 students, 10 students say they prefer hot cereal and 20 say they prefer cold cereal. Based on this survey, how many people out of 300 would you expect to prefer cold cereal?

(Lesson 11) Use any strategy to solve.

11. Suppose you are playing a game in teams of 8 people. A team A person calls out the name of a team B person. If you are on team B, what is the probability that your name will be called?

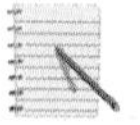

12. Journal Suppose you had a spinner like the one shown next to **8–9.** You spin 50 times. Predict how many outcomes would be odd numbers. Explain your prediction.

Skills Checklist

In this section, you have:

- ☑ Explored Likely and Unlikely
- ☑ Explored Fairness
- ☑ Listed Possible Outcomes
- ☑ Explored Probability
- ☑ Explored Predictions
- ☑ Solved Problems by Solving a Simpler Problem

Choose at least one. Use what you have learned in this chapter.

1 The Right Match

From the numbers below, find three pairs that have quotients of about 6. For each pair, tell which number is the divisor and which is the dividend. You may work with a partner.

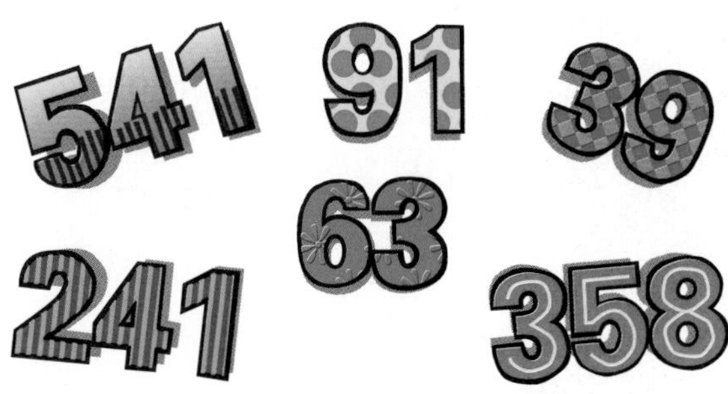

2 Marbles Game

Make up your own probability game with marbles. Use at least 3 different color marbles. Play the game with a friend.

3 Rock, Scissors, Paper

Explain the game Rock, Scissors, Paper to someone who has never played before. If you allow each player three turns, what are the possible combinations the player might get?

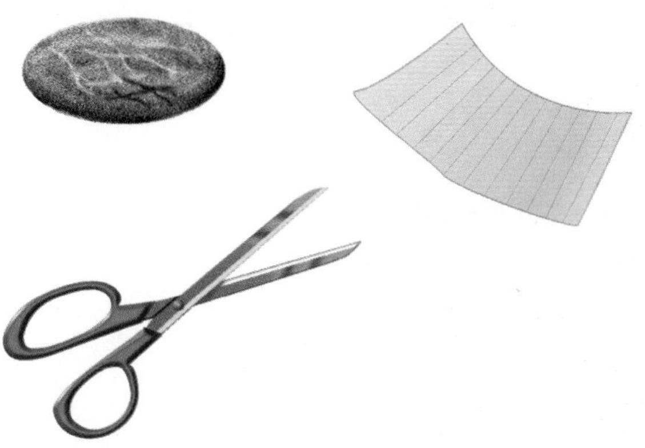

4 Weather Predictions

At Home With a friend or family member, check the weather in the morning. Is it likely or unlikely your classmates will be carrying umbrellas? Wearing hats? Wearing sandals? Check when you get to school!

Is it likely or unlikely that the weather in a different hemisphere is different from the weather in your hemisphere? Use **www.mathsurf.com/4/ch12** to find the weather in cities in the southern hemisphere.

CHAPTER 12

Review/Test

(Lesson 1) Mental Math Find each quotient.

1. $120 \div 20$
2. $270 \div 30$
3. $540 \div 90$
4. $60 \div 30$
5. $360 \div 40$
6. $480 \div 80$
7. $630 \div 70$
8. $160 \div 40$

(Lesson 2) Estimate each quotient.

9. $91 \div 29$
10. $245 \div 31$
11. $363 \div 91$
12. $257 \div 63$
13. $576 \div 72$
14. $189 \div 61$
15. José hiked about the same distance each day for 12 days. If he hiked a total of 67 miles, about how many miles a day did he hike?

(Lessons 3 and 4) Divide and check.

16. $181 \div 60$
17. $229 \div 70$
18. $499 \div 80$
19. $636 \div 69$
20. $169 \div 32$
21. $83\overline{)671}$
22. $94\overline{)849}$
23. $21\overline{)89}$
24. $53\overline{)438}$
25. $37\overline{)248}$

(Lesson 6) Read each statement. Write whether the event is impossible, unlikely, likely, or certain.

26. The next person you meet will be from France.
27. It will snow this winter in Alaska.
28. The month after December will be February.

(Lesson 7) Write whether each game is fair or unfair. If it is unfair, explain why.

29. A box contains 8 digit cards—4 even and 4 odd. Emily chooses a card without looking. She wins if the card is even. Katie wins if it's odd.
30. Jinny and Jon turn on a TV set. Jinny wins if a commercial is playing. Jon wins if a commercial is not playing.

(Lesson 8) List all the possible outcomes.

31. A counter has a 4 on one side and a 6 on the other. A second counter has a 3 and a 5.

(Lessons 9 and 10) Write the probability of each outcome as a fraction.

32. Spinning a 3
33. Spinning a 1 or 4

REVIEW/TEST

CHAPTER 12

Performance Assessment

A. Division

A store manager asks you to pack marbles into bags with an equal number of marbles in each bag and none left over. The bags should contain more than 30 but fewer than 60 marbles. You count 990 marbles.

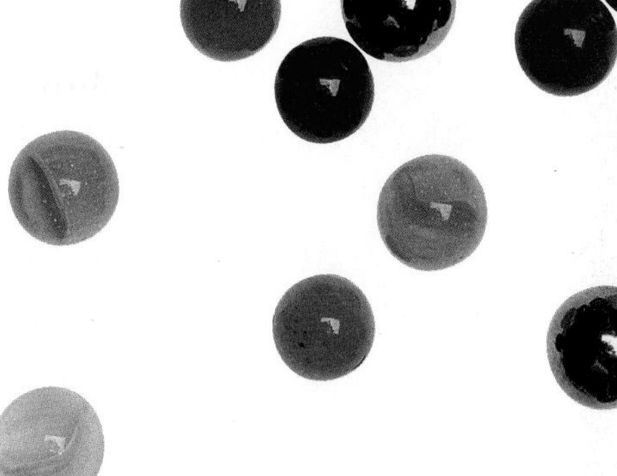

1. **Decision Making** How many bags will you make? How many marbles will be in each bag?
2. **Recording Data** Make an organized list to find all the ways you can pack the marbles.
3. **Explain Your Thinking** How did you find how many marbles to pack in each bag?
4. **Critical Thinking** What if you found another 10 marbles, how would you pack the marbles?

B. Probability

Some dominoes have already been played in a set with 55 dominoes. If you draw a domino from a pile of 35 remaining dominoes, what is the chance you'll get the domino you need?

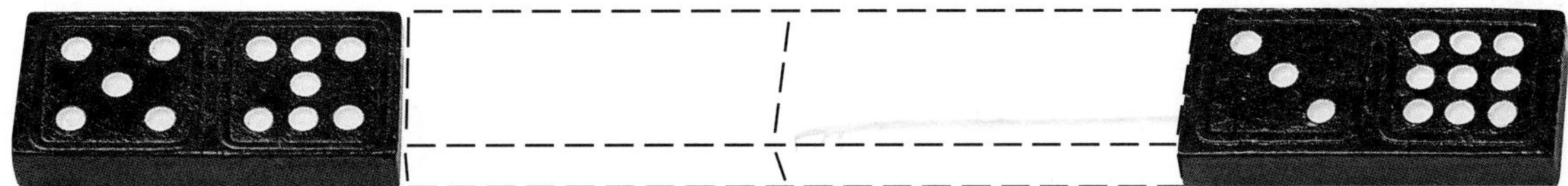

1. **Decision Making** Use the table. You need a 9 or a 5 to continue the game. What is the chance of drawing a 9 or a 5? Of not drawing a 9 or a 5?
2. **Explain Your Thinking** How did you use the table to figure out the chance you'll get one of the dominoes you need?
3. **Critical Thinking** In which direction is the domino game more likely to go?

Probability of Getting a Domino with the Number:	
9	8 chances in 35 draws
8	4 chances in 35 draws
7	2 chances in 35 draws
6	6 chances in 35 draws
5	2 chances in 35 draws

REVIEW/TEST

Math Magazine

Moving Pictures

How many hooves does a galloping horse place on the ground at any single moment? Looking for the answer to that question helped lead to the invention of the movies.

In the 1870s, the photographer Eadweard Muybridge took pictures of horses and other animals in motion. He set up 24 cameras along a straight path. He attached thread to each camera and stretched it across the path. As the horse passed by, it snapped the thread, which caused the camera to take a picture.

Muybridge used a toy called a zoetrope (ZOH-uh-trope) to project the pictures. The zoetrope showed the pictures quickly, one after the other. The horse in the still pictures looked as if it was moving. Those pictures were one of the first movies!

In the movies today, 24 still pictures, or frames, are projected in every second of film. Our eyes "fill in" the spaces between the still pictures. So what we see looks like real motion.

Try These!

1. How many seconds of film will you see in:

   a. 120 frames? **b.** 360 frames?

   c. 480 frames? **d.** 720 frames?

2. How many still pictures are in a movie that lasts 90 minutes?

CHAPTERS 1–12

Cumulative Review

Test Prep Strategy: Read Carefully!

Watch for tricky problems.

The length of one side of a square desk top is 3 units. How much paper will you need to cover the desk top?

Ⓐ 9 square units Ⓑ 6 square units Ⓒ 9 units Ⓓ 10 units

To cover a surface you need to know its area. To find area, multiply. The area should be in square units. The answer is Ⓐ.

Write the letter of each correct answer. Read carefully or use any strategy to help.

Test Prep Strategies

- Read Carefully
- Follow Directions
- Make Smart Choices
- Eliminate Choices
- Work Backward from an Answer

1. School ends at 3:45 P.M. and it takes you 25 min to walk home. What time will you get home?
   Ⓐ 3:70 P.M. Ⓑ 5:10 P.M. Ⓒ 4:10 P.M. Ⓓ 25 min
2. If you have 7 quarters, 3 dimes, and 12 pennies in your pocket, how much money do you have?
   Ⓐ $2.17 Ⓑ $7.42 Ⓒ $1.75 Ⓓ not here
3. If you and 6 of your friends have 1 dozen marbles each, how many marbles do you have all together?
   Ⓐ 8 Ⓑ 56 Ⓒ 72 Ⓓ 84
4. How many seconds are there in 11 min?
   Ⓐ 60 Ⓑ 66 Ⓒ 660 Ⓓ 600
5. You are asked to hand out 36 counters to 9 students so that each student has an equal number. How many counters will each student get?
   Ⓐ 36 Ⓑ 1 Ⓒ 4 Ⓓ 9
6. The floor of a square room is 6 meters long on one side. What is the perimeter of a carpet that will cover the floor of that room?
   Ⓐ 6 m Ⓑ 24 m Ⓒ 36 sq m Ⓓ 6 sq m
7. Which fraction is the simplest form of $\frac{16}{48}$?
   Ⓐ $\frac{4}{12}$ Ⓑ $\frac{8}{24}$ Ⓒ $\frac{6}{18}$ Ⓓ $\frac{1}{3}$
8. What is the sum of 16.3, 0.23, and 13.03?
   Ⓐ 29.29 Ⓑ 29.59 Ⓒ 13.33 Ⓓ 29.56

Set 1

Find each sum or difference.

1. $8 + 8$	**2.** $6 + 7$	**3.** $4 + 6$	**4.** $2 + 7$	**5.** $5 + 5$
6. $12 - 3$	**7.** $6 - 5$	**8.** $9 - 4$	**9.** $13 - 7$	**10.** $10 - 2$
11. $1 + 7$	**12.** $6 + 5$	**13.** $2 + 8$	**14.** $3 + 4$	**15.** $9 + 8$
16. $9 - 6$	**17.** $14 - 7$	**18.** $11 - 8$	**19.** $3 - 3$	**20.** $15 - 9$
21. $9 + 9$	**22.** $6 + 8$	**23.** $4 + 7$	**24.** $5 + 9$	**25.** $3 + 8$
26. $17 - 8$	**27.** $10 - 5$	**28.** $8 - 2$	**29.** $11 - 6$	**30.** $13 - 5$
31. $1 + 8$	**32.** $3 + 7$	**33.** $5 + 9$	**34.** $9 + 7$	**35.** $4 + 6$
36. $16 - 7$	**37.** $12 - 5$	**38.** $8 - 3$	**39.** $14 - 6$	**40.** $6 - 4$
41. $9 + 3$	**42.** $6 + 7$	**43.** $4 + 8$	**44.** $3 + 2$	**45.** $5 + 2$
46. $14 - 5$	**47.** $11 - 2$	**48.** $7 - 4$	**49.** $8 - 6$	**50.** $10 - 3$
51. $6 + 6$	**52.** $8 + 7$	**53.** $2 + 4$	**54.** $5 + 8$	**55.** $7 + 5$
56. $11 - 7$	**57.** $8 - 8$	**58.** $13 - 9$	**59.** $9 - 3$	**60.** $7 - 5$
61. $2 + 7$	**62.** $5 + 7$	**63.** $8 + 4$	**64.** $9 + 8$	**65.** $3 + 3$
66. $10 - 6$	**67.** $8 - 4$	**68.** $4 - 3$	**69.** $14 - 8$	**70.** $12 - 6$
71. $6 + 9$	**72.** $7 + 3$	**73.** $5 + 4$	**74.** $9 + 4$	**75.** $6 + 5$
76. $13 - 6$	**77.** $9 - 2$	**78.** $6 - 3$	**79.** $7 - 6$	**80.** $15 - 8$
81. $4 + 5$	**82.** $6 + 8$	**83.** $9 + 6$	**84.** $7 + 7$	**85.** $6 + 3$
86. $16 - 9$	**87.** $12 - 4$	**88.** $9 - 7$	**89.** $5 - 3$	**90.** $15 - 7$
91. $7 + 9$	**92.** $3 + 8$	**93.** $6 + 2$	**94.** $8 + 5$	**95.** $3 + 4$
96. $12 - 9$	**97.** $9 - 5$	**98.** $8 - 1$	**99.** $10 - 4$	**100.** $14 - 9$

Set 2

1. The park is 8 blocks from Emily's house. Emily walked 3 blocks to meet her friend. Then together they walked to the park. How many blocks did Emily walk with her friend?

2. Alonso plans to draw some insects in his scrapbook. On one page he will draw 8 ants. On another page he will draw 4 grasshoppers. How many insects does he plan to draw?

Set 1 For use after page 11.

Use the Data File on page 7.

1. How many kangaroos jumped 40 feet?
2. How many more kangaroos jumped 40 feet than 41 feet?

Set 2 For use after page 15.

Use the line graph.

1. How many books did Ron read when he was 8?
2. How old was Ron when he read 30 books?
3. How many more books did Ron read when he was 12 than when he was 8?

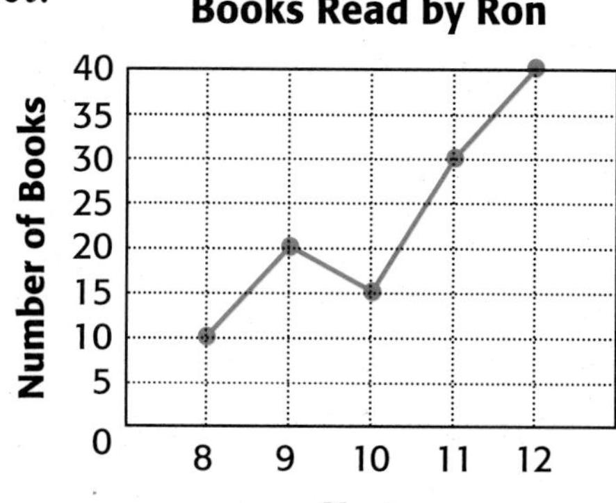

Set 3 For use after page 19.

Use this stem-and-leaf plot.

1. What is the difference in time between the shortest and longest bus ride?
2. How many bus rides are 21 minutes long?

	Bus Ride (minutes)
1	4 9
2	1 8 7 5 1 5 3 0 1
3	2 0 1 9 0 2 4

Set 4 For use after page 27.

Copy and complete the bar graph of the trees.

Type of Tree	Elm	Oak	Fir
Number of Trees	10	25	30

1. How many more firs are there than elms?

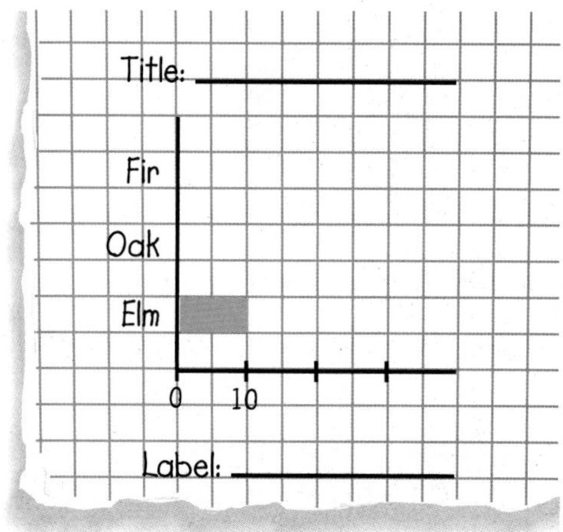

Set 5 For use after page 31.

Use the data of judges' scores.

1. Find the range.
2. Find the median.
3. Find the mode.

Scores for a Gymnastic Event								
8	10	7	9	7	7	8	9	10

Set 6 For use after pages 23 and 39.

1. **(Page 23)** Jim has 34 pine cones. He gives 15 to Andrea. How many pine cones does Jim have now?
2. **(Page 39)** Jo finds 9 fossils. There are 3 more leaf fossils than insect fossils. How many are leaf fossils?

Set 1 For use after page 57.

Write the standard form or word name for each number.

1. Five million, six thousand, two hundred
2. 407,209
3. One million, sixty-four thousand, five hundred
4. 9,180,033

Set 2 For use after page 69.

Order the numbers from least to greatest.

1. 83,182, 162,180, 160,800, 161,208
2. Write a number that is between 18,010 and 18,100.

Set 3 For use after page 71.

Round each number to the nearest hundred.

1. 692
2. 348
3. 123
4. 460
5. 939

Round each number to the nearest thousand.

6. 7,305
7. 1,642
8. 3,880
9. 4,444
10. 8,511

Set 4 For use after page 75.

Write each time two ways.

1. 

2. 

3. Draw an analog and a digital clock for twenty minutes to seven.

Set 5 For use after page 79.

Write each elapsed time.

1. 12:00 P.M. to 7:15 P.M.
2. 8:05 A.M. to 11:58 A.M.
3. 9:24 A.M. to 2:46 P.M.
4. 10:38 P.M. to 6:39 A.M.

Set 6 For use after pages 61 and 83.

1. **(Page 61)** William has red, white, yellow, and purple shirts. He has gray and black pants. How many different outfits can he wear?
2. **(Page 83)** It is 3:30 P.M. Does Helena have time to practice the drums for half an hour and do homework for 20 minutes before soccer practice at 4:45 P.M.? Explain.

Set 1 For use after page 109.

Find each sum. Estimate to check.

1. 37 + 8 + 23
2. 492 + 89 + 270
3. 98 + 305 + 217
4. 670 + 839 + 226
5. 1,430 + 6,864 + 3,728

Set 2 For use after page 113.

Subtract.

1. 5,825 − 3,604
2. 7,709 − 1,802
3. 8,124 − 7,319
4. 6,526 − 835
5. 3,270 − 1,290

Set 3 For use after page 115.

Find each difference.

1. 500 − 325
2. 7,800 − 718
3. 6,009 − 4,507
4. 4,000 − 1,363
5. 8,010 − 291

Set 4 For use after page 129.

Add or subtract. Estimate to check.

1. $5.69 + 2.40
2. $2.43 − 1.35
3. $42.71 + 37.89
4. $3.17 − 0.59
5. $27.88 − 14.92

Set 5 For use after page 131.

Copy and complete the table.

Cost	$1.95	$0.89	$13.21	$27.46	$35.03
Amount Given	$5.00	$10.00	$14.00	$40.00	$50.03
Change					

Set 6 For use after pages 101, 119, and 137.

1. **(Page 101)** Mark has a $10 bill. Can he buy 4 tickets that cost $2.25 each? Explain.

2. **(Page 119)** **Time** Jared borrows a computer for 2 hours. So far he has spent 30 minutes drawing and 45 minutes writing. How much more computer time does he have left?

Copy and continue the pattern. Describe the rule.

3. **(Page 137)** 324, 325, 327, 330, 334, ■, ■, ■

Set 1 For use after page 153.

Find each product.

1. 9×4 2. 5×3 3. 4×0 4. 3×7 5. 8×4

6. 3×3 7. 4×5 8. 2×4 9. 3×6 10. 8×3

11. 4×4 12. 9×3 13. 4×7 14. 3×4 15. 4×6

Set 2 For use after page 157.

Find each product.

1. 6×5 2. 7×7 3. 8×4 4. 6×6 5. 7×9

6. 8×6 7. 4×8 8. 7×3 9. 8×8 10. 6×3

11. 7×8 12. 9×7 13. 6×4 14. 8×9 15. 5×7

Set 3 For use after page 159.

Find each product.

1. 10×9 2. 11×8 3. 5×12 4. 11×0 5. 10×4

6. 2×12 7. 3×10 8. 6×11 9. 6×12 10. 10×8

11. 11×2 12. 3×12 13. 10×9 14. 7×11 15. 12×0

Set 4 For use after page 163.

1. Jessica earns \$3 an hour delivering papers. Ethan earns \$2 an hour walking a dog. How much can Jessica and Ethan earn if they both work 5 hours?

2. Ned has 4 bags of apples. Maggie has 5 bags. There are 10 apples to a bag. How many apples do Ned and Maggie have?

SKILLS PRACTICE BANK

Set 5 For use after page 171.

Find each quotient.

1. $2\overline{)14}$ 2. $5\overline{)40}$ 3. $9\overline{)36}$ 4. $2\overline{)12}$ 5. $9\overline{)81}$

6. $5\overline{)20}$ 7. $2\overline{)2}$ 8. $9\overline{)45}$ 9. $5\overline{)30}$ 10. $9\overline{)54}$

11. $16 \div 2$ 12. $18 \div 9$ 13. $35 \div 5$ 14. $4 \div 2$ 15. $10 \div 2$

16. $25 \div 5$ 17. $9 \div 9$ 18. $6 \div 2$ 19. $8 \div 2$ 20. $5 \div 5$

21. $3\overline{)9}$ 22. $2\overline{)2}$ 23. $9\overline{)72}$ 24. $5\overline{)15}$ 25. $9\overline{)63}$

26. **Money** How many nickels are there in a quarter?

Set 6 For use after page 179.

Find each quotient.

1. $6\overline{)36}$ 2. $8\overline{)48}$ 3. $7\overline{)35}$ 4. $6\overline{)42}$ 5. $6\overline{)6}$

6. $7\overline{)49}$ 7. $6\overline{)54}$ 8. $7\overline{)14}$ 9. $8\overline{)32}$ 10. $7\overline{)42}$

11. $56 \div 8$ 12. $28 \div 7$ 13. $40 \div 8$ 14. $64 \div 8$ 15. $21 \div 7$

16. $24 \div 8$ 17. $7 \div 7$ 18. $24 \div 6$ 19. $63 \div 7$ 20. $16 \div 8$

21. $8\overline{)8}$ 22. $6\overline{)18}$ 23. $5\overline{)40}$ 24. $4\overline{)28}$ 25. $6\overline{)12}$

26. $3\overline{)21}$ 27. $9\overline{)72}$ 28. $6\overline{)30}$ 29. $9\overline{)54}$ 30. $3\overline{)27}$

Set 7 For use after page 189.

Use any strategy to solve each problem.

1. Peter and Juan were sharing a tape player with new batteries. The batteries ran out after 12 hours of use. If Peter used the player 2 more hours than Juan, how long did each use the player?
2. Jean has 4 pairs of different colored shoes. What is the least number of shoes she can take out of a dark closet and be sure of having a matching pair?

Set 1 For use after page 203.

Find each product.

1. 9×50
2. 400×6
3. 3×70
4. 100×10
5. $8 \times 2{,}000$
6. 300×9
7. $4 \times 8{,}000$
8. 500×7
9. $9 \times 6{,}000$
10. $7{,}000 \times 8$
11. 7×90
12. 800×8
13. $5 \times 6{,}000$
14. 30×8
15. 9×900

Set 2 For use after page 213.

Find each product. Estimate to check.

1. 42×3
2. 18×5
3. 23×7
4. 57×6
5. 84×4
6. 96×8
7. 51×4
8. 37×2
9. 64×8
10. 79×5
11. 48×9
12. 22×7
13. 35×4
14. 73×6
15. 17×3

Set 3 For use after page 215.

Multiply.

1. 306×4
2. 235×3
3. 510×8
4. 627×5
5. 809×9
6. 763×7
7. 221×3
8. 405×6
9. 617×5
10. 747×8
11. 204×7
12. 469×3
13. 888×4
14. 711×9
15. 590×3

Set 4 For use after page 217.

1. Doug bakes cupcakes. His pan holds 12 cupcakes. How many cupcakes can he make in 6 batches?
2. A pizza recipe takes 20 minutes to prepare, 45 minutes for the dough to rise, and 15 minutes to bake. Melissa's guests will arrive in an hour. Can she make the pizza and have it ready for the guests when they arrive? Explain.

Set 5 For use after page 225.

Find each product.

1. $\begin{array}{r}\$3.64\\ \times\quad 5\\ \hline\end{array}$
2. $\begin{array}{r}\$8.25\\ \times\quad 4\\ \hline\end{array}$
3. $\begin{array}{r}\$6.06\\ \times\quad 8\\ \hline\end{array}$
4. $\begin{array}{r}\$2.43\\ \times\quad 7\\ \hline\end{array}$
5. $\begin{array}{r}\$9.95\\ \times\quad 6\\ \hline\end{array}$
6. $\begin{array}{r}\$5.99\\ \times\quad 3\\ \hline\end{array}$
7. $\begin{array}{r}\$1.78\\ \times\quad 2\\ \hline\end{array}$
8. $\begin{array}{r}\$6.17\\ \times\quad 9\\ \hline\end{array}$
9. $\begin{array}{r}\$0.87\\ \times\quad 6\\ \hline\end{array}$
10. $\begin{array}{r}\$5.08\\ \times\quad 7\\ \hline\end{array}$
11. $\begin{array}{r}\$4.50\\ \times\quad 4\\ \hline\end{array}$
12. $\begin{array}{r}\$3.29\\ \times\quad 9\\ \hline\end{array}$
13. $\begin{array}{r}\$7.04\\ \times\quad 5\\ \hline\end{array}$
14. $\begin{array}{r}\$2.22\\ \times\quad 6\\ \hline\end{array}$
15. $\begin{array}{r}\$4.12\\ \times\quad 3\\ \hline\end{array}$
16. $4 \times \$9.35$
17. $9 \times \$6.17$
18. $8 \times \$8.29$
19. $3 \times \$4.18$
20. $2 \times \$5.31$

Set 6 For use after page 231.

Find each product.

1. $(3 \times 8) \times 5$
2. $6 \times (4 \times 3)$
3. $(9 \times 8) \times 2$
4. $7 \times (5 \times 4)$
5. $(7 \times 7) \times 7$
6. $(9 \times 5) \times 6$
7. $4 \times (4 \times 3)$
8. $(1 \times 2) \times 8$
9. $3 \times (12 \times 4)$
10. $(4 \times 5) \times 6$
11. $8 \times (9 \times 1)$
12. $(3 \times 1) \times 7$
13. $5 \times 5 \times 5$
14. $4 \times 8 \times 6$
15. $5 \times 3 \times 2$
16. $2 \times (4 \times 4)$
17. $8 \times 6 \times 5$
18. $(3 \times 2) \times 9$
19. $11 \times 3 \times 3$
20. $7 \times (6 \times 4)$

Set 7 For use after page 237.

1. Rivka needs 8 inches of ribbon for bows to decorate each pocket on a pair of overalls. Each pair of overalls has 3 pockets. How much ribbon does she need for 6 pairs of overalls?

2. If your pattern has 4 triangles, how many Power Polygons pieces will it have in all?

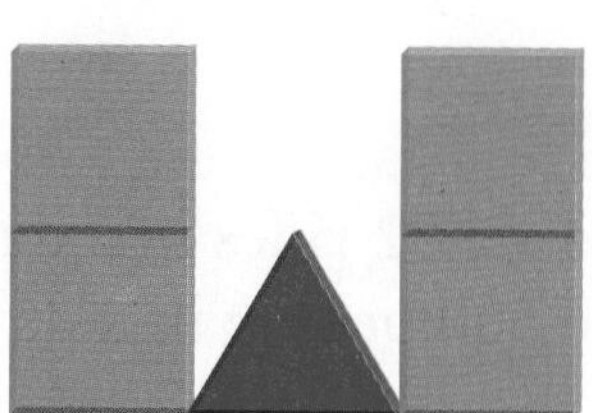
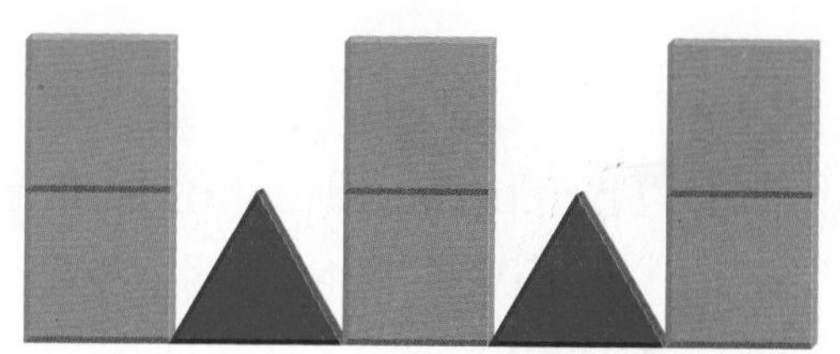

SKILLS PRACTICE BANK

Set 1 For use after page 255.

Find each product.

1. 40×52
2. 65×30
3. 74×10
4. 80×29
5. 20×18
6. 92×90
7. 60×21
8. 34×70
9. 80×50
10. 90×42
11. 78×30
12. 89×40
13. 30×75
14. 40×41
15. 63×80

Set 2 For use after page 263.

Find each product. Estimate to check.

1. 25×17
2. 68×34
3. 47×81
4. 93×55
5. 36×72
6. 84×67
7. 36×23
8. 71×15
9. 28×46
10. 55×32
11. 65×12
12. 81×43
13. 73×84
14. 42×54
15. 71×81

Set 3 For use after page 265.

Estimate each product.

1. 287×31
2. 113×56
3. 670×44
4. 249×15
5. 819×82
6. 961×73
7. 95×98
8. 206×39
9. 474×62
10. 736×45
11. 69×11
12. 78×39
13. 74×82
14. 37×51
15. 67×84

Set 4 For use after page 271.

1. The Ferris wheel holds 68 riders. There are 92 rides in a day. Can the Ferris wheel carry more than 6,500 people in a day? Explain.
2. Groups of 25 people can explore the Fun House at a time. If 56 groups tour the Fun House in an afternoon, how many people explored the Fun House?

Set 5 For use after page 267.

Find each product.

1. 521 × 42	2. 172 × 26	3. 5,000 × 30	4. 3,862 × 49	5. 4,736 × 85
6. 458 × 16	7. 973 × 32	8. 3,311 × 53	9. 3,082 × 22	10. 5,699 × 13
11. 321 × 14	12. 518 × 43	13. 2,507 × 28	14. 7,000 × 60	15. 4,212 × 35
16. 822 × 15	17. 304 × 72	18. 4,000 × 90	19. 3,050 × 44	20. 8,161 × 29

Set 6 For use after page 275.

Multiply. Estimate to check.

1. $3.15 × 18	2. $8.63 × 24	3. $10.49 × 31	4. $15.77 × 46	5. $28.04 × 32
6. $8.04 × 11	7. $2.45 × 16	8. $12.36 × 27	9. $17.81 × 33	10. $25.99 × 54
11. $6.32 × 12	12. $4.65 × 18	13. $53.21 × 74	14. $49.72 × 48	15. $19.45 × 38
16. $4.99 × 10	17. $7.35 × 25	18. $19.75 × 52	19. $34.05 × 22	20. $46.15 × 91

Set 7 For use after page 281.

1. Bernie has 48 autographed baseball cards that he wants to frame. What are the different ways he can arrange the cards in rows so that there are the same number of cards in each row?

2. Alison is the middle musician in a marching band. There are the same number of musicians in each row. Alison has 4 musicians to the left of her, 4 to the right, 3 directly in front of her, and 3 directly behind her. How many musicians are there?

Set 1 For use after page 305.

Divide. Check your answer.

1. $3\overline{)51}$ 2. $4\overline{)56}$ 3. $2\overline{)62}$ 4. $6\overline{)96}$ 5. $3\overline{)64}$

6. $5\overline{)79}$ 7. $4\overline{)47}$ 8. $8\overline{)96}$ 9. $9\overline{)97}$ 10. $7\overline{)90}$

11. $7\overline{)91}$ 12. $6\overline{)83}$ 13. $9\overline{)91}$ 14. $2\overline{)32}$ 15. $8\overline{)99}$

16. $68 \div 5$ 17. $79 \div 7$ 18. $72 \div 4$ 19. $89 \div 8$ 20. $37 \div 2$

Set 2 For use after page 311.

Divide. Check your answer.

1. $3\overline{)222}$ 2. $5\overline{)465}$ 3. $4\overline{)528}$ 4. $2\overline{)384}$ 5. $6\overline{)531}$

6. $7\overline{)684}$ 7. $9\overline{)436}$ 8. $8\overline{)944}$ 9. $5\overline{)697}$ 10. $9\overline{)775}$

11. $4\overline{)345}$ 12. $6\overline{)696}$ 13. $8\overline{)756}$ 14. $2\overline{)837}$ 15. $5\overline{)678}$

16. $384 \div 6$ 17. $257 \div 3$ 18. $436 \div 9$ 19. $152 \div 7$ 20. $128 \div 4$

Set 3 For use after page 315.

Divide. Check your answer.

1. $5\overline{)509}$ 2. $2\overline{)181}$ 3. $6\overline{)485}$ 4. $4\overline{)282}$ 5. $3\overline{)321}$

6. $6\overline{)723}$ 7. $8\overline{)865}$ 8. $5\overline{)547}$ 9. $9\overline{)998}$ 10. $4\overline{)830}$

11. $3\overline{)609}$ 12. $7\overline{)842}$ 13. $9\overline{)633}$ 14. $8\overline{)878}$ 15. $7\overline{)986}$

16. $602 \div 3$ 17. $657 \div 6$ 18. $484 \div 8$ 19. $622 \div 3$ 20. $263 \div 4$

Set 4 For use after page 317.

1. Andre invites 15 people to his party. He wants to buy a party hat for each person. If there are 6 party hats in a package, how many packages should Andre buy?

2. If 15 guests at Andre's party each drink one soda, how many six-packs of soda will they use? How many guests could drink more than one soda?

Set 5 For use after page 323.

Divide. Check your answer.

1. $3\overline{)\$4.74}$ 2. $5\overline{)\$8.15}$ 3. $2\overline{)\$9.74}$ 4. $7\overline{)\$6.16}$ 5. $6\overline{)\$9.12}$

6. $8\overline{)\$6.48}$ 7. $4\overline{)\$4.16}$ 8. $3\overline{)\$8.40}$ 9. $7\overline{)\$0.63}$ 10. $8\overline{)\$8.40}$

11. $9\overline{)\$9.63}$ 12. $4\overline{)\$8.72}$ 13. $6\overline{)\$6.84}$ 14. $8\overline{)\$9.84}$ 15. $2\overline{)\$1.52}$

16. $5\overline{)\$6.50}$ 17. $3\overline{)\$5.88}$ 18. $9\overline{)\$0.81}$ 19. $6\overline{)\$9.00}$ 20. $7\overline{)\$9.94}$

21. $2\overline{)\$8.94}$ 22. $5\overline{)\$7.05}$ 23. $4\overline{)\$0.28}$ 24. $6\overline{)\$7.68}$ 25. $8\overline{)\$8.96}$

Set 6 For use after page 331.

Copy and complete. Test each number to see if it is divisible by 3, 5, 6, or 9. If it is, write the quotient.

		30	45	66	75	180
1.	By 3?	10				
2.	By 5?	6				
3.	By 6?	5				
4.	By 9?					

5. Without dividing, tell whether you can put 159 pennies in 3 equal piles.
6. Write an even number that is divisible by 9.
7. Write an odd number that is divisible by 5.

Set 7 For use after page 333.

1. Daniel used an 8-ounce package of chocolate chips for a trail mix. He used an unmeasured amount of nuts. He weighed the mix and found it weighed 20 ounces. What was the weight of the nuts he used?
2. Anita mixed 32 ounces of orange juice with some seltzer. She filled seven 8-ounce glasses and had 4 ounces remaining. How much seltzer did she use?

Set 1 **For use after page 347.**

Write the name of each polygon.

1. 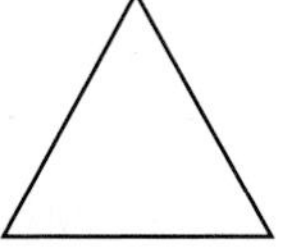

2. 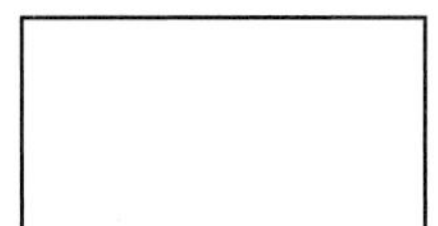

3. 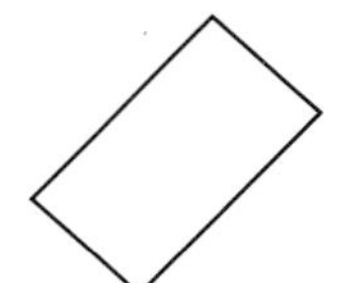

4. 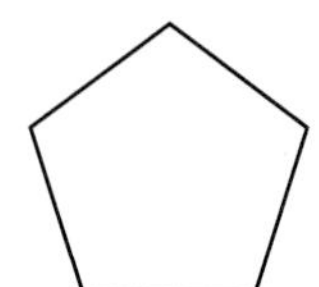

Set 2 **For use after page 351.**

Name each triangle as right, acute, or obtuse.

1. 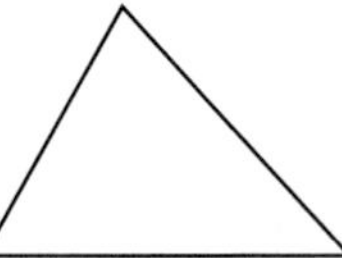

2. 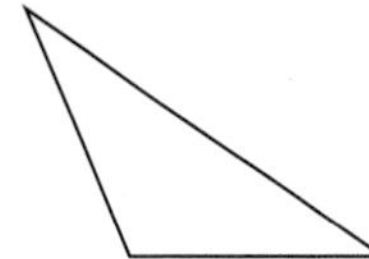

3. 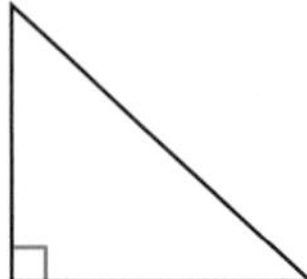

4. 

Set 3 **For use after page 363.**

How many lines of symmetry for each? You may trace each figure.

1. 

2. 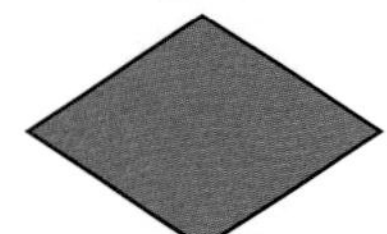

3. 

4. 

Set 4 **For use after page 371.**

Find the area of each rectangle.

1. 

2. 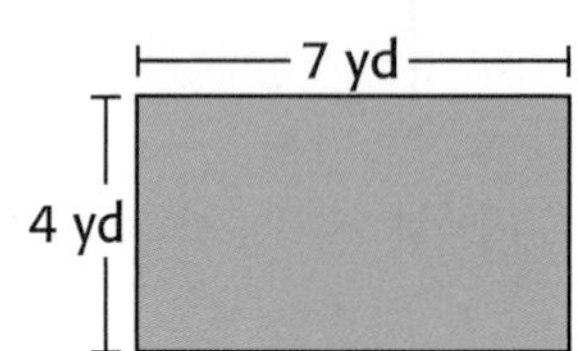

3. 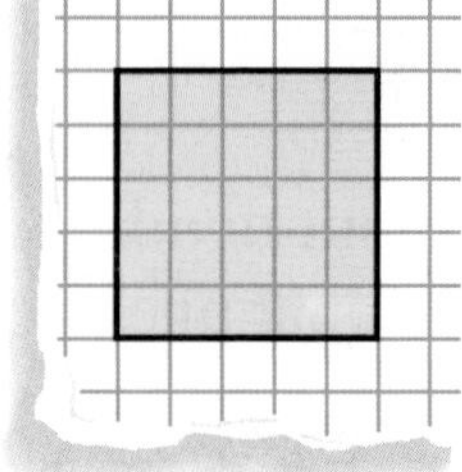

Set 5 **For use after page 373.**

Find the volume of each rectangular prism.

1. 

2. 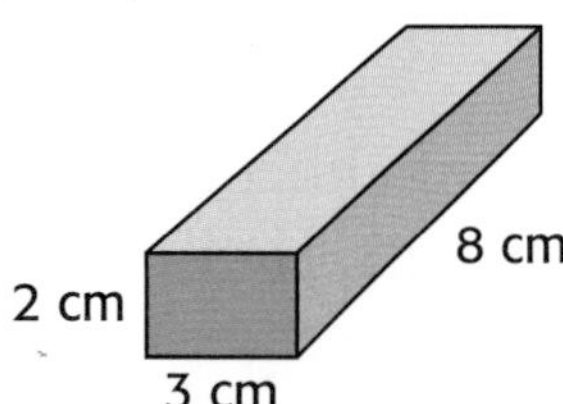

3. 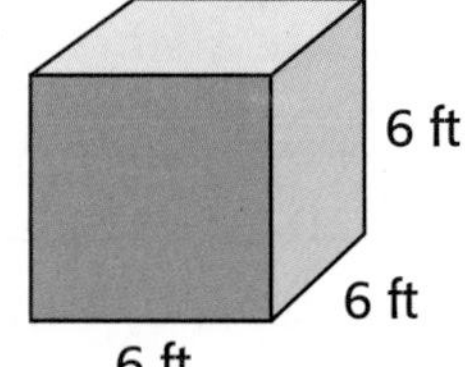

Set 6 **For use after pages 365 and 375.**

1. **(Page 365)** Andy is measuring a square garden plot. He measures one side in 15 steps. What is the area of the garden in steps?
2. **(Page 375)** A rectangle has an area of 50 square inches. If the length is 10 inches, what is the width? What is the perimeter?

Skills Practice Bank Chapter 9

Set 1 For use after page 389.

Write a fraction that compares the different balls to the whole set.

1. Basketballs **2.** Tennis balls **3.** Baseballs **4.** Soccer balls **5.** Round balls

Set 2 For use after page 393.

Write each improper fraction as a whole or mixed number. Use fraction strips or draw pictures to help.

1. $\frac{5}{3}$ **2.** $\frac{8}{4}$ **3.** $\frac{9}{4}$ **4.** $\frac{10}{2}$ **5.** $\frac{7}{2}$

Write each mixed number as an improper fraction.

6. $1\frac{1}{4}$ **7.** $2\frac{2}{3}$ **8.** $3\frac{3}{4}$ **9.** $1\frac{5}{6}$ **10.** $6\frac{1}{2}$

Set 3 For use after page 403.

Is each fraction in simplest form? If not, write it in simplest form.

1. $\frac{10}{20}$ **2.** $\frac{3}{7}$ **3.** $\frac{4}{6}$ **4.** $\frac{3}{9}$ **5.** $\frac{5}{8}$

6. $\frac{8}{10}$ **7.** $\frac{9}{16}$ **8.** $\frac{15}{25}$ **9.** $\frac{12}{18}$ **10.** $\frac{23}{24}$

Set 4 For use after page 409.

Find the number for each fraction of a set. You may use counters to help.

1. $\frac{1}{2}$ of 16 **2.** $\frac{2}{3}$ of 12 **3.** $\frac{1}{4}$ of 20 **4.** $\frac{3}{5}$ of 15

5. $\frac{1}{8}$ of 24 **6.** $\frac{3}{4}$ of 16 **7.** $\frac{2}{7}$ of 21 **8.** $\frac{5}{6}$ of 18

Set 5 For use after page 419.

1. Jackie walks 450 feet. If she walks 10 times as far, will she walk more or less than a mile? Explain.

Set 6 For use after page 421.

1. One block has 15 recycling containers. There are three more paper containers than plastic containers. How many paper containers are there? How many plastic containers?

Set 1 For use after page 435.

Draw pictures to help find each sum. Simplify.

1. $\frac{1}{2}+\frac{1}{4}$ 2. $\frac{1}{2}+\frac{1}{8}$ 3. $\frac{1}{6}+\frac{1}{2}$ 4. $\frac{2}{3}+\frac{1}{6}$ 5. $\frac{1}{4}+\frac{5}{8}$ 6. $\frac{1}{4}+\frac{3}{8}$

Set 2 For use after page 437.

Find each sum. Simplify.

1. $\frac{1}{5}+\frac{2}{5}$ 2. $\frac{1}{10}+\frac{4}{5}$ 3. $\frac{1}{3}+\frac{2}{9}$ 4. $\frac{1}{6}+\frac{5}{12}$ 5. $\frac{2}{3}+\frac{3}{9}$

Set 3 For use after page 449.

Find each difference. Simplify.

1. $\frac{7}{9}-\frac{5}{9}$ 2. $\frac{5}{6}-\frac{1}{3}$ 3. $\frac{9}{10}-\frac{3}{5}$ 4. $\frac{7}{12}-\frac{1}{6}$ 5. $\frac{11}{12}-\frac{3}{4}$

Set 4 For use after page 459.

Choose the best estimate for each capacity.

1. Tall glass of milk
   Ⓐ About 1 pint Ⓑ About 1 tablespoon
2. A sink
   Ⓐ About 12 ounces Ⓑ About 12 gallons
3. 5 raindrops
   Ⓐ About 2 cups Ⓑ About 2 teaspoons

Set 5 For use after page 461.

Copy and complete. Use the Table of Measures on page 575.

1. 5 c = ■ fl oz 2. 12 qt = ■ gal 3. 2 T = ■ lb 4. 64 oz = ■ lb
5. 7 ft = ■ in. 6. 15 yd = ■ ft 7. 8 pt = ■ qt 8. 10 pt = ■ c

Set 6 For use after pages 453 and 463.

1. **(Page 453)** Georgia spent $\frac{1}{3}$ of an hour studying her spelling words. Frances spent $\frac{5}{6}$ of an hour studying her spelling words. How much longer did Frances spend studying spelling than Georgia?

2. **(Page 463)** At the bagel shop you get one free bagel for every dozen you buy. A dozen bagels cost $4.50. How much would it cost if you ordered 65 bagels?

Skills Practice Bank Chapter 11

Set 1 For use after page 483.

Copy and complete. Write >, <, or =.

1. 1.7 ● 1.72 2. 50.1 ● 5.08 3. 0.24 ● 0.33 4. 9.9 ● 9.90

Order the decimals from least to greatest.

5. 2.06, 2.6, 1.96, 2.09, 1.9 6. 0.93, 9.03, 0.39, 0.09, 0.99

Set 2 For use after page 487.

Write the decimal for each fraction. Find an equivalent fraction in tenths or hundredths or draw a grid to help.

1. $\frac{9}{10}$ 2. $\frac{3}{5}$ 3. $\frac{47}{100}$ 4. $\frac{11}{50}$ 5. $\frac{13}{20}$ 6. $\frac{6}{25}$ 7. $\frac{3}{4}$

Set 3 For use after page 499.

Find each sum or difference. Estimate to check your answer.

1. $\begin{array}{r} 24.84 \\ +\ 7.19 \\ \hline \end{array}$ 2. $\begin{array}{r} 4.51 \\ -\ 2.80 \\ \hline \end{array}$ 3. $\begin{array}{r} \$67.25 \\ -\ 47.85 \\ \hline \end{array}$ 4. $\begin{array}{r} 13.9 \\ +\ 20.66 \\ \hline \end{array}$ 5. $\begin{array}{r} 90.30 \\ -\ 5.42 \\ \hline \end{array}$

Set 4 For use after page 509.

Copy and complete.

1. 7 m = ■ cm 2. 28 cm = ■ m 3. 299 cm = ■ m 4. 0.3 m = ■ cm

5. 6.08 m = ■ cm 6. 5 cm = ■ m 7. 87 m = ■ cm 8. 4,460 cm = ■ m

Set 5 For use after page 515.

Choose the better estimate for each.

1. Winter day in Antarctica
   Ⓐ –30°F
   Ⓑ 50°F
2. Paper burning
   Ⓐ 64°C
   Ⓑ 234°C
3. Ice cube
   Ⓐ 32°F
   Ⓑ 40°F
4. Hot chocolate
   Ⓐ –30°C
   Ⓑ 35°C

Set 6 For use after pages 481 and 517.

1. **(Page 481)** Suppose you have 19 coins, all quarters and dimes, that total $2.35. How many of each coin do you have?

2. **(Page 517)** Tanya has a rectangular garden that is 9 meters long and 6.8 meters wide. How many meters of fence does she need to enclose her garden?

Set 1 For use after page 529.

Find each quotient.

1. $80 \div 40$ 2. $100 \div 20$ 3. $90 \div 30$ 4. $120 \div 30$
5. $540 \div 90$ 6. $48{,}000 \div 60$ 7. $1{,}600 \div 80$ 8. $360 \div 60$

Set 2 For use after page 533.

Divide and check.

1. $20\overline{)89}$ 2. $40\overline{)215}$ 3. $50\overline{)191}$ 4. $90\overline{)642}$ 5. $60\overline{)435}$
6. $30\overline{)203}$ 7. $60\overline{)554}$ 8. $80\overline{)467}$ 9. $70\overline{)618}$ 10. $20\overline{)78}$

Set 3 For use after page 535.

Divide and check.

1. $23\overline{)111}$ 2. $62\overline{)246}$ 3. $35\overline{)180}$ 4. $47\overline{)329}$ 5. $81\overline{)560}$
6. $18\overline{)151}$ 7. $59\overline{)437}$ 8. $74\overline{)147}$ 9. $98\overline{)613}$ 10. $60\overline{)195}$

Set 4 For use after page 545.

1. Emily can get 10 or 20 points when she tosses a bean bag at the first target. She can get 5, 15, or 25 points when she tosses a bean bag at the second target. Make a tree diagram to show the possible outcomes after two tosses.

Set 5 For use after page 549.

1. Kim plans to toss a number cube numbered from 1 to 6. What is the probability of rolling:

   a. an even number? b. a 5 or 6? c. a 7?

Set 6 For use after page 551.

1. In Mr. Henri's class, there are 3 people wearing red T-shirts, 10 people wearing blue T-shirts, 5 people wearing yellow T-shirts, and 6 people wearing purple T-shirts. What is the probability that a person picked at random is:

   a. wearing a yellow T-shirt? b. wearing a red T-shirt? c. wearing a purple or blue T-shirt?

2. The shirt store has 3 T-shirt styles and 4 cap styles. How many T-shirt and cap combinations can you buy?

Table of Measures

Customary Units of Measure

Length

1 foot (ft)	= 12 inches (in.)
1 yard (yd)	= 36 inches (in.)
	= 3 feet (ft)
1 mile (mi)	= 5,280 feet (ft)
	= 1,760 yards (yd)

Area

1 square foot (ft^2)	= 144 square inches (in^2)

Volume

1 cubic foot (ft^3)	= 1,728 cubic inches (in^3)

Capacity

1 tablespoon (tbsp)	= 3 teaspoons (tsp)
1 fluid ounce (fl oz)	= 2 tablespoons (tbsp)
1 cup (c)	= 8 fluid ounces (fl oz)
1 pint (pt)	= 2 cups (c)
1 quart (qt)	= 2 pints (pt)
1 gallon (gal)	= 4 quarts (qt)

Weight

1 pound (lb)	= 16 ounces (oz)
1 ton (T)	= 2,000 pounds (lb)

Fahrenheit Temperature

32°F	= freezing point of water
98.6°F	= normal body temperature
212°F	= boiling point of water

Metric Units of Measure

Length

1 centimeter (cm)	= 10 millimeters (mm)
1 decimeter (dm)	= 100 millimeters (mm)
	= 10 centimeters (cm)
1 meter (m)	= 1,000 millimeters (mm)
	= 100 centimeters (cm)
	= 10 decimeters (dm)
1 kilometer (km)	= 1,000 meters (m)

Area

1 square meter (m^2)	= 10,000 square centimeters (cm^2)
	= 100 square decimeters (dm^2)

Volume

1 cubic decimeter (dm^3)	= 1,000 cubic centimeters (cm^3)

Capacity

1 liter (L)	= 1,000 milliliters (mL)

Mass

1 gram (g)	= 1,000 milligrams (mg)
1 kilogram (kg)	= 1,000 grams (g)
1 metric ton (t)	= 1,000 kilograms (kg)

Celsius Temperature

0°C	= freezing point of water
37°C	= normal body temperature
100°C	= boiling point of water

Time

1 minute (min)	= 60 seconds (sec)
1 hour (hr)	= 60 minutes (min)
1 day (d)	= 24 hours (hr)
1 week (wk)	= 7 days (d)
1 month (mo)	= about 4 weeks (wk)
1 year (yr)	= 365 days (d)
	= 52 weeks (wk)
	= 12 months (mo)
1 decade	= 10 years (yr)
1 century	= 100 years (yr)

Glossary

A.M. (p. 74) Times from midnight to noon.

acute angle (p. 350) An angle that is less than a right angle.

acute triangle (p. 350) A triangle with all angles less than right angles.

addend (p. 108) A number added to find a sum.
Examples: $2 + 7 = 9$
↑ ↑
Addend Addend

addition (p. 22) An operation that tells the total number when you put together two or more numbers.

analog clock (p. 74) A clock that displays time using hands.

angle (p. 350) Two rays with a common endpoint.

area (p. 370) The number of square units needed to cover a closed figure.

array (p. 148) Objects arranged in rows and columns.

average (p. 326) The number found when the sum of two or more numbers is divided by the number of addends. Also called the *mean.*

bar graph (p. 10) A graph that uses bars to show data.

benchmark (p. 390) A known measurement that is used to estimate other measurements.

capacity (p. 512) The amount a container can hold.

centimeter (cm) (p. 505) A unit for measuring length in the metric system. *See also* Table of Measures, page 575

1 centimeter

certain (p. 541) Definitely will happen.

chances (p. 540) The probability that a particular event will occur.

change (p. 129) The amount of money you receive back when you pay with more money than something costs.

circle (p. 347) A plane figure in which all the points are the same distance from a point called the center.

Center → · ← Circle

circle graph (p. 404) A graph in the form of a circle that shows how the whole is broken into parts.

cluster (p. 16) Data that group around one value of a line plot.

compare (p. 66) To decide which of two numbers is greater.

composite number (p. 185) A whole number greater than 1 with more than two different factors. *Example:* The composite number 6 has factors of 1, 2, 3, and 6.

cone (p. 345) A solid figure with a curved surface and one circular flat surface.

congruent figures (p. 353) Figures that have the same size and shape.

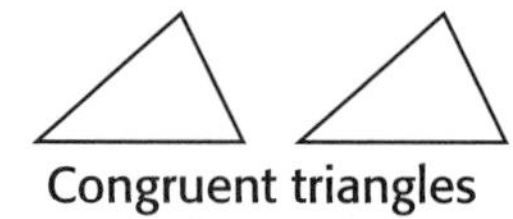

Congruent triangles

coordinate grid (p. 12) A graph used to locate points.

cube (p. 345) A solid figure whose 6 faces are all squares.

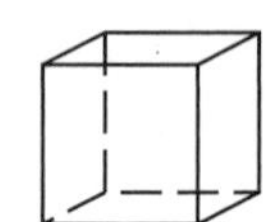

cubic centimeter (p. 373) A cube with 1 centimeter edges; Unit for measuring volume.

cubic inch (p. 373) A cube with 1 inch edges; Unit for measuring volume.

cubic unit (p. 372) A cube with 1 unit edges; Unit for measuring volume.

cup (c) (p. 458) A unit for measuring capacity in the customary system. *See also* Table of Measures, page 575

customary units of length, weight, capacity, and temperature *See* Table of Measures, page 575

cylinder (p. 345) A solid figure with a curved surface and two congruent circular flat surfaces.

data (p. 10) Information used to make calculations.

decimal (p. 476) A number that uses a decimal point to show tenths and hundredths. *Example:* 4.15

decimal point (p. 126) A symbol used to separate the ones place from the tenths place in decimals, or dollars from cents in money. *Example:* 4.57
↑ Decimal point

decimeter (dm) (p. 505) A unit for measuring length in the metric system. *See also* Table of Measures, page 575

degree Celsius (°C) (p. 514) A unit for measuring temperature in the metric system. *See also* Table of Measures, page 575

degree Fahrenheit (°F) (p. 514) A unit for measuring temperature in the customary system. *See also* Table of Measures, page 575

denominator (p. 388) The bottom number of a fraction that tells the number of equal parts in the whole. *Example:* $\frac{7}{8}$ ← Denominator

diagonal (p. 363) A line segment other than a side that connects two vertices of a polygon.

difference (p. 95) The number that is the result of subtracting one number from another. *Example:* $6 - 4 = 2$ ← Difference

digits (p. 52) The symbols used to show numbers: 0, 1, 2, 3, 4, 5, 6, 7, 8, and 9.

digital clock (p. 74) A clock that displays time using numbers.

display (p. 404) The window on a calculator that shows the numbers as they are entered and the results of the calculations.

dividend (p. 170) The number to be divided in a division number sentence. *Example:* $63 \div 9 = 7$
↑ Dividend

divisible (p. 330) Can be divided by another number without leaving a remainder. *Example:* 18 is divisible by 6.

division (p. 166) An operation that tells how many groups there are or how many are in each group.

divisor (p. 170) The number by which a dividend is divided. *Example:* $63 \div 9 = 7$
↑ Divisor

edge (p. 344) A line segment where two faces of a solid figure meet.

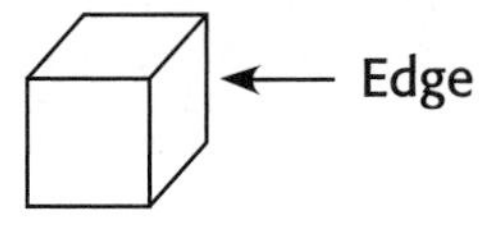

elapsed time (p. 78) The difference between two times.

endpoint (p. 358) A point at the start of a ray or ar either end of a line segment.

equally likely (p. 541) Just as likely to happen as not to happen.

equation (p. 22) A number sentence that uses the equals sign (=) to show that two expressions have the same value. *See also* number sentence *Example:* $9 + 2 = 11$

equilateral triangle (p. 349) A triangle with three equal sides.

equivalent fractions (p. 399) Fractions that name the same region, part of a set, or part of a segment. *Example:* $\frac{1}{2}$ and $\frac{2}{4}$

estimate (p. 70) To find a number that is close to an exact answer.

even number (p. 180) A whole number that has 0, 2, 4, 6, or 8 in the ones place; A whole number divisible by 2.

expanded form (p. 52) A way to write a number that shows the place value of each digit. *Example:* 9,000 + 300 + 20 + 5

experiment (p. 146) A test or trial.

face (p. 344) If a solid figure has only flat surfaces, then we call each surface a face.

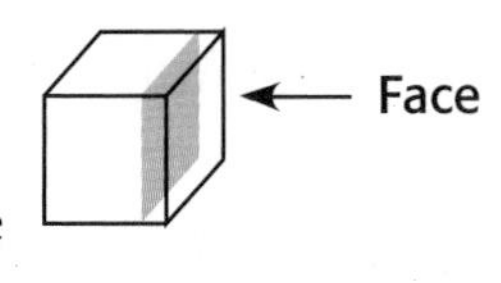

fact family (p. 169) A group of related facts using the same set of numbers.
Example: $4 + 3 = 7$
$3 + 4 = 7$
$7 - 3 = 4$
$7 - 4 = 3$

factors (p. 148) Numbers that are multiplied together to obtain a product.
Examples: $7 \times 3 = 21$
Factor ↑ ↑ Factor

fair game (p. 543) A game where each player has an equal chance of winning.

flip (reflection) (p. 353) To turn a plane figure over.

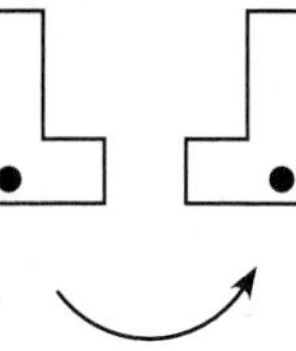

fluid ounce (p. 459) A unit for measuring capacity in the customary system. *See also* Table of Measures, page 575

foot (ft) (p. 415) A unit for measuring length in the customary system. *See also* Table of Measures, page 575

fraction (p. 387) A way to compare equal parts to a whole. *Example:* $\frac{3}{10}$ is 3 equal parts out of 10 equal parts.

front-end estimation (p. 108) A way to estimate a sum by adding the first digit of each addend and adjusting the result based on the remaining digits.

gallon (gal) (p. 458) A unit for measuring capacity in the customary system. *See also* Table of Measures, page 575

gram (g) (p. 511) A unit for measuring mass in the metric system. *See also* Table of Measures, page 575

graph (p. 10) A picture that shows data in an organized way.

greater than (>) (p. 66) The relationship of one number being farther to the right on a number line than another number. *Examples:* $7 > 3$

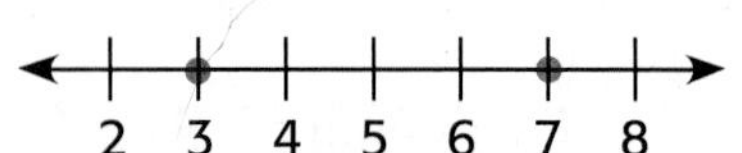

"Seven is greater than three."

grouping (associative) property (p. 230) When the grouping of addends or factors is changed, the sum or product stays the same.
Examples: $(5 + 2) + 3 = 5 + (2 + 3)$
$(3 \times 2) \times 1 = 3 \times (2 \times 1)$

hexagon (p. 347) A polygon with six sides.

hundredth (p. 476) One out of 100 equal parts of a whole.

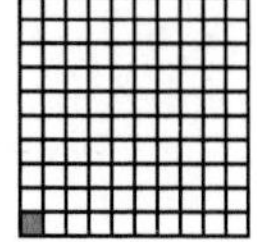

impossible (p. 541) Cannot happen.

improper fraction (p. 392) A fraction in which the numerator is greater than or equal to the denominator.

inch (in.) (p. 415) A unit for measuring length in the customary system. *See also* Table of Measures, page 575

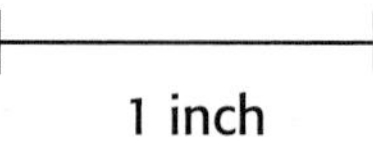

intersecting lines (p. 358) Lines that cross at a point.

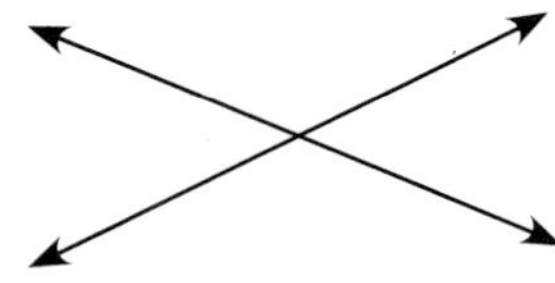

isosceles triangle (p. 349) A triangle that has at least two equal sides.

key (p. 10) Part of a pictograph that tells what each symbol stands for. *See also* symbol

kilogram (kg) (p. 511) A unit for measuring mass in the metric system. *See also* Table of Measures, page 575

kilometer (km) (p. 506) A unit for measuring length in the metric system. *See also* Table of Measures, page 575

leaf (p. 18) The part of a stem-and-leaf plot that shows the ones digit of a number.

less than (<) (p. 66) The relationship of one number being farther to the left on a number line than another number. *Examples:* $3 < 7$

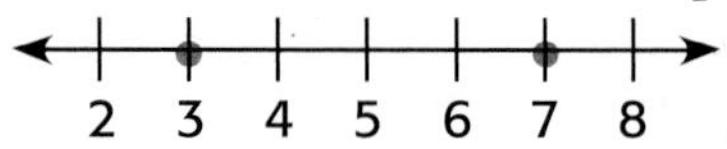

"Three is less than seven."

likely (p. 541) Probably will happen.

line (p. 358) A straight path that is endless in both directions.

line graph (p. 14) A graph that connects points to show how data changes over time.

line of symmetry (p. 363) A line on which a figure can be folded so that both halves are congruent. Line of symmetry

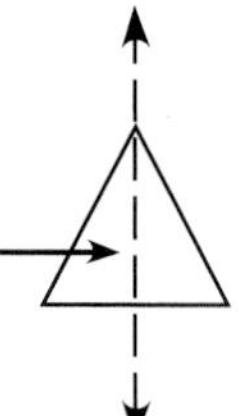

line plot (p. 16) A graph that shows data along a number line.

line segment (p. 358) Part of a line that has two end points.

liter (L) (p. 512) A unit for measuring capacity in the metric system. *See also* Table of Measures, page 575

mass (p. 511) The amount of matter that something contains.

mean (p. 327) The number found when the sum of two or more numbers is divided by the number of addends. Also called the *average.*

median (p. 31) The middle number when data are arranged in order.

mental math (p. 120) Performing calculations without using pencil and paper or a calculator.

meter (m) (p. 505) A unit for measuring length in the metric system. *See also* Table of Measures, page 575

metric units of length, weight, mass, capacity, and temperature *See* Table of Measures, page 575

mile (mi) (p. 419) A unit for measuring length in the customary system. *See also* Table of Measures, page 575

milliliter (mL) (p. 512) A unit for measuring capacity in the metric system. *See also* Table of Measures, page 575

millimeter (mm) (p. 505) A unit for measuring length in the metric system. *See also* Table of Measures, page 575

mixed number (p. 392) A number that has a whole-number part and a fractional part. *Example:* $2\frac{3}{4}$

mode (p. 31) The number or numbers that occur most often in a set of data.

multiple (p. 150) The product of a given whole number and any other whole number.

multiplication (p. 148) An operation that tells the total number when you put together equal groups.

number line (p. 16) A line that shows numbers in order using a scale.

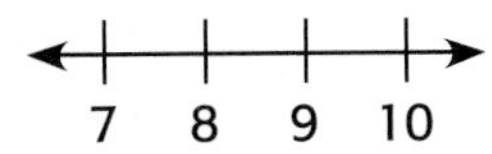

number sentence (p. 22) A way to show a relationship between numbers. *See also* equation
Examples: $2 + 5 = 7$
$6 \div 2 = 3$

numerator (p. 388) The top number of a fraction. It tells the number of equal parts compared to the number of equal parts in a whole.
Example: $\frac{7}{8}$ ← Numerator

obtuse angle (p. 350) An angle that is greater than a right angle.

obtuse triangle (p. 350) A triangle with one angle greater than a right angle.

octagon (p. 347) A polygon with eight sides.

odd number (p. 180) A whole number that has 1, 3, 5, 7, or 9 in the ones place. A whole number not divisible by 2.

one property (p. 151) In multiplication, the product of a number and 1 is that number. In division, a number divided by 1 is that number. *Examples:* $5 \times 1 = 5$
$3 \div 1 = 3$

operation (p. 22) Addition, subtraction, multiplication, and division.

order (p. 68) To arrange numbers from least to greatest or from greatest to least.

ordered pair (p. 12) A pair of numbers used to locate a point on a coordinate grid.
Example: (3, 5)

order (commutative) property (p. 151) Changing the order of addends or factors does not change the sum or product.
Examples: $8 + 5 = 5 + 8$
$3 \times 6 = 6 \times 3$

ordinal number (p. 80) A number used to tell order.
Examples: First, thirteenth, 1st, 4th

ounce (oz) (p. 457) A unit for measuring weight in the customary system. *See also* Table of Measures, page 575

outcome (p. 543) A possible result of an experiment.

P.M. (p. 74) Times from noon to midnight.

parallel lines (p. 358) Lines that do not intersect.

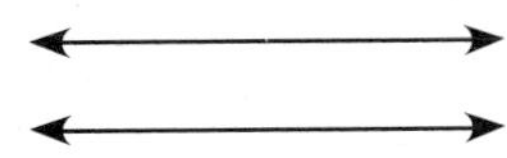

parallelogram (p. 360) A quadrilateral with two pairs of opposite parallel sides.

pattern (p. 136) A list of objects, events, or ideas that repeat.

pentagon (p. 347) A polygon with five sides.

perimeter (p. 368) The distance around a closed figure.

period (p. 52) A group of 3 digits in a number, separated by a comma.

perpendicular lines (p. 358) Two lines which form right angles where they intersect.

pictograph (p. 10) A graph that uses symbols to show data.

pint (pt) (p. 458) A unit for measuring capacity in the customary system. *See also* Table of Measures, page 575

place value (p. 52) The value given to the place a digit has in a number. *Example:* In 6,928, the place value of the digit 9 is hundreds.

plane figure (p. 347) A figure that lies on a flat surface.

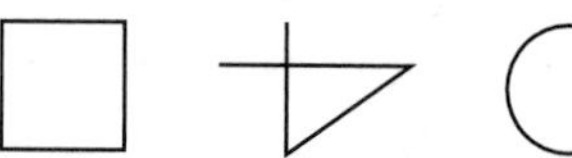

point (p. 358) An exact position often marked by a dot or named by an ordered pair.

polygon (p. 347) A closed plane figure made up of line segments.

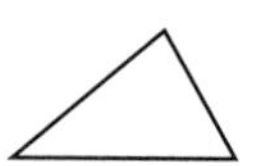

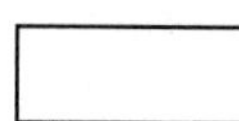

possible (p. 540) Able to happen.

pound (lb) (p. 457) A unit for measuring weight in the customary system. *See also* Table of Measures, page 575

prediction (p. 548) An educated guess about what will happen.

prime number (p. 185) A whole number greater than 1 that has only two factors, itself and 1.

probability (p. 547) The chance that an event will happen.

problem solving guide (p. 20) A process for solving a problem: Understand, Plan, Solve, Look Back.

product (p. 148) The number that is the result of multiplying two or more factors.
Example: $5 \times 6 = 30$
↑ Product

pyramid (p. 345) A solid figure whose base is a polygon and whose faces are triangles with a common vertex.

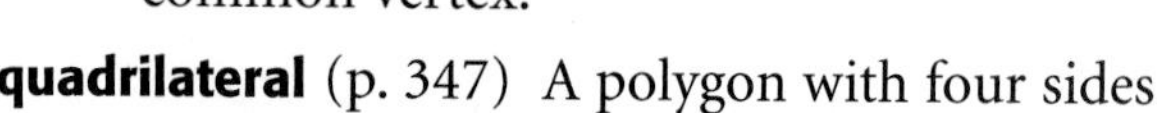

quadrilateral (p. 347) A polygon with four sides.

quart (qt) (p. 458) A unit for measuring capacity in the customary system. *See also* Table of Measures, page 575

quotient (p. 170) The number other than the remainder that is the result of dividing.
Example: $63 \div 7 = 9$
↑ Quotient

range (p. 31) The difference between the greatest and least numbers in a set of data.

ray (p. 350) Part of a line that begins at a point and is endless in one direction.

rectangle (p. 360) A quadrilateral with four right angles and opposite sides parallel and the same length.

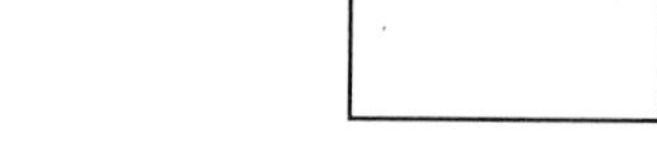

rectangular prism (p. 345) A solid figure whose six faces are all rectangles.

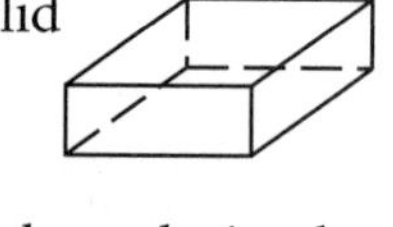

regroup (p. 104) To name a whole or decimal number in a different way. *Example:* 28 is 2 tens and 8 ones. 0.3 is 0.30 or 0.300.

remainder (p. 297) The number less than the divisor that remains after the division is complete.
Example: $31 \div 7 = 4$ R3
↑ Remainder

rhombus (p. 360) A quadrilateral with two pairs of parallel sides and all sides the same length.

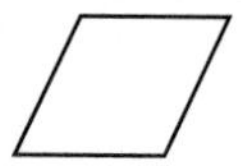

right angle (p. 350) An angle that forms a square corner.

right triangle (p. 350) A triangle that has one right angle.

Roman numerals (p. 88) Numerals in a number system used by ancient Romans.
Examples: I = 1
IV = 4
V = 5
VI = 6

rounding (p. 70) Replacing one number with another number that tells about how many or how much.

sample (p. 526) A representative part of a large group.

scale (p. 10) Numbers that show the units used on a graph. Also, (p. 456) an instrument used to measure an object's weight.

scalene triangle (p. 349) A triangle with no equal sides.

schedule (p. 82) A list which shows the times events occur.

similar figures (p. 355) Figures that have the same shape and may or not have the same size.

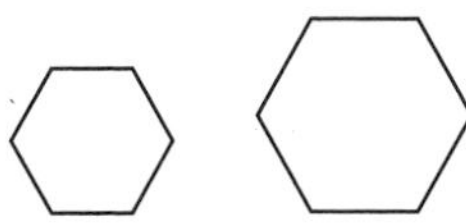

Similar hexagons

simplest form (p. 402) A fraction in which the numerator and denominator have no common factors other than 1.

slide (translation) (p. 353) To move a plane figure in one direction.

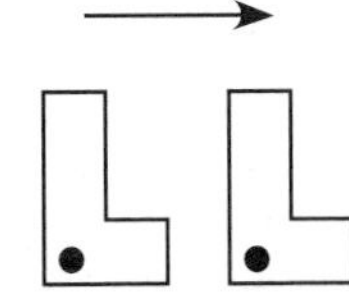

solid figure (p. 344) A figure that has length, width, height, and volume.

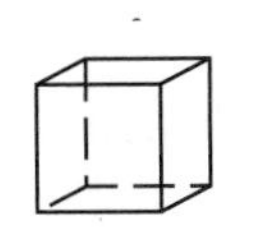

Cube

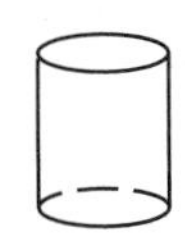

Cylinder

sphere (p. 345) A solid figure that has the shape of a round ball.

square (p. 360) A quadrilateral that has four equal sides and four right angles.

square centimeter (p. 371) A square with 1 centimeter sides; Unit used for measuring area.

square inch (p. 371) A square with 1 inch sides; Unit used for measuring area.

square number (p. 155) The product of a number multiplied by itself. *Example:* 6 × 6 = 36
Square number ↑

square unit (p. 370) A square with 1 unit sides; Unit used for measuring area.

standard form (p. 52) A way to write a number that shows only its digits. *Example:* 9,325

stem (p. 18) The part of a stem-and-leaf plot that shows all but the ones digit of a number.

stem-and-leaf plot (p. 18) A graph that uses place value to organize numbers in data.

straight angle (p. 350) An angle that forms a straight line.

strategy (p. 4) A plan or method used to solve a problem. *Example:* Guess and Check

subtraction (p. 22) An operation that tells the difference between two numbers, or how many are left when some are taken away.

sum (p. 95) The number that is the result of adding two or more addends.
Example: 7 + 9 = 16
↑ Sum

survey (p. 8) Question or questions answered by a group of people.

symbol (p. 10) A picture in a pictograph that stands for a given number of objects.

symmetry (p. 363) A figure has symmetry if it can be folded along a line so that both parts match exactly. *See also* line of symmetry

tablespoon (p. 459) A unit for measuring capacity in the customary system. *See also* Table of Measures, page 575

tally mark (p. 7) A mark used to record data.

/ = 1
~~////~~ = 5

teaspoon (p. 459) A unit for measuring capacity in the customary system. *See also* Table of Measures, page 575

tenth (p. 476) One out of 10 equal parts of a whole.

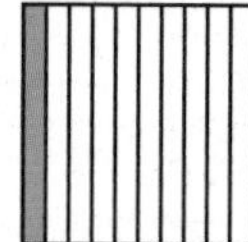

ton (p. 457) A unit for measuring weight in the customary system. *See also* Table of Measures, page 575

trapezoid (p. 360) A quadrilateral that has exactly one pair of parallel sides.

tree diagram (p. 544) A diagram showing all possible outcomes of an event.

triangle (p. 347) A polygon with three sides.

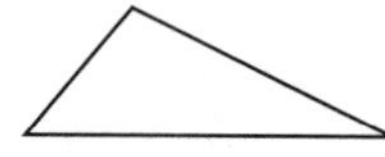

turn (rotation) (p. 353) To rotate a plane figure.

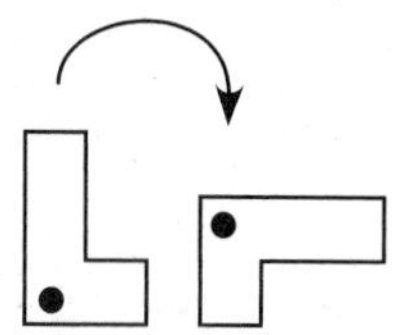

unit (p. 77) A quantity used as a standard of measure.

units of time (p. 77) *See* Table of Measures, page 575

unlikely (p. 540) Probably will not happen.

variable (p. 32) A letter that stands for a number or a range of numbers.

vertex (plural, vertices) (p. 344) The point where two or more edges meet. *See also* (p. 350), the common endpoint of two rays forming an angle.

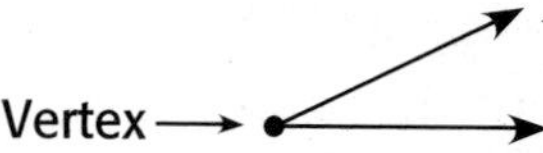

volume (p. 372) The number of cubic units needed to fill a solid figure.

word name (p. 52) A way to show a number using words. *Example:* Nine thousand, three hundred twenty-five

yard (yd) (p. 415) A unit for measuring length in the customary system. *See also* Table of Measures, page 575

zero property (p. 151) In addition, the sum of a number and 0 is that number. In multiplication, the product of a number and 0 is 0. *Examples:* $7 + 0 = 7$
$7 \times 0 = 0$

Photographs

Cover Steve Ewert*

Front Matter **iiiTL** Gail Shumway/FPG International **iiiBR** Runk-Schoenberger/Grant Heilman Photography **viiT** FOTOPIC/West Stock **xiiTL** Katrine Naleid* **xiiTR** Katrine Naleid* **xiiB** Katrine Naleid* **xiiiT** Corbis-Bettmann **1T** Zig Leszczynski/Animals, Animals **1CL** Adrienne McGrath **1CR** Dan Toulgoet **1B** Dan Feicht/Cedar Point Park **2T** Lloyd Litsey* **2B** Steven Jessmore*

Chapter 1 **6TL** Wisniewski/ZEFA/H. Armstrong Roberts **6TR** Gail Shumway/FPG International **6BR** Runk-Schoenberger/Grant Heilman Photography **6–7** ZEFA GERMANY/ The Stock Market **7** Superstock **8T** Konrad Wothe/Ellis Nature Photography **8TC** Art Wolfe/ Tony Stone Images **8C** Gerry Ellis/Ellis Nature Photography **8BC** Daniel J. Cox/Tony Stone Images **8B** Gerry Ellis/Ellis Nature Photography **9** James Keyser* **10T** Matt Meadows/Peter Arnold, Inc. **10B** Hamblin/Liaison International **11T** Neal Mishler/FPG International **11B** Steve Gettle/Ellis Nature Photography **12** Louis Psihoyos/Matrix **13** Francois Gohier/Photo Researchers **14** James Keyser* **15** ZEFA-VIRDEE/The Stock Market **16B** Gerry Ellis/ Ellis Nature Photography **17** Runk-Schoenberger/Grant Heilman Photography **18** Stuart Westmorland/Tony Stone Images **19T** Renee Lynn/Photo Researchers **22T** Jeff Lepore/Photo Researchers **22B** Info Hund/ Kramer/Okapia/Photo Researchers **23T** Lynn M. Stone/The Image Bank **23B** Joseph Van Wormer/Bruce Coleman Inc. **25** Rick Dole* **26L** S. J. Krasemann/Peter Arnold, Inc. **28B** Erwin and Peggy Bauer/Bruce Coleman Inc. **29T** Tom Brakefield/DRK Photo **29C** FPG International **29B** ZEFA GERMANY/The Stock Market **30** Rick Dole* **37** Norman Owen Tomalin/Bruce Coleman Inc. **39** Roy King **40L** M. H. Sharp/Photo Researchers **41** Kenneth H. Thomas/Photo Researchers **46TL** Hans Pfletschinger/Peter Arnold, Inc. **46TR** Alan D. Carey/Photo Researchers **46CL** N. H. (Dan) Cheatham/Photo Researchers **46B** Martin Harvey/NHPA

Chapter 2 **49B** Superstock **51** Mike Peters* **58** Mike Peters* **59** Mike Peters* **60** Art Resource, NY **65T** Kevin Anderson/Midwestock **65B** The History Museum for Springfield - Green County **68** Laura Ingalls Wilder Home Association **70TL** Runk-Schoenberger/Grant Heilman Photography **70TR** Runk-Schoenberger/Grant Heilman Photography **70TCL** Runk-Schoenberger/Grant Heilman Photography **70TCR** David Higgs/Tony Stone Images **70BC** Michael Fogden/Bruce Coleman Inc. **70B** Runk-Schoenberger/Grant Heilman Photography **71T** Kjell B. Sandved/Photo Researchers **71C** AH Rider/Photo Researchers **71B** Simon D. Pollard/Photo Researchers **73T** David Pollack/The Stock Market **73BL** Jose Luis Banus/FPG International **73BR** ZEFA **75B** Corbis Media **77** Dan Suzio/Photo Researchers **81** Mike Peters* **83** Penny Tweedie/Tony Stone Images

Chapter 3 **91T(1)** Lori Adamski Peek/ Tony Stone Images **91T(2)** Michael A. Keller/ The Stock Market **91T(3)** David Young Wolff/ Tony Stone Images **91T(4)** Debra P. Hershkowitz/ Bruce Coleman Inc. **91T(5)** Chuck Savage/ The Stock Market **91T(6)** Blair Seitz/Photo Researchers **91T(7)** Anthony Edgeworth/ The Stock Market **93** Copyright: STAR TREK: DEEP SPACE NINE © 1993 by Paramount Pictures. All Rights Reserved. Photo by Robbie Robinson **97L** Barbara Alper/Stock, Boston **97LC** Barbara Alper/Stock, Boston **97R(background)** Bill Ross/Westlight **97RC** Robert Landau/Westlight **97R** Bill Ross/Westlight **98** Copyright: STAR TREK: DEEP SPACE NINE © 1993 by Paramount Pictures. All Rights Reserved. Photo by Robbie Robinson **100** James Keyser* **102** Brian Parker/Tom Stack & Associates **103L** Thor Swift **104T** Beverly Barton **104BL** Phyllis Ha **105L** Karen Evans **105R** Phyllis Ha **106** Gordon Smith **107T** Wide World Photos **108** Greg Kiger* **110** Bill Frakes* **114L** Thor Swift* **114R** Larry Kanfer* **116** Joe Quever* **120** Patrick Ward **121L** Peter Davey/Bruce Coleman Inc. **122T** Thor Swift **123** Thor Swift **125** Dede Hatch **126R** Dede Hatch **128** Rachel Holland* **130R** Joe Quever* **142R** Michele Burgess/The Stock Market

Chapter 4 **147** Lori Adamski-Peek **152T** Caryn Levy* **153** Culver Pictures, Inc. **154** Lori Adamski-Peek **156** Hulton Getty **157** David Simson/Stock, Boston **159** Jeff Weiner Photography **165** David Brownell **166** David Brownell **167** David Brownell **170** Steve Payne* **175** Lloyd Litsey* **176** Steve Winter/National Geographic Image Collection **177** Milo Stewart, Jr./Baseball Hall of Fame Library, Cooperstown, NY **178** Lloyd Litsey* **179** Paul J. Sutton/Duomo **183C** Marco Fontes/ Kino Fotoarquivo **194L** Culver Pictures, Inc.

Chapter 5 **197T** FOTOPIC/West Stock **199** Steve Winter/National Geographic Image **201** Herbert W. Booth III/Liaison International **204** Steve Winter/National Geographic Image **209** Focus on Sports **213** Superstock **216** Mike Zerby **218** Focus on Sports **227** Wayne Lynch/DRK Photo **229T** Stephen Dalton/NHPA **229B** Runk-Schoenberger/Grant Heilman Photography **230** Rachel Holland* **234TR** Rob Levine* **234B** Rob Levine* **236B** Renee Lynn* **237L** Museum of N. Arizona, Flagstaff **237R** Chuck Place Photography

Chapter 6 **248** Hans Pfletschinger/Peter Arnold, Inc. **249** Dan Toulgoet **251** Dallas & John Heaton/Stock, Boston **252** Stacy A. Harris/ Miami Valley RTA, Dayton, Ohio **253** The Telegraph Colour Library/FPG International **254R** Dan Toulgoet **256** Corbis-Bettmann **259** Steven Jessmore* **260T** Steven Jessmore* **262** Corbis-Bettmann **264** Andrew Wallace* **266** The Dong -A Ilbo Company/Seoul, Korea **269** Scala/Art Resource, NY **270** Dan Feicht/ Cedar Point Park **271** Dan Feicht/Cedar Point Park **273** Neal Preston* **274T** Neal Preston* **278** Dugald Bremner/Tony Stone Images **280** Steven Gottlieb/FPG International **281** Tony Demin/International Stock **285** A. Ramey/Woodfin Camp & Associates **286T** Holt Studios International (Irene Lengui)/ Photo Researchers

Chapter 7 **291** Rick Friedman* **294** Dan Dancer/Sipa Press **295BL** Cover from "Ozma of Oz," by L. Frank Baum, illustrated by John R. Neill. Permission from Morrow Junior Books, a division of William Morrow and Company, Inc. Photo by Cheryl Fenton* **295BR** Illustration from "Ozma of Oz," by L. Frank Baum, illustrated by John R. Neill. Permission from Morrow Junior Books, a division of William Morrow and Company, Inc. Photo by Cheryl Fenton* **296T** Rick Friedman* **296C** Rick Friedman* **299** Win Kryda* **302T** Robert Overton* **302B** Jane Grushow/Grant Heilman Photography **305** Robert Overton* **306** Win Kryda* **307T** Courtesy of Carolrhoda Books. Copyright 1991 by Carolrhoda Books. All Rights Reserved. Photo by Cheryl Fenton* **309** Gary Gengozian **310T** Rick Dole* **311** William Felger/Grant Heilman Photography **312TR** Greg Kiger* **314** Barry L. Runk/Grant Heilman Photography **316T** Chef John Folse & Company **316B** José Garcia II/Chef John Folse & Company **319** David Leeson* **322L** David Leeson* **338T** Eric Valli & Diane Summers **338C** Grant Heilman/Grant Heilman Photography

Chapter 8 **340BL** Adrienne McGrath **341TL** Bill Gallery/Stock, Boston **341TC** Lewis Bloom/Liaison International **341TR** George DiSario/The Stock Market **341B** Robin Smith/ FPG International **343** Photo by Tom Powel **344T** Jeff Heger/FPG International **346** Jessica Ehlers/Bruce Coleman Inc. **347L** Sotographs/ Liaison International **347R** J. C. Carton/Bruce Coleman Inc. **348T** Mondrian, Piet. *Broadway Boogie Woogie.* 1942–43. Oil on canvas, 50" × 50" (127 × 127 cm). The Museum of Modern Art, New York. Given anonymously. Photograph © 1998 The Museum of Modern Art, New York. **350** Photo by Tom Powel **356BL** Bruce Forster/ Tony Stone Images **357** Graphic Eye/Tony Stone Images **363T** Kjell B. Sandved/Photo Researchers **363CC** Science Source/Photo Researchers **363CR** Frank Krahmer/Bruce Coleman Inc. **364T** Larry Ulrich/Tony Stone Images **365T** Wayne R. Rilenduke/Tony Stone Images **367** Michael Simpson/FPG International **368T** Dennis Hallinan/FPG International **372T** Steven Burr Williams/Liaison International **374TL** Arthur Tilley/FPG International **374TR** Elyse Lewin/The Image Bank **374B** Mark Romine/Liaison International **377B** Laguna Photo/Liaison International **379** Tony Velez **380** Chip Simons/FPG International

Chapter 9 **385** Robie Price* **388T** Robie Price* **390L** Bob Daemmrich/Stock, Boston **390R** Bob Daemmrich/The Image Works **394TL** Bob Daemmrich/Stock, Boston **394TR** Bob Daemmrich/Stock, Boston **394BL** Bob Daemmrich/Tony Stone Images **394BR** Tom Bean/The Stock Market **397** Patrick Pfister* **400B** Clermont County Public Library/ Clermont Senior Services Inc. **401** Clermont County Public Library/Clermont Senior Services Inc. **402** Patrick Pfister* **403** Barry L. Runk/ Grant Heilman Photography **404-405** Michael Schlueter* **406R** Nan Ramey **408T** Renee Lynn* **409** Mask - "Untitled," 1997, acrylic on wood by Gregory Lomayesva. Wheelright Museum of The American Indian. Photo by Renee Lynn* **413** T. E. Levy **415** Harald Sund/The Image Bank **416TL** T. E. Levy **416TR** T. E. Levy **418** North Ridge Primary School **419** Texas Department of Transportation **421** Karen Preuss/The Image Works **426L** Giulio Andreini/ Liaison International

Chapter 10 **428** Katrine Naleid* **429** Katrine Naleid* **430T** The Research Libraries, New York Public Library **430B** White House Historical Association **432T** Katrine Naleid* **435** Shahn Kermani/Liaison International **436B** Steve Grubman/The Image Bank **437** Fritz Prenzel/OKAPIA/Photo Researchers **443** Marc Pokempner*

[illegible]okempner* **446C** Gabe Palmer/ [illegible]arket **446B** Michael A. Keller/ [illegible]Market **447** Guy Marche/FPG [illegible]nal **449** Wide World Photos [illegible]ge Grall/National Aquarium in Baltimore **455([illegible]et)** Zig Leszczynski/Animals, Animals
460 Max Gibbs/Animals, Animals
467 Geoffrey Nilsen* **470T** Katrine Naleid*
470BL Gavin Hellier/Tony Stone Images
470BC GJ Images/The Image Bank
470BR Steve Vidler/Tony Stone Images

Chapter 11 Corbis-Bettmann
472BR Christoph Burki/Tony Stone Images
474B Archive Photo **474T** AFP/Corbis-Bettmann
475 Doug Pensinger/Allsport **476** Doug Pensinger/Allsport **477** David Madison/Duomo **478T** Paul J. Sutton/Duomo **479** Paul J. Sutton/ Duomo **480** Chris Cole/Duomo **482** Helmets courtesy of Giro Sports Design. Photos by Geoffrey Nilsen* **484** Wide World Photos **485** Tom Strattman/Wide World Photos **487T** Manoj Shah/Tony Stone Images **488TR** T. Zimmerman/ FPG International **488BR** William R. Sallaz/ Duomo **489** James Randklev/Tony Stone Images **491L** UPI/Corbis-Bettmann **491R** Paul J. Sutton/Duomo **492T** Mike Powell/Allsport **496** Clive Brunskill/Allsport **497** Michal Heron/The Stock Market **499** Simon Bruty/ Allsport **502** William R. Sallaz/Duomo **503** Dr. Ward Ransdell **504** Michael Probst/ Wide World Photos **505** Focus on Sports **506** Courtesy of Kathyrn Zimmerman **507** Ben Van Hook/Duomo **508TL** David Sailors/ The Stock Market **508TR** ZEFA-Cutouts/ The Stock Market **508B** Katrine Naleid* **510T** Courtesy of Kim Brownfield **512T** Frank Augstein/Wide World Photos **514** David Madison/Duomo **516T** Ronald Sheridan/ Ancient Art & Architecture Collection **516BL** Katrine Naleid* **516BR** Katrine Naleid* **522L** Marvin Newman/Sports Illustrated ©Time Inc. **522R** Katrine Naleid*

Chapter 12 **532** Hugh Grannum* **535** Renee Lynn/Photo Researchers **536T** Robie Price* **536B** F. Pedrick/The Image Works **536–537** F. Pedrick/The Image Works **537** Robie Price* **539** Lloyd Litsey* **542** Lloyd Litsey* **546TR** Michael DeYoung/AlaskaStock **546CL** Michael DeYoung/AlaskaStock **546BL** Danny Daniels/AlaskaStock **550** Steve Payne* **556T** Edward J. Muybridge/Stanford University

Cheryl Fenton* viT, xivL, 95, 104BR, 107B, 111, 122B, 126L, 127, 130L, 134B, 135, 136, 142C, 145T, 146, 149, 152B, 163, 168T, 171, 183T, 189, 191, 223TL, 223TR, 223CR, 223BL, 232TL, 232TCL, 232TCR, 232B, 238, 239, 265, 274B, 276TL, 276TR, 286C, 288C, 288–289, 295T, 296B, 303, 307B, 310B, 312TL, 312B, 317, 322R, 323, 333, 386TC, 386B, 388B, 389, 391T, 391B, 398T, 400T, 406L, 416C, 416BL, 416BR, 417, 526, 544T, 547, 548T, 548BL, 555, 556C **George B. Fry III*** viiiL, ixT, xiT, xiBL, xiBR, 247, 249(inset), 254L, 255, 288L, 289, 300, 329T, 382, 383, 426R **GHP Studio*** xT, 19B, 49T, 197BL, 197BR, 198, 234TL, 234TCL, 234TCR, 235, 236T, 340TL, 347CR, 352BL, 352BC, 352BR, 355L, 355C, 356TC, 356BC, 363B, 364B, 366, 372BL, 372BC, 372BR, 373, 376 **Ken Karp*** iiiTR, iiiBL, ivT, vT, vB, viC, viB, viiC, viiB, ixB, xC, xiiiB, xivR, 4T, 4C, 4B, 5, 6BL, 26R, 28T, 32, 40R, 45, 46CR, 48, 49CL, 49CC, 49CR, 54, 56, 62, 76, 79, 82, 90, 91B, 118, 134T, 142L, 144, 145B, 148, 150, 158, 162, 168B, 169, 172, 180, 184, 186, 188, 194R, 196T, 196TC, 200, 202, 214L, 215, 220, 223CL, 224, 228, 232TR, 238–239, 250, 260B, 276B, 277, 286B, 292, 315, 320, 324, 325, 326, 328, 329B, 330, 332, 338B, 340TR, 344B, 345, 347CL, 348CL, 348BC, 348CR, 351, 352T, 353, 354, 355R, 356TL, 356TR, 356BR, 359, 360, 362, 363TR, 365B, 368B, 369, 375, 386TL, 386TR, 392, 398B, 404, 408B, 410, 411, 414, 431, 432B, 434, 436TL, 436TR, 438, 438–439, 439, 444, 456, 458, 462, 464, 472T, 472BL, 473, 478B, 486, 487B, 488L, 494, 500, 510B, 512B, 517, 522C, 524, 525, 527, 528, 530, 534, 540, 544B, 546BR, 548BR, 556B **Parker/Boon Productions and Dorey Sparre Photography*** ivB, xB, 52, 57, 74, 80, 88, 94, 96, 210, 214R, 217, 244, 340–341, 370, 377T **Jenny Thomas*** viiiR, 16T, 38, 121R, 141, 206, 246, 340BLC, 340BRC, 340BR, 363BL, 440T, 440–441.

*Photographed expressly for Addison Wesley Longman, Inc.

Illustrations

John Amoss 50b, 85e, 88b, 88d, 129a, 133a, 133b, 275a, 279a, 283a, 283c, 388b, 389a, 389e, 392a, 392b, 392c, 423a, 423b, 428b, 429a, 429c, 461a, 461c, 466a–c, 470a, 499c–e, 519a, 524d, 553a, 553b **Scott Angle** 389f, 393c, 415a, 415b, 415c, 415d, 415e, 415f, 423c, 513f, 515i, 540a, 547c, 551a, 553d **Pamela Becker** 269a **Johnee Bee** 496b **Christine Benjamin** 19b, 48c–g, 290b, 340a, 383a–b, 384b–c, 525b, 548a, 548b **Ken Bowser** 53a, 99a, 130b, 161a, 161b, 228b **Cameron Eagle** 19c, 35a, 35b, 35c, 35d, 162b, 188c, 188d, 191a, 493a **Rob Ebersol** 89a, 89b, 161c, 169a, 193a, 240a, 507a–c **Eureka Cartography** 428c **Frank Frisari** 33b, 422a, 422b, 422c, 422d, 463a, 481a, 513a, 513b, 513c, 513d, 513e, 543d **Derek Grinnell** 223a, 516b **Tim Haggerty** 92b, 92c **Gary Hallgren** 15b, 36a, 56a, 60a–c, 66a, 81c, 85a, 85c, 139a, 139c, 241b, 241c, 335a, 335b, 451a, 451b, 457d–f, 461b, 467c, 519b **Barbara Hoopes Ambler** 20a, 31c, 420a, 452b, 453a, 534a **Dave Jonason** 27b, 33a, 77a, 137e, 219a, 243a, 309b, 337a, 390f, 390g, 391a, 391b, 396d, 396e, 396f, 396g, 396h, 448a, 457a–c, 459c–e, 463b, 468a–c, 477g, 505a, 505b, 505c, 505d, 505e, 505f, 511c, 511d, 511e, 511f, 518a, 518b, 518c, 521b, 521c, 539b, 542b, 543c **Paul Koziarz** 10b, 10c, 10f, 12b, 38b, 43b, 43c, 45a, 45b, 58b, 76a, 76f, 84a, 84d, 84e, 425a, 482b **Joe LeMonnier** 73a **Masami Miyamoto** 283b **Laurie O'Keefe** 12c, 21b–d, 27d **Kathleen O'Neill** 476b **William Pasini** 12a, 23c, 37b, 69a, 82a, 101a, 107b, 156b, 183a, 191b, 205a, 213a, 256a, 262a, 267a, 276b, 333b, 335c, 359d, 369b–d, 379b, 416a, 419b, 448b, 452a, 496c, 514b, 541b **Ann Pickard** 11a, 227a, 241a **Gary Pierazzi** 289a, 289b, 289d **Precision Graphics** 172a, 208a, 349d–f, 416e, 416h, 416i, 464a, 465a–f, 509a, 511b **Pronk & Associates** All currency art **QYA Design Studio** 16c, 17b, 26b, 28a, 150c, 458a–d, 459a–b, 467a–b, 469a, 515a, 515b, 515c, 515d, 515e, 515f, 515g, 515h **Saul Rosenbaum** 107c, 112a, 224b, 225a, 225b **Rosiland Solomon** 55c, 55d, 304a **Rob Schuster** 202a, 263a, 390c, 390d, 390e, 424b, 483c, 485b, 490d, 492b, 498a, 504b, 506b, 514c **Bill Thompson** 168b **Joe VanDerBos** 30b, 43a, 57b, 61a, 64a, 85b, 85d, 87b, 109a, 118b, 124a, 419c, 425b, 499b, 507d, 521a **Thomas Ward** 31a, 113a, 394a, 394b, 394c, 394d, 395a, 531a, 553c **Jil Weil** 144c, 145c, 146b, 194c, 197a, 246b, 248a, 342a, 380e–g, 404a, 411b, 474c
Precision Graphics, Paul Koziarz, QYA Design Studio, Jil Weil All technical artwork throughout; all generated electronically

Text and Art

Chapter 10 p. 469, Excerpts from *LUCKY LUCKY LUCKY ME* by Milton Berle and Buddy Arnold. (New York: Santly-Joy, Inc., 1950). Copyright ©1950 by Santly-Joy, Inc. Used by permission.

CREDITS

Index

D

INDEX

E

F

N

O

INDEX

Q

R

S

INDEX